HARVARD ECONOMIC STUDIES
VOLUME CXII

The studies in this series are published by the Department of Economics of Harvard University. The department does not assume responsibility for the views expressed.

THE
CANADIAN ECONOMY
Prospect and Retrospect

By

RICHARD E. CAVES
RICHARD H. HOLTON

HARVARD UNIVERSITY PRESS
Cambridge, Massachusetts
1961

Library of Congress Catalog Number 59–14734
Printed in the United States of America

Preface

During the past decade or so the world has seen an interest in economic growth which probably matches the prewar interest in the business cycle. Concern for the welfare of the low-income countries has generated an impressive output of development plans for individual countries, writings on development by economists, and pleas for measures to aid development by th world's political leaders. And now economic aid to und developed areas has become one of the more prominent policy instruments of the "cold war."

Through much of this discussion runs a particular conception of the end product of development. The developed country is one with a high income per capita. It has a "balanced" economy, with a manufacturing sector grown to thrive side by side with agriculture and other primary production. Manufactured goods are important exports and the country is self-sufficient in a significant proportion of the goods it uses. In brief, the developed country is one such as the United States, Great Britain, France, Germany, or the Scandinavian countries.

One reason the Canadian economy holds great fascination is its failure to match this concept of the developed economy, despite its having the world's second highest income per capita. Canada produces many manufactured goods, but she is a net importer of manufactures. She imports capital as heavily and exports proportionally as many raw and semimanufactured materials as she did many years ago. Her economic growth has been extremely rapid and shows no sign of slackening.

Along what route has the Canadian economy come, and where will it go from here? Will Canada continue to ship her raw materials to the factories of the industrialized countries? Or will she industrialize to the point where she exports primarily fully manufactured goods? Is she going to be a kind of mineral frontier for the United States and Great Britain, processing these minerals only enough to minimize transportation costs? Or are factor costs and markets going to shift in such a way as to call for production of the final goods in Canadian factories? What factors historically have shaped the Canadian economy and given it the structure it now displays? Does a study of these determinants provide a basis for projecting Canadian economic growth and structure for a decade or so? Just what are the prospects for the Canadian economy?

These are the broad questions which this book attempts to answer.

The future of the Canadian economy holds interest not only for Canadians and for students of economic growth. The United States is becoming more concerned with her neighbor to the north. In part, this is due to the importance of Canadian minerals for the United States, which has almost no nickel and has always drawn virtually all of its supply from Canada. Substantial quantities of the base metals as well have come from Canada. Now that the better ores of the famed Mesabi range are depleted, the United States even looks to Canada for high-grade iron ore. Canada is also an important reservoir of uranium, oil, and natural gas.

But the jet age has underscored Canada's importance to the United States for reasons other than her natural resources. The possibility of trans-Arctic air attack has led to the establishment of the DEW (Distant Early Warning) line of radar stations across northern Canada, financed by both the Canadian and United States governments. Canada's insistence on a St. Lawrence Seaway has forced the United States to work with her in this long-delayed venture. In recent years, too, the United States has listened with at least outward displays of sympathy to Canadian complaints about surplus wheat disposal programs which disrupt normal trade channels and aggravate Canada's grain marketing problem. With the development of the Alberta oil and gas fields, the flow of United States venture capital into Canada, and the negotiation over natural gas transmission and exportation have helped make the United States more conscious of Canada and her problems. Disagreement over United States oil import quotas and over the control of the Columbia River has served the same end.

Why a long-range forecast of Canadian economic growth? Economists are famous for their lack of success in forecasting. At the end of World War II the most carefully prepared forecasts showed a serious depression to be imminent for the United States. The unprecedented boom which actually developed, much to the embarrassment of the seers, provided the most glaring recent example of faulty prognostication by economists. With this unimpressive record, why should one dare attempt a long-range economic forecast?

The cynic might point out that long-range forecasting is safer than short-range forecasting. It is longer before the prediction can be proved wrong. Furthermore, by the time the forecast turns out false most people will have forgotten all about it. Short-period predictions lack these virtues.

The trouble is that long-term forecasts must be made. The action of some agent today often puts some constraint on his behavior in the future. He must have some conception of the circumstances to be faced in the future in order to evaluate the wisdom of the present decision. Otherwise he is acting on either pure whim or an ill-founded belief in predestination. Firms, governments, and individuals constantly face decisions which are affected by the prospects of the future. If these agents have some clear-cut objectives which these decisions aim to secure, then the decisions *must* rest on at least implicit forecasts of the future. Given the objectives, a particular decision is not likely to be optimal except for a small range of the many possible sets of events which can subsequently happen. Granting the logical necessity of a forecast, implicit or explicit, one need not be a child of the Age of Reason to believe that better-laid plans will result if the forecast is explicit and prepared with reasonable care. This is true even if best-laid schemes "gang aft agley."

This point can bear the stress of a few examples, because it provides the central justification for long-range forecasting. Consider the firm deciding on the location of a new plant. One location will prove, over the lifetime of the plant, to have been better than another only if labor market conditions, transportation cost, location of markets, and power and raw material supplies all work out in the future as expected when the decision was made. Any sort of capital investment, whether public or private, involves a similar set of assumptions. A public power project, a municipal water plant, an improvement in harbor facilities, a rapid transit system — all projects of this sort require some estimate of future conditions.

When capital is committed without explicit recognition of the forecasting problem, usually the decision is based on only present-day conditions. It is not uncommon for some projects, for example, public schools, to be built to meet current, rather than future, needs. But even in this case it is clear that a school district's decision to build for today's classes is the wisest decision only if tomorrow's classes are duplicates or near-duplicates of today's.

We are left in the position, then, of recognizing that a great many private and public policy decisions involve at least implicit estimates of future conditions. Once this proposition is granted, there can be no question that one is better off to attempt careful forecasts of these conditions rather than merely to make some casual assumptions. Since even an imperfect forecast is likely to be better than no forecast at all, the errors that are virtually certain to appear in the projections can be tolerated.

However, the useful long-range forecast of an entire economy should do more than provide estimates of the gross national product and its components, the output of individual industries, the regional distribution of income, and so on. A careful forecast must also establish the causal relations among the economic variables which go into the prediction. In order to estimate the extent and direction of economic change, one is forced to seek out the causes of economic change so that the guesswork can be minimized. The understanding of the determinants of economic change is not only necessary for intelligent forecasting but also more valuable, perhaps, than the forecasts of the economic magnitudes themselves. The specific forecasts will probably be out of date after a few years. But the analysis of economic growth should provide the knowledge and insight which can be applied to the appraisal of the significance of developments which throw off the forecast of the economic magnitudes.

The purpose of this long-range forecast of the Canadian economy, then, is really twofold. It is intended to project a picture of the Canadian economy several years hence: to be specific, in 1970. But a prerequisite to such a forecast is an understanding of the causes of Canadian economic growth. So we will attempt to explain the historical development of the Canadian economy in order to assess more accurately the importance and role of the causal factors which will shape Canada through the 1960's. The framework of the analysis can thus be used to up-date the specific projections as this becomes necessary in the future.

The selection of 1970 as the target year is largely arbitrary. The Royal Commission on Canada's Economic Prospects (the Gordon Commission) was set up in 1955 and concentrated on Canadian development to 1980. A twenty-five-year time span is, of course, more unwieldy than a ten- or fifteen-year span, and on this count 1970 is preferable to 1980 as a target year. Presumably, too, because of the greater uncertainty surrounding the more distant years, more individuals and firms and government units will be interested in a forecast for 1970 than for 1980.

For these same reasons a 1965 forecast would be more desirable than one for 1970. But because the study was initiated to provide a background for long-term capital budgeting, we concentrate on long-run forces. As the projection span is shortened the cyclical forces become more important relative to the secular forces. In order to focus on long-run development, then, we have chosen to project to 1970.

The 1970 estimates do not take into account the probable status of the business cycle in that year. Rather the forecasts are to be interpreted as estimates of trend values for 1970. So even if the forecasts do yield accurate trend values for that year, the actual magnitudes may be above or below the trend depending on whether boom or recession conditions are operative.

Predicting trend values rather than actual values for the economic variables in 1970 means that the accuracy of the estimates cannot be evaluated until well after 1970. No one can ascertain for the current year what the trend value of, say, the gross national product might be. Data for at least some future years as well as the past years are required to estimate the actual trend. Nevertheless, the "sustainable level" or "trend value" is a more useful and presumably more reliable figure for any economic variable than in the cyclical value. It is paradoxical that this trend value should be more useful for private and public long-range planning in spite of its being less realistic than the cyclical value.

This study was begun in the summer of 1955 for the Canadian Pacific Railway Company. Its goal was to furnish guidance for the firm's investment decisions. Its end product was to be an estimate of the demand for transportation in Canada in 1970, deduced from a comprehensive estimate of the volume and location of economic activity in that year. The reports which were subsequently submitted to the Canadian Pacific form the basis for Part II of the present volume. They have since been shorn of a good deal of detail and bolstered with the academic armor of analytical and historical material. However, many of our numerical estimates, including the crucial population and income forecasts, have not required changing since their conception. Some of them are approaching the age of three years, fortunately without having grown grotesque in the eyes of their creators. The historical analysis of Part I was written more recently, although we reached the conclusions set forth there in the early days of plotting our forecasting strategy.

Interest in the future of the Canadian economy is now great both inside and outside of Canada. Our glances into the crystal ball of Canada's future have often met nothing but the refracted stares of other forecasters. The most determined of these have been the members of the staff of the Royal Commission on Canada's Economic Prospects, which was officially charged with the task of producing comprehensive forecasts of the economy's future. These, it turned out, differ little from our own either in scope or in specific conclusions. In preparing our forecasts we had access to a quantity of useful material contained in submissions to the commission. Our statistical estimates, however, were made entirely independently of the commission's work, which has been appearing in the form of reports and staff studies only as our manuscripts reached the final stages of revision. Thus it is that only a few isolated portions of the Royal Commission's final product have served as grist for the present study. Perhaps it is only fair to indicate why we have brought our product into the market place when the Royal Commission's wares are already available, especially since their labors were sustained by a budget approximately 100 times as large as our own. We feel able to claim two advantages to be placed against the breadth and thoroughness of the commission's information-gathering efforts. First, our work makes much more elaborate use of cross-checks for internal consistency. Second, we have been much more explicit than the commission in pinning our outlook for the future onto our interpretation of Canada's past.

Nonetheless, the scarcity of resources available for the present project forced some conscious optimizing behavior upon its authors. It is safe to say that no fact about the Canadian economy is totally irrelevant to such an extensive effort as appears below. The available resources for marshalling these facts, however, were distinctly limited. They were limited first by the budget allowed by the supporting agency, the Canadian Pacific Railway Company, and later by the time the authors could let elapse before some of the material became hopelessly outdated. We have tried to equate the marginal productivity of effort in the various lines of inquiry, giving the most attention to keystone estimates and to those less essential variables for which past experience seems to contain clear-cut lessons for the future. The same limited-resources problem affects the final form in which our results are presented. The advancement of knowledge would no doubt benefit if all published empirical studies enjoyed the "reproducibility" properties of Raymond Goldsmith's recent work on saving in the United States. This involves presenting basic data and methodology in enough detail that an alert and determined reader could reproduce on his own the study's results. Alas, this is terribly expensive in publishing costs, as Goldsmith's study again shows. We have tried to indicate clearly our data sources and the general nature of our assumptions throughout. Not nearly all of the detail involved in calculating individual forecasts is presented, however.

Several procedural matters remain to be mentioned. The authors have collaborated to some degree on nearly all parts of the study. However, primary responsibility can be indicated for all chapters, though a few are nearly inseparable joint products. Mr. Caves is primarily responsible for Chapters 2 through 4, 7 through 9, 11, 13, 14, and 17, as well as the final versions of 10, 12, and 15. Mr. Holton, who originally planned the methodology of the projections and organized the project, has taken principal charge of Chapters 1, 5, 6, 16, and 18 through 20.

To reduce the space occupied by footnotes and bibliography we have made regular use throughout the study of the following abbreviations:

AER   *American Economic Review*
CJAE   *Canadian Journal of Agricultural Economics*
CJEPS   *Canadian Journal of Economics and Political Science*
EJ   *Economic Journal*
JASA   *Journal of the American Statistical Association*
JPE   *Journal of Political Economy*
LE   *L'Actualité économique*
OEP   *Oxford Economic Papers*
QJE   *Quarterly Journal of Economics*
RES   *Review of Economics and Statistics*
DBS   Dominion Bureau of Statistics (Canada)
RCCEP   Royal Commission on Canada's Economic Prospects
RCDPR   Royal Commission on Dominion-Provincial Relations

The last two abbreviations are used even when they appear in the titles of publications, for reasons which will be obvious to any browser of the bibliography.

We have run up a heavy overdraft of debts during the preparation of this volume. The first and foremost is to the Canadian Pacific Railway, whose executives not only provided financial support but also made a patient, interested, and effectively critical audience for the results. The second major debt is to John A. Pincus, who served as a full-fledged collaborator in the early stages of the work. He was to have been a co-author of the final volume, but other commitments have kept him from lending a hand. Countless individuals in Ottawa have been of assistance at critical points; we are particularly indebted to John A. Sawyer of the Dominion Bureau of Statistics and to O. J. Firestone of the Department of Trade and Commerce. We have told our troubles at various times to members of the staff of the Royal Commission on Canada's Economic Prospects, especially William C. Hood, S. S. Reisman, David W. Slater, and Anthony D. Scott; and to colleagues attached to the Canadian Pacific project — John Kenneth Galbraith, John D. Black, John R. Meyer, John Stenason (all of Harvard University), and David L. MacFarlane of Macdonald College, McGill University. The School of Business Administration and the Bureau of Business and Economic Research of the University of California, Berkeley, have assisted in typing the final manuscripts. Constance M. Holton edited the manuscript and improved it markedly. She also served admirably as emergency typist, a fate familiar to so many academic wives.

Finally, we should acknowledge a broad if amorphous debt to Canada itself. Canadians have long lamented their drab reputation on the international scene, resulting from their conspicuous shortage of revolutions, cabinet crises, Communists, and quaint peasant costumes. As non-Canadians setting out to crack an effective home-market monopoly in Canadian economic research, we have been continually gratified by the good sense and good statistics generally prevailing north of the border. And we take no offense at the persistent refusal of our United States colleagues to believe that we were not Canadian-born. All peoples, of course, have certain conceits and preconceptions; the Canadians are no exception. The principal form these take in Canadian economic research circles is what we have come to think of as Great Canadian Clichés, a handful of phrases worn smooth by the ceaseless washing of economic harangue. We have attempted to use each of these exactly once in the present volume.

R. E. C.
R. H. H.

Berkeley, California

CONTENTS

FIGURES

TABLES

PART I
RETROSPECT

I

The Problem of Long-Range
Forecasting

Prediction in either the natural sciences or the social sciences is possible only because of the stability of cause and effect relations among the variables with which the fields are concerned. But there is a vast difference in the degree of this stability in the two fields. In the social sciences prediction is possible only because people are likely to behave in the future more or less as they have behaved in the recent past. If they were to behave exactly as they have behaved in the past, social scientists would have a much easier time of it. But one of the prime distinctions between the fields of, say, chemistry and economics is that in the former the raw materials consist of the elements whose behavior is eminently stable, whereas the raw material of the latter consists largely of human beings, whose behavior is shaped by various factors the effect of which is not wholly predictable. The chemist is almost certain how oxygen will react when introduced into an atmosphere of hydrogen in a ratio of one to two by volume at standard temperature and pressure and then ignited. The economist, on the other hand, has only a crude idea as to how the work force participation rate in Canada would react to, say, a sustained drop of 5 per cent in the national income in the mid-1960's. He may know what happened to this rate the last time the national income dropped 5 per cent or he may know how the rate has behaved in other countries in the past. But this information has limited predictive value. (The chemist would face the same difficulty as the social scientist if to form water one atom of oxygen were to combine with two atoms of hydrogen today in Canada, with one in 1965 in Canada, and with four in Scandinavia!) Were social scientists ever to develop a scheme comparable to the chemists' table of atomic weights so that human responses to given stimuli could be predicted with accuracy, economists and sociologists would most assuredly face mass unemployment, and the task of drawing up long-range economic projections could be satisfactorily relegated to the less competent of the statistical clerks.

Even if the impact of one economic variable on another, such as the increase in per capita income on the demand for meat, were highly predictable, economic forecasts would still be less than fully accurate. Many economic variables are shaped by noneconomic forces, witness the political influences which determine the nature and extent of taxes, tariffs, and subsidies. The decision to maintain a large-scale defense establishment, for example, has an obvious effect on the pattern of industrial output, yet this decision is based on many noneconomic factors. Unless one is an adamant defender of economic determinism, one must admit that a country's economic future is the result of countless noneconomic forces.

Thoroughly reliable economic forecasting, then, clearly requires prediction of noneconomic as well as economic behavior since the former affects the latter. And since no nation is completely and permanently isolated from other nations, the economic future of any single nation can be affected by economic and noneconomic developments outside its boundaries. A long-range economic forecast for any country, therefore, is based ultimately on a forecast of the political and economic behavior of other countries as well. This puts the economist in the embarrassing position of having to predict everything in order to predict anything.

Painted in these colors, the task of long-range economic forecasting appears more formidable than it really is. The economic future is the result of countless forces and it is well to recognize this as a fact. But there is a degree of consistency in human behavior which does make it possible to predict. If it were otherwise there would be no such field as the social "sciences." What we must do is utilize the limited degree of consistency we find in cause and effect relations to construct a long-range forecast. For the central problem remains: a long-range economic forecast is unavoidable as a preliminary step for many kinds of decisions. We must work out what we consider the "most probable" picture of the economy for the target year, stressing always the causality of economic growth as well as the final estimates themselves.

Kuznets has noted that one of the major problems in economic projections rests on the absence of a satisfactory theory of the economic growth of nations. We do not have "a tested theory of the economic growth of nations which demonstrates that long-term changes in national product invariably follow a specific pattern expressible by a given curve; that this pattern is securely founded upon a causal explanation that traces it to underlying factors that in turn display persistent patterns of change — say, trends as clear-cut and as invariant as in the growth processes of a biological species." [1] Forecasts go wrong because we are aware only of *some* of the causal relations in the growth process. Only if we knew with precision the relations between dependent and independent variables and only if we knew the laws of growth of the independent variables would we have a really satisfactory theory of economic development.

Statistical analysis of historical time series tries to establish the relation between dependent and independent variables so that at least pieces of a theory of economic growth can be identified. But the student of economic growth needs always to remind himself that a high correlation between A and B establishes only that the data are not inconsistent with the hypothesis that A has caused B in the past. Using the relation as a basis for prediction presumes not only that the relation historically has been a causal one but also that no new factors determining the level of B will arise to swamp the effect of A. A really complete theory of growth not only would explain why any such new factors might arise, but also would provide a framework for predicting whether they actually would appear.

One of the great difficulties caused by the lack of a generalized theory of economic growth concerns the relevance of available historical data. Suppose that variables A and B show a distinct and stable relation to each other for the period 1900–1940 but that since the end of World War II the relation has shifted. Which set of coefficients is going to apply for the period of the projection? If one thinks of economic growth as the result of relations which are stable for long periods of time, then the postwar data might be considered as short-term aberrations. But

[1] Simon Kuznets, "Concepts and Assumptions in Long-Term Projections of National Product," in Conference on Research in Income and Wealth, National Bureau of Economic Research, *Long-Range Economic Projection* (Princeton, N.J., 1954), p. 13.

on the other hand the new pattern may be far more applicable than the long-run pattern simply because it does reflect circumstances closer in time to the target year. The problem is essentially one of determining whether the current data reflect only short-run changes or indicate a change in the direction of trend.

This dilemma is familiar to anyone who has attempted even casual long-range projections and it need not be belabored here. It does serve to underscore the importance of viewing economic projection as an exercise in the rationale of growth rather than simply a matter of curve-fitting. When the researcher is faced with this problem he must compare the theory of growth which apparently fits the 1900–1940 data with the theory which is suitable to the postwar experience. Has there really been a structural change in the system? Or can he switch to a broader, more general model which covers both cases? Much of the value of the forecast lies in this search for proper causal explanations — at least as much as in the magnitude of the actual forecasts.

THE ASSUMPTIONS

We have stressed that innumerable variables conceptually should be taken into account in a long-range forecast, and that forecasting really requires a projection of a multitude of non-economic as well as economic forces. One means of simplifying this overwhelming problem is to make the prediction contingent on the assumption that certain conditions will prevail in the future rather than to attempt an absolute forecast, an absolute forecast being one which includes forecasts of all conditions surrounding the economic projection. For example, we will assume in this study that no major war will occur before 1970. This is in the nature of an assumption rather than a forecast. But we must agree with Kuznets that such a tactic may not be cricket.[2] The forecaster is supposedly setting forth what he considers to be the combination of circumstances which seems most likely to prevail in the target year. If he chooses to assume that no war will intervene, he is really forecasting the absence of war without justifying the forecast. This can be interpreted as cheating a bit, perhaps, but the only alternative is an impossibly ponderous and at least partially amateurish study. The basic fact is that there are some matters on which the economist simply does not wish to

---

[2] Kuznets, p. 20.

prepare forecasts because they lie outside his discipline. Consequently, he merely makes assumptions about these matters with a minimum of justification.

The assumed level of employment

Of the many assumptions which one must make in order to draw up a long-range forecast of Canadian economic growth, none needs more careful examination than that involving the level of employment. The estimated size of the gross national product in 1970 can vary over a wide range depending on whether high-level employment is anticipated with only minor interruptions over the intervening years or whether some intermediate pattern combining prosperous periods and depressed years is assumed.

A multitude of alternative patterns of prosperity and depression could be established for the span. These alternative patterns might vary not only in the timing and magnitude of the departures from full employment; they might differ also in origin and nature. It is conceivable that an individual sector might be depressed while the rest of the economy operates nearly at capacity. Such was the case in the 1920's when agriculture was depressed but the rest of the economy was enjoying prosperity. An extended slump in construction in the United States and Canada might retard the forest and forest products industries in Canada more than other industries. Or a capital goods recession might slow the development of central Canada more than the development of British Columbia.

Because there are an infinite number of variations of boom and slump which might be assumed and because it is an ambitious task to develop more than one detailed model of the 1970 economy with the resources available for this study, a single assumption about the level of employment is used throughout this report. We assume that a high level of employment will be obtained in most but not all of the period to 1970; that over-full employment will be rare; that minor recessions, including inventory recessions, will occur, and that they will cause but brief departures from high employment levels. Thus, Canadian industries are not expected on the average to maintain for the coming years a rate of growth quite as rapid as that experienced since the end of the war.

In other words, the projections of the following chapters anticipate no serious or extended departure from high employment levels. Mild cyclical fluctuations in the level of business activity are likely, however. Since the end of the war, cycles roughly three years in length have been common in the advanced countries. Among the several causes of these cycles have been the fluctuations in inventory levels. Inventories may be built up in anticipation of sales levels which do not materialize, bringing on mild recessions during which firms attempt to work off their excess stocks. Since these inventory fluctuations seem to influence the periodicity of the cycles which have appeared since the end of the war, we can anticipate that something like these three-year cycles is probably going to operate during the period covered by the forecast.

However, it might be repeated that in estimating the 1970 gross national product we have not attempted to determine whether an inventory boom or inventory recession will be experienced in that year. The projections to 1970 should be considered as estimates on the trend line rather than as estimates of the cyclical values above or below that trend line.

This high-level employment assumption is not only the simplest assumption which can be made, it also seems to be the most easily justified. The level of national income in the developed countries is now recognized as subject to some degree of manipulation by means of monetary and fiscal policy. The experience and attitude of the United States is at least as relevant here as that of Canada, not only because most policies employed in the United States can also be used in Canada but also because the level of national income in the United States is an important determinant of the level of business activity in Canada. The United States now has had more than ten years of experience with the Employment Act of 1946 in which for the first time Congress clearly recognized that the policies of government should be directed toward maintaining a high level of employment. Considering the vociferous objections to government intervention in economic affairs in the United States in the 1930's, the acceptance of the basic objectives of the 1946 Employment Act in the 1950's is truly impressive. That the government can and should institute policies which encourage stability and growth is now a wholly reasonable view to the business community in the United States, and the debate concerns only the various alternative methods which might be instituted. There is particular concern over avoiding continually rising prices in the face of full employment. But the basic proposition that we can, through public policy, avoid extended depressions seems widely accepted by business leaders.[3]

The government of Canada also took as a "primary object of policy" the maintenance of "a high and stable level of employment and income" in an April 1945 white paper. The Canadian business community has widely and readily accepted this point of view, as evidenced by the attitude of the Conservatives toward public spending during the 1957 recession.

However, in spite of the presence of these strong indications that the governments of Canada and the United States can *and will* so react during periods of falling income as to revive the economy, this proposition has not as yet faced a severe test. We cannot be positive that the possible recovery measures would be strong enough or would be instituted soon enough to prevent a depression of some magnitude. But the very existence of the belief that conscious policy can halt depressions helps to maintain the business community's confidence and thus increases the likelihood that long-run investment plans will not be altered by fluctuations in the short-run outlook. Furthermore, our experience of the last twenty years would seem to argue for the plausibility of this belief.

Unfortunately, Canada can apply monetary and fiscal measures less successfully to avoid extended periods of low income and employment. Being an open economy, she is highly sensitive to the export market. If the United States and the United Kingdom, Canada's big customers, fail to maintain high employment levels, Canada's employment is put under particularly great pressure. Therefore, our high-level employment assumption for Canada really presumes that the United States and the United Kingdom will for the most part succeed in maintaining a high level of income over the period of our forecast. Again, the experience of the

[3] See, for example, Gerhard Colm, ed., *The Employment Act Past and Future, A Tenth Anniversary Symposium* (Washington, 1956), particularly the statements by Harry A. Bullis, Chairman of the Board, General Mills, Inc.; Meyer Kestnbaum, President, Hart Schafner and Marx, Inc.; Fred Lazarus, Jr., President, Federated Department Stores, Inc.; and Herman W. Steinkraus, President, Bridgeport Brass Company.

last fifteen years seems to indicate that this assumption is more readily justified than any of the infinite number of employment-level patterns one might assume for these two countries.

A final reason for working with what may seem an optimistic employment level assumption involves Canada's unique position among the high income countries of the world. The nation's rate of growth may give it a buoyancy which helps it weather recessions more successfully than mature countries with weaker pressures for growth. In 1949, for example, the Canadian gross national product rose by about 4 per cent in the face of a 1 per cent *drop* in United States output.

Other assumptions

The 1970 forecasts of this study have been drawn up presuming that there would be no major war but that continuing international tensions would cause defense expenditures to remain at their present levels in terms of dollars, shrinking as a proportion of the gross national product. This would not exclude a minor war such as the Korean affair was to Canada. If an outbreak of this sort were to occur before 1970, then the high-level employment assumption would prove all the more justified. Such an outbreak would not only raise defense expenditures in the United States and the United Kingdom, causing an expanded demand for Canadian minerals, but it would also raise Canada's own defense expenditures, putting a strain on the country's manufacturing capacity.

It is also presumed that there will be no wave of trade restrictions sweeping across the world in the next decade or so, although there may be some slight movement toward freer trade in some commodities between some countries. This is saying only that we anticipate on balance some advance toward removal of trade restrictions of all sorts, but the extent of the change may not be significant for Canada. The impact of the European Common Market plan and the related Free Trade Area, although significant for the member countries and for some outside countries as well, will not be especially great for Canada. Her volume of trade with the Common Market countries is small and her United Kingdom trade consists primarily of raw materials and semimanufactured goods unlikely to be greatly affected by the proposed regional freeing of trade.

That trade restrictions will not be increased follows in part from our assumption that high-level employment will be the rule in the major industrial countries. More precisely, if a country is able to maintain a high level of employment by means of monetary and fiscal policy, it need not resort to trade restrictions to keep its domestic industry busy. Rather than to attempt a justification of this assumption at this point, it might be wiser to indicate briefly how the conclusion of this report should be altered were the assumption to prove erroneous.

If trade barriers were to be raised in the world before 1970, the primary products export industries (agriculture excepted) would probably suffer least. Import restrictions generally are applied to manufactured goods rather than raw materials because the country instituting the controls wishes to perform its own processing of raw materials. Since foreign countries are less likely to find new sources of raw materials than means of processing them, trade restrictions abroad are more likely to reduce Canada's exports of manufactures than her exports of raw materials. Agriculture should probably be excluded from this statement, however. Protectionist measures applied to agricultural commodities may become more rather than less common because the pressure on world agricultural prices caused by surpluses in the United States and Canada may force more countries to devise means of insulating their farmers from low world prices. If trade restrictions were to increase, then, one would expect Canada's primary producers to be hurt least, her manufacturers (and processors of local raw materials) to be hurt most, and the Canadian producers of import-competing goods might benefit the most. The latter conclusion follows if one considers that reduced Canadian exports will so affect exchange rates as to raise the price of imports. The import-competing producers would also benefit because labor and other resources released from the depressed export industries could be available at lower prices than if the export industries were booming.

If, on the other hand, freer trade were to prevail, the manufacturing industries selling part of their output on the world market would be affected more than raw material producers. Again this is based on the notion that imposition or relaxation of trade barriers is likely to influence the flow of manufactured goods more than the flow of raw materials. If trade barriers are lowered,

Canadian producers of import-competing goods may suffer a good bit as the increased flow of Canadian exports leads to greater imports.

With respect to government policies, other than those already discussed, and their impact on the country's growth, we assume few significant changes. There is no doubt that if Ottawa were to wish it, the rate and nature of Canadian development could be altered by public policy. The nation's history provides so many illustrations of this point that they need not be reviewed here. It is assumed that there will be no new, large subsidy program applied to any major industry nor will the tax structure be altered to retard or accelerate the growth of any major industry significantly. Thus the projections assume that no government encouragement of any development ventures of the magnitude of the railway networks or the St. Lawrence Seaway will be forthcoming before 1970. Our only justification for this assumption is that no projects of such magnitude are now being discussed and the planning and construction time on such projects is generally so long as to preclude completion, by 1970, of any massive schemes not yet contemplated.

The assumptions that employment will hold to a high level and that international tensions will continue give rise to forecasting problems which deserve some special attention. We have noted that economic projections are based on the continuity between the past and the future; only if there is such continuity is the experience of the past relevant in forecasting the future. By positing that the defense budget will remain large and that a high level of employment will be maintained, we are setting up conditions which have not been encountered, except for brief periods, in Canada's past. The relevance, then, of past experience must be examined. What new problems are likely to arise because of these assumptions?

The most obvious problem is that of chronic inflation. Although it is conceivable that public policy can now be designed to maintain employment at high average levels, it is not clear that this can be achieved without a secular increase in the price level. The evidence points in the opposite direction. The accepted means for dealing with inflation, instituting fiscal and monetary measures, have been notably unsuccessful. It can be argued that they have not been used vigorously enough, that Ottawa failed to run a surplus sufficiently large or that the Bank of Canada failed to set the structure of interest rates high enough. Yet from January 1956 to August 1957 the yield on three-month treasury bills rose from 2.6 per cent to 4.0 per cent and the federal government ran a budget surplus of about $280,000,000 in fiscal 1957 on total expenditures of about $4,900,000,000. Despite these strong actions the consumer price index rose in the same one and one-half year period from 116.8 to 122.6.

It is commonly argued that the usual anti-inflationary measures will not work because the inflation of recent years has been "different." Generally it is stressed that the inflation stems not from an excess of market demand but rather that it is a "cost-push" inflation or "wage" inflation or a "wage-profits" inflation. In its simplest terms, the argument runs thus. Even when aggregate demand is just sufficient to support full employment, wage increases are likely to be granted by employers because the cost increases can be passed on as price increases. With little market restraint on wage increases, unions are tempted to ask for wage increases without regard for productivity increases. Employers will announce price increases forthwith, using the wage increase as an excuse but raising prices sufficiently to cover the increases in nonwage costs as well. With these price increases built into the price structure in the entire economy, the cost of living rises, providing the basis for another wage increase, and so on.[4]

We need not dwell on the causes of inflation here. It is necessary only to realize that inflation is likely to be a recurring problem, regardless of the exact nature of the causality, simply because a high employment level is likely to be a primary goal of public policy. But we must devote some attention to the effect of "creeping inflation" on the pattern of Canadian economic growth.

A major objection to inflation is the resulting redistribution

[4] It has been suggested that in a full employment economy inflation will result even if the wage increases in manufacturing do no more than match the productivity increases in the manufacturing industries. Such increases touch off parallel wage increases in other industries, especially distribution and the services, in which productivity is not increasing as rapidly as in manufacturing. So the labor costs per unit of output may remain stable in manufacturing but rise in other industries, thus necessitating price increases. See "Inflationary Stability," *The Economist*, 181:878–879 (December 8, 1956).

of income. Fixed income recipients see their real income fall; creditors lose and debtors gain. But the dangers go beyond the redistribution effect. Thrift is supposedly discouraged because the purchasing power of savings declines continuously. Inflation gives rise to speculation in assets, especially land, and price rises cause further price rises. Exports drop if the exchange rate is pegged; otherwise the currency depreciates in response to balance of payments troubles, feeding the forces of inflation. At the very worst, the type of inflation encountered by Germany in 1921–1923 is envisioned, leading to thorough currency reform and perhaps rigid controls until the economy is readjusted.

But the galloping inflation of postwar Germany went so much further than one involving a price level rising at 1 or 2 per cent per year as to constitute a difference in kind rather than degree. Hansen has suggested that we distinguish between moderate price increases, which may be only an "expansionary force," and what he proposes we call "pure inflation," meaning price level increases which appear without any corresponding increase in physical output. He argues that the economy and the general welfare are not likely to be injured if the increase in aggregate output exceeds the increase in prices.[5] He would view moderate price increases as a permissible means of encouraging continued expansion of the economy. He suggests that in an emergency a percentage increase in prices greater than the percentage increase in output might be wise if it is necessary as a means of avoiding a depression.

Is a moderate annual increase in the price level likely to discourage personal saving? If the decision to save is viewed as a decision to buy future goods rather than present goods, then the effect of a steadily rising price level is to raise the expected prices of future goods relative to present goods, so saving is discouraged and the percentage of income spent on current consumption increases. But this line of reasoning, frequently used implicitly if not explicitly, presumes that the demand for future goods has more than unit elasticity with respect to price or that the savings cannot be held in the form of claims the monetary value of which

---

[5] Alvin H. Hansen, *The American Economy* (New York, 1957), p. 43. For a similar view and an excellent rebuttal to the argument that "creeping" inflation is evil, see Sumner H. Slichter, "On the Side of Inflation," *Harvard Business Review*, 35:15–36, 162–170 (September-October 1957).

moves upward with the price level. If such claims are available as an investment outlet for savings, then moderate inflation does not increase the price of future goods relative to present goods. Furthermore, if the demand for future goods is inelastic, the threat of continually rising prices may cause the individual to increase his rate of savings. This is particularly likely to hold in the case of saving for retirement, for education of one's children, and for similar purposes with high priority.

Evidence on the effect of expected inflation on the level of saving seems to indicate that inflation may change the attitude toward saving very little if at all. It is not even clear that people hasten their purchases of goods if they are expecting price increases in the near future.[6] Goldsmith's outstanding study of saving in the United States has concluded that saving rates have been generally insensitive to extended declines in the purchasing power of the dollar.[7] A recent study of the impact of income taxes on incentives also sheds some light on this problem. G. F. Break has reported that about as many respondents in his sample of self-employed in England reported that they were working harder because of income taxes as reported that they were working less.[8] If one looks on continuous moderate inflation as having the effect of an income tax on that portion of income reserved for

[6] See Robert Ferber, "The Role of Planning in Consumer Purchases of Durable Goods," *AER,* 44:854–874 (December 1954), especially pp. 865 and 871; John B. Lansing and Stephen B. Withey, "Consumer Anticipations: Their Use in Forecasting Consumer Behavior," pp. 381–453 in Conference on Research in Income and Wealth, National Bureau of Economic Research, *Short-Term Economic Forecasting* (Princeton, N.J., 1955), pp. 400–402; L. R. Klein and J. B. Lansing, "Decisions to Purchase Consumer Durable Goods," *Journal of Marketing,* 20:109–132 (October 1955), especially pp. 113 and 115. Ferber found more purchase plans among those who expected prices to fall than among those who did not expect lower prices, but among those respondents who had actually fulfilled their plans to buy appliances the fulfillment of major plans seemed greater among those planners who expected price increases than among other planners. Lansing and Withey found little relation between price expectations and plans to buy. Klein and Lansing found downward price expectations were associated with relatively frequent buying of durables for spending units earning less than $3000, but in income groups above $3000 those respondents expecting prices to go up were more likely to buy durables than those who expected prices to drop.

[7] Raymond Goldsmith *et al., A Study of Saving in the United States* (Princeton, 1955), Vol. I, p. 22.

[8] G. F. Break, "Income Taxes and Incentives to Work: An Empirical Study," *AER,* 47:729–549 (September 1957).

future spending, Break's study indicates the distinct possibility that the prospect of inflation may motivate people to work more in order to maintain some rate of saving.

It seems certain that the form in which savings are held would be altered by continuous moderate inflation, as savers would turn toward the equity capital and away from fixed obligations. But this is saying only that contractual interest rates will rise if moderate inflation is taken for granted.

Since inflation penalizes creditors to the benefit of the debtors, the rational consumer might choose to go into debt more readily to buy consumer durables. Consumer debt, then, might stand at a higher level relative to current income than would be the case in the absence of inflation. The higher interest rate accompanying inflation would partially offset this influence, not because consumers would be conscious of the higher interest cost of debt but rather because they would see the monthly payments swell to cover the higher interest payments.[9] The greater repayment of debt, being a form of saving, could serve to keep the rate of saving at least as high as in the absence of inflation.

Corporate saving in the national income accounts consists of depreciation charges plus retained earnings. In any particular year that depreciation charges are given, dividends depend primarily on an historical percentage pay-out or absolute dividends per share, leaving corporate retained earnings as the difference between the net sales and the operating costs plus dividends and taxes. So the current price level clearly affects current corporate saving through its influence on the level of sales. But we need to know whether the level of corporate saving is influenced by price *expectations*. We must isolate the effect of expectations on the general price level, forgetting about the relative price of the firm's product. The expectation of a rising price level will buoy up the firm's profit outlook, lifting the marginal efficiency of capital in monetary, though not real, terms. The firm's investment expenditures may, therefore, run at a slightly higher level than they would if stable prices were expected. However, it has been established now that the Keynesian argument that the level of investment depends on the marginal efficiency of capital and the rate of interest is incomplete. The role of the rate of interest has been

[9] See Jean Mann Due, "Consumer Knowledge of Installment Credit Charges," *Journal of Marketing*, 20:162–166 (October 1955).

questioned for some time since such a high proportion of corporate investment expenditures is financed by internal funds subject
only to in-pocket interest costs.[10] In a recent study, Meyer and
Kuh have found that the most common factor limiting investment on the upturn has been the availability of internal funds.[11]
It may be, then, that the effect of inflation is to bring firms up
against this investment ceiling a bit sooner than in the absence of
inflation. In the expectation of brighter profit prospects and rising replacement costs, firms may attempt to hold down their
dividend pay-out in order to have the internal funds needed for
replacement and expansion. On balance, then, it would seem most
realistic to expect corporate saving and investment expenditures
to run at slightly higher levels secularly if moderate inflation were
to continue.

The burden of the evidence on inflation and decisions to save
and to invest indicates that an annual increase in the price level
of 1 or 2 per cent is likely to affect either type of decision but
slightly, probably keeping investment and saving rates just a bit
higher than they otherwise would be. What about the redistributional effect of "creeping inflation"? Bach and Ando in a recent
article have shown that in the United States the inflation since
1939 has not decreased wage earners' share of the national income
and increased the share going to profits, as neoclassical business
cycle theory has indicated.[12] The authors argue that no significant
shift in the shares of the major functional groups has taken place
although within functional groups some subgroups have been
affected. Teachers, pensioners, and executives, for example, have
seen their incomes lag behind increases in the price level. Inflation has very definitely redistributed the burden of debts, however. Households have been penalized largely to the benefit of
government, the major debtor.

Yet another consequence of moderate price inflation might be
mentioned. The price-regulated industries, particularly the utilities, may suffer unless some means is found for adjusting rates

[10] For a summary discussion of current problems in investment theory, see
E. M. Hoover, "Some Institutional Factors in Business Investment Decisions,"
AER, 44:201–213 (May 1954).
[11] John R. Meyer and Edwin Kuh, *The Investment Decision* (Cambridge,
Mass., 1957).
[12] G. L. Bach and Albert Ando, "The Redistributional Effects of Inflation,"
RES, 39:1–12 (February 1957).

more quickly in accordance with increases in the price level. The development of "social overhead" capital facilities, then, may be slowed perceptibly if firms have difficulty raising capital funds for expansion because of poor earnings records.

Continuous but moderate inflation, therefore, seems unlikely to cause any serious distortions of the growth process. The decisions to save and to invest probably will not be greatly affected. The interest rate structure may well be higher than would otherwise be the case. Government interest expense would reflect the higher rates and investment portfolios would reflect the price level expectations. The redistributional effects would be of little importance to long-run growth.

To summarize, the assumptions discussed to this point are five: (1) that a high level of employment will generally be maintained; (2) that there will be no major war although the "cold war" will continue; (3) that there will be no wave of trade restrictions but instead a gradual freeing of trade; (4) that no large new governmental policies aimed at accelerating economic growth will be instituted; and (5) that any inflation will be moderate and will not affect the rate of development except insofar as it will help maintain a high level of employment.

The institutional environment

A sixth assumption deserves special attention. The forecast of this study presumes that the institutional environment in Canada will remain essentially unchanged. This condition calls for special comment, not because it is more problematical than the other assumptions, but because the character of the people and their way of thinking and of running their affairs is a critical factor in the development process in any country, and therefore warrants some discussion.

Resources have been the key to Canada's rapid economic growth, but without the efforts of an ambitious populace they would remain unexploited. Here indeed lies the great contrast between Canada and other areas of the globe with large reserves of unexploited resources. For British settlers planted in Canada an "acquisitive society" almost ideally suited for rapid economic development. It was largely lacking in the traditional rigidity and elaborate structure of its European parent, traits which (whatever their virtues) do not easily mold to the requirements of rapid economic change. Immigrants by definition are people willing to give up their old patterns of living for new opportunities. The migrant spirit has persisted in the willingness of Canadians to move west to newly opened wheat lands, or north to new mineral developments, or out of the Maritime provinces as economic opportunity there has become relatively restricted. Canadians have occasionally portrayed themselves as cautious curators of their great land area who have stood by while freewheeling foreign enterprise has seized the initiative in their economy.[13] Yet compared to other countries which have had the assistance of foreign capital, Canadians have been uniquely successful in first attracting the aid of foreign capital and then integrating it into the economy. Again, the reason for this lies in the character of Canada's population. Highly educated and with few cultural differences to isolate them from the populace of more mature economies, Canadians have faced no major bars in rising to high positions in foreign-established firms, learning skills imported from foreign technological reserves, and in participating in the ownership of foreign-built firms. Frequently ownership of individual business enterprises has shifted back and forth between Canadian and foreign control.[14] Thus, Canadians have not only been ambitious workers and bold enterprisers, they have also been able to attract from abroad and successfully integrate with their own efforts massive assistance in the tasks of economic development.

Analysts of Canadian character frequently contrast the desire of English-speaking Canadians for progress with French-speaking citizens' quest for stability in economic and social matters. This contrast itself illustrates the way the character of Canadian society has fostered economic development. No nation-wide economic enterprises are under predominantly French-speaking management, and indeed much of the natural resource development in Quebec province has been under English management. Most significant of all, it has been the English-speaking segment of the economy which has proved the dominant attraction over the years to non-English-speaking immigrants, who would not logically have any intrinsic preference for English-speaking over

[13] See, for example, A. R. M. Lower, *The North American Assault on the Canadian Forest* (New Haven, Conn., 1938) ; especially ch. xiii.
[14] N. Islam, "Studies in Foreign Capital and Economic Development," unpublished Ph.D. thesis, Harvard University, 1955.

French-speaking culture. Yet these two nationality groups, each making its unique cultural contribution, have been loyally "Canadian." [15]

As a nation, Canada is a geographic oddity, a thin line of settlements lying along the northern boundary of the United States. The difficulties of assembling a nation from these pieces became clear enough in the years immediately following Confederation, the union of Ontario and Quebec with New Brunswick and Nova Scotia in 1867. Canadians have at all subsequent times been in tacit agreement that they must maintain a "constructive nationalism" and a common striving to achieve national economic integration. This consensus has registered itself politically in such measures as the protectionist "National Policy" of the nineteenth century and the immigration restrictions of the twentieth. It explains that commonly cited paradox of Canadians' apparent conservatism in their dealings with the outside world in contrast to their boldness with respect to domestic social and economic development. Government enterprise in Canada, so frighteningly common to certain Americans, reflects not the Canadian's mistrust of private enterprise but his knowledge that when many of the tasks requisite to national economic development have presented themselves private enterprise has not yet been able to undertake them. By being "nationalistic" in these bloodless and nearly costless ways, Canadians have provided a strongly favorable climate for economic growth.

It is also important to look away from the economic behavior of individual Canadians to the effect on economic development of the total political and legal structure they have built. Politically, Canada has achieved both democracy and stability, successfully adapting to a relatively new country the institutions evolved in centuries of British experience. The resulting stability of the general legal and political framework has encouraged capital formation and economic development by giving business a stable environment in which to make long-run plans. There have never been periods of such open hostility between business and government in Canada as have occasionally plagued countries like the

[15] This would seem to be true despite the fact that Mayor Houde of Montreal was actually interned by the Canadian government in 1940 because of his outspoken opposition to conscription. It was apparent that Houde's sentiments were not shared by a very substantial portion of Quebec. See "Seizure of Houde Backed in Quebec," *The New York Times*, August 7, 1940, p. 4.

United States and United Kingdom. Beneath the level of such broad political considerations, many specific qualities of Canada's legal framework have encouraged long-run economic development. To mention just one of contemporary importance, the highly concentrated control of mineral rights in western oil lands in the hands of the provincial governments and a few large private landholders greatly enhances the chances of establishing a conservation policy to provide optimum long-run extraction policies for Canada's petroleum and natural gas resources.[16] In contrast, the United States' mineral rights situation was at least partly responsible for tragic waste of billions of barrels of crude oil in the 1930's and for the failure of that country ever to establish a "conservation" policy for crude oil and gas amounting to more than an awkward price-fixing scheme.

These very fortunate environmental circumstances have in large measure been responsible for the development of the Canadian economy. In projecting that country's growth to 1970, we are surely on safe ground in assuming that the institutions and attitude of the Canadians will continue to encourage development as they have in the past.

THE METHODOLOGY OF THE PROJECTIONS

Although some economic projections are found to have little explicit theoretical content, long-range forecasts imply some theory of economic growth. In the Canadian case we wish to take special pains to make clear the basic forces shaping economic growth. Indeed, as we have stressed earlier, we are at least as interested in this causality as in the projections themselves.

It is a well-known fact that Canadian economic history is the history of successive exploitation of various natural resources. First came the fisheries off her eastern coast and the fur-bearing animals in her forests. Permanent settlement later brought the agricultural land and forests of the St. Lawrence Valley into use. As the nineteenth century closed, a wheat economy sprang from the prairie soil. In the twentieth century, pulpwood joined saw-logs in the contribution of Canada's forests. Hydroelectric power was developed to assist all industrial processes. And vast mineral discoveries gave rise to a new boom as Canada's habit of discov-

---

[16] N. E. Tanner, "Petroleum Development," in L. B. Pearson, *et al.*, *Canada: Nation on the March* (Toronto, 1953).

ering her mineral wealth accidentally while building railroads
gave way to practices of systematic exploration.[17]

Canadian scholars have developed an able and comprehensive
explanation for these waves of natural resource exploitation and
their effects in the well-known staple theory of Canadian economic growth. The staple theory emphasizes the role of world
demand for resource-based Canadian products and discoveries of
resources and resource technology. It stresses the rapidity with
which resource development and general economic growth have
proceeded because export booms have attracted capital and population to Canada. Foreign capital has moved in to supplement
domestic saving at the same time that immigration has expanded
the labor force, providing a growing domestic market and pushing
back the frontier of settlement. In manifold ways resource development has supported growth of other segments of the economy
and thereby generated a "filling in" process which has made
Canada look less and less like a national mining operation. This
"filling in" process has manifested itself in roughly three ways,
listed in order of their historic importance. First, the increasing
number of Canadians — with increasing average per capita income — has supported a growth of consumer goods industries
much more steady than staple production or the general level of
business activity. Second, in almost all of Canada's lines of resource-based production for export, there has been a tendency
for an increased amount of processing to be performed in Canada before exportation takes place. Admittedly, the main stimulus
to this sort of development was the condition of strained facilities
abroad produced by World Wars I and II. Third, the high level
of saving and capital formation in Canada has given sporadic
stimulus to investment goods production at home. Here the
development has not been of a steady sort. Construction, of
course, is an industry which serves the domestic market and the
domestic market alone. But the producers of Canadian investment goods have not enjoyed any systematic change in fortunes
compared to their foreign competitors. This is not so much a
cause for alarm as a reflection of Canada's continued success at
profiting from an international division of labor. The "filling in"
process will always remain incomplete, because the industries en-

---

[17] See, for example, A. W. Currie, *Canadian Economic Development* (Toronto
1942).

couraged by staple export growth must compete against the staple industries themselves for Canada's factors of production. And barring catastrophic declines in foreign demand for Canada's exports the competing power of these industries will remain strong indeed.[18]

THE ORDER OF PROCEDURE

Within the framework of this general view of Canadian economic development, how can one proceed step-by-step to construct a forecast of the Canadian economy in 1970? Briefly stated, we start by estimating the total size of that economy in terms of its population and real gross national product (GNP). Then we proceed to more detailed estimates, filling in the structure and composition of this total amount of economic activity. As we proceed to sketch in these details, we develop numerous ways of checking the consistency of the details with one another and of testing the reasonableness of the original gross magnitudes, GNP and population.

In Part II of this volume, in which the actual projections are worked out, the first problem is to project Canada's population to 1970. Here we follow a methodology which has become standard in such projections. The birth rates among women in each age group are projected to 1970. These rates, combined with projected death rates and net immigration rates, provide the basis for the 1970 population estimate. The next step is to estimate the size of the work force in 1970 by applying estimated participation rates for each age group of men and women, again basing these rates on historical experience and expected departures from this experience.

This brings us to one of the various ways in which gross national product can be estimated. The simplest and most obvious method is based only on aggregate data and consists of applying to the estimated size of the 1970 work force a forecast of output per worker in that year. This requires a forecast of productivity per worker, again based on historical trends.[19] A second method

---

[18] Chapters 2 and 3 review in much greater detail selected long-run and short-run aspects of the staple theory.

[19] This is the method used by the United States President's Materials Policy Commission, *Resources for Freedom* (Washington, 1952), and by J. F. Dewhurst and Associates, *America's Needs and Resources, A New Survey* (New York, 1955).

of GNP forecasting, which is not likely to be entirely independent of the first, involves projecting the output of the individual industries in the economy to the target year, then estimating each industry's value added and summing these for all industries to reach an estimate of the GNP. A variant of this second method would be to project the value added for the individual industries directly. The disadvantages inherent in both of these approaches have necessitated a combination of the two methods, which fortunately turn out to yield almost identical results.

Possessing forecasts for Canadian population and GNP in 1970, plus the available body of historical evidence, we proceed to estimating the four major categories of final demand. Personal consumption expenditures can be estimated by combining our knowledge of the historic relation between consumption patterns, personal disposable income, and other variables with our estimate of personal disposable income and the age distribution of the Canadian population in 1970. Gross domestic investment is forecast by reconciling two different methods. The first works with the historical marginal capital-output ratio for the economy as a whole. The second projects the demand for various components of total investment (residential construction, machinery and equipment expenditures, and so forth). Government expenditures are forecast by various *ad hoc* procedures and the pattern of future foreign trade is developed from trends in world trade structure and the prospective income growth rates in Canada's major foreign markets. These estimates of final demand in 1970 appear in Chapters 10 through 13.

From the estimated pattern of final demand we next proceed to identifying the composition of industrial activity for 1970. What levels of output must emerge from each sector of the Canadian economy to satisfy the forecast volume of final demand? To answer this question we employ the interindustry table for Canada recently prepared by the Dominion Bureau of Statistics.[20] The exact nature of this table and its use are described in Chapter 14. Here we can indicate only the basic strategy, which was to extract the information the table conveys about the technology of Canadian production in 1949, project this information on the basis of technological trends in Canada and the United

[20] Canada, DBS, *The Inter-Industry Flow of Goods and Services, Canada, 1949* (Ottawa, 1956).

States, and finally transform it to allow computation of the industry outputs needed to supply our estimate of 1970 final demand.

This is one method for arriving at a forecast of the GNP and the industrial make-up of the economy. The alternative method, mentioned above, consists of projecting the output of the individual industries in the economy to the target year. Chapters 15 through 19 develop this approach, moving from the agricultural sector to the minerals, forestry, fisheries, manufacturing, and service industries. Developing this second set of industry projections has two main uses. First, it affords a check on the reasonableness of our over-all estimate of GNP, productivity growth, and the labor force. Second, it permits careful consideration of the probable influence of "supply" factors on 1970 industry outputs to see whether such forces as real cost trends and resource availabilities indicate that each industry will just supply the estimated 1970 demand, or whether it will tend to grow more or less rapidly than this demand would indicate.[21]

At least three basic methods for projecting the growth of the individual industries are available. Simple correlation using time as the independent variable (projection of trend) is the simplest but conceptually the least satisfactory method. It presumes that the complex of forces which actually have determined the rate of growth will all continue to behave with respect to time just as they have in the past. Simple correlation of the industry's output with some other independent variable is generally more satisfactory, and multiple correlation, in which the industry's growth is expressed as a function of two or more independent variables, generally is even more satisfactory if the data permit this type of analysis.

But even the latter method cannot be satisfactorily applied in some instances. It may be that an industry is too young for its output to show a reliable correlation with any set of variables. Or, if it has been systematically related to certain variables in the past, there may be good reason to think that the relation will not hold in the future. In Canada, where so many industries sell an important part of their output on the export market, this is particularly likely to be true. A change in a major buyer's tariff

---

[21] The meaning of this comparison for future relative prices in Canada is quite obvious.

or quota restrictions, a discovery of a competing source of a mineral, technological change which displaces a particular type of product (to say nothing of wars and depressions and the consequent distortions) — these are the kinds of disturbances which frequently obscure whatever basic relation one might except to find under more stable conditions. If any such changes are expected before the target year or if such changes have clouded the historical data, correlation may be of little help and one may have to rely heavily on a subjective appraisal of the probable importance of the forces which will work to alter the level of output of the industry in question.

Because various methods may be used for projecting the individual industries, one cannot be certain that the resulting forecasts for the separate sectors are consistent with each other. Perhaps the projected size of the steel industry, say, is too small considering the expected growth of all the steel-using industries. The check on this internal consistency of the sector projections is provided by the interindustry table, for in that table the projected sales of each industry to every other industry are shown explicitly. If a sector's output as projected by the industry-by-industry method does not agree with that sector's projected output in the interindustry table, either the projected input coefficients in the table are in error, or the projected sales of the sector in question to final buyers is off or else the forecast by the industry-by-industry method is wrong.

In this study we have not attempted to juggle the industry-by-industry estimates into identity with the industry estimates coming out of the interindustry table. Rather we have used the two methods as partial checks on each other, letting the sector approach illuminate the magnitude and direction of probable error in the interindustry table. This approach would seem to be more revealing and certainly more honest than any attempt to force the two methods to yield exactly the same forecasts.

Another virtue of the two-fold approach to the forecast lies in the check on the productivity estimates which it provides. The individual industry forecasts include employment estimates. These must sum to the estimated size of the work force as deduced from the projections of the population and the participation rates. If these two estimates are not consistent with each other, the weighted average of the productivity increases in the individual industries is not equal to the aggregate productivity increase used to compute the GNP from the work force estimate.

The industry-by-industry approach does not provide a completely independent check on the GNP estimate. In projecting the individual industries, one finds in many instances that the output of the industry depends primarily on the size of the gross national product. This is particularly true of those industries, such as chemical and allied products, which sell a substantial proportion of their output to other industries rather than to final buyers.

Another advantage of the industry-by-industry approach lies in the estimates of geographical distribution which it makes possible. In the studies of the individual industrial sectors the probable shifts in regional distribution of each industry have been worked out. These are summarized in Chapter 20. It would be possible, of course, to project regional growth by forecasting regional population, work force, and productivity, just as in the national projections. But with the regional as with the national estimates, it is very desirable to check the industrial make-up for consistency with the aggregate projection.

To economists versed in modern econometric methods, the methodology used in this study will no doubt have a strongly old-fashioned flavor. First of all, it is quite generally agreed now that forecasts should be presented in the form of probability distributions rather than single values. Actually we have prepared high and low as well as best-guess estimates for population and the gross national product, and we have made extensive use of tests of significance in the statistical-historical work for establishing the best forecasting model. But the great bulk of our forecasts are presented only as single-valued estimates.

Let us consider the problems involved in developing probability distributions of predicted variables. Hurwicz has shown that, where *no* structural changes are expected between the period of our historic experience and the target date for the forecast, conventional least-squares regression possesses optimal properties for developing the probability distribution of the predicted variables on the basis of their historic relation to their predictors. Even where a well-defined set of structural changes is expected, the modified structure of historic relations will still yield the best estimate of the probability distribution of the predicted variable, although least-squares is no longer sufficient and structural estimation must be employed.[22] Unfortunately, this is not much help. We foresee considerable structural change in the Canadian economy between the period for which good national statistics exist (1926 to date) and the year of our forecast (1970). This should be clear from the assumptions made above and will emerge more clearly in later chapters. But the whole trouble is that there is no way of knowing definitely the structural changes to be expected. These structural changes are themselves predicted and are subject to uncertainty. Their variance is unknown and unknowable. Hence any attempt to indicate the variance of a forecast variable would imply that these structural changes have been better defined than is actually the case.

Nor have we chosen to follow the currently popular practice of placing a phony confidence interval around our forecasts by relating them to a year "around 1970." The trouble is that we must make a best guess for 1970 without knowing what degree of probability to attach to this best guess. The trouble is *not* that we possess 100 per cent certainty about our forecasts but are not sure to what year they pertain.

Another aspect of our work which may annoy the statistically sophisticated is seeming infractions of the rules of significant digits. We have set forth to forecast the whole pattern of the Canadian economy in 1970, not just a few isolated variables. We have drawn up forecasts of both very large aggregates and some of their very small components. The main claim to novelty of this study is the use of varied checks for the internal consistency of these estimates of wholes and parts. In some cases nonsignificant digits have been retained to allow completing these checks. If a definite statement is desired, one can think of most of the estimates made in this study as containing two or three significant digits. However, the whole problem of assumptions and structural changes with unknown variances renders any elaborate concern with significant digits fairly pointless.

The additional details of the methodology are provided in the chapters of Part II. The remaining chapters of Part I deal with various aspects of Canadian economic development in order to provide the background for the projections. Chapter 2 develops

---

[22] L. Hurwicz, "Prediction and Least Squares," *Statistical Inference in Dynamic Economic Models* (New York, 1950), pp. 266–300.

the staple theory as an explanation of Canadian development and Chapter 3 shows how the short-run adjustments in national income have been brought about and how the nature of the adjustment process is consistent with the staple theory. Chapter 4 is devoted to some special statistical studies in the structure of the Canadian economy. The regional growth of Canada is then reviewed within the framework of the staple theory in order to establish a basis for forecasting regional development to 1970. The background of government revenue and expenditures is taken up in Chapter 7.

2

Strategic Factors in Canadian Development

A careful and conscientious forecast cannot grow from any simple projection of past trends, though much unscrupulous projection in the guise of forecasting comes from seers equipped only with rulers and log paper. There is a broader sense, though, in which all forecasting is extrapolation. The workaday economist, denied the luminous truth of clairvoyance and revelation, must fashion his vision of the future from wisps of the past. Knowledge of the past, plus "theory" which guides him in ordering that past, constitutes the sum of his resources.

The purpose of this chapter is to prepare the way for forecasting Canada's long-range economic development by studying a few strategic aspects of her previous growth. What follows will not be a broadside effort at surveying Canada's economic development. Several able scholars have already performed this task. We only wish to isolate certain trends and habits of the Canadian economy which have key importance for an intelligent guess about its probable future behavior.

The first of these features is the best known—the crucial role the extraction and export of primary products have played in Canadian economic development. Branded the "staple theory," this interpretation of Canadian development has won almost unanimous acceptance among scholars and the general public as well. True, it is not always clear what is thought to be determined by changes in Canada's staple exports. One infers that, for the early years at least, the usual answer to this question is "everything." But the staple theory, as a few recent writers have emphasized, is more than anything else a theory of capital formation and industrial location. As such, it still plays a crucial part in any interpretation of the Canadian economy.

A second aspect of the Canadian economy to be studied is the pattern of population growth and its economic absorption. Because of the crucial role of population forecasting for the success of our whole network of projections, it is vital to know as much as possible about the connection between staple development and population changes. The historic evidence of the absorption of immigrants into the Canadian economy tells a good deal about Canada's potential for economic growth. Drastic shifts in the age distribution of the population such as are occurring today possess their counterparts in the past. Understanding the historic effects of such changes may augment our ability to foresee their meaning for the future.

A third topic which will receive attention in this chapter is the movement of the Canadian economy toward maturity. This familiar if distressingly vague notion has a good deal of importance for long-range forecasting — if it possesses any measurable counterpart in the historic record of Canadian growth. That record must be searched for evidence.[1]

STAPLE EXPORTS AND THE CANADIAN ECONOMY

Following the great work of Harold A. Innis, the economic history of Canada has regularly been written in terms of the rise (and, occasionally, fall) of her exported staple products. Fisheries first lured Europeans to the shores of Canada. Furs drew them inland. The production of timber and agricultural staples pervades the story of settlement and early nationhood. Grain trade spurred the filling of the West. More recently, pulp and paper, metals, and metallic ores have carried on the tradition and now lend some validity to the popular practice of referring to new frontiers in the Canadian North.

What is a staple? It is a product with a large natural resource content. Some part of its fabrication must take place at the spot, even if only in the trivial sense of seizing it away from Nature. The staple is a product which does not require elaborate processing involving large quantities of labor or rare skills. (This does not preclude its using large amounts of capital, as indeed most of Canada's staples have.) The staple is a product which will bear transport charges and which is in international demand. All of Canada's successful staples have thrived on vigorous export markets.

[1] Logically, this chapter might be expected to contain a review of capital formation in Canadian economic growth. However, because we have little to add to the existing secondary sources, a study of the pattern of investment is deferred to Chapter 11.

We need to know how these staples have fitted into the general pattern of Canadian development. First, what has caused their establishment? What forces have determined that a staple should develop at a certain time? What has limited or restrained the growth of a staple once established? Second, what have been the effects of staple development on Canadian national income, other outputs, investment, population, and the like? Why has one staple had different effects from another?

Prerequisites of staple development

Historically, three sorts of forces have governed the establishment of Canada's major staple industries. There is little use in speculating about one of these — discovery, the finding of previously unknown resources. When an accessible resource in widespread demand is found, exploitation follows as rapidly as known techniques permit. One can analyze the process after the event; there is no hope of foretelling it. Two of Canada's most important mineral deposits, Sudbury and Cobalt, were uncovered accidentally in the process of railroad construction. The fact has an aura of historical romance but little predictive value, less predictive value than the story of the way the railroads and the mineral deposits later stimulated each other's development. Nonetheless the significance of discovery as a random process in economic history must not be overstressed. People generally find things because they have been looking for them, and this fact throws the emphasis back upon the demand for a resource-intensive product and the availability of technology for exploiting it. In Canada's earliest times discoveries of furs and fisheries available for exploitation were generally made by adventurous individuals hoping for profits from just such trade. In Canada's most recent times Alberta's oil and gas were unearthed by major petroleum producers well aware of the heavy and rising requirements for these fuels. And another point worth noting about the role of discovery in Canadian economic development is that ostensibly accidental discoveries have often occurred incidental to some other systematic process of development. In the earliest days of Canadian history the fur resources came to light in the search for fishing grounds, and in later years railroad construction regularly unearthed mineral deposits in the Ontario portion of the Canadian Shield. In this way good demand and profit prospects for any of Canada's major staple products have assisted the discovery and development of others.

Thus changes in technology and changes in demand, broadly conceived, have been the mainsprings of much Canadian staple development. The rise of large scale timber exports came with a shift in the demand situation — Britain's fear of the loss of continental supply sources in the Napoleonic Wars. Wheat depended on both demand and technology in the development of rust-resistant, fast-growing wheats, a major rise in the world price in the mid-1890's, and, finally, the closing of the American frontier. The pulp and paper industry awaited the massive appetites of the United States daily newspapers and the discovery of the sulfite process in the United States and Europe. Much of Canada's present-day mining industry owes its rise not so much to discovery of mineral deposits as to major technical development in mining machinery which occurred in the United States around the turn of the century. Today, discovery itself is being propelled by the hand of technology, as aerial surveying has greatly reduced the labor and the hit-or-miss character of returns in prospecting for mineral resources.

Let us look at some of these developments in more detail. Canada's second great staple, furs, grew to importance only following a shift in European tastes toward the products of beaver fur in the latter half of the seventeenth century. For many years fur trade had only been an activity incidental to fishing. In the nineteenth century, growth of Canada's timber trade was a clear case of the influence of foreign market developments. As Easterbrook and Aitken declare: "Naval timber was, up to 1862, as essential an element in war and diplomacy as oil is today."[2] From the early eighteenth century, bounties were given for North American mast-timber production. From this base of the mast-timber trade, the general British demand for lumber supported growth of commerce in a wide range of lumber products. Revolution in the American colonies forced an emergency shift of timber supply sources from New England to Nova Scotia, for the first time bringing Canadian woodlands into this trade. The cost of Canadian timber was several times that of the Baltic product, and only naval mast production for export could have withstood

[2] W. T. Easterbrook and H. G. J. Aitken, *Canadian Economic History* (Toronto, 1956), pp. 40, 187.

an unrestrained competitive process. But war again intervened. As the Napoleonic blockade imperiled Great Britain with her worst timber crisis of all time, a heavy tariff preference was created in 1804 to support a permanent and secure Canadian source. At the same time, Canadian timber production switched from the Maritimes toward Quebec, where it developed rapidly along with the settlement of the St. Lawrence valley.[3]

Overseas demand was also the main factor in the establishment of Canada's staple foodstuff exports. These developed in two periods when British demand for imported foodstuffs was expanding rapidly — at the middle and at the end of the nineteenth century. The former years saw the first growth of grain exports from the St. Lawrence region, following rapid extension of settlement and improvement of transportation facilities. Corn Law repeal initially resulted in depressed conditions for Canadian commercial circles, but the St. Lawrence wheat farmer continued to improve his position for a number of years as the volume of exports continued to grow.

Another period of rising demand at the end of the nineteenth century saw the opening of the prairie wheat economy and the expansion of exports of meat and dairy products (mainly bacon and cheese) from the St. Lawrence valley. The rise of exports of high-value foodstuffs from the St. Lawrence came with a notable improvement of the standard of living of the English worker. Rapidly rising real incomes during these years meant large increases in the total expended on such luxuries as meat and dairy products. Likewise, rising foreign demand was a major prelude to the great wheat boom following 1900. World wheat prices rose irregularly from 1896 to 1920, and the total freight costs of transporting wheat to Liverpool fell steadily through the years until 1911. In the two decades 1893–1913, Canada's exports of grain and grain products grew four-fold,[4] and wheat production rose 300 per cent in the first decade of the twentieth century. Total wheat acreage reacted very sensitively to year-to-year wheat price changes. With only one exception it grew sharply following every year of rising wheat prices in this period and marked time following years of falling prices.[5]

[3] Easterbrook and Aitken, pp. 187–200.
[4] K. W. Taylor, "Statistics of Foreign Trade," in *Statistical Contributions to Canadian Economic History* (Toronto, 1931). Vol. II, pp. 40–45.
[5] Kenneth Buckley, *Capital Formation in Canada, 1896–1930* (Toronto, 1955), pp. 19–21.

A very important but less conspicuous force behind the growth of the wheat economy was technological change. As Penelope Hartland has pointed out: "If summer fallow and dry farming techniques had been used extensively earlier, if Marquis wheat had been adopted or developed sooner, it seems probable that yields would have been sufficiently sizable and quality sufficiently good to compensate for the higher railroad and transportation rates which prevailed in the 1890's." Although the chilled steel plow and roller method of flour milling were already known, they could not make a massive wheat development possible without the new techniques of cultivation.[6]

Another vital causal factor in the growth of the wheat economy, a rising tide of international migration after the turn of the century, does not seem to fit into the categories of demand and technology. Yet ultimately it reflects their workings in a deeper fashion. Given the state of world demand and technology for a staple product, its production will be allocated among countries according to their relative production costs, viewing costs as dependent in a very broad fashion on the physical traits of various regions. Thus the wave of European migration in the 1880's had by-passed Canada to populate the Great Plains of the United States; yet after the turn of the century the filling up of desirable land in the United States and the technological trends in Canada's favor succeeded in turning the tide. Another example of the same sort of shifting of relative cost in the world economy would be the rise of the Canadian timber trade. Canada benefited from the rising cost of Baltic supplies in the highly relevant sense of the excessive risk to Great Britain of depending on timber supplies from that area.

Let us now turn to the other staples of the twentieth century. Two factors which dominated the development of the wheat economy continue to guide the formation of Canadian staple industries. No doubt the last has not been seen of these factors. One is technological developments which swing the profit balance in favor of exploiting certain Canadian resources. The other is the exhaustion or occupation of all free or readily available resources in the United States. Consider these influences in the growth of the Canadian pulp and paper industry. Rapidly rising

---

[6] P. E. Hartland, "Factors in Economic Growth in Canada," *Journal of Economic History*, 15:19 (No. 1, 1955).

foreign demand nourished the newsprint industry during the first three decades of this century. In the United States, per capita newsprint consumption swelled from eight pounds per person in 1890 to thirty pounds in 1913 and a peak of sixty-two pounds in 1929. Total tonnage consumed in the United States rose from 200,000 tons in 1890 to 3,800,000 tons in 1929 as American dailies poured forth an endless stream of extras, department store ads, Sunday supplements and the like.[7] Canada was ideally equipped to become a major newsprint producer. She had ample sources of pulpwood, excellent water and power sites, and good transport facilities both from forest to mill and from mill to market. All of these were located quite close to major American markets.

Exhaustion of United States pulpwood supplies and technological developments in newsprint machinery set the date when these resources would come into use. By 1910, United States mills were faced with the clear necessity of turning to Canadian sources of pulpwood — an expensive proposition because of high transport costs. At the same time, development of bigger and better newsprint machines was conferring a large competitive advantage on new mills. These factors gave the necessary boost to establishment of a Canadian industry. Political factors lent an assist in the form of various restrictions placed on the taking of pulpwood by Ontario and Quebec between 1900 and 1913. By the latter date, both Canadian and United States restrictions on newsprint production and trade had fallen, and an unhampered North American market was in existence. Between 1913 and 1920, Canadian pulp production (all types) rose from 850,000 tons to 1,850,-000 tons. The largest increase was in sulfite pulp, where technology again assisted Canadian staple development as the sulfite process, discovered in the United States and developed in Europe, came into use.[8]

The growth of Canadian mining provides a very clear case of the joint work of the forces of technology and rising demand. With the exception of gold, most of Canada's major nonferrous metal deposits have been known for some time before they were

[7] J. A. Guthrie, *The Newsprint Paper Industry: An Economic Analysis* (Cambridge, 1941), p. 234.

[8] See V. W. Bladen, *Introduction to Political Economy* (Toronto, 1946), pp. 145–158.

worked on a large and successful scale. Often they have lain untouched for years because they were not of high enough grade to guarantee profits under existing technology.[9] The Sullivan Mine of Consolidated Mining and Smelting was discovered in 1892, and the Flin Flon deposits came to light in 1914. But neither of these came into its own until development of the selective flotation processes in the 1920's allowed the effective handling of Canada's complex ore bodies.[10] Canadian mining technology drew very heavily on the United States. Since 1890, American skills in the manufacture of heavy machinery plus American experience in mining a wide variety of materials had produced a continuous stream of improvements, most of which were adapted to Canadian use. The machine drill, a great labor-saving device, had first been made in the United States around the middle of the nineteenth century, and later the United States was the source of almost all major types of gold mining equipment, thus supplying the gold mining industry which long stood in the fore of Canadian mining.[11]

Improved technology had much to do with the rise in production reflected in Canadian nickel and silver exports which jumped from $2,000,000 in 1896 to $26,000,000 in 1913. Developments on the demand side were equally favorable. Throughout these years, world demand for nonferrous metals was expanding very fast, due mainly to increasing production of electrical machinery and of armament requiring nickel steel. World War I naturally expanded these uses immensely, and high prices caused great acceleration of Canadian mining development. The working of low-grade ore bodies became profitable and several major technical problems gave way as Canadians devoted more ingenuity to their solution. Between 1913 and 1918 Canada's major nonferrous metals showed the following output increases: copper, 54 per cent; nickel, 86 per cent; lead, 36 per cent; zinc, from a negligible quantity to 35,000,000 pounds a year. In value terms, production of these four metals increased from $29,000,000 in 1913 to $74,-000,000 in 1918. Canadian mining was permanently and solidly

[9] O. W. Main, *The Canadian Nickel Industry, A Study in Market Control and Public Policy* (Toronto, 1955), ch. 2.

[10] A. Skelton, "The Canadian Mining Industry Today," in "Features of Present-Day Canada," ed. R. H. Coats, *Annals of the American Academy of Political and Social Science,* 253:67 (September 1947).

[11] E. S. Moore, *American Influence in Canadian Mining* (Toronto, 1941), pp. 90–95; Hartland, p. 20.

established. "The high prices disappeared after the War but
the growth of interest in mining, the improved techniques, and
the greater resources accumulated by mining companies out of
profits were permanent gains to the industry." [12]

Even depressions have had relatively little effect on the Canadian nonferrous mining industry. Because her major nonferrous
deposits all contain both precious and nonprecious metals, Canada has a geological built-in stabilizer of a sort not commonly
known to monetary theorists. In bad times the fixed prices of
the precious metals have sustained companies whose main profit
sources were undercut by slumping prices of industrial nonferrous
metals.[13]

In analyzing the causes of staple development in Canada it is
just as important to understand what forces have halted or
reversed the growth of particular staples. Why have staples
turned sour for the Canadian economy and suffered declines either
of their export volume or total production? One important answer has been declining foreign demand, itself due to several
ultimate causes: (1) Shifting of foreign tastes away from the
staple commodity. This was the fate of Canada's fisheries in their
later years. (2) Changing trade regulations of foreign governments, such as the loss of the British tariff preference for Canadian timber. (3) The rise of effectively competitive sources of
supply, such as the European producers of agricultural specialties
which were partly responsible for displacing several exports of
the St. Lawrence region in the late nineteenth century.

Not only have foreign developments put the brakes on Canadian staple production, but also Canada's growth has itself
blocked the growth of some staple products, or at least removed
them from export channels. An obvious case of this has been the
depletion of the underlying natural resources. Fur-bearing animals, white pine forests in the Ottawa Valley, and the petroleum
reserves in Ontario have simply been exhausted by the home and
foreign demands placed upon them. More interesting and more
important, however, has been the phenomenon of growth in one
segment of the Canadian economy interfering with the develop-

[12] Canada, RCDPR, *Report,* Vol. I, pp. 91, 77.
[13] E. S. Moore, "The Mining Industry and the Depression," *The Canadian Economy and its Problems,* ed. H. A. Innis and A. F. W. Plumptre (Toronto, 1934), pp. 34–38.

ment or maintenance of trade and production of some staple item.

The most dramatic example has been the effect of settlement upon the fur trade. Maintaining an ample stock of fur-bearing animals grew more difficult in direct proportion to the rise in settlement. This conflict played no minor part in the disputes leading up to the American War of Independence, due to colonial wrath over the Quebec Act of 1774 reserving vast blocks of territory west of the Appalachians from settlement to maintain the fur trade.[14] The same conflict reappeared three quarters of a century later as settlement encroached upon Hudson's Bay Company activities on the Pacific coast. The company had not encouraged settlement in its territories except for raising agricultural produce needed by the company itself. Pressures for broader development and settlement in the region finally brought down this policy in 1863 when the Grand Trunk Railway bought control of the Hudson's Bay Company to gain access to land for a transcontinental rail route. After that change, the company became a land office first, a fur trading enterprise second.[15]

Harold Innis' famous essay on "Unused Capacity as a Factor in Canadian Economic History"[16] traced relations between Canadian settlement and staple production operating in earlier years. The critical connection was unused capacity — specifically, the search for balanced cargoes for trans-Atlantic shipping. The fur trade produced very light east-bound cargoes compared to the supplies which had to be brought in to support it. It allowed no shipping space for settlers and their effects. The opposite was true of the timber trade. Wood not only produced a bulky east-bound cargo, but in effect transported itself through the encouragement it gave to shipbuilding. The timber trade generated considerable shipping capacity for settlers. Moreover, not only did the timber trade pull settlers into Canada by supplying transportation in timber ships returning to Canada, but also the flow of settlers increased the supply of exportable timber as trees were removed from the land to make room for agricultural settlement. Thus the increasing stream of migration to Canada en-

---

[14] Easterbrook and Aitken, pp. 130 ff.
[15] Easterbrook and Aitken, pp. 324-334, 343-346.
[16] *CJEPS*, 2:1-15 (February 1936), reprinted in *Essays in Canadian Economic History* (Toronto, 1956).

couraged the development of timber as a staple export while it interfered with the production of furs.

Important for the future of Canada's foreign trade is the effect of increasing Canadian population and expanding domestic markets for raising home demand for Canadian staple products. The rate of expansion of staple production is often limited because of its natural-resources content, or, in the more familiar terms of economic statics, diminishing returns and rising real costs appear as production expands. Thus rising home demand for a staple, while it in no way means an "interference" with Canada's overall growth, nonetheless can reduce the volume or growth rate of exports and induce broad changes in the economy.

The lumber industry provides the clearest example. In 1842 the loss of a substantial tariff preference in the British market produced the usual signs of distress in the Canadian lumber industry. The growth of towns in the St. Lawrence valley, however, was rapidly creating a local market for lumber at this time, starting the timber export staple on its long road to becoming mainly a domestic industry.[17] After 1900, the effects of Canada's national economic growth on the timber industry became more dramatic. First, growing lumber demand in the prairie regions put an end to export shipments from the Manitoba and western Ontario lumber industry. Soon American logs were imported from Minnesota as the Canadian industry faced, for the first time, "a domestic market of large dimensions, where demand outran supply."[18] The second major effect of Canadian growth on lumber as an export staple was an adverse change in the labor supply. Through the nineteenth century, the industry had depended on a French-Canadian labor force which was by temperament marvelously well adapted to the industry's needs. At the turn of the century, the combination of rising urban employment opportunities and heavy immigration of unskilled labor displaced this force with what proved to be a much less satisfactory one drawn from newer migrant groups. The position of the lumber industry as a competitor for Canada's factors of production had clearly deteriorated.[19]

[17] Easterbrook and Aitken, pp. 200–202.
[18] A. R. M. Lower, *The North American Assault on the Canadian Forest, A History of the Lumber Trade Between Canada and the United States* (New Haven, 1938), pp. 153–164.
[19] *Ibid.*, pp. 189–192.

Another twentieth-century impact of Canada's growth on the lumber industry was the effect of increasing interregional competition on older areas of exploitation. With the opening of the Canadian Pacific Railway, British Columbia seized the prairie lumber market from Eastern Canada; later, the Panama Canal allowed British Columbia lumber to compete on the east coast of the continent. Only the simultaneous rise of the pulp and paper industry in the St. Lawrence region averted major problems of readjustment.[20]

This sort of displacement of foreign buyers of Canadian staples by a rising domestic market has not been common in Canadian history. This has been the case for many reasons, the most prominent being the accidents of timing in the appearance of new resources and new technology. But this force may become more important in the future for a rapidly growing nation exporting many natural-resource-based products.

Effects of staples on the Canadian economy

We turn now from the forces determining changes in staple production and exports to review a few of the ways in which staple development has fashioned the pattern of Canadian economic growth.

Discussions of the effects of staple production on the Canadian economy often have a diffuse air about them. So many effects vie for scholarly attention — effects on factors of production, income levels, location of economic activity, cyclical instability, political and social institutions — that orderly selection grows difficult. Before trying to isolate the lessons these effects teach for the future of the Canadian economy, let us pause to arrange the order of inquiry. One broadly useful way of looking at the economic effects of staple production is in terms of the production functions of the various staple commodities.[21] By this we mean the type and quantity of land, labor, capital, and other commodities needed to produce a quantity of some staple product. An example of the interpretive uses of this approach is the often-made comparison between the effects of gold mining and fur

[20] Bladen, *Introduction to Political Economy,* pp. 145–146.
[21] For a general discussion of the importance of production functions to patterns of economic development, see R. E. Baldwin, "Patterns of Development in Newly Settled Regions," *Manchester School,* 24:161–179 (May 1954).

production on general economic development. Both had very high
value per unit of weight and hence required very little transportation service. Therefore they both created major problems of
unused capacity in the transportation systems which served them.
Production of both goods was quite mobile and could quickly
become established in a new region. Neither gold nor furs required much specialized capital in the sense of capital goods with
great durability and few alternative uses. Producers of both
staples, at least in earlier centuries, operated on the assumption
that their main natural resource was in fairly short supply and
would soon be exhausted. They were seldom wrong in this belief.
Therefore there was no incentive to build any permanent plant.
Furthermore, no single intermediate good was needed in large
quantities for either product — rather the general line of supplies
demanded as trading stock by the fur factor and as subsistence by
the gold miner. The transient nature of production meant that
these were usually shipped into current areas of exploitation,
rather than coming from stimulation of any local production. A
notable exception, of course, was the Hudson's Bay Company's
efforts to supply itself with agricultural produce. There was one
major difference between the production functions for gold and
furs — namely in the relative amounts of capital and labor required. Gold extraction in the "rush" days was a highly labor-
intensive process which required only small amounts of capital in
the way of tools and worker's subsistence. The fur trade, by contrast, demanded considerable circulating capital relative to the
labor supply (excluding Indians). Thus, while neither activity left
much residue in the form of permanent settlement and a nucleus
for a self-sustained economy, the fur trade offered much greater
problems of commercial organization. As Innis's work has demonstrated, it was problems of controlling a far-flung apparatus and
dealing with vast problems of uncertainty which tested entrepreneurial mettle — first in the rivalry between English and
French, later in the struggle between the Hudson's Bay Company
and their Montreal-based rival, the North West Company.[22]

The story of input requirements for the wheat economy is a
much different one. It not only took considerable supplies of
capital, both directly and in transport facilities, but also fixed

[22] Compare W. T. Easterbrook, "Uncertainty and Economic Change," *Journal
of Economic History,* 14:355–356 (Autumn 1954).

this capital firmly on the spot in highly specialized and durable forms. Recently Buckley has provided estimates of prairie farm capital formation from 1901 to 1930. He shows how this investment stream showed first an extensive phase of spending on buildings and inventories as farms spread across the prairies, later an intensive phase as machinery and motor vehicles were substituted for human and animal labor. In the half-decade 1901–1905, prairie farm investment was one-sixth of Canadian gross domestic investment.[23] A very large portion of investment in the first phase was in construction, and hence it comes as no surprise that the value of Canadian sawmill products, which in 1901 barely exceeded the 1891 figure, had doubled by 1911.[24]

The production function for wheat dictated a stupendous volume of investment not just in the prairie farms themselves but also in transportation equipment required to serve them. The period of settlement of the Canadian prairies coincided with the last great extensive phase of Canadian railroad construction. The second and third transcontinental railways came into being. With the benefit of hindsight, one can readily exclude these from any catalogue of investments necessary to develop the wheat economy. But these years also saw heavy construction of branch lines in the prairies, an activity which continued into the 1920's. Net additions to Canadian railway mileage were 1,680 miles in 1896–1900, 2,830 miles in 1901–1905, 4,244 miles in 1906–1910, and 10,151 miles in 1911–1915.[25] Over half of the increase in railway mileage during the first two decades of the twentieth century occurred in the prairie provinces.[26]

Canadian industries producing manufactures needed in wheat culture naturally underwent spectacular growth. Between 1900 and 1910, production of agricultural implements doubled, and the output of railway rolling stock increased four-fold.

Of course the most important "input" of the wheat economy, for its total effects on the Canadian nation, was labor. Providing subsistence for the great inflow of population into the prairies demanded a near-revolution in the economic structure of eastern Canada. Previously, there had been little in the way of division

---

[23] Buckley, *Capital Formation in Canada,* pp. 21–25.
[24] Lower, *North American Assault,* p. 187.
[25] Buckley, *Capital Formation in Canada,* pp. 28–30.
[26] W. A. Mackintosh, *The Economic Background of Dominion-Provincial Relations* (Ottawa, 1939), p. 27.

of labor and major exchange of goods among Canada's regions. Now central Canada could switch in part from the role of exporter of farm produce to Europe to supplier of manufactures to the prairies.

This change has been well documented in the report of the Royal Commission on Dominion-Provincial Relations. The essence of the story is that the wheat boom finally caused the Canadian policy of high tariffs and "all-Canada transportation" to yield the desired pay-off of a large industrial sector. The net value of production of manufactures was $214,500,000 as recorded in the census of Canada in 1901. By the time of the 1911 census, this figure had grown to $564,500,000, an increase of 163 per cent for the decade and a fantastic compound annual rate of 11.1 per cent. Despite the size of the labor flow into the prairie provinces, the portion of Canada's populace engaged in manufacturing stayed almost constant. The expansion of manufacturing was great not just for those goods employed in prairie farm production (as already noted) but extended over all segments of Canadian industry. Almost no major class of manufactures failed to double in value of net output over the decade.[27]

Finally, consider the major staples which have spurred Canadian economic growth in recent years, particularly newsprint and mine products. In weighing the impact of their production on the Canadian economy one notes two shifts of emphasis which set them apart from most of the major staples of earlier years. First, with Canadian factor supplies growing more diversified and its national markets more unified, the problem of securing inputs has come to be less and less of an element in the story of staple expansion. Not a small part of the explanation of this is the great capital intensity of staple exploitation in recent decades, which has meant in turn small labor requirements and little significant settlement associated with staple production in new areas. The second contrast between the effects of twentieth-century staples and their predecessors is in the industries most encouraged by the growth of staple output. Secondary expansion stirred by earlier staples appeared mostly in industries supplying the staple producers; now the most important impact quantitatively seems to be upon those industries which are themselves supplied by the staple output.

The mining industry particularly reveals this shift in the impact

[27] Canada, RCDPR, *Report,* Vol. I, pp. 66–74.

of staple production. Thus, in his study, *Settlement and the Mining Frontier,* H. A. Innis found the significant effects of early mining development in new markets for southern Alberta horse farms, new areas of farm settlement supplying food to mining camps, new and improved transportation routes and the like.[28] New towns, farms and railroads still accompany the establishment of new mining operations in Canada. But with the history of settlement largely a closed book their significance shrinks beside the meaning which these developments hold for the *aggregates* of Canadian income, production and trade. Thus E. S. Moore, summing up the significance of Canadian mining in the 1930's, stressed the number of jobs dependent on mining. One-seventh of Canada's population, he concluded, depended for support on workers employed directly in mining or indirectly in processing, transportation, and distribution of the products of mining activity.[29] These facts now hold much more significance for the economy than the local impact of changes in mining activity on the patterns of settlement.

The mining industry also shows the switch in the impact of staple development from industries supplying to industries supplied by staple production. Between World Wars I and II there was a great expansion in the industries smelting, refining, and fabricating Canada's primary nonferrous metals output, so that on the eve of World War II the bulk of the smelting and refining was being carried on in Canada and fabricating industries were just beginning to develop. In Skelton's words, "This was a long stride from the position on the eve of the previous World War, when Canada was only a relatively small shipper of ores and concentrates to foreign refineries." [30]

Other staple developments show this same tendency toward inducing large investments in processing facilities. A conspicuous postwar development has been the petro-chemical plants which have come to the prairies to manufacture sulphur, ammonia, cellulose acetate, and the like from available natural gas supplies.[31] People in a position to make good guesses are suggesting

[28] Vol. IX, Part II, of "Canadian Frontiers of Settlement," ed. W. A. Mackintosh and W. L. G. Joerg (Toronto, 1936), pp. 257–259, 311–312, and *passim.*
[29] "The Mining Industry and the Depression," pp. 39–40.
[30] Skelton, p. 68.
[31] Easterbrook and Aitken, p. 552; J. D. Gibson, "The Changing Influence of the United States on the Canadian Economy," *CJEPS,* 22:423 (November 1956).

that research on new uses for the products and byproducts of Canada's pulp and paper industry will produce more subsidiary manufacturing operations in that quarter.[32]

One final intriguing development in the interindustry impact of staple production is that there are strong complementary effects among Canada's current staple industries. The fuel resources of Alberta may promote an expansion of metal smelting and refining in western Canada. Sulphur extracted from natural gas at the wellhead can provide the sulfite for pulp production.

These new directions in the impact of staple production of course do not deny the presence of the effects on location and regional development stressed in Innis's research on the older staples. The appearance of so much of Canada's current dynamic staple growth in Ontario and Quebec contrasts sharply to the era of prairie wheat expansion. The older period made Canada much more of an east-west economy, the prairies depending on European markets and eastern Canada depending on prairie purchasing power. Now the demand for capital and consumers' goods rising from staple growth lies within the two great manufacturing provinces themselves, and the relevant foreign market is that of the United States.[33] Once again the habitual tendency of the Canadian economy toward a north-south trade pattern reappears, a development reinforced by changes in the trade of the prairie provinces resulting from the past decade's oil and gas discoveries.[34] But the point merits repeating that settlement has clearly taken a back seat as the crucial aspect of staple development. This is not just because agricultural settlement and expansion is now a closed chapter in Canadian history. Even more so it is because of the great capital requirements and small labor inputs demanded by the present-day technology of mining and smelting, newsprint production, and the like. The new mining towns of the Shield will remain isolated settlements, even though they are far cries from the mining camps of former years. The great wealth brought to the prairie provinces by oil and gas discoveries will have a surprisingly small impact on the prairies' long-run share of Canada's total population. The only important

[32] H. L. Keenleyside, *The Place of the Forest Industry in the Canadian Economy* (Vancouver, 1950), pp. 12–16 and *passim*.

[33] Bladen, *Introduction to Political Economy*, p. 146.

[34] For extensive discussion of trends in regional development, see Chapters 5 and 6.

exception to these generalizations seems to be the continuing high labor requirements of woods operations, but even here the prospects are for rapidly increasing mechanization.

All of these effects of staple development hold particular interest for the economic forecaster — the impact of autonomous developments in primary production on the location of industry, the level of employment, the composition of foreign trade, and the growth rate of investment and income. Yet these are only the current manifestations of a centuries-old pattern of Canadian development.

POPULATION GROWTH AND CANADIAN DEVELOPMENT

Since population growth is an essential ingredient of long-run economic growth, understanding its pattern is essential to any successful attempt at long-range forecasting. Economists, however, find themselves in doubt over such fundamental questions as whether population growth determines income growth or vice versa. The purpose of this section is to collect evidence on the relation of population change to the general pattern of Canadian development.

First, consider the decade-to-decade record of percentage increases in Canada's population since 1851, as shown in Table 1. These figures reflect several major long-range trends. First, international migration has made but a slight net contribution to Canada's population. Only in prosperous decades — the 1850's, 1900's, 1910's, 1920's, 1940's — has heavy immigration exceeded the steady trickle of emigrants going mainly to the United States. Furthermore, decades of heavy gross immigration are usually followed by decades of heavy gross emigration. Percentage additions to Canada's population by natural increase — the excess of births over deaths — and net immigration have been very highly correlated. Looking at pairs of successive decades of Canadian history, we see that these two sources of population growth have changed in the same direction in every decade but one, the 1890's. And this uniformity shows even before we take account of such disturbances as wartime periods. When opportunities have come for the Canadian economy to undertake major new phases of expansion, the effect of rising economic opportunity on population growth has been striking indeed.

Beyond this general picture, four special phases of Canadian

Table 1.   Canadian population growth, 1851–1950 (thousands).

Period	Births (1)	Deaths (2)	Immigration (3)	Emigration (4)	Pop. at end of period (5)	Natural increase No. (6)	Natural increase % (7)[a]	Net immigration No. (8)	Net immigration % (9)[a]	Total percentage change (10)
1851–1860	1,281	611	209	86	3,230	670	27.5	123	5.0	32.5
1861–1870	1,369	718	187	377	3,689	651	20.2	−190	−5.9	14.3
1871–1880	1,477	754	353	439	4,325	723	19.6	−86	−2.3	17.3
1881–1890	1,538	824	903	1,110	4,833	714	16.5	−207	−4.8	11.7
1891–1900	1,546	828	326	505	5,371	718	14.9	−179	−3.7	11.2
1901–1910	1,931	811	1,782	1,067	7,207	1,120	20.9	715	13.3	34.2
1911–1920	2,338	868[b]	1,592	1,480	8,788	1,470	20.4	112	1.6	22.0
1921–1930	2,403	917	1,198	1,095	10,377	1,486	16.9	103	1.2	18.1
1931–1940	2,248	1,006	149	262	11,507	1,242	12.0	−113	−1.1	10.9
1941–1951[c]	3,283	1,186	676	632	13,648	2,097	18.2	44	0.4	18.6

[a] Percentage of population at beginning of period.
[b] Does not include World War I dead.
[c] Newfoundland not included.

Source: N. Keyfitz, "The Growth of the Canadian Population," Population Studies, 4:47–63 (June 1950), Table 11; 1940–50 corrected by official figures from 1951 Census.

population growth require inspection. The first is the long-run and short-run determinants of the natural increase of the Canadian population. The second is the impact of migration on the Canadian economy and the determinants of immigration and emigration. The third is the history of the Canadian "population pyramid" and its economic significance. The fourth is the inter-action between population flows, the labor force, and capital formation.

Canada's vital rates

Analyzing the components of Canada's net natural increase of population requires studying two primary time series, with side glances at a third. These are birth rates, death rates, and marriage rates. Any way one slices the available data on Canadian births and deaths, one finds a slow and steady downward drift of death rates and an irregular, generally downward movement of birth rates from the time of the Confederation at least to World War II. Two standard measures of birth rates are available, the so-called crude birth rate (number of live births per thousand population per year) and an alternate measure which relates the number of children aged 0–4 years to the number of women between 15 and 44. The latter has two advantages for analyzing long-run trends. First, its basic data come from census records and hence are not affected by the occurrence of births which are never officially registered. Second, even when demographic statistics are highly accurate, as in modern-day Canada, this measure has the advantage of taking partial account of changes in the structure (age and sex distribution) of the population. Long-run birth rate calculations for Canada have been produced in both ways, and W. B. Hurd has developed a method of further correcting the ratio of children 0–4 to women 15–44 to take account of shifts in the age-distribution of women within the child-bearing ages.[35]

Both types of birth rate data tell the same story. Birth rates have drifted gently but steadily downward ever since Confederation except for periods of considerable prosperity — the 1900's, the years immediately following World War I, and the decade

---

[35] See W. B. Hurd, "The Decline in the Canadian Birth-Rate," *CJEPS,* 3:41–42 (February 1937); P. Veyret, *La Population du Canada* (Paris, 1953), especially p. 102.

which has followed World War II. After each of these periods, the secular decline has set in again at about the same steady rate. W. B. Hurd fixes this long-run rate of decline at about 0.5 per cent, a result consistent with Firestone's figures.[36]

Hurd's study of Canadian birth rates is of great interest because it focused on the 1920's, a period as fruitful as any for the lessons Canadian history may teach about current population changes. The fall through the 1921–1930 census decade was 14.4 per cent, and the rate of decline in the 1930's to the bottom of the depression was no greater than that during the prosperous 1920's. Hurd shows that one-sixth of the decline was due to the fact that the age distribution of women between 15 and 44 became less favorable during the decade. The rest was due to factors touched by the economic situation of the time. Hurd ascribes half of the decline to the falling marriage rate. Of the remaining one-third of the decline, a large amount seems to have been due to rapid urbanization during the 1920's, for not only were rural birth rates higher than urban in general, but those in smaller urban centers were greater than those in the larger cities.

Against this picture of the 1920's we can place the experience of the post-World War II decade. One similarity between the two periods strikes one immediately — namely, the decline in the crude marriage rate. The 1933 crude marriage rate was one-fourth below the 1921 rate; the 1955 figure was almost one-fifth below that for 1945–1947. Yet the crude birth rate has not been behaving at all like that of the 1920's. In 1955 it was about the same as in 1947, and the 1950's as a whole average higher than the late 1940's. This astonishing display of fertility has proceeded in the face of a very unfavorable age structure of the population. That is, if birth rates for each specific age group of mothers had stayed constant in Canada over the last decade, the crude birth rate would have slumped sharply. The relatively small numbers of Canadians in the 20–29 years age groups today clearly explain the fall in the marriage rate and create all the more curiosity over the cause of the high birth rates. The trends in birth rates

[36] Hurd, "The Decline in the Canadian Birth-Rate," p. 56; O. J. Firestone, *Canada's Economic Development 1867–1953, With Special Reference to Changes in the Country's National Product and National Wealth* (London, 1958), Table 3; see also N. B. Ryder, "Components of Canadian Population Growth," *Population Index,* 20:75 (April 1954). Firestone's extremely important work has been available to us only in the form of galley proofs and consequently all references to it in the present work must be to sections or tables rather than pages.

for specific age groups of mothers tell the story. The rates for women aged 15–24 have *doubled* since the mid-1930's, and the rate for the 25–29 group has risen one-third. In short, the birth rates among the most productive groups of Canadian women have risen steadily in the post-World War II decade, while they fell steadily during the 1920's.

The trend in death rates is a much more stable factor in the population picture than the birth rate. The decline of the mortality rate has been steady over the last century, so that the crude death rate (annual deaths per thousand population) is just half of what it was at Confederation. Most of this improvement has come in the twentieth century, and it shows no sign of slackening. When one looks at the death rates for specific age and sex groups of the Canadian populace, some important differences appear. Death rates have been falling only slightly for all male age groups over 50 and all female groups over 60. Most of these older groups have experienced roughly stable death rates, or even distinctly rising rates for men between 50 and 64. For all younger age groups, though, the trend is sharply downward. Mortality rates for persons under 20 have in the past been much higher in Canada than her racial composition and income levels would suggest. But if the trends of the last one and one-half decades continue, this situation will not persist much longer. Indeed, improvement of survival for some of these groups could not go on long at the same absolute pace for some groups without their death-rates going to zero.[37]

In summary, the decade-by-decade rate of natural increase of the Canadian population has stood at or near 20 per cent in each prosperous decade since Confederation (see Table 1). This stability of the rate of natural increase cloaks a continuous decline in death rates, accelerated in recent years, and a continual decline of the birth rate, interrupted on several occasions but never halted so dramatically as in the past decade.

Immigration, emigration and Canadian growth

Probably the biggest barrier to studying Canada's international migration position is the quality of the statistics. No direct records of emigration exist. Some shaky hints appear in United

---

[37] Statistics giving rise to these conclusions appear in United Nations Statistical Office, *Demographic Yearbook, 1953,* p. 178. See *infra,* pp. 258–269.

States immigration and census data, since the United States has been the near-exclusive recipient. But emigration has to be estimated as a residue after other components of population change are measured. Hence it reflects errors of estimation in all the other components of population change. The best available estimates are those of Nathan Keyfitz, which seem to do about all that one can about underregistration problems.[38] If we correct Keyfitz's figures for the 1940's decade by inserting the results of the 1951 census, then they reveal total immigration into Canada, 1851–1950, of 7,790,000 persons, coupled with emigration of 7,260,000. The net gain of the Canadian nation from the great waves of migrants crossing her borders then amounts to only half a million persons. Some earlier migration estimates show smaller totals on both sides of the balance than those of Keyfitz but all agree that the net addition has been positive but very small. There is a very noticeable relation between the size of the immigration and emigration flows over time. With fair regularity, a decade of high immigration into Canada has been followed by one of high emigration.[39]

Ryder's series of figures for net annual immigration since 1921 shows several interesting short-run trends. The depression of 1921 was immediately followed by three years of significant net emigration, with net departures in 1922 erasing one-third of the net natural increase. In the prosperous late 1920's the situation reversed, with net immigration making a substantial contribution to population growth. In the 1930's the world-wide character of the depression and particularly its catastrophic hold on the United States kept both immigration and emigration very small, but there was a net emigration during every year of the decade, ranging as high as one-sixth of the (diminished) net natural increase. The net outflow continued during World War II and was clearly reversed only in 1946 as Canada furnished asylum to the victims of European chaos. Still, immigration for the whole decade only slightly exceeded emigration. In the 1950's, however, with domestic prosperity and heavy immigration, net immigration has made a greater contribution to population growth than at any other time since World War I. In several years it has added

[38] "The Growth of Canadian Population," *Population Studies*, 4:47–63 (June 1950).
[39] R. H. Coats, "Statistics Comes of Age," *CJEPS*, 2:280 (August 1936).

almost one-third as many people to the Canadian nation as the remarkably large net natural increase.[40]

Canadians have picked out the near-equality between immigration and emigration over the long run as the main talking point in analyzing Canadian migration. It was first emphasized by the 1931 census of Canada, which declared that over the period 1851–1931 "the increase in population due to immigration . . . about balances, in point of numbers, the loss of Canadians to the United States and other countries." [41] Furthermore, the statistics clearly showed that large waves of immigration had coincided with, or had been closely followed by, heavy emigration. In the midst of the depressed 1930's, surrounded by urban mass unemployment and the threat of rural famine, Canadian scholars understandably read from these figures what was branded the Displacement Theory. Crudely stated (as it usually was), the theory held that employment opportunities in Canada could grow little more rapidly than the natural rate of population increase. Consequently immigration merely created unemployment and drove out of Canada a corresponding number of emigrants. "Decade-by-decade analysis shows that the United States served as a safety valve drawing off excess population as circumstances required." [42]

The Displacement Theory should be conceded as a plausible explanation of a certain set of facts. The long-run immigration-emigration parity and the timing of these movements (emigration never leading changes in immigration) agree nicely with the theory. But it is open to two overwhelming attacks. One of these exposes its absurdity when viewed in a broader perspective; the other shows that the pattern of Canadian settlement in the United States does not accord with the Displacement Theory's predictions.

As Paul Veyret declares in his splendid study of Canada's population, "Canada has never exercised on the imagination of Europeans a fascination comparable to that of the United

[40] Ryder, p. 75.
[41] Canada, DBS, *Census of Canada, 1931,* Vol. I, p. 99.
[42] W. B. Hurd, "Demographic Trends in Canada," in "Features of Present-Day Canada," ed. R. H. Coats, *Annals of the American Academy of Political and Social Science,* 253:10 (September 1947); for a survey (unsympathetic) of the Displacement Theory, see Mabel F. Timlin, *Does Canada Need More People?* (Toronto, 1951), pp. 14–20.

States." [43] Canada's turn-of-century immigration wave had to await the near-exhaustion of unsettled farm land below the border and the growing political hostility to mass immigration into the United States. Whatever noneconomic fascination the States may have for foreigners, there should be no mystery about their economic interest for Canadians. The delay in the settlement of the Canadian prairies was certainly not unaffected by the fact that Canadian land was more expensive or more difficult to secure than a free United States homestead. Apart from the attractiveness of western settlement, the United States has always had a noticeably higher average income per capita. Two careful examinations of income per capita in Canada and the United States put the Canadian figure between two-thirds and three-fourths of the American one.[44] It is certain not only that this difference has persisted for some time, but also that it has probably been greater at most times in the past than it is now. Throughout the twentieth century, Canada seems to have enjoyed at all times income growth rates at least equal to those of the United States. Thus the United States has always had a little more to offer the immigrant than Canada, and a heavy flow across the border of both native Canadians and the foreign-born should not seem strange.

A second difficulty with the Displacement Theory appears when one looks at the new locations Canadians have selected within the United States. No less an authority than R. H. Coats sought to bolster the Displacement Theory by citing the alleged fact that the Canadians pushed out of Canada by new immigrant arrivals cluster just south of the border in *emigré* communities. By his reckoning, only 5 per cent of Canadian emigrants to the United States were "fortune-seekers" who had moved to fast-growing United States areas in search of greater opportunities. Of the remainder, 30 per cent represented the original outflow from Quebec and Ontario in the decade following Confederation, and another 60 per cent consisted of friends and relatives who had followed these original emigrants to their new communities just across the border. "These Canadians have not gone to the parts

---

[43] Veyret, p. 38.

[44] J. H. Young, "Comparative Economic Development: Canada and the United States," *AER*, 45:85–86 (May 1955); J. M. Due, "Consumption Levels in Canada and the United States, 1947–50," *CJEPS*, 21:174–181 (May 1955).

of the United States which were expanding most rapidly, unless by accident: they have not been straws sucked into a vortex." [45]

Brinley Thomas has examined this view in his study of migration in the North Atlantic economy. In the decade 1920–1930, the states of California, Florida, Michigan, New Jersey, Ohio, Oregon, and New York had the largest total population gains through internal migration of white persons. These states received 57 per cent of the net immigration of Canadians into the United States. Thus "the majority of Canadian emigrants did go to those parts of the United States which were expanding most rapidly: they *were* straws sucked into the American vortex." The Coats hypothesis holds much better for the French-Canadians settling in New England, but Thomas points out that in addition to being near Quebec the New England states were one of the last areas where farms could be bought cheaply.[46] Likewise, Mabel Timlin has argued convincingly from the same 1920's data that Canadian migration to the United States normally reflects just the same forces as migration from the country to the city. The vastly greater urban development of the United States then would readily explain a large amount of movement south.[47]

Further information came to light in the two studies of population exchange between Canada and the United States which appeared in the Carnegie Endowment's series of monographs on the relations between the two countries. Leon Truesdell's careful examination of the United States census information showed a close positive correlation of differences between the total population growth rates of the two countries with the pattern of population exchange. Broadly speaking, the United States enjoyed the faster population growth in the nineteenth century, Canada in the twentieth. The Canadian-born in the United States increased rapidly to the turn of the century, reaching a peak of one-fourth of Canada's native population in 1900. From then on, this *emigré* population took on a much more static character. By contrast,

[45] R. H. Coats, "Two Good Neighbours: A Study of the Exchange of Populations," *Proceedings* of Canadian-American Affairs Conference at Queens University, 1937, pp. 116–117.

[46] Brinley Thomas, *Migration and Economic Growth, A Study of Great Britain and the Atlantic Economy* (Cambridge, 1954), p. 137.

[47] Timlin, *Does Canada Need More People?* pp. 84–87.

after 1900 the American-born in Canada began increasing sharply for the first two decades of the century.[48]

Another interesting datum for Truesdell's study was the occupational distribution of Canadian-born in the United States. In sixteen states where they were most numerous, Canadians turned up in larger proportions in skilled and semi-skilled positions than did all gainfully employed workers. They were noticeably scarce among the farm labor force. These facts suggest, though of course they do not prove, that a major reason for Canadian emigration was higher rewards to skilled work prevailing in the more highly developed American industries.[49]

The debate stirred by the Displacement Theory has turned up some very important features in Canadian emigration to the United States for anyone concerned with the future of such movements. First, as Miss Timlin has pointed out, if Canada in the past has lost much of its surplus farm population to the coruscating enclaves of America's cities, then the growth of Canada's own urban centers will help cut this loss (or even reverse it).[50] Second, the age distribution of Canadian emigrants to the United States has shown a definite trend with important meaning for the future. In the nineteenth century, persons under 40 years of age constituted the great bulk of those admitting Canadian birth to United States census-takers. But in the 1920's persons between 50 and 70 made up a larger portion.[51] Perhaps in the future Canada will send its aged to Indian Lake, rather than its youth to New York.

Age structure of the Canadian population

Changes in the age structure of a population are certainly one of the gentler forces of economic change. Nonetheless, they are a fundamental determinant of the rate of growth of the labor force relative to total population and thus to the size of the total bundle of standard-of-living goods demanded relative to the labor

[48] Leon E. Truesdell, *The Canadian Born in the United States, An Analysis of the Statistics of the Canadian Element in the Population of the United States, 1850 to 1930* (New Haven, 1943), pp. 4–10; R. H. Coats and M. C. Maclean, *The American-Born in Canada, A Statistical Interpretation* (Toronto, 1943), pp. 55–57.
[49] Truesdell, p. 6 and ch. 12.
[50] Timlin, *Does Canada Need More People?* p. 87.
[51] Thomas, p. 251.

available to produce it. As such, population age distribution gets less attention than it deserves from students of long-run economic change.

Consider the "population pyramids" for Canada in census years since 1881. The population pyramid is the demographer's tool for plotting the percentage distribution of the population by sex and (usually five-year) age groups. Between 1881 and 1901, the pyramid is quite regular in form; any given age group is less numerous than every younger one. The pyramid is much wider at the base than in the adult age groups, indicating a sustained birth rate and high mortality. By 1911, immigration has brought considerable change. On the female side, the pyramid keeps its staircase ordering of age groups. On the male side, however, the decade's heavy immigration swells the 20–35 age groups considerably. A secondary distortion comes in the unusually large 0–4 group, a reflection of the decade's high birth rate.

No major changes appear in the 1921 pyramid. The disturbance of the previous decade's immigration shows less conspicuously in the male 20–40 age groups. Emigration to the United States has already taken a large toll. The decline of the birth rate from the 1910 peak shows, as the 0–4 age group is scarcely more numerous than the 5–9 group. By 1931 the effects of immigration are barely visible, but the uneven pattern in the age groups under 20 becomes quite marked. The 5–9 year olds are more numerous than the 0–4 group. The 1941 pyramid accents the peculiarity of the past two decades' birth rates. The 15–19 group is larger than any of the three below it, and the 5–9 group barely exceeds young adults 20–24. The 0–4 group announces some revival of the birth rate but is still less numerous than the 10–14 year olds.[52]

The population pyramid for 1951 shows at a glance that immigration in the postwar years has not lessened the peculiarities of the 1941 pyramid. The 25–29 group is still much more numerous than the two groups immediately below it, although normal mortality plus the bloodshed of World War II have reduced it to equality with the 10–14 year old group. The two youngest groups, however, are much greater than any higher ones, giving the 1951 pyramid a remarkably wide base.

Figure 1 is helpful for showing the effect of these changes over

[52] The preceding two paragraphs summarize results given by Veyret, pp. 119–120.

the last 70 years on the Canadian labor force and its relation to total population. If we take the portion of the population aged 20–60 as roughly approximating the potential labor force, then the long-run trend has obviously been an increase in the portion of the population available for work. Persons 20–60 years of age

Fig. 1. Age distribution of Canada's population, 1881–1951 (percentages).

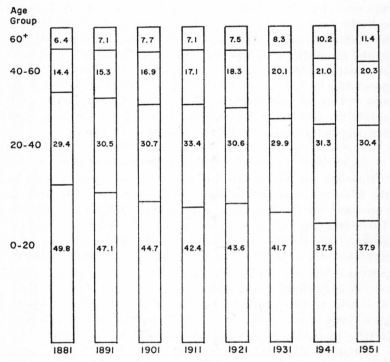

Age Group

	1881	1891	1901	1911	1921	1931	1941	1951
60⁺	6.4	7.1	7.7	7.1	7.5	8.3	10.2	11.4
40-60	14.4	15.3	16.9	17.1	18.3	20.1	21.0	20.3
20-40	29.4	30.5	30.7	33.4	30.6	29.9	31.3	30.4
0-20	49.8	47.1	44.7	42.4	43.6	41.7	37.5	37.9

Source: Paul Veyret, *La population du Canada*, Publications de la Faculté des Lettres de l'Université de Grenoble, VII (Paris, 1953), p. 133; *Canada Year Book, 1956*, p. 162.

were 43.8 per cent of the total in 1881; they were 52.3 per cent in 1941. However, a reversal — and a rather sharp one, at that — had cut this percentage down to 50.7 in 1951. If present birth rates continue, this percentage will go on falling until near the middle of the 1960's, at which time it will start rising rapidly. This situation is much more marked in Canada than in the United States, which has a larger fraction of its population in the older age groups and a smaller fraction in the younger groups than Canada.[53]

In the 1930's, it seemed to students of population in Canada and the United States that the falling birth rate portended a rise in the proportion of the population of labor-force age far beyond what aggregate demand could normally keep employed. Canada will again face such a situation in the 1970's because of the present odd population pyramid, and almost regardless of what the birth rate is doing at that time. Hence there is some reassurance in the calculations of demographers that even if the birth rate of a nation stabilizes at quite a low level, the portion of the population in the ages 15–59 can never exceed 60 per cent for long.[54] This proportion was reached in Canada at the end of the 1930's. It might be reached again in the future, but its appearance can only be transitory.

Population, labor force, and capital formation

How has the fraction of Canada's population participating in the labor force changed over time? This question stands for an important link between population changes and economic growth. Taken in connection with the population age distribution and the length of the work week, the share of the population in the labor force governs the total labor supply over time. The number of persons in the labor force per thousand population has risen quite considerably since Confederation. In 1870, 317.5 persons of every 1000 held or were seeking jobs. This figure was up to 347.5 by 1900, 392.3 in 1929, 408.9 in 1939. It hit a wartime peak of 432.3 in 1945, then dropped off rather sharply to 376.5 in 1952.[55]

Not nearly all of these changes reflect the desires of the average Canadian adult for work rather than leisure. As the preceding discussion of the population pyramid over time showed, the fraction of Canada's people in the working age groups has changed tremendously. The portion of Canadians in the 20–60 age brackets provides almost all of the pool from which the labor force is drawn, and this portion has suffered major long-run changes (see Figure 1).

[53] J. V. Grauman, "Effects of Population Trends upon Age Structure, With Application to the Americas," *Estadistica*, 14:278 (June 1956).

[54] Grauman, p. 278.

[55] Firestone, *Canada's Economic Development*, Table 6.

We have tried to make allowance for changes in the fraction of the Canadian populace of working age, to see whether Canadian preferences for work have changed systematically among Canadians of the normal working ages. Depressions and wars cloud the historical record; both, paradoxically, tend to raise the proportion of the population in the labor force. But the portion of adult Canadians seeking work seems to have risen from Confederation to the turn of the century, reached its peak sometime between then and 1920, and then declined slightly and irregularly to the present. The last phase — the decline — is actually the least certain of the three.

Since the end of World War II, data have become available estimating the fraction of each age and sex group of the population in the labor force.[56] Even over this short period, some striking changes come to light. The participation rate in the labor force for men over 65 fell almost a third in the decade following the war. Earlier retirement and the shift of labor out of agriculture have had marked effects here. Males 15–19 have also tended less and less to enter the labor force in favor of continuing their education. There is one striking increase in group participation rates — that for women aged 45 to 64. Here two factors have been at work. On the one hand, the tendency for women to marry and have families earlier in life has meant that many mothers are still willing and able to work when their family duties are discharged. On the other hand, the rapid growth of the service sector of the Canadian economy and the steady decline of prejudice against women in business has greatly boosted their employment opportunities. Under generally prosperous conditions, all the trends observed in postwar participation rates seem quite stable and likely to persist for some time.

THE MATURING OF THE CANADIAN ECONOMY

Taking a broad view of the growth of Canada's national output, the economist often explains it by reference to the nation's growing stock of factors of production and increases in the productivity of all those factors. If he is generous with his definitions of factor supply and productivity, these two concepts will prove sufficient to explain the growth of real output. This is a

[56] Canada, DBS, *The Labour Force, November 1945-January 1955* (Ottawa, 1955), pp. 21–22, 28–29.

dangerous practice, however, because of the weight the concept of productivity must bear.[57] It performs its usual chore of indicating the effect of innovations in product and technology which increase the economic fruits of a given flow of factor inputs. But productivity increases also reflect a number of other changes. Two very important ones of these will concern us in the following pages — the achievement of economies of scale in the process of economic growth, and improvement in the efficiency of the economy through rising allocative efficiency of factor markets and through utilization (as contrasted to discovery) of superior technology. Is there evidence that these components play an important role in Canadian economic growth? If so, should special provision be made for them in our forecasting procedure?

Tackling these questions is not an attractive chore in a study using statistical methods and aiming at numerical results. Yet both popular and academic discussions of Canadian economic development regularly convey the conviction that they are important. Take, for example, the concept of economic maturity commonly encountered in such discussions. Canadians show complete lack of agreement on whether their nation has achieved its economic adulthood. On one hand, there stands the sentiment embodied in one of Canada's great national clichés: "The time has arrived when we are to decide whether we will simply be hewers of wood and drawers of water." [58] This view has retained its popularity for eighty years while the economy has persisted in exporting a heavy volume of primary products and refusing to achieve the national self-sufficiency implied by "maturity." On the other hand, optimistic viewers of Canada's future often identify a wholesome maturity by applying a different test. They argue that some time in the twentieth century the economy reached a critical size and extent of settlement at which the gains through economies of scale were sharply accelerated.

These views have a vague and inchoate air to them. Nonetheless, the issues they raise for the long-range forecaster cannot be ignored. Due to such factors as economies of scale and changes in

---

[57] No doubt it is dangerous for other reasons as well. We shall neglect here the problems of identifying and measuring the effective quantities of factors of production and of accounting for changes in the international terms of trade within this framework.

[58] Quoted in the RCDPR *Report*, Vol. I, p. 51.

allocative efficiency, bends, angles, nonlinear trends, and the like
may appear at some points in a nation's economic development.
Many students have associated structural changes in the Canadian economy with some process of maturation, thereby implying
more or less identifiable points in time where breaks occur in
long-run trends. Economic forecasting is necessarily a matter of
projecting trends, the difference among forecasts lying in the
sophistication with which the trends are identified and measured.
Hence an understanding of any such critical points in the pattern
of structural change is highly important for successful analysis
and forecasting.

First, let us examine the evidence on the role of economies of
scale in the long-run growth of Canadian productivity. At least
three sorts of evidence might seem relevant. (1) Certain real
unit costs of social and economic overhead facilities are commonly
believed to become less burdensome to the economy as a whole
as its total size increases. There may be a possibility of detecting
this effect in the long-run pattern of Canadian employment. (2)
As a complex of secondary industries develops, certain economies
of scale external to the firm and industry seem to be won through
the sharing of a skilled labor pool, distribution facilities, financial
and other service functions, and finally the creation of a broad
market for standardized goods. There may be certain critical
stages in this process where the "maturity" concept has descriptive
value. (3) Finally, the Canadian economy may be gaining economies of scale of a sort through the rapid growth of internal
commercial circuits cutting the economy's short-run dependence
on foreign economic happenings and conferring some ability to
carry on independent national economic policies. One can test
this possibility by checking the sensitivity of the economy over
time to prosperity and depression in other countries and the
structural connections between domestic income and employment
levels and Canada's international trade and payments. Let us
look in turn at each of these three hypotheses and the relevant
evidence.

Changes in Canadian employment patterns

Looking at long-run changes in the composition of employment
is a highly unsatisfactory way of getting at the working of
economies of scale in economic development, but it is justified on

the positive grounds that economies of scale are often held to be visible in labor-force changes and on the negative grounds that none of the alternatives is particularly appetizing. It is well, how-ever, to be aware how far the historic record of labor inputs stands from the desired record of economies of scale. The hypothesis states that growth of the total Canadian economy or portions thereof has allowed some or all sectors to produce more goods and services relative to the amount of all inputs supplied. The historic size and distribution of the labor force gives us only the record of one sort of factor input. There is a chance, though, that it may suffice as a crude index of total input for some sectors which pro-vide a relatively fixed output or service to the economy as a whole.

Long-run changes in the number of Canadians employed in various sectors of the economy appear in Table 2. Percentage declines, computed from data in this table, in three sectors are very striking. In 1881, 48.0 per cent of Canada's labor force was employed in agriculture, 2.1 per cent in fishing and trapping, and 15.5 per cent in construction. By 1951, these figures had fallen respectively to 19.4 per cent, 0.7 per cent, and 6.8 per cent. Each of these sectors is less than half as prominent as before in the occupational pattern. One might argue that much of the activity of each of these sectors is a fixed charge on Canada's ability to produce. Both agriculture and fishing produce subsistence goods, the demand for which is not greatly affected by changes in na-tional income per capita. This is important, but it has nothing to do with economies of scale either in these industries themselves or in the economy as a whole. Canadian agriculture and fishing have not been perpetually depressed and inefficient economic backwaters, but rather successful export sectors. Their relative decline has not come through any awakening of the economy but rather through the simple working of technological advance and shifts in consumer spending patterns with rising incomes. The ongoing importance of the transfer of labor from these sectors to other lines of activity comes in its contribution to the aggregate productivity growth rate of the economy, as we shall see below. One might also take construction activity to be a fixed charge on Canada's productive facilities and infer a working of economies of scale in the fall in the share of the labor force thus engaged. But again appearances are deceptive. It is true that settling a new region involves heavy demands for housing, transportation

Table 2.   Number of persons employed in various sectors of Canadian industry, by census years, 1871–1951 (thousands).

| | Primary | | | | | Secondary | | | Tertiary | | | |
Year	Agri-culture	Fishing, trapping	Mining	Forest operations	Total primary	Manufac-turing	Construc-tion	Total secondary	Public utilities	Other tertiary	Total tertiary	Total Total
1871	566	—	—	—	—	148	—	—	—	—	192	1,130
1881	662	29	7	8	706	190	215	405	—	—	267	1,378
1891	735	30	16	13	794	260	163	423	—	—	389	1,606
1901	717	27	29	17	790	309	188	497	—	—	496	1,783
1911	934	35	63	43	1,075	541	198	739	—	—	911	2,725
1921	1,042	29	51	40	1,162	556	284	840	—	—	1,171	3,173
1951	991	38	85	88	1,202	1,356	353	1,709	440	1,804	2,244	5,155

Source: O. J. Firestone, *Canada's Economic Development, 1867–1953, With Special Reference to Changes in the Country's National Product and National Wealth*, Income and Wealth Series VII (London, 1958), Part II, Section 9, Table 65.

facilities, public works, and all kinds of commercial property which are extremely durable. After an initial push in a new region, a much smaller fraction of the labor force can take care of replacements and improvements. But there is little or no connection with economies of scale, which could exist only because larger buildings were more efficient or (more likely) because a larger economy could use its stock of buildings more efficiently. The decline of the portion of the labor force in construction probably reflects rather the technology of its product — the fact that even in a capital-scarce region it is often most efficient to build a structure which is extremely durable and larger than the current level of demand would warrant.[59]

There are a few other portions of the labor force which may service fixed charges on the economy and where a decline in the percentage of the labor force occupied may indeed reflect economies of scale. They are, however, hard to dig out of available statistics. The most conspicuous case is Canada's railway network. Apart from the enormous original cost of constructing it, keeping it in operation requires a current drain on Canada's factors of production which is quite independent of the actual volume of traffic being carried. Dramatic increases in traffic can take place without anything approaching proportional expansion of current inputs, as World War II showed. Likewise, over the long run, the system will serve the growing demands placed upon it by growing population and incomes without proportionate increases in real costs. The same is true, though less spectacularly so, of many other facilities. Many government services, especially below the federal level, depend for their "input requirements" on the fact of their existence much more than on the volume of economic activity which goes on within their jurisdiction.[60]

The same phenomenon shows up in many commercial enter-

[59] Whether the explanation turns on technology or economies of scale, the declining share of the labor force engaged in construction has considerable interest for the forecaster. One could concoct a mathematical model of economic growth which would predict the fraction of the labor force engaged in construction to fall rapidly at first, then slowly, and finally approach a constant percentage value. The share of Canadian labor in construction fell rapidly in the nineteenth century but has only wavered erratically downward since then. It may be nearing the time when no secular trend will be visible.

[60] Compare A. Maddison, "Productivity in an Expanding Economy," *EJ*, 62:592 (September 1952).

prises. Modern technology frequently imposes very high minimum efficient outputs upon many production processes. These businesses, once established, can steadily increase their output without proportionate increase of physical inputs. Probably the most important instance of this outside of transportation is Canada's distribution system, which, in the absence of geographic shifts of population, has almost always been expanded well beyond the requirements of current flows of commodities. The burden of accumulating inventories to sustain the flow of commerce has clearly declined since the beginning of the century. As we shall see in Chapter 11, inventory accumulation absorbed 3 per cent or more of gross national product during 1901–1915, less than 2 per cent during 1936–1940 and 1946–1955. Of course this is an economy of scale which saves capital inputs but not necessarily labor. The portion of total employment in the distributive sector has been rising, but consumer preferences have clearly been shifting toward paying for extra distributional conveniences, so no inference concerning economies of scale and the labor force is possible.

There are, then, a few signs of economies of scale and of a process of maturing in Canada's labor force changes. But one must remember that the oft-heard gains of economies of scale through the filling out of the economy will probably affect only a few industries. Many deceptive appearances tend to encourage a stronger view. Finally, where economies of scale from expansion of the national economy are visible there is nothing to portend any sudden variations in the rate of structural change, and hence nothing which needs to be noted independently in establishing a long-range forecast.[61]

Filling out the Canadian manufacturing sector

Statistical evidence tells us that for the last forty years, at least, Canada has slowly but steadily been developing a complete manufacturing sector, producing at least part of domestic purchases of most kinds of processed goods. This development shows up

---

[61] One possible exception, discussed in Chapter 9 is an eventual falling off of the rate of transfer of labor away from Canadian agriculture. *Ceteris paribus,* a decline in this transfer would reduce the over-all rate of growth of labor productivity in Canada because output per man in agriculture stands well below that for the rest of the economy. But since this slowing down will not be a major feature in the situation by 1970, we do not stress the point.

qualitatively in the types of industries flourishing in Canada and quantitatively in the portion of Canadian purchases of manufactures and intermediate goods made from Canadian firms.

The classic principle of comparative advantage tells us that a country normally does not best serve its own welfare by establishing *every* type of economic activity within its borders. This doctrine certainly implies limits to how many of Canada's factors of production should be allocated to domestic manufacturing as a whole. This issue, however, must in practice be regarded as a closed one. Not only is the National Policy as strongly entrenched in popular sentiment as ever (as time and progress still the voices of its opponents on prairie farms and in Maritime cities), but also the Canadian tariff serves as rationally as ever the purpose for which it was designed. The threat to the Canadian economy of heavy labor migration to the United States, taken in connection with the low labor-intensity of Canada's major export industries, gives the Canadian tariff a clearer justification than that of almost any other nation.[62] If Canada is still in the stage of gaining economies of scale from increased population, it is not certain that the average Canadian would benefit from lower tariffs and more extensive export production, at least so long as United States tariffs keep their present character.

Granting that Canada has probably been justified economically in promoting domestic manufacturing, the question remains why this structure has become so diversified and whether and how its growth reflects any gain of economic maturity. In an economy with a growing population, good supplies of skilled labor and capital and reasonable social and political stability, the manufacturing sector tends for several reasons to fill out over time, sometimes in apparent defiance of comparative cost considerations. Product differentiation in the consumer goods area usually favors domestic firms in close touch with tastes in the home market. Such effects are not absent from the producer and intermediate goods sectors. Second, some sectors of manufacturing and all of the related service facilities are "sheltered" industries in that their outputs are for various practical reasons not traded internationally. Third, almost any manufacture or processed raw material

[62] For an excellent evaluation of Canadian tariff policy in the light of modern tariff theory, see C. L. Barber, "Canadian Tariff Policy," *CJEPS*, 21:513–530 (November 1955).

available in a country serves as an intermediate good for other manufacturing establishments, actual or potential. Establishment of some manufacturing sectors then has a supply effect favoring the establishment of still others in the domestic economy, once the effects of transfer costs on location are recognized.

Some evidence turned up in the famous 1936 study of Canadian-American industry reflects these trends. One hundred and twelve Canadian branch firms gave in answer to a questionnaire the "Canadian content" of their products for the period 1926–1933. For the group, the figure was 69 per cent in 1926, 72 per cent in 1929 and 81 per cent in 1933.[63] Part, and quite possibly all, of the change from 1929 to 1933 was due to the impact of the Great Depression on Canada's foreign trade. International adjustments, however, could hardly explain the change for the years 1926 to 1929.

More recently, the first study of the interindustry structure of the Canadian economy has offered reliable and global figures for the Canadian content of Canada's industries. These hold considerable interest, despite the fact that they exist only for one year (1949) and hence are no help on gauging the trend. The following figures show the Canadian content of total output (total input) for seven broad segments of Canadian manufacturing: food, beverage and tobacco industries, 94 per cent; clothing and household goods industries, 84 per cent; forest products industries, 97 per cent; metal products industries, 89 per cent; electrical apparatus and supplies industry, 90 per cent; mineral products industries, 79 per cent; miscellaneous manufacturing industries, 93 per cent.[64] Unfortunately these figures are in no way comparable with those presented in *Canadian-American Industry*.

Other evidence of the expansion of Canada's manufacturing sector appears in the portion of exportable raw materials processed in Canada and in changes in the market share of major import-competing industries. Harry E. English has computed indexes of the net value of Canadian production and imports of selected manufactured goods for 1949, based on the 1926–1929 average. As shown in Table 3, taken from his figures, Canadian production

---

[63] H. Marshall, F. A. Southard, Jr., and K. W. Taylor, *Canadian-American Industry, A Study in International Investment* (New Haven, 1936), pp. 233–234.

[64] Calculated from Canada, DBS, *The Inter-Industry Flow of Goods and Services, Canada, 1949* (Ottawa, 1956), Table 1.

Table 3.   Indexes of net value of Canadian production and imports
of selected manufactures for 1949 (1926–1929 = 100).

Industry	Domestic production	Imports
Textiles:		
primary	371	—
clothing	325	200
Chemicals	408	374
Iron and steel	354	239
Industrial machinery	438	408
Agricultural machinery	355	610
Automobiles and parts	470	229
Electrical apparatus	527	288

Source: H. E. English, "The Role of International Trade in Canadian Economic Development since the 1920's," (Unpublished Ph.D. thesis, University of California, 1957), Table 25, p. 192.

has grown faster than imports for all sectors except agricultural machinery, where an important tariff change occurred. It should be pointed out again that these figures represent the complex outcome of the processes of international adjustment and not just the abilities of Canada as a manufacturing nation in any simple sense. Canada's chemicals and industrial machinery have made the poorest showings against import competition during the two-decade period in question. Both produce a variety of specialized products and hence suffer from the small Canadian market compared to the United States; in many lines of production, economies of scale for the plant continue to accrue up to outputs which are large even in comparison to United States markets.

While the maturity of Canada's manufacturing industry seems to show up in the Canadian content of current inputs, the same is not true for the machinery and equipment used in Canadian factories. In 1929, imports made up one-fifth of all Canadian machinery and equipment purchases; around 1950, the figure had risen to one-third. In both periods, about 90 per cent of machinery and equipment imports came from the United States.[65] These figures reflect again the great and continuing dependence of Canada upon United States technology. In general, Canadians

[65] Canada, Department of Trade and Commerce, *Private and Public Investment in Canada, 1926–1951* (Ottawa, 1951), pp. 22–23.

seem to produce their own capital goods only for processes where technology is relatively simple or relatively stable or, alternately, for export industries where Canada is a leading world producer.[66]

Of the remaining industries, automobiles and electrical apparatus became established Canadian industries only during the period covered. But no such factor explains the market share gains of Canadian textiles and iron and steel. "It would appear that some factor other than age has been of predominant importance in explaining the distinctive behavior of these industries." [67]

Canada now processes more of her nonferrous metals production at home than in the 1920's, although the changes are not spectacular. Again, of course, heavy foreign demand for Canadian metals is reflected just as much as Canada's ability to create and support processing operations. The portion of Canadian copper exported fell from 94 per cent in 1926–1929 to 75 per cent in 1948–49. The figure for lead has fallen slightly. Canada now uses at home one-fifth of her aluminum production.[68]

The report of the Royal Commission on Dominion-Provincial Relations and subsequent work by O. J. Firestone at the Department of Trade and Commerce have detailed the growth in the types of industrial operations carried on in Canada, thereby providing a direct picture of the filling-out process. Two influences stand out among the catalytic agents behind the formation of new Canadian industries. One is the effect of wars and preparation for wars, the other is the effect of changing energy sources and power technology. Neither has much to do with economies of scale directly.

World War I both advanced the growth of the rising staple industries of the day and spurred the establishment of totally new industries. Nonferrous metals and pulp and paper production grew rapidly, both because the war swelled demands for their products and because hydroelectric power supplies (especially important for pulp and paper) increased greatly. As the hostilities cut off the flow of manufactured imports into Canada, central Canada consolidated its position as the heartland of Canadian manu-

[66] Moore, *American Influence in Canadian Mining,* pp. 95–98.

[67] H. E. English, "The Role of International Trade in Canadian Economic Development since the 1920's" (unpublished Ph.D. thesis, University of California, 1957), pp. 194–195.

[68] English, pp. 156–160.

facturing and of commercial and financial services. Overseas munitions orders were of course a temporary stimulus, but, in the eyes of the Royal Commission, "the demands imposed and the facilities required to meet them resulted in a considerable increase in technical and mechanical efficiency." The demand for military goods also incited diversification of Canada's basic steel industry, which had been heavily specialized to serve the needs of railways and other forms of heavy construction.[69] The important fact for the long run, of course, is that the vitality and potential of the Canadian economy were such that war-swollen productive apparatus could easily be absorbed into the peacetime economy.[70] The Royal Commission fulfilled its obligation for moral piety by abhorring the suggestion that Canada was better off than if the war had not occurred. The nasty truth remains, however, that World War I advanced Canada's industrial facilities and skills in ways which would have taken much longer under normal peacetime stimuli.

World War II brought the same sort of changes to the Canadian economy as did its grim predecessor. In no normal year of the interwar period did manufacturing furnish more than 45 per cent of total value added for Canada. In 1943, this percentage reached a peak of 57 per cent and in 1950 it stood at 50 per cent. "Expansion of productive capacity in manufacturing was particularly striking in such fields as tool making, electrical apparatus, chemicals and aluminum . . . Entire new industries were created, making for example roller bearings, magnesium and artificial rubber . . . Advances were made in the production of finished goods and equipment, some of which were of a type quite new to Canadian industry and which had previously been imported, such as optical glass, high octane gasoline, penicillin and sulfa drugs." [71] The Department of Reconstruction and Supply estimated that roughly two-thirds of the special wartime industry structure was adaptable to peacetime uses, and the reconversion was quickly accomplished by the end of 1947.[72]

---

[69] Canada, RCDPR, *Report*, Vol. I, p. 108.

[70] B. H. Higgins and A. Lerner, "Trends and Structure of the Economy," in *Canada*, ed. G. W. Brown (Berkeley and Los Angeles, 1950), pp. 251–253.

[71] Canada, Department of Trade and Commerce, *Private and Public Investment in Canada*, pp. 36–37.

[72] Canada, Department of Reconstruction and Supply, *Encouragement to Industrial Expansion in Canada, Operation of Special Depreciation Provisions, November 10, 1944-March 31, 1949* (Ottawa, 1948), pp. 13–15.

During the twentieth century, resource discovery and technological change have been exceedingly kind to Canada. Not the least of their blessings has been making feasible a much larger and more complex manufacturing industry than would otherwise have developed. In and around the 1920's, the development of hydroelectric power and the gasoline engine helped to overcome Canada's handicaps of poor coal resources and great internal distances. The rising importance of nonferrous metals overcame her disadvantages in basic iron and steel production. Both types of developments furthered many branches of manufacturing which had previously not been feasible.[73]

Since World War II, Canada has seen a similar expansion based on new technology and new resources. Before the late 1940's a prudent long-range forecaster would have seen Canada's growth potential as distinctly limited by a scarcity of energy sources. Today, the discoveries of oil and natural gas in the prairies have done much to remove this limitation. Developments in the way of new products and new technology have been widespread, although there have been few changes so sweeping as those of the 1920's. The Department of Trade and Commerce cites the following sorts of "rounding out" in the postwar years: many firms in the metals and chemicals fields have integrated backward or forward to undertake new types of processing activities; other firms have expanded horizontally to add to their selling lines products new to Canadian industry; new technology has allowed more efficient processing and use of by-products in many fields (for example, waste pulp) and widened product varieties in others (for example, synthetic yarns). Commodities manufactured in Canada for the first time in the postwar years include "jet aircraft, diesel locomotives, gas turbines, roller bearings, a wide range of automobile parts and various kinds of heavy machinery and equipment, such as special types of pulp machinery, road building equipment, oil well equipment, and heavy agricultural implements."[74]

What does all this evidence mean in terms of economic maturity and future growth prospects? New lines of business have opened in Canada for three central reasons — secular growth of the

[73] Canada, RCDPR, *Report*. Vol. I, pp. 115–116.
[74] Canada, Department of Trade and Commerce, *Private and Public Investment in Canada*, pp. 41–42.

market to a size consistent with low-cost operations, growth of the supply of some important input or raw material, and temporary exclusion of foreign supplies during wartime. In the absence of war and depression and in the presence of steady population growth, this proliferation of the industrial structure seems to continue at a slow rate. Probably that rate is much less rapid than in the late nineteenth century; a slower growth rate for the total population of business enterprises may indicate that this is the case. But there is no obvious tendency for this expansion of the economic structure to slow down, and so the trend can safely be taken as a constant one for moderately long-range forecasting. No appeal to any critical stage of economic maturity seems in order.

A final sort of evidence which may have something to do with the maturity of the Canadian economy concerns the sensitivity of Canadian income and employment levels to economic changes abroad, particularly income fluctuations in the United States. This evidence appears in detail in the following chapter where short-run changes in income and its components are studied extensively. The conclusions reached there are, briefly, that (1) no clear trends in the structure of the Canadian economy establish a reduction in dependence on foreign economic changes over the last three decades, but nonetheless (2) the actual sensitivity of Canadian economic activity to prosperity and depression in the United States seems to have diminished over a long period of time. Here again is slight evidence of a steady trend toward greater economic maturity, but nothing in the way of critical changes.

In sum, the Canadian economy reveals little in the way of critical turns in its growth except from such external forces as the swing in the tide of migration at the turn of the century and the two world wars. This leaves rather little ground for employing any descriptive concept of maturity to the economy on the basis of trends in the securing of economies of scale. There remains, however, the other special sort of productivity gain which we shall treat in this section, stemming from improved efficiency of factor allocation or utilization of better technology. Now these are fairly nebulous matters to discuss. The allocative efficiency of an economy will improve as transportations costs decline, as employment information of all sorts is diffused more widely,

as a willingness to move in response to economic incentives grows
more prevalent among labor force members, and so forth. Better
technology will be used as education and physical skills are
more and more diffused among the population, as contact with
foreign owners of advanced technology increases, as an optimistic
business outlook makes businessmen more willing to replace
obsolete machinery, etc. One could note copious evidences of all
these conditions in the Canadian economy, but still end with little
quantitative information.

Let us try a slightly different technique for getting at the same
material. Economists often attempt to judge the performance
of an industry by placing it against a set of criteria for optimal
functioning derived *a priori* from economic theory. Perhaps the
same sort of technique could be used in rough fashion on nations
to evaluate the income levels and growth rates they achieve
subject to their physical circumstances. An acceptable theoretical
norm would be hard to come by for this purpose, but a theoretical
norm is not the only possibility.

Let us pursue this line of thought with special reference to the
Canadian economy. Canada has at her southern doorstep the
wealthiest nation in the world, one which continues to achieve
great economic gains through effective and steadily improving
technology, both in the narrow realms of production and distribution methods and in the broader realms of social and economic
organization. Subject to the limitations of geography, climate, and
the like, has Canada followed as fully as possible the paths of
economic advancement blazed by the United States? Specifically,
does the Canadian economy display any inferiority in productivity
and technology to the United States not explained by fixed
physical factors? Quite a bit of evidence exists on this question.

Because Canada and the United States share the same language,
the same culture, and to a large degree the same business enterprises, Canada's economy would have to be ranked immature if it
uses less advanced technology or shows lower productivity in
comparable situations. Generally the same sorts of input combinations bear slightly fewer fruits north of the border, this much is
certain. Is this only because of the smaller Canadian market
rubbing against very extensive economies of scale? Or does Canadian productivity and skill suffer infirmities which will demand
more than the growth of markets as a palliative?

One does not observe a nation's stock of technology or its efficiency in fact or allocation directly, only their results. There are two factors reflecting (*inter alia*) technology and skill which we can check for signs of Canadian inferiority to the United States, size of establishment and labor productivity.

There are two convenient sources of information on the relative size of United States and Canadian manufacturing establishments — an older study by V. W. Bladen using 1923-24 data and a recent one by Gideon Rosenbluth based on 1947-48 data. Bladen developed a comparison of the distribution in the United States and in Canada of employment by size of establishment. In the United States, he found, 40 per cent of all employees work in establishments employing over 500, while in Canada only 20 per cent of all employees are in such large plants. In each country, 21 per cent of the labor force is in establishments employing 201-500 workers; that is, this medium-sized establishment is equally common in both countries.[75] As Bladen points out, we do not know whether this pattern arises because the Canadian establishment typically serves a smaller market or because Canada specializes in production where small firms are relatively efficient. Looking at particular industries, indeed, Canadian establishments average larger than American ones in several key cases — flour milling, pulp and paper, and cotton yarn and cloth. The opposite is true for electrical apparatus, bread and bakery products, and slaughtering and meat packing.[76]

Rosenbluth's data come in a different form. For fifty-three manufacturing industries, selected for comparability, he shows the ratio of employment per firm (not establishment) in the United States to employment per firm in Canada. The median United States industry is ten times as large as its Canadian counterpart. The median United States industry has eight times as many firms. Therefore, the median ratio of average firm size is only 1.2 to 1. In twenty of the fifty-three industries, the average United States firm is smaller.[77] For drawing inferences about technological similarity, such information would be more useful on the basis of establishments rather than firms, since the

[75] V. W. Bladen, "The Size of the Establishment in Canadian and American Industry," *Contributions to Canadian Economics* (1928), p. 68.
[76] *Ibid.*, pp. 56-59.
[77] G. Rosenbluth, *Concentration in Canadian Manufacturing Industries* (Princeton, 1957), pp. 82-84.

establishment is the unit embodying the restraints of technology, and since the average number of establishments per firm no doubt differs between the United States and Canada. Nevertheless, Rosenbluth's figures offer strong support for the hypothesis that United States and Canadian establishment sizes are normally quite similar. If one makes the very plausible guess that the average Canadian firm has fewer establishments than its United States counterpart, then the ratio of United States to Canadian *establishment* size must be less than 1.2 to 1.

Rosenbluth himself presses the argument farther on intuitive grounds. He concedes that the small size of the Canadian market and the unprofitability of fully integrated production may restrain the use of the most advanced United States technology in Canada. But he holds that otherwise the two countries will tend to use the same methods of production.

Specialized machinery, which could not be produced for the Canadian market alone, can be easily imported from the United States, and what is perhaps more important, repair services, parts, and facilities for training technical and administrative personnel are easily accessible. In these ways production techniques dependent on the external economies resulting from the large United States markets have been made available to the much smaller Canadian market. Hence the difference in plant and firm sizes in the two countries is slight.[78]

If Canadian enterprise does suffer because of a smaller domestic market, then, the reason is not because establishments are smaller than those which United States firms find efficient. There are, of course, many other possible ways in which the smaller market could put Canadian firms at a disadvantage, of which one of the most important is probably the smaller amount of product specialization possible within the typical Canadian plant. This is certainly true for Canadian textiles and fine papers.[79]

The upshot of the evidence seems to be that Canada generally draws upon the same stock of technology as the United States. Any inferiority in her ability to use it must be due to such factors as harsher physical circumstances and a smaller domestic market.

[78] Rosenbluth, *Concentration in Canadian Manufacturing Industries,* pp. 84–85.
[79] English, pp. 197–220; Canadian Pulp and Paper Association, *Submission to the Royal Commission on Canada's Economic Prospects* (Montreal, 1956), pp. 54–58; compare Young, p. 91.

This conclusion itself suggests a look at some further data, namely, the relative levels and growth rates of productivity in the United States and Canada. One might reason in the following way. It is quite unlikely that economies of scale of all sorts are so extensive that they continue to accrue to the United States economy as fast as to the Canadian economy when both are growing at the same rate. Thus if economies of scale account for part of Canada's lower physical productivity of labor, at least in a few industries, then Canadian labor productivity should be gaining on that of the United States over reasonably long periods of time.

This in fact seems to be the case in recent decades. G. D. Sutton's study shows that average annual Canadian production in 1929–1933 per employed person was 73.9 per cent of United States production for the period, but by 1946–1950 it had risen to 78.4 per cent. This rise was visible in both the productivity of employed persons in agriculture (Canada rose from 57.8 to 67.0 per cent of the United States) and in nonagricultural industries (Canada rose from 83.0 to 86.1 per cent of the United States).[80]

Sutton suggests that three factors explain the remaining 14 per cent difference between Canadian and United States productivity outside of agriculture: (1) the smaller scale of the Canadian market and consequently the smaller scale of production; (2) the fact that many specialties which are imported into Canada from the United States come from high-productivity industries; (3) the greater burden for Canada of transportation, storage, and communication charges.[81] Putting these elements together — Canada's more rapid rate of gain in productivity and the causes of her remaining backwardness — one concludes that Canada does not lag behind the United States except from elements associated with the smaller size of her market, and that this disadvantage is steadily receding in importance. Sutton points out that one indisputable source of future Canadian gains relative to the

---

[80] G. D. Sutton, "Productivity in Canada," *CJEPS*, 19:197 (May 1953), Table IX.

[81] *Ibid.*, pp. 197–198. Three other studies which generally support these conclusions are A. Maddison, "Productivity in Canada, the United Kingdom, and the United States," *OEP*, 4:235–242 (October 1952); F. W. Dresch, *Productivity in Manufacturing in the Post War Period in Canada, Western Europe and the United States* (Palo Alto, 1953); and J. B. Heath, "British-Canadian Manufacturing Productivity," *EJ*, 67:665–691 (December 1957).

United States lies in the fact that Canada still has further to go in transferring labor from agricultural to nonagricultural pursuits.[82]

In short, there is a significant sense in which the Canadian economy has achieved considerable economic maturity at some time in the past, if one will accept as a condition of maturity a technology and factor utilization pattern which compares favorably with that of the United States. Allowing for the restraints of climate and geography Canada has turned in a record of economic performance which definitely meets this test. Nor are the uses of this fact only liturgical; the forecaster can proceed somewhat more boldly to examine trends in United States technology, productivity, and the like with hope that his findings will also be relevant to Canadian experience.

[82] Sutton, "Productivity in Canada," pp. 200–201.

3
Short-run Changes in Canadian Income

Long-run economic changes are the subject of this study. Yet the long run, whether past or future, is the sum of a series of short periods. No theory of long-period change in the past is likely to be valid if it is inconsistent with what we know about historic patterns of short-period change. No such long-period theory can safely be placed in the hands of the long-run forecaster. Lord Keynes' famous pronouncement on human mortality and the long run has become common currency among economists. Its moral, however, has usually been read as a call to jettison the long run rather than as an injunction to reinterpret it. This chapter surveys the short-period process which determines Canada's gross national product and its components. Its purpose is to show the consistency between the long-run model implied by the staple theory and the historic chronicle of short-period income changes. The argument breaks logically into two steps. First, we argue that the short-period mechanism of income adjustment in the Canadian economy has been unchanged for five decades, except for explainable special features. Second, we argue that this short-period mechanism is consistent with the long-run staple theory, in that when the short-run forces work themselves out the results will mirror the predictions of the long-run theory. Thus, long-run forces steer the economy in the short run, subject to the jars and jolts of random, transitional factors.

A MODEL OF INCOME DETERMINATION

Before surveying the supporting evidence, let us set down, in the fashion of a short story, the process of Canadian income adjustment. The most fundamental variable is the level of exports of goods and services. Insofar as any measurable variable determines Canadian gross domestic investment in plant and equipment, it is Canada's exports. This relation operates, on the average, with a one-year lag. Investment is the main determinant of current gross national product unless major changes are occurring in the level of government purchases of goods and services. The level of gross national expenditure normally moves at the same pace as personal disposable income, which in turn determines Canadian consumer expenditures. This relation also operates partly with a one-year lag; this year's consumption reflects not only this year's income but also past habits of consumption reflected in last year's consumption level. Imports bear a rather complex relation to income, since they depend in different ways on investment and consumption. The income elasticity of Canada's demand for imports is quite high, so that rising personal disposable income usually forces a sharp rise in some classes of imports. Another large chunk of Canadian imports is investment goods, depending heavily on the level and composition of gross domestic investment. Thus, total imports do not correlate closely with income, consumption, or investment separately. Changes in consumption and investment, however, jointly explain them very well.

Several cross-currents normally disturb this mechanism. First of all, inventory accumulation chronically makes belated adjustments to changes in the level of income. Canadian businesses appear habitually unable to maintain inventories in any hypothetical desired relation to current income. The data suggest that inventories "hunt" some desired level with about a one-year lag. When income rises very rapidly, inventory accumulation falls behind. When income growth suddenly slacks off, or when income slips back, inventories usually keep on growing for at least a year. Thus one part of gross domestic investment changes independently of the current or immediate past level of exports.

Another cross-current affecting investment levels arises from the current rate of population growth and change in the age composition of the population. The immediate determinants of business investment usually appear to be the level of business liquidity and the state of expectations. Lagged exports affect the former clearly enough, but they obviously share with a good many other factors the role of determining expectations. A prominent partner in the function of determining investors' outlook for long-term capital formation is population growth. Especially in industries serving the home market, businessmen forming their long-term investment plans seem to base their decisions heavily on the prospects for growing markets reflected in current population growth. This conjecture is hard to demonstrate statistically, but it is also impossible to disprove. Population growth, of course, directly affects another category of business investment — residential construction. However, this is a complicated relation because of the powerful influence of the existing stock of dwellings. The historic record of the building cycle in Canada bears witness to the influence of this stock.

In the next section, we shall have to elaborate upon this story, showing how the Canadian economy is imbedded in an international network of trade, capital, and population movements. Before facing that extra complication, let us review the statistical evidence behind the model already presented.

The first stage is the relation between exports and gross domestic investment, and between exports and gross national product. Two studies published in the 1940's uncovered extremely close relation during the interwar period between one year's commodity exports from Canada and the following year's national income. Gilbert Jackson found a correlation of 0.923 between exports and lagged national income, both measured in current dollars.[1] In a more careful study, Munzer found that, between 1923 and 1938, correlations between commodity exports and lagged national income produced stood between 0.987 and 0.989, whether current or constant dollar values were employed. On the average, Munzer found a value of the export multiplier during this period of 1.67, a $1.00 change in exports producing a $1.67 change in income during the following year.[2] He also found that this multiplier seemed to vary with the level of income, taking a much higher value when income stood at depression levels than during years of prosperity.[3] Fortunately, he did not lay much stress on this difference. Many hypotheses would explain this result even without reference to the peculiar conditions of the 1930's (which Munzer notes), and some of these hypotheses have nothing to do with causal connections between exports and income.

Why should Canada's national income correlate so highly with

[1] Gilbert Jackson and Associates, *Exports and National Income* (1945).

[2] Edward Munzer, "Exports and National Income in Canada," *CJEPS*, 11:36–38 (February 1945).

[3] *Ibid.*, p. 39. Interesting comments on the exports-investment connection in time of depression appear in F. W. Burton, "The Business Cycle and the Problem of Economic Policy," *The Canadian Economy and Its Problems*, ed. Harold A. Innis and A. F. W. Plumptre (Toronto, 1934), p. 156.

the previous year's exports? Certainly we expect a high correlation between exports and current income, if only because exports are part of current income. But a high correlation between exports and next year's income suggests that some important behavioral factor may be at work. The obvious answer is the correct one, judging from available information. The level of exports has a major effect on current decisions by businessmen to increase their plant and equipment, and hence it affects gross domestic investment when these plans materialize as additions to Canada's capital stock.

Two pieces of evidence back this generalization. First, English has calculated for the years 1926–1950 (omitting 1942–1945) the correlation between commodity exports and gross domestic investment in Canada, both with and without a one-year lag. The correlation between exports and current gross domestic investment was 0.91; that between exports and gross domestic investment the following year was 0.95. The only significant deviations in the latter relation were for the years 1946 and 1947, when variations in government spending and the postwar disruption of foreign trade severed the normal connection. As English recognizes, the chance of observing such a difference in correlation coefficients when the true parameters are identical is as high as one-third.[4] But ample evidence exists of the effect of rising exports on investment in particular industries to sustain the view that this lag is both a significant and a durable one.

One can develop a piece of indirect proof of the significance of the export-investment relation by checking the correlation between exports of goods *and services* (the total of current account credits) and current gross investment. The reasoning behind this test is as follows: The close relation between *commodity* exports and lagged income and investment might exist solely because of the normal correlation between exports and current income, taken along with the well-known autocorrelation of national income series from year to year. If this were the case, then there should also be a high correlation between total current account credits and both current and lagged income and investment. But all of these correlations are noticeably lower, and the correlation be-

[4] Harry E. English, "The Role of International Trade in Canadian Economic Development Since the 1920's," unpublished Ph.D. thesis (University of California, Berkeley, 1957), pp. 49–51.

tween goods and services exports and current business investment (gross domestic investment minus residential construction) is only 0.69 for the period 1926–1956 minus the war years, far too low to suggest a causal relation. Thus the much higher correlations between commodity exports and investment are consistent with the working of some powerful accelerator-type mechanism or at least a strong connection between the level of exports and the state of business expectations.

Several writers have studied the income-consumption relation for Canada. Their results agree nicely on the form of the function as it affects short-term income determination. The main determinant of aggregate consumption is of course the current year's disposable personal income. But memories of the past also influence consumer behavior. Modigliani has produced a Canadian consumption function revealing a very good fit for the interwar years which incorporates both current and highest previous gross national product.[5] More recently, T. M. Brown has argued in an excellent paper that the influence of memory on current consumption operates through habit persistence and an incomplete adjustment of last year's consumption pattern to this year's (changed) income. This hypothesis implies that current consumption will show a positive relation not just to current income but also to last year's consumption. The 1926–1949 data fit this pattern very closely. As Brown points out, one could foresee this upon realizing that the residuals from a simple regression relating consumption to current income are negative when Canadian income is rising, positive when it is falling.[6] As their paychecks rise, Canadian households require time to make the full upward adjustment of their consumption standards to the usual average relation to income. During years of falling incomes, belt-tightening comes about only with a lag.

This income-consumption relation has important consequences for the working of the multiplier in the Canadian economy (whether the exogenous force be exports, government spending,

[5] Using these variables plus the previous year's GNP, he gets a correlation coefficient of 0.97 for the years 1923–1939. See Franco Modigliani, "Fluctuations in the Saving-Income Ratio: A Problem in Economic Forecasting," in Conference on Research in Income and Wealth, *Studies in Income and Wealth,* Volume Eleven (New York, 1949), pp. 392–395.

[6] T. M. Brown, "Habit Persistence and Lags in Consumer Behavior," *Econometrica,* 20:355–371 (July 1952).

or domestic investment). Because of the persistence of consumer habits, the marginal propensity to consume will be lower, the shorter the reaction time allowed. This in turn means that the multiplier will take a higher value over long periods than over short ones,[7] and it offers some grounds for expecting that Canadian boom periods would be slow starters. It also suggests that at the end of boom periods personal consumption would appear as an "element of strength."

Another plausible hypothesis about the relation between consumption and income in Canada made its appearance about the same time as Brown's research. In a study of income changes during the decade of the 1920's, V. W. Malach was faced with the problem of explaining a fall in personal consumption expenditures in two consecutive years when investment, exports, and income were all rising. The hypothesis he put forth was that these two years saw a heavy income redistribution to profits and away from wages and salaries, and that the difference in the average propensity to save of these two groups of income recipients was enough that the redistribution cut total consumer spending. Plotting the average propensity to consume (the anual ratio of consumption to income) against the wage-salary share of national income, he found a very close relation between the two for the years 1919–1935.[8] Unfortunately, Malach has developed no econometric model to test this highly plausible suggestion. Actually, some of Brown's experimental equations will do for the purpose. Using both least squares and limited information techniques, Brown has tested this same hypothesis (which he attributes to L. R. Klein, its best-known proponent). Each type of estimating procedure yields about the same conclusion — that a dollar of extra wage-salary income yields almost twice as much extra consumption expenditure as does an extra dollar of profit income. In all cases, these relations are statistically significant.[9] Where does

---

[7] *Ibid.*, pp. 366 ff. This is also implied by Modigliani's results.

[8] V. W. Malach, "Internal Determinants of the Canadian Upswing, 1921–9," *CJEPS,* 16:184–187 (May 1950).

[9] For the regression coefficient of consumption on wage income, Brown gets 0.5929 by least squares and 0.6061 by limited information estimation. For the regression coefficient of consumption on profit income, he calculates 0.3419 via multiple regression least squares and 0.2828 by limited information. Each of these coefficients contains its standard error at least 4.2 times. Brown's best-fitting least squares equation, however, contains as independent variables both the two income components and lagged consumption. This equation explained

this leave our inquiry into Canadian income-consumption relations? Statistically speaking, neither hypothesis can be ruled out. There is a good economic reason why both hypotheses explain the historic record of consumption changes quite well. Typically, the wage-salary share of national income slumps sharply at the beginning of a boom, then rises slowly as the boom continues, and then rapidly as recession sets in. When this pattern prevails, the impact of income redistribution on consumption would make the relation of consumption to income lie below its long-run average at the beginning of booms and above its long-run average at the beginning of recessions. But that is also exactly what the habit-persistence hypothesis predicts. As a practical judgment, one can say that these two hypotheses will seldom predict different behavior for consumption under ordinary circumstances. Hence, our inability to tell which is the correct or the *more* correct interpretation of Canadian consumption habits *may* not make too much difference.

A large volume of impressionistic evidence and casual opinion holds that Canada's imports bear a significant relation to both personal consumption and gross domestic investment. A typical bundle of Canadian imports contains both a wide range of consumers' goods, mostly manufactured, and a wide variety of producers' equipment items. Analyzing this view statistically is difficult because of the well-known problem of the absence of any reliable breakdown between imports of these two different types. And the multicollinearity problem, due to the high correlation between investment and consumption, blocks any attempt at sorting out their separate influence on the total flow of imports. One possible procedure is to calculate the year-to-year changes (first differences) of imports, consumption, and gross domestic investment. When this is done, and simple correlations are calculated between the import series and the consumption and investment series separately, investment appears to have significantly more to do with year-to-year changes in imports than does consumption.[10] The respective correlation coefficients are 0.80 and 0.63. A check on this conclusion appears in some of English's calcula-

---

99.8 per cent of the variance of consumption, suggesting that both habit persistence and the income distribution must receive attention for short-term forecasting of consumption.

[10] The investment series used here was gross domestic investment less inventory changes. The war years 1942–1945 were excluded.

tions, where he finds a correlation between investment and imports
as high as that between exports and imports — two variables held
closely in line by international short-term adjustment mechanisms.[11] In any case, it is plain that the over-all income elasticity
of Canada's demand for imports is fairly high; Chang places it at
1.75, a little higher than the world's income elasticity of demand
for Canadian exports.[12]

Making statistical sense out of the historic pattern of inventory
accumulation is not a simple task. The problem is that of de-
ducing people's economic desires or preferences from their observed actions or, to use the economist's terms, to deduce *ex ante*
propensities or schedules from *ex post* statistical results. In some
aspects of national income adjustment, the inference is fairly safe.
Except in periods of wartime, inflation, or other disrupting
events, consumers are most likely to spend over a reasonable period of time just about that portion of their income they intend
to spend. With inventory accumulation, the situation is different.
The purchases which expand business inventories can be planned
and controlled by businessmen, but the sales which deplete them
lack the element of contractual stability of consumer's incomes.
Hence the actual change in inventories during a period of time reflects not only the planned changes in purchases but also un-
planned changes in sales. Thus the early stages of Canadian business cycles are often marked by increases in the rate of inventory
accumulation. Yet these increases are quite compatible with desires on the part of the whole business community to reduce inventory holdings. Therefore, inventory accumulation does not
move along with other components of Canadian gross domestic
investment. It correlates much better with the other components
of domestic investment when lagged one year than when both
variables are taken for the same year.

CANADA IN THE WORLD ECONOMY

Because of its great dependence on foreign trade, Canadian national income adjustment has to be viewed in relation to Canada's
position in the world economy. Only in this setting do some of the

[11] English, pp. 52–55.
[12] T. C. Chang, *Cyclical Movements in the Balance of Payments* (Cambridge,
1951), pp. 200–201. Not much significance can be attached to these figures,
which cover only the years 1926–1938.

most important determinants of the growth and fluctuation of Canadian income emerge. Only in this setting do significant patterns show up in the total saving offsets to Canadian capital formation.

Again, let us begin by surveying the terrain. Over the past three decades, Canada has conducted a fairly constant 80 per cent of her trade with the United States and the United Kingdom. Foreign influences on Canadian incomes normally arrived from one of these centers. More and more the connection with the United States has become the central concern of students of Canadian income and business cycles. The American share of Canada's trade has risen from its depression low of 42 per cent to about 67 per cent today. As Canada's exports to the United States have switched more and more toward materials basic to the American economy, this trade flow has come to bear a highly stable relation to gross national product. The same of course is true of Canadian income and imports from the United States. The net result of these two relations is that Canada's current account balance tends strongly to depend on the direction and size of the difference between rates of income change in the two countries.

Taken by itself this fact would seem to mean that international transactions furnish a stabilizing factor for the Canadian economy. The trade deficit arising during a period of rapid income growth in Canada creates an extra leakage from the income stream and slackens inflationary pressure. Likewise, a positive trade balance tends to mitigate a Canadian recession when American income declines less rapidly.

The trouble with this view is that it does not reckon with the effect of long-term capital movements. Common generalizations taken from foreign trade multiplier theory are often dangerous in practice because that theory makes special assumptions about the capital account offset to a nation's current account balance. They must come in the form of some capital movement which does not affect the level of gross domestic investment within the country. Canadian long-term capital movements, however, normally create a direct increase in domestic investment. They do this insofar as they permit private or public investment which could not or would not have been undertaken solely on the basis of Canadian saving.[13] Now suppose, for the sake of argument, that a current account deficit is entirely financed through long-term capital imports, which serve to raise gross domestic investment by this same amount. Then the income leakage from the current account deficit is just offset by the income injection of the extra investment.[14] And indeed it could be more than offset if an injection of foreign investment regularly induces complementary investment by Canadians. In several recent writings on the Canadian economy the heavy adverse trade balance has been listed as a cause of inflation. On the face of it this statement is roundly false. But, where long-term capital imports act in the fashion just described, the view may ultimately turn out to be true.[15]

In the context of the Canadian situation all of this means that a rapid rate of economic growth brings not just an adverse current account balance, but also heavy net capital imports which offset the income leakage through the current account and increase the rate of real capital formation. Thus two major items in the capital account of Canada's foreign trade balance — direct foreign investment and net new securities issues — have major stabilizing effects on the total Canadian balance of payments. Another capital item is important because it plays the same sort of payments-stabilizing role — net new issues of Canadian securities. This flow has been shown to depend strongly on the difference between Canadian and United States long-term interest rates and, thereby, on their relative rates of income growth. Thus it too furnishes a reliable offset to swings in the current account balance of the Canadian balance of payments.

There remains the relation between the pattern of Canadian foreign trade and patterns of investment and saving within Canada. In the previous section, we established a clear connection between Canadian merchandise exports and the level of gross

---

[13] Through increased voluntary personal saving by Canadians, increased business earnings retention, increased use of taxation to finance public investment, or "forced saving" accomplished by credit creation and inflation.

[14] A qualification may be necessary here if investment financed by foreign saving has a higher import content than investment financed by Canadian saving. Investment funds borrowed abroad and spent entirely on imports would create no net injection of Canadian income and, taken by themselves, would be a purely neutral factor in the balance of payments.

[15] Some considerations rather similar to those of this paragraph appear in Fritz Machlup's *International Trade and the National Income Multiplier* (Philadelphia, 1950), ch. viii.

domestic investment. It makes a difference, however, whether the United Kingdom or the United States is the principal recipient of the increased exports. The commodity bundles taken by Canada's two best customers differ significantly, America's purchases running toward much more capital-intensive goods than Britain's, although both draw heavily on Canada's natural resources. On the side of savings it is hard to show any clear stable relations among the components of Canadian domestic saving. However, it is definitely true that net foreign saving (capital imports) makes up a regularly higher portion of the sources of Canadian investment as the investment figure rises to higher levels. Without the flexibility of Canadian corporate finance and capital imports, such rapid spurts of investment as 1956's 20 per cent increase over the preceding year could not occur.

Available research studies document almost every point of this account. First, consider the connection between United States economic activity and American imports from Canada. Imre de Vegh's study covering the period between World Wars I and II [16] examines both this relation and the corresponding one between Canadian income and imports from the United States. Over the years 1919–1938, using short-period time series, de Vegh found a high income elasticity for American imports of Canadian goods. A 1 per cent change in American GNP usually coincided with a change of 1.35 per cent or more in imports from Canada.[17] Another study, prepared for the New York Federal Reserve Bank, shows that not only does a strong trading relation exist between the United States and Canada, but also that American trade with Canada is much more stable than her trade with other nations. First, looking at the structure of United States imports from all countries, imports from Canada have fared much better than those from any other nation. Between 1923 and 1949, variations in the over-all price of United States imports from all countries except Canada were closely related to opposite changes in the quantity of imports, quantity declining as price rose. Only for Canada did the secular movement of American demand toward Canadian goods and materials swamp the effect of rising prices of those goods, causing postwar imports from Canada to stand much

---

[16] Imre de Vegh, "Imports and Income in the United States and Canada," *RES*, 23:130–146 (August 1941).

[17] *Ibid.*, pp. 139–140.

above prewar imports in physical quantity.[18] Second, the correlation between Canadian raw and semimanufactured exports to the United States and the American index of industrial production was 0.99, and every 1 per cent increase in industrial production called forth a 1.20 per cent increase in primary imports from Canada. No other country or group trading with the United States enjoyed such an expansion of her exports relative to American industrial production. These facts establish the increasing dependence of the United States on Canada, a dependence fast becoming as fundamental as that of Canada on the United States.[19] A Canadian Department of Trade and Commerce writer recently summed up this trend. This dependence is growing

not only because the United States is buying a much larger quantity of Canadian goods than before the war, but also because some Canadian and American industries are now more closely integrated than in the pre-war period . . . Many new developments have been undertaken to ensure adequate supplies for the United States market. American financing means a common interest in the future of these undertakings, thus establishing closer ties. As a result of these and numerous other agreements arising out of the increased volume of trade, there are closer relationships now between the two economies and Canadian exports to the United States appear to be on a more secure footing than in the pre-war period.[20]

Canadian imports from the United States bear the same sort of close relation to Canadian national income. De Vegh's investigation shows during the years 1926–1940 that a 1 per cent increase in Canadian income normally was associated with a 2.20 per cent increase in imports from the United States, a value which does not vary significantly from the average value for the corresponding United States elasticity.[21]

These close correlations between the trade flows between Canada and the United States and the income levels of the respective purchasing countries support the contention that Canada's trade balance will normally be passive during periods of relatively rapid growth and active during periods of relatively slow income growth

[18] John H. Adler, Eugene R. Schlesinger, Evelyn van Westerborg, *The Pattern of United States Import Trade Since 1923, Some New Index Series and Their Application* (New York, 1952), p. 25.

[19] *Ibid.*, pp. 45–46, 70–71.

[20] "Canadian Exports to the United States: A Comparative Study," *Foreign Trade*, 105:8 (21 January 1956).

[21] De Vegh, pp. 139–140. He calculates values for the United States elasticity ranging from the 1.35 already mentioned to 5.6.

or during cyclical slumps. They, of course, do not prove that one can forecast the trade balance from looking at Canada's income level alone. It *might* be systematically true that when Canada's income grows rapidly the incomes of her trading partners grow *more* rapidly. Then the balance of payments would be normally favorable during Canada's more prosperous years. But this is in fact not the case, either at the present time[22] or during the nineteenth century. K. W. Taylor's famous study of Canadian foreign trade statistics from 1872 to 1929 shows a strong inverse correlation between prosperity in Canada and the balance of trade.[23] His explanation is quite the proper one. He rests the case squarely on the role of capital imports. "Expansion means construction, construction means foreign borrowings, and foreign borrowings mean heavy imports of capital goods, raw materials, and the necessities and decencies of life for the thousands of men engaged in capital construction work." Thus the level of investment in Canada has a powerful effect on both the level of income and the volume of imports.

Evidence on short-run changes in the pattern of Canadian saving is scattered and inconclusive. Radford has pointed out that foreign saving (capital imports) tends strongly to lag behind movements of gross domestic investment by one or two years, citing as examples 1929–1931, 1934–1936 and 1945–1948.[24] Within gross domestic saving, depreciation allowances bear a remarkably stable relation to gross national product during all phases of the business cycle and over long periods of time.[25] Since investment is more volatile than gross national product, other sources of gross

[22] Chang (p. 204) estimates for the years 1926–1938 that a 1 per cent change in world income normally was accompanied by a 1.57 per cent change in Canadian income.

[23] Kenneth W. Taylor and H. Michell, *Statistical Contributions to Canadian Economic History* (Toronto, 1931), Vol. II, pp. 3–4. Taylor gives a correlation coefficient between his indexes of prosperity and the trade balance of −0.66. His prosperity index, though not the best, is probably acceptable for the period covered. It is an unweighted average of moving averages of a number of fairly good cyclical indicators, including railway freight traffic, bank deposits, physical production, and the volume of employment. One wishes he had not chosen a seven years moving average, which can lead to curious distortions if the business cycle is itself around seven years in length, but his results do not seem subject to serious question.

[24] R. A. Radford, "Canada's Capital Inflow, 1946–53," *International Monetary Fund Staff Papers*, 4:228–229 (February 1955).

[25] Kenneth Buckley, *Capital Formation in Canada, 1896–1930* (Toronto, 1955), p. 63.

saving fluctuate much more sharply than do depreciation allowances. Retained corporate earnings likewise fluctuate with the level of general economic activity, and hence with gross national product. However, their swings are naturally much more violent.

Studying the behavior of personal saving is largely the other side of studying the behavior of personal consumption expenditures. The Brown habit-persistence hypothesis implies that, apart from its close relation to current personal disposable income, saving will tend to be high when income rises rapidly or when it has just started to rise after a slack period. Malach's income-distribution theory of Canadian consumption implies roughly the same behavior for personal saving. Both views, as noted above, are consistent with the available data. Finally, one additional study is available which tries to explain personal saving on the basis of the level of employment. Maywald has suggested that saving will relate closely to the difference between actual employment and normal full employment. He holds that, in conditions of over-full employment, saving from extra wages will be quite high, while the onset of unemployment will see a drawing down of savings by the unemployed in attempting to maintain their consumption standards, sharply cutting the total volume of saving. Since the level of employment and the level of personal disposable income are almost perfectly correlated, Maywald's hypothesis boils down to the hypothesis that (1) consumption relates closely to the level of current personal disposable income, and (2) the marginal prospensity to consume is low. Thus his work carries us no further in analyzing personal saving than that of Modigliani and less far than Brown and Malach in their treatment of other variables which have a significant influence on the short-run level of consumption and saving.[26]

At the present time available information on Canadian saving is not good enough to allow any confident conclusions about the effect of saving on the level of investment and thereby on other

[26] See Karel Maywald, "National Savings and Changing Employment in Canada, 1926–54," *CJEPS*, 22:174–182 (May 1956). Maywald does not test his hypothesis statistically, though he does calculate a range of saving levels for plausible values of the (uncomputed) regression coefficient of saving on the employment level. When one plots his figures for the percentage of net national product saved against the actual figures, the residuals are obviously not random. This fact just substantiates Brown's contention that the lagged response of consumers to income changes must be considered.

portions of national income.[27] Hence, the following generalizations are impressions rather than proved hypotheses. Aggregate
intended saving does not seem to be a powerful determinant of
short-run investment levels. This does *not* mean sources of saving
are not important for maintaining high-level investment. It means
rather that the sources of saving for Canadian investment are
sufficiently diverse and elastic to wield little influence in the short
run on the volume of investment. The main exception to this
generalization probably lies in the role of corporate retained earnings. At least in the United States, corporate liquidity seems to
be a significant determinant of business investment. This fact implies that business investment will depend on the amount of
saving through retained earnings. But for most firms the dividend
pay-out ratio from current earnings is very stable, so this volume
of retained earnings does not really reflect a decision to save
which can be sorted out from the influence of the current rate of
profit and current and past decisions on investment. Thus, even
this apparent dependence of investment on savings is probably
unimportant in practice.

If anyone has doubted the short-run elasticity of the supply of
saving and credit in Canada, the last few years should have re-
lieved much concern. From the beginning of 1955 to the beginning
of 1957, the Canadian banking system expanded its general loans
(excluding mortgages and special category loans) by nearly 50
per cent from $3,250,000,000 to $4,500,000,000. True, the reduction in bank holdings of government bonds necessary to expand
the credit superstructure could not go on forever.[28] But such
great short-run flexibility seems to rule out saving as an important investment determinant in the short run. With its access to
foreign saving and its high level of potential saving by busi-

[27] Two pieces of research now in preparation should do a good deal to eliminate this lack of information. One is a study of the financing of economic
activity in Canada prepared by the staff of the Royal Commission on Canada's
Economic Prospects. Another is a forthcoming sample study of corporation
finance prior to publication of corporate taxation statistics by the Department
of National Revenue in 1946. For a good discussion of the problems of analyzing
the causal role of saving in national income determination, see "Financing a
Decade of Corporate Investment," Bank of Nova Scotia *Monthly Review*
(September 1956).

[28] "The Squeeze on Liquidity," Bank of Nova Scotia *Monthly Review* (April
1957).

nesses and individuals Canada's income level depends far more strongly on the effects of market prospects on the decision to invest.

SHORT-RUN GROWTH PATTERNS

If these generalized descriptions of short-term economic adjustment in Canada have any practical use, then they should agree fairly accurately with actual short-term changes in twentieth-century Canada. Such agreement will go no further toward "proving" the hypotheses wrapped up in these models. However, it will underscore their general consistency with the facts and (more important) reveal any tendency for changes to occur in the basic structure. This section will examine short-term changes in the Canadian economy during its three periods of rapid growth during the twentieth century — 1900–1913, 1920–1929, and 1946–1956.[29]

For the first period of rapid Canadian economic growth after the turn of the century, the statistical evidence of national income adjustments is naturally quite meager. There are no reliable annual GNP estimates, only the shakiest sort of industrial production estimates and some painstaking but still dubious annual investment figures. Only for the international sector can we be fairly confident of the available data. Even so, we can infer quite a lot about short-range income adjustments. And they turn out to follow nicely the events outlined in our two-stage descriptive model.[30]

The years 1900–1913 furnish a clear case of the same basic forces governing both the long-run rate of economic growth and short-run changes in national income and investment. At the beginning of the decade, the dominant force of the period was already at work — improving terms of trade in the form of rising prices for Canada's primary products exports in general and grain in particular. The harvests of 1901 and 1902 were both excellent,

---

[29] High-quality official statistics on year-to-year economic changes of course date back only to 1926. However, a number of excellent published studies yield enough information on the earlier years to permit use of a common approach in surveying them.

[30] Three handy sources of information on the period are Jacob Viner's famous study, *Canada's Balance of International Indebtedness, 1900–1913* (Cambridge, 1924); W. A. Mackintosh, *The Economic Background of Dominion-Provincial Relations,* Appendix 3 of the RCDPR *Report* (Ottawa, 1939), pp. 24–31; and A. K. Cairncross, *Home and Foreign Investment, 1870–1913, Studies in Capital Accumulation* (Cambridge, 1953), ch. iii.

and the value of Canada's wheat crop rose from $55,600,000 in 1900 to $85,300,000 in 1901 and $93,600,000 in 1902.[31] This state of affairs, plus the exhaustion around this time of the last good free land in the United States, turned the tide of trans-Atlantic migration away from the United States and toward Canada. Immigrant arrivals were about 42,000 in 1900. By 1903 they had risen to almost 139,000.[32] The annual level of domestic investment had apparently been rising steadily since 1896. Total construction (new and repair) averaged a little over $70,000,000 annually during 1896–1898, $119,000,000 during 1900–1901. It was over $200,000,000 by 1904. Total fixed domestic investment (that is, excluding inventory changes) rose from around $180,000,000 annually in 1900–1901 to around $280,000,000 annually in 1903–1904. This rapid expansion from the beginning of the decade did not reflect solely the subjection of the prairies to the plow. In the years 1901–1904 the index of industrial production rose by one-fourth, and population growth in the prairie cities was as rapid as that on prairie farms.[33]

A minor recession appeared in Canada in 1904 as a result of short wheat crops in 1903 and 1904. Despite rising wheat prices due to a similar crop failure in the United States, the value of the wheat crop fell 26 per cent from 1902 to 1904. The value of exports dropped in the latter year, apparently triggering a minor business recession. Investment was slightly affected; machinery and equipment investment fell in 1904, though construction did not. Imports showed no increase.[34] The keynote of the early years thus was the response of domestic investment to changing exports. It was not a simple relation of current investment to current exports, though. It was a response to increasingly favorable export *prospects*, operating both directly and through the increased immigration stream and the effect of extra population on investment incentives.

After 1905 the Canadian economy entered a new phase of sus-

[31] Cairncross, pp. 46, 49.

[32] Canada, DBS, *Canada Year Book, 1936*, p. 186.

[33] Buckley, p. 128; Cairncross, p. 45 (annual gross fixed investment figures taken from Buckley); League of Nations, Economic, Financial and Transit Department, *Industrialization and Foreign Trade* (New York, 1945), p. 135. Not much weight can be placed on the industrial production index appearing in the League of Nations study, since year-to-year changes are interpolations based on coal consumption.

[34] Cairncross, pp. 45–49.

tained growth which did not run its course until World War I broke out in Europe. The outstanding economic trait of these years was an immense inflow of capital to support a rapid growth of domestic investment. In the first years of the decade, prairie farm investment had been the most important portion of total capital formation, by way of offering a stimulus to other forms of spending. Prairie farm investment was 17.2 per cent of total investment during 1901–1905, but only 15.9 per cent during the last half of the decade.[35] Prairie farm investment directly fixed in capital goods the real savings of settlers and immigrants. This could not be financed from outside the country. But by the middle of the decade the Canadian economy had demonstrated its credit-worthiness to the satifaction of British investors and American business firms. Plumptre and later critics of Viner's study of the Canadian capital inflow have rightly stressed the effect of the rising value and volume of Canadian exports. "Capital imports came in to take advantage of the new opportunities associated, directly or indirectly, with the expansion of exports — in the expectation that exports would continue to grow." [36]

During the years 1900–1904 net long-terms capital movements into Canada were generally below $50,000,000 annually, less than one-fourth of gross domestic investment. From 1905 to 1910 the inflow of foreign capital swept almost steadily upward from about $100,000,000 to about $300,000,000 annually, finally reaching a peak at $541,700,000 in 1913, when it financed roughly two-thirds of Canada's gross domestic investment.[37]

Exports continued during the rest of the period to play a dominant role in short-run changes. They bore at least some relation to the 1907–1908 recession. The growth of exports in 1907 was quite small, due to a poor harvest and declining markets for Canadian lumber and raw materials in the United States and Great Britain. Had this decline not occurred, the tight money situation which prevailed from the last quarter of 1906 on would not have been much of a deterrent to domestic investment. Borrowings

[35] G. M. Meier, "Economic Development and the Transfer Mechanism: Canada, 1895–1913," *CJEPS*, 19:8 (February 1953).

[36] A. F. W. Plumptre, "The Nature of Political and Economic Development in the British Dominions," *CJEPS*, 3:492n. (November 1937); cited by Meier, p. 8.

[37] Figures are from F. A. Knox, *Dominion Monetary Policy 1929–34, A Study Prepared for the RCDPR* (Ottawa, 1939), p. 93 (based on Viner's estimates), and Cairncross, p. 45.

from abroad dropped about 10 per cent in 1907, contributing to a credit shortage and helping to explain the tight position in which the Canadian banks found themselves. A recession of the "commercial crisis" species was under way, which possibly could have been averted had 1907 commodity export earnings been good enough. The indicators which fell in 1908, compared to those which fell in 1907, represented areas of the economy sensitive to interest rates and capital availability — construction and railway investment. Logically enough, imports declined. Immigration was much smaller in 1908, a fact which no doubt slowed the investment rate because of the labor shortage problem which plagued Canadian investors throughout this period.[38] Nonetheless, this recession was quite short lived. The scene was quickly set for revival as continued heavy borrowing from abroad increased the foreign reserves of the Canadian banks. Later on, during 1911–1913, when the absorption of borrowed capital reached its peak, the banks' outside reserves were drawn down sharply. Indeed, many foreign purchases came to be made by Canadian firms in anticipation of the proceeds of loans yet to be floated.[39]

The years 1905–1913 reveal to a striking degree the growth possibilities open to Canada through her place in the world economy. Home investment levels reflected the continued strong export prospects and improving terms of trade, but with the level of gross domestic investment strongly affected by capital inflows. For both the period 1906–1910 and 1911–1915 gross domestic investment was about 27 per cent of gross national product. Capital imports financed respectively one-third and one-half of these inflows. Imports adjusted very closely to changes in the rate of capital inflow and the rate of investment because many investment goods were secured abroad. Often the same companies were responsible for both capital and commodity import transactions.

The rapid growth of total investment in the years after 1904 reflected only to a small degree investment in export industries. The second and third transcontinental railroads played a major part, as did investment in many sorts of manufacturing and other facilities geared to the needs of a rapidly expanding population.

---

[38] Cairncross, pp. 55–56; Buckley, pp. 128, 130, 136; Canada, Board of Inquiry into the Cost of Living in Canada, *Report of the Board* (Ottawa, 1915), Vol. II, Part I, secs. (5) and (6).

[39] Viner, pp. 189–190.

During the 1901–1905 half-decade, transport investment was only 14.2 per cent of gross domestic investment; for 1906–1910 it was 24.1 per cent. The tremendous growth recorded for many manufactured products during the latter part of the decade reflects the increases in capital stock which they must have installed during the last years of the decade.[40]

As far as we can tell, the 1900–1913 period does not violate the model of income adjustment developed above. We know nothing about consumption and its changes during these years, nothing about year-to-year changes in gross national product or inventory investment, and we possess only moderately reliable estimates of year-to-year changes in fixed investment. Certain patterns are clear, such as the dependence of home investment on exports (subject to the sweeping special influence of inflows of people and capital) and the dependence of import demand on the growth of Canadian investment and income.[41]

Let us now turn to the 1920's to survey Canada's second period of rapid economic expansion under peacetime conditions. The task of analyzing short-run changes becomes much easier now, as we encounter official national income figures and a quantity of useful information turned up by students of the Canadian business cycle.[42]

[40] Meier, Table II and pp. 9–11; Board of Inquiry into the Cost of Living, *Report*, Vol. II, p. 1058; Canada, RCDPR, *Report*, Vol. I, pp. 74–76.

[41] The discussion here has omitted the substitution effect which also acted to increase Canadian imports through the more rapid rise in domestic than in imported prices; see Viner, p. 229.

Another piece of research on the 1900–1913 period which shows the close investment-imports connection is James C. Ingram, "Growth in Capacity and Canada's Balance of Payments," *AER*, 47:93–104 (March 1957). By assuming a fixed simultaneous multiplier and marginal propensity to import, he calculates a series of hypothetical import figures (from Buckley's annual investment series) which fit the actual import series quite well. In fact, the fit is even better than Ingram's Figure 1 indicates, because in Table II he has mislaid a minus sign, which throws off his hypothetical import series for 1909–1913.

The rest of Ingram's computations are of questionable merit. He also calculates hypothetical exports on the assumption that any of this year's extra output (from last year's investment increase) which does not go to increasing investment this year will be exported. Actually, during the 1900's, harvest variations and foreign income changes had much more to do with the export level from year to year, so it is no surprise that changes in Ingram's hypothetical export series are negatively correlated with the actual annual changes in exports.

[42] Almost all major DBS statistical series make their first appearance for the year 1926. For Malach's results, see *International Cycles and Canada's Balance of Payments, 1921–33* (Toronto, 1954); "External Determinants of the Canadian Upswing, 1921–9," *CJEPS*, 17:50–64 (February 1951); "Internal Determi-

As in the United States, the 1920's decade got off to a bad start with a short, sharp depression during 1920–21. The downswing in Canada seems to have been more intensive than in most other countries. The index of industrial production for Canada (1913 = 100) stood at 99.1 in 1920, fell to 89.4 in 1921, then rose to 99.0 and 108.3 in the subsequent two years.[43] Hence her merchandise imports fell more than did her exports, and the current account balance became less passive.[44] Part of the reason for the brevity of this recession no doubt lies in the fact that much of the slump came in lower prices and attempted inventory liquidation, rather than durable investment. The annual rate of inventory investment in railways, manufacturing, and public utilities fell by $357,000,000 from 1920 to 1921, although in constant 1935–1939 dollars it rose by $43,000,000.[45] This fact neatly confirms W. A. Mackintosh's characterization of the immediate postwar boom of 1919–20: "It was marked by feverish and vastly over-extended investment, not in fixed capital goods . . . but in inventories of goods at various stages of processing." [46]

The subsequent general expansion of the Canadian economy lasted until 1929, marred only by a slight recession in 1923–24 (Canada missed the United States recession of 1927). It is convenient, however, to break the period into two phases covering 1922–1925 and 1926–1929 respectively. The first of these saw only a moderate recovery spurred by increasing exports and domestic investment undertaken to utilize new developments in technology. Between 1921 and 1925, Canadian exports rose by a little more than 50 per cent while imports fluctuated irregularly and in 1925 stood only about 5 per cent above their 1921 level. The balance of commodity trade rose from −$27,400,000 to $368,-700,000, while the total current account balance rose from −$196,-

---

nants of the Canadian Upswing, 1921–9," *CJEPS*, 16:184–198 (May 1950); "The Mechanism of Adjustment in Canada's Balance of Payments, 1921–9," *CJEPS*, 18:303–321 (August 1952); "The International Business Cycle and Canada, 1927–39," *CJEPS*, 21:88–100 (February 1955).

[43] League of Nations, *Industrialization and Foreign Trade*, p. 135.

[44] Malach, "The International Business Cycle and Canada, 1927–39," p. 89.

[45] Clarence L. Barber, "Inventory Fluctuations in Canada, 1918–50," *CJEPS*, 18:375 (August 1952), Table II. Barber argues convincingly that, insofar as inventory changes wield an influence of their own on business decisions, a money illusion persists which makes changes in the value of inventory holdings more important than the change in their volume. Available information on the inventory accounting methods of Canadian firms accords with this view.

[46] Mackintosh, p. 38.

700,000 to $284,800,000.[47] The sustained rise in exports, however, did not come until 1924–25, and depressed export trade in grain and livestock during the first few years of the decade gives much of the explanation for the slow rate at which the boom developed.[48]

Gross domestic investment increased much more sharply between 1921 and 1925 (187 per cent), with about two-thirds of the recovery coming between 1921 and 1923. While three-quarters of the total increase in gross domestic investment took the form of increased inventory accumulation, plant and equipment investment was a major force in encouraging high spending levels throughout the economy. The adoption of new products and new technology explained heavy growth in such industries as non-ferrous metals (especially lead), electric power, newsprint, and automobile production.[49]

Malach, who leans heavily on the multiplier-accelerator model as an analytical framework, makes much of the fact that, in the face of rising investment and net foreign balance, Canadian consumption fell during 1923 and 1924 in both real and monetary terms. T. M. Brown's "habit persistence" hypothesis would predict a slower growth of income than of the autonomous elements during these years, but not a decline. Malach's own hypothesis that the average propensity to consume depends mainly on the distribution of income does much better, for the share wages and salaries claimed of GNP fell about 5 percentage points between 1921 and 1925.[50] This is as much as the statistical evidence will reveal, though one may wonder on *a priori* grounds whether an income redistribution of this size can reasonably explain a fall of the annual average propensity to consume of 13 percentage points. At any rate, the upward adjustment of Canadian consumption lagged severely behind the rise in the more autonomous elements of exports and gross domestic investment.

One more feature of the first half of the 1920's merits comment. Another student of the Canadian business cycle, Edward Mar-

[47] Malach, *International Cycles and Canada's Balance of Payments,* pp. 86–88.
[48] *Ibid.,* pp. 20–21.
[49] Malach, "Internal Determinants of the Canadian Upswing, 1921–9," pp. 193–196; Canada, RCDPR, *Report,* Vol. I, pp. 115–116.
[50] Malach, *International Cycles and Canada's Balance of Payments,* p. 22; *idem,* "Internal Determinants of the Canadian Upswing, 1921–9," pp. 184–187.

cus,[51] has placed considerable stress on the relations among Canadian gross domestic investment, net borrowing abroad as a source of finance, and high levels of imports as a source of capital goods. Net long-term borrowing, it was argued above, has great importance for holding the Canadian foreign exchanges steady in times of heavy domestic investment. Malach argues that foreign borrowing does not, however, have much causal significance for the level of home investment because of the size and flexibility of domestic sources of saving.[52] Specifically, during the years 1922–1925, net new issues of Canadian capital in the United States fluctuated in rather random fashion, while the level of investment in Canada was rising steadily. Canadian domestic investment could not have depended in any simple way on the quantity of new capital supplied from abroad; if anything, the direction of causation ran the other way.[53]

The latter half of the 1920's (1926–1929) took on quite a different character in Canada. The slow recovery from the 1920–21 recession finally gave rise to a very rapid expansion of income, based on a massive construction boom and heavy investment in industries enjoying a high and stable export demand. In 1925 the value of Canadian exports leaped to 20 per cent above the previous year's value and sustained this level through 1929. The later 1920's saw not so much the effect of a steadily rising export level as a high and stable export volume. Instead, important shifts in the composition of exports caused a fairly constant export total to place a steadily increasing investment incentive before the Canadian economy. By 1929, exports of pulp and paper and nonferrous metals were 30 per cent of Canada's total exports; in 1920 they had made up 19 per cent.[54] During these years the dependence of Canada's exports on United States income levels was reaching its present high level. Malach found that, for the 1920's as a whole, national income of the United States explains 93 per cent of the variation of Canadian exports to the United States, while United

---

[51] Edward Marcus, *Canada and the International Business Cycle, 1927–1939* (New York, 1954), ch. ix and *passim*.

[52] As we shall see later, this is more nearly true of the 1920's than of other periods.

[53] Malach, "The International Business Cycle and Canada, 1927–39," pp. 90–91.

[54] Canada, RCDPR, *Report*, Vol. I, p. 116.

Kingdom income explains only 70 per cent of the variation of Canada's exports to the United Kingdom. Most of the latter exports were standard of living goods which did not stand to gain much from rising income levels abroad; most of the former were basic industrial goods which would necessarily advance with the level of industrial production in the United States.[55] Besides, the investment incentive furnished by extra sales of the typical goods sent to the United States was clearly stronger than that of extra exports to Britain. "Investment in the pulp and paper and nonferrous metal industries led in turn to increased investment in other capital-intensive industries such as construction materials, explosives, chemicals, electric power, electrical equipment and machinery. On the other hand, the increased wheat and animal exports to Britain do not seem to have stimulated an investment boom of similar proportions." [56]

In short, the dependence of Canadian investment on exports held very great importance for explaining income changes and growth patterns during the 1920's. But the relation was not a simple linear simultaneous one. First, there was a lag between the major rise in export volume at the middle of the decade and the responding rise in investment during its latter half, because the massive investment required in the new export industries had a longer gestation period than the one-year lag suggested by the model explored previously. Second, in the latter half of the decade the export stimulus to investment worked not through changes in the total level of exports but through shifts in their composition.

Let us look in more detail at Canadian gross investment during the years 1926–1929. This period is one of the few in Canadian history readily comparable to the decade following World War II and hence bears great interest for the long-range forecaster. Making an accurate comparison of the investment volume in these years to that of the first half of the 1920's is difficult because the current official national income figures begin only in 1926. We have, however, Buckley's estimate for capital formation in the quinquennia 1921–1925 and 1926–1930. Gross domestic investment was 60 per cent higher in the second half of the decade; of its major components, construction was up 36 per cent, machinery

---

[55] Malach, "External Determinants of the Canadian Upswing, 1921–9," pp. 59–60.

[56] Malach, *International Cycles and Canada's Balance of Payments, 1921–33,* p. 21; *idem,* "External Determinants of the Canadian Upswing, 1921–9," p. 62.

and equipment 73 per cent.[57] It is helpful to have a more accurate idea of the distribution of gross domestic investment among industries, such as appears in Table 4. Unfortunately it is not pos-

Table 4. Percentage distribution of Canadian gross domestic investment (excluding inventories) by industry, selected years, 1926–1956.[a]

Industry	1926–1929	1947–1950	1953–1956
Agriculture, fishing, and trapping	11.6	13.6	8.7
Forestry	0.6	1.1	1.0
Mining, quarrying, and oil wells	2.7	3.9	6.6
Manufacturing	28.5	19.7	19.1
Construction	2.1	2.1	2.6
Transportation, storage, communication, public utility operation	22.9	21.9	23.6
Trade	4.0	6.2	6.3
Finance, insurance, and real estate	22.9	25.7	26.5
Service	4.8	5.8	5.7
Total[b]	100.0	100.0	100.0

[a] Total investment figures for the period, converted to percentages.
[b] Columns may not add to 100 due to rounding errors.
Source: Computed from DBS, *National Accounts, Income and Expenditure, 1926–1950,* Table 25; *ibid., 1950–1956,* Table 25.

sible to compare the industry-by-industry distribution of investment with that of the early 1920's, so instead Table 4 presents corresponding figures for the years 1947–1950 and 1953–1956.

This evidence tells us much about the determinants of investment in the late 1920's. First, a fairly small portion was in industries heavily dependent on export markets. Investment in agriculture, forestry, and the mining sector was less prominent in total investment than in the post-World War II period. For the latter two sectors (forestry and mining), no doubt investment during the early 1920's was relatively heavier than during the years 1926–1929. Elsewhere in the economy, only pulp and paper and electric utilities investment bore a close relation to export markets or prospects. The two sectors where investment was abnormally heavy in the late 1920's, manufacturing and residential construction (included in Table 4 as "Finance, insurance, and real estate"), both rested on economic prospects at home.

[57] Computed from Buckley, Table H, p. 135.

A rapid increase in residential construction was not one of the main features of the later 1920's. However, housing construction in the first half of the decade had been high by comparison to the long-run trend; if one grants the existence of long cycles in residential construction, then the 1920's clearly span the peak of a thirty-year cycle.[58] During the whole 1920's decade, Canada's housing stock increased by a little more than 20 per cent. In 1929, the stock of dwellings was 8.5 per cent *greater* than the total number of families; twenty years later, in 1949, it was 0.9 per cent *less*.[59] How much relation was there between this burst of residential construction and the other national income components of the 1920's? There are several distinct connections. First, the demand for new construction does not depend on the total number of families so much as the number of families in income brackets where they could exert an *effective* demand for new housing. This fact no doubt goes far to explain why construction proceeded so rapidly in the early recession years of the decade; those years saw a major gain in the relative income position of persons other than wage and salary recipients — by and large the upper income groups. With their income position improved, and with liquid savings accumulated during World War I, they readily sustained the demand for new residential construction. A second connection between construction and general economic activity arises from the fact that the demand for new housing will depend on how much people are moving from region to region.[60] During the late 1920's, internal migration within Canada was particularly heavy, a reflection of the growing prominence of the auto and the suburb and also of the great differences in the fortunes of Canada's various regions during the decade.

The same sorts of changes which so much marked the demand for residential construction in the latter 1920's — changes in tastes, the adoption of new goods and technology and heavy changes in the location of economic activity — sustained a high level of manufacturing investment. The strength of these forces can be seen in Table 4 in the great difference between the share of manufacturing investment in gross domestic investment for the

[58] *Ibid.*, p. 40.
[59] O. J. Firestone, *Residential Real Estate in Canada* (Toronto, 1951), Table 46, p. 201.
[60] Buckley, pp. 40–49, establishes this generalization for Canada from evidence covering a much longer span of time.

1920's and the 1940's. Not until the early 1950's did investment in Canadian manufacturing exceed the 1929 figure in real terms.

Let us turn to other aspects of national income determination in the late 1920's. In contrast to its behavior during 1923 and 1924, consumption in the late 1920's ran ahead of its long-run trend relation to disposable income. This fits either the Brown or the Malach hypothesis about Canadian consumption. Another candidate for the role of explanation is an illusion of soaring wealth enjoyed by holders of common stocks and other speculative assets. This effect has been noted frequently by students of United States consumption patterns in the late 1920's.

The result of stable exports and high investment and consumption in the 1926–1929 period was a growing current account deficit as imports rose rapidly. The international mechanism of adjustment then followed the traditional gold standard pattern. The Canadian dollar tended to depreciate, and nearly every year saw exports of monetary gold and imports of short-term capital. In contrast to the 1950's, Canada was exporting rather than importing capital on long-term account during these years. Canada's growth was not noticeably faster than that of the United States, or at least not enough faster to blot out for the world's investors the cynosure of the American stock market.[61]

The decade 1946–1956 bears an interesting similarity to the short-term pattern of the 1920's. The first and second halves of each decade show sharply differing traits; for the post-World War II years, the break comes between 1946–1949 and 1950–1956. In each case the rate of income growth is fairly slow during the first period but quite rapid in the second. In each case a residential construction boom appears in the later period along with rapidly rising total investment in all types of economic activities. Here, however, most of the similarity ends. We shall argue that the recent decade conforms to the model of short-run income adjustment developed above, as did the 1920's. But various special factors stamp their character strongly enough upon the two decades to color them quite differently. Indeed, several writers have argued from quite solid reasoning and observation that the post-World War II period bears more resemblance to the 1900's than to the 1920's. We shall refer to this suggestion again later.

[61] See Malach, *International Cycles and Canada's Balance of Payments, 1921–33*, p. 24 and Table XI, pp. 86–90; Marcus, pp. 47–53.

During the late 1940's Canada sustained a high level of employment but not a satisfactory rate of economic growth. She missed the 1948–49 United States recession, but the years 1946–1948 bear the marks of the major readjustments following the war. The readjustment process thus came more easily than that following World War I (compare the 1920–21 recession) but was still not an easy one due to the size of the changes necessary and the presence of a first-class balance of payments crisis.

In 1946 and 1947, both exports and government purchases of goods and services fell as military expenditures were reduced both at home and abroad. Consumption and gross domestic investment both showed sharp autonomous rises, respectively because of heavy asset backlogs in consumers' hands and wartime maintenance deferrals by business. At the same time the labor force was readjusting from the overemployment levels of wartime. Output per man year outside of agriculture fell every year from 1945 through 1949, except for a tiny rise in 1948, although productivity per man hour fell only during 1948 and 1949.[62] The combined impact of these forces brought a sharp inflation, the price level advancing about 10 per cent from 1946 to 1947.[63] An easy credit policy allowed the economy to sustain a very high investment level. This helped bring on the balance of payments difficulties by curtailing the goods available for export. Likewise, the remedy in the form of direct import controls artificially controlled consumption and permitted the high level of investment to persist.[64] Thus, autonomous shifts in all areas of the economy cloud the working of the basic mechanism of income determination during the early postwar years 1946–1948. And regulation of imports and foreign exchange prevented the normal adjustments in the balance of payments.

By 1949, most of the postwar adjustments had run their course, and one might again expect to find the normal peacetime functional relations governing national income to assert themselves. Liquid assets had ceased to burn holes in the pockets of Canadian consumers, annual reductions in holdings of Government of Canada market securities took on a more normal appearance,

[62] G. D. Sutton, "Productivity in Canada," *CJEPS*, 19:191–194 (May 1953).
[63] Canada, DBS, *National Accounts, Income and Expenditure, 1926–1950*, p. 22.
[64] H. C. Eastman, "Recent Canadian Economic Policy: Some Alternatives," *CJEPS*, 18:140 (May 1952).

and the public's holdings of other bonds and stocks rose again to normal levels.[65] Inventories were restored to levels appropriate for the general level of economic activity. Personal saving and undistributed corporate profits increased. The Canadian price level had caught up with those outside of the country, so that pressure on Canadian prices through international commodity movements diminished. Inflation slowed to a manageable rate, if not to a standstill.[66]

The year 1951 saw the first significant postwar increase in the real volume of Canadian exports. They rose 10 per cent in 1951 and again in 1952, although because of the 1953–54 recession they did not increase by another 10 per cent until 1956. Growth of exports, actual and prospective, had a normal effect on gross domestic investment. In real terms, the 1950 investment figure was 20 per cent above the plateau of 1947–1949, and the rise continued through the next six years until the 1956 investment volume was almost double the late 1940's figures. Government expenditure in real terms shifted up sharply in 1951 and 1952 but remained relatively passive in the following years. Since the buying spree of the Korean War, personal consumption has increased in proportion to income, no more.

The distribution of investment by sector of the economy tells much of the story (see Table 4). Comparing 1953–1956 with 1947–1950, three shifts stand out. First, the portion of gross investment going into the agricultural sector fell very heavily. The prairie provinces, as we shall see, bore almost the whole burden of the 1953–54 recession. Second, the share of investment accounted for by mining, quarrying, and oil wells rose by an equally spectacular amount. This is where the export stimulus in conjunction with resource discoveries really mattered. Third, investment in basic social facilities such as housing and public ultilities increased somewhat in relative importance, largely in response to the strongly maintained rate of population growth and level of employment and the increasingly obvious inadequacy of many existing facilities. An excellent example of the working of all these forces would be the heavy investment in electric power generating facilities in central Canada.

[65] See the direct estimates of personal saving produced by the Bank of Canada in Bank of Canada, *Statistical Summary, Financial Supplement, 1955*, p. 55.
[66] Canada, DBS, *National Accounts, Income and Expenditure, 1926–1950*, p. 23.

Because of the broad foundations of the 1950's investment boom, it is worth inquiring what forces caused the momentary halt of the 1953–54 recession. This recession clearly traveled along the channels of foreign trade. Its infection was significant in the wheat economy of the prairie provinces, but almost nowhere else in Canada. In volume terms, Canadian exports dropped very slightly from 1952 to 1953, then fell 4 per cent from 1953 to 1954. In value terms, the fall was greater in both years. Total farm income in these three years was respectively $2,849,000,000, $2,776,000,000, and $2,378,000,000. The prairies witnessed a sharp decline in retail sales, sales of automobiles, and farm equipment. The rest of the economy showed some effects of this recession. Gross domestic investment excluding inventories fell $174,000,000 from 1953 to 1954, but the drop in agricultural investment accounted for almost all of this. Gross national product, excluding net farm income, fell after the third quarter of 1953 and did not significantly exceed this level until the final quarter of 1954. Inventory accumulation dropped in the last quarter of 1953, showed what was probably an "unintended" increase in the first quarter of 1954, and then dropped through the remaining three-quarters of that year. In 1954 all major classes of production fell except the export-dependent mining industry. However, personal incomes rose slightly due to wage increases at the end of 1954, expansion in the finance and services trades, and sharply increased government transfer payments; personal consumption increased 4 per cent. The recession was only a transitional and partial disturbance to the mechanism of economic expansion.[67] Exports were a leading factor in the recovery from this recession and the 1955 increase in capital expenditures was greatest in such industries as minerals and forest products which had the best export recovery. The significance of this fact is limited, however, because these industries were also the ones whose long-run export prospects were viewed most favorably.[68]

[67] For a good summary of the course of this recession, see Great Britain, Board of Trade, *Canada: Economic and Commercial Conditions in Canada* (London, 1957), pp. 37–44.

[68] Compare the following statement from the Bank of Nova Scotia *Monthly Review* (March 1956): "More than at any previous time since the war, the trend of Canadian business during the past year and a half has been clearly linked with the demand for basic export products. The marked upturn in sales

Such spectacular events have occurred in Canada's international transactions recently that the international accounts have come to be watched with fascination and horror by economists and the public alike. The reason, of course, is the volume of capital imports entering Canada in the last half-decade and the associated colossal deficits in the current account. It is the capital inflow which gives the post-World War II years a resemblance to the 1900's and creates a major difference from the 1920's.[69] As at the beginning of the century, Canadian prosperity had to run for several years before really large capital inflows started to appear. We can safely confine our attention to three types of capital movement into Canada: direct investment in Canada, new issues of Canadian securities abroad, and net sales abroad of outstanding issues. Direct investment did not become substantial until 1950. In that year and all since, direct investment in Canada has been at least $200,000,000. In the earlier years of the postwar period it was below $100,000,000. Trade in outstanding securities has been erratic — very high in 1946, 1950, and 1956, but otherwise rather random in its movements. The explanation, of course, is that this trade often reflects short-term capital transactions more strongly than it does the working of long-term investment motives. Canadians tend to sell off their securities holdings to foreigners in years when domestic expenditure or imports or both expand sharply. This selling off comes in the general process of reducing certain assets in years when the level (or even just the growth rate) of personal saving declines. New issues of Canadian securities abroad, on the other hand, have been high ever since 1946. In no postwar year have they been much below $100,000,-000, and in 1956 they reached a breathtaking $681,000,000. Before 1950, however, the government of Canada was a heavy borrower abroad, and provincial and municipal governments and corporations imported capital only sporadically. Since then these latter agencies have borrowed heavily for investment projects of many sorts, so that new issues abroad since 1950 have been much

---

of lumber and base metals in the second half of 1954, the accelerated growth in shipments of pulp and paper, and the improvement in export market prospects in general exerted their traditional influences upon the Canadian domestic economy."

[69] Compare G. S. Watts, "The Canadian Balance of International Payments, 1950–2, and the Mechanism of Adjustment," *CJEPS,* 20:20 (February 1954).

more clearly a source of financing real capital accumulation.[70]

One of the most remarkable aspects of the recent capital flows into Canada is the way they have brought about their own adjustments in the balance of payments. This has occurred in two principal ways. First, several parts of international portfolio investment, particularly net new issues, have varied in close relation to the difference between long-term interest rates in Canada and the United States. (Since the United States has been the source of the great bulk of Canada's capital imports, the reason for this is obvious.) But the Canadian long-term interest rate has been closely related to the state of Canadian prosperity and Canada's demand for imports. Thus a rising demand for imports has coincided with a high Canadian interest rate, a tendency toward a higher differential from the United States long-term rate, and hence a heavier movement of long-term securities out of Canada. Thus long-term capital imports have tended to rise and fall with imports, contributing to a stable exchange rate for the Canadian dollar.[71] A second connection between Canada's capital and current accounts is much more direct and much more important. In the last few years direct investment has made up at least half of Canada's long-term capital imports. Major portions of direct investment by American firms have been directly connected with movements of imports from the United States to supply the physical counterpart of the direct investment flow. Figures recently prepared by the Bank of Canada clearly illustrate this. Table 5 shows the percentage of Canada's commodity imports classified as industrial materials, investment goods, and consumer goods. There is a moderately clear tendency for the share of investment goods to rise over the period for which figures are available, 1950–1956. More important, the highest share for investment goods appears in the years 1953 and 1956, when direct investment in Canada was highest. It is lower for 1955, when other factors besides investment were important in the revival of income growth from the 1953–54 recession.[72]

The last two columns of Table 5 show the relation between

[70] Statistical evidence summarized here can be found in Bank of Canada, *Statistical Summary, Financial Supplement, 1956,* and Canada, DBS, *The Canadian Balance of International Payments in the Post-war Years, 1946–1952.*

[71] Radford, p. 235 and Chart 6.

[72] See E. P. Neufeld, "Canada's Economy Now," *The Banker,* 107:437 (July 1957).

Table 5.   Distribution of Canadian imports by end use, 1950–1956.[a]

Year	As percentages of total imports			Ratio of investment-goods imports to domestic investment[b] (per cent)	Ratio of consumer-goods imports to personal consumption (per cent)
	Industrial materials	Investment goods	Consumer goods		
1950	31.6	22.1	29.8	21.9	7.8
1951	33.5	25.2	26.9	27.0	8.3
1952	28.1	29.8	27.5	28.2	7.7
1953	26.8	30.4	29.5	27.5	8.6
1954	26.0	29.8	30.9	26.1	8.0
1955	27.1	30.1	30.3	26.9	8.3
1956	27.0	32.7	28.6	28.2	8.8

[a] The first three columns do not add up horizontally to 100 per cent because a few items are not accounted for in this classification — fuels and lubricants, military goods, settlers' effects, and Canadian goods returned.
[b] Excluding inventory changes.
Source: Calculated from Bank of Canada, *Statistical Summary, Financial Supplement 1956*, pp. 98–99, and DBS, *National Accounts, Income and Expenditure, 1950–1956*, pp. 18, 35.

total Canadian gross domestic investment and personal consumption and the respective flows of imports to these end-uses. Between 1950 and 1956, the percentage for consumption goods has been quite stable, and its year-to-year variations are consistent with an income-elasticity of import demand just slightly higher than unity. The percentage for investment-goods imports as a share of gross domestic investment (excluding inventories) suggests about the same generalization, at least if we ignore 1950. In short, the relation between imports and domestic economic activity during the current boom reveals no significant "import buying sprees" but rather a highly stable relation between total spending of each sort and imports for the corresponding end-use.

One more fact should be noted about Canadian income and trade levels in the postwar decade. The current-account balance pattern has been highly consistent with the hypothesis that Canada's balance on current account depends on the difference between United States and Canadian income growth rates. Generally speaking, Canada got off to a slower start than the United States until the time of the latter's 1948–49 recession, but subsequently it has shown a uniformly higher rate of growth of real income. The current-account balance was active during 1946–1949, then turned heavily passive except for 1952.

In general, the post-World War II period conforms well to our model of short-run income determination in Canada. Growth of investment and income have been closely geared both to the current level of exports and to the general outlook for export industries bolstered by a remarkable series of natural resource discoveries. Consumption has followed its normal lagged pattern of adjustment, except when disturbed by consumers' efforts to convert extra assets into extra goods after World War II. Imports have closely followed domestic levels of consumption and investment. Finally, the trade balance and long-term capital movements have reflected differences in the income growth rates of Canada and the United States.

THE STABILITY OF SHORT-RUN PATTERNS

This chronicle of short-run changes very strongly supports the view that the same income-determination mechanism has been at work in each of Canada's major growth phases in the twentieth century. Furthermore, this mechanism agrees very well with that suggested in the first two sections of this chapter, with one glaring but scarcely surprising exception. The critical connection between the level of exports and the level of investment never has resembled anything so simple as a linear relation with a constant lag. As Plumptre argued so brilliantly twenty years ago, the inducement to undertake major new investments on the prospect of export-based markets is never a matter of neat calculations of revenues and costs. Such decisions emerge only after several years of favorable signs, such as the rising wheat prices of the 1900's, export demand for metals and newsprint in the 1920's, and sustained United States industrial growth after World War II. When these investment decisions do emerge, they come in a rush and halt only when strongly adverse factors appear (World War I, the world depression of the early 1930's).

The differences between these three periods result from easily identifiable special circumstances. The inflow of factors of production in the 1900's was incomparably greater than in later periods. But this inflow did not occur because of any narrow shift in advantage between Canada and other regions deficient in mobile factors. The nations of Europe had been steadily exporting an overflow of their factors of production to unpopulated areas of the globe for many years.[73] The lands ready to receive them in the nineteenth century had been vast; the order in which they were filled had been relatively arbitrary. Around the turn of the century, the United States' unfilled land resources came to an end, and the outflow of European factors of production turned next to Canada. In Skelton's famous words, "At last Canada's hour had struck." In the 1920's and 1950's, with the frontier of totally unused resources closed, Canada's claim to the world's capital supply depended upon a much closer balancing of advantages at the margin. Indeed, this marginal balancing explains much of the peculiar character of the 1920's. In contrast to the other two periods, Canada did not achieve a clearly greater growth rate than the United States during the latter part of the 1920's. And she failed to attract any significant inflow of foreign capital from the United States. The reason of course lies in nothing so abstract as income growth rate differences, but rather in the palpable and hard-breathing American investment and securities boom. During the years 1926–1929 Canada imported long-term capital from Great Britain but exported it to the United States. Direct investments in Canada by United States firms were niggardly, much lower (in *current* dollars) than United States direct investments in Canada during 1910–1913, and insignificant beside the direct investments of the 1950's.[74] Moreover, large amounts of Canadian funds fought their way to Wall Street, arriving in ample time for the great debacle. In the 1950's, the balance has swung the other way, on the strength of Canada's wealth of natural resources and growing domestic market.

One other sort of difference seems to distinguish these three periods of rapid growth. That is the distribution of investment between home market and export industries. It has become a fairly commonplace generalization that the 1920's were a period when capital formation was directed primarily toward satisfying the needs of domestic production, while investment both in the post-World War II years and at the beginning of the century

[73] For a splendid study of the mechanism governing migration in the Atlantic economy, see Brinley Thomas, *Migration and Economic Growth, A Study of Great Britain and the Atlantic Economy* (Cambridge, 1954).
[74] Canada, DBS, *The Canadian Balance of International Payments, 1926 to 1948* (Ottawa, 1949), pp. 164–165; Viner, p. 134; Bank of Canada, *Statistical Summary, Financial Supplement*, 1956, p. 91.

tended more strongly to go into industries serving (directly or indirectly) Canada's export markets. Admittedly, many changes in tastes and technology in the 1920's called for heavy expansion of capital goods serving Canadian purchasers. Electric power investment, assorted public works and buildings, and all the different sorts of investment requirements created by the automobile can be cited to support this view.[75] The point is hard to prove from the available statistics. We have nothing resembling the present-day breakdown of investment by industry for either the 1900's or the 1920's, only the extremely unreliable census figures on capital employed in various (ill-defined) sectors of the economy. Even if we had reliable figures for industries defined consistently in all three periods, there would still be the problem that some of the most important capital-using industries serve both home and export-producing industries. Thus investment in electric power generation during the 1920's clearly accounted for a larger share of total investment than it has in the past decade. But much of the expansion of electric power during the 1920's went to serve the power needs of the mining and pulp and paper industries, themselves heavily dependent on export markets. Likewise the 1900–1913 period saw heavy growth not just of farm investment and transport facilities to carry farm products to market, but also in domestic manufacturing and various sorts of social capital. It has not proved possible to produce investment statistics comparisons worthy of quotation, but the impression remains that none of these periods clearly stands out from the others in terms of the importance of export-oriented investment.

Some writers have tried to guess on the basis of short-run income behavior whether Canada has been growing more or less dependent on foreign trade as a growth stimulus. Very commonly this question turns up in studies of the vulnerability of the Canadian economy to external fluctuations. Thus, English, in an unpublished dissertation, has given tentative acceptance to the view that export dependence has diminished, and Walton has ended a less elaborate inquiry in a state of uncertainty.[76] Recently Rosenbluth in an orderly and luminous study has found a

[75] Mackintosh, pp. 42–43.
[76] English, p. 16; E. A. Walton, "The Vulnerability of the Canadian Economy," CJEPS, 20:12 (February 1954).

statistically significant decline in the power of the United States business cycle to create disturbances in the Canadian economy. He concludes that "the amplitude of Canadian fluctuations exceeded that in the United States before 1914, was frequently about the same in the 1920's, was usually lower in the 1930's and was often lower after 1946." [77] The most common explanation of this trend runs in the following terms. In the absence of wars, domestic investment and exports are twin determinants of income levels in the fashion indicated by the multiplier theory of modern macroeconomics. Investment may be partly dependent on export levels, but it is also partly autonomous or determined by long-run prospects for the domestic economy. This is reflected in Rosenbluth's finding that the Canadian economy has followed the United States economy more closely in business downturns than in periods of expansion. Hence a rise in the relative importance of investment compared to exports may mean a lessening of vulnerability to changes abroad.[78]

English and Walton both note that in the 1950's domestic investment seems to have grown in importance relative to exports, compared to the situation in the late 1920's. The year 1956 helps their view considerably; gross domestic investment sneaked ahead of exports in total value during 1955, but in the following year exceeded them by 20 per cent. Nonetheless, interpreting this to show decreasing export dependence is very risky for two reasons.

First, such a generalization about the falling importance of exports will not extrapolate backward from the 1920's. From the turn of the century to World War I gross domestic investment

---

[77] G. Rosenbluth, "Changes in Canadian Sensitivity to United States Business Fluctuations," *CJEPS*, 23:480–503 (November 1957), especially p. 489.

[78] Rosenbluth summarizes this argument and also points out the possibility of constructing a counterargument on the following points: (1) Canadian exports seem to be growing more and more specialized, both in terms of concentrating on a few commodities and emerging from a few particular regions of Canada, thus increasing the chance of Canada being badly burned by the onset of a world depression; (2) the long-term tendency for Canadian manufactures to replace formerly imported items may be transferring cyclically unstable items to the domestic production pattern and reducing the stabilizing effect of import variations for total Canadian employment. See Rosenbluth, pp. 480–483. The second point of this argument would imply a decline for Canada of J. J. Polak's "reflection ratio," a trend commonly associated with increasing maturity for a national economy.

ran far ahead of exports. These two quantities then bore the following percentage relationships to gross national product:

	Gross domestic investment	*Exports*
1901–1905	24.2%	22.0%
1906–1910	29.0	20.2
1911–1915	29.0	21.8 [79]

This pattern, of course, resulted from the immense capital inflows of the earlier period. But that fact only re-emphasizes the connection between levels of investment and export prospects, present and future.

The second difficulty in assessing the significance of foreign trade for income determination is that the relations are numerous and complex and do not depend just on the level of exports or their value relative to home investment. It would be very helpful to know whether the Canadian economy is equally sensitive to equal variations in exports and investment. The possibility that it is *not* equally sensitive can be tested in several ways. First, one can compare the correlation coefficients of gross national expenditure on exports and upon gross domestic investment. English's calculations, using undeflated variables, give respectively values of 0.96 to 0.97 for exports and 0.95 for investment.[80] The difference is obviously not statistically significant. Anyhow, since the interesting question is really the trend in the corresponding regression coefficients and not the absolute degree of correlation, one can try computing regression coefficients for early and late portions of the years since 1926. This was done in the present study by regressing year-to-year changes in these same variables (that is, first differences) separately for the years before and after World War II. No change appeared in the dependence of income on exports, while its dependence on investment appeared to drop in the post-World War II period because of the increasingly important role of changes in government purchases of goods and services.[81]

Even if statistical tests do not reveal a decreased sensitivity of

[79] Calculations based on figures given by Buckley.

[80] English, pp. 45–47.

[81] A covariance test was used to determine whether the prewar and postwar regression coefficients could be regarded as the same for these two relationships. There was no significant change in the relation between export changes and income changes, while the decline in the dependence of income changes on investment changes was significant at the 95 per cent confidence level.

the Canadian national income to export fluctuations, it still might be true that gross domestic investment has become less strongly influenced by export changes. English's work shows that the closest export-investment relation lies between one year's investment and the previous year's exports, an obvious reflection of the gestation period of investment projects. One can check whether this relation was closer before or after World War II. The statistics do seem to show the connection between investment and previous export levels to be a little less close in the postwar years. But one wonders whether this would have been true if government purchases of goods and services had stayed relatively stable in the past decade.[82]

Assembling all this evidence, can one say that the short-run income determination pattern in Canada has changed to reduce export dependence? Has an unwritten declaration of economic independence come into force? During none of Canada's twentieth-century growth periods has investment depended in any rigid way on export levels. But it has always depended in a gross sense on export prospects. None of the tests employed in the preceding pages controvert that view.

We can grant, then, that the pattern of short-term adjustment has been quite stable during comparable portions of the twentieth century. The final question concerns the degree of similarity between this short-run pattern and the long-run growth pattern described by the staple theory. Let us compare them piece by piece. The staple theory declares that rapid capital formation and rising per capita incomes depend jointly on strong foreign demand for resource-based, mass-producible commodities and upon technological developments making such production feasible. The short-term theory of income determination holds that rate of investment closely reflects the demand for exports, current and prospective. Although the fact has not been stressed in the preceding pages, in the short run technological changes have often altered the response of investment to export demand. Cases would

[82] The scatter diagram of the exports-to-lagged investment relation looks extremely random, when the variables are first differences of constant-dollar exports and investment in non-residential construction and machinery and equipment. The scatter of investment on exports lagged one year (same variables, but not first differences) shows a linear relationship with a reasonably high correlation. The most interesting thing about it, though, is that the postwar observations are scattered much more widely than those for the interwar period 1926–1940.

be the expansion of the prairie wheat economy as new varieties of wheat became available, and the expansion of the mining industry in the 1920's and 1930's as new processes made the use of low-grade ores feasible. The staple theory emphasizes the connection between export-based growth and expansion of the domestic economy, the income (and often population) increases induced by staple development broadening the domestic market and encouraging domestic production to satisfy consumers formerly dependent on imports. In the short run, heavy export-based investment goes hand-in-hand with heavy investment in capital partly or entirely serving the domestic economy. Indeed it often seems that boom periods induce more and more investment of the home-market type as they reach their maturity. In the short run, import-replacing investment does not coincide closely with export expansion; on the contrary, imports always increase most rapidly at such times because of the strong demand for imported machinery and short-run increases in consumers' demand for imports. Yet this very enlargement of the market for imports raises the inducement to enter import-competing industries. This process cannot be traced well within the three boom periods of the twentieth century, but it can be inferred in the ease with which wartime excess productive capacity has been absorbed into the Canadian structure of production.

The staple theory stresses the role of optimistic outlook and over-building in establishing new export-based industries. The fact that Canada's booms boom so loudly in the short run reflects this, as does the fact that they tend to gather momentum and at their peaks yield faster growth rates than those which most other countries enjoy. The staple theory stresses the quantity of saving adjusting itself to the passions of investment demand in times of rapid staple growth through capital imports, government-financed investment, credit creation, and direct saving by the investors (for example, prairie farmers in the 1900's). The short-term income model explains the way in which improving export prospects induce capital imports and substantiates the view that saving generally conforms to desired investment by failing to turn up any conspicuous cases of capital shortages hampering investment for more than very short periods.[83]

[83] This conclusion seems consistent with the explanations for Canada's cyclical turning points developed by Malach, Marcus, and others.

What features of the short-term income adjustment model does this leave unaccounted for? Little remains except the effect of inventory fluctuations, the habit-persistence lag in consumer behavior, several other one-year lags, and certain features of the balance-of-payments adjustment process. But these are all transitory phenomena. Even over a period as short as a decade it seems unlikely that they could significantly change the pattern of economic growth. Hence it follows that the staple theory interpretation of Canadian economic growth is consistent with what we know about patterns of short-run change in Canada. This fact furnishes one more prop for the use of the staple theory in both analyzing and forecasting Canadian economic development.

4

Structure of the Canadian Economy: Statistical Studies

This chapter presents two special investigations into the structure of the Canadian economy. They elaborate and confirm conclusions reached at several other points in this study and are set apart here because they employ special analytical tools which demand a measure of explanation. The first of these investigations employs interindustry analysis to explore the structure of the Canadian economy, especially with respect to its foreign trade. The second develops an extremely simplified long-run statistical model of the economy for purposes of limited testing of some well-known hypotheses about Canadian economic development.

CANADA'S INTERINDUSTRY STRUCTURE[1]

Much of Canada's economic history is written in terms of interindustry relations. As was emphasized in Chapter 2, one of the vital connections between staple production and Canada's general economic growth has been through the staple industries' demand for intermediate goods. The Canadian farm machinery and mining machinery industries bear adequate testimony to this. Each of the two great wars of the twentieth century has greatly expanded Canada's manufacturing sector via demand transmitted through interindustry channels. Thus, for background to forecasting the future development of Canada it is well to have some information on the interindustry structure of the economy.

The most common sort of information interindustry analysis provides is the relative impact of personal consumption, gross domestic investment, exports and government purchases of goods and services — the "final demand" sectors — on different indus-

[1] Portions of this section are reprinted from "The Inter-Industry Structure of the Canadian Economy," *CJEPS*, 23:313–330 (August 1957).

tries in the economy. For this tool can tell us not just how final demand is distributed among the various industries of the economy but also how this distribution affects total output of the various industries. This is precisely because interindustry analysis traces purchases of intermediate goods through the economy. Of course, one could not have full knowledge of the connection between one industry's level of sales and its purchases from all other industries without a great deal of information about that industry's technology, output mix, input-substitution possibilities, and so forth. Interindustry analysis sweeps all this aside with the strategic, simple, and often plausible assumption that one can suppose one industry's purchases from any other industry to be proportional to the former's total output and not dependent on any other variable. While not theoretically defensible, this assumption has proved sufficiently serviceable to assuage any qualms which arise for most of its users.

We can use this technique of analysis on the Canadian economy because the Dominion Bureau of Statistics has recently completed the arduous work of preparing an interindustry table for Canada in 1949. It is a form of national accounting which embodies not only the conventional national expenditure and product accounts but also all interindustry sales and purchases among forty-two separate producing sectors of the Canadian economy.[2]

Table 6 gives us some notion of the relation between the composition of Canada's final demand for goods and services and the production levels of sixteen large producing sectors of the economy. The comparisons are made in the following way. Suppose one portion of final demand for goods and services, such as personal consumption, were to rise by $100,000,000 while some other portion, such as gross domestic investment, falls by the same amount. Aggregate spending in the economy remains the same; no complications are introduced through multiplier effects and changes in the level of total employment. However, the total outputs of all industries change, because in general the total requirements of a particular industry's output to satisfy $100,000,-000 worth of personal comsumption will not be the same as its

[2] Canada, DBS, *The Inter-Industry Flow of Goods and Services, Canada, 1949* (Ottawa, 1956). See also J. A. Sawyer, "The Measurement of Inter-Industry Relationships in Canada," *CJEPS*, 21:480–497 (November 1955).

Table 6. Changes in total Canadian outputs caused by shifts of final
demand, by sectors (millions of dollars).

Sector	Consumption rises, investment falls by $100 million (1)	Government rises, investment falls by $100 million (2)	Exports rise, consumption falls by $100 million (3)
1. Agriculture	7.1	4.0	15.5
2. Forestry	−1.9	−1.1	6.7
3. Fishing, hunting, trapping	0.7	0.2	0.7
4. Coal mining, crude petroleum, natural gas	0.9	−0.1	−0.4
5. Other mining and quarrying industries	−1.1	−1.1	15.8
6. Food, beverage and tobacco industries	12.9	6.9	−0.2
7. Clothing and household goods industries	23.4	−1.0	−22.1
8. Forest products industries	−7.8	−4.7	25.0
9. Metal products industries	−19.6	−25.9	0.2
10. Electrical apparatus and supplies industry	−3.9	−5.8	−2.6
11. Mineral products industries	−1.6	−2.2	1.9
12. Miscellaneous manufacturing industries	2.3	4.0	−1.9
13. Construction	−50.0	−30.8	−5.4
14. Transportation, storage, trade	4.4	4.4	5.9
15. Communication, finance, insurance, real estate, public utility operation	12.5	2.7	−9.6
16. Other service industries	9.2	70.1	−14.0

Source: Calculated from Canada, DBS, *The Inter-Industry Flow of Goods and Services, Canada, 1949* (Ottawa, 1956), Table I.

output required to satisfy the same amount of gross domestic investment. The difference is a matter of $8,000,000 for the forest products industry, $9,000,000 for the miscellaneous service industries, and so forth.[3]

[3] To make these calculations we have assumed that the change in gross domestic investment is spread across the various sectors of the economy in proportion to the value of their total sales into domestic investment in 1949. The same assumption will be made for government expenditure and exports below. For personal consumption, however, a more elaborate approach was followed through assuming that the distribution of the $100,000,000 expenditure change is that which would be implied by cross-sectional elasticities of demand. For a full description, see "The Inter-Industry Structure of the Canadian Economy," p. 316 and note 12, and Chapter 10, Table 43 *infra*.

Considering that the total final demand remains unchanged, the variations in output by industry are quite large. The total value of construction (sector 13) would decline by $50,000,000, half the amount of the assumed reallocation of expenditure. The output of the metal products industries (sector 9) would drop nearly $20,000,000; new automobiles have a high income elasticity but also a high import content. The largest net increases in expenditure would be on clothing and household goods (sector 7), the foods group (sector 6), and the public utilities group (sector 15). The *composition* of output, of course, might change greatly in this situation for some sectors whose total output stays fairly stable. For example, the small decline in mineral products output (sector 11) would cloak a large decline in cement production and a large increase in cosmetics. An interesting property of the figures in Table 6 is that, if the autonomous change were the opposite of the one assumed, that is, reallocation of $100,000,000 expenditure from consumption to investment, then the resulting changes in gross output would have the same numerical values but opposite signs.

Column (2) of Table 6 deals with the effect of a hypothetical increase in government expenditures to offset an autonomous decline in gross domestic investment. Interpreting a change in government activity requires some care. First, only government purchases of goods and services appear in the interindustry table, so we are assuming that the increase in expenditure involves no change in transfer payments. Second, governments appear both as final purchasers and as producers of goods and services. Government business enterprises (railroads, for example) are treated in the same way as other business enterprises; they create no problem. Government agencies of public administration and defense, however, are defined as "selling" their total output to the government final demand sector, this "product" being the total cost of providing these services. Most of this output appears in sector 16, with minor amounts in sectors 15 and 14.[4] In interpreting the changes shown in column (2) we must remember that parts of the changes for these sectors directly reflect the chang-

[4] In 1949, governments purchased their own production of $1,279,300,000 of government service and $282,000,000 of community service from sector 16 of our condensed table, $8,000,000 of communication from sector 15, and $500,000 of transportation and $2,000,000 of trade from sector 14 (figures furnished by Mr. Sawyer of DBS).

ing level of government activity, and that other parts reflect the increased demand of government from the private portion of the economy. A change in the level of government activity would thus cause the greatest increase in sector 16. The pattern of government expenditure is weighted fairly heavily toward the producers' goods industries but not sufficiently to compensate them for an offsetting change in total gross domestic investment.

The third column of Table 6 shows the effect of an increase in exports offsetting a decline in Canadian personal consumption. If exports were to expand while consumption declined (owing, say, to depreciation of the Canadian dollar), the significant gainers would all be primary industries — sectors 1, 8, and 5. This experiment suggests which sectors of the Canadian economy are strongly dependent on foreign markets, that is, which sectors would show declining total outputs following a slump in export demand even if total spending stayed constant. Canada's agriculture, forestry, and mining (other than energy sources) depend heavily on foreign markets and would present problems of "structural disequilibrium" even in a prosperous economy if exports were lowered.

It is useful to condense the information on Canada's interindustry structure even further. Table 7 displays the interindustry

Table 7.   Canadian interindustry relations of primary, secondary, and tertiary sectors (millions of dollars).

| Sector where total output affected | Sector where final demand increases by $100 million | | |
| | Primary | Secondary | Tertiary |
	Agriculture, fishing, etc. (1)	Extractive industries (2)	Manufacturing and construction (3)	All services (4)
Primary				
Agriculture, fishing, hunting, trapping	104.5	2.8	11.4	4.2
Extractive (mining, forestry)	1.6	102.2	6.1	2.7
Secondary				
Manufacturing, construction	32.8	24.8	145.6	33.0
Tertiary				
Services and unallocated	34.6	38.8	41.9	125.5

Source: Calculated from Canada, DBS, *The Inter-Industry Flow of Goods and Services, Canada, 1949,* Table 1.

connections among four broad groups of Canadian industries, two primary sectors (one including agriculture and fishing, the other all mining and forestry), a secondary sector including all manufacturing and construction,[5] and a tertiary sector including all the service industries and also the unallocated items. The inverse of the structural matrix derived from the condensed table tells how much on the average each of the large sectors purchases from each of the others per unit of its sales to the final demand sector. It is this inverse which appears in Table 7. We can interpret Table 7 as follows: when final demand for an industry listed in one of the column headings increases by $100,000,000, the total output of the industries listed at the side of the table will increase by the amounts appearing in that column.

Much interest attaches to the effect of growth in the primary sectors on the level of output in the secondary and tertiary industries. The last two figures in columns (1) and (2) give this information. If these figures are contrasted with the first two figures in columns (3) and (4), it will be seen that the secondary and tertiary sectors are much more sensitive to changes in final demand for primary output than the latter is to changes in the former. Moreover, inspection shows that the secondary and tertiary sectors are quite sensitive to given changes in final demand for each other's output; on the other hand, derived demand relating the two primary sectors is extremely slight. Some care is necessary in interpreting these results. They tell little about the degree to which one sector's *total* output depends on the level of output of another; that dependence varies with the proportion of the total output of the first which is sold to the other. The results provide only an *absolute* measure of the changes in the output of one sector induced in the short run by changes in the demand for another.

The evidence of Table 7 confirms some well-known patterns in Canadian history. Rising primary products output has been a tremendous stimulus for the rest of the economy because of the strong interindustry connection revealed in the table as well as through consumers' typically high income elasticities of demand

[5] It should be noted here that the primary sector includes nonferrous smelting and refining, and the manufacturing sectors include the tertiary industries which repair and service their respective products. See Canada, DBS, *The Inter-Industry Flow of Goods and Services, Canada, 1949*, pp. 30, 31.

for manufactured goods. Conversely, the expansion of Canada's manufacturing and service sectors as an independent force affords comparatively little growth stimulus to the rest of the economy through interindustry demand.

Another use of interindustry analysis is giving some content to the notion of Canada's vulnerability to external economic changes. In the past, particularly in the interwar period, the volume and value of international trade fluctuated more violently over the world business cycle than did the incomes of most nations. Canada derives almost one-fifth of her national income from foreign trade and has nearly the highest foreign trade per

Table 8.   Proportion of total Canadian outputs by industry depending directly and indirectly on exports.

Sector	Fall in total output if all exports ceased (millions) (1)	Column (1) as percentage of total output of each sector (2)	Ratio of column (2) to weighted average (3)
1. Agriculture	$ 952.1	30.7	3.0
2. Forestry	289.9	64.4	6.4
3. Fishing, hunting, trapping	55.8	42.5	4.2
4. Coal mining, crude petroleum, natural gas	54.2	14.8	1.5
5. Other mining and quarrying industries	653.6	80.4	7.9
6. Food, beverage and tobacco industries	529.9	13.4	1.3
7. Clothing and household goods industries	173.2	7.1	0.7
8. Forest products industries	1,112.0	55.4	5.5
9. Metal products industries	744.4	21.8	2.1
10. Electric apparatus and supplies industry	61.7	9.6	0.9
11. Mineral products industries	395.9	20.5	2.0
12. Miscellaneous manufacturing industries	108.4	12.1	1.2
13. Construction	112.7	4.0	0.4
14. Transportation, storage, trade	1,044.1	23.2	2.3
15. Communication, finance, insurance, real estate, public utility operation	301.3	10.6	1.0
16. Other service industries	76.2	2.0	0.2

Source: Calculated from Canada, DBS, *The Inter-Industry Flow of Goods and Services, Canada, 1949* (Ottawa, 1956), Table 1.

capita of any nation in the world. It is frequently argued from these two facts that Canada is somehow particularly vulnerable to economic shocks transmitted from elsewhere in the world economy — that the burden of economic readjustment imposed on Canada is somehow particularly great. Interest seems to be concentrated on two loci of adjustment — aggregates of income and output and the balance of payments.

Interindustry analysis readily reveals the portion of each sector's total output which depends upon Canadian exports (either as direct export sales or as inputs into export production). These calculations appear in Table 8. Column (1) shows the value in millions of dollars of the portion of each sector's total output which, in the 1949 economy, depended (directly or indirectly) on the level of exports. In column (2) these values appear as percentages of the total output of each sector, and in column (3) each percentage is converted to a ratio to the weighted average of all the percentages, the weights being the actual total outputs. Thus column (3) gives clearly defined evidence of the vulnerability of Canada's primary sectors. In terms of this method of measurement, sector 5 is nearly eight times as vulnerable to external shocks as the whole economy, sectors 2 and 8 six times, sector 3 four times, and sector 1 three times. It should be noted that these calculations ignore the changes in imports that would be necessary to maintain balance of payments equilibrium.

The second locus of vulnerability in Canada's economic struc-

Table 9.   Direct and indirect effects on Canadian imports of increases in final demand, by sectors (millions of dollars).

Sector where increased demand of $100 million originates	Increase of imports		
	Direct (1)	Indirect (2)	Total (3)
1. Consumption	18.0	10.7	28.7
2. Investment	17.2	13.0	30.2
3. Government purchases of goods and services	0.0	8.6	8.6
4. General exports	0.0	14.5	14.5
5. Exports to United States	0.0	14.1	14.1
6. Exports to United Kingdom	0.0	10.4	10.4

Source: Calculated from Canada, DBS, *The Inter-Industry Flow of Goods and Services, Canada, 1949* (Ottawa, 1956), Table 1.

ture is the balance of payments. In countries such as Canada which depend on importation for many essential goods there is considerable interest in the effect on imports of changes in domestic expenditure. How much do imports rise with increased personal consumption or gross domestic investment? How much does an investment boom tend to weaken the trade balance from the import side? Under the restrictive assumption that the share of all markets held by imported goods remains constant (that is, that fixed coefficients govern import requirements) interindustry analysis can reveal what adjustment in the demand for imports is generated by any such change. Table 9 shows the direct and indirect requirements for imports generated by increases of $100,000,000 in each of the final demand sectors. "Direct" requirements for imports when consumption (item 1) increases are simply the portion of the increased consumption spent on imports. The indirect requirements are those imports needed by Canadian industry in order to produce goods for domestic consumers; hence, a growth of consumption creates a demand for such goods only indirectly. Column (3) shows that in the short run a shift in final demand of the magnitude of $100,000,000 away from investment (item 2) and toward consumption (item 1) would cut the demand for imports by $1,500,000. Stepping up government expenditure on goods and services (item 3) to offset declining consumption or investment would have a much stronger tendency to reduce import demand; the amount of the reductions would be respectively $20,000,000 and $21,600,000. Thus, it is true that a reduction in the portion of the Canadian national product that is devoted to capital formation would in the short run reduce the demand for imports, though the difference is not marked.

A slightly different set of problems concerning economic structure and balance-of-payments stability arises for some countries from the fact that some imports serve as intermediate goods for producing exports. Writers have frequently noted that where the import content of exports is high, as in countries like the United Kingdom which import raw materials and export finished goods, larger fluctuations in the exchange rate are necessary to requite balance-of-payments disequilibria of a given size. If all world prices stay constant, then part of the country's import purchases will rise in proportion to the increase in exports; depreciation must be sufficient to place the whole burden of adjustment on imports for domestic use.

As item 4 of Table 9 shows, an increase of $100,000,000 in Canadian exports would raise Canada's import requirements by $14,500,000 in order to satisfy the technical requirements for the production of exports.[6] Reflection on the working of the foreign trade multiplier of course makes it plain that the import-inducing effects of rising exports do not stop there. Increased exports may generate higher domestic incomes through the multiplier mechanism; these in turn induce higher consumption and more imports, both directly as consumer goods and indirectly as producer goods to increase output capacity. Polak has published figures which, though of dubious accuracy, can be taken as a rough indication of the size of the total effect on imports of a change in exports. His computations suggest that the *total* effect of an increase of $100,000,000 in exports would be an increase of $68,000,000 in imports.[7] That is, the increase in imports owing to their being used up to produce exports ($14,500,-000) would be about 21 per cent of the total increase in imports.

A LONG-RUN STATISTICAL MODEL OF THE CANADIAN ECONOMY

As a check and supplement to our view of the historic pattern of Canadian economic development, we have prepared an extremely simplified statistical model of the Canadian economy, 1901–1955. We present it here not because it gives a very satis-

[6] Standing alone, this figure is difficult to interpret. For the United States, Leontief has provided a comparable figure of 3.2 per cent as the change in imports occasioned by a given change in exports; see W. W. Leontief, "Factor Proportions and the Structure of American Trade," *RES,* 38:394–395 (November 1956), Table 1, note 3. No completely comparable figure seems to exist for a European country, although one of Billewicz's methods of deriving the import content of British exports seems roughly similar to interindustry analysis. His figures of 16.4 per cent for the United Kingdom in 1938 and 14.0 per cent in 1946 are probably a little low. See W. Z. Billewicz, "The Import Content of British Exports," *Economica,* 20:162–169 (May 1953).

[7] J. J. Polak, *An International Economic System* (Chicago, 1953), pp. 123–126, gives 0.68 as the value for Canada's "reflection ratio," which is equal to the product of the foreign trade multiplier (2.13) and the marginal propensity to import (0.32). These figures can be taken only as suggestive because the data consist of short time series of annual observations during the most abnormal years of the 1930's. One should note that Polak's method of calculating the foreign trade multiplier lumps together both the direct effect of changing exports on income through the conventional multiplier mechanism and the indirect effect operating through the accelerator effect of exports on investment and the effect of investment on income through the multiplier.

Table 10. List of variables and identities used in statistical model of the Canadian economy, 1901–1955.

	Variable	Units	Type
P	Population	Thousands	Endogenous
R	Immigration	Thousands	Endogenous
S	Emigration	Thousands	Endogenous
B	Births	Thousands	Endogenous
D	Deaths	Thousands	Exogenous
L	Labor force	Thousands	Endogenous
Y	Gross national output	1935–39 billions	Endogenous
I	Gross domestic investment	1935–39 billions	Endogenous
I_r	Gross residential construction	1935–39 billions	Endogenous
I_b	Gross domestic investment ex. housing	1935–39 billions	Endogenous
K	Capital stock	1935–39 billions	Endogenous
X	Exports of goods and services	1935–39 billions	Endogenous
M	Imports of goods and services	1935–39 billions	Endogenous
Y_f	Foreign gross national output[a]	1935–39 = 100	Exogenous
t	Time	1901–05 = 1 1906–10 = 2 etc.	Exogenous
u_i	Error terms allowing for random shocks		

Identities

(1)	Capital stock	$K = K_{-1} + I_{-1}$
(2)	Population	$P = P_{-1} + (B_{-1} - D_{-1}) + (R_{-1} - S_{-1})$
(3)	Investment	$I = I_r + I_b$

[a] This is a synthetic variable constructed by computing indexes of United Kingdom and United States real gross national output or industrial production and weighting them by the normalized share of Canada's exports going to each country. For recent years the official figures were used for both countries; Robert Martin's figures were used for earlier years in the United States and Prest's for the United Kingdom [*EJ*, 58:58–59 (March 1948)].

factory fit or because it can be used to forecast future economic changes in Canada, but rather because it provides a rough sort of test of certain common generalizations about Canadian economic growth. We shall not stress the dynamic properties of the over-all model, because it is too simplified (particularly by the complete absence of price variables) to hold much interest for such purposes.[8]

[8] For a considerably more elaborate and interesting model for the United States, see S. Valavanis-Vail, "An Econometric Model of Growth, U.S.A. 1869–1953," *AER*, 45:208–221 (May 1955). This article has been a source of many ideas for developing a long-run model for Canada.

The variables appearing in the model are listed in Table 10. Note that they concentrate almost entirely on Canada's foreign trade, supplies of factors of production, population, and general level of real output. The data are used in the form of five-year totals from 1901–1905 to 1951–1955. Thus there is a maximum of eleven observations for each series. The reason for using five-year totals of course is that Kenneth Buckley's figures for capital formation and gross national product before 1926 come only in this form.[9] Without Buckley's figures, constructing a satisfactory statistical model of long-run economic growth in Canada is impossible. Whether it becomes possible with Buckley's figures in hand remains an open question. The short time series furnish the first major obstacle to constructing a statistical model. If one explains eleven observations of a dependent variable by more than a very few independent variables, the result will be a good fit and a high coefficient of multiple correlation, but there will also be a good chance that the fit is quite spurious and indicates no connection between the independent and dependent variables. Hence, none of the equations in this system contains more than two independent variables.

The method of solving the model has been by least squares rather than the more high-brow limited-information method. A number of reasons conditioned this choice. First, as indicated above, the model was desired mainly for descriptive purposes and as a check on other work rather than a solitary and independent system for testing hypotheses. Because of this and the rough quality of some of the data, the fact that limited-information is not an efficient estimating procedure (that is, the estimator does not have minimum variance in large samples) weighed against its use. Statisticians frequently recognize that such considerations can at times justify the use of an inconsistent estimator such as that given by the least-squares procedure.

The second reason for using least-squares estimation has to do with the nature of the Canadian economy. The main problems of statistically fitting economic relations arise because Walrasian interdependence is supposed to pervade economic systems. The notion of this interdependence has become quite dominant in economic thinking, particularly in the theoretical work of English-speaking economists. A number of Scandinavian economists are

[9] K. A. H. Buckley, *Capital Formation in Canada, 1896–1930* (Toronto, 1955).

hold-outs from this orthodoxy, however. They insist that in many contexts systems of economic relations are not interdependent but *recursive*, the variables connected to each other in the fashion of a chain rather than that of a network. This possibility is particularly obvious in a dynamic setting where time lags assume importance in the decisions made by economic agents. With regard to statistical fitting, Herman Wold has pointed out that systems of stochastic equations may be shown to be recursive, the first depending only on variables exogenous to the system, the second only on exogenous variables and endogenous variables in the first equation, and so on.[10] Then the case for an estimating procedure more complicated than least squares disappears. Our contention is that the long-run development of the Canadian economy can as a rough approximation be depicted in this way, and the equations of our system displayed in Table 11 satisfy these conditions for recursiveness. Part of the reason, as we shall see, is the location in time of available measurements of certain stock variables. But the substance of Canadian economic relationships is also at issue.

Exports from Canada have a powerful effect on gross domestic investment, but investment in turn only affects exports after a substantial lag. The main determinant of the movement of both goods and people out of the country is the level of income in regions outside Canada, an exogenous variable. Via the birth rate and immigration Canada's population depends on the domestic level of investment and rate of income growth. Population will of course ultimately influence these variables, but only through a roundabout process. The long-run output level depends on the size of the labor force, even if short-run production planning (and no doubt some long-run investment) depends on the current birth rate. Even investment can be included in these chainwise relations. Residential construction in the long run is frequently held to depend on past population growth, particularly lagged immigration, the current birth rate, and the existing stock of dwelling space. Other components of gross domestic investment (which we shall call "business investment" for convenience) depend heavily on exports. In neither of these cases are the re-

---

[10] H. Wold and L. Juréen, *Demand Analysis, A Study in Econometrics* (New York and Stockholm, 1953); for an excellent brief summary, see W. C. Hood, "Empirical Studies of Demand," *CJEPS*, 21:314–317 (August 1955).

Table 11. Equations and parameter estimates, statistical model of the Canadian economy, 1901–1955.

Dependent variable	Parameter estimates	Coefficient of multiple correlation
1. Emigration	$S = -1462.7 + 0.4922R_{-1} + 1499.3\,Y_t/Y_{t-1} + u_1$ $\phantom{S = -1462.7 + {}}(0.0760)\phantom{R_{-1} + {}}(391.7)$	0.3538
2. Exports	$X = -1.4703 + 0.0744Y_t + u_2$ $\phantom{X = -1.4703 + {}}(0.0090)$	0.9156
3. Labor force	$L = -497 + 0.3074P + 0.4319(K/P) + u_3$ $\phantom{L = -497 + {}}(0.0404)\phantom{P + {}}(0.1833)$	0.9946
4. Output	$Y = 20.52 + 3.004K - 0.0214L + u_4$ $\phantom{Y = 20.52 + {}}(0.127)\phantom{K - {}}(0.015)$	0.9724
5. Birth rate	$(B/P) = 0.177 + 0.0011(Y/P)/(Y/P)_{-1} - 0.00416t + u_5$ $\phantom{(B/P) = 0.177 + {}}(0.0114)\phantom{(Y/P)/(Y/P)_{-1} - {}}(0.0007)$	0.5539
6. Residential construction	$I_r = -0.5366 - 0.00002R_{-1} + 0.00114B + u_6$ $\phantom{I_r = -0.5366 - {}}(0.00010)\phantom{R_{-1} + {}}(0.00012)$	0.9218
7. Other investment	$I_b = 6.1119 + 0.5368X - 4.9017(Y/P)/(Y/P)_{-1} + u_7$ $\phantom{I_b = 6.1119 + {}}(0.0805)\phantom{X - {}}(13.918)$	0.6775
8. Imports	$M = 1.052 + 0.2807I + 0.6386X + u_8$ $\phantom{M = 1.052 + {}}(0.0904)\phantom{I + {}}(0.0835)$	0.9888
9. Immigration	$R = 419.0 + 133.2I_b - 75.84t + u_9$ $\phantom{R = 419.0 + {}}(14.1)\phantom{I_b - {}}(12.23)$	0.7175

Note: figures in parentheses give the standard error of each slope coefficient.
Source: See text. All estimates are calculated by least-squares procedure.

verse relations particularly significant. Finally, the movement of goods and people into Canada is determined by many variables within the Canadian economy but has little causal power in determining the economy's pattern except over long periods. All of these relations, which are simply verbal statements of the hypotheses embodied in the equation system of Table 11, illustrate the importance and generality of recursiveness in the Canadian economy.

As mentioned above, one feature of data availability also had a good deal to do with the recursive structure of the model. The stock variables capital and population (or labor force) can be measured only by adding net flows onto bench-mark estimates. For population, the bench-mark estimate is the decennial census; but for earlier years the information on annual changes in population through net natural increase and net migration is poor enough that we have preferred to take our population estimates as of the beginning of the five-year time periods covered by the flow variables. The only remotely plausible bench mark for an estimate of capital stock in the economy was the 1929 DBS estimate of $31,276,000,000 (current prices). Capital stock could be estimated before 1926 only by subtracting out Buckley's five-year gross investment totals, reduced by a rough estimate of depreciation. Adding to this uncertainty by interpolating to find the average capital stock during each five-year time period seemed one straw too many, and so the capital stock variable was also taken at the beginning of each time period. Note that this dating of the stock variables gives a peculiar interpretation to some of the equations. Equation (4) hypothesizes that a five-year total real output is a function of the labor supply and the capital stock existing at the *beginning* of the period.

Let us turn again to Table 11 and survey the statistical results. There the standard error of each slope coefficient appears in parentheses below it, while the coefficient of multiple correlation appears at the right. In terms of the correlation coefficients, four of the nine equations exhibit notably bad fits. Equations (1) and (9), emigration and immigration, have obviously been subject to very potent excluded variables such as national policy changes and wars. The equations for the birth rate and for business investment are also poor, the determinants of these variables always being statistically difficult to isolate. Three slope coefficients clearly have signs which are perverse according to normal theoretical expectations. Output appears negatively related to the size of the labor force in the output equation (4), a solid case of multicollinearity. In the residential construction equation (6), the previous half-decade's immigration appears to have a negative influence, contrary to commonly heard opinions. And, in the equation for business investment (7), the growth rate of per-capita national product has a negative coefficient, which will surprise at least those with great faith in a long-term accelerator effect. Several other regression coefficients have standard errors so large as to lack any statistical significance, and several of the intercept coefficients have magnitudes which are out of line with common sense, notably those in equations (4) and (7).

As a general statistical description of Canadian economic growth, then, the model is scarcely a resounding success. Nonetheless, a good deal can be learned by comparing the actual values for the explained variables of Table 11 with the values estimated for them by the equations. Table 12 facilitates this by presenting the percentage by which each observation of each explained variable exceeds (+) or falls short of (−) its predicted value. Using this table, let us briefly consider each of the equations in the system.

1. The emigration equation relates gross emigration in each half-decade to the previous half-decade's gross immigration and to the rate of growth of foreign gross national output.[11] The equation thus embodies two well-known hypotheses about Canadian population changes, the Hurd-Lower displacement theory (heavy immigration displaces Canadians because of the economy's limited ability to support population) and the theory that emigration largely responds to economic opportunity outside of Canada, and particularly in the United States. It would have been desirable to take into account the growth of foreign income relative to Canadian income, but this would have complicated the structure of the model seriously. The results do not reject either of these hypotheses; the standard errors of both regression coefficients are fairly low. One thing clearly shown by the size and direction of the residuals for equation (1) is the powerful de-

[11] The latter is a synthetic variable which was described in a footnote to Table 10.

Table 12. Percentages by which actual Canadian economic variables deviated from predicted values, 1901–1955.

Time period	Emigration	Exports	Labor force	Output	Birth rate	Residential construction	Other investment	Imports	Immigration
1901–1905	133.8	−39.6	−5.7	−17.5	−3.4	−0.4	−3.6	−16.4	−10.0
1906–1910	19.8	−37.2	0.6	33.6	−1.8	41.6	73.3	−2.4	56.3
1911–1915	64.2	−29.4	4.8	58.6	2.4	13.5	53.0	9.8	69.2
1916–1920	−51.5	35.2	−0.4	3.4	−6.2	−14.4	−18.7	6.1	−34.0
1921–1925	94.2	43.9	−3.3	4.6	−1.3	−19.5	−21.4	6.4	18.8
1926–1930	−7.6	9.2	−1.8	−4.9	−17.6	26.0	−16.4	5.6	41.3
1931–1935	−72.6	−7.3	2.0	−29.1	−25.5	−24.2	−62.4	−2.2	−40.7
1936–1940	−61.3	9.3	4.6	−8.1	−27.6	8.9	−2.0	−8.0	−79.0
1941–1945	−61.1	a	−1.6	4.9	−14.8	−24.4	−42.1	1.2	−48.8
1946–1950	−27.7	6.5	1.7	8.9	7.4	4.6	9.2	−7.1	−32.1
1951–1955	28.3	7.9	−2.5	−3.4	13.6	4.2	59.5	2.6	−28.7

a Data unavailable.

Source: Calculated by dividing actual magnitudes by corresponding estimates predicted from equations in Table 11. Figures represent percentage by which actual variables exceeded or fell short of predicted variables.

terring effect war and depression have on international movements of population.

2. Because of the method of constructing the independent variable, "foreign gross national output," the export equation would be expected to have a high correlation coefficient. By weighting the indexes of United States and United Kingdom real income by the distribution of Canadian exports between the two, we automatically build a positive correlation into the relation. Taking this into account, the correlation of 0.9156 is not particularly high. More interesting is the large negative constant, reflecting the high long-run income elasticity of demand for Canadian exports in their principal markets. The equation seriously underestimates Canadian exports during the years 1901–1915 due to the impact of heavy capital movements and rapid domestic growth during those years. It is interesting that it does not notably overestimate exports for 1931–1940. In real terms foreign purchases of Canadian exports did not fall so much more than in proportion to the drop in real income.

3. The size of Canada's labor force is almost entirely explained by the size of the total population and the quantity of capital per head, though one could argue that the sign of the coefficient relating to the latter variable is perverse. According to the equation, a rise in the stock of capital per head increases the portion of the population in the labor force. One might *a priori* expect a many-sided substitution effect which would produce a negative coefficient here. But, on the contrary, just as good an *a priori* argument can be made that the long-run labor supply has a positive elasticity, with more of the population going to work when real wages are rising (due in part to the increase in capital or circumstances which normally accompany it). One suspects that the really significant forces here lie in the realm of social change — the urbanization of Canadian society and the steady erosion of hostility to the employment of women. The residuals are of little interest; it should be remembered that they reflect the situation at the *beginning* of each of the eleven half-decade periods and thus fail to reflect the influence of such features as wars and depressions except for the 1936–1940 period.

4. The residuals from the output equation are likewise of little interest because of the multicollinearity encountered there. The difficulty could probably have been tempered by using half-decade

figures for the average number actually employed. But these would be extremely hard to secure in accurate form for the earlier years and, furthermore, would undermine the identity of the equation as a production (output) equation by interjecting the relation determining the level of employment in the short run.

5. The birth rate equation incorporates two hypotheses which hold considerable interest for this study — that of the secular birth rate decline in an industrializing society and that of a "positive income elasticity of demand for offspring," which seems necessary to explain post-World War II developments. Actually, what explanatory value the equation possesses derives almost entirely from the time trend variable. The coefficient relating the birth rate to the rate of growth of per capita income *is* positive, but is much smaller than its standard error and therefore not significant. Much more of the variation of the birth rate could no doubt have been explained by substituting an index of the per cent unemployed. The equation seriously underestimates the birth rate only for the post-World War II decade. One striking case of overestimation is the period 1926–1930, when a period of considerable prosperity and high employment was accompanied by a sharp decline in the birth rate, possibly due to rapid urbanization and economic distress in some farming areas.

6. We attempt to explain residential construction by the current number of births — an index of the crowding the typical family will be experiencing — and the previous period's immigration. The logical significance of this lag may not be immediately apparent; after all, Canadian immigrants typically have not lived outdoors while saving enough to buy a new dwelling. However, one can argue that on first arrival immigrants compete for housing space with other low-income groups in the society, with neither group providing immediately much effective demand for new dwelling space. This does come later, though, as immigrant families work their way up in the income distribution and as extra competition for housing space affects higher income groups. Examining the components of the estimating equation suggests that this explanation has some merit for the first twenty years of the period, although over the whole fifty-five-year period the relation becomes insignificant. The residuals of the equation clearly suggest the influence of major omitted variables, particularly the size of the stock of existing housing. This would help

to explain the substantial underestimation for the periods 1911–1915 and 1926–1930.

7. The business investment equation attempts to relate gross domestic investment less residential construction to exports and to the growth rate of per capita GNP. The former relation is easy to spot in the annual data, as was indicated in Chapter 3. But although the relation is still significant in the long run it dominates the scene less thoroughly. The growth rate of per capita GNP proves to be an unsatisfactory index of the economic growth prospects which clearly influence long-run investment decisions. The regression coefficient is negative due to a small negative partial correlation coefficient connecting the two variables business investment and per capita income growth. In recent years econometricians have had some luck at isolating the determinants of investment demand in the short run, but isolating its long-run determinants in the form of statistical time series still seems a hopeless task. It is interesting to note that the equation underestimates business investment more for the years 1951–1955 than for 1911–1915.

8. The equation relating imports to current gross domestic investment and current exports yields a very high correlation but its explanatory significance is a bit obscure. Exports clearly should be included as a determinant of imports because of the strength of the balance of payments adjustment mechanism, but they also powerfully affect the import level in other ways, among them through influencing the level of investment. In view of the common belief that in the short run Canada's import demand is highly elastic with respect to domestic income and investment, it is curious that the intercept in equation (8) should be positive and large. The pattern of residuals suggests that other components of Canadian economic activity are important excluded variables. The equation underestimates imports during periods when personal consumption or government purchases of goods and services have run ahead of their long-run trend values. This fact confirms the usual view about the sensitivity of imports to income changes and suggests an alternative interpretation of the high intercept. The partial elasticity of imports to export changes when income remains constant may be very low, as it no doubt is in the absence of exchange rate adjustments.

9. The immigration equation, relating gross movement of

persons into Canada to current business investment and time, offers no particular surprises. The time trend roughly approximates the steady rise of world-wide barriers to block the international movement of people in response to economic motives. The level of business investment gives an index of employment opportunities, which seem to be the strongest force drawing migrants into a new land. The residuals in the equation have a high positive correlation with gross domestic investment. The equation, despite the presence of the time trend, consistently overestimates immigration from 1931 on. The fact itself is no surprise, but the amount of the overestimation in the postwar period is quite striking.

The reader may wonder whether the relatively poor results of this statistical study of Canadian economic growth are due to skimping on the resources devoted to the effort. With respect to long-run models, the authors doubt that this is the case. Any attempt to elaborate this long-run model further seems likely to get tangled in considerable difficulties. An obvious step would be to incorporate a long-run consumption function, but not the slenderest sort of consumption estimates are available before 1926 except for isolated years. The determinants of investment might be more fully explored, but immediately one runs into great problems of quantifying variables. What statistical series independently measures producers' beliefs about the long-run future demand for nonferrous metals? One might include various price and factor wage levels, but the highly regionalized nature of the Canadian economy, especially before World War I, seriously impugns the wisdom of this step.

A more fruitful use of econometric talent would be to develop an ambitious model based on annual data since 1926. The resources of the present project were not sufficient to allow efforts in this line, since the chances seemed slim that such a model could be used directly for forecasting purposes. We have substituted instead the piecemeal approach of Chapter 3. However, the excellent statistics available for Canada since 1926 and the many interesting structural properties of the economy suggest that such endeavors might yield quite interesting results.[12]

[12] The only generally available study of this sort is T. M. Brown, "Habit Persistence and Lags in Consumer Behavior," *Econometrica*, 20:355–371 (July 1952).

5
The Growth of Canada's Eastern Regions

A study of Canadian economic growth must be in part a study of the growth of the disparate regions which comprise the country. The marked geological, climatic, geographical, and cultural differences among the regions provide quite different historical pictures. Since these areas are now growing — and will continue to grow — at different rates and for different reasons, no serious survey of the prospects for Canadian economic development can afford to ignore this aspect of the country's history.

Chapters 2 and 3 have discussed the growth of Canada within the framework of the staple theory. The working hypothesis has been that the waves of Canada's economic development have been due to the exploitation of a series of staple commodities for export: first fur and fish, then timber, then wheat and pulp and paper, and now minerals. These staples, in demand abroad, provided the foreign exchange with which Canada financed her capital expansion and the importation of her manufactured consumer goods. The growth of the other sectors of the economy then followed from the development of the export industries. As the population and investment opportunities increased due to the growth of the export industries, the size of the market grew sufficiently to support an increasing number of manufacturing industries producing goods formerly imported. Some of the agricultural resources which had been devoted to production for export turned to supplying the domestic market. Processing industries developed, as did utilities, retail and wholesale trade, and the various services. All this activity can be traced ultimately to the great export staples.

The staple theory is basically an explanation of regional growth. The region, however, can range in size from the township to the nation. As a result, one of the great advantages of the staple theory is that it can be used to explain not only the growth of a nation but the growth of the regions within the nation as well. In contrast with the staple theory, the better known theories of economic development which prevailed prior to World War II posited a closed economy. Since regions are less likely to be isolated from each other than are countries, the closed economy assumption is not appropriate to the analysis of regional growth. Indeed, the closed economy assumption, although it may have been realistic in the days of primitive and costly transportation, can scarcely be used in the explanation of the growth of Canada or any of the other "young" countries of the world. The technology of transportation and communication nearly precludes isolated development. Furthermore, modern technology applied to production may lead to more intense specialization among nations than would be the case if technological advance had been halted for the last century (although technological change under certain circumstances can also reduce a country's comparative advantage). Since specialization implies trade, isolated development may be less likely now simply because of these production techniques, transportation costs aside. For all these reasons, the staple theory is useful in understanding the growth of regions of all sizes in the present-day world.

Although "regional economics" and "regional analysis" have attracted a great deal of attention among professional economists, especially since the end of World War II, comparatively little has been said about the determinants of regional growth. The limited work in this area points to two groups of theories. Edgar M. Hoover has summarized one school of thought in saying that "as a rule" regions are initially self-sufficient because of high transport costs; higher living standards are brought about only when trade develops, and trade must await "reduction of transfer costs and increased specialization of production, involving shifts of resources to new uses."[1] Since agricultural output in a given geographical area has a limit even if more intensive methods are used, the argument runs, incomes cannot rise indefinitely without turning to industries other than agriculture.[2] "Similar limitations

[1] Edgar M. Hoover, *The Location of Economic Activity* (New York, 1948), pp. 187–188. This view of regional development he also spells out in Edgar M. Hoover and J. L. Fisher, "Research in Regional Economic Growth," in *Problems in the Study of Economic Growth* (New York, 1949), pp. 180 ff.

[2] Denmark and New Zealand are cited as countries which have to date specialized in agricultural production for export. It is implied that even these two areas must eventually industrialize if growth is to continue.

apply to forestry and fishing but not to manufacturing," it is stated, "nor to mining, which exploits ground resources in all three dimensions." [3] So if a region is to show an increase in income per capita it must eventually industrialize, he concludes.

An alternative theory of regional growth, the staple theory, has been put in its most explicit form by Plumptre and by North.[4] North complains that the more common "stages" theory just outlined does not fit the facts for many regions, especially those in North America. Some areas never went through the self-sufficiency stage but rather were opened up to exploit some commodity which could be exported in exchange for the goods necessary to support the workers in the export industry. The Pacific Northwest was initially exploited for its furs, then its wheat, and then its lumber.[5] Corbett has argued for the same point of view in discussing the opening of the Canadian prairies. "Favourable factors of technology, resources and markets made possible an inflow of population into primary production . . . expansion in this sector called forth an even greater relative expansion in secondary industries; and the production by the settlers of a staple for export made possible the importation of capital upon which industrial and agricultural expansion were [sic] based." [6]

A shotgun wedding of these two theories is not impossible. The staple theory holds for regions which were uninhabited prior to the establishment of the export trade in the staple good. The region which is initially self-sufficient may shift to production for export as transfer costs fall and thus become dependent on a staple export for further growth. Such a region's development would fit the "stages" theory outlined by Hoover. But this union of the two theories is somewhat forced. The staple theory puts much greater emphasis on the nature of the genesis of growth, namely, the development of a major export commodity, than does the more common theory of development. The staple theory also stresses the influx of settlers whereas the stages theory implies

[3] Hoover and Fisher, pp. 181–182.
[4] A. F. W. Plumptre, "The Nature of Political and Economic Development in the British Dominions," *CJEPS*, 3:489–507 (November 1937), and Douglass C. North, "Location Theory and Regional Economic Growth," *JPE*, 63:243–258 (June 1955).
[5] See North, p. 246.
[6] D. C. Corbett, "Immigration and Economic Development," *CJEPS*, 17:360–368 (August 1951).

that population growth will be essentially internal. But there is also a difference in the conception of the mature economy under the two theories. North argues that the region may remain primarily dependent on exports for its livelihood, with income per capita rising secularly, while the "stages" theory implies that the mature economy is a self-sufficient economy and that therefore a country which is not self-sufficient or nearly so is in some sort of disequilibrium.[7]

The staple theory presupposes that transportation costs are lowered enough to permit trade among regions and between regions and foreign countries. The regions of Canada were opened up by means of new transportation routes and techniques which lowered transportation costs. Thus it has often been said that the history of Canada is the history of its transportation. This common observation, familiar to every Canadian schoolboy, strongly implies that the staple theory is the more appropriate vehicle for the analysis of Canada's regional growth.

CANADA'S REGIONS

Canada can be divided quite neatly into five regions. The Maritime provinces and Newfoundland will be referred to as the "Atlantic Provinces," a term which seems to be coming into use since Newfoundland's union with Canada in 1949. Quebec and Ontario constitute central Canada. The provinces of Manitoba, Saskatchewan, and Alberta make up a third region. Frequently British Columbia and the Yukon and Northwest Territories are treated as one region, but for our purposes it is preferable to treat British Columbia separately from the northern territories.

Although this particular regional breakdown is often used in discussion of Canadian problems, some justification is nonetheless required, especially for considering Quebec and Ontario as a single region.

Regions are delineated in economic research only to help in the analysis of some particular problem. Thus the regional breakdown found most useful by the agricultural economist may bear little resemblance to that preferred by the student of labor market problems. Here we are concerned with the nature of Canadian economic growth. It has been argued earlier that Canadian growth can be traced to her great export commodities. Since

---

[7] North, pp. 251–256; Hoover and Fisher, pp. 183–184.

these commodities have been identified with particular regions, it follows that the division most useful for our purposes would distinguish regions by the homogeneity of their productive resources. If the productive resources of two contiguous provinces are such that the two have a comparative advantage in the same kinds of goods, they should be included in the same region.

Although the homogeneity criterion is conceptually neat, some areas are nevertheless difficult to classify. Area X may be similar to Area A in some respects but similar to Area B in others. Generally one can determine whether Area X is more nearly like Area A than like Area B, but the classification may not be altogether satisfactory. As a result, one occasionally must drop the regional scheme in order to handle a particular problem conveniently.

The Maritimes and Newfoundland are distinguished, of course, by their proximity to the Atlantic and the resource-use and trade patterns which this location has dictated. The fisheries caused the initial settlement of the area. The trade pattern was similar for all the Atlantic provinces. It is true that Newfoundland never developed the lively timber trade which Nova Scotia and New Brunswick enjoyed in the early decades of the nineteenth century nor did commercial agriculture ever really develop there. Yet Newfoundland is similar to the Maritimes in that the role of the fisheries and the Atlantic trade has been of overwhelming importance. Newfoundland as well as the Maritimes faces problems of transportation disadvantages vis-à-vis central Canada. The entire area faces a declining growth rate and looks largely to new mineral development for future growth.

Ontario appears vastly different from Quebec. But if non-economic characteristics are set aside, the similarity of the two provinces is clear. Both were originally exploited for their furs and both went through a period when timber was the major export commodity. In both provinces agriculture has followed roughly the same development path. Subsistence farming and farming to supply the timber camps was followed by the production of wheat and then of dairy products for export. As urban centers developed in the region, agricultural output shifted to supply the needs of the cities and towns. Exports from both Quebec and Ontario came to supply the rest of Canada rather than customers abroad. Together the two provinces constitute the industrial heart of Canada, and pulp and paper and hydro-electric power loom large in both economies. Both provinces, too, have experienced mineral booms since the end of the war.

The prairie provinces constitute a well-defined region geographically. That portion of the pre-Cambrian shield north of Lake Superior is nearly as inhospitable to settlement as are the Rockies which separate the population centers of Alberta from those of British Columbia. Manitoba, Saskatchewan, and Alberta, however, are not duplicates of each other by any means. Saskatchewan is the "wheat province"; Alberta has enjoyed a much greater oil boom than has either of the other two provinces; and Manitoba is the manufacturing center for the prairies market.[8] But all three provinces were opened up by the construction of the Canadian Pacific Railway in 1885; all three concentrated initially on wheat production for export; and all have been dependent on distant urban cities for the bulk of their manufactured goods. Consequently, in reviewing the history of Canada's regional growth, the three prairie provinces will be treated as a single region.

Because of its topography and its location between the Rockies and the Pacific, British Columbia has had an economic history quite distinct from that of the prairies. Not agriculture but furs and gold first attracted settlers to British Columbia and, with the development of the province's forest resources, the basis for its growth has continued to be quite different from that of the prairies.

The Yukon and Northwest Territories can be lumped into a single region because the resources are largely unknown rather than because they are known to be similar. The whole area is so sparsely populated, there being but 31,000 persons reported in the region in 1956, that we will ignore it in these two chapters. Our prime concern is the explanation of the growth of the various regions in Canada and so our defense of this decision can be based on two arguments. First, the Yukon and the Northwest Territories involve such small economic magnitudes as to warrant the feeling that they have scarcely begun to grow; second, the growth

---

[8] Veyret has characterized the prairie provinces as "a true family," with Manitoba the elder and more sedate son and Saskatchewan and Alberta being twins, Saskatchewan impetuous and rough, Alberta slower but more solid. Paul Veyret, *La population du Canada* (Paris, 1953), p. 31.

which has appeared has been such a palpable example of the staple theory that we should devote our time and talents to the more complicated aspects of Canadian economic development. This is not to say that the future of the area is bleak, but rather that its history has been simple. With the hope that this attitude toward the northland does not seem too cavalier, we will concentrate on the development of the four major economic regions of Canada.

Our treatment of the economic growth of these four regions is not intended to be well-balanced and thorough because we are really interested only in selected aspects of this economic history. A number of good works on Canadian economic history already exist and our space does not permit a careful review. We have chosen merely to cover for each region the broader developments by examining first the pattern of growth prior to the region's becoming a part of Canada. Next, the year of the fifth census, 1911, is used as a stopping-place where the changes in the scene up to about the time of World War I can be summarized. In one final leap the changes to 1951 are examined, again largely by a kind of phrenological exercise with the census data. Although such a breezy pace prohibits even mentioning many factors and critical periods in the economic development of the regions, it does permit concentration on certain underlying forces which have given each region its unique economic configuration. This condensed overview also allows an examination of a few special topics. While surveying the history of the Atlantic provinces and central Canada, we will focus on the economics of retarded regional growth in an attempt to add to what has been said in the past about the economic relation between the two eastern regions. The study of the Prairie Provinces includes an analysis of the contrast between the wheat boom and the oil boom in Alberta. The discussion of the growth of British Columbia is concluded with a note on the province's special attributes which caused such a rapid growth from 1939 to 1955. So this chapter and the following one lack detail, but it is hoped that they contribute a bit to an understanding of Canadian economic history nonetheless.

THE ATLANTIC PROVINCES

At one time the Atlantic Provinces were blessed with a combination of resources and locational advantages which made the area the economic heart of what is now Canada. But technological innovation, shifts in population centers, changes in trade policies abroad, and the expansion of employment opportunities in surrounding areas have all so buffeted the Atlantic Provinces over the last seventy-five years that the area now has a personal income per capita one-third lower than the national average.

The Atlantic Provinces were brought into the economy of the western world at the outset of the sixteenth century because of their fisheries, and those fisheries set the pattern of the region's economic life for four centuries. A natural resource exploited for export beyond North America, the fisheries were to be followed, though not displaced, by forestry, minerals, and to some extent agriculture. In the days of the sailing ships the forestry resources were used in local shipbuilding, it is true, but the ships themselves were for the most part sold in Britain. Even now most of Nova Scotia's steel output goes to the United Kingdom and Europe. So all through its history Atlantic Canada has lived primarily by exploiting its natural resources for export. For many years this meant export to Europe and the tropics. But in the past two decades the significance of the United States market has grown, especially as a buyer of minerals and pulp and paper.

Although the schoolboy may learn that Cabot in 1497 was the first man to touch the North American continent, the fishing grounds off Newfoundland were probably known before that famous voyage.[9] Whether or not this conjecture is justified, it is known that, after news of Cabot's discovery had spread, English, French, Portuguese, and Spanish ships all came to pursue the cod. Catholic Europe demanded fish not only for religious reasons but also because of the chronic shortage of meat. At the outset the English were overshadowed in the New World fisheries by the French and Portuguese. Protestant England offered a limited market for cod, and the English fishing captains were at a cost disadvantage because they had to import their salt for curing. The French and Portuguese had plenty of cheap salt, thanks to the climate of their home countries. But, in spite of this initial disadvantage, the English came to dominate the Atlantic provinces.

Several factors brought this about. Perhaps of greatest sig-

[9] At least the Portuguese think so. In 1955 Portuguese fishermen held a pageant in St. John's commemorating 500 years on the Banks.

nificance was the development of the dry-curing technique by the English. By drying the catch on the beaches in the sun, they found that they could cut their salt requirements substantially. Also, the dry cured fish kept better and longer and so was more desirable for trade with the tropics than was the cod which the French and Portuguese salted down "green" in the hold. Consequently, by the end of the sixteenth century the English had settlements in Newfoundland since someone had to tend the drying catch. The French cured their catch on board. This helps explain why the British by 1700 had a population of about 1500 in Newfoundland, the French had only about 500.[10]

As the West Indian plantations developed, the demand for dried cod expanded and the French established some bases, notably Placentia on the Avalon peninsula in Newfoundland and Port Royal in Nova Scotia.[11] But the French attempt to establish a three-cornered trade between Newfoundland, the West Indies, and France never really succeeded. The strong position of the British in Newfoundland and Nova Scotia, developed during the seventeenth century, was consolidated by the Treaty of Utrecht in 1713, according to the terms of which Newfoundland and Nova Scotia became British territory with the exception of Cape Breton.

The fisheries remained the *raison d'etre* of Newfoundland and of what is now Nova Scotia until the American Revolution. During the 1700's the population of Newfoundland grew from about 1500 (in 1698) to over 26,000 (in 1806).[12] Meanwhile, St. John's became an important *entrepot* for several trading routes. For example, supplies from New England were unloaded there by Boston ships and cod was picked up for the West Indies, molasses being brought back to New England as raw material for her rum. Nova Scotia's fisheries expanded to some extent during the first sixty years of the eighteenth century but were handicapped by the proximity to the French at Louisburg in Cape Breton. The Treaty of Paris of 1763 removed this deterrent to the area's growth.

It is scarcely an exaggeration to say that the American Revolu-

---

[10] *Census of Canada, 1870–71* (Ottawa, 1876), Vol. IV, pp. 44, 45.

[11] In order to avoid confusion for those less familiar with the geography of Canada we will, at the expense of historical accuracy, usually refer to the various regions of Canada prior to 1867 by the provincial names which now apply.

[12] *Census of Canada, 1870–71*, Vol. IV, pp. 44n. and xliv.

tion served as midwife for the economic birth of Nova Scotia. Loyalists from the rebellious colonies swelled the tiny population. During the fifty years following the Treaty of Utrecht in 1713, the population of Nova Scotia rose from about 1800 to something over 8000; but between 1762 and 1817 the population rose from 8000 to over 81,000.[13] Agriculture and the fisheries benefited from the greater labor supply and the increased domestic market. The loss of the American colonies also caused the British to attempt to develop Nova Scotia as a substitute for New England in the triangular trade with Great Britain and the West Indies. Meanwhile, shipbuilding for Great Britain was stimulated by England's loss of the American shipping capacity and by the Napoleonic wars.

But Nova Scotia never developed into a supply base for the West Indies on the scale to which it had aspired. This has been attributed in part to a stunted agricultural development.[14] But it was also due to the fact that Nova Scotia, unlike the New England states, had little oak for the barrel staves so essential to the West Indies. Nor was Nova Scotia close enough to assure that the more perishable goods would survive the long trip.

Meanwhile New Brunswick was developing its own export staple, timber. After a period of producing masts for the British following the American Revolution, high transportation costs plus the inaccessibility cut the province's timber output after 1800 until Great Britain in 1808 and 1809 instituted duties on Baltic naval timber. Later these duties were raised, improving New Brunswick's competitive advantage in the British market. Until Confederation in 1867 the export of timber and of ships to Great Britain and the export of various forms of sawn lumber to the West Indies were the major activities in New Brunswick. Growth of the industry was halted, however, after the British tariffs on timber were reduced several times in the 1840's.

[13] *Census of Canada, 1870–71,* Vol. IV, pp. 49, 61 and 82.
[14] W. T. Easterbrook and H. G. J. Aitken, *Canadian Economic History* (Toronto, 1956), p. 146. The factors other than limited agricultural possibilities would seem to have been more important, however. In 1827 the population stood at 124,000, roughly ten times the population in 1766. Yet potato production was more than seventy times greater than in 1766 (over 3,200,000 bushels compared with 45,400 bushels), grain production eighty times greater, and sheep numbers were about twenty-five times greater than in the earlier year. The surplus was providing extensive supplies to the West Indies in the latter year since the carrying trade was then partially foreclosed to the Americans.

Wars frequently prove to be catalytic agents in economic development. During the Napoleonic wars shipbuilding began to flourish in New Brunswick and Nova Scotia. Britain's increased demand for ships led to the use of the Maritimes' timber in ship construction in the provinces rather than in the British Isles. While New Brunswick specialized in producing for the British and European market, the Nova Scotia ships were typically smaller, designed for the coasting trade. The shipbuilding industry continued to thrive until Confederation.

The period immediately preceding Confederation is known in the Maritimes as the "golden years," a term still applied by some to stress the error that was Confederation. This prosperity was due in part to the Reciprocity Treaty of 1854. In the latter half of the 1840's the timber trade was seriously depressed because of the collapse of the railroad boom in Britain, which cut the demand for ties, and because of Britain's reduction of the tariff on timber from the Baltic. Meanwhile, the United States had raised its tariff on timber and consequently exports even to this market slowed up. With the British market gone, the Maritimes grew particularly eager to regain access to the United States market. Consequently they joined those forces in what was then Canada (now Ontario and Quebec) who favored reciprocity with the United States. The enthusiasm in the Maritimes was snuffed out, however, when it developed that in exchange the United States wanted access to the inshore fisheries. Conveniently for the rest of Canada, the Maritimes had little to say in the matter since the mother country was doing the negotiating, and the Reciprocity Act of 1854 went through. Presumably, there were grumblings then, too, about one's heritage being bartered away.

Yet the Maritimes fared quite well during reciprocity. Between 1854 and 1859, exports from the Maritimes rose some 150 per cent, considerably more than did her imports.[15] But, in addition, the period during which reciprocity was in force (1854–1866) was one during which world trade was expanding and, consequently, the demand for ships remained strong. The Crimean War of 1854–1856 stimulated exports, but it was the Civil War in the United States which provided the greatest stimulus to the Maritimes.

---

[15] Easterbrook and Aitken, p. 248.

Confederation to World War I

In 1864, the demise of reciprocity was imminent, and a conference of Maritime premiers was held in Charlottetown to discuss the possibilities of forming a Maritime union in order to deal more effectively with a whole series of problems common to the three colonies. Retreat from reciprocity would clearly mean reduced trade with the United States and certainly the British market did not appear promising. Discussion of this trade problem and others led, quite unexpectedly but not illogically, to consideration of union with Canada, and in the same year a conference in Quebec was held to discuss the situation. The result was the British North America Act of 1867, commonly referred to as Confederation, under the terms of which Quebec (formerly Lower Canada), Ontario (formerly Upper Canada) and New Brunswick and Nova Scotia united as provinces within the Dominion of Canada.[16]

Confederation represented a great turning point for the Maritimes in terms of the economic orientation of the economy. Prior to Confederation they had ignored the rest of what is now Canada, relying almost exclusively on trade with Britain, the West Indies, and the United States for their livelihood. The Maritimes looked to the west not only because of the end of Britain's colonial preferences in the timber trade, the end of reciprocity, and the close of the Civil War in the United States but also because of the coming of the railroads. The building of the first railroad in the Maritimes in the 1850's held the promise of a network which would provide the eastern provinces with a hinterland which hitherto they had lacked. This geographical about-face was to let the Maritimes funnel goods into and out of the rest of Canada. The ice-free ports of Halifax and Saint John would become Canada's New York and Boston. It was this thinking which caused the Maritimes to lay down as a condition for Confederation the construction of a railroad linking them with the interior. Construction was to be started within one year after Confederation, but the project, the Intercolonial Railway, was not completed until 1876.

Confederation offers an opportunity to survey the structure of the economy of what are now the Atlantic provinces. Newfound-

[16] Prince Edward Island did not join Canada until 1873. Newfoundland was not a party to any of these conferences and did not become a part of Canada until 1949.

land, which was not to become a part of Canada for another 80 years, had a population of about 147,000 compared with 94,000 on Prince Edward Island, 286,000 in New Brunswick and 388,000 in Nova Scotia.[17] Fishing and trade, plus a small amount of subsistence agriculture, supported the people of Newfoundland. Prince Edward Island was engaged almost exclusively in agriculture and was exporting food to the other Maritimes and to England. New Brunswick was more dependent on her forests than on fishing. Although the export of timber fell off precipitously during the decade prior to Confederation, the export of deals, boards and planks, shingles and sugar-box shooks plus shipbuilding kept the province looking to its forest. In Nova Scotia, on the other hand, fishing was much more important than forestry. In 1871, about three times as many men were engaged in fishing in Nova Scotia as in New Brunswick, but in the latter province, about two and one-half times as many men were engaged in the sawmills as in Nova Scotia.[18] Neither Nova Scotia nor New Brunswick had been able to develop a thriving agriculture. This has been ascribed to the farmers' attempts to augment their income by making timber in the winter. Such a casual attitude, which resulted in just part-time farming, made for a more primitive and retarded agricultural sector than climate and soil would have dictated. A limiting factor of greater significance, however, was simply the shortage of good farm land in New Brunswick and Nova Scotia. As for mineral production, only in Nova Scotia was mining of any consequence. There some 1500 men were engaged in gold mining and 3000 in coal mining at the time of Confederation.[19] This was about one-fourth the number engaged in fishing.

The manufacturing sector was of some importance both in Nova Scotia and in New Brunswick at the time of the 1871 census. Table 13 shows that the structure of this sector was about the

[17] The Newfoundland figure is for 1869, Prince Edward Island's population for 1871. *Census of Canada, 1870–71*, Vol. IV, pp. 370, 390. The New Brunswick and Nova Scotia data are from *Census of Canada, 1870–71*, Vol. I, Table 1, p. 83.

[18] *Census of Canada, 1870–71*, Vol. III, Table 26, p. 268 and Table 33, p. 346. The relative importance of fishing is also reflected in the fact that in 1865 only about 8 per cent of New Brunswick's exports were accounted for by the fisheries whereas the corresponding figure for Nova Scotia was about 40 per cent. Compare S. A. Saunders, "The Reciprocity Treaty of 1854; a Regional Study," *CJEPS*, 2:48 (February 1936).

[19] *Report of the Chief Commissioner of Mines for the Province of Nova Scotia, for the Year 1867* (Halifax, 1868), pp. 45–57.

Table 13. Ten leading manufacturing industries in Nova Scotia and New Brunswick by value of product and by number of employees, 1871.

Industry	Value of product (thousands)	Industry	Number of employees
Nova Scotia			
Shipyards	$1,635	Sawmills	2,858
Sawmills	1,398	Shipyards	2,058
Flour and grist mills	1,073	Lumber products[a]	2,019
Boots and shoes	1,058	Boots and shoes	1,313
Lumber products[a]	1,022	Blacksmithing	1,226
Tanneries	770	Tailors and clothiers	579
Blacksmithing	593	Tanneries	547
Foundries and machine working	484	Foundries and machine working	455
Tailors and clothiers	428	Carriage making	428
Bakeries	396	Flour and grist mills	416
New Brunswick			
Sawmills	6,576	Sawmills	7,134
Shipyards	1,087	Lumber products[a]	1,587
Flour and grist mills	1,049	Shipyards	1,364
Boots and shoes	976	Boots and shoes	1,187
Tailors and clothiers	827	Tailors and clothiers	1,072
Lumber products[a]	773	Blacksmithing	866
Foundries and machine working	602	Foundries and machine working	650
Tanneries	597	Carriage making	472
Ship material making	541	Tanneries	341
Blacksmithing	513	Flour and grist mills	311

[a] The lumber products industry did not appear under this title in the 1871 Census, the component industries being shown instead. In order to provide better comparability with the 1911 Census the components were aggregated here. Note that shipyards, however, are not included in the lumber products industry.

Source: Census of Canada, 1870–71, Vol. III, Table 55, pp. 458–463.

same in the two provinces except that sawmills were of relatively greater importance in New Brunswick than in Nova Scotia, while shipyards were the leading industry in the latter province by value of product. Otherwise the manufacturing in the two provinces exhibited the attributes of the comparatively simple economy oriented toward the forests and the sea. Prince Edward Island's manufacturing consisted exclusively of grist mills, sawmills, tanneries, brick kilns and the like, producing primarily for the local market.[20]

[20] *Census of Canada, 1870–71*, Vol. IV, pp. 398–399.

How had the face of the Atlantic economy changed by World War I? And why had those changes taken place? Did the old staples retain their importance or did these provinces develop as manufacturing centers for the hinterland brought within reach by the railroads?

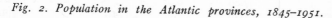

Fig. 2. Population in the Atlantic provinces, 1845–1951.

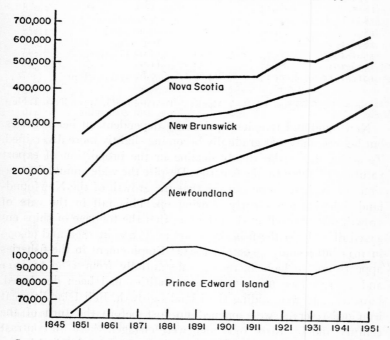

Source: *Census of Canada, 1870–71,* Vol. IV, pp. 160, 174, 224, 232, 246, 332, 344, 358, 370; *Canada Year Book, 1956,* pp. 1236–1237; *Census of Newfoundland and Labrador, 1911* (St. John's, 1914), Vol. I, p. vi; Government of Newfoundland, *Submission to the RCCEP* (n. p., 1955), p. 22.

The population changes for this period are shown in Figure 2. The retardation in the rate of growth is immediately obvious, with the rise and then fall in the population of Prince Edward Island being most noticeable. Since after 1900 the prairie provinces were growing at an especially fast rate, this slow growth in the east is not surprising.

Table 14. Percentage distribution of value of exports by commodity group, Newfoundland, 1871–1875 to 1911–1915.

	Fishery and other marine products	Forest products	Mineral products	Furs and game	All other products
1871–1875	97.09	0.07	2.50	0.11	0.23
1876–1880	91.49	.23	7.63	.18	.47
1881–1885	95.54	.24	3.94	.17	.11
1886–1890	92.84	.22	6.45	.31	.18
1891–1895	89.93	.65	9.02	.26	.14
1896–1900	87.05	1.33	10.88	.45	.29
1901–1905	83.73	2.13	13.00	.73	.41
1906–1910	84.40	2.54	11.99	.73	.34
1911–1915	74.13	14.61	9.81	.98	.47

Source: Newfoundland, ed. R. A. MacKay (Toronto, 1946), Appendix A, Table 3.

Newfoundland remained primarily dependent on her fisheries, but her economy was gradually becoming slightly more diversified. Table 14 shows the steady decline in the proportion of export value represented by the fisheries. Despite the wide annual fluctuations in the catch, one can see that the growth of the Newfoundland fisheries was clearly slowing up. This fall in the rate of growth was also reflected in the fact that the tonnage of ships engaged directly in the fisheries stood at 46,000 in 1869 and 66,000 in 1911 but at only 40,000 in 1921.[21] Employment in the fisheries appears not to have increased substantially from 1869 to 1911 and 1921.[22] Two new export commodities had been developed, however, and were aiding the island's growth. Bell Island's great iron ore reserves were opened up just before the turn of the century and by 1910, 1900 men were engaged there, in contrast with 50,000 in the fisheries. Pulp and paper production had begun in Newfoundland in 1909 and by 1921 was employing nearly 2300 workers. Sawmills accounted for another 2900 persons.[23]

[21] Census of Newfoundland and Labrador, 1921 (St. John's, 1923), Table II, p. vi; and Newfoundland: Economic Diplomatic, and Strategic Studies, ed. R. A. MacKay (Toronto, 1946), Appendix A, Table 12 (not paged).

[22] The census of Newfoundland data indicate a decline in employment in the fisheries from 58,000 in 1869 to just under 54,000 in 1911 and 1921. Data for the latter years, however, seem to omit employment in salmon and herring fishing and other minor types of fishing. See Census of Canada, 1870–71, Vol. IV, p. 374; Census of Newfoundland and Labrador, 1911, Vol. II, pp. 442–447; and Census of Newfoundland and Labrador, 1921, Vol. II, pp. vi–x.

[23] Census of Newfoundland and Labrador, 1921; and Government of the Province of Newfoundland, Submission to the RCCEP (n. p., 1955), p. 35.

Table 15.   Selected census data, Nova Scotia and New Brunswick,
1871 and 1911 (thousands).

	Nova Scotia		New Brunswick	
	1871	1911	1871	1911
Population	387.8	492.3	285.6	351.9
Labor force:				
Agriculture	49.6	48.7	40.3	45.7
Fisheries:				
Primary occupation in fisheries	10.8	14.7	1.7	2.8
Total employment in fisheries[a]	18.2	26.6[b]	6.0	22.7[c]
Manufacturing	15.6	28.8[d]	18.4	24.8[e]
Mining	4.5[f]	17.1	—[g]	0.8
Coal production (tons)	657.5	6561.3	13.5	124.4
Gypsum production (tons)	96.5	350.6	13.6	91.5
Iron ore production (tons)	0	0	3.1	24.5

[a] Includes persons primarily engaged in pursuits other than fishing, such as farmers.

[b] Includes 4,988 persons in "canneries and fish houses."

[c] Includes 6,502 persons in "canneries and fish houses."

[d] Includes 4,388 persons in "preserved fish" industry.

[e] Includes 3,265 persons in "preserved fish" industry.

[f] Estimated from *Report of the Chief Commissioner of Mines for the Province of Nova Scotia for the Year 1867* (Halifax, 1868), pp. 45-57.

[g] Not available.

Source: *Census of Canada, 1870-71*, Vols. II and III; *Census of Canada, 1911*, Vols. III, V, VI, except as noted.

Small scale manufacturing of such things as boots and shoes and rope for the local market also employed well over 10,000 workers.

Prince Edward Island by 1911 was, of course, still primarily agricultural, but fish and butter and cheese were export industries of some consequence. The remainder of the manufacturing was for the local market.

In Nova Scotia, meanwhile, the most striking change was the development of a primary iron and steel industry to complement a thriving coal mining industry. Fishing was still very important, for employment in this industry, defined to include fish processing, had grown about 45 per cent between 1871 and 1911 as the census data of Table 15 show. But, whereas in 1871 the fisheries accounted for more employment than manufacturing, by 1911 these positions were reversed. The number of farmers had actually

Table 16. Ten leading manufacturing industries in Nova Scotia and New Brunswick by value of product and by number of employees, 1911 and 1951.[a]

Industry	Value of product (thousands)	Industry	Number of employees
	Nova Scotia, 1911		
Log products	$7,928	Log products	5,558
Fish, preserved	4,766	Fish, preserved	4,488
Iron and steel products	3,896	Iron and steel products	1,327
Foundry and machine shop products	1,967	Foundry and machine shop products	1,249
Lumber products	1,548	Lumber products	882
Bread, biscuits, and confectionery	1,322	Bread, biscuits, and confectionery	766
Boots and shoes	1,098	Cottons	686
Cottons	1,036	Boots and shoes	534
Flour and grist mills	817	Boilers and engines	512
Boilers and engines	679	Ships and ship repairs	453
	Nova Scotia, 1951		
Primary iron and steel	$39,512	Primary iron and steel	4,837
Fish processing	38,819	Fish processing	4,003
Railway rolling stock	23,581	Sawmills	3,312
Sawmills	21,534	Shipbuilding	2,128
Pulp and paper	18,574	Railway rolling stock	1,213
Shipbuilding	10,866	Pulp and paper	1,143
Butter and cheese	8,598	Sash, door, and planing mills	972
Miscellaneous iron and steel products	8,183	Miscellaneous iron and steel products	905
Sash, door, and planing mills	7,020	Confectionery	818
Bread and other bakery products	6,768	Bread and other bakery products	763
	New Brunswick, 1911		
Log products	12,199	Log products	9,037
Cottons	2,673	Fish, preserved	3,393
Car repairs	2,102	Cottons	1,828
Foundry and machine shop products	1,725	Foundry and machine shop products	1,163
Fish, preserved	1,613	Car repairs	1,160
Flour and grist mill products	1,324	Wood pulp, chemical and mechanical	692
Bread, biscuits, and confectionery	1,202	Printing, publishing, and bookbinding	591
Wood pulp, chemical and mechanical	1,149	Bread, biscuits, and confectionery	574
Iron and steel products	1,031	Men's clothing	560
Leather, tanned, curried, and finished	916	Lumber products	529

Table 16. Continued.

Industry	Value of product (thousands)	Industry	Number of employees
	New Brunswick, 1951		
Pulp and paper	94,066	Pulp and paper	3,807
Sawmills	22,125	Sawmills	3,098
Fish processing	18,590	Fish processing	3,004
Slaughtering and meat packing	13,870	Sash, door, and planing mills	1,093
Miscellaneous food preparations n.e.s.	10,185	Bread and other bakery products	774
Butter and cheese	8,511	Heating and cooking apparatus	690
Sash, door, and planing mills	8,342	Printing and publishing	611
Bread and other bakery products	6,409	Butter and cheese	429
Feeds, stock and poultry prepared	5,972	Slaughtering and meat packing	379
Heating and cooking apparatus	4,962	Biscuits	378

[a] Since data for industries with fewer than three establishments are not published by DBS, certain industries might be omitted from this table because of the disclosure rules. The industries in Nova Scotia for which data are not published for 1951 are: breweries; cotton yarn and cloth; machinery, household, office and store; wire and wire goods; petroleum products; coke and gas. For New Brunswick the industries affected are: breweries; sugar refineries; cotton yarn and cloth; synthetic textiles and silk; railway rolling stock; shipbuilding; brooms, brushes and mops; brass and copper products; and gypsum products.

Source: Census of Canada, 1911, Vol. III, Table 1; and DBS, *General Review of the Manufacturing Industries of Canada, 1951.*

declined slightly. The changes within the manufacturing sector were particularly indicative of the change in the economy. The number of men in the shipyards had declined from just over 2000 in 1871 to only 450 in 1911, demonstrating graphically the impact on Nova Scotia of the passing of the wooden ship. Employment in iron and steel production had risen to the point where it was second only to the log products, in which employment had nearly doubled, among the manufacturing industries (see Table 16).[24] Cotton textile production was also coming to be of some importance. Judging from this picture, Nova Scotia was emerging from her dependence on a single export staple and was

[24] If fish processing is included in the manufacturing sector rather than with the fisheries, iron and steel production would rank third.

becoming a more diversified economy with coal and primary iron and steel as the new exporting industries.

It has been stressed that, in 1871, Nova Scotia was much more dependent on the fisheries than on her forests while, in New Brunswick, just the reverse was true. In the period to World War I, the forest products industry in Nova Scotia grew faster than the fisheries. Conversely, in New Brunswick, where lumbering was the leading activity in 1871, employment in the fisheries had more than tripled by 1911, whereas employment in lumbering had risen by less than 50 per cent.[25] As in Nova Scotia, the ship-yards' employment had dropped to a tiny figure after having been second only to the sawmills as a source of employment at the time of Confederation. But cotton textile manufacturing had grown to major proportions, with the foundry and machine shop products and railroad car shops close behind. As in the case of Nova Scotia, it seemed that New Brunswick was developing a stronger, more diversified economy. Even within the fisheries considerable diversification had occurred for by 1910 less than 5 per cent of the value of the catch in the Maritimes was accounted for by cod, since lobsters, smelts, haddock, sardines, and salmon had all become more significant in the industry.

What forces had wrought these changes? First, Confederation had given the Maritimes a market in the interior. Although the railroad which was promised them was not complete to Quebec until nine years after Confederation, nevertheless, it was finally built, giving the Maritimes their hinterland. Coal, textiles, the fisheries, and iron and steel all turned toward this new market. Second, the major industries there were aided by the "National Policy" and the resulting tariff of 1879. This put a fifty cents per ton tariff on coal, thus swelling the market for the Nova Scotia product. Textiles and iron and steel products were given special attention. Since the rate on consumer goods in common use was put as high as 30 per cent, the Maritimers felt that they were being asked to subsidize the inefficient manufacturers of Central Canada, but they had to grant that their own industries were certainly helped as well. The growing markets in Central Canada

[25] This estimate is based on the fact that in the 1871 census among the manufacturing industries the "saw mills" category shows 7,134 employed, and in 1911 the "log products" category, apparently comparable, shows a reported employment of 9,037. *Census of Canada, 1870-71*, Vol. III, pp. 268, 462, and *Census of Canada, 1911*, Vol. III, p. 12.

increased their purchases of Cape Breton coal steadily from about 1,200,000 short tons in 1880 to just under 8,000,000 tons in 1913, the peak year. A third factor during this period in the Maritimes' history was, of course, the demand for steel occasioned by the booming railroad expansion in Canada. Nova Scotia's pig iron production increased from 19,000 long tons in 1889 to 25,000 in 1900 and to 428,000 long tons in 1913. The happy coincidence of Bell Island's mammoth iron ore reserves and Nova Scotia's coal both so near water made steel production at Sydney especially attractive. Fourth, even the decline of the timber trade with Britain had its brighter side in that the timber ships were no longer bringing back so much British coal at cheap rates to compete with the local product. And the coming of the steamship, which hit the shipyards so hard, meant faster schedules and consequently the province's apples could reach Britain in better shape and potatoes could get to the West Indies in proper condition.

World War I to the 1950's

The war years brought frenzied activity to the Maritimes since they were now the focal point for much traffic as well as productive effort. But the postwar adjustments, the international trade difficulties of the past three decades, plus the development of central Canada have left the Maritimes in the backwater of Canadian development. The promising years of 1900–1920 slipped away, and the rest of the country was growing but not pulling the Atlantic provinces along with it. While the population of Canada nearly doubled, rising from 7,200,000 to 14,000,000, the population of New Brunswick rose by only 47 per cent; Nova Scotia, 31 per cent; Prince Edward Island, 5 per cent; and Newfoundland, 33 per cent.

The census data of Table 17 show the retarded rate of growth. Most striking is the drop in employment in agriculture in Nova Scotia and New Brunswick. In Nova Scotia the decline was greater than 50 per cent of the 1911 figure. This was a continuation of the movement noted in comparing the 1911 and 1871 census figures. As the Canadian West was opened up, competition in grain production appeared, and the Maritimers concentrated more on production for the local market. The number of farms dropped substantially in all three provinces. Area in farms

Table 17. Population and distribution of the labor force in Nova Scotia, New Brunswick, Prince Edward Island, and Newfoundland, 1911 and 1951[a] (thousands).

	Nova Scotia		New Brunswick		Prince Edward Island		Newfoundland[a]	
	1911	1951	1911	1951	1911	1951	1911	1951
Population	492.3	642.5	351.9	515.7	93.7	98.4	242.6	361.4
Labor force:	173.4	220.8	119.8	169.0	31.9	34.1	—	106.5
Agriculture	48.7	23.3	45.7	26.5	19.7	13.0	2.9[a]	3.5
Fishing and hunting	14.7	9.8	2.8	4.5	1.4	1.7	109.1[a]	18.5
Mining	17.1	15.6	0.8	1.2	—	—	2.3	3.7
Forestry	3.2	5.9	4.4	16.1	—	0.3	2.8	10.5
Manufacturing	26.1	36.9	20.2	31.2	2.6	3.5	10.3	14.6
Construction	12.6	16.4	11.8	10.1	1.7	1.9	—	7.3
Personal and domestic service	14.2	14.0	9.1	10.1	1.9	1.8	—	4.9
Trade	13.7	30.1	9.7	22.2	1.9	3.9	1.3	14.3
Transportation	11.4	18.2[b]	8.0	16.7[b]	1.1	2.1[b]	—	10.0
Government	4.7	22.9	2.1	8.7	.3	2.3	1.5	9.5
Other services[c]	7.0	27.8	5.1	21.8	1.3	3.7	—	8.8

[a] Minor differences between the 1911 and 1951 classification schemes may prevent accurate comparison of the Census data for the two years. For example, in 1911 the class "building trades" was used but in 1951 we find the class termed "construction." The two groups may not be strictly comparable. For the most part, however, the Census groups for the two years appear to be comparable. An exception is Newfoundland. Most of the classes seem to be comparable with the 1951 Census data except agriculture and fisheries. The Newfoundland Census for 1911 reports 2,915 "farmers," 40,880 "fishermen and others who cultivate the land," 67,040 persons "catching and curing fish," and 1,204 persons "engaged in the fisheries." A substantial portion, at least 40,880, of the 109,124 persons in the last three groups carried on part-time farming.

[b] Includes storage and communication. Employment in the latter industry in 1951 was 2,569 in Nova Scotia; 1,652 in New Brunswick; 226 in Prince Edward Island; and 642 in Newfoundland.

[c] Includes mostly professional services, unclassified workers, and, in 1951, electricity, gas, and water.

Source: Census of Canada, 1911, Vol. VI, Table 2; Census of Canada, 1951, Vol. IV, Table 16; and Census of Newfoundland and Labrador, 1911, Vol. I, pp. xvii, xxiii, xxx.

fell a full 40 per cent in New Brunswick and even declined 9 per cent in Prince Edward Island, a province with little nonagricultural activity. In Prince Edward Island and New Brunswick, wheat acreage fell off drastically and mixed grains and potatoes became much more important. The depression troubles of the apple, potato, and silver fox producers had encouraged adjustments away from export markets.[26] All three provinces shifted production significantly toward dairy and poultry products, and Prince Edward Island also raised its hog numbers very substantially. Although the census data for 1951 do not permit accurate comparisons with earlier years, it is apparent that even the numbers of fruit trees declined over the 1911–1951 period.

Outside of agriculture, even the fisheries suffered reduced employment in Nova Scotia, although in New Brunswick and Prince Edward Island the work force increased substantially as the industry diversified and shifted away from cod. In Nova Scotia, mining also provided fewer jobs in 1951 than in 1911 because of the reduced demand for the area's coal. In New Brunswick, base metal finds helped push mining employment upward.

What industries were providing the new jobs for the growing work force? The most startling increase in Nova Scotia was in government employment, where nearly 15,000 of the 23,000 persons working for all government units were in the federal armed services. Between 1911 and 1951, employment in trade, an industry in which freedom of entry permits ready absorption of workers during depressed times, more than doubled in Nova Scotia. Transportation, forestry, construction, and manufacturing absorbed the remainder.

In New Brunswick the spectacular change was in employment in forestry, thanks largely to the increase in pulp and paper production in the province. As in Nova Scotia the increases in employment in trade, transportation, and government were also striking. The same increase in employment in the tertiary sector is found in Prince Edward Island, where nearly all the decline in agricultural employment was absorbed by the service industries.

Table 17 shows a monumental decline in employment in the Newfoundland fisheries. The decline is exaggerated because some

[26] For a discussion of this and other aspects of the Maritimes' difficulties during the depression years, see S. A. Saunders, *The Economic History of the Maritime Provinces, A Study Prepared for the RCDPR* (Ottawa, 1939), esp. pp. 45–58.

41,000 of the persons in the fisheries were part-time farmers. Nonetheless the fall in the number of persons engaged in agriculture plus fisheries seems to have been on the order of 80 per cent. Forestry (largely for pulp and paper operations) helped cushion this decline but again we see the tertiary sector providing most of the new jobs.

A comparison of the leading manufacturing industries as of 1911 and 1951 in the two larger provinces is hampered by the difference in the classification scheme employed in the census in the two years and by the effects of the disclosure rule. Nonetheless Table 16 gives the impression that Nova Scotia's manufacturing sector in 1951 looked very much as it did in 1911. Perhaps primary iron and steel and the manufacturing based on this industry had become more significant, but the change was not marked. Pulp and paper had also risen to prominence. Yet the changes were not nearly so great as in the manufacturing sector in New Brunswick. There, as in Nova Scotia, sawmills and fish processing retained their old stature but the growth of pulp and paper was much more pronounced. Also, New Brunswick's manufacturing in 1951 was clearly oriented much more than in 1911 toward serving an agricultural community which was in turn producing for urbanites.

Central in the explanation of the slow rate of population growth in the Atlantic provinces over the forty-year period we are concerned with is the role of agriculture. In Nova Scotia about 49,000 persons were in agriculture in 1911 compared with but 29,000 in manufacturing. By 1951 the agricultural work force requirements in the province had fallen by 25,000. What other sectors could replace these jobs and provide enough more for substantial growth? Not the primary industries, as we have seen. The secondary industries took up some of the slack, but the services provided the real refuge. The Atlantic provinces lacked the big new export industries which marked many of the other parts of the country.

The economics of retarded regional growth

The economic history of the Maritimes since Confederation has been shaped by a combination of forces which come into operation in a region growing more slowly than the national economy of which it is a part. It is common to refer to such a region as a "declining" area. Frequently, however, the area is not actually declining but rather is growing more slowly than the surrounding regions. This relatively slow rate of growth gives rise to some self-reinforcing pressures which make recovery of the region extremely difficult. Because the Maritimes are a region of the sort described, it might be rewarding to examine the generalized case of the "declining" area.

Let us posit that Region A, dependent on the export market for a large share of its total income, encounters both a declining rate of growth in its major export markets and increased competition for those markets, so that its own exports stop expanding. Let us suppose that the unworked natural resources of Region A other than those producing for export are definitely limited. In adjoining Region B, however, there are unexploited natural resources which can be used to produce either for the export or for the regional domestic market.

Even when the problem is put so simply, one result can already be foreseen. The difference between Region A and Region B lies in the availability of productive resources relative to markets. The marginal product of labor and of capital being higher in Region B than in A, new capital and labor arriving from outside both regions will favor Region B over A. Also, some capital and labor will shift from Region A to Region B. Given the usual assumptions about factor mobility, the flow of capital and labor into Region B would continue until the marginal products are equated in both regions.

Stated in these gross terms, the model implies that income per capita should tend toward equality among regions. But of course we know that regional income differentials persist over long periods of time. How must the model be altered in order to explain the case of continuing regional income differentials?

First, the regional income differential will persist if there is a persisting difference in the proportion of the population in the work force. Income per worker may be as high in Region A as in Region B, but if each worker in Region A supports more people outside the work force than does each worker in Region B, income per capita of course will be lower in Region A.

Second, even if regional income *per member of the work force* is higher in Region B than in Region A, the difference might persist just because of differences in skills or degree of training of the average member of the work force. In the higher-income areas of a country one finds more doctors and lawyers and other professional people and perhaps more highly skilled industrial workers as well. So it is conceivable that wage rates might be the same, occupation by occupation, in two regions, yet the average annual earnings in one region might be considerably higher than in the other because of a higher proportion of workers in the well-paid occupations.

A third factor might be property income per person in the region. Personal income per capita may be higher in Region B than in Region A because capital per person is greater in B.

In many instances various imperfections in the labor market operate to perpetuate income differentials between regions over time. The mere cost of moving may be a deterrent, for example, or the lack of information about the nature of the alternative job opportunities elsewhere may prevent people from moving to take advantage of wage differentials.[27]

A fifth explanation of income differentials may rest on the differences between money income and psychic income. Region A may be such a delightful place to live that its residents are willing to sacrifice some money income in order to remain there rather than move to Region B and earn better wages.

These are the major reasons why we might expect to find income differentials between two regions persisting over time. The two areas might be in equilibrium with respect to each other, that is, there may be no flow of labor in one direction or the other in the presence of such differentials as those just named.

At least some of these factors do explain the lower income per capita in the Atlantic provinces. In 1954 each member of the work force was supporting 3.35 people, including himself. In none of the other regions was the figure above 3.0. In Ontario for each worker there were only 2.55 people in the population, in Quebec 2.79, and in British Columbia as in the prairies the figure was 2.94. That the occupational "mix" was so different in the Atlantic provinces as to influence the personal income figures is a bit difficult to prove conclusively from the available data. It is clearly implied, however, in that 7.1 per cent of the work force in all Canada was engaged in the professions whereas the proportion

---

[27] For a summary discussion of the labor mobility problem in the United States, see Herbert S. Parnes, *Research on Labor Mobility* (New York, 1954).

Table 18.   Personal income per capita and average hourly earnings in certain industries of Newfoundland, Nova Scotia, and New Brunswick expressed as percentages of the averages for Canada as a whole, 1954.

	Newfoundland	Nova Scotia	New Brunswick
Personal income per capita	53	75	66
Hourly earnings:			
in coal mining	—	94	—
in manufacturing	98	88	89
in buildings and structures	84	77	74
in highways, bridges, and street construction	—	83	81

Source: DBS, *Review of Man-Hours and Hourly Earnings,* 1945–1954; and DBS, *National Accounts, Income and Expenditure,* 1950–1955.

stood at only 6.1 per cent for the Atlantic provinces. Then, too, Table 18 shows that a substantial proportion of the difference in income per capita between the eastern provinces and the rest of Canada must be based on factors other than wage differences.[28] This is to say that one must look well beyond the relatively low wages in the Atlantic provinces in order to explain the lower per capita income there.

The last few paragraphs have discussed the major reasons for income differentials between two regions existing at any point in time. The same causal factors might work to keep income per capita or per member of the work force growing indefinitely at a slower rate in Region A than in Region B. For example, the industries growing in Region B may require more highly skilled workers than industries growing in Region A, or nonwage income per person might grow faster in Region B than in A.

But the rate of growth is measured by indexes other than income per capita or income per member of the work force. The most obvious of these is total regional income, the areal counterpart of national income. This measure is, of course, influenced not only by the income per member of the work force but also by the size of the work force. In our simple model we have assumed that the resources and the availability of markets for Regions A and B are such as to give a higher marginal produc-

[28] Table 18 covers only those industries cited in Canada, DBS, *Review of Man-Hours and Hourly Earnings,* 1945–1954.

tivity of labor and of capital in Region B than in Region A. As long as this condition holds, new capital and labor from outside the country will be attracted to Region B rather than to Region A, and capital and labor will migrate from A to B. Savings in Region A will be invested in Region B rather than in A. Since increased investment provides increased employment opportunities, the difference in regional income between A and B grows. Residents of Region A enjoy the return on their investments in Region B and so interest income in A is greater than it would be if their savings were invested in A. But the labor income arising because of the investments is income to residents of Region B. Ignoring momentarily the role of interregional trade, the multiplier effect, operating regionally just as it would nationally, may widen the differential in regional incomes. In Region B the increase in regional income is some multiple of the increase in investment expenditures there. In Region A, local savings exceed local investment expenditures and the multiplier works in reverse, reducing regional income by some multiple of the decline in investment. The size of the multiplier depends primarily on the marginal propensity to save in the region. A's regional income will fall, as a result of the depressing effect of the multiplier, until annual intended savings are reduced to equality with the annual intended investment expenditures. The decline in regional incomes may be reflected either in wage levels or simply in employment levels, wages remaining constant, or there may be a bit of both. The worker in Region A sees his annual income cut as a consequence and he (or more probably his son) will migrate to Region B.

Interregional trade will dampen the effects of more rapid growth in Region B, however. The multiplier as just discussed assumes that the new expenditures (caused by the increase in income) in Region B will be spent in Region B. If this region is contiguous to Region A, however, and if Region A is the older of the two, some of Region B's income increase will probably be spent on imports from A. We can visualize the extreme case in which Region B produces only an export staple and imports all its consumer goods from Region A while Region A's imports from Region B remain constant. In that case the multiplier would have a value of one in Region B and more than one in Region A. Ignoring the further impact of A's growth on B's exports, investment in B could cause a greater growth of income in A than in B. If Region A can produce capital goods at lower costs than can Region B, Region A will feel the accelerator effect of the new growth as well.[29]

The effect of the development of Region B on Region A, then, will depend on Region A's ability to produce Region B's requirements (and to transport them to Region B) more cheaply than can Region B. Firms which plan to sell to Region B may establish in Region A if factor costs are sufficiently lower in Region A to yield full costs, plus transportation costs, which are lower than full costs in Region B. Plants already established in Region A can forestall new competition in Region B if *marginal* costs in the former region plus transportation costs are less than full costs in the second region.

Casting the Maritimes in the role of Region A and central Canada in the role of Region B, we know that the older region failed to keep pace with the newer part of the country. Between 1871 and 1951 the population of Nova Scotia plus New Brunswick increased by just over 70 per cent while that of Ontario and Quebec increased by more than 200 per cent. Let us turn now to the history of the development of the latter two provinces to complete this examination of the differential in the rate of growth of the two big regions in eastern Canada.

QUEBEC AND ONTARIO

It is striking that a modern country of the size and importance of Canada should have had half its history shaped by an item as inconsequential in the affairs of men as the beaver hat. Yet for more than two centuries central Canada was exploited by the Europeans primarily for its fur. There seems little doubt that the concentration on this first great export staple retarded the development of what is now Quebec and Ontario.

It was the French, rather than the English, who first moved up the St. Lawrence Valley, because their disadvantageous position with respect to the English in the development of the dry-cure cod fisheries forced them to explore the marginal areas. One such area was the Gulf of the St. Lawrence. When the beaver hat came into fashion in Europe in the second half of the sixteenth

---

[29] Great Britain of the nineteenth century provides an illustration of this point.

century, the French developed a lively fur trade. This trade was dependent on the natural transportation system afforded by the St. Lawrence drainage basin, which deposited furs from the interior at Quebec. But this trade was soon encroached upon, first by the Dutch (followed by the English), who channeled fur from the Great Lakes area down the Mohawk and Hudson Rivers to New York, then by the Hudson's Bay Company which, after its founding in 1670, monopolized the fur trade of the Hudson's Bay drainage basin. The French survived between these two hostile groups until the Seven Years War and the Treaty of Paris of 1763 effectively removed them from North America.

France failed to maintain a foothold in North America in part because the fur trade was inconsistent with settlement. French ships east-bound had excess capacity, for they carried valuable but compact furs. On the return trip to New France, however, the ships were packed tight with goods to be traded with the Indians in exchange for the furs, so there was little room for immigrants and their goods. Carrying settlers would only worsen the imbalance in this trade.[30] Furthermore, the settlers were thought likely to compete with the company which had brought them. So the French were reluctant to comply with the agreements in their government charters to encourage settlement of land. New France failed to develop into the agricultural and commercial center which was supposed to function in the French colonial empire as New England did in Britain's.

The French were succeeded in the St. Lawrence valley by English, Scottish, and American traders. Amalgamation of the competing trading companies into the North West Company soon began, for the economics of the fur trade encouraged monopolization. Collusion among competitors was fairly simple since the furs all went to London rather than to scattered markets. Furthermore, the enormous quantities of working capital required to keep the traders in goods prevented easy entry into the industry. And, since the Indians were not organized, it was apparent that merging the trading companies would work to the disadvantage of the Indians and no one else. So the North West Company came to be the monopoly trader in the St. Lawrence

---

[30] Harold A. Innis, "Unused Capacity as a Factor in Canadian Economic History," *CJEPS*, 2:1–15 (February 1936). Reprinted in Innis, *Essays in Canadian Economic History* (Toronto, 1956), pp. 141–155.

basin. But the competition between the Hudson's Bay Company and the North West Company became so intense that amalgamation resulted there, too. In 1821 the two companies united. Thereafter virtually all the fur going out of central Canada went by way of the shorter and cheaper Hudson's Bay route. The trade in the first great export staple of the St. Lawrence Valley was suddenly diverted.

The timber trade

Britain's use of a preferential tariff on timber during the Napoleonic wars not only revived lumbering in New Brunswick, as we have seen, but also accelerated the exploitation of timber lands in Quebec and Ontario. Since the timber trade, like the fur trade, was dependent on the natural transportation routes afforded by the rivers, lumbering began along the banks of the St. Lawrence and then pushed up the Ottawa River. The town of Hull, opposite the Ottawa of today, shipped out timber as early as 1806. As the accessible stands along the St. Lawrence were eventually "lumbered out," the Ottawa Valley became the great timber supply area. Timber continued to be the main export staple of the area until the 1860's, by which time the agricultural sector had grown so large that its exports rivaled those of timber.[31] By Confederation in 1867, the Province of Canada was clearly an agricultural province. Timber was no longer the major staple.

How had this shift from timber to agriculture come about? First of all, the timber trade, in marked contrast to the fur trade, encouraged immigration and settlement.[32] The bulky timber cargoes to Britain meant excess capacity on the west-bound trip. So the timber ship captains were happy to bring back immigrants at a very low rate (some 30 shillings plus food and bedding[33]) which reflected the miserable accommodations as much as the existence of excess capacity. Despite the suffering and death com-

[31] D. G. Creighton, *British North America at Confederation,* Appendix 2 of RCDPR *Report* (Ottawa, 1939), p. 16.

[32] See Innis, *Essays in Canadian Economic History,* p. 147; also Innis, "An Introduction to the Economic History of Ontario from Outpost to Empire," pp. 108–122 in the same volume, originally published in *Papers and Records of the Ontario Historical Society,* 30:111–123 (1934).

[33] A. R. M. Lower, *Colony to Nation: A History of Canada* (London, 1946), p. 182.

mon on these voyages, the east-to-west flow of human beings on
timber ships contributed heavily to the "Great Immigration" of
1820–1850. Augmented by refugees from Britain's industrial problems and especially from Ireland's famine, the population of the
province of Canada increased from about 575,000 to nearly 1,850,-
000, an increase of about 220 per cent.

This wave of immigrants of course expanded the agricultural
base of central Canada. Earlier, agricultural settlement along
the St. Lawrence and Lake Ontario had been accelerated right
after the American Revolution by the influx of loyalists from the
south. They were given land so located that they might supply
the garrisons at Montreal, Kingston, Niagara, and Detroit.
Around 1800, these farmers began producing a wheat surplus and
the military and civilian demand led to the production of more
livestock, potatoes, peas, and other foodstuffs.[34] The clearing of
new land was encouraged by the export market for timber, and
agricultural settlement was encouraged by the possibility of part-
time employment "making timber." When lumbering moved up
the Ottawa, farming followed, attracted by the markets provided
by the lumber camps. But unlike the agriculture of the St. Lawrence and Lake Ontario lowlands, which was established prior
to the lumber trade, the Ottawa farms, which followed the lumber, were too poor and too far from markets to survive after the
lumbering moved on.

By 1867 the prosperous agricultural sector of Ontario and
Quebec was no longer exporting wheat and flour in such quantities. The United States market was growing, particularly after
the completion of the Ogdensburg railroad made Boston a market for Ontario produce and so encouraged diversification. In
1852, it was reported that New York and New England were
more important as markets for Ontario than was Montreal.[35]
Meanwhile the local market was expanding. After the collapse of
the timber trade with Britain in the late 1840's, exports of planks
and boards from Quebec and Ontario to the rapidly growing
United States market fortunately were accelerated so that the
total export demand for lumber was growing again in the 1850's.[36]
The rate of growth of the United States market for planks and

[34] R. L. Jones, *History of Agriculture in Ontario* (Toronto, 1946), pp. 23–31.
[35] Jones, p. 188.
[36] Lower, p. 211.

boards is reflected in the fact that in 1851 the total exports of boards and planks, most of which went to the United States, amounted to 120,000 M. feet, while by 1867 this figure had grown to over 530,000 M. feet.[37] The construction of the Grand Trunk required vast numbers of ties, and the lumber workers plus the railroad workers provided Ontario agriculture with a strong local demand.

Wheat exports to Europe had been very large during the middle 1850's, owing largely to the Crimean War. But continual wheat farming was exhausting the soil and the annual production was dropping in spite of the fact that the wheat acreage in Quebec and Ontario expanded until 1881. Constant difficulty with rust and midge was cutting down on the export market both in the United States and in Great Britain. Farmers were discouraged with wheat also because of the frequent winter-killing and the vagaries of the export market. With less competition from wheat, dairying and livestock production expanded rapidly to meet the demand stemming from the Civil War in the United States and from Canada's own urban centers and from Great Britain. In both Quebec and Ontario this diversification and reorientation toward the United States market took place, but the change was more pronounced in Ontario.

By Confederation, Quebec and Ontario had seen the forest industries decline to second place in importance behind a diversified agriculture which was now exporting primarily livestock, dairy products, and wheat. The expanding export markets generated a demand for manufactured products and so industrialization of these two provinces was well under way by 1867. In contrast with Nova Scotia and New Brunswick, where there were 3.3 and 3.9 persons in manufacturing (sawmills excluded) per thousand population, Quebec and Ontario reported 4.6 and 4.5 persons, respectively. If the shipyards in New Brunswick are dropped out of the manufacturing sector for purposes of this comparison on the grounds that they were producing for export rather than for the domestic market, the contrast is even greater. Quebec and Ontario were clearly stronger industrially than the Maritimes. Central Canada's industrial lead, which was to plague the Maritimes and their later development, was already established.

Since we are so concerned with the determinants of regional

[37] Creighton, p. 17.

growth, we must pause to examine why Quebec and Ontario were already leading the Maritimes in industrial development by Confederation. It is common to hear that the Maritimes are too far from markets, too barren of resources, too much oriented toward shrinking markets abroad to enjoy much industrial vigor. These reasons are of varying degrees of validity, but some additional insight can be gained by looking at the beginnings of the industrialization of Central Canada.

Could distance from Canadian markets have played any part in the slower industrialization of the Maritimes by 1871? We know that the populations of Ontario and Quebec were 1,600,000 and 1,200,000, respectively, compared with but 286,000 and 388,-000 for New Brunswick and Nova Scotia plus about 150,000 in Newfoundland and 94,000 in Prince Edward Island. But total population figures must be used with care here since cause and effect need be clearly distinguished. Does population attract industry, because of the markets afforded by that population, or does industry attract population because of the employment opportunities? Obviously both forces are at work.

To disentangle this interdependence we will revert to our simplified model involving Regions A and B. Let us assume the following: (a) that the residents of both areas earn income solely by producing for export beyond the two regions; (b) that the geographical density of incomes and population is equal at all points within each region; (c) that the two regions are contiguous; and (d) that all consumer goods are imported. Now suppose we introduce a consumer goods industry, one which uses a ubiquitous raw material. The industry, then, is exclusively market oriented. Where will the industry locate? If the economies of scale are sufficiently great, the new industry will consist of but one firm, which can establish a monopoly in the total market consisting of both Regions A and B. The firm will locate to minimize average transportation costs. But if the total market is large enough to support several optimum-sized plants, the new firms will be scattered throughout the two markets.

Now let us alter the assumptions. Suppose Regions A and B are separated geographically by a vacant "no-man's land." If the size of the market in A, even though it is smaller than in B, is larger than necessary to support a plant of optimum size, plants will be located in both regions. There may be some shipment from one region to the other but only in amounts less than an optimum firm could produce. But, if the economies of scale are so great that the total market afforded by Region A *plus* Region B can support but one optimum plant, then the firm will locate in the larger Region B. But since it will attempt to minimize transportation costs to consumers, some of which are in Region A, it will locate away from the center of Region B, in the direction of Region A.

Before returning to the actual case at hand, let us examine one variation on the model. Suppose Region B becomes geographically larger, the poulation and income remaining stable but population density falling. This pulls the optimum location of our single plant toward the center of Region B because transportation to customers in B becomes relatively more costly. As the geographical size of Region B expands, thereby reducing the density of population and income, the optimum location moves toward the center of Region B.

It appears that the population of central Canada was more widely dispersed than that of New Brunswick and Nova Scotia if we consider only the population dependent on export markets. Agriculture was much more labor intensive in New Brunswick and Nova Scotia than in Ontario and Quebec. It will be seen later than in Ontario and Quebec in 1871 there were 51 and 48 acres of improved land per occupier,[38] whereas in New Brunswick and Nova Scotia the corresponding figures were only 38 and 35. In Ontario and Quebec lumbering might have been more widely dispersed than in the Maritimes, giving a lower population density. Certainly the prominence of fishing in the Maritimes resulted in a population concentrated along the seacoast.

This exercise leads to the conclusion that "proximity to markets" in 1871 caused faster industrialization in central Canada than in the Maritimes only in the case of those industries in which the economies of scale were so great that but one plant could meet the requirements of both regions. With the bulk of consumer goods produced in 1871, however, the economies of scale were quite limited. The largest consumer goods industries by gross value of product in the four provinces were flour mills, boots and shoes, bakeries, tailors and clothiers, wool cloth making, and distilleries. (The latter two were prominent only in Ontario.)

[38] Defined as owner, tenant, or employee.

If employment rather than gross value of product is used as the index of size, one must add carriage making and cabinet and furniture making to the list. Economies of scale appear to have been insignificant in all cases except wool cloth making and distilleries. These two industries, which were far more important in Ontario than in the other provinces, nevertheless had plants small enough relative to the population to permit location anywhere in the four provinces if markets alone were to determine location. They were concentrated in Ontario not because of the proximity to markets but rather because they were materials-oriented.[39]

So proximity to markets can explain little of the difference in the degree of industrialization found in Quebec and Ontario as compared with the Maritimes. Other differences between the two regions were much more significant. First of all, agriculture in Ontario and Quebec had a larger capital input relative to land and labor than in the Maritimes. Table 19 shows that as one moved west across these four provinces in 1871 the acres of improved land per occupier rose steadily. Generally speaking, there was more equipment per thousand acres and per thousand occupiers in Ontario and Quebec than in the Maritimes. In areas where land is plentiful we expect to find lesser amounts of labor *and capital* applied per acre than where land is less plentiful. So at first glance Ontario and Quebec appear to be odd cases when compared with the Maritimes for they show more capital equipment per acre but less labor per acre than do the Maritimes. The reason for this is, of course, that the agriculture of the two regions differed in ways other than the degree of intensity of cultivation and that, the more extensive farming is, the more easily some capital equipment can be used. For example, over 15 per cent of the improved land in Ontario was in wheat, compared with 1 per cent in Nova Scotia.

The greater capital intensity of central Canada's agriculture provided a greater market for agricultural implements than did

---

[39] The distilleries were reasonably large firms. Twenty were in operation in 1871 (18 of them in Ontario), with an average employment of 23 persons. Of the 2,036 woolen mills, 1,702 were in Ontario. The average employment was but 13. Although in both cases employment per establishment was well above the average, it seems apparent that the scale was still small enough to have permitted a more general geographical distribution were it not for the fact that these industries were materials-oriented.

Table 19. Acres of improved land per occupier and implements per thousand acres and per thousand occupiers in Ontario, Quebec, New Brunswick, and Nova Scotia, 1871.

Province	Acres of improved land per occupier[a]	Implements						
		Light carriages	Reapers and mowers	Vehicles for transport	Ploughs, harrows & cultivators	Horse rakes	Threshing mills	Fanning mills
		Number per thousand acres of improved land						
Ontario	51.3	23.3	4.2	33.9	32.8	5.2	1.6	13.7
Quebec	48.3	42.1	.9	71.0	36.2	1.8	2.7	6.5
New Brunswick	37.5	23.7	.7	53.0	33.2	2.3	.8	4.5
Nova Scotia	35.1	24.7	.8	46.8	23.8	2.3	.3	2.9
		Number per thousand occupiers						
Ontario		1,197	214	1,738	1,680	268	80	701
Quebec		2,033	44	3,429	1,750	88	131	316
New Brunswick		889	28	1,988	1,247	85	31	168
Nova Scotia		866	28	1,644	836	80	11	102

a "Occupiers" are owners, tenants, and employees.
Source: Census of Canada, 1870–71, Vol. III, pp. 101, 118.

the Maritimes. In 1871, 85 per cent of the total output of agricultural implements was accounted for by Ontario and nearly the whole of the remainder by Quebec. The presence of the agricultural implement industry undoubtedly helps explain the disproportionate size of the foundries and machine-working industry in Ontario.

It is conceivable that the capital intensity not only of agricultural production but of all manufacturing production was greater in central Canada than in the Maritimes, thus making for a greater degree of industrialization in the former region. Although capital data are notoriously unreliable, those available for 1871 do show capital per worker in manufacturing to be slightly greater in Ontario and Quebec than in the Maritimes. The ratio of capital to gross value of product, however, is much greater in Nova Scotia than in either of the other three provinces if all manufacturing industries are included. If only the ten leading industries are included, Quebec shows the highest capital-output ratio. The data are shown in Table 20. Since we are measuring the degree of industrialization by the ratio of manufacturing employment to population, capital per worker would seem to be the more relevant measure. If the capital data are adequate, the greater capital equipment per worker might help to explain the greater degree of industrialization in central Canada as contrasted with the Maritimes.

Another explanation for the greater degree of industrialization in central Canada than in the Maritimes lies in the difference in the extent to which goods were processed before export. In Quebec

Table 20. Capital per worker and ratio of capital to value of product in all manufacturing and in the ten leading industries, Ontario, Quebec, New Brunswick, and Nova Scotia, 1871.

	Capital per worker		Ratio of capital to value of product	
Province	All manufacturing	Ten leading industries	All manufacturing	Ten leading industries
Ontario	$434	$457	0.33	0.31
Quebec	421	357	.36	.45
New Brunswick	326	312	.34	.35
Nova Scotia	387	254	.49	.43

Source: Census of Canada, 1870–71, Vol. III, Table 55, pp. 458–463.

and Ontario, there were 81 men in the wood products industries for every 100 in the sawmills; but in New Brunswick and Nova Scotia there were but 70. (This was despite the fact that in Nova Scotia the shipyard employment was large enough to bring the employment in wood products in that province up to 143 per 100 in the sawmills.) Central Canada was closer to the export market which was buying wood products, namely the growing central plains of the United States. And undoubtedly the faster growth of central Canada tempered the importance of employment in wood products relative to employment in sawmills. Furniture

Table 21. Ten leading manufacturing industries in Quebec and Ontario by value of product and by number of employees, 1871.

Industry	Value of product (thousands)	Industry	Number of employees
		Quebec	
Flour and grist mills	$9,898	Sawmills	11,848
Sawmills	9,549	Boots and shoes	9,865
Boots and shoes	9,074	Lumber products^a	7,154
Lumber products^a	5,403	Blacksmithing	3,311
Tanneries	4,398	Tailors and clothiers	3,193
Sugar refineries	4,069	Iron and steel products	2,435
Bakeries	3,284	Shipyards	2,164
Iron and steel products	2,819	Carriage making	2,118
Tailors and clothiers	2,666	Foundries and machine working	1,862
Furriers and hatters	2,303	Tanneries	1,735
		Ontario	
Flour and grist mills	27,116	Sawmills	13,851
Sawmills	12,734	Lumber products^a	8,057
Lumber products^a	6,374	Boots and shoes	6,354
Tailors and clothiers	5,425	Tailors and clothiers	6,248
Boots and shoes	5,025	Blacksmithing	4,810
Foundries and machine working	4,632	Carriage making	4,780
Wool cloth making	4,589	Foundries and machine working	4,686
Distilleries	3,876	Iron and steel products	3,778
Iron and steel products	3,778	Wool cloth making	3,696
Tanneries	3,420	Flour and grist mills	2,759

^a The lumber products industry did not appear under this title in the 1871 Census, the component industries being shown instead. In order to provide better comparability with the 1911 Census the components were aggregated here. Note that shipyards, however, are not included in the lumber products industry.

Source: Census of Canada, 1870–71, Vol. III, Table 55, pp. 458–463.

and cabinet making, for example, in the Maritimes must have been producing largely for replacement, whereas in central Canada a high proportion of this industry's output must have gone into the homes of new arrivals.

But easily the most obvious explanation for the greater industrialization of central Canada is that the major primary products in the Maritimes did not lend themselves to as much processing as did those of central Canada. This is reflected in Table 13 and 21. In Nova Scotia, New Brunswick, Quebec, and Ontario, flour and grist mills were among the ten leading industries, but the value of output in Ontario was over $27,000,000 as compared with less than $10,000,000 in Quebec and but $1,000,000 in New Brunswick and Nova Scotia. (Since wheat production in Ontario was about seven times that of Quebec, some Ontario wheat must have been milled in Quebec as it moved east to the export markets.) Tanneries, meat curing, and wool cloth making reflect the role of livestock in Ontario. And in Quebec the tanneries showed a larger value of product relative to the Maritimes than the population differentials would account for. The role of the distilleries in Ontario reinforces the point that the type of primary products in central Canada were more suitable for further processing than were those of the Maritimes. There was no fish processing as yet in the Maritimes, and the apples and potatoes which later came to be so important there could not be processed in any quantity. Lumber was clearly an exception in the case of Nova Scotia. And cooperage was one of the ten leading industries in Nova Scotia, providing another illustration. But, for the most part, Tables 13 and 21 show the importance of the processing of local primary products in central Canada and the absence of this processing in the Maritimes.

This discussion has shown that central Canada was industrializing more rapidly than the Maritimes not only because of the usual reasons cited by the Maritimers but also because central Canada's primary products were of a sort which could be processed further before being exported whereas in the Maritimes this was not true except for lumber in Nova Scotia. Furthermore, the kind of manufacturing in central Canada may have required more capital per worker than was the case in the eastern provinces, thus giving rise to more supporting industries than was general in the Maritimes. Certainly the agriculture was more capital intensive in Ontario than elsewhere and so the production of agricultural implements came to be centered there.

We have been taking here a very static view of the differential in the degree of industrialization between these two regions. But surely at least two dynamic factors influenced the degree of industrialization. First, capital goods production in a closed economy is a function of the rate of investment. Therefore, even if two economies have identical economic structures at "birth" and "maturity" (however defined), they would probably have different structures at any one point in time if one is younger than the other; the younger would be devoting a greater portion of its output to capital goods.

Of more relevance, though, is the role of expectations. Even at Confederation, talk of expansion to the west was heard. The prospect for growth was surely greater in central Canada than in the Maritimes and manufacturers may well have been more attracted to Ontario and Quebec because of the growth prospects than by the market as it stood at that time.

We can now turn to certain differences within central Canada. The role of immigration in the population growth in the two provinces can be determined from the 1871 census data on place of birth. In Ontario just 70 per cent of the population had been born in Ontario but in Quebec 92.5 per cent had been born in that province. Of the Ontario population 23 per cent were born in the British Isles while only 5 per cent of the Quebec residents were from the British Isles. There were about six times as many people from the British Isles living in Ontario as in Quebec. This reinforces the point that the British policy on immigration into Canada had directed population into Ontario rather than into Quebec. Quebec's growth, then, was primarily internal whereas Ontario's was due largely to immigration.[40] Even New Brunswick and Nova Scotia, older than Quebec, showed a lower percentage of locally born and a higher percentage of immigrants among the population than did Quebec.

Other differences between the two provinces should be mentioned. Cattle, sheep, and wheat were considerably more important in Ontario than in Quebec. Although meat curing in Ontario accounted for a larger value of product relative to Quebec than the population difference would warrant, the tanneries were more

[40] Veyret, pp. 17–21.

prominent in Quebec. This is presumably explained by the
marked concentration of the production of boots and shoes in
Quebec. The concentration of flour and grist mills and of foundries and woolen goods production in Ontario is also clear. Ontario's manufacturing employment was slightly greater, relative
to agricultural employment, than was that of Quebec. Not only
was she processing her agricultural products, as was Quebec, but
Ontario was also building up some basic industries to supply her
capital goods requirements. The foundries and machine working
output and the employment in agricultural implements are especially noteworthy in Table 21. The processing of export staples
was still important but was fading relative to the manufacturing
of goods for the domestic market. Central Canada was industrializing.[41]

Central Canada at World War I

Between 1871 and 1911 the population of all Canada rose by
nearly 100 per cent. The prairies were filling up rapidly, especially after 1900, and of course Ontario and Quebec grew more
slowly than the nation as a whole. Ontario's population increased
by only 56 per cent as against 68 per cent for Quebec. The
prairies were attracting more people from the former province,
thus retarding its rate of growth a bit. The 1911 census reported
that nearly seven times as many people in the three prairie provinces were born in Ontario as in Quebec (227,000 compared with
34,000).

The great westward movement generated an extensive demand
for the products of central Canada. In Ontario, the percentage
increase in manufacturing employment was nearly three times as
great as the percentage increase in population while in Quebec
manufacturing employment increased less than twice as much as
did the entire population. In marked contrast to this experience

---

[41] But the degree of industrialization should not be exaggerated. One writer
has said: "About the middle of the nineteenth century, the Province of Canada
was transformed from a raw, staple-producing area to a rounded, integrated
economy that might be called metropolitan . . . Signs of the change were visible
in 1830, unmistakable in 1840. By 1850 change had gone too far to be turned
back, and 1860 and 1870 can denote only the filling out of a home market exchange economy already implicit." (H. C. Pentland, "The Role of Capital in
Canadian Economic Development before 1875," *CJEPS*, 16:457–474 [November
1950].) The degree of self-sufficiency implied in this statement appears to be
unjustified.

stood New Brunswick. There the ratio of the percentage increase in manufacturing employment to the percentage increase in population was only 1.5. However, in Nova Scotia, which developed its iron and steel industry between 1871 and 1911, manufacturing employment increased about three times as much as did the population.

In order to sketch the developments of the four decades prior to 1911, let us review developments in the primary products fields and then note the developments in the manufacturing sector. Lumbering had taken on quite a different character over this period. The old square timber trade, declining since the 1880's, disappeared soon after 1900. Sawn lumber had filled the gap and was still growing. The railroad boom brought a demand for ties. and the burgeoning towns south of the Great Lakes provided a continuing demand for lumber.

But a still greater demand on the forests was developing. The growing demand for newsprint in the United States and Canada was reflected in the expansion of pulpwood production. Until about 1910, the United States was able to supply most of its own pulpwood requirements and Canadian production was largely for the domestic market. Even so, pulpwood production accounted for a substantial proportion of total lumber output.[42] In 1911, paper production was among the top ten manufacturing industries in Quebec in terms of both value of product and employment.[43] The industry was just beginning to develop, thanks in large part to an embargo on the export of pulpwood from Quebec's crown lands imposed in 1910. Ontario had imposed such an embargo in 1900. As a result of this and other later measures, the proportion of pulpwood which was exported fell from about two-thirds in 1908 to 18 per cent in 1936.[44]

Mining in Quebec was still insignificant at the turn of the century except for the asbestos in Quebec's eastern townships.[45] Asbestos production rose from less than 11,000 tons in 1896 to just over 100,000 tons in 1911. In the latter year cement was sec-

---

[42] By 1907, about one-third of the timber cut in Quebec was for pulpwood. Province of Quebec, *Report of the Minister of Lands and Forests of the Province of Quebec, 1908*, p. 32a.

[43] See Table 22.

[44] V. W. Bladen, *An Introduction to Political Economy* (Toronto, 1946), p. 150.

[45] These lie between the St. Lawrence River and New England.

ond to asbestos in value of product in Quebec even though cement production had been started after 1900.[46] Limestone and brick production were of considerable importance, but the output of metallic minerals was as yet inconsequential.

But in Ontario mining was developing much more rapidly. A bit of iron ore was mined in that province prior to 1845, but the bulk of the minerals were not developed until the second half of the century. The great Sudbury deposit of nickel and copper was discovered when the Canadian Pacific Railway was being built. By the end of the century over a million dollars worth of matte was being produced and shipped annually from Sudbury.[47] The southwestern part of the province was also producing oil valued at something over a million dollars a year, but output was falling off rapidly after having hit a peak of more than 800,000 barrels in 1895.[48] Pig iron, gold, silver, and salt were also produced in substantial quantity. By 1906, Ontario's mineral production totaled over $22,000,000 compared with just over $5,000,000 for Quebec.

By 1911 the complexion of agriculture in central Canada had changed dramatically. No longer was wheat the region's export staple. Wheat "mining" had declined for several reasons. The difficulties with disease and winter killing, mentioned earlier, had continued and now the western lands in both Canada and the United States were opening up, producing wheat in abundance for the world market. Perhaps of greater importance in the decline of wheat, however, was the rise in the opportunity cost of producing the grain. The growing urban centers generated a demand for meat and dairy products and garden truck which encouraged diversification away from wheat. Furthermore, improvements in trans-Atlantic steamship handling of livestock had made it possible to ship live cattle to Britain with very small losses.[49] This had accelerated the breeding of better cattle and the general expansion of livestock production until Britain placed an embargo

[46] F. D. Adams, "History of Mining in the Province," in *Canada and Its Provinces,* ed. Adam Shortt and Arthur G. Doughty (Toronto, 1914), Vol. 16, p. 595.

[47] Canada, Department of Mines, *Report on the Mining and Metallurgical Industries of Canada, 1907–08,* p. 308.

[48] R. B. Harkness, "Petroleum in 1930," in Ontario Department of Mines, *Fortieth Annual Report, 1931,* p. 54.

[49] H. A. Innis and A. R. M. Lower, *Selected Documents in Canadian Economic History, 1783–1885* (Toronto, 1933), pp. 554–555.

on live cattle imports in the 1890's. Meanwhile the McKinley tariff of 1890 had effectively cut off the export of livestock to the United States. This trade had already been severely reduced by a 20 per cent *ad valorem* duty imposed shortly after the end of reciprocity.

These difficulties in the export market for livestock in turn hastened the growth of dairying and of cheese production in particular. The introduction of the first cheese factories in 1864 was followed by a rapid growth in cheese production. By 1871 there were 353 cheese factories in Ontario and Quebec and by 1911 there were 3390 factories. Meanwhile the value of product of these factories had multiplied by about twenty times and employment by nearly six times over the 1871–1911 period. Cheese had become the major export staple, generally exceeding even wheat exports in the two decades preceding World War I.[50]

The shift in central Canada's agriculture from grain to live-stock is clearly reflected in the census data for 1871 and 1911. The acreage sowed to wheat declined by 70 per cent in Quebec and by 30 per cent in Ontario.[51] Production of feed grains and hay expanded greatly, with Ontario, for example, producing four times as much oats in 1911 as in 1871. The number of milch cows increased by 70 per cent. Expanding local demand for meat increased the number of cattle other than milch cows by 100 per cent and of the number of swine by 115 per cent.

The make-up of the manufacturing sector in 1911 differed in several important respects from that of 1871. Comparing Table 22 with Table 21 shows that Ontario's ten leading industries, ranked by value of product, no longer included tailors and cloth-iers, boots and shoes, wool cloth making, distilleries, tanneries, and carriage making. Lumber products had slipped several places down the list. Foundry products and iron and steel products had risen, as had slaughtering and meat packing, agricultural implements, butter and cheese, and printing, publishing and book-binding. In terms of employment foundry products; agricultural implements; printing, publishing, and bookbinding; furniture; and hosiery had all risen on the list or come onto it. Lum-

---

[50] A. W. Currie, *Canadian Economic Development* (Toronto, 1942), p. 140.

[51] But production, which fell by more than 50 per cent in Quebec, actually increased by 40 per cent in Ontario. *Census of Canada, 1870–71,* Vol. III, p. 202, and *Census of Canada, 1911,* Vol. IV, Tables 6, 14.

Table 22.   Ten leading manufacturing industries in Quebec and Ontario by value of product and by number of employees, 1911.

Industry	Value of product (thousands)	Industry	Number of employees
		Quebec	
Log products	$26,670	Log products	22,076
Boots and shoes	22,662	Boots and shoes	11,552
Men's clothing	16,826	Men's clothing	8,331
Cottons	16,741	Cottons	8,137
Butter and cheese	16,157	Car repairs	8,749
Car and car works	12,775	Foundry and machine	
Tobacco, cigars, and		shop products	4,998
cigarettes	11,921	Lumber products	4,627
Flour and grist mill		Paper	4,542
products	11,095	Tobacco, cigars, and	
Paper	10,971	cigarettes	4,438
Lumber products	10,010	Cars and car works	4,354
		Ontario	
Flour and grist mill		Log products	21,738
products	52,227	Foundry and machine	
Log products	36,014	shop products	18,015
Foundry and machine		Women's clothing	11,770
Shop products	28,515	Printing, bookbinding,	
Iron and steel products	21,938	and publishing	9,754
Slaughtering and meat		Men's clothing	8,969
packing	20,935	Agricultural implements	8,929
Agricultural implements	19,116	Lumber products	7,061
Butter and cheese	18,149	Iron and steel products	6,587
Lumber products	17,075	Furniture and uphol-	
Printing, publishing,		stered goods	6,490
and book binding	15,002	Hosiery and knit goods	6,320
Leather, tanned, curried,			
and finished	14,736		

Source: Census of Canada, 1911, Vol. III, Table 1.

ber products had declined in relative terms, as had wool cloth making. Cottons, car repairs, and car works as well as tobacco products were not on the list. In Quebec, flour and grist mills fell on the list in terms of value of product, as did lumber products, tanneries, sugar refineries, baking, and foundries. Paper now appeared on the list for the first time, along with butter and cheese, tobacco, cottons, and car works. Among the ten leading industries in terms of employment we see that shipyards, carriage making, tanneries, and flour mills had dropped off the list completely and lumber products had declined from third to seventh place.

These comparisons show several forces at work in the region. First, among those industries producing primarily for the domestic market, the heavy industries were gaining at the expense of the lighter industries in Ontario, whereas the reverse appears to have been happening in Quebec. In the latter province, iron and steel products and the foundries dropped from the list, cotton textiles and tobacco products had become established, and the clothing and boots and shoes industries remained prominent, unlike the Ontario experience.[52] This reflects the greater availability of labor in Montreal and Quebec than in Ontario since the latter area was industrializing a little more rapidly and, more important, was sending more emigrants into the prairies than was Quebec.

Second, the old staples were declining in importance. For example, flour and grist mill output even in Ontario, where it was still the leading product in terms of value, no longer led the pack by such a huge margin. In 1871 the three leading industries accounted for 60 per cent of the value of product of the leading ten in Ontario; in Quebec the corresponding figure was 53 per cent. By 1911 these two percentages had fallen to 48 and 43, respectively. So the manufacturing sector was clearly becoming more diversified.

Third, a regrouping of the staple-processing industries was under way. The role of butter and cheese has already been discussed. Paper, too, had risen by this time enough to place on Quebec's list of leading industries. Meanwhile the industries processing the old staples, timber and wheat, were no longer of overwhelming significance to the economy.

To some extent this industrialization was a result of the National Policy and the tariff of 1879. The depression of 1873–1879 had reinforced the arguments of the protectionists. The hope was that by expanding her industry Canada could reduce her reliance on export markets. The textile industry and iron and steel seem to have expanded at least in part as a result of the special attention given them in the 1879 tariff, although the impact of the

---

[52] These changes are more apparent in the value of product list than in the employment list for an obvious reason: heavy industries by definition have lower labor costs per dollar of output.

Table 23.   Population and distribution of the labor force in Quebec and
                      Ontario, 1911 and 1951 (thousands).

	Quebec		Ontario	
	1911	1951	1911	1951
Population	2,006	4,056	2,527	4,598
Labor force	653	1,472	991	1,885
Agriculture	205	195	307	201
Forestry	11	45	11	23
Fishing and hunting	4	5	4	2
Mining	6	20	17	31
Manufacturing	142	453	231	615
Construction	68	103	83	127
Transportation	43	107[a]	76	127[a]
Trade	71	173	112	267
Government	18	62	28	117
Personal and domestic service	54	94	79	105
Other services[b]	31	216	45	268

[a] Includes communication and storage.
[b] Includes in 1951 labor force in electricity, gas, and water of 12,617 in Quebec
and 30,704 in Ontario.
Source: Census of Canada, 1911, Vol. VI, Table 2; and Census of Canada, 1951.
Vol. IV, Table 16.

tariff is not altogether clear.[53] Fully manufactured industrial
equipment and machinery were protected by tariffs of about 25
per cent and the duty on consumer goods ranged up to 30 per
cent. The tariff on goods not specifically included in other categories was raised from 17.5 per cent to 20 per cent.[54] It is quite
apparent that, although some of the growth of industry in central
Canada can be attributed to the growth of the local market, the
protective tariff must be considered to have been very effective.

Central Canada after World War II

By 1951, Ontario and Quebec were well established as the industrial heart of Canada. The two accounted for 81 per cent of the
total manufacturing employment in the country. In large part the
predominant position resulted from central Canada's producing
the bulk of the consumer goods for the rest of the economy. But
one of the most interesting characteristics of the 1911–1951 period of growth for these two provinces was the importance of new

[53] See Chapter 7, p. 236.
[54] Easterbrook and Aitken, p. 393.

export staples. Three forces are apparent during this period: the rise of new consumer goods industries, the decline of old export staples, and the rise of new export staples. Both light and heavy industries expanded rapidly during the period. Agriculture, which in 1911 had provided the export staple, was reoriented during these four decades to serve the needs of an urban, industrial economy. Meanwhile pulp and paper and mineral production and processing rose to commanding positions, reinforcing the point that the export staples are of strategic significance even in the most industrialized region in the country.

The magnitude of the shift toward industrialization in Quebec and Ontario is shown in the work force distribution figures in Table 23. The proportion in agriculture declined from 31 per cent to 13 per cent in Quebec and from 32 per cent to 11 per cent in Ontario. The manufacturing sector had expanded meanwhile from 21 per cent to 31 per cent of the work force in Quebec and from 23 to 33 per cent in Ontario. Mining in Quebec had expanded in terms of work force requirements from 0.9 to 1.4 per cent while this percentage remained stable in Ontario.

What had happened to the agricultural sector, which had been such a prominent exporter in 1911? Briefly put, agriculture had responded to the growth of population and incomes on the domestic market. It is curious that in the face of a 90 per cent increase in population, the total improved land in the two provinces actually declined slightly.[55] So even if there had been no change of any sort other than the population increase we would expect a decline in exports because of the apparent inelasticity of supply of agricultural land in the region. In Ontario the acreage in field crops had declined by all of 13 per cent. The percentage distribution of the acreage among the various field crops had changed very little, the continuing decline of wheat and the growth of tobacco acreage in Ontario being the two major changes worth noting. Easily the most significant agricultural development of the period was the growth of poultry and egg production. The number of hens and chickens on farms doubled in Quebec and nearly doubled in Ontario while egg production of course followed a parallel path. Milk production, meanwhile, nearly doubled in Quebec and rose by a little less than 20 per cent in Ontario.

[55] The population of Canada as a whole increased by 94 per cent from 1911 to 1951, that of Quebec by 102 per cent and of Ontario 81 per cent. The increase for the two provinces taken together was 91 per cent.

Table 24. Ten leading manufacturing industries in Quebec and Ontario by value of product and by number of employees, 1911[a] and 1951.

Industry	Value of product (millions)	Industry	Number of employees
		Quebec, 1911	
Log products	$27	Log products	22,076
Cars, car works, and car repairs	24	Cars, car works, and car repairs	12,103
Boots and shoes	23	Boots and shoes	11,552
Cottons	17	Cottons	8,137
Butter and cheese	16	Clothing, men's, factory	6,499
Clothing, men's, factory	13	Foundry and machine shop products	4,998
Tobacco, cigars, and cigarettes	12	Lumber products	4,627
Flour and grist mill products	11	Paper	4,542
Paper	11	Tobacco, cigars, and cigarettes	4,438
Lumber products	10	Butter and cheese	3,255
		Quebec, 1951	
Pulp and paper	524	Pulp and paper	24,449
Nonferrous metal smelting and refining	307	Clothing, women's, factory	18,800
Petroleum products	246	Cotton, yarn, cloth	18,161
Slaughtering and meat packing	192	Clothing, men's, factory	17,838
Cotton yarn and cloth	182	Railway rolling stock	15,572
Clothing, men's, factory	136	Synthetic textiles and silk	13,016
Clothing, women's, factory	134	Footwear, leather	12,188
Railway rolling stock	125	Miscellaneous electrical apparatus and supplies	11,905
Butter and cheese	112	Sawmills	10,763
Tobacco, cigars, and cigarettes	109	Furniture	9,047
		Ontario, 1911	
Flour and grist mill products	$53	Log products	21,738
Log products	37	Foundry and machine shop products	18,015
Slaughtering and meat packing	34	Clothing, women's, factory	9,115
Foundry and machine shop products	29	Agricultural implements	8,929
Iron and steel products	22	Cars, car works, and car repairs	7,133
Agricultural implements	19	Lumber products	7,061
Butter and cheese	18	Iron and steel products	6,587
Lumber products	18	Furniture and upholstered goods	6,490
Leather, tanned, curried, and finished	15	Hosiery and knit goods	6,320
Bread, biscuits, and confectionery	14	Clothing, men's, factory	6,336

Table 24. Continued.

Industry	Value of product (millions)	Industry	Number of employees
		Ontario, 1951	
Motor vehicles	729	Motor vehicles	29,413
Pulp and paper	387	Machinery, heavy elec-	
Primary iron and steel	359	trical	23,956
Slaughtering and meat		Primary iron and steel	22,670
packing	356	Motor vehicle parts	20,205
Nonferrous metal smelt-		Pulp and paper	18,348
ing and refining	353	Agricultural imple-	
Rubber goods	257	ments	16,022
Motor vehicle parts	255	Rubber goods	15,825
Machinery, heavy elec-		Bread and bakery	
trical	212	products	14,379
Agricultural implements	161	Furniture	13,953
Petroleum products	154	Printing and publishing	12,496

[a] Data for 1911 have been regrouped in some instances to provide better comparability with 1951.

Source: Census of Canada, 1911, Vol. III, Table 1; and DBS, General Review of the
Manufacturing Industries of Canada, 1951.

But not only had the size and nature of the domestic market
altered the structure of agriculture, developments on the export
market were also influential. After satisfactory methods for refrig-
erating in transit had been devised, the Argentine, New Zealand,
and Australia began to supply meat and dairy products to the
United Kingdom.[56] The growth of the domestic market thus coincided with increased competition abroad. Domestic demand
for milk and butter grew with the increase in incomes, improved
transportation, and more sanitary production. Creameries and
condensed milk factories expanded at the expense of cheese factories. Beef and pork production expanded only slightly compared with population, again causing a reduction in agricultural
exports.

In the industrial sector the rise of the new and the decline of
the old export staples had altered the ranking of major industries. In 1911 the export of newsprint and pulp and paper to the

[56] See Innis, Essays in Canadian Economic History, p. 217. This essay, "The
Historical Development of the Dairy Industry in Canada," appeared originally
in J. A. Ruddick et al., The Dairying Industry in Canada, ed. H. A. Innis
(Toronto, 1937), pp. 1–11.

United States was just beginning to be significant. By 1951 pulp and paper in Quebec showed a value of product more than half again as great as the second industry, while in Ontario pulp and paper placed second. (See Table 24.) Nonferrous metal smelting and refining was the second industry in Quebec, the fifth in Ontario. The role of these new export commodities in the two provinces is clear. The old staples of the 1911 list had declined at least relatively. In both provinces log products (sawmills) had dropped off the value of product list, as had flour and grist mills. Butter and cheese factories had disappeared from the leading ten industries in Ontario and had dropped from fifth to ninth place in Quebec. The relative decline of railway rolling stock is also apparent.

By 1951 a pronounced difference in the make-up of manufacturing in Quebec and Ontario had appeared, a difference which in 1911 had been just barely perceptible. By 1951 the heavy industries were concentrated in Ontario, the light industries in Quebec. Among the ten leading industries in Ontario were motor vehicles, primary iron and steel, heavy electrical machinery, and agricultural implements. None of these was among the leading ten in Quebec. There we find cotton yarn and cloth, men's clothing, women's clothing, butter and cheese, and tobacco products among the ten leading industries. Yet none of these was among the leading ten in Ontario.

This marked difference in the pattern of industrialization in the two provinces is explained largely by the difference in the availability of fuel and power. Neither Quebec nor Ontario has any coal deposits worth noting. Canadian coal unfortunately is located predominantly in the Maritimes and in Alberta and British Columbia, far from central Canada. As a result, Quebec and Ontario have been importing coal heavily from the United States for many years. Nova Scotian coal can compete with the United States product only with the aid of government subventions. Proximity to the Appalachian coal fields has given Ontario the locational advantage for industries dependent on large quantities of heat. But central Canada does boast large quantities of hydroelectric power. In this resource Quebec holds a substantial edge over Ontario, installed capacity in the former province being roughly twice that of the latter.[57] Since electricity is a far less

[57] *Canada Year Book, 1955*, p. 542.

efficient producer of heat than is coal, the heavy industries, with substantial fuel requirements, have chosen to locate in Ontario. On the other hand, the so-called light industries, in which the stress is on the need for power rather than heat, have become the more significant industries in Quebec. Dales has shown in a simple but illuminating model that, under certain simplifying assumptions, a region must have at least 50 per cent of the materials requirements (defined to include power and food needs) if industry is to develop.[58] Central Canada appears to have, by crude estimate, about 60 per cent of the materials requirements of light industry. It would not meet this 50 per cent requirement for industrial development, however, were it not for the availability of hydro power. But just as hydro power is a necessary prerequisite to central Canada's industrialization, by Dales' estimates, so also are food resources and forest resources.[59] This amounts to saying that industrialization of central Canada has occurred only because of the fortunate juxtaposition of water power, agricultural resources, *and* forest and mineral resources.

The rise of the new primary products in Quebec and Ontario was little short of spectacular between 1911 and 1951. In terms of employment the growth of pulp and paper production was most outstanding. Taking the two provinces together, employment in pulp and paper production was nearly five times as great in 1951 as in 1911, while the total employment in the two provinces had just doubled. Employment in forestry had more than tripled. The growth of the great metropolitan areas in the United States, with their expanding daily newspapers gobbling up increasing quantities of newsprint to carry advertisements to the consuming public, had provided the market for a new export staple which central Canada was ideally suited to produce.

But the performance of mineral output in central Canada was nearly as impressive as that of pulp and paper. Nickel production was about eight times as great (by quantity) in 1951 as in 1911 while copper output was nearly twenty times as large. Lead and zinc were now being produced in substantial quantity in Quebec, and gold production had risen from a negligible figure to over 3,500,000 ounces. Ontario's iron ore production had also risen,

---

[58] John H. Dales, *Hydroelectricity and Industrial Development, Quebec 1898–1940* (Cambridge, 1957), pp. 156–181.

[59] Dales, p. 175.

from virtually zero to nearly 3,000,000 tons. Aluminum production, based on neither raw materials nor markets but rather on hydro power, was launched in Quebec at the turn of the century after the first aluminum plant in the country was built at Niagara Falls in 1895. In 1910 the output of aluminum amounted to 4900 tons. By 1951 output stood at 447,000 tons. So unquestionably central Canada's economic strength is still largely based on primary production.

6

The Growth of Canada's
Western Regions

THE PRAIRIE PROVINCES

The geography of the prairies has been of such towering importance in the development of the region that a review of the area's historical development must begin with some notes on soil and climate.[1] The prairies are isolated from eastern Canada by the huge pre-Cambrian shield, that enormous body of igneous rock which covers almost one-half of Canada's total land area. The thin, usually sandy soil and the countless small lakes and swamps in that part of the shield separating central Canada and the prairies have discouraged agriculture except for occasional pockets where mining or lumber camps or pulp and paper production provide a local market. The unattractiveness of the shield was all too apparent as central Canada developed and it was seen as an enormous barrier to the extension of the nation into the prairies and on to the Pacific.

For years there was some question, too, whether the prairies themselves could sustain extensive settlement. It was argued by Captain John Palliser in 1863 that the prairie country which he had explored for the British government was too arid for settlement. This region was bounded on the south by the United States border, on the west by the Rockies, on the north by a line running due east and west about sixty miles north of Calgary, and on the east by a line running southeasterly from near Saskatoon to a point in Manitoba on the United States border about seventy-five miles inside the Manitoba-Saskatchewan border. The area came to be known, through a quite casual application of geometry, as "Palliser's Triangle." But Palliser considered the area bordering this region on the north and east, forming a crescent from the present location of Winnipeg northwesterly to the Rockies, quite suitable for agriculture. This zone, known as the

---

[1] The following paragraphs are drawn largely from W. A. Mackintosh, *Prairie Settlement: The Geographical Setting* (Toronto, 1934).

Park Belt, has one of the richest soils of the prairies. Two other exploration parties, sent out by the Canadian government in 1857 and 1858, were at least as optimistic as Palliser about the prospects of settlement in the fertile belt. North of the Park Belt are the timber soils, less suitable for farming.

The first settlement of note in the prairie provinces was established at the Red River near the present site of Winnipeg by Lord Selkirk, a stockholder in the Hudson's Bay Company. The company had granted Selkirk the land partially to comply with the obligation under its charter to encourage settlement and partially to establish a source of supply for the fur trade. The colony, established in 1812, was caught in the conflict between the Hudson's Bay Company and the North West Company until the two groups merged in 1821. In the years that followed, the settlers supported themselves not only by means of their planned function of supplying the company but also by developing, ungratefully, a lively private fur trade with Red River settlements in the United States in violation of company regulations.

This north-south trade at Red River is worth noting because it shows the difficulty of welding a single economic unit out of the area that is now Canada. In British Columbia, too, the trade was almost exclusively with the United States. With the disappearance of British tariff preference in the 1840's, it became more apparent that trade with the United States would play a decisive role in Canadian development. In the late 1840's the movement for union with the United States was gathering considerable momentum. One Upper Canadian businessman is quoted as having written, in 1849, that "I would willingly remain a subject of Her Majesty if I could afford it; but having built my hopes upon the continued prosperity of Canada and that foundation having failed, the reflection that I am a British subject does not afford substantial relief." [2]

Sentiments such as this led to the Reciprocity Treaty with the United States in 1854. To offset the north-south pull on trade and to strengthen the St. Lawrence and Montreal as an export route, railroads were built almost feverishly during the 1850's. At the beginning of the decade there were but 66 miles of railway in all British North America. By 1860 the Grand Trunk connected Sarnia, Montreal, and Portland and there were 2065 miles of rail

[2] Easterbrook and Aitken, p. 293.

laid down.[3] One objective, to capture for Montreal the export trade from the American West which was moving through New York, was not achieved, but certainly the cohesiveness of the St. Lawrence economy was enhanced substantially. By Confederation, however, only 213 additional miles had been constructed and there was neither a railroad to the Maritimes nor to the west beyond Sarnia.

It is the extension of the railroad network westward into the prairies that concerns us here. Especially after the explorations of the prairies in the late 1850's there had been a growing interest in linking eastern Canada with the colony on the west coast by means of a railroad. Edward W. Watkin, president of the Grand Trunk, in the early 1860's considered expansion to the Pacific as an answer to the road's financial problems. The Hudson's Bay Company owned the land between the province of Canada and British Columbia and refused to cooperate in any such venture since settlement of its territory would ruin its fur trade. But Watkin arranged for the sale of the Company to the International Finance Society, which was controlled by friends of Watkin's who were more favorably inclined toward settlement. Negotiations aimed at bringing the Hudson's Bay territory into the dominion culminated in the Manitoba Act of 1870, under the terms of which the company surrendered its charter to the dominion. British Columbia then joined the dominion in 1871.

Though the way was cleared now for extending the Grand Trunk to the Pacific, the Canadian government insisted on a route north of Lake Superior whereas the Grand Trunk was adamant in arguing that the line should run south of the lakes, through the United States. At last in 1881 a solution was found when the Canadian Pacific Railway Company, formed by a St. Paul group, struck an agreement with the Canadian government and was chartered. Considering the distance and the terrain, the construction was completed in incredibly short time: the line was finished in November 1885, and the first passenger train from Montreal to Vancouver went through the following spring.[4]

The Canadian Pacific Railway was originally to be laid through the fertile belt bordering Palliser's Triangle on the east and north. However in 1880 a botanist, John Macoun, reported to the

[3] Easterbrook and Aitken, p. 316.
[4] Easterbrook and Aitken, p. 432.

engineer-in-chief of the Canadian Pacific that the prairies were much more likely to support settlement than Palliser and the other explorers had indicated. Because of this advice and because the prairie route would be shorter, cheaper to build, and more competitive with American roads, the line was laid across Palliser's Triangle rather than around the top of it.

As a consequence of this route, it was the arid prairie rather than the fertile Park Belt which was settled first. There being no local markets of any consequence, settlement was tied to the railroads. Mackintosh has shown very clearly that the land was taken up in bands along the projected rights of way as well as along the existing rights of way but that there was considerable development of Park Belt lands in spite of the Canadian Pacific Railway location. From 1901 to 1906, however, settlement raced well ahead of the railroads and the bulk of Alberta and Saskatchewan farmland was more than ten miles from a railroad, the grain frequently being hauled thirty to fifty miles to a station or siding.[5] This was the period of the great rush into the prairies. In 1901 there were about 420,000 persons in the prairie provinces but by 1911 this population had swollen to over 1,300,000. The improved acreage meanwhile quadrupled, jumping from 5,600,000 to 23,000,000 acres.

There are several reasons why the prairie economy should have experienced its boom in the years after 1900 rather than before. We have stressed the necessity of transportation for the export staple. But that transportation was available as early as 1885, yet the growth in the following ten years was at a slow rate compared with the years after the turn of the century. One major force accelerating expansion into the prairies was the new burst of industrialization in Europe and the consequent demand for more food. The price of wheat had been falling since the 1870's and in 1893 it stood at 64¼ cents, reportedly the lowest since the fourteenth century.[6] But then it began a long rise until 1920. The American West had filled up, meanwhile, and the Canadian West was the new frontier for agricultural expansion. To encourage this expansion, the dominion government negotiated with the Canadian Pacific a reduction in export grain rates out of the prairies in return for an $11,000 per mile subsidy on a rail line

---

[5] Mackintosh, pp. 46–53.
[6] A. R. M. Lower, *Colony to Nation* (Toronto, 1946), p. 420.

Table 25.   Distribution of the labor force in Manitoba, Saskatchewan, and Alberta, 1911 and 1951 (thousands).

	Manitoba		Saskatchewan		Alberta	
	1911	1951	1911	1951	1911	1951
Agriculture	69.9	73.7	133.0	147.7	80.5	115.0
Forestry	0.3	1.5	0.5	0.7	0.7	1.7
Fishing and hunting	0.4	1.6	1.8	1.4	0.9	1.0
Mining	0.9	4.0	0.7	1.7	5.2	15.7
Manufacturing	17.7	49.0	7.6	18.7	9.6	35.6
Construction	18.6	17.1	14.2	11.6	12.2	25.7
Transportation	17.1	29.6	14.2	24.0	17.3	26.9
Trade and merchandising	23.4	47.6	14.7	34.1	14.0	46.8
Government	4.9	18.0	4.1	11.7	4.5	22.2
Personal and domestic service	15.7	17.0	11.7	16.0	10.8	20.9
Other services[a]	24.9	39.6	17.7	34.5	16.4	42.4
Total	178.1	298.5	208.5	302.1	161.2	353.9

[a] Includes employment in 1951 in "Electricity, gas and water" of 3.4 in Manitoba, 1.8 in Sakatchewan, and 3.4 in Alberta.

Source: Census of Canada, 1911, Vol. VI, Table 1; and *Census of Canada, 1951,* Vol. IV, Table 16.

to be built through Crow's Nest Pass. This amounted to about a 20 per cent reduction in freight rates.[7] The rates on settlers' effects were also substantially reduced. Shipping rates across the Atlantic fell after 1900 and more efficient grain handling methods were devised and instituted. But one of the most significant developments came with the introduction of Red Fife and Marquis wheat. The Marquis, which was perfected after Red Fife, shortened the growing period by about a week and gave a higher yield as well. In an area where early frosts frequently ruined the crop, a week's shorter growing time could mean a great deal. The new varieties of wheat, combined with the rising world price of wheat, the reduced transportation costs, the closing of the American West, and improved handling methods all contributed to the tripling of the population in the single decade of 1901–1911.

The prairie provinces in 1911

By 1911 Palliser's Triangle was settled, though but thinly in many places, and the Peace River country in northwestern Alberta was being opened up. The Park Belt was now served by

[7] A. W. Currie, *Canadian Economic Development* (Toronto, 1942), p. 179.

Table 26. Ten leading manufacturing industries in Manitoba, Saskatchewan, and Alberta by value of product and by number of employees, 1911 and 1951.

Industry	Value of product (thousands)	Industry	Number of employees
Manitoba, 1911			
Flour and grist mills	$11,660	Car repairs	4,093
Slaughtering and meat		Lumber products	1,187
packing	6,821	Brick, tile, and pottery	1,106
Car repairs	5,518	Flour and grist mills	625
Lumber products	3,080	Iron and steel products	631
Cotton bags	1,770	Printing and publishing	795
Iron and steel products	1,754	Slaughtering and meat	
Bread, biscuit, and		packing	536
confectionery	1,675	Log products	525
Liquors, malt	1,637	Clothing, men's,	
Foundry and machine		factory	516
shop products	1,133	Dyeing and cleaning	506
Printing and publishing	1,172		
Manitoba, 1951			
Slaughtering and meat		Railway rolling stock	6,065
packing	$118,519	Slaughtering and meat	
Railway rolling stock	35,949	packing	2,758
Flour mills	27,703	Clothing, men's,	
Butter and cheese	27,106	factory	2,438
Petroleum products	21,062	Clothing, women's,	
Misc. food preparations	21,000	factory	1,764
Clothing, men's,		Printing and publishing	1,626
factory	18,077	Butter and cheese	1,535
Bread and other bakery		Bread and other bakery	
products	12,999	products	1,530
Pulp and paper	12,589	Printing and book-	
Clothing, women's,		binding	1,478
factory	11,414	Furniture	1,383
		Primary iron and steel	1,000
Saskatchewan, 1911			
Flour and grist mill		Car repairs	952
products	$1,459	Log products	680
Car repairs	1,228	Brick, tile, and pottery	389
Lumber products	654	Lumber products	286
Log products	764	Printing and publishing	201
Butter and cheese	385	Flour and grist mill	
Brick, tile, and pottery	274	products	161
Printing and publishing	286	Liquors, malt	70
Liquors, malt	225	Butter and cheese	47
Aerated and mineral		Aerated and mineral	
waters	113	waters	45
Foundry and machine		Foundry and machine	
shop products	101	shop products	40

Table 26. Continued.

Industry	Value of product (thousands)	Industry	Number of employees

Saskatchewan, 1951

Industry	Value of product (thousands)	Industry	Number of employees
Petroleum products	46,903	Butter and cheese	1,218
Flour mills	44,396	Slaughtering and meat packing	1,212
Slaughtering and meat packing	39,050	Printing and publishing	1,127
Butter and cheese	27,328	Sawmills	866
Breweries	8,093	Bread and other bakery products	956
Bread and other bakery products	7,992	Petroleum products	764
Printing and publishing	5,910	Flour mills	710
Sawmills	4,497	Sash, door, and planing mills	451
Sash, door, and planing mills	2,641	Breweries	365
Feeds, stock and poultry, prepared	2,635	Carbonated beverages	275

Alberta, 1911

Industry	Value of product (thousands)	Industry	Number of employees
Slaughtering and meat packing	$4,030	Log products	1,135
Flour and grist mill products	2,526	Car repairs	1,110
Lumber products	1,880	Brick, tile, and pottery	759
Car repairs	1,492	Lumber products	717
Liquors, malt	959	Slaughtering and meat packing	488
Log products	955	Printing and publishing	341
Brick, tile, and pottery	891	Flour and grist mill products	249
Butter and cheese	557	Liquor, malt	227
Printing and publishing	395	Stone, cut	128
Awnings, tents, and sails	278	Foundry and machine shop products	101

Alberta, 1951

Industry	Value of product (thousands)	Industry	Number of employees
Slaughtering and meat packing	104,631	Sawmills	3,872
Petroleum products	62,722	Slaughtering and meat packing	2,860
Flour mills	41,615	Railway rolling stock	2,130
Butter and cheese	32,080	Sash, door, and planing mills	1,700
Sawmills	22,668	Butter and cheese	1,656
Sash, door, and planing mills	18,406	Bread and other bakery products	1,466
Bread and other bakery products	13,426	Printing and publishing	1,103
Railway rolling stock	12,796	Petroleum products	1,028
Breweries	11,485	Flour mills	799
Misc. food preparations	9,945	Clothing, men's, factory	751

Source: Census of Canada, 1911, Vol. III, Table 1; and General Review of the Manufacturing Industries of Canada, 1951, Tables 11, 12, and 13.

the railroads and the population density there had increased substantially. The census data for 1911 present the picture of an area producing a single agricultural export staple, wheat. Yet each province had its own distinguishing characteristics.

Manitoba had a smaller proportion of the work force in agriculture than did Saskatchewan or Alberta, 39 per cent as compared with 63 per cent and 53 per cent. (See Table 25.) Manitoba, the oldest of the three provinces, was the distribution and manufacturing center for the prairies, to the extent that there was any manufacturing. Ten per cent of her work force was in manufacturing, as compared with 4 per cent in Saskatchewan and 6 per cent in Alberta. In trade and merchandising Manitoba reported 13 per cent of the work force as against 7 and 9 per cent in Saskatchewan and Alberta. The manufacturing was of a sort one might expect in a young, agricultural region dependent on rail transportation. Railway shops, lumber products, brick plants, flour mills, and meat packing were the big industries in terms of employment, as Table 26 shows. At this point there was very little processing for export. The manufacturing was almost exclusively for the local market, although undoubtedly some of the flour and perhaps some of the meat was exported. Neither Manitoba nor Saskatchewan reported any significant proportion of the work force in mining, but Alberta's coal fields in the vicinity of Lethbridge had been opened up and over 3 per cent of her work force was reported in mining.

But of course the great concentration was on wheat. In Manitoba 46 per cent of the improved land (60 per cent of the land in field crops) was devoted to wheat; in Saskatchewan about 44 per cent and in Alberta nearly 38 per cent of the improved land was in wheat. Oats accounted for about half as much acreage as wheat for the prairie provinces as a whole, the proportion being a bit less than one-half in Manitoba and more than one-half in Alberta. Alberta had a much more balanced agriculture, for cattle, hogs, and sheep were all more important, relative to wheat, in that province than in the other two. Already it was becoming apparent that the brown prairie soil of southern Alberta was better suited to ranching than to wheat production.

Although for the other regions in Canada 1911 and 1951 may be useful points at which to stop to note the pattern of economic development, this is not so true of the prairie provinces. In 1911 the area was in the midst of its period of most rapid agricultural growth and consequently we should look at the region in 1921 to see how the economy had been shaped by World War I and the end of its greatest expansion. By 1921 the population of the three provinces stood at just under 2,000,000 compared with only 400,000 in 1901 and 1,300,000 in 1911. The area in occupied farms increased even faster than the population, rising from 15,400,000 acres in 1901 to nearly 88,000,000 acres in 1921. Wheat acreage accounted for about the same proportion of the total improved land in the region in 1921 as in 1911, this proportion having dropped in Manitoba but having increased in Saskatchewan and Alberta. The make-up of agriculture as between grains and livestock remained reasonably stable in Saskatchewan between 1911 and 1921. In Manitoba, however, there was a definite substitution of feed grains for wheat as the wheat acreage declined even in absolute terms. Meanwhile the number of hogs, horses, and especially sheep and cattle increased substantially relative to improved acreage in that province. But livestock production was still not so important relative to the grain acreage or to total improved acreage as in Alberta.

The prairie provinces in 1951: the new export economy

By 1951 the prairie economy had felt the impact of two developments of immense significance. First, the region had gone through the painful depression years, years which demonstrated the vulnerability of a one-crop economy to the vicissitudes of markets and weather. By the mid-1920's, the price of wheat stood at about one-half the level of 1917–1920. But in the period 1925–1929 there was considerable recovery of the price and the prairie population rose substantially again. It was after 1928 that the disastrous decline in the wheat economy began. Saskatchewan, being the province most dependent on wheat, saw the estimated net income from wheat sold off the farms drop from $218,000,000 in 1928 to $42,000,000 in 1933 and in 1937 to a dismal low of only $18,000,-000, about 8 per cent of the 1928 figure.[8] The price of cattle fell in Saskatchewan from $53.00 per head in 1928 to $18.00 in 1934.[9] The need for diversification of the agriculture of the prairies was apparent and, with the advent of World War II, controls were

[8] Easterbrook and Aitken, p. 493.
[9] G. E. Britnell, *The Wheat Economy* (Toronto, 1939), p. 72.

Table 27. Percentage of gross agricultural revenue derived from wheat in
Manitoba, Saskatchewan, and Alberta, 1924–1928 and 1951.

Period	Manitoba	Saskatchewan	Alberta
1924–1928 average	33	64	48
1951	32	78	49

Source: DBS, *Canada Year Book, 1930;* and DBS, *Canada Year Book, 1954.*

instituted to prevent the return of the wheat boom and bust.
During the war there was a marked shift away from wheat and
toward livestock. But by 1951 wheat was clearly again king, as
Table 27 shows.[10]

In Saskatchewan, the "wheat province," the wheat acreage in
1951 was about 18 per cent greater than in 1924–1928 yet cattle
and hog numbers had both declined slightly. The percentage of
Saskatchewan's field crop acreage which was devoted to wheat was
actually greater in 1951 than in 1924–1928, having risen from 67
per cent to 71 per cent. In Manitoba the wheat acreage was
virtually the same in 1951 as in 1924–1928, both in absolute terms
and as a percentage of total field crop acreage. Cattle and hog
numbers were also nearly unchanged from 1924–1928, although
there had been a marked increase in poultry production. In short,
agriculture in Manitoba and Saskatchewan was no more diversified
in 1951 than in 1924–1928. In Alberta, on the other hand, there
was at least a slight move out of wheat and into livestock over
the period, for wheat acreage as a percentage of all field crop
acreage fell from 57 per cent to 49 per cent and cattle and hog
numbers increased substantially.[11]

[10] It is true that 1951 was a very good wheat year. Canadian production had
reached 553,000,000 bushels as compared with 366,000,000 for the 1945–1949
average. Yet the 1951 production in the prairies was only slightly above the
1951–1955 average (530,000,000 bushels as compared with the 1951–1955 average of 523,000,000).

[11] This conclusion seems in conflict with the statement by Easterbrook and
Aitken to the effect that "it was clear that in the process of adjustment [to
wartime and then postwar conditions] the dependence of the economy on this
staple had been permanently reduced. Governmental policies directed to the
marketing of wheat through international negotiations now have stability as
their primary objective. Export sales of wheat no longer determine the state of
the economy even though their contribution to the national income is still a
matter of national concern" (p. 495). The contribution of wheat to the national
income, if still a matter of national concern, would certainly seem to be a matter of concern, too, to the region specializing in its production. Government

Thus the depression of the 1930's seems not to have affected the product structure of prairie agriculture significantly except in Alberta. The effect of the depression and the subsequent recovery of the prairie economy was especially great insofar as the work force engaged in agriculture is concerned. Between 1921 and 1951 the agricultural work force dropped in Manitoba from 87,000 to 74,000 and in Saskatchewan from 174,000 to 148,000, while in Alberta it climbed slightly from 114,000 to 115,000. For the three provinces the agricultural work force had fallen by about 10 per cent while the total work force in the region had increased by about 36 per cent. Wheat may have been just as important to prairie agriculture in 1951 as in the 1920's, but agriculture was no longer so important to the total region's economy as before.

It seems not to have been the mineral development, however, which altered the industrial distribution of the work force in the region, or even in Alberta, where oil production was concentrated. Between 1911 and 1951, our two major bench-mark years, the proportion of the work force engaged in agriculture in the three provinces dropped substantially, from 52 per cent to 35 per cent for the three provinces combined. But the sectors which expanded employment most in absolute terms were manufacturing, trade and merchandising, and transportation, not mineral extraction. "Mining, quarrying, and oil wells" showed an increase of only 15,000 in these forty years while the total work force increased by 406,000.

If we focus only on the decade 1941–1951, however, we find that the increase of 5500 workers in mining, quarrying, and oil wells accounted for nearly half of the total increase (12,100) in the work force in the region in that period. Nevertheless these 5500 workers constituted but 0.5 per cent of the total work force. In Alberta, where the oil boom had been under way for four years, the mining, quarrying, and oil well industry accounted for 4.4 per cent of the total work force in 1951. The part of the work force in mineral extraction for the three provinces combined was 2.1 per cent.

Because of the small number of persons involved in mining, quarrying, and oil wells, then, it is tempting to conclude that the

---

policies might minimize instability of wheat revenues but this is not the same thing as reducing prairie agriculture's dependence on wheat revenues.

oil boom in Alberta and the rest of the prairie region is but a midget when compared with the giant wheat boom of 1900–1920.

Wheat boom and oil boom in Alberta

We can examine this proposition more carefully by studying Alberta, where the oil development activity has been concentrated. Between 1941 and 1951, Alberta's population increased by 18 per cent, compared with 6 per cent in Manitoba and an 8 per cent decrease in Saskatchewan. By 1951 only 5800 persons in Alberta were engaged in the production of natural gas and crude oil; and another 2900 were reported in oil prospecting, giving a total of 8700 persons. In contrast, in 1911 over 80,000 were reported in agriculture in Alberta and by 1921 this number had swollen to 114,000. Even if one takes into account the probability that there were more construction workers on oil projects per hundred production workers in 1951 than there were in agriculture in 1911 or 1921, the contrast is still marked. In 1951 there were but 26,000 construction workers in all of Alberta. Thus, in terms of the work force directly involved, the oil boom in Alberta was far less significant than was the wheat boom earlier in the century.

Even after allowing for the indirect employment effects of the oil boom on tertiary production, the developments since 1947 have had surprisingly little impact, considering all the publicity given the oil and gas finds in Alberta. Tertiary employment is greater now relative to all other employment than in the years of the wheat boom. An examination of the 1911 and 1951 census data shows that in the earlier year about 32.5 per cent of the work force in Alberta was engaged in three sectors: service, trade, and transportation and communication. In 1951 this percentage stood at nearly 41. This implies that, for a given increase in the work force exclusive of these three sectors, the increase in the number of persons employed in these sectors would have been nearly half again as great in 1951 as in 1911. Nonetheless, with about one-tenth as many persons engaged directly in oil production in 1951 as were in agriculture in 1911, even allowing for the greater tertiary employment multiplier, which is operative today, the employment effect of the post World War II oil boom is minor when compared with the wheat boom.

The above version of the employment multiplier omits the employment effects in the manufacturing sector, however. Here, three separate effects must be distinguished. Manufacturing employment may rise because output of consumer goods is increased due to the expansion of the local market; or it may rise because the output of the new primary industry is processed locally; or it may rise because new factories spring up to supply the growing sector with some of its input requirements. At any one point in time, supposedly a given increase in income earned in one primary industry will cause an expansion of manufacturing output for the local market just as large as would an equal increase in income earned in another primary industry. Hence this portion of the employment multiplier should be about the same for agriculture as for oil, *ceteris paribus*. The employment in those manufacturing industries supplying the new primary producers in the present case is probably negligible. The more relevant question for our purposes, then, is whether employment in the extraction stage relative to employment in the processing stage is significantly larger in the case of crude petroleum and natural gas than in the case of agricultural output.

With respect to the ratio for crude petroleum and natural gas, the industry in Alberta is still too immature to argue this point with complete confidence. However a look at the data for Texas is illuminating, since in terms of the economic structure of the area and its distance from markets Texas is very roughly comparable with Alberta. (The availability of water transportation, however, puts Texas closer to markets cost-wise than Alberta for many products.) In Alberta, the 1951 census indicates that there were about four workers in the production of (and prospecting for) crude oil and natural gas for every worker in "petroleum refining and products." One would expect this ratio to fall precipitously as the province's petroleum complex matures. But the Texas data, to the extent that they are relevant, suggest that the fall may not be so great. There the related industries have had a longer time to develop and yet the 1954 United States *Census of Manufactures* indicates that in Texas there were about 3.4 persons in the production of crude oil and natural gas for every worker in the manufacture of petroleum products. Even if we consider the entire chemical products industry in Texas to be petroleum-based, which it is not, the ratio drops only to about 1.8. If we say that Alberta's prospects for the development of related industries are roughly indicated by the Texas experience, it seems reasonably certain that the oil boom will not bring in its wake a great wave of jobs in the processing of petroleum and gas. In view of Texas' location more proximate to markets than Alberta's, the extraction to processing employment ratio in Texas is probably higher than can be expected for Alberta.

That the effect of the oil boom on the manufacturing sectors of the prairie provinces is limited can be seen in Table 26. In Alberta in 1951 petroleum products ranked but eighth and in Saskatchewan only sixth in terms of employment. But in terms of the gross value of product this industry ranked first in Saskatchewan, second in Alberta, and fifth in Manitoba. The industry does well enough in Manitoba, which has a large manufacturing sector than the other two provinces, but no crude production. Thus, petroleum refining is market-oriented to a considerable degree. Consequently, one can argue that the importance of petroleum products in Alberta and Saskatchewan is due at least in part to the presence of the markets rather than the presence of the raw materials.[12] Again, the relatively minor effect of crude oil resources on local manufacturing is apparent.

Unfortunately work force data by province are not sufficiently detailed to permit an intensive examination of the make-up of the work force in Alberta beyond 1951.[13] But it is enlightening to note at least the change in the employment in crude petroleum and natural gas extraction, 1951–1955, as compared with the change in output of that industry and the change in the employment in petroleum products. Employment in crude petroleum and natural gas production, plus contract drilling for fuels, increased only from 7087 to 7515, or by about 6 per cent. Output of crude,

[12] In 1941, 683 persons in Alberta reported themselves as occupied in the manufacture of petroleum products. By 1951 this figure had risen to 2114, an increase of about 210 per cent. The output of crude had increased in Alberta over the same period from 9,900,000 barrels to 45,900,000 barrels, an increase of about 360 per cent. The contrast in these two percentages offers further support for the above argument. An estimate of the employment in petroleum products and refining which can be considered as dependent on the local market can be constructed by assuming that if Alberta were self-sufficient in petroleum products she would have the same percentage of her work force in this industry as the country as a whole. By this measure, 1261 of the 2114 workers in this industry in Alberta could be considered as producing for export from the province, leaving about 850 as the number producing for the local market.

[13] The DBS publication, *Annual Review of Employment and Payrolls*, falls short of providing the necessary detail by industry and by province.

meanwhile, increased by about 145 per cent and the output of natural gas nearly doubled. Employment in Alberta's petroleum products industry increased from 1028 to 1803 persons, leaving the ratio of employment in extraction to employment in processing at better than four to one.[14] To put it differently, employment in drilling, extracting, and manufacturing petroleum products has increased only from about 8100 to 9300 persons, a 15 per cent increase, while crude oil production increased by 145 per cent.

We can now put together a very crude approximation of an employment multiplier. For every 100 persons in the work force we can expect about 42 workers in the tertiary sector[15] and another 33 workers in petroleum products, if we put the probable long-term ratio of employment in extraction to employment in processing at three to one, which ratio is probably too low. The manufacturing industries producing for the local market will also expand employment as the local market grows. In 1951 in Alberta there was 1 person in manufacturing for every 10 persons in the total work force. It is estimated that about 2800 of the total

[14] These data indicate for 1951 a ratio of nearly seven to one, in contrast with the four to one ratio mentioned earlier as taken from 1951 census data. The seven to one ratio is based on data from three annual DBS reports, *The Crude Petroleum and Natural Gas Industry*, *The Petroleum Products Industry* and *Contract Drilling in the Mining Industry*. The employment data in these reports are "average employment" figures whereas the census data are "labor force" figures. Furthermore the census includes an important category, "oil prospecting," which is not identified as such in any of the DBS annual industry reports. To confuse matters further, the DBS category, "Contract Drilling in the Mining Industry," has no counterpart in the census industry classification. Among the other causes of the discrepancy are the following: (1) The census data include the unemployed in the industry's labor force whereas the DBS reports show only "average employment"; and (2) the DBS reports on crude petroleum and natural gas cover only companies with operating wells. Considerable difference in coverage also causes a marked difference between the census and the DBS industry reports on employment in petroleum products. The 1951 census reports 2114 persons in Alberta's "petroleum refining and products" industry whereas the DBS *Petroleum Products Industry* for 1951 reports employment of but 1028 persons. We will emphasize the 1951 census figures since they are explicitly designed to account for the industrial distribution of the work force.

[15] Defined here to include public utilities; finance, insurance, and real estate; trade; transportation, communication, and storage; and service. For purposes of computing the employment multiplier, however, we have omitted from the service employment figures those persons in the federal defense services, the reasoning being that this is essentially an exported service, the demand for which would not grow with the local market.

manufacturing employment of 35,635 were producing for export to other provinces, however.[16] Manufacturing for the local market appears to account for about 9 per cent of the work force. This set of assumptions yields an estimated multiplier of 2.71, meaning that every 100 jobs in oil and gas extraction generates 171 jobs in other sectors of the economy.[17]

This estimate is probably a bit too high. Daly estimated that, in thirteen areas of England, for each new job in "unimpeded" (that is, not tied to markets) industries, 1.042 new jobs were created in the "localized" industries.[18] The multiplier was computed by regressing increases in employment in the localized industries, 1921–1931, on increases in employment in the unimpeded industries for the thirteen areas. Daly notes (p. 250) that his classification of the industries yields a conservative multiplier. One might ask, too, whether the changes in employment in the two groups of industries between 1921 and 1931 might have been

[16] The only two important manufacturing industries which might have produced for export from the province in 1951 were slaughtering and meat packing and petroleum refining and products. The employment effect of the latter has already been discussed, leaving just slaughtering and meat packing to concern us. To arrive at a crude estimate of the number of workers in this industry which might be considered as producing for export, the national ratio of employment in the industry to total work force was applied to the Alberta work force, giving an estimate of the persons in the industry who were producing for the local market. The residual employment was considered to be producing for export. Employment in sawmills was presumed to be dependent on the local market exclusively, as was employment in the railroad and rolling stock equipment industry. In the former case it was presumed that the geographic location of Alberta and the ample supplies of lumber in the neighboring provinces prohibited exportation of sawmill products in any significant volume. In the latter case, Alberta has less than its proportionate share of employment in railroad and rolling stock equipment, and so again it was presumed that the employment could be considered as oriented toward the provincial, rather than the national, economy.

[17] The employment multiplier is defined here and in the paragraphs which follow as the number of jobs created in the economy as a whole per job in the sector in which employment was initially increased. If x = the increase in employment in industries other than oil and gas extraction per person employed in that industry, then

$$x = 0.33 + 0.42 (x + 1) + 0.09 (x + 1) = 1.71$$

and the multiplier is $1 + x$, or 2.71. This method for estimating the multiplier, simple though it is, seems distinctly preferable to any method based on time series because adequate employment data are available only for census years in Alberta.

[18] M. C. Daly, "An Approximation to a Geographic Multiplier," *EJ*, 50:248–258 (June-September 1940).

warped by the business cycle to give a higher multiplier than one would expect for a more nearly normal period because of the depression shift of workers into the tertiary sector.

Hildebrand and Mace computed an employment multiplier for Los Angeles county, 1940–1947, of 2.248.[19] This estimate was based on monthly data for 1940–41 and 1946–47. Moore and Petersen estimated employment multipliers for Utah by means of the interindustry model for the state in 1947.[20] They did not distinguish between "export" industries and industries producing for the local market. Instead, they computed for each sector the employment response in the state as a whole to an increase of demand, in the given sector, great enough to increase that sector's employment by one man-year. This interindustry approach yielded multipliers ranging from 1.75 for "utilities, trade and services" to 5.40 for nonferrous metals. The multipliers for the other four sectors ranged only from 2.13 to 3.18. The multiplier for nonferrous metals is so much larger than the others because that industry is very capital-intensive whereas its major supplier, copper mining, is very labor-intensive, judging from the input coefficients.[21]

Isard and Kuenne, in studying the impact of new steel producing facilities on a region, built up an employment multiplier of about 20.[22] This astronomical figure is explained in large part by the attraction of steel-fabricating industries to steel mills. The authors estimated that for each worker in basic steel there would be 6.7 workers in steel fabrication. Thus the multiplier would be 7.7 even before allowing for expansion of those industries supplying inputs to the expanding industries or of those industries producing consumer goods and services for the residents of the region. One reason, then, for the huge difference between the multiplier coming out of the Isard-Kuenne study and that computed above for Alberta is that each new job in oil and gas production in Alberta we estimate to generate about 0.33 jobs in

[19] G. H. Hildebrand and Arthur Mace, Jr., "The Employment Multiplier in an Expanding Industrial Market: Los Angeles County, 1940–47," *RES*, 32:241–249 (August 1950).

[20] F. T. Moore and J. W. Petersen, "Regional Analysis: An Interindustry Model of Utah," *RES*, 37:368–383 (November 1955).

[21] Moore and Petersen, Table I (following p. 372).

[22] Walter Isard and R. E. Kuenne, "The Impact of Steel upon the Greater New York-Philadelphia Industrial Region," *RES*, 35:289–301 (November 1953).

processing, whereas Isard and Kuenne would anticipate that each new person employed in steel production gives rise to 6.7 jobs in processing. Once one allows for the induced effects of this new direct employment, the difference in the final multiplier becomes understandable.

For obvious reasons the Moore-Petersen study of Utah provides a better check on our Alberta employment multiplier than do any of the other studies mentioned. Two of the sectors for which Moore and Petersen computed employment multipliers are metallic and other mining, and coal and coke. For these two sectors the multipliers were 2.88 and 3.18. Considering that these two industries are, like Alberta's oil and gas producing industry, regional export industries in an area which imports the bulk of its manufactured goods, the multiplier of 2.71 we have computed for Alberta's oil and gas industry seems reasonable.

In contrast with this multiplier, the employment multiplier for agriculture in Alberta during the wheat boom was only about 1.4.[23] Even now the employment multiplier for agriculture in Alberta is considerably below that for oil and gas since employment in the processing of agricultural products for export is so small. In 1951 there appeared to be only about 7 persons in the entire food and beverages industry per 100 workers in agriculture, as compared with the rough long-term ratio of 33 to 100 in oil and gas.

To summarize the employment effect of the oil and gas boom as compared with the wheat boom in Alberta, we have seen that, although the employment multiplier seems to be substantially larger in the case of oil and gas than in the case of agriculture, the number of workers directly engaged in agriculture in Alberta between 1900 and 1920 was so very large as compared with the number of oil workers that the population effect of the latter, even after allowing for the much larger multiplier, is distinctly minor. In 1951, there were 115,000 persons reported employed in agriculture in Alberta but only 5800 persons in oil and gas produc-

[23] The 1911 census reports 38.4 persons out of every 100 in the work force were in those industries clearly producing for the local economy and not for export. This includes the entire manufacturing employment, since none of the industries, with the exception of brick and clay products, reported as employing a larger proportion of the provincial work force than was true for the country as a whole. This was taken as prima facie evidence that these industries were on an import basis. Employment in brick and clay products exceeded the national ratio but slightly and, since the number of workers involved was small, this case was ignored.

tion plus another 2900 in oil prospecting. But with a multiplier of 2.71 operating, these 8700 jobs in oil and gas production and prospecting are responsible for almost 15,000 additional jobs. In other words, the total work force in Alberta must be about 23,700 larger than it would have been in the absence of oil and gas. This figure is to be contrasted with a total work force in 1951 of about 354,000. In short, considerably less than 10 per cent of the work force in Alberta seems to be dependent either directly or indirectly on oil and gas.

If such a small proportion of the work force is involved in this new boom, why has it attracted so very much attention? The pelf rather than the people has caused the uproar. The capital and the profits are considerably greater in this boom than in the wheat boom. One need look only at the gross value of product per worker in agriculture and oil and gas production for a clue to this distinction. In the three years 1950–1952, gross farm income (that is, before deduction of expenses) per person employed in agriculture in Alberta averaged a little under $4900 if production for inventory is included as income, $4300 if it is not.[24] By contrast, crude petroleum production in Alberta in 1951 was valued at just under $40,000 per worker, or more than eight times as much as in agriculture. By 1956 this crude petroleum figure had passed $100,000 per worker. The difference between the two industries can be expressed in yet another way: in 1956 the crude petroleum industry produced a gross value of product of $356,000,000 with 3500 workers in Alberta while the agriculture in the province produced $527,000,000 in gross value product with between 110,000 and 115,000 workers. So agriculture used about thirty times as many workers to produce about half again as much gross value of product as did crude petroleum.

In terms of the gross value of product involved, crude petroleum production in 1956 was about two-thirds as large an industry as was agriculture in the province. What can we say about what happened to this huge amount of money from the crude oil

[24] We have averaged three years here rather than used 1951 alone because of the variation in the gross income and the inventory accumulation from year to year. In 1951 gross income was $631,000,000 as compared with but $432,000,000 in 1950, for example, but in 1951 the gross income included $114,-000,000 increase in inventory as contrasted with but a $24,000,000 increase in in 1950. See DBS, *Quarterly Bulletin of Agricultural Statistics*, January-March 1953, p. 13.

industry? Of the $356,000,000 gross value, about $8,000,000 was paid out for fuel and electricity and process supplies and another $18,400,000 was paid out as wages and salaries. This leaves about $329,000,000, or more than 92 per cent of the gross value, to cover depreciation profits and the other expenses, primarily royalties.[25] Net income to farm operators (from farming operations) in Alberta in 1956 amounted to $345,000,000 before deduction of rental payments or depreciation. Total income to the rentier and entrepreneurial elements in the two industries, then, is about the same.

Unfortunately the provincial data on the two industries do not permit any but the most casual conclusions about the proportion of the rentier and entrepreneurial income paid to nonresidents in the two industries. There would surely be little opposition, though, to the conclusion that a substantially higher proportion of the crude petroleum industry's royalties and profits move out of the province than is the case with agriculture. Indeed, the publicity given Alberta oil and gas development in the rest of Canada and in the United States is in itself evidence of the interest of nonresident firms and individuals in this boom.

We can now make some summary observations about the effect of the oil and gas discoveries on the economy of Alberta as contrasted with the years of really great population growth preceding World War I. First, the "oil era," if we can call it that, seems likely to have relatively little effect on the population of the province. Not only is there but a small number of workers engaged in oil and gas prospecting and production, but the employment multiplier is low, as compared with regions closer to markets, because (1) there is likely to be relatively little processing of petroleum in the province and (2) the processing of petroleum has a low labor-output ratio anyway. Second, even though this em-

---

[25] The Alberta government receives a sizable piece of this. The province in fiscal 1956 estimated its revenue from rentals, fees, royalties, and so forth on petroleum *and* natural gas to be $36,000,000 and from the sale of crown leases to be $26,000,000. The latter amount cannot be viewed as a cost of production for the industry in fiscal 1956 because it is an outlay to be amortized over a period of years. These two sources of income covered more than one-third of the provincial government's estimated fiscal 1956 expenditures of $180,000,000. Province of Alberta, *Estimates of Revenue and Amounts to Be Voted for the Public Service of Alberta for the Fiscal Year April 1st, 1955, to March 31st, 1956* (Edmonton 1955), pp. 3, 12.

ployment multiplier is low as compared with other industries or with the petroleum industry in other regions, it is still substantially higher than for the province's agriculture. The processing of locally produced agricultural output for export is decidedly minor. Third, the economic glamour of the oil and gas discoveries stems primarily from the amount of money involved rather than the number of people. Gross value of product per worker in crude petroleum production is about twenty times as great as in the province's agriculture. The rentier income and entrepreneurial profits in crude petroleum are of the same magnitude as in agriculture and they are growing rapidly. Yet the province may not feel much impact from this new source of income within its boundaries, because of the probably high proportion of entrepreneurial profits accruing to nonresidents.

It is fairly clear, then, that the local repercussions of the petroleum and gas development are likely to be distinctly limited. There may be a great deal of capital involved, but a substantially smaller percentage of it probably stays in the province than in the case of the agricultural sector.

The discussion above has been based on the Alberta experience exclusively but the conclusions about the effect on employment and income probably can be extended to Saskatchewan and Manitoba, where oil and gas production has developed largely since 1950.[26]

In general, the prairie provinces' manufacturing complex has remained that of an area which produces primarily for the local market. But there were some exceptions. In Manitoba, pulp and paper production had appeared among the top ten industries by gross value of product, obviously an export industry. Slaughtering and meat packing, flour mills, and butter and cheese production in Manitoba were apparently exporting part of their output. In Saskatchewan, the manufacturing sector had the same configuration as in Alberta. Despite the new mineral discoveries, the prairies seem destined to remain essentially agricultural.

[26] In 1950, Manitoba reported no crude oil production but in 1951 about 11,000 barrels were produced and, in 1956, 5,787,000 barrels. In Saskatchewan output rose from just over 1,000,000 barrels in 1950 to more than 21,000,000 barrels in 1956. Over the same period Alberta's production rose from 27,500,000 barrels to 144,000,000. DBS, *The Crude Petroleum and Natural Gas Industry,* 1956.

BRITISH COLUMBIA

The modern history of British Columbia really began in 1778 when the intrepid Captain James Cook, who had already circled the globe twice, dropped anchor in Nootka Sound on the west coast of Vancouver Island in the course of searching for a north-west passage.[27] The Indians displayed a great variety of furs and the value of these, especially the sea otter fur, became apparent when Cook's men, after their leader's death in the Hawaiian Islands, sold the furs in Macao on their way back to England. One would have expected the fur trade in the new area to come into the hands of the British immediately, in view of their interest in the fur trade in the rest of the continent. In fact, however, British interests were slow to develop the trade partially because of trouble with Spain but probably too because trade with other parts of the world was more attractive. The East India Company had monopoly rights to the British Pacific trade but chose to neglect it. Besides, Napoleon so commanded the attention of the British as to slow the growth of the North Pacific trade.

Meanwhile in 1793 the famous Alexander Mackenzie reached the Pacific via the overland route for the North West Company, but the firm chose not to develop the area. In 1804–05, however, the Lewis and Clark expedition pushed from St. Louis to the mouth of the Columbia, and the fear that the fur trade of the Pacific might go to the Americans forced the North West Company into action. Simon Fraser was sent into New Caledonia to make the claim of the North West Company stick. Later David Thompson also explored the area. Fraser did not reach the mouth of the Columbia, and Thompson reached it shortly after John Jacob Astor's Pacific Fur Company men had begun construction of a fort. Competition between the North West Company and the Pacific Fur Company in the area was intense but the North West Company gained the upper hand and in 1813 bought out the American firm. In 1821, when the North West Company was in turn merged into the Hudson's Bay Company, the latter was trading on the Pacific coast from Alaska to California. But the

---

[27] Much of the material which follows is based upon Easterbrook and Aitken; "The Period of Exploration," by T. G. Marquis; and "Colonial History, 1849–71," by R. E. Gosnell, in *The Pacific Province*, Vol. XXI of *Canada and Its Provinces*, ed. Adam Shortt and Arthur G. Doughty (Toronto, 1914); and Hubert Howe Bancroft, *History of British Columbia* (San Francisco, 1887).

company did not have a monopoly in the Oregon Country — the Americans were at a disadvantage because their trading goods were inferior, but as settlers they caused the company great discomfort. In the early 1840's the "54–40 or Fight" cry rose in the United States and in 1846 the southern boundary of Canada on the west coast was put at 49 degrees latitude.

By the early 1850's the rate of migration into Oregon and California had made it abundantly clear to the Hudson's Bay Company that British Columbia would have to be colonized in order to keep it from falling eventually to the Americans. The Hudson's Bay Company had a long history of discouraging colonization since, as one writer put it, "it was becoming a pretty well established fact that foxes, beavers and native hunters do not dwell long in apple orchards." [28] The company faced then two painfully unattractive prospects: colonize and see the fur trade ruined, or not colonize and lose the land to immigrants from the south. Apparently operating on the hypothesis that colonization of some order of magnitude was inevitable, the company chose to sponsor the colonization itself and so control it. The company already held exclusive rights to traffic with the natives in the region. It applied for and in 1849 was granted title to Vancouver Island for purposes of colonization. The grant committed the company to apply 90 per cent of their returns from the sale of the land and minerals to public improvement. But the company made only a gesture toward colonization of the island, and in 1854 there were only about 450 settlers on the island and not more than 500 acres were cultivated. In 1857 a Select Committee of the House of Commons recommended compliance with Canada's request that areas suitable for settlement be ceded to her. So Vancouver Island passed from the hands of the Hudson's Bay Company in 1858 but the company retained exclusive trading rights. The Hudson's Bay Company now considered the possibility of an influx of settlers to be quite unlikely, and the 1858 agreement left the company with the profitable trade but without the bothersome responsibilities of government. The 1858 agreement spelled out the boundaries of British Columbia nearly as they stand today, with Vancouver Island being excluded.

The great initial influx of settlers into British Columbia occurred in 1858 when the news of gold on the Fraser, Thompson,

[28] Bancroft, p. 206.

and Columbia attracted immigrants by the thousands. Some gold had apparently been mined as early as 1852 but the exaggerated reports of gold along the Thompson in 1857 seem to have been directly responsible for the rush of 1858.[29] But the major excitement was transferred immediately to the Fraser. Then in 1860, 1861, and 1862 the mining spread into the Cariboo country, roughly the area between the headwaters of the Fraser and its tributary the Thompson. Gold mining remained the basis of the economy through the 1860's and 1870's. Coal mining, too, was well established at Nanaimo on Vancouver Island by the 1870's.

British Columbia in 1881

British Columbia was united with Canada in 1871 and was not included in the census of Canada for 1871. A census of the colony in 1870 gives a crude idea, however, of the make-up of the economy for there were some 2300 men in mining, 1800 in agriculture, 1300 in trade, and but 400 in manufacturing.[30] Data on exports from the province are available for 1872 and these show unmistakably the importance of the export staple. "Products of the Mine" accounted for $1,389,585 worth of exports, 75 per cent of the total exports of the province. The fisheries exported about $38,000 worth of goods, and animals and animal products accounted for another $215,000.[31] About $214,000 worth of forest products were also exported.

By 1881 mining was of considerably less importance in the export picture, accounting now for just under 60 per cent of the total. The big increase had occurred in the export of fisheries products, which were more than ten times as great in 1881 as a decade earlier. Nor was 1881 a unique year for the British Columbia fisheries. In 1882 and 1883 and again in 1888, fisheries products exports exceeded $1,000,000, compared with $400,000 in 1881. The exports of forest products were rising slowly but 1881 was an abnormally low export year for this sector. The ex-

[29] Bancroft, pp. 348 ff.

[30] *Census of Canada, 1870–71,* Vol. IV, p. 377.

[31] The forestry sector was an important one at an early point in the history of British Columbia not only because of the export market but also because of the lumber needs of the mining towns. This source of demand for lumber was especially great after shaft mining developed in the Kootenay region, generating a need for pit props. See H. A. Innis, *Settlement and the Mining Frontier* (Toronto, 1936), especially chs. v-vi.

ports of animals and animal products had increased about 50 per cent. In short, the exports from the mines had done little better than hold their own over the period in absolute terms, while the exports of fisheries products and animal products were rising rapidly.[32]

In 1881 there were between 2600 and 2800 persons engaged in each of the main export industries — mining, fishing, and agriculture. Agriculture had been altered a bit since the days when its sole function was to serve the mining camps, and it now produced a substantial amount of livestock. By 1881, too, the manufacturing sector had grown to the point where nearly 2900 persons were reported as employed in industrial establishments. Nearly half of these were reported in the "preserved articles of food" industry, mostly fisheries products.[33] About 400 more persons were working in the sawmills and the remainder were scattered among the various types of small scale manufacturing which one expects to find in a new economy, such as boots and shoes, foundries, carpentering, blacksmithing, flour and grist mills, and so on. Between 1870 and 1881, then, we find the kind of change in the structure of the economy which has been apparent in some of the other regions: a relative shift from the export staple which was the original cause for the region's growth, accompanied by the development of a new export staple and the emergence of a manufacturing sector of some importance.

British Columbia in 1911

Between 1881 and 1911 the population of British Columbia jumped nearly 700 per cent, from 50,000 to 392,000, while the country as a whole grew by about 67 per cent. This was not as rapid an expansion as that experienced in the prairies, but it is impressive nonetheless. What caused this rapid growth?

First, the completion of the transcontinental railroad and the expansion of the prairies were themselves partly responsible, for British Columbia served as a gateway through which some of the trade of the prairies passed. In 1911 more than 14 per cent of the work force in the province was engaged in transportation as compared with but 10 per cent for all of Canada. But British

[32] Economic Council of British Columbia, *Statistics of Industry in British Columbia, 1871 to 1934* (Victoria, 1935), Table T-1 to T-8 (not paged).
[33] See Bancroft, p. 748.

Columbia was still relying primarily on the extractive industries. Of the extractive industries, lumbering apparently expanded the most. The 1881 and 1911 occupational data in the Census are not comparable, but the information on manufacturing establishments provides some evidence. In 1881 there were but 27 sawmills reported but by 1911 there were 224 firms indicated in "log products." Employment in these firms had risen from 393 to nearly 15,400.[34] Despite the fact that there were five times as

Table 28. Ten leading industries in British Columbia by value of products and by number of employees, 1881, 1911, and 1951.

Industry	Value of product (thousands)	Industry	Number of employees
	1881		
Preserved articles of food	$592	Preserved articles of food	1,449
Sawmills	550	Sawmills	398
Fittings and foundry working	183	Boots and shoes	112
Flour and grist mills	179	Dressmaking and millinery	95
Boots and shoes	151	Fittings and foundry working	70
Carpenters and joiners	115	Carpenters and joiners	78
Bakeries of all sorts	113	Tailors and clothiers	62
Sash, door, and blind factories	88	Blacksmithing	60
Tailors and clothiers	87	Bakeries of all sorts	44
Opium factory	79	Flour and grist mills	47
Blacksmithing	70	Printing offices	41
	1911		
Log products	19,753	Log products	15,379
Smelting	11,715	Fish, preserved	5,788
Fish, preserved	4,469	Lumber products	1,862
Lumber products	3,827	Smelting	1,282
Foundry and machine shop products	2,100	Car repairs	1,148
Car repairs	1,801	Foundry and machine shop products	881
Liquors, malt	1,519	Housebuilding	464
Electric light and power	1,302	Ships and ship repairs	443
Coke	1,302	Brick, tile, and pottery	517
Bread, biscuits, and confectionery	1,260	Bread, biscuits, and confectionery	387

[34] "Log products" in the 1911 census apparently included little else than sawmills since "lumber products" constituted a separate industry. It seems apparent that even after any conceivable adjustments in the data to assure comparability, one would still find employment in the industry in 1911 being roughly thirty times as great as in 1881.

Table 28. Continued.

Industry	Value of product (thousands)	Industry	Number of employees
		1951	
Sawmills	347,147	Sawmills	29,462
Nonferrous metal smelting and refining	215,329[a]	Nonferrous metal smelting and refining	4,849[a]
Pulp and paper	141,503	Fish processing	4,168
Fish processing	84,122	Pulp and paper	5,778
Slaughtering and meat packing	59,081	Shipbuilding	3,484
Veneers and plywood	43,202	Veneers and plywood	3,416
Petroleum products	41,903	Printing and publishing	2,752
Sash, door, and planing mills	41,331	Sash, door, and planing mills	2,770
Miscellaneous food preparation	36,614	Bread and bakery products	2,621
Fertilizers	30,810	Fruit and vegetable preparations	2,355

[a] Because there are fewer than four establishments in this industry, data for the province are not published in the DBS, *General Review of Manufacturing, 1951*. The employment figure is the occupational figure from the *Census of Canada, 1951*. The gross value of product estimate presumes British Columbia to have the same share of the country's gross value of output as of employment in this industry. There may be a substantial error involved here, but probably not great enough to alter its rank in the list.

Source: *Census of Canada, 1880–81*, Vol. III, Table 61; *Census of Canada, 1911*, Vol. III, Table 1; and *General Review of the Manufacturing Industries of Canada, 1951*, Table 14.

many miners in 1911 as in 1881 in British Columbia, lumbering had expanded so much more rapidly that both industries accounted for between 15,000 and 16,000 workers in the latter year. Employment in agriculture had apparently expanded considerably faster than in mining, rising from about 2600 to over 24,000. The fisheries recorded the least rate of increase in employment among the extractive industries, with but a 65 per cent increase. Although one can raise questions about the dissimilarity in classification methods in the two censuses, the data are at least satisfactory in indicating the rough magnitudes of change. In brief, the rise of lumbering between 1881 and 1911 was spectacular, leaving lumbering on a par with mining in terms of employment; but agriculture employed about half again as many workers as lumbering or mining, and the fisheries about one-third as many as mining.

The change in the relative importance of the various extractive industries is reflected in the change in the make-up of the manufacturing sector between 1881 and 1911. As Table 28 shows, the canneries had slipped in relative importance, for now preserved fish was outranked in value of product by log products and smelting. In terms of employment, however, it was second to log products. The role of Vancouver and Victoria as transportation terminals is also apparent in the data. The industries which had disappeared from the ten leading industries list, including (alas!) the opium factory, had all been producing for the local market. By 1911 British Columbia's manufacturing had become much more involved in trade with other areas.

The province's agriculture by 1911 had shifted away from beef cattle somewhat and toward wheat and dairy cattle. The number of beef cattle rose by nearly 60 per cent but the number of dairy cattle more than tripled. Wheat acreage doubled. One really spectacular change in British Columbia's agriculture reflected the livestock economy, however: the production of oats, according to the census, was thirty times as great in 1911 as in 1881, while the hay acreage was about seventeen times as great. In the former years only about 10 per cent of the field crop acreage was in hay, but in 1911 nearly 60 per cent was in hay. The pressure of a growing cattle population on the available open range land was apparently the cause of this shift. The second significant development in British Columbia's agriculture was the expansion of fruit and vegetable production. In 1911 there was about six times as much acreage devoted to this use as in 1891, and in 1910 the value of fruit and vegetable production was about one-third as great as the value of all field crops and about two-thirds as great as the value of all livestock sold. The bulk of this expansion in fruit and vegetable production occurred between 1901 and 1911.

The character of mining in the province, too, had been altered considerably by 1911. Gold mining was most prominent in 1881, for the Vancouver Island coal mines, which had been producing at least since 1850, yielded but 268,000 tons in 1881 according to the census. In 1911, however, over 2,500,000 tons were produced and the value of output was roughly half again as great as for gold.[35]

[35] Economic Council of British Columbia, Table M-5. In 1910 and 1912, production exceeded 10,000,000 tons, the 1911 output being affected by a strike. See E. Jacobs, "Mines and Mining," in Canada and Its Provinces, ed. Adam Shortt and Arthur G. Doughty (Toronto, 1914), p. 574.

Copper, first mined in quantity in the late 1890's, ranked with gold in terms of dollar value of output by 1911 and employed about five times as many workers. Lead and silver were of lesser importance.

In 1911, then, we see that British Columbia was no longer dependent on the exports of the single commodity but had diversified its mineral production. Nor was it so dependent on imported manufactured goods, for now the province had quite a respectable manufacturing sector of its own. Some 35,000 persons were reported in manufacturing employment; this was more than were employed in mining, forestry, and fishing combined and about 10,000 more than were employed in agriculture. Over 17,000 workers, or nearly half of the manufacturing employment, were reported in log products and lumber products. The preserved fish industry accounted for another 5800 and smelting for 1300. The manufacturing sector in 1911 was so large, then, because of the processing of goods for export rather than because of the production of goods for local consumption.

British Columbia, 1911–1951

The most spectacular growth during this period was recorded in lead and zinc and in pulp and paper production. Again it was production of an export staple which seemed to accelerate the province's growth. The population rose from 392,000 to 1,165,000, the work force from 206,000 to 444,000.[36] How was this increase in the work force divided up among the various sectors of the economy and what seems to have been the nature of the growth in more detail?

Table 29 shows the growth of employment in the extractive industries. It is apparent that only about 5 per cent of the increase in the work force can be attributed directly to the extractive sector. The really huge increases in employment occurred in manufacturing, in the services, and in trade. Of the increase in total work force of 238,000, manufacturing accounted for 68,000, the various services (excluding government but including public utilities) accounted for 66,000, and trade accounted for 48,000.[37]

[36] Note the change in the number of persons, besides himself, which each worker had to support: from 0.9 in 1911 to 1.6 in 1951.

[37] The employment data in the census of 1951 are not strictly comparable with those of 1911. We have not attempted any reconciliation of these two series since we are interested only in the approximate magnitude of the changes.

Table 29. Distribution of the labor force among the primary industries in British Columbia, 1911 and 1951.

Industry	1911	1951
Agriculture	24,442	27,659
Forestry	11,831	24,911
Mining	15,569	11,442
Fishing and hunting	4,580	4,836
Total	56,422	68,848

Source: Census of Canada, 1911, Vol. VI, Table 1; and *Census of Canada, 1951*, Vol. IV, Table 16.

Expressed in relative terms, the work force more than doubled but the services (defined as above) and the trade sectors more than tripled in size and the manufacturing sector nearly tripled. Employment in government nearly tripled, also. The economy appears to have "filled up" in the sense that the secondary and tertiary sectors expanded in response to the growth of the local market and the availability of raw materials.

Let us examine these changes in more detail. In mining, coal output had fallen by about 40 per cent and the number employed in coal mining dropped even more drastically, from about 7000 to 2000. Due mostly to the price increase but partially to a quantity increase, the value of gold output rose over this period so that it was about equal to that of coal in 1951.[38] But the star performers in mining in British Columbia over these four decades were, of course, lead and zinc. The expanding automobile and electrical goods industries during the 1920's helped pull lead production in the province up from about 40,000,000 pounds in the early 1920's to 320,000,000 pounds in 1930. After a depression dip, lead production rose to a wartime peak of about 480,000,000 pounds, but it has since fallen back to about the 1930 level. Zinc output followed a similar path, since it is found with lead. In dollar terms, lead output was no less than 50 times as great in 1951 as in 1911 and zinc output was more than 500 times as great. In 1951 the value of output of these two metals was on the order of 5 and 6 times

[38] In 1951, about 280,000 ounces of gold were produced. After World War I output fluctuated between 100,000 ounces and 250,000 ounces until about 1933. Output then rose to a peak of nearly 600,000 ounces in 1939–40 but fell down to the 200,000 ounce level and below by the end of the war. British Columbia, *Annual Report of the Minister of Mines, 1951*, p. A21.

the value of output of gold and of coal. These changes were accompanied by an absolute decline in the number of persons reported in mining, from 15,600 in 1911 down to 11,400 in 1951. The
doubling of the work force, then, was not caused by the minerals.

Forestry production in British Columbia over this period was
undergoing quite a different type of experience. Employment in
this sector more than doubled. The most spectacular growth in this
sector was recorded by pulpwood production, which rose from 150
cords in 1911 to 860,000 cords in 1951. The former year's output
was unusually low, however; total pulpwood used in the province
in the four years 1909–1912 was (in cords) 1316, 440, 150, and
35,000. Pulpwood production was just getting under way during
the first decade of the century and output, or at least the recording of output, was erratic. Nonetheless in 1951 the bulk of the
timber cut still was used for purposes other than pulp; only about
12 per cent of the production by quantity was cut for pulpwood.

In agriculture two types of change had taken place side by side
over these forty years. One would anticipate that the growth of
population would have given rise to the usual kind of shift
toward more dairy and poultry products as well as more beef
and pork relative to the grains. However, the data for the province
indicate that among the field crops barley and wheat acreage
increased most rapidly. Barley acreage rose by a factor of nearly
12 and wheat by a factor of 7. The explanation of this phenomenon
is that the Peace River country in the northeastern part of the
province had been opened up after 1911. This region is agricul-
turally an extension of Alberta, and so a type of prairie agriculture
expanded in British Columbia during the 1911–1951 period. In
1951, 25 per cent of the improved farm area of the province was
in Division 10, the Peace River country, but about 70 per cent
of the wheat acreage, 56 per cent of the oats acreage, and nearly
70 per cent of the barley acreage in the province lay in this one
division. The southern part of the province was engaged in an
entirely different sort of agriculture, oriented much more toward
cattle and fruit. In the area around Vancouver in 1950 nearly 90
per cent of the value of all field crops was accounted for by fodder
crops. Fruit and vegetable production in that year was about
two-thirds as valuable as the output of all field crops. Farther
east, the tree fruits become of overwhelming importance. The
province's cattle are in the central and southwestern regions

rather than in the Peace River country, with the dairy cattle concentrated around Vancouver.

In the manufacturing sector, employment grew over the 1911–1951 period at nearly twice the rate of total employment in the province. This growth in manufacturing was not so much the result of the processing of new staples but rather a growth of the processing of the old staples plus the development of a very substantial amount of smaller scale manufacturing scattered among several industries. Table 28 reflects at least the first of these two aspects. In 1951 the leading manufacturing industries were still based on lumber, fishing, and smelting, just as in 1911. Pulp and paper had come of age and more wood-using industries had developed. However, the forest products industries as a group recorded a substantially smaller percentage increase in employment than did manufacturing as a whole. Due to the large absolute employment in this group of industries, however, its relatively small percentage increase nonetheless represented more than one-third of the total increase in manufacturing employment over the 1911–1951 period. The food processing industries showed the second largest increase in employment in absolute terms, but here, too, the percentage growth was slower than for manufacturing as a whole. The manufacturing industries which grew at particularly high rates during four decades were transportation equipment (the census defines this industry to include garages), iron and steel products, smelting, shipbuilding, printing and publishing, commercial bakeries, clothing, chemical products, and leather products. The growth of manufacturing in British Columbia, 1911–1951, was accounted for in large part by this "filling out" of the manufacturing sector by means of the growth of industries which were, for the most part, market oriented rather than materials oriented.

Table 30 helps give a clearer picture of the province's manufacturing sector compared with that of Canada as a whole. If we assume that a region showing a greater proportion of its work force engaged in a particular industry than is true for the country as a whole must be on an export basis with respect to that industry, we see that British Columbia is on an export basis only in food and beverages, wood and paper products, nonferrous metal products, and petroleum and coal products. So, despite the fact that the highest rates of growth in the 1911–1951 period were in

Table 30.   Number of employees in manufacturing industries per thousand persons in the labor force, Canada and British Columbia, 1951.

Industry	Canada	British Columbia
Food and beverages	28.9	30.9
Tobacco and tobacco products	1.6	—
Rubber products	4.2	.1
Leather products	7.4	2.6
Textile products	15.8	1.8
Clothing	23.1	5.2
Wood products	28.1	91.4
Paper products	17.4	17.8
Printing, publishing, and allied industries	12.1	12.1
Iron and steel products	38.7	20.2
Transportation equipment	36.0	25.2
Nonferrous metal products	10.0	14.1
Electrical apparatus and supplies	13.7	2.4
Nonmetallic mineral products	6.8	3.1
Products of petroleum and coal	2.6	2.9
Chemical products	10.0	4.2
Miscellaneous manufacturing	6.0	3.4

Source: *Census of Canada*, 1951, Vol. V, Table 16.

the other manufacturing industries, the province is still on an import basis with respect to those products. This supports the view that in recent decades the most rapid rates of growth have been in those types of manufacturing catering to local demand.

We have seen, now, that the extractive industries accounted for but 12,000 of the 240,000 increase in the work force over the 1911–1951 period and that manufacturing, which accounted for another 67,000 of the increase, grew not only because of the processing of the old staples but also because of the expansion of those types of manufacturing which produced for the local market. The really huge increases occurred in trade, transportation, and the services. Excluding construction from the tertiary sector of the economy, employment in British Columbia in this sector rose from about 90,000 to over 230,000 over the 1911–1951 period.

More than one-half of this increase occurred in the distributive trades alone. The census classifications differed in 1911 and 1951 and so it is impossible to tell exactly how the increase in employment in trade was distributed among the different types of retailing and wholesaling. Even so, it is easy to see that the major increases were in such lines as automobiles, food, apparel, lumber, and drugs. The growing importance of most of these types of business reflected either the increase in the standard of living or the increased proportion of consumer goods going through the market place (rather than being produced and consumed at home) or both.[39] The increase of more than 11,000 in employment in transportation, storage, and communication is explained primarily by the increase in employment on the railroads and in truck transportation.[40] Government employment skyrocketed from about 10,000 to 30,000, but about half of the increase is explained by increases in the number of people in the armed forces. Although the census categories in the 1911 and 1951 censuses are not strictly comparable for our present purposes, it appears that the number of persons engaged in medicine and in various aspects of medical care accounted, too, for a substantial proportion of the increase in the work force, as one would expect.

But even in 1911 British Columbia reported quite a high proportion of its employment in the tertiary sector. Whereas the country as a whole devoted almost exactly one-third of its workers to this sector, in British Columbia the proportion was 44 per cent. The difference then could be attributed mostly to the greater (relative) employment in transportation and in government in British Columbia. By 1951 the difference had narrowed but was still substantial, the proportions being 45 per cent for all Canada and 53 per cent for British Columbia. The percentage difference in employment in transportation was no longer as great as earlier; the province showed a quite consistent tendency in all tertiary industries to show an employment percentage greater than did the country as a whole. The difference was greatest in the services and in trade, the latter being a large sector in part because of the export trade.

The causes of growth since 1939

From 1939 to 1955 the population of Canada rose by 39 per cent. The population of British Columbia rose by an astronomical 70 per cent. This raises an interesting question, for we have been

[39] See George J. Stigler, *Trends in Employment in the Service Industries* (Princeton, 1956), ch. viii, for a fuller discussion of the forces increasing employment in the service industries.

[40] Automobile repair services are not included in this sector in the census but rather are considered as a manufacturing industry under "transportation equipment."

made aware of the oil boom in Alberta, yet there the population rose only at the national rate. In British Columbia, which experienced no single new resource development, what pushed the population up so rapidly?

A piece of the answer lies in the ratio of the population to the work force. Since it was a younger region, British Columbia for a long while showed fewer persons being supported per member of the work force than was true for the country as a whole. But this figure has been creeping upward. It was but 2.27 in 1931, compared with 2.64 for the whole country, whereas in 1955 it stood at 2.97 in contrast with 2.83 for the country. Had the province's ratio but come up to the national one by 1955, the 1939–1955 population increase would have been 60 rather than 70 per cent.

For a fuller explanation, however, one must look at the nature of the particular industries which expanded most rapidly during the 1939–1955 period. Beyond this, we must consider, too, certain unique features of the province's economy as it existed in 1939.

Table 31.   Percentage increase in undeflated value of product and in number of employees in selected sectors, British Columbia, 1939–1955.

Sector	Value of product	Number of employees
Forestry	616	60
Manufacturing	569	115
Fisheries	243	—ᵃ
Agriculture	237	—ᵃ
Mining	166	−10

ᵃ Not available.

Source: British Columbia, Bureau of Economics and Statistics, Department of Industrial Development, Trade and Commerce, British Columbia Facts and Statistics, Vol. X (1956), passim; and DBS, Annual Review of Employment and Payrolls, 1951 and 1955, Table 7.

Table 31 shows the percentage increase in the value of product of the major primary and secondary sectors of the economy. Unfortunately the employment data are based only on firms employing fifteen or more persons and are not available for some sectors. The increase in the output of forestry products is immediately apparent, but the repercussions of that increase are not quite so obvious from the above data alone. In 1955 there were over 13,000 persons employed in logging in the province.[41] But there were several times that many people in the manufacturing sector engaged in various wood products industries. There were 31,300 in sawmills, 6700 in pulp and paper, 5400 in veneers and plywood production, 3600 in sash, door, and planing mills, and 1970 in furniture plants, to mention only the major wood-processing industries. In these industries alone, then, there were about 370 workers for each 100 workers in logging. This ratio stands in marked contrast with the corresponding one for Alberta's oil industry, where the long-term prospects are for only about 33 workers in processing oil and gas per 100 workers in primary production of oil and gas. To put the proposition in other words, in British Columbia's wood processing industries there are about ten times as many workers per worker in the primary industry as is true of Alberta's oil and gas products industry. This is one major reason why British Columbia's population has expanded so much more rapidly than has Alberta's over the 1939–1955 period.

But a second reason is at least as important as the first. In British Columbia the total employment in manufacturing industries expanded by only 41 per cent in 1939–1955, as compared with a 74 per cent increase in Alberta. This fact taken by itself seems out of keeping with the increase in total population, which favored British Columbia so strongly. The answer to this enigma can be found in the structure of the two economies in 1939. Alberta was devoting nearly one-half of its work force to agriculture, whereas in British Columbia only one-seventh or one-eighth of the work force was so engaged.[42] Alberta's manufacturing sector, on the other hand, was far smaller than British Columbia's.[43] In Alberta, then, the farm population was able to provide workers to the manufacturing sector over the ensuing years in substantial numbers. In British Columbia, the farm population was too small relative to the industrial work force for the labor requirements of the latter to be filled in the following years from

[41] British Columbia, Department of Industrial Development, Trade and Commerce, Bureau of Economics and Statistics, *British Columbia Facts and Statistics*, Vol. X (1956), p. 19.

[42] Detailed employment data by province and by sector are not available for 1939. In the 1941 census, however, the proportion of the work force reported in agriculture stood at 47 per cent in Alberta and but 13 per cent in British Columbia.

[43] In 1941, the census reported about 21 per cent of the British Columbia work force in manufacturing compared with but 8 per cent in Alberta.

the rural labor group. A quick look at the 1941 and 1951 census work force data shows what was happening. In Alberta the persons engaged in agriculture dropped by nearly 33,000, or 22 per cent. The labor force in manufacturing increased by no less than 40 per cent over this period, but in absolute terms this amounted to only about 10,000 workers. In British Columbia, on the other hand, the agricultural sector shrank much more than in Alberta percentage-wise (37 per cent as compared with 22 per cent) yet this provided only about 16,000 workers to a manufacturing sector in which employment increased by over 30,000. Mining, quarrying, and oil wells employment dropped by 25 per cent in British Columbia in the 1941–1951 decade, but this provided fewer than 4000 workers to the expanding sectors of the economy. Clearly British Columbia had to attract immigrants in order to fill its labor requirements. Alberta, with its much greater agricultural sector and much smaller manufacturing sector, could staff its rapidly expanding manufacturing industries primarily with people leaving agriculture.

One other contrasting feature of the two economies helps explain the much greater rate of population growth in British Columbia. For every 100 workers in the primary and secondary sectors in British Columbia in 1951 there were about 113 in the tertiary sector. In Alberta there were but 79 in the tertiary sector for every 100 workers in primary and secondary industries.

To summarize, British Columbia's 70 per cent increase in population, 1939–1955, was the result of at least four forces: (1) an increase in the number of people dependent on each member of the work force; (2) the expansion of the export market for forest products, which not only increased employment in primary production but also generated more jobs in wood processing than in primary production itself; (3) the limited "slack" in the economy in 1939, meaning that the sectors of the economy in which employment could shrink were too small to provide the growing sectors with enough workers, thus necessitating immigration to fill the labor force requirements; and (4) the relatively large number of persons British Columbia has in the tertiary sector, due in part to the export trade, relative to the primary and secondary sectors, thus giving a higher employment multiplier than would be expected in Canada as a whole.

Certain inadequacies in the data on the manufacturing sector have necessitated our stressing the forest products industries more than is probably justified. The disclosure rule prohibits the publication of data for the nonferrous smelting and refining industry, in which employment was increased substantially by the opening of a new aluminum plant at Kitimat. The company has reported that the work force was about 1300 in 1956.[44] But this kind of development, like the oil development in Alberta, has but limited repercussions in the economy because of the small employment multiplier. British Columbia's primary export staple is one which lends itself to extensive processing prior to export, and this processing is fairly labor intensive. It is this feature of the economy, so in contrast with that of Alberta, which largely explains the very rapid growth since the beginning of World War II.

[44] Aluminum Company of Canada, Ltd., *Submission to the RCCEP* (Montreal, 1956), p. 14.

7

Government and Canadian Economic Development

Ever since Confederation, the majority of Canadians have echoed the call of nineteenth-century liberalism for a restriction of government activities to the minimum of socially necessary functions. But for Canada this minimum has been far from miniscule, and necessity has been a fecund mother of political inventions. In short, governments have taken a major part in furthering Canadian economic development. Qualitatively as well as quantitatively that role has changed a good deal between 1867 and the present time. For the purpose of economic forecasting, it is valuable to know the direction this change has taken. Thereby one can get some notion of the probable net impact of government actions in the future as well as the response to be expected from the body politic to any economic maladjustments which may crop up over the next decade.

GOVERNMENT AND THE ECONOMY TO WORLD WAR I

Imputing a conscious policy-forming mind to the measures adopted by a democratic government is a labor of questionable morality but occasional practical usefulness. Many students of federal and provincial government activities before World War I have seen a common objective in the creation of a unified east-west economy out of a thin string of scattered settlements. In tackling this task these governments had three sorts of resources at their command — their general powers of regulation and control, certain real property in the form of land and mineral rights, and finally their fiscal powers to tax, borrow, and spend. All of these were thrown into the breach. Historical interpreters have generally classed the results as disappointing, at least up to 1896 and the beginning of the wheat boom.[1]

Indeed in the historic Canadian setting governments have made

[1] Compare, for example, Kenneth Buckley, *Capital Formation in Canada, 1896–1930* (Toronto, 1955), p. 5.

much headway at furthering economic development only when the general climate was clearly favorable. Nonetheless the policies and achievements of the early years after Confederation had a powerful effect on economic growth then and later.

Let us recall the major government actions taken in the pre-World War I period which clearly fall into the class of development policies. Expansion of Canada's transportation network was not only the most conspicuous portion of dominion development policy during this period, it also reflects the conflicting objectives such policies sought to gain. Canada wanted not just a transportation system, but a transportation system with an added kick for national political objectives. Many of the difficulties in securing railroad linkage from the Atlantic to the Pacific lay in political insistence on all-Canada routes in preference to less costly lines passing through northern New England and below Lake Superior. Financial difficulties before the time of Confederation soured governments on guaranteeing the interest on private firms' debts as a means of promoting major projects. Consequently the major railroad projects of the 1870's and 1880's, the Intercolonial and the Canadian Pacific, grew from direct government investment and encouragement to private companies through land grants and cash subsidies, certain monopoly privileges, and freedoms from regulation.[2] The next major railway project, the Canadian Northern, was assembled piecemeal over three decades and with help from a variety of governments which were induced to grant many varieties of aid. The federal land grant policy ended in 1894, but the road received land at various times from the dominion as well as from Ontario and Quebec. Cash subsidies from the dominion, Ontario, Quebec, and Manitoba totaled more than the federal contribution to the Canadian Pacific.[3] The final transcontinental rail line, as first planned, involved even more government participation than the first two, with the federal government to build the National Transcontinental from Winnipeg to the Atlantic to link with the Grand Trunk Western's line to Prince Rupert. Furthermore, the entire cost of the western section was to be financed by bonds ultimately guaranteed by the government. Eventually still greater expenditures were needed as the govern-

[2] W. T. Easterbrook and H. G. J. Aitken, *Canadian Economic History* (Toronto, 1956), pp. 420–422, 428–432.
[3] *Ibid.*, pp. 435–438.

ment was forced at the time of World War I to combine into the Canadian National system all of these railways except the Canadian Pacific, incurring extra expenses of further construction and buying out private interests.[4]

While government natural resources policy helped subsidize transportation improvements by means of land grants, its greatest importance lay in its influence on prairie settlement and later upon commercial development of Canada's natural resources. The "Dominion Lands Policy" was established shortly after Confederation, when title to much of the Canadian West was transferred from the Hudson's Bay Company to the dominion. The Dominion Lands Act of 1872 fixed the basic settlements terms of a free 160-acre homestead upon payment of a $10 registration fee, title to be secured after three years if certain cultivation requirements had been met.[5] Although Canada's land offer found few takers until the closing of the United States frontier, from the 1890's on it facilitated the rapid populating of the West. Also of importance before World War I was provincial control over Canada's forest resources. This authority was heavily used by the provinces during the first decade of the twentieth century to enforce Canadian sawmilling of logs destined to supply United States lumber needs.

A final link in the important government policies of the pre-World War I period was the much-studied Canadian tariff. W. A. Mackintosh has argued that up to 1879, when the National Policy assumed its capital letters and became a permanent feature of the Canadian scene, tariff policy had created few protected jobs.[6] By contrast, the 1879 legislation introduced substantial, broadside tariff protection for manufactures and many raw materials. There was little conscious economic selection among industries to be given infant-industry assistance; the tariff-making process, in nineteenth-century Canada as in most times and places, was unselective and politically conditioned to mollify assorted sectional interests. The average *ad valorem* rate of duty rose from

[4] *Ibid.*, pp. 438–444; G. P. de T. Glazebrook, *A History of Canadian Transportation* (Toronto, 1938), ch. x.

[5] Easterbrook and Aitken, p. 390; C. B. Martin, "Dominion Lands Policy," *Canadian Frontiers of Settlement,* ed. W. A. Mackintosh and W. L. G. Joerg, Vol. II (Toronto, 1938).

[6] W. A. Mackintosh, *The Economic Background of Dominion-Provincial Relations* (Ottawa, 1939), pp. 17–18.

21.4 per cent in 1878 to 26.1 per cent in 1880. Subsequently it reached a peak of 31.9 per cent in 1889 before slipping off slightly in the next decade. More important than the changes in the treacherous average duty rate were the increases on various major articles. Many sorts of woolens and cotton goods enjoyed nearly doubled protection after the 1879 legislation, while numerous iron and steel articles previously admitted free or nearly free now bore moderate rates of duty. Agricultural implements and machinery (except textile) moved up to a 25 per cent duty rate. Nova Scotia coal and Ontario petroleum received substantial protection.[7]

What came of this major shift in tariff policy? Did it succeed in its overt goal of speeding Canadian industrialization? We know that the gross value of production in six major groups of industries increased by 50 per cent in the decade preceding the tariff change, no more than 50 per cent in the decade following it, and distinctly less than 50 per cent in the second decade following (1890–1900). Only in the first decade of the twentieth century did Canadian manufacturing output double in value, then due to the obvious influences of rapid settlement and export-induced prosperity. Mackintosh concludes that the new protectionist policy "fostered manufacturing development in Ontario and Quebec on a larger scale than hitherto." O. J. Firestone, while conceding this much, argues that during the 1880's and 1890's cheaper ocean transportation and the new rail network which made Canadian raw materials more available were much more substantial stimuli to the development of manufacturing.[8] As with the other major governmental aids to economic development during this period, the National Policy was not enough by itself. It had to await the changed economic conditions of the new century.

A glance at the fiscal side of government policy before World War I reveals a powerful constraint on development expenditures in the limits to the funds available to Canadian governments. Before Confederation, heavy development loans to various transportation projects has thrown the provinces heavily into debt. By

[7] Canada, RCDPR, *Report,* Vol. I, p. 51; *Canada Year Book, 1924,* p. 383; Mackintosh, pp. 19–20.

[8] O. J. Firestone, *Canada's Economic Development, 1867–1953, With Special Reference to Changes in the Country's National Product and National Wealth,* (London, 1958), Part II, Sec. 9, especially Table 78; Mackintosh, pp. 20–21.

1866 debt charges absorbed 21 per cent of the current annual revenue of Nova Scotia, 28 per cent of New Brunswick's, and 30 per cent of the revenues of the province of Canada.[9] These debts, taken over by the dominion at the time of Confederation, were the start of a gross national debt which grew at an average rate of $9,000,000 a year in the subsequent twenty years. The average annual debt increase thus was 1 to 2 per cent of gross national product. Five-sixths of the dominion's capital expenditures during this period were for transportation projects, and 61 per cent went to railroads alone. Between 1867 and 1875 the task of completing the Intercolonial Railway cost $34,000,000 and expanded the national debt by $22,000,000. Later the Canadian Pacific accounted for even larger sums, bringing capital expenditures to a new peak in 1883. Thus by 1887 the dominion faced debt charges of nearly $10,000,000 against tax revenues of less than $29,000,000. "The growing burden of the debt charge, coupled with the desire to maintain the credit of Canada in the London market, impressed opinion with the advisability of checking new borrowings for government capital expenditures."[10] The increase in gross national debt averaged only $6,000,000 annually and total federal government expenditure increased little until economic conditions showed a massive improvement after 1896. Dominion ordinary revenues at this time depended heavily on customs duties and hence showed no tendency to increase, for customs revenue depended on the volume of imports, and neither booming exports nor significant capital imports appeared before the turn of the century to expand the flow of dutiable imports. The provinces also had little fiscal elbowroom during these years. In the 1890's they imposed corporation and inheritance taxes to broaden their tax base beyond the royalties and fees derived from the then static staple exports.

Likewise, the improving fiscal situation around 1900 had a lot to do with the massive public development projects appearing after 1907. Rapidly rising imports after 1903 yielded rising customs revenue for the dominion treasury and, after a decent lag, supported higher provincial subsidies and new capital im-

[9] A. E. Buck, *Financing Canadian Government* (Chicago, 1949), p. 170; RCDPR, *Report*, Vol. I, p. 38.

[10] S. Bates, *Financial History of Canadian Governments* (Ottawa, 1939), pp. 32–36.

provement projects. Prairie settlement created an obvious demand for new railways, canals, and post offices, but the budgetary surpluses after 1906 certainly did much to encourage such schemes as the grandiose blueprints for railroad development. Surpluses continued to pile up for the federal government even in years when heavy capital expenditures were charged to current accounts; the 1912–13 surplus was nearly double the gross revenues of the dominion in 1896.[11] Characteristically, these surpluses were not used to retire outstanding debt but were plowed back into the economy to finance new improvement projects.

Some clear patterns emerge from this survey of pre-World War I developments. On the surface, public efforts seemed to play a major role in fostering economic growth. Certainly the dominion used all public powers available for this purpose, and certainly public expenditures were massive compared to the young nation's resources. Yet when one reaches the adding up, public policies at no point seem to have shifted the direction of the underlying economic forces. Aside from speeding the formation of a national transportation network, they had little impact until the turn of the century when the basic economic climate turned strongly favorable. Again excepting the early contributions to a transport network, public investment had relatively minor visible effect either as a short-run pump-priming or as a long-run stimulus to complementary private capital formation. The most massive waves of public capital formation were actually stimulated by heavy private investment which swelled the dominion's tax take and hence the stock of funds available for public investment projects. Finally, the clear internal consistency among the dominion's nineteenth-century development projects — settlement, transport, and industrialization — was perhaps less the fruit of cool-headed planning than a lucky coincidence of sectional interests. This accidental coherence becomes more and more apparent from the perspective of the interwar years, when luck ran out for comprehensive dominion promotion of economic development.

WAR FINANCE AND THE INTERWAR YEARS

World War I had a tremendous impact on Canadian public finance and government policies generally. On the one hand, it

[11] Buck, p. 171; Bates, pp. 36–48.

greatly broadened the tax base and caused the dominion to discover that it had substantial abilities to borrow from Canadian holders of loanable funds. On the other hand, it created a range of economic conditions which greatly hampered the return of government to the role of development promotion in later years.

The coming of the war found Canadian public finance far from ready to face the task of financing massive assistance to Great Britain. "Hitherto the federal Government had obtained about 90 per cent of its total revenues from customs duties and excises on liquor and tobacco. It had no system of general taxation or machinery for directly taxing the net incomes, profits, and wealth of individuals." [12] It had never borrowed substantially in the home money market; in 1914 less than $800,000 of the federal funded debt was payable in Canada. The government's early plans for financing the war included mainly borrowing in London (and later New York), increased excises on a variety of domestic articles, and inflation through increased fiduciary issue and other measures. These quickly proved inadequate. During fiscal 1915–16 the arrangements for British financing of Canadian war costs broke down as the pound sterling became heavily strained, and the British indicated that they would be forced to depend on Canadian financing in the future for part of the military goods orders placed with Canadian producers. At the same time, dominion efforts to raise revenues through increased excises were proving clearly inadequate. Thus in the autumn of 1915 the dominion resorted to its first domestic war loan, a $50,000,000 issue which to the surprise of the authorities yielded double that amount. Thereafter heavy emphasis, perhaps too heavy emphasis, was placed on domestic borrowing.[13] The reasons for its success seems to be closely connected with an inflation-induced income redistribution. Selling prices rose faster than almost all classes of primary costs, with the result that many salaried employees, some wage-earners, and those living on interest and rents at fixed rates suffered a considerable reduction in real income. Heavy profits surpluses piled up.

[12] J. J. Deutsch, "War Finance and the Canadian Economy, 1914–1920," *CJEPS,* 6:527 (November 1940).

[13] *Ibid.,* pp. 528–532; Bates, pp. 51–54. Only about one-fourth of the loans seems to have been subscribed by individuals of modest means, and the heavy participation by banks in the remainder meant that borrowing created substantial inflationary pressure.

The war left two major legacies for Canadian public finance and general government action in the 1920's. One was a greatly expanded tax base. Besides the new excises tried in the first year of the war, 1916 had seen the coming of a business profits tax and 1917 a personal income tax. The sales tax which made its first appearance in 1920 was part of the same series of changes, growing from the realization that in peacetime borrowing would be an inappropriate way of meeting what looked like a permanently higher expenditure level.[14] By 1921 customs revenue, while slightly larger than before the war, furnished only 33 per cent of total dominion tax revenue compared to 82 per cent in 1913.[15] The other major legacy of World War I was a set of fixed spending commitments which greatly limited the freedom and flexibility of dominion action in the following years. The most obvious of these was the interest transfer on the national debt. Net debt charges were as high as 41 per cent of total expenditure in 1925. In that same year, another 14 per cent went for pensions growing out of wartime obligations. Stuart Bates calculated that "net debt charges, pensions, subsidies, and other small uncontrollable expenditures, had formed only 18 per cent of total expenditure before the War, but averaged between 50 per cent and 60 per cent after the War, becoming much higher when the depression added to net debt charges, railway deficits and relief costs." [16] Although not a result of the war itself, nationalization of half of Canada's overexpanded railways came at the same time and, with it, dominion assumption of their operating deficits. From the public finance viewpoint, the Canadian railway deficit became even more burdensome than the fixed charges, for it tended to be much higher in years of high unemployment, which also saw dominion tax revenues shrink alarmingly.

Against this background, it is clear why the dominion largely

[14] Bates, pp. 53–54; J. Harvey Perry, *Taxes, Tariffs, and Subsidies, A History of Canadian Fiscal Development* (Toronto, 1955), Vol. I, pp. 150–165, 199–206.

[15] Bates, p. 78.

[16] *Ibid.*, pp. 80–81. Compare the following passage from Perry (p. 163), who uses a slightly different method of classification: "The Dominion debt had increased from $½ billion to over $3 billion, and debt charges, railway subsidies, and pensions, which formed slightly more than one-third of the Dominion budget before the war, had increased to two-thirds. Of this fixed burden most was paid to bondholders and pensioners tax-free, since interest on the war bonds and war pensions was exempt from income tax."

abandoned its earlier policies for promoting economic expansion during the interwar years. First, with the heavy burden of fixed obligations and the popular expectation that the new wartime taxes would be at least partly relaxed, it would have taken a major decision to tax or borrow more if any bold new measures were to be financed. Second, no bold new measures were forthcoming. The objectives of the National Policy of earlier days had largely been won. Settlement of the West was largely complete. The railroad system was finished — more than finished, as it then appeared — except for links and feeder lines in the western half of the country. The nation had been successfully defended, and the view in those idyllic days was that the task needed doing but once.[17] Many of the dominion programs of the 1920's were mopping-up operations on these older policies. The Hudson Bay Railway was completed, along with feeder lines for the Canadian National. The Welland Ship Canal was finished, and terminal grain elevators were constructed at Prescott, Prince Rupert, and Churchill. Dominion use of natural resource policy as a booster for economic development was officially closed out in 1930 with the transfer of authority over natural resources to the Prairie Provinces.[18]

The positive aspects of government action in the 1920's went in a different direction from the old National Policy, to a direction which placed provincial and municipal governments in the leading position as a result of the constitutional division of powers. The appearance of greater stratification in the society gave rise to demands for enlarged social services, especially protection of citizens against unemployment, sickness, and old age. The age distribution of the population was changing to enlarge those groups most dependent on these sorts of services. In a variety of ways the industrial adjustments and relocations following the war increased the requirements for social welfare services. Industrialization and urbanization tested the resourcefulness of the provincial and municipal governments which had to foot the cost of building paved highways, public hydroelectric plants, grain elevators, and communications systems, plus all the expensive adjuncts of a modern municipality.[19]

[17] Canada, RCDPR, *Report*, Vol. I, p. 112. See also V. C. Fowke, "The National Policy — Old and New," *CJEPS*, 18:277–279 (August 1952).
[18] Fowke, pp. 278–280.
[19] Bates, pp. 61–65; Perry, chs. xv, xvi.

The dominion government was extremely slow to take a part in filling these new social needs.[20] The bare figures on changes in total expenditure tell the story: between 1921 and 1930 dominion expenditures increased by only 10 per cent while provincial current expenditures increased by 106 per cent.[21] The first sign of dominion initiative in these new areas came only late in the 1920's with the Old Age Pension Act of 1927, the first of a series of relatively clumsy grants-in-aid tenders to provinces which would pass enabling legislation.

Actions by Canadian governments in the 1930's largely continued the new trend revealed in the 1920's of a movement of emphasis from economic development to economic stabilization and to more equitable distribution of wealth and income, increasing tension in dominion-provincial relations, increasing diversity of revenue sources, and increasing budgetary weight of relatively inflexible programs and obligations. The economic environment of government action of course sank from the bliss of the New Era to the despair of the Great Depression, but these changes in the role of government in the economy antedate the befouling of the economic climate.[22] Specifically, to the 1927 federal old age assistance program the 1930's added first a series of annual emergency grants to the provinces, beginning in 1930. Then in 1935 came Mr. Bennett's "New Deal" legislation, a diverse bag consisting of four labor measures, two industrial control bills, and two agriculture bills. The main concern at the time of their passage was not whether they were good but whether they were constitutional. This was not an idle concern; and, as things turned out, by judicial decisions on various grounds the labor bills and one agricultural measure were held *ultra vires* of the federal legis-

---

[20] Compare Fowke (p. 278): "The first decade and a half between the wars show as little trace of policy at the national level as one could find in a century of Canadian history." Likewise, Bates declares (p. 76): "The history of Dominion expenditure and tax charges in the post-war period indicates that the Dominion fiscal position was dictated mainly by the economic conditions ruling from year to year, and that fiscal action was limited to what prevailing economic conditions seemed to permit."

[21] Bates, p. 68.

[22] In his interesting essay on "The National Policy — Old and New," Fowke suggests that the years since World War I be interpreted as revealing the rise of a new National Policy, emphasizing public welfare, agricultural adjustment and monetary policy. The notion is intriguing, though hardly likely to offer salvation to the economic forecaster.

lature.[23] Faced with these decisions as well as complete uncertainty about the chances for amending the British North America Act of 1867 (Canada's constitution) to circumvent them, the dominion government was rendered impotent in many major fields and the problem of dominion-provincial relations reached a terrible impasse on the eve of World War II.[24]

WORLD WAR II AND ITS AFTERMATH

Canada's second great war demanded a heavier economic effort than had its predecessor, but it produced fewer significant changes in public finance and economic policy. In both wars public expenditures by the dominion government rose over a half-decade to five or six times their previous peacetime level.[25] But on entering World War I the dominion had to transform the taxation system of a relatively pastoral trading nation into that of a modern industrial society. In World War II it was more a question of the prudent use of existing fiscal weapons.

The financing of World War II was an outstanding success, compared either to Canada's performance in World War I or to any other country's fiscal efforts in the recent conflict. Canadian authorities recalled the lesson learned from the heavy reliance on borrowing during the 1915–1918 period — that rapid inflation is almost certain to result. Perry has calculated that during World War II the dominion scraped up revenue to cover 56.6 per cent of its total expenditures; during World War I the figure was only 42.8 per cent.[26] The results are plain to see. During World War I the Canadian cost of living rose 74 per cent, while during World War II the increase was confined to a mere 18 per cent.[27] Widely assorted taxes were adopted in World War II as rapidly as the need arose. The major changes included increased excises on a wide range of goods, increased corporate and personal income taxes (with reduced exemptions on the latter), higher customs

[23] F. R. Scott, "The Privy Council and Mr. Bennett's 'New Deal' Legislation," *CJEPS,* 3:234–241 (May 1937).
[24] Fowke, pp. 281–285.
[25] For the relevant figures, see Bates, p. 66; Deutsch, p. 540; Perry, Vol. II, p. 328.
[26] Perry, p. 328. World War I figure calculated for fiscal years ending March 31, 1915–1920 from Deutsch, p. 540.
[27] Buck, p. 188. Heavier dependence on borrowing during World War I is of course not the whole explanation.

duties, and an excess profits tax. In addition there appeared a "national defense tax" taking the form of a payroll tax and a foreign exchange tax to curtail civilian imports. Borrowing of war-swollen Canadian savings was done with considerable success. Issues to the public grew larger and larger as the war went on, but were regularly oversubscribed. Over the whole period only 20.6 per cent of the total bonds issued had to be placed with the Bank of Canada and the chartered banks. At least one careful study has concluded that Canada was more successful than the United States in selling war bonds outside of the banking system and in keeping them there.[28]

This enviable record of financing World War II reveals administrative skill rather than policy innovation, except in one important regard. The idea became generally accepted that taxation policy should be used as a sensitive and flexible tool to accomplish a multitude of economic objectives of economic stabilization and control beyond the basic role of financing desired government activities.[29] This change becomes clearly visible in the postwar bargaining between the dominion and the provinces over the control and distribution of Canadian tax revenues. To this, the dominant issue of Canadian public finance in the last two decades, we now turn.

As often happens with marriages of convenience, dominion-provincial relations in Canada since 1867 have never been completely harmonious. This is one aspect of Canadian society where the United States observer draws parallels from American experience only at considerable risk. The issues of dominion-provincial fiscal relations in Canada are bound up with the general legal question of the distribution of powers between the two layers of govenment, which in turn contrasts to the United States picture in two essential ways: (1) the distribution of powers long tended to move not toward but away from the federal government; (2) the underlying issues have become not less but more unsettled during the last four decades.

Canada's constitution took shape during the years of the American Civil War, and its creators drew from the war a hearty

---

[28] *Ibid.*, pp. 198–200. For good general accounts of Canadian public finance during World War II, see Buck, ch. ix, and Perry, chs. xxi–xxiii.

[29] Compare Perry, p. 327: "Pre-war thought . . . had hardly accepted taxation as a dynamic instrument of economic policy; but in the urgency of the war years the role came to be recognized without question."

respect for the virtues of a strong central government. As a result they placed in the hands of the dominion government a general residual power to legislate for "the peace, order, and good government of Canada," plus a list of specific functions designed as illustrations of its proper functions "for greater certainty, but not so as to restrict the generality" of the residual grant.[30] The provincial legislatures retained authority over fifteen enumerated matters largely of purely local interest, but including one which later proved to have crucial importance, "property and civil rights in the province." A local residual clause granted exclusive jurisdiction to the province over "all matters of a merely local or private nature in the province." Since the authors of the constitution put the major and costly tasks of government in the federal realm, they gave the federal government first claim on the major tax revenue sources of that day. By the letter of the constitution, the federal government held either exclusive or concurrent power over all fields of taxation, rendering it legally unlimited in taxing powers. All indirect taxes, the vast bulk of revenue sources in nineteenth century Canada, were the exclusive area of the federal government. The provinces were left only concurrent jurisdiction over direct taxation, then a form so unpopular in all areas but Ontario that it was not expected ever to have much importance. As recompense for this weak fiscal position, the federal government assumed all provincial debts and was bound to pay to the provinces an annual unconditional subsidy based on their population. This subsidy arrangement was blithely billed as a "full and final" settlement of provincial claims on the dominion.[31]

To make a very long story very short, two forces have worked almost continually to undermine these constitutional arrangements, judicial interpretations and economic change. The former have effectively rewritten the British North America Act to the point where the provincial power to regulate property and civil rights has tended to usurp the residual power in the constitution.

[30] For a convenient description of the Canadian constitution and its federal arrangements, see R. M. Dawson, *The Government of Canada* (Toronto, 1952), Part II. Surveys of the financial history of dominion-provincial relations are given by J. A. Maxwell, *Federal Subsidies to the Provincial Governments in Canada* (Cambridge, 1937), and A. Milton Moore and J. Harvey Perry, *Financing Canadian Federation, The Federal-Provincial Tax Arrangements* (Toronto, 1953).

[31] Moore and Perry, pp. 5–6.

The dominion has been largely confined to its enumerated specific powers, although these were originally written only as illustrations of its general legislative role. Economic change has affected the balance of dominion-provincial power by reversing the relative importance of direct and indirect taxes. Since World War I, indirect taxes have suffered a relative decline from their pre-1913 significance. More and more, governments have concentrated on the direct personal and corporate income taxes which in Canada are subject to concurrent jurisdiction and therefore to the possibility of disputes and interprovincial inequities.

During the 1930's these two forces affecting the dominion-provincial power balance came to a head as the depression brought new needs for social services lying by prevailing legal interpretation under provincial control but obviously best served at the national level. At the same time, both provincial and dominion governments were scurrying about for new revenue sources and running head on into the problems of concurrent jurisdiction.[32] During the eight-year period 1930–1937, the provinces' combined revenues were short of total relief and current expenditures by over $750,000,000, and by 1937 even with extensive emergency subsidies from the dominion one-fifth of the total municipal-provincial revenues went to meet the interest on non-self-supporting debts.[33]

This situation produced an intensive inquiry into dominion-provincial relations centering around the famous Rowell-Sirois Commission. Established in 1937, it recommended two years later a bold and logical general solution to the problems of Canadian federalism — a solution too bold and perhaps too logical for immediate acceptance. The Commission urged that the dominion take over from the provinces relief to the involuntarily unemployed (including agricultural relief) and all outstanding provincial debts, that it receive the sole right to tax personal and corporate incomes and inheritances, and that it pay "National Adjustment Grants" to the less wealthy provinces.[34] This solution

---

[32] R. B. Bryce, "Federal Provincial Tax Arrangements," *Report of Proceedings of the Tenth Annual Tax Conference, 1956* (Toronto, 1957), p. 300. See also J. A. Corry, *Difficulties of Divided Jurisdiction* (Ottawa, 1939), and L. M. Gouin and B. Claxton, *Legislative Expedients and Devices Adopted by the Dominion and the Provinces* (Ottawa, 1939).

[33] Canada, RCDPR, *Report,* Vol. I, pp. 151–177.

[34] Canada, RCDPR, *Report,* Vol. II, summarized at pp. 269–279.

immediately faced poor prospects of adoption for at least two reasons. First, amending the Canadian constitution is an unusually touchy task, with no agreed procedure despite a recent change clarifying jurisdiction over amendment.[35] As F. R. Scott has declared, "Amending the constitution is one of those complexes in the Canadian psyche which we prefer to thrust down deep into our political subsconscious." [36] Second, the coming of World War II provided both the need and the opportunity for an interim solution even though provincial-rights sentiment at the time would not stomach the full set of Rowell-Sirois reforms.[37] Indeed, the expedients adopted at this time have never been fundamentally changed, and show every likelihood (we shall argue) of continuing into the foreseeable future.

During World War II, the provinces vacated all income and succession duties on an emergency expedient basis to allow the dominion a free hand in wartime finance. In return they received payments containing some element of fiscal need subsidy. The postwar period saw a lengthy and contentious attempt by the government of Canada to establish a broad and uniform version of these wartime arrangements on a permanent basis. The dominion's proposals would have involved no loss of provincial constitutional rights, but did feature a variety of conditional grants, federal assumption of certain social security burdens and continued wartime tax rental agreements, all in return for continued subsidies to the provinces incorporating a definite element of fiscal need. After protracted discussions a uniform agreement with all provinces proved impossible, but every province except Ontario and Quebec negotiated a separate agreement, in almost all cases winning some extra concessions from the federal government. Again, income and succession duties were rented to the federal government except for a small, uniform income tax collected for the provinces by the dominion.

Well before the end of the 1947 tax rental period in 1951, it became clear that this device would continue in use. It avoided

[35] The British North America Act (No. 2), 1949. *Brit. Statutes,* 13 George VI, ch. 81, reprinted in Dawson, p. 646. A concise discussion of the problems of constitutional amendment in Canada appears in D. C. Rowat, "Recent Developments in Canadian Federalism," *CJEPS,* 18:10–16 (February 1952).

[36] F. R. Scott, "The Constitutional Background of Taxation Agreements," *McGill Law Journal,* 2:1 (Autumn 1955).

[37] Bryce, p. 300.

double tax payments on personal and corporate incomes and was thus popular with the average taxpayer. The provinces were acquiring sufficient revenue even after giving up control of the major direct taxes, especially since recent court decisions had classed the sales or commodity tax rather miraculously as a direct tax and therefore within the concurrent jurisdiction of the provinces.[38] Furthermore, the agreements were to be renewed in 1952 and thus were renegotiated during the heavy phases of Korean War preparation, when the need for such arrangements was hard to refute.[39]

The 1952–1956 agreements revealed relatively minor changes from their 1947–1951 predecessors, such as an increase in the guaranteed minimum payments and a change in the formula for calculating payments to the provinces.[40] A tax abatement on corporation income taxes made its appearance to allow the provinces an independent option on enacting a 5 per cent tax; this innovation proved important in the most recent renegotiation of the agreements. With these changes the provinces which were party to the 1947 agreements approved speedily. To the surprise of many, Ontario also agreed to an arrangement similar to that adopted with the other provinces. Quebec remained a truculent insurgent.[41]

In the 1955 negotiations for a new round of tax rental agreements to start in 1957, some new and more systematic arrangements were made. The major policy objectives served by the agreements were specifically recognized and separated into equalization grants to meet the fiscal needs of the poorer provinces, stabilization grants to help combat recession when necessary, and, finally, the regular tax rental and collection payments which serve to simplify the taxing process. All grants are to be unconditional and will be calculated from impersonal formulae. The equalization payments are designed to boost total receipts *per capita* of the poorer provinces to the standard set by the two with

---

[38] A leading case is *Atlantic Smoke Ships v. Conlon* (1943) A.C. 550.

[39] Rowat, pp. 8–9; Moore and Perry, pp. 38–41. The Korean crisis also forced the government to curtail the conference agenda and eliminate consideration of expanding social security programs and the like.

[40] Thus the rental fees paid to nine provinces under the new agreements in 1952 came to $303,000,000, compared to $96,000,000 under the old agreements in 1951. *Canada Year Book, 1956,* p. 1071.

[41] Moore and Perry, pp. 41–51; Bryce, p. 303.

the highest yield *per capita* from certain standard taxes. Abatements of the taxes rented to the federal government (personal and corporate income taxes and succession duties) are used throughout to maintain equitable treatment of citizens in nonrenting provinces compared to those in the renting provinces. All provinces except Ontario and Quebec have again agreed to rent all income and succession duties to the federal government until 1962. Ontario has again entered on a limited basis, this time choosing to rent only the personal income tax, not the corporate income tax or succession duties.[42]

How good is the tax rental arrangement? What does it contribute to the general role of government in Canadian economic expansion? Canadian Tax Foundation writers argue strongly and convincingly that the tax rental arrangement is a highly satisfactory device and that it is likely to continue. First, given the Canadian constitutional framework of concurrent jurisdiction over the most important areas of taxation, federal collection is by far the most efficient system. The tax rental agreements are more efficient than some alternatives; other alternatives have major disadvantages of different sorts. For example, sharing tax fields involves duplicate collecting staffs and added inconvenience for the taxpayer. Rigidly allocating all tax fields to one government or another can leave some governments in a severe pinch when economic conditions change, given the fact that the constitutional division of governmental responsibility is also fixed. The tax rental agreements form a simple and easy method of making regional income redistributions within the country. The body politic in a country such as Canada often concedes the virtue of some such transfers, and equally efficient and painless ways of making them are hard to find. Finally, the temporary and flexible nature of the tax rental arrangements is by itself an advantage. Similarly, the stabilization grants authorized under the 1957–1961 agreements could prove an important tool for helping provincial government finance to play a stabilizing role in the national economy — another difficult problem of public finance. Compare the expedients in use to the Rowell-Sirois recommendations, which

[42] See Bryce, pp. 304–307, and Canadian Tax Foundation, *The National Finances, An Analysis of the Programme of Revenues and Expenditures of the Government of Canada, 1957–58* (Toronto, 1957), pp. 108–111. For some recently announced minor developments, see "Fact and Opinion," *Canadian Tax Journal,* 6:6 (January-February 1958).

would have made a permanent and constitutional change in the distribution of revenue sources and responsibilities between the provinces and the federal government. The tax rental arrangements, by contrast, are flexible and can be recontracted in the face of changing circumstances. As Moore and Perry argue, "When the circumstances of the nation and the functions performed by governments are constantly in flux, there can be no permanent financial settlement that will remain for long satisfactory, and any step which reduces the flexibility of financial arrangements must be undesirable." [43]

Numerous astute observers have argued that there is no reason why one should not expect the tax rental arrangements to continue indefinitely. Rowat holds that "it is probable that the tax transfer arrangement, though adopted as a 'temporary' agreement, will become a permanent feature of federal-provincial finance." [44] The volume of funds covered by the agreements will certainly grow if economic stabilization remains a periodic problem and if the provinces continue as significant organs for welfare services.

Before attempting a general evaluation of the role of government in present and prospective Canadian economic development, let us note some of the more positive development-promoting policies of recent years. The outstanding case has been the St. Lawrence Seaway, a gigantic navigation and power project strongly reminiscent of Canadian transportation policy of the nineteenth century. The dominion will have spent $200,000,000 on the navigation portion of the project, while Ontario Hydro, the provincial electrical authority, will contribute considerable investment in hydroelectric generating capacity. Less conspicuous, but important in total, have been postwar investments by Quebec Hydro and other provincial government agencies. Certainly large-scale investments by organs of the provincial governments will play a major role in the future. The federal government has never been reluctant to start public enterprises, and the last two decades have brought several vigorous public corporations which

---

[43] Moore and Perry, pp. 62–63 and Part III generally; J. A. Maxwell, *Recent Developments in Dominion-Provincial Fiscal Relations in Canada* (New York, 1948), especially pp. 51–56. For a discussion of the relation of tax rental to provincial autonomy, see J. N. Wolfe, "Tax Rentals and Provincial Autonomy," *Canadian Tax Journal*, 2:359–362 (November-December 1954), with rejoinders by Moore and Perry.

[44] Rowat, p. 15. Compare Moore and Perry, p. 73.

have helped boost postwar economic development. In 1937 Trans-Canada Airlines came into being as the dominion became impatient with private efforts.[45] The defense requirements of World War II put the Canadian government into the business of producing natural rubber, mining and refining uranium, and, more recently producing atomic energy. The author of one study of Canadian public enterprise has concluded:

> The years since the onset of World War II have witnessed a merger of the national development theme with that of national defense. Each reinforces the strength of the other. Does it aid defense or development more when, for example, public corporations mine and refine uranium or build transportation and electric power systems in remote, primitive areas of the country? The pace of events still outruns the capabilities of private interests in conquering Canadian geography alone. . . .[46]

Other measures adopted by Canada have been tried to encourage development by lubricating the capital market. The National Housing Act of 1954 went far beyond its predecessors of 1935, 1938, and 1944 by admitting the chartered banks to N.H.A. mortgage lending and creating a secondary mortgage market in these loans where individuals and other investors could participate. This has been an important step toward eliminating the historic isolation between the mortgage market and the rest of the Canadian capital market.[47] Another such policy was the establishment of the Industrial Development Bank in 1944, an agency with maximum reserves of $100,000,000 acting as a lender of last resort to businesses, particularly small enterprises, which could be expected to succeed in a high employment economy.[48] Again, the objective was to fill a blank spot in the Canadian capital market existing because the popularity of the commercial loan theory of banking makes medium- and long-term capital hard for small firms to acquire.

[45] C. D. Howe, then minister of transport, told the House of Commons at the time: "Our task in Canada is to set up this service without all the lost motion that has been expended during the past ten years." Such sentiments fall much more easily from Canadian lips than from those of United States politicians.

[46] L. D. Musolf, "Canadian Public Enterprise: A Character Study," *American Political Science Review*, 50:405–421 (June 1956), especially p. 409.

[47] J. V. Poapst, "The National Housing Act, 1954," *CJEPS*, 22:234–243 (May 1956).

[48] For a study of the first three years of the bank's operations, see D. A. Fergusson, "The Industrial Development Bank of Canada," *Journal of Business of the University of Chicago*, 21:214–229 (October 1948).

Can we get from this record any firm indications of the future role of government in economic development? That record chronicles two sharply different periods in Canadian history with the break coming at World War I. Previously the federal government in particular had taken the initiative with massive development projects lying at the heart of economic growth in the new country. After World War I these development promotion activities broke off sharply, giving place to social welfare and adjustment programs undertaken first by the provinces in the 1920's and later by the dominion in the face of the greater needs of the 1930's. The years since World War II have not brought a really sharp break from the character of the interwar period, but it seems fair to conclude that promoting economic development has been much more fashionable than in the 1920's. To a degree there has been a synthesis of the development promotion programs of the pre-World War I era and the economic stabilization programs developed since then. At least one writer, Maurice Lamontagne, has tried to explain and interpret this pattern in terms of changes in Canada's economic climate.[49] In periods when market forces generate a socially acceptable rate of economic growth on their own, governments refrain from development efforts and devote themselves to economic stabilization. When private investment prospects are inadequate, government investment bulks larger to take its place while government stabilization efforts recede into the background.[50] Given the excellent economic prospects for the coming decades, he foresees government activity in coming decades confined largely to short-run economic stabilization.

On close examination this interesting argument proves unacceptable. The weakest part of it is the assumption that the normal course of political action in Canada has been for government to take measures to promote long-run development only when private investment *in the aggregate* was inadequate. The opposite assumption would be just as easy or easier to defend out of the history books, for the major development projects have ridden waves of enthusiasm and not solaced waves of gloom. True, in

[49] M. Lamontagne, "The Role of Government," in *Canada's Tomorrow*, ed. G. P. Gilmour (Toronto, 1954), pp. 117–152.

[50] Lamontagne holds the rather optimistic view that, unlike private investment, government investment will not automatically generate business cycles (p. 135).

the post-Keynesian era public investment for development promotion has been seen to serve the uses of economic stabilization as well, and if Canada faces prolonged high unemployment in the future public investment will undoubtedly be stepped up. But this conjecture does not rule out government actions for promoting economic development just because the prospects for private action promise to be rosy.

How active can we expect government to become in promoting economic development? Certainly it will not return to its role in the 1900's. Canada has had national development policies in the past not because development became a national ideology, but because it lay in the interest of particular groups able to gain their political wishes.[51] J. A. Corry has pointed out that where this is the case government projects are likely to assume massive proportions only where the structure of political interests is fairly simple so that it will yield something near únanimity on policies such as railroad construction or prairie land settlement. Turning the point around, in a complex and diversified economy and society it is very unlikely that sufficient special interests will line up to institute really major government projects.[52] Clearly the latter case is the broadly relevant one for present-day Canada. Yet the Canadian willingness to undertake public projects guarantees that government will go on aiding economic development in less showy but still significant ways. Opening up northern Canada for mining and forestry, long-distance transportation of oil and natural gas, maintaining an adequate supply of low-cost electric power, utilizing the promise of atomic energy — one can safely count on Canadian governments undertaking these tasks if private enterprise proves insufficient or slow.[53] This view is supported by the outcome of the postwar dominion-provincial financial arrangements, which have settled the responsibility for economic stabilization firmly at the federal level, where it can be coordinated much better with the aims of long-run economic

---

[51] A. Brady, "The State and Economic Life," in *Canada,* ed. G. W. Brown (Berkeley and Los Angeles, 1950), pp. 353–371, especially p. 354.

[52] J. A. Corry, *The Growth of Government Activities since Confederation, A Study Prepared for the RCDPR* (Ottawa, 1939), p. 5.

[53] Compare Musolf, p. 409. Speaking of federal public corporations, he declares: "In view of world events and Canada's own ambitions, it is evident that continued government action of this sort will be needed in the foreseeable future."

development. Furthermore, as F. R. Scott points out in surveying the whole federal-provincial relations question, social insurance is closely related to industrial development, and the latter is operated at the national and indeed the international level. "The big risks go with the big industries and there too are to be found the chief sources of wealth which must pay for the protection. National economic policy and national insurances [*sic*] cannot easily be separated." [54]

Thus projecting the historic record of public policy in Canada implies a continued synthesis of efforts at economic stabilization and economic development. The development efforts will certainly be there and, while they will not change the course of Canadian economic development, they may do much to smooth that course. It takes no clairvoyance to see that a main problem of wise public policy will be devising ways of making the same policies serve the ends of both stabilization and development.

[54] F. R. Scott, "Constitutional Adaptations to Changing Functions of Government," *CJEPS*, 11:336 (August 1945).

PART II
PROSPECT

8

Prospects for Canada's Population

Projecting population growth is not a pastime recommended for the faint of heart. The history of population forecasting is so strewn with disasters as to make the uninitiated wonder whether the game is worth the candle. For example, J. G. Gardiner in 1937 forecast that by 1950 Canada's population would amount to 25,000,000. In 1931 C. L. Burton estimated that the population of Canada could increase to as much as 35,000,000 by 1956, thus overshooting the mark by something more than 100 per cent.[1] At the other end of the spectrum, a very careful 1939 study by W. B. Hurd indicated that the population even in 1971 would be no greater than 15,400,000.[2] Predictions for shorter periods have scarcely been more successful, considering that the less distant target date leaves less room for error.

Needless to say, poor population forecasts have by no means been a Canadian monopoly. The Scripps Foundation in the United States predicted in 1928 that the United States population would hit a peak in 1970 at 145,000,000 and would decline thereafter.[3] Colin Clark in 1942 predicted a United States work force of 58,700,000 for 1960;[4] the actual figure in 1955 was approximately 65,000,000. The 1950 census showed the United States population to be 152,000,000 and the following five years alone saw an increase of an additional 13,000,000 persons. Even projections prepared in 1947 predicted a maximum population in 1950 of only 148,000,000 and but 162,000,000 by 1960.[5]

This shabby record is brightened considerably by one amazing prediction of the United States population which was accurate for sixty years. One Francis Bonynge, writing in 1852, presumably

---

[1] Steven Cartwright, *Population: Canada's Problem*, Canadian Institute of International Affairs (Toronto, 1954), pp. 9-10.

[2] W. B. Hurd, "Some Implications of Prospective Population Changes in Canada," *CJEPS*, 5:492–503 (November 1939).

[3] W. S. Woytinsky and E. S. Woytinsky, *World Population and Production, Trends and Outlook* (New York, 1953), pp. 251–253.

[4] Colin Clark, *The Economics of 1960* (London, 1942), p. 80.

[5] U. S. Bureau of the Census, *Forecasts of the Population of the U. S., 1945–1975*, p. 41.

with the knowledge of the 1850 census figure of 23,300,000, predicted for 1910 a population of 96,400,000, less than 5,000,000 off the mark, simply by assuming definite rates of annual increase in the number of white persons, slaves, and free colored persons.[6]

Despite the unfavorable odds one faces in attempting to construct reasonably accurate long-range population projections, for some problems there is no alternative. Research designed to estimate the demand for any commodity in the future, or any major national income aggregate, must first establish a studied estimate of the number of consumers expected to exist at the future date in question. The simple trend extrapolations which often pass for forecasts of single economic variables must implicitly rest on some assumption about population changes or the range of possible changes. It is far wiser to make the population estimate specific and establish it with care.

Because of the absence of satisfactory alternative assumptions, social scientists must rely heavily on the proposition that there is considerable stability in human behavior over time. Therefore, population projections presume that future birth rates, mortality rates, and migration rates will be stable or will in some degree follow recent trends. Extraneous events such as wars or serious depressions which will disrupt such trends generally cannot be foreseen, of course; the population projections drawn up in the 1930's could hardly have been expected satisfactorily to prophesy the impact of World War II on Canada's population. Even now, more than a decade after the close of the war, it is difficult to discuss with much confidence the impact of World War II on Canadian population growth. Because it is so difficult to discern whether or not the higher birth rate is transitory, it is now perhaps more difficult to predict future population growth than it will be, say, five years from now.

THE EXPECTED BIRTH RATES

Population projections can best be constructed by careful analysis of trends in the birth rates, mortality rates, and immigration rates for the country in question. The postwar population projections both for the United States and Canada have been quite wide of the mark (considering that most of the projections were relatively short range) primarily because the anticipated return

---

[6] Woytinsky and Woytinsky, p. 245.

of the birth rate to prewar levels has not yet materialized. The crude birth rate, that is, births per thousand persons in the population, gradually declined by more than 10 per thousand from its peak following World War I down to a low of 20.1 per thousand in 1937. This secular decline in the birth rate had characterized all the major industrial powers in recent decades, so it was generally considered that the decline would be resumed soon after the return of normal peacetime conditions. Actually, the birth rate had climbed back to 24.3 in 1945 and to 28.9 in 1947 and has not been below 27 since that time.

Figure 3 shows the Canadian crude birth rate and also specific birth rates (births per thousand women of the specified age

Fig. 3. Crude birth rate and birth rates per thousand women of specified ages, 1926–1956.

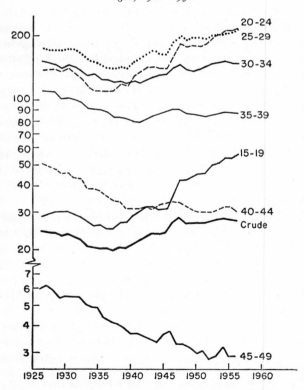

Source: DBS, *Vital Statistics, 1956* (Ottawa, 1957), pp. 89–93.

groups) from 1926 through 1956. Note the steadiness of the
plateau reached by the crude birth rate since 1947. Several students of Canadian population changes have claimed that the
bulk of the postwar birth rate increase reflects family formation
deferred during World War II.[7] But such a factor could hardly
explain a decade of birth rates only a little short of those
achieved in two or three years after World War I. The crude
birth rate zoomed to 32.2 in 1921, but then fell steadily to 29.0
in 1924 and 25.8 in 1928. The effect of deferred family formation
could explain such a pattern as that of the 1920's, but not the
sort seen in Canada during the last decade.

The specific birth rates tell much of the story behind the pattern of the post-World War II years. As was noted in Chapter 2,
the great force behind the high crude birth rate has been the
rising specific birth rates among women aged 20–29. But during
the 1950's only the rate for women over 45 has failed to rise
steadily. The specific birth rates for all age groups of women show
peaks some time during the 1945–1947 period, thus giving some
interpretive significance to the deferred family formation doctrine. But the rise of birth rates in all classes since 1949–50
cannot be laid at the doorstep of World War II. Because it appears in nearly all age groups, the rise cannot be attributed to a
preference for having children at an earlier age. The only obvious
explanation consistent with the data behind Figure 3 is that the
cumulative effect of a decade of rising incomes and steady employment have given Canadian families sufficient confidence in their
economic futures to commit themselves to the burden of rearing
more children.

Giving the correct interpretation to this apparent trend is absolutely vital to successful long-range forecasting. Granted, the
Canadian labor force for 1970 has already been born. But the
inducement to invest depends so heavily if indirectly on the birth
rates of the present and immediate past that these rates must be
studied carefully if either the size or the composition of Canada's
1970 income is to be estimated with any accuracy.

At the outbreak of World War II demographers foresaw a continuing decline in the birth rate of the industrialized countries of
the world. They had good reason to hold this opinion. In western

[7] N. B. Ryder, "Components of Canadian Population Growth," *Population
Index*, 20:77 (April 1954).

Europe the birth rate had declined steadily from the level of about 30 per thousand in the middle of the nineteenth century to 15 per thousand in 1940, and in the United States the rate had been dropping steadily since the turn of the century.[8] Since this rate of decline would indicate for the United States and western Europe a birth rate surprisingly near zero by the year 2000, it is understandable that we have seen prosperity bring an increase in the birth rate.

A number of reasons can be cited for expecting the crude birth rate to remain in the 25 to 28 per thousand range rather than falling much toward the depression rate of 20 and 21 per thousand. As we have seen, the pattern of specific rates is consistent with only one obvious explanation — that in a state of high confidence about their economic future Canadians prefer larger families than they have in the past. If this confidence escapes the ravages of unemployment and other major disturbances, there is no reason to think that specific birth rates must turn downward drastically within the next decade. Under conditions of continuing prosperity, Canadians may go on using some of their increased income to buy not only longer married lives and longer parenthood but also bigger families.

The expansion of employment opportunities for women in the economy would seem to lend support to this hypothesis. Industrialization is making it increasingly easy for women to find work. Further, continued mechanization of existing industry and the rapid development of light industry would open up increased opportunities for women even if the degree of industrialization were to remain stable.[9] The expansion of these employment opportunities for women might be interpreted as likely to retard the marriage rate since the single woman now can more easily support herself, but on the other hand certainly a tremendous number of marriages have been hastened because the married woman could work and would not be completely reliant on her

[8] Woytinsky and Woytinsky, pp. 143–144.
[9] Recently this trend has been so pronounced even in year-to-year labor force changes as to attract attention. Between September 1956 and September 1957, the increase in Canada's labor force consisted of nearly equal numbers of men (144,000) and women (131,000). But the increase of males with jobs was only 42 per cent of the increase of men in the labor force, while the increase of women with jobs was 89 per cent of the female labor force increase. See "Save Your Tears, Watch the Girls," *Financial Post*, November 16, 1957, pp. 1, 8.

husband for support. The advent of the "working wife" and the "working mother" may very well mean a continuation of early household formation, early families, and larger families.

The family allowance plan would also seem to operate to retard any secular decline in the birth rate, at least in that it makes large families less burdensome for the poor than would be the case in the absence of the family allowances. Because of the relatively brief experience with the family allowances, however, it is extremely difficult to assess with any degree of confidence the extent to which they are likely to influence the birth rate.

Another bit of questionable but intriguing evidence in support of a continued high birth rate hypothesis can be cited. A recent careful survey of families in one United States city revealed that family size and family income were inversely correlated for the entire group. The high income families typically had fewer children than the low income families. Nevertheless, among those families who planned their family size, the correlation was positive, meaning that the larger the income the larger the family size.[10] Although generalization on the basis of this one study can scarcely be accepted with much confidence, it does raise the distinct possibility that over time our society may see rising incomes causing larger families, even though at any one point in time the poor families are larger than the well-to-do families.

The bi-cultural nature of the Canadian population is another factor which may augur a continued high birth rate. The rate of natural increase among French Canadians has been so much greater than among the British ethnic group that from 1921 to 1951 the ratio of non-French to French Canadians fell from two to one to about one and one-half to one.[11] Still more telling, perhaps, is the fact that although there are three times as many British as French among the Canadians age 65 and above, there are but 20 per cent more British than French in the under-20 age group. An increase in the proportion of Canadian families with a high birth rate heritage exerts an upward pressure on the rate for the country as a whole.

This effect can be exaggerated, however, since the birth rate among French Canadians is clearly falling. The province of

---

[10] C. V. Kiser and P. K. Whelpton, *Social and Psychological Factors Affecting Fertility* (New York, 1949), p. 413.

[11] Ryder, p. 78.

Quebec is becoming industrialized, rather belatedly, and the St. Lawrence Seaway will supposedly assure that this type of economic development will continue. Industrialization has brought the usual urbanization, higher incomes, and shifts from agricultural to industrial and commercial occupations, and the birth rate has responded to these changes. In 1937 the birth rate in Quebec was 16 per cent greater than for all of Canada; by 1954 the rate for that province was but 8 per cent above the rate for the rest of the country. The largest declines in French birth rates have been in the upper age groups of women, a phenomenon often viewed by demographers as a sure sign of a long-run decline in birth rates. Quebec's marriage rate has fallen over the last half century relative to that of the rest of Canada. In 1891, Quebec had the highest marriage rate among the provinces; in 1941 it occupied the lowest rank, and the proportion of the population married had fallen.[12] High rural French Canadian birth rates have been shown to depend on the need for farm labor, the possibility of exporting surplus offspring to urban employment, and a definite pattern of rural traditionalism.[13] None of these forces can persist long in urban centers. Even if family formation patterns stay unchanged among rural French Canadians, the total effect will be a continued decline in French Canadian birth rates.

In short, the French Canadian birth rate situation has two effects on the total Canadian birth rate pattern. First, it tends to raise that rate as the French make up a growing share of the total population, for their birth rates are above the birth rates for the non-French populace. On the other hand, French birth rates are themselves declining. What will be the net result? It is fairly clear that French rates are still so much higher than non-French rates that the urbanization of Quebec will not deal a major blow to Canada's population increase. Table 32 shows the specific birth rates for Canadians of British and of French origin at the time of the 1951 Census. The French still have a marked excess in all but the lowest age group (15–19).

Although at least some of the arguments for sustained high

---

[12] Jacques Henripin, "Observations sur la situation demographique des Canadiens français," *LE*, 32:565–569 (janvier-mars 1957).

[13] Horace Miner, "The French-Canadian Family Cycle," *American Sociological Review*, 3:700–708 (October 1938).

Table 32.   Specific birth rates of Canadians of British and of French origin,
1951 (births per thousand women).

Female age group	British origin	French origin
15–19	57.8	36.2
20–24	178.4	194.8
25–29	176.3	229.4
30–34	123.1	180.6
35–39	66.4	123.7
40–44	20.1	51.1
45–49	1.4	5.6

Source: J. Henripin, "Observations sur la situation démographique des Canadiens français," *LE*, 32:562 (janvier–mars, 1957).

birth rates are persuasive indeed, a decline from the present level of specific birth rates is not hard to defend. First of all, the Canadian marriage rate is falling. The marriage rate climbed from a depression low of 6.0 per thousand in 1932 and 1933 to 11.0 in 1942 and 10.9 in 1946. Since then, however, it has been declining steadily and in 1955 stood at 6.7.[14] To the extent that the marriage rate can be taken as a harbinger of the birth rate, a decline in the crude birth rate at least would seem to be ahead. Secondly, it is still virtually undisputed that industrialization of a country is associated in the long run with lower birth rates. If the industrialization and urbanization of Canada continue, therefore, we can expect to see the birth rate drift downward. Some forecast of this decline is evidenced by the fact that the discrepancy between the birth rate in Canada and that of the United States has been declining from about six to eight births per thousand in the 1920's to about three or four per thousand in the years since World War II. Finally, Canada's current birth rate is the highest of any developed country and therefore might be expected to move over the coming years toward the average for the older industrialized nations.

Instead of choosing some sort of median birth rate projection

[14] Some of the fall in the crude marriage rate since World War II can be attributed to the change in the age distribution of the population. The unusually low birth rates of the 1930's have resulted in a relatively small number of persons entering marriageable ages in the 1950's and the unusually high birth rates of the war and postwar years have increased the total population; consequently, the number of marriages per thousand population is temporarily distorted.

and basing a single population projection on that rate, the present study uses a high, a low, and a medium birth rate for each age group to compute three alternative population projections. This tactic makes it possible to discern the margin of error in the 1970 population estimate arising from any poor prognostications of the birth rate. Figure 4 shows the method, using the

Fig. 4. Diagrammatic comparison of high, low, and medium birth rate assumptions, 20–24 age group.

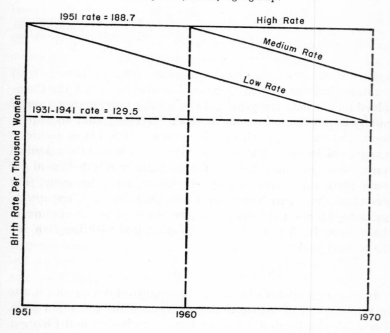

20–24 age group as an illustration. The high birth rate projection assumes that the 1951 rate of 188.7 will continue for this group to 1970. It is considered that this is a reasonable maximum expectation, since the crude birth rate has not been more than the 1951 crude rate for any extended period since the first half of the 1920's. The low birth rate assumption, on the other hand, presumes first of all that a high level of employment will be maintained in Canada in most years, and that therefore the birth rate is not likely to fall below that of the years of lowest unemployment immediately prior to World War II. The low birth rate assumption for the 20–24 age group therefore presumes that the rate will decline in a linear manner from the 1951 level, descending by 1970 to 129.5 per thousand, the birth rate of the 1939–1941 period. Crude birth rate data through 1956 indicate that this decline has not yet started, so the low birth rate assumption allows for quite a sharp drop in the 1960's decade.

For setting a "best guess" somewhere between the high and low birth rate assumptions discussed above, two possibilities come to mind. The first is a linear decline from the 1951 levels to a higher birth rate in 1970 than obtained in 1939–1941. The second possibility presumes that the 1951 rates will continue until 1960, and that thereafter the rate of decline will be the same as in the low birth rate assumption discussed above. The latter assumption squares with facts to date and, moreover, can be rationalized by granting that the current high level of employment will be sustained for the next few years both by sizable defense expenditures and by large private investment expenditures on plant and equipment, and that the birth rate is in part a function of the level of national income. The decline after 1960 presumes a limited retreat from sustained full employment and a return toward the lower birth rates indicated by the long-run prewar trend. The second of these two possibilities was used for the "best guess" estimate. Figure 4 illustrates for the 20–24 group the nature of the medium birth rate projection as compared with the high and the low projections.

THE EXPECTED DEATH RATES

In marked contrast with variations in birth rate, the death rate in Canada has, of course, followed a much more stable course. The crude death rate for Canada since 1921 is shown in Figure 5, and the specific mortality rates for males and females are charted in Figure 6 for selected years since 1926. It is evident that while there has been a steady decline in the death rate for the country as a whole, the rate of decline has differed among age groups. Infant mortality has been reduced most substantially, and the percentage reduction in the mortality rate since 1940 falls as one moves up through age groups. In other words, the life expectancy of young people is increasing all the while, but the life expectancy of persons over 60 is increasing but slowly. There is an interesting differential in the rate of decline in the death rate for

Fig. 5. *Crude death rate per thousand population, 1921–1956.*[a]

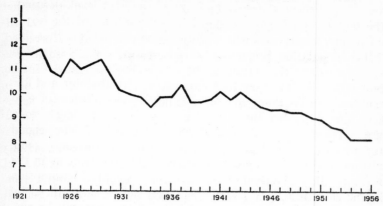

[a] Rates are per thousand mid-year population and are exclusive of the Yukon and Northwest Territories and Newfoundland to April 1, 1949, and of Quebec to 1926.

Source: DBS, *Vital Statistics, 1956* (Ottawa, 1957), p. 14.

Fig. 6. *Death rates per thousand persons of specified age and sex, selected years, 1926–1956.*

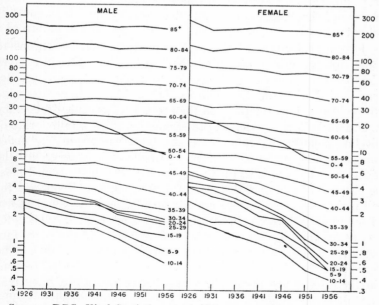

Source: DBS, *Vital Statistics, 1956* (Ottawa, 1957), pp. 110–113.

men in the 40 to 55 age groups in contrast with women of those ages. This differential would seem to support the hypothesis that the high tempo of present day business life causes physical ailments and weaknesses which are not easily avoided or corrected.

The population projection, of course, must make some presumption about the pattern of these mortality rates in the future. Not only is it necessary to decide whether the rate of decline in the crude rate is likely to continue, but a judgment is also necessary about whether the pattern of specific death rates will continue. There is general agreement on the causes of the twin features of Canadian death rate history, that is, falling mortality rates among the young and relatively stable rates among the old. First, public and private medical care, especially maternity and infant care, has been greatly improved over the years. Second, the conquest of the major communicable diseases has removed what was once a major cause of mortality in the lower age groups. Other factors, difficult to evaluate but surely of considerable importance, are the general improvement in diets and hence in resistance to disease and the long-run improvement in working conditions in industry. The slow rate of change in the mortality rate among those over 60 testifies to the relatively intractable nature of the diseases of organic degeneracy — cancer, heart and circulatory diseases, and so forth.

Linear projections of the 1926–1956 death rate reductions to 1970 by age groups are unrealistic since this procedure gives death rates of zero before 1970 for some of the age groups. Because of the inevitability of some deaths in all age groups (due to accidents, for example, and the problem of organic degeneracy mentioned above) it seemed preferable to assume a falling rate of decline in mortality rates for each of the age groups for males under 50 and for females under 55. In the higher age groups the death rate has fallen so little since 1921 that it was deemed most appropriate to assume the present death rate would continue for all males age 50 and above and for all females age 55 and above. The growing interest in heart disease and related aspects of geriatrics may possibly result in some reduction in the death rate by 1970, but it is assumed that such a reduction would not be significant by that date. The relatively small number of persons in these older age groups in a growing population assures that any errors in this assumption would have but a minute effect on the total 1970 estimate.

It is appropriate to point out parenthetically that the crude death rate in Canada in recent years probably has been lower than can be sustained for any extended period. At first, such a statement might seem to presume a reduction in average life expectancy contrary to the long-run trend. Actually, an increase in the crude death rate would occur simultaneously with increased life expectancy if the rate of growth of the population were to fall sufficiently. If the Canadian population were to remain fixed at its present level, for example, the current death rate of less than nine per thousand population could continue only if the average age at death were 110 years! Thus we know that the very low crude death rate of recent years has been caused in part by the large influx of young immigrants which increased the population size more, proportionally, than it increased the absolute number of deaths.[15]

IMMIGRATION

Greater uncertainty surrounds the forecast of net immigration than either the birth rate or the death rate, although the final population projection would be affected far less by, say, a 20 per cent error in the migration forecast than by a 20 per cent error in the birth rate. The unique nature of Canada's immigration history makes forecasting in this area particularly hazardous. Historically, Canada has provided Europe with one of its great population safety valves. Between 1821 and 1932, some 54,000,-000 immigrants poured into the Americas, 34,000,000 of these coming into the United States. Canada and Newfoundland attracted more than 5,000,000 of the remaining 20,000,000.[16] However, for the period 1851 to 1941 the number of emigrants from Canada came within about 5 per cent of the number of immigrants to the country. This remarkable fact has led a few writers to espouse the "displacement theory" of Canadian immigration.[17] It is regrettable that this theory is not acceptable, for if it

---

[15] Compare the discussion of the effects of Canada's changing population pyramid in Chapter 2.

[16] Woytinsky and Woytinsky, p. 72.

[17] See Chapter 2.

were we could quickly set down a forecast of zero net immigration by 1970 and move on to the next problem. But the displacement theory, which was particularly popular during the days of net out-migration during the 1930's, rests on the assumption that Canada's resources are limited and cannot support a larger population for any length of time unless the standard of living is reduced, that is, that the "optimum population" has a stable and narrowly defined value. The inadequacies of this reasoning have been discussed in Chapter 2.

If we admit that surely some net migration will occur over the coming decade, it remains to examine the determinants of immigration and to decide how these determinants are likely to behave. A review of the history of international immigration in general and of immigration into Canada in particular makes it quite clear that the differential in living standards has been, as one might expect, the primary factor influencing the movement of people over international boundaries, although political and social turmoil were also of some influence. The potato famine in Ireland and depressed conditions in the British Isles in general caused extensive migration to the United States and Canada in the 1840's. Political disturbances on the continent also were responsible for some out-migration to the Americas during the latter part of the 1840's and through the 1850's. Immigration into Canada fell from 310,000 between 1851 and 1860 to 290,000 during the next decade, and but 220,000 people entered Canada during the 1870's. During the next twenty years approximately 6,000,000 more immigrants came into the country. The annual migration rate then more than tripled for the great years of Canadian expansion, 1900–1920. The decline in immigration to Canada which applied to the period from 1860 to 1900 can be attributed to the depressed conditions which the major countries were experiencing during much of this period. Some attention is given below to the role of the business cycle in international migration; it suffices to say here that when all countries are suffering under depression conditions, migration is low simply because relatively few people can afford to move. The huge immigration into Canada in the first twenty years of the twentieth century definitely occurred primarily because differentials in economic opportunity appeared simultaneously with prosperity in the countries of emigration. Not only did Canadian policy encourage immigration at this time, but also the revolution in ship technology permitted substantially reduced fares.

The history of migration into countries other than Canada also testifies to the importance of the differential economic opportunity as the factor of primary importance in determining the direction and rate of migration. Although it is impossible to construct and compare satisfactory measures of average real income for different countries because of the difficulty of comparing diverse living standards, a crude indication of differences in average real incomes has been constructed for several prewar years by Colin Clark.[18] He expressed the average income received by families in the various countries for which data were available in terms of International Units, an International Unit being defined as the amount of goods and services which one United States dollar would purchase in the United States over the period 1925–1934. At the top of the list of average real incomes for the 1925–1934 period is the United States with 1771 International Units, followed by Canada, New Zealand, Great Britain, Argentina, Switzerland, and Australia, all with average real incomes of about 1,000 International Units. Near the bottom were Rumania, Lithuania, India, and China, with 100 to 120 International Units. It is clear that, with the exception of Great Britain and possibly Switzerland, the countries at the top of the list attracted immigrants from the countries with lower average real incomes: Great Britain and Switzerland lost emigrants to countries with higher incomes.

The basic work on the relation of migration and the business cycle corroborates the hypothesis that differentials in economic opportunity generally (although not always) determine the direction and rate of migration.[19] Before the United States took steps seriously to restrict immigration from Europe in 1921, cyclical fluctuations in economic activity in the United States generally coincided with the business cycle in other countries. It is interesting, however, that the migration was considerably greater when the country losing emigrants and the country receiving immigrants were both enjoying boom conditions. It seems that during the prosperity phase of the cycle people can afford to migrate,

[18] Colin Clark, *The Conditions of Economic Progress,* 2nd ed. (London, 1951), ch. iii.

[19] Harry Jerome, *Migration and Business Cycles* (New York, 1926).

and they do migrate in spite of the high employment in the country of emigration. At such times, their relatives in the country of immigration are also better prepared to help finance the trip.

That migration depends primarily on the differential in economic opportunity assumes the absence of any significant barriers to the international movement of persons. Since the early 1930's, Canada and the United States have legislated restrictions on the number of immigrants. We must therefore qualify the conclusion that the flow of migrants into Canada will depend on the economic prospects in that country as contrasted with others by adding that a ceiling on this flow may be imposed by Canadian immigration policy. During the early 1930's it became quite apparent that Canadians would not tolerate unlimited immigration when unemployment prevailed at home. In the prosperous years since the war, however, Canadian immigration policy has been more lenient. It appears that historically those in the British ethnic group and management generally have preferred a liberal immigration policy while the French Canadians and the labor unions have favored a more restrictive attitude. At present, it would seem probable that a very favorable attitude toward immigration will prevail, at least while prosperity lasts.[20] Parliament, however, can prevent what it considers an excess of immigration merely by reducing the appropriation for immigration examiners while leaving untouched the prevailing immigration legislation. Thus, immigration could be slowed simply because the staff would be inadequate to process the applications while the political repercussions of restrictions are minimized because there has been no ostensible change in the legislative policy.

Emigration, on the other hand, is not likely to be brought under control, and significant numbers have been leaving Canada in the postwar years for the United States at an annual rate of about 23,000 persons. The yearly figures have covered a range of from 20,400 in 1946 to 33,400 in 1952. Since the ratio of United States per capita income to Canadian per capita income has shrunk only from about 1.5 in 1931 to about 1.4 in 1953, the his-

[20] See, for example, "More Immigrants Needed by Canada," *New York Times,* August 28, 1955. Business groups and liberals in Canada have often been critical of Canadian immigration authorities for restricting their overseas prospecting for migrants to a search for skilled labor of types in short-run shortage in Canada.

tory of migrations suggests a continuing net movement southward. Variations in this rate of flow to the United States may in turn influence immigration policy significantly, for in a sense sizable emigration to the United States is a substitute for restricted immigration. Thus a minor recession may not bring a change in immigration policy if emigration increases significantly; however, the fact that any immigration seems so clearly to increase the competition for scarce jobs may make restricted immigration a political necessity regardless of the changes in emigration.

Given a liberal immigration policy except under depression conditions and given the hypothesis that migration is a function of income differentials between Canada and the other countries of the world (especially the other members of the Commonwealth), some progress toward a defensible migration rate assumption can be achieved. In view of the announced policy — in Great Britain and the United States as well as Canada — of using the federal budget as a means of maintaining a high level of employment, it does not appear unreasonable to assume that prolonged or serious departures from a high level of employment will not be experienced by any of the major western powers in the foreseeable future. It is widely granted that our understanding of the causes and cures of depressions has been advanced to the point where we can make this assumption with a fair degree of confidence. At least it seems more likely than any specific alternative pattern. With the gradual return to settled conditions in Europe, the primary source of Canadian immigrants is expected to provide a shrinking number of persons each year. However, disturbances such as the "Suez affair," which sent British emigration rocketing, can change the picture greatly.

Underlying any discussion of potential immigration is some preconception about whether population growth in general, as well as migration in particular, is a result of or a cause of increases in the country's national income. In this study natural population increase is considered to be independent of the growth of the national income if a reasonably high level of employment is maintained. Migration, on the other hand, is rather clearly determined in part by the rate of increase in the national income contrasted with the rate of increase in the incomes in other countries. It is considered much more difficult, therefore, to forecast migration rates than birth rates and death rates. If Canada's natural resources continue to show distinct cost advantages over reserves of the same resources elsewhere, it is easy to visualize a strong export market and a steadily rising income to the country. On the other hand, if newsprint from bagasse becomes a major threat or if other Canadian exports suffer similar accidental curtailment, export demand may not run as great, incomes may not rise as fast, and immigration may not be as great as in the first instance. In brief, Canada's absorptive capacity is determined primarily by the absorptive capacity of her export industries and the industries dependent on them; and the performance of the export industries will be determined largely by world prices. Thus, it is more hazardous to express firm views about the magnitude of the immigration into Canada than to forecast changes in the rate of natural increase.

Because so much of the postwar immigration was due to the war itself, rather than to the income differentials which normally determine migration, it is generally granted that migration will decline. It remains to establish a "best guess" migration rate for 1970. Assuming that no serious recessions will be experienced by any of the major industrial powers of the West is to assume that the postwar immigration wave will prove to have been unique and that migration hereafter will play but a minor role again in Canadian population growth. In 1951, the net immigration was 120,000 and now appears to be at about 100,000 per year. If this rate of decline were to continue, net immigration would be approaching zero in 1970. Considering the world's growing needs for the minerals and other raw materials which Canada appears to have at her disposal, a return to a zero net migration within the next decade or so does seem most unlikely. Recent mineral discoveries would seem to portend a continued net immigration of significant amount, although not as great as in the immediate postwar years. High, low, and medium immigration rate assumptions were, therefore, drawn up as follows. The low immigration rate assumption considers the net rate to decline linearly from 120,000 in 1951 to 30,000 in 1970; the medium rate assumes a linear decline to 40,000 a year in 1970; and the high rate assumes the rate to hit a 1970 low of 50,000.

In order to forecast the total impact of immigration on Canadian population, it is also necessary to set up assumptions about the age and sex composition of the immigrants as well as the birth rates and death rates applicable to them. Two alternative assumptions about age-sex composition were considered. First, the appropriate age-sex distribution might be that of 1926–1929 since that was the last period of high level immigration during peacetime. The second argument is that the 1951–52 age-sex distribution of immigrants is more appropriate since the immigrants entering that year and in the years immediately following will constitute such a large proportion of the total anticipated over the next decade. Also, immigration policy may well operate to maintain this age-sex distribution among immigrants. The latter procedure was used, although the effect on the final projection would not be great. Finally, the age-sex distribution of the emigrants is considered to be the same as for the immigrants, and the birth rates and death rates applicable to the immigrants are taken to be the same as for native Canadians. Any errors resulting from these last two assumptions are no doubt small.

THE FINAL PROJECTIONS

In computing the three alternative population forecasts, the low birth rate assumption was used in conjunction with the low immigration assumption, and the high birth rate and the high immigration rate both were used in preparing the high population estimate. The underlying rationale for this procedure is the feeling that both these rates are high or low depending on the level of national income, and therefore they will be high or low together.

The calculating procedure is simple in theory although extremely laborious in practice. First, consider those Canadians who were living in 1951 (the year of the most recent census). Of every age and sex group, a certain fraction will survive to comprise the age groups 20 and over in 1970. The number of these survivors can be calculated using our assumed rates of change in death rates. Each year, each age group is assumed to be decreased through mortalities and increased through immigration. Applying this procedure for all age groups gives the base population for the next year's calculation, adjusting for the fact that everyone becomes one year older. The age distribution of the female population which comes out of these calculations lets us compute the number of births each year, using the assumed specific birth rates.

Fig. 7. *Population of Canada, 1871–1951, with projections to 1970.*

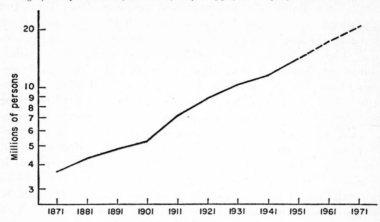

Source: *Canada Year Book, 1956*, p. 149.

It is remarkable how close together the resulting high, low, and medium 1970 estimates are, considering the spread between the high and low birth rate assumptions. The medium rates lead to an estimate of 20,984,000, the low to an estimate of 20,190,000, and the high to an estimate of 21,515,000. That is, the high and low estimates are only about 4 per cent above and below the medium estimate. The historical and projected population figures

Table 33.   Population of Canada by age groups for selected years
(thousands).

Age group	1951	1955	1960	1965	1970
0–9	3,120	3,604	4,118	4,410	4,601
10–19	2,189	2,462	3,017	3,672	4,029
20–29	2,220	2,360	2,392	2,565	3,022
30–39	2,042	2,266	2,493	2,603	2,559
40–49	1,613	1,837	2,129	2,293	2,472
50–59	1,243	1,360	1,531	1,768	1,993
60+	1,592	1,743	1,918	2,118	2,308
Total*a*	14,009	15,634	17,598	19,429	20,984

a Columns may not total due to rounding errors.

Source: 1951 — Actual figures from *Canada Year Book*, 1953. 1955 — Estimates by Canadian Economic Research Associates. 1960, 1965, and 1970 — See text, pp. 275.

are plotted in Figure 7. The age distributions are shown in Table 33.

These estimates point, therefore, to an increase by 1970 of about 50 per cent over the 1951 population. This is an annual rate of increase of about 2.25 per cent which, if maintained, would cause the 1951 population to double about 1980. This rate of increase compares with a rate of about 1.75 per cent for Canada for the period 1911–1951.

Population estimates computed independently of those above are available as a crude check on our own. The Canadian Economic Research Associates have published a group of 1970 estimates ranging from a low of 20,900,000 to a high of 22,400,000.[21] Probably working from the same material, the Royal Commission on Canada's Economic Prospects has recently forecast a 1970 population between 21,160,000 and 22,130,000, depending on whether immigration averages 50,000 or 100,000 annually during the intervening years.[22] The private forecast of a large Canadian manufacturer's market research department is 20,200,000 in 1965, compared with our 19,400,000. Mr. J. E. Coyne of the Bank of Canada has estimated the 1975 population at about 23,000,000, which would mean about 21,000,000 in 1970.[23] Van der Valk also expects the population to reach 23,000,000 sometime in the 1970's.[24] Compared with these four projections, the population expectations of this study are a bit on the conservative side.

For Canada, a growing population can help to insure prosperity for a number of reasons. First of all, a growing population means a continued demand for new housing and for all the consumer durable goods, such as refrigerators, washing machines, and heating plants, which a demand for housing generates. A growing population assures a growing demand for certain services, and consequently private investment expenditures in the service industries should help sustain a high level of aggregate demand. These increases in demand are in addition to the increases in the demand for consumer goods in general.

[21] Canadian Economic Research Associates, *The Future Population of Canada* (Toronto, 1955), unpaged.
[22] Canada, RCCEP, *Preliminary Report* (Ottawa, 1956), pp. 14–18.
[23] J. E. Coyne, "Some Possible Features of Economic Growth and Investment in Canada, 1955–1975," remarks before the annual meeting of the Dominion Mortgage and Investment Association, May 5, 1955, p. 3.
[24] H. M. H. A. van der Valk, *The Economic Future of Canada* (Toronto, 1954), p. 169.

Of particular interest is the prospective change in the age distribution of the population. Although the total population by 1970 is expected to be about 50 per cent greater than in 1951, the increase in the number of school age children will be about 70 per cent, or nearly half again as great as the percentage change for the entire country. If the change in the 20–24 age group is taken as indicative of the change in college age people, an increase of just over 60 per cent is expected. It is clear that Canadians must anticipate a continuing school facilities shortage unless they are prepared to increase per capita expenditures on schools by about one-half by 1970. This differential between the rate of increase of the school age population as compared with the total population also makes it apparent that if the Canadian government seriously pursues a high employment policy, one of the most commendable means of maintaining employment expenditures in times of recession would be to build more school facilities. The increase in the college-age population also forebodes a strain on the country's educational plant even without allowing for an increase in the percentage of the college-age population which will actually go to college.

The number of persons of retirement age, that is, 70 and over, will increase at about the same rate as the total population. The numbers in this group will increase from the 1951 level of about 650,000 to about 940,000 by 1970.

Even though the 70-and-over group will increase by almost 45 per cent, the average age in Canada will fall slightly over the coming years because of the current high birth rates. In 1951, the average age was 30.4; this will fall to 30.1 by 1970. This is but another expression of the increase expected in the younger age groups. (It might be noted that this sizable increase does not extend to the very youngest age group, in which, because of the declining birth rate assumption, an increase over 1951 of scarcely 30 per cent is expected by 1970, compared with the over-all increase of 50 per cent.) The consuming public, therefore, will remain young, so to speak, and certain shifts in the types of goods and services demanded are, of course, implied by this when one considers the continuing reduction in the work week. For example, we can expect the demand for sport clothes and boating equipment to increase more rapidly than the demand for wheelchairs, and so on.

Of greatest significance for purposes of the present study is the change in the absolute size of the work force and in the ratio of the work force to the total population. This is the subject of the following chapter.

9
Labor Force and Gross National
Product in 1970

Now that the population estimate has been established, the expected growth in the labor force can be deduced. By applying the expected rate of increase in productivity of the labor force, the gross national product expected in 1970 then can be estimated. This chapter therefore deals with three topics: (1) the growth in the labor force anticipated over the next decade; (2) the annual increase in productivity which can be expected over that period; and (3) the gross national product which will result if the labor force and productivity projections are correct.

TRENDS IN CANADA'S LABOR FORCE

For the most part the projection of the labor force to 1970 is a straightforward exercise, but a few of the developments in recent years cloud the long-run trends a bit. The available data indicate the percentage of each age group by sex in the work force annually since 1946. Some of these percentages, commonly referred to as participation rates, have stayed nearly constant and can be assumed so for forecasting purposes. But for other groups it is necessary to surmise the reasons for the changes in the rates in order to estimate whether or not the changes can be expected to continue and, if so, to what degree.

A review of the recent trends and their probable causes will facilitate an estimate of the expected movements for the next decade. Two developments are very clearly indicated by the data in Table 34. First, the participation rate among the men 65 and over has declined by about one-third over the nine-year period. This is due in part to the shift out of agriculture into industry, for in agriculture the older man can continue to work if he wishes whereas commonly in industry he is required to retire. The expansion of public and private pension plans also makes early retirement more attractive and feasible than formerly was the case. The second striking development is the increase of about

Table 34. Average annual labor force participation rates in Canada, 1946–1954, and the expected rates for 1970[a] by age and sex (percentages).

Age group	1946	1947	1948	1949	1950	1951	1952	1953	1954	1970[b]
Male										
14–19	60.1	60.1	57.9	58.1	55.8	55.2	52.0	53.1	51.2	39.6
20–24	88.9	90.6	92.1	93.5	93.0	93.0	92.7	92.8	91.6	88.0
25–44	97.0	97.4	97.9	97.9	97.4	97.9	97.8	97.6	97.2	97.6
45–64	93.4	92.7	92.5	93.0	91.9	92.0	91.6	91.8	91.1	92.2
65 and over	47.5	44.8	44.0	42.9	40.5	37.8	36.4	34.8	33.3	17.5
Female										
14–19	37.8	36.6	33.4	35.1	32.9	34.1	33.2	33.6	34.3	26.5
20–24	48.1	45.3	45.4	45.7	46.4	46.8	47.1	47.0	46.4	46.5
25–44	23.2	22.9	22.8	22.9	22.4	22.8	23.3	23.0	23.0	26.0
45–64	15.3	13.5	16.2	15.3	16.4	17.0	17.5	17.0	18.1	25.0
65 and over	5.0	5.7	5.0	4.7	4.3	4.0	4.3	3.7	3.7	3.7

[a] Each annual percentage figure expresses a ratio of labor force to civilian noninstitutional population as estimated by survey procedures, each quarterly survey weighted by estimated population.

[b] It is interesting to compare these forecasts with a comparable set which appeared after our study was completed in the excellent work by William C. Hood and Anthony Scott, *Output, Labour and Capital in the Canadian Economy* (Hull, 1957), p. 184. Their 1970 participation rates are significantly higher than ours for males 15–19, 20–24, and 65 and over, lower for females 45–64. The element of guessing in any such estimates is so great that one cannot say precisely why such differences exist. However, it seems fair to say that we have been bolder than Hood and Scott in assuming that trends apparent in the postwar data will continue and that Canadian labor-force participation will come nearer to resembling the pattern in the United States.

Source: DBS, Reference Paper No. 58, *The Labour Force, November, 1945–January, 1955* (Ottawa, 1955), pp. 21–2, 28–9; for 1970, see text, pp. 285–286.

one-fifth in the participation rate among women between the ages of 45 and 64. This pronounced trend presumably is accounted for partially by the greater number of employment opportunities for women. Not only have the jobs for women in the white collar occupations increased but, in the course of the country's economic development, light industry in which women can work at less arduous tasks has been expanding steadily. The growing use of labor-saving appliances in the home has reduced the time required to run a household to the point where a full-time job in industry does not preclude the housewife from managing her home well. The trend toward earlier marriages and earlier families means that the children are grown before the mother is too old to find work, and so more women join the work force because their parental responsibilities are lessened at an earlier age than formerly. The expansion of formal education is also a factor; women, increasingly better trained, are easier to employ.

The participation rate for males in the 14–19-year-old group is marked by a steady downward trend since 1946. One might ascribe this to the increasing proportion of the group attending high school and college. However, the trend is probably influenced a bit by conditions unique to the postwar years. Since the participation rates are for the civilian noninstitutional population, it might be argued that with demobilization the servicemen in this age bracket who returned to civilian life probably chose to continue their education rather than to enter the labor force, thus momentarily reducing the participation rate. Also it is widely recognized that for some age brackets the participation rate is influenced by the number of jobs to be had. When jobs are readily available, men under 20 and over 65 as well as women in the older age brackets decide to go to work and so are counted as part of the work force; then when jobs become scarce, college-age boys will decide to go to school instead of to work and older men and women will go back to living on their pensions. Since they are no longer working or seeking work, they are not part of the labor force as it is currently defined. This may explain some of the decline in the participation rate among the 14–19-year-old group in the immediate postwar years. However, the level of unemployment rose so little after the war that this can hardly be cited as a major factor. The continuity of the decline over the entire nine year period implies that the long-run trend is the basic explanation. The two influences above were surely slight. Not only does the influence of longer education affect the rate for this age group but also the movement of the population out of agriculture into industry makes it more difficult for at least the 14- and 15-year-olds to be members of the labor force.

As with the males, the females in the 14–19-year-old group are reducing their participation in the labor force. Besides reflecting the increased proportion of girls attending high school and college, this reduced participation rate is the counterpart of the rapidly increasing birth rates for this group, discussed above.

The male 20–24-year-old participation rate climbed from about 89 per cent in 1946 to almost 94 per cent in 1949 and 1951 and then began to decline. The rise in the participation rate may be explained by the gradual reduction in the number of this age group who were still in school. That is, immediately after the war a higher than usual proportion of this group was in college, but this proportion was gradually reduced. Since 1951 the trend has been downward, possibly because of the long-run increase in the length of professional training and in the number of men getting such training.

It is quite enlightening to compare Canadian labor force participation rates with those for the United States, since any trends which are continually remolding Canadian society in the image of her southern neighbor will likely push Canadian work habits in the direction of current United States patterns. The differences are notable indeed. Below the age of 25, Canadian participation rates are distinctly higher. For men 20–24 the Canadian rate in 1950 was 93 per cent, compared to only 82 per cent for the United States. The corresponding figures for women were 46 and 43 per cent. Differences of the same order exist for the 14–19 group.[1] These figures, of course, reflect the higher pro-

[1] United States figures are from Department of Commerce, *Statistical Abstract of the United States, 1957* (Washington, 1957), p. 196. The 1950 figures rest on a 20 per cent sample taken in connection with the 1950 census and, hence, are considerably more reliable than the Canadian rates. One must keep in mind two conceptual differences between the Canadian and United States participation rates: (1) the United States rates are on the basis of total population, the Canadian rates on the basis of civilian noninstitutional population; (2) the United States rates count military personnel as employed, the Canadian rates do not. Were the Canadian rate for a particular group calculated on the United States conceptual basis, it would appear higher because of both of these prac-

portion of Americans receiving higher education. The other major difference appears in the figures for women 25–64, where United States rates are uniformly and significantly higher than those for Canada. For the 25–44 group the United States rate is half again as high as the Canadian; for the 45–64 bracket it is two-thirds higher. The lower Canadian rates reflect partly cultural factors which will alter slowly if at all. But certainly they are partly due to the slower rate at which Canadians have accepted the employment of women and Canadian family patterns have adjusted to the working mother.

Another possible source of information on Canadian participation rates is the figures for the portion of the population gainfully occupied drawn from the census of Canada. It would be extremely desirable for long-term forecasting to have an idea of long-term trends in participation rates. Unfortunately, various accidents render the census of Canada labor force data unusable for this purpose. In 1951 a change in the definition of the labor force was adopted and the old concept of "gainfully occupied" was dropped. Yet that concept had been the basis of employment figures collected in earlier censuses so that the 1951 information is not comparable with any earlier year.[2] There is not much use in looking at participation trends in earlier censuses, because those of 1931 and 1941 came in years when labor force patterns were clearly distorted one way or another.

For the United States, however, Harold Wool has presented consistent long-run census data covering the period 1920–1950 which can be checked for consistency with the short-run trends observed in Canada.[3] There is no case of significant contradiction in the direction of trends for a particular age-sex group between the long-run United States and post-World War II Canadian patterns except for women over 65. However, for two groups in

---

tices, though only slightly higher due to the United States method of handling military personnel.

[2] *Census of Canada, 1951,* Vol. IV, p. xiv. No information seems to have been published on the differences, but when one lines up the data for 1951 and earlier censuses some major shifts are immediately apparent which probably have to do with changes of definition rather than economic reality; see *Canada Year Book, 1954,* pp. 694–695, for the relevant statistics.

[3] H. Wool, "Long-term Projections of the Labor Force," in *Long-Range Economic Projection, Studies in Income and Wealth, Volume Sixteen* (Princeton, 1954), pp. 51–62.

the Canadian labor force the participation rate has changed more sharply since World War II than it has in the long-run for their United States counterparts. These groups are males 14–19 and over 65. At the same time the Canadian short-run trend for women 25–64 has proceeded more slowly than the United States long-term trend.

Combining the information on postwar trends in Canadian participation rates with the prospects implied by Canada–United States differences, we have forecast the participation rates shown in the last column of Table 34. In three categories, namely males 25–44 and 45–64 and females 65 and over, the stability of Canadian rates and their magnitude relative to United States rates seemed to indicate a best guess of no change by 1970. For both males and females 14–19 it was assumed that the linear rate of change for the postwar decade would continue to 1970; and for males 65 and over, whose participation rate dropped one-third in the decade after World War II, it was assumed that the same percentage rate of change would continue.[4] For males 20–24, Canadian postwar experience is quite inconclusive, and the Canada–United States difference was given considerable weight in setting a 1970 rate significantly below the 1946–1954 average. Likewise the Canada–United States difference caused the rates for women 25–44 and 45–64 to be set higher than the Canadian trend alone would justify. For the former group there was an additional reason for such a change because the abnormally high postwar birth rates have reduced the portion of this group participating in the labor force, an effect which should be redressed in the 1960's if we are correct in supposing that specific birth rates will return to something like their levels immediately before World War II. A further ground for justifying such an adjustment of the Canadian trend is the probable effect of urbanization in French Canada on female participation rates. The 1951 census showed that the portion of married women employed in Canada (11.1 per cent) stood well below the United States percentage (26.6 per cent) at least partly because of the very low figure for Quebec (7.3 per cent).[5]

---

[4] That is, the forecast was based on a simple regression of the logarithms of the participation rate series on time.

[5] See N. Zay, "Analyse statistique du travail de la femme mariée dans la province de Québec," *LE,* 32:492–493 (octobre-decembre 1956).

In any case, the adjustments we have made of past trends are quite modest, for they rest on the workings of social factors which can be sticky over long periods of time.[6]

Applying these forecast participation rates to the projected population, after allowing for persons expected to be institutionalized or in the armed forces in 1970, gives a civilian labor force of 7,230,000 persons, an increase of slightly more than 30 per cent over 1954.[7]

HISTORIC EVIDENCE ON PRODUCTIVITY

To move from the projection of the work force to the projection of the gross national product expected in 1970 requires an estimate of production per member of the work force in 1970. This estimate in turn must rest on the historic record of productivity growth. We shall examine the rather frail statistics available for Canada and some slightly more substantial ones covering a longer period for the United States.

Table 35 shows the GNP of Canada per worker per year in constant 1935–1939 dollars for the period 1926–1955. The increase from $1307 worth of output per worker in 1926 to $2371 in 1955 represents an increase of almost 2 per cent compounded annually, but the range of the annual changes runs all the way from a decrease of 8.9 per cent in 1946 to an increase of 15.1 per cent in 1942.[8] These figures of course represent weighted averages of

---

[6] The reader may notice that we attribute most of the task of determining changes in participation rates to economic and social factors rather than to demographic factors except the most basic one of changes in the age-sex composition of the population. Studies of long-term changes in participation rates in the United States seem to support such a procedure. See S. L. Wolfbein and A. J. Jaffe, "Demographic Factors in Labor Force Growth," *American Sociological Review*, 11:392–396 (August 1946), and J. D. Durand, *The Labor Force in the United States, 1890–1960* (New York, 1948).

[7] It was assumed that the armed forces would account for 100,000 persons and the institutional population for another 150,000. The former estimate is a relatively arbitrary figure felt to be consistent with our basic assumption of no major war but no significant relaxing of international tension. The latter estimate assumes that the institutional population will grow in proportion to the total population. The age distribution of the institutional population had to be assumed in the absence of information on the matter, but since the total number amounts to less than 1 per cent of the civilian noninstitutional population the chances of significant error arising here are negligible.

[8] The data in Tables 35 and 36 parallel Tables III and VII in G. D. Sutton, "Productivity in Canada," *CJEPS*, 19:185–201 (May 1953). For the years after 1930 the figures in the present study were computed independently from the

Table 35. Gross national product of Canada per member of the employed
civilian work force, annually, 1926–1955 (1935–1939 dollars).

Year	GNP (millions of dollars)	Employed work force on June 1 (thousands)	GNP per member of employed work force (dollars)	Change in GNP per worker (per cent)
1926	4548	3477	1307	—
1927	4926	3606	1366	4.4
1928	5330	3790	1406	2.9
1929	5337	3983	1340	—4.7
1930	5127	3869	1325	—1.1
1931	4475	3630	1233	—6.9
1932	4096	3432	1193	—3.2
1933	3772	3411	1106	—7.3
1934	4208	3666	1148	3.8
1935	4530	3736	1213	5.7
1936	4738	3852	1230	1.4
1937	5201	4070	1278	3.9
1938	5246	4022	1304	2.0
1939	5664	4075	1390	6.6
1940	6487	4138	1568	12.8
1941	7481	4224	1771	12.9
1942	8941	4385	2038	15.1
1943	9374	4447	2108	3.4
1944	9721	4445	2187	3.7
1945	9315	4411	2112	—3.4
1946	9045	4699	1925	—8.9
1947	9165	4823	1900	—1.3
1948	9438	4915	1920	1.1
1949	9722	4970	1956	1.9
1950	10330	5037	2051	4.9
1951	10935	5172	2114	3.1
1952	11677	5222	2236	5.8
1953	12134	5356	2265	1.3
1954	11725	5297	2212	—2.3
1955	12941	5458	2371	7.2

Source: DBS, *National Accounts, Income and Expenditure, 1926-1950, 1950-1956;* and DBS, *Canadian Statistical Review,* various issues.

productivity levels in all Canadian industries, and it is useful
to look at the productivity level for one particular sector,

same basic data; thus they show a few minor variations from Sutton's results,
some of which may be due to differences in rounding practices.

Table 36. Output per man-year in Canadian agricultural and
nonagricultural employment, annually, 1926–1955 (1935–1939 dollars).

Year	Agricultural employment[a]		Nonagricultural employment[b]	
	Output (dollars per man-year)	Percentage increase over previous year	Output (dollars per man-year)	Percentage increase over previous year
1926	492	—	1688	—
1927	501	1.8	1759	4.2
1928	530	5.8	1786	1.5
1929	355	−33.0	1746	−2.0
1930	342	− 3.7	1745	0.0
1931	244	−28.7	1723	−1.3
1932	282	15.6	1698	−1.5
1933	217	−23.0	1615	−4.9
1934	273	25.8	1608	−0.4
1935	301	10.3	1690	5.1
1936	253	−16.0	1730	2.4
1937	263	4.0	1767	2.1
1938	345	31.2	1786	1.1
1939	409	18.6	1883	5.4
1940	488	19.3	2078	10.4
1941	474	− 2.9	2292	10.3
1942	756	59.5	2483	8.3
1943	547	−27.6	2625	5.7
1944	689	26.0	2695	2.7
1945	551	−20.0	2652	−1.6
1946	496	−10.0	2449	−7.7
1947	560	12.9	2326	−5.0
1948	567	1.3	2346	0.9
1949	597	5.3	2347	0.0
1950	617	3.4	2434	3.7
1951	776	25.8	2434	0.0
1952	839	8.1	2537	4.2
1953	841	0.2	2560	0.9
1954	609	−27.6	2542	−0.8
1955	757	24.3	2613	2.8

[a] Agriculture contribution to national income deflated by wholesale index of farm prices of agricultural products.

[b] GNP deflated less agriculture contribution to national income, the agriculture contribution having been deflated by farm prices index.

Source: DBS, *National Accounts, Income and Expenditure,* and DBS, *Canadian Statistical Review,* various issues.

agriculture, which is known to differ greatly from the national average. (Later we shall encounter some good reasons for not pushing an industry break-down of productivity trends any further than this.) The productivity of labor in Canada's agricultural and nonagricultural sectors is shown in Table 36 and Figure 8 for the years 1926–1955. The value of output per

Fig. 8. Agricultural and nonagricultural production per man-year, 1926–1955 (1935–1939 dollars).

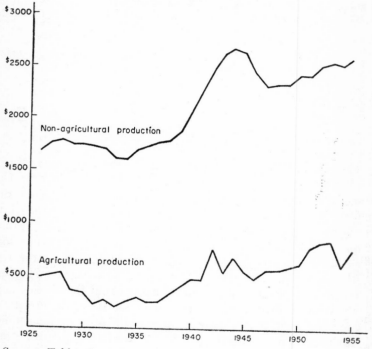

Source: Table 36.

worker of course has been much higher in the rest of the economy than in agriculture throughout the period. Agricultural productivity growth acted as a drag on productivity expansion for the whole economy to 1938 due to poor crops and markets and other conditions associated with the depression. Since then these forces have reversed and agricultural productivity has outstripped that in the rest of the economy. Most striking are the years 1950–

1952, in which the economy's over-all productivity growth rate of 4 per cent per annum undoubtedly depended on excellent harvests and a continued decline in the farm labor force. Even if agricultural and nonagricultural productivity always grew at the same rate, however, it would be important to examine them separately because of the continuing impact of the transfer of labor away from low-productivity farming to other sectors where productivity typically is higher.[9]

Table 37. Compound annual increase in output per man-year in agricultural employment, in nonagricultural employment, and in all industries of Canada for selected periods, 1926–1955.

	1926–1950	1926–1954	1926–1955	1935–1954
All industries	1.95	1.87	1.99	3.20
Agricultural employment	0.95	0.77	1.50	3.78
Nonagricultural employment	1.55	1.47	1.52	2.17

Source: Derived from Tables 35 and 36.

The data of Table 37 indicate that for the 1926–1955 period productivity per worker in agricultural employment increased at about the same annual rate as in nonagricultural employment, namely 1.50 per cent. Probably because one is accustomed to considering employment in agriculture to be less productive than employment outside agriculture, it is startling to learn that agriculture has enjoyed as great a rate of increase as the rest of the economy. Undoubtedly mechanization in agriculture contributes much of the explanation behind this, but the development of the large scale, efficient agriculture of the West, the growth of the average farm to a more efficient size, the growing importance of high value crops and livestock in Canadian agriculture, and the declining number of workers in agriculture have also been important factors. Notice, however, that output per worker in agriculture is still scarcely one-third as great as in the other sectors.

Let us consider the year-to-year changes in the productivity series for the nonagricultural sectors of the economy given in Table 36. The fact that the rate of change was actually negative

[9] Compare Sutton. pp. 193–195.

in some years may be explained in several ways. During the depression years employers might have maintained their work forces at higher levels than sales volume would warrant, not to be charitable so much as to keep the skilled employees on hand. Reduction of the work week but not the work force would account for a lowering of the output per man-year even though output per man-hour might have been maintained. Also production may have decreased faster than the work force simply because maximum production per worker is commonly possible only when the plant operates at or above a certain minimum percentage of capacity.

With respect to phases of the business cycle, the evidence seems consistent with Sutton's conclusion that productivity normally seems to rise slowly or drop at the top of the cycle and during the downswing, showing sharp gains at the bottom of the cycle and during the rise or, also, in response to any special stimulus such as an armament boom. Sutton's explanation of the cycle pattern is a psychological one: at the bottom of the cycle the extra cost-consciousness of employers and the extra fear of discharge held by workers spurs both of them to extraordinary efforts.[10] Frederick C. Mills has found just about the same generalization to apply to the United States. Over ten peacetime business cycles, output per man-hour grew on the average three times as fast during the expansion phase as the contraction phase.[11]

The negative rates of increase in Canadian nonagricultural productivity in 1945, 1946, and 1947 call for some explanation. In 1946 and 1947 the decline apparently was due to reduced hours because production per man-*hour* in nonagricultural employment seems to have increased in both of those years.[12] But in 1945 and 1948 and 1949 productivity per man-*hour* outside

---

[10] Sutton, p. 193.

[11] F. C. Mills, "The Role of Productivity in Economic Growth," *AER*, 42:547 (May 1952).

[12] Sutton, p. 191. We place main emphasis here on the man-year series instead of man-hour productivity measurements because the Canadian data seem better in the former case. As Sutton indicates, the index of man-hours worked is calculated by dividing an index of total labor income by an index of wage rates. Thus it would indicate spurious productivity changes whenever any change occurs in the level of wage relative to salary income, and it would systematically underestimate productivity to the extent that total wages include extra payments for overtime work.

agriculture declined. Some of this fall in output per man-hour in industry in 1948–1949 might possibly have been caused by the installation of new capital equipment; when new equipment is installed in large quantities (as was the case in 1948–1949), it is not uncommon for productivity per worker to decrease until the workers and the entire plant layout and production process are adjusted to utilize the new equipment to the best advantage. A certain digestion period is necessary before productivity increases due to new equipment begin to manifest themselves.

Another possible explanation of these facts, urged by H. C. Pentland, is that Sutton's figures understate the productivity gains realized in the postwar years in manufacturing and mining. By using physical volume of production as an output indicator for these sectors he concludes that in the postwar period in question both mining (1942–1952) and manufacturing (1945–1952) achieved productivity growth rates per man-year in excess of 1 per cent. For the whole period covered in his study, 1935–1952, he finds an average compounded rate in manufacturing of a little under 1.5 per cent and a rate in mining a little under 1.75 per cent. The explanation he suggests for the understatement resulting from Sutton's procedure is that the gross national product which Sutton deflates and uses as an output measure is constructed in a way which conveys an implicit assumption of no productivity growth in services and construction.[13] Although Pentland's contribution does not settle the issue, it does offer some assurance that Canadian productivity growth has not suffered any real crisis in the postwar years.

This information on Canadian productivity over the last three decades does not provide a particularly sound foundation for long-range forecasting. Recent evidence on United States productivity growth covers more than half a century in detail and most of a century in general fashion. Moreover, it takes the highly desirable step of computing the productivity of all primary inputs rather than imputing the whole gain in physical efficiency to labor. Let us look briefly at this material.

Jacob Schmookler has published a study of long-run changes in the efficiency of the American economy. His basic strategy, shorn of its qualifications, is to calculate indexes of physical inputs

[13] H. C. Pentland, "Physical Productivity in Canada, 1935–52," *EJ,* 64:399–404 (June 1954).

of land, labor, and capital since 1869 for each of Kuznets' over-lapping decades. Then he weights each of the three indexes by the income received by the three factors in an arbitrarily chosen period to get a single index of factor inputs into the American economy. By comparing this to an index of output he derives the desired figures for the contribution to rising real output made by improvements in the technical utilization of all factors.[14] Schmookler finds that the major increases in efficiency for the United States economy came in the years 1874–1888 and 1919–1933. This fact is strikingly significant for the student of the Canadian economy, for the only scraps of information available on long-run Canadian productivity growth yield a similar impression. These are Firestone's computations of annual growth rates for real gross national expenditure per worker, which show more rapid increases before 1910 and after 1930 than during the intervening period.[15] If productivity growth is due mainly either to technological innovations or to the business cycle mechanism, then there is good reason for thinking that periods of rapid productivity growth in the United States and in Canada would be closely associated. Both countries effectively draw upon the same pool of technology, and their business cycle patterns show remarkable similarity for major movements.[16] In any case, this similarity between the United States and Canadian productivity growth patterns suggests further examination of United States productivity information.

By far the most thorough study of productivity undertaken in the United States is that in progress at the National Bureau of Economic Research, preliminary findings for which have been reported by J. W. Kendrick.[17] In the private domestic economy, Kendrick finds that output per unit of labor input has grown at an average annual rate of 1.9 per cent over the period 1899–1953 while the productivity of all factors has risen at a rate of 1.75

[14] J. Schmookler, "The Changing Efficiency of the American Economy: 1869–1938," *RES*, 34:214–231 (August 1952).

[15] O. J. Firestone, *Canada's Economic Development 1867–1953, With Special Reference to Changes in the Country's National Product and National Wealth* (London, 1958), Table 11.

[16] These two similarities are examined respectively by P. Hartland, "Factors in the Economic Growth in Canada," *Journal of Economic History*, 15:13–22 (No. 1. 1955), and G. Rosenbluth, "Changes in Canadian Sensitivity to United States Business Fluctuations," *CJEPS*, 23:480–503 (November 1957).

[17] "Productivity Trends: Capital and Labor," *RES*, 38:248–257 (August 1956).

per cent. Since real product has grown at 3.3 per cent annually during the same period, productivity growth has actually accounted for more than half of the total growth of real output.[18] In industry groups for which separate figures are available (those *other than* trade, service, finance, and construction), the growth of total factor input productivity has been 2.0 per cent, confirming the common view that productivity gains have been relatively modest (less than 1.5 per cent) in the service sectors. Another evidence of the general importance of productivity growth in the American economy is the fact that real output has grown faster than the capital stock. Thus, it is not correct to say that in the net sense capital accumulation has been responsible for part of the growth of output per worker. Innovations have been capital-saving as well.[19]

Kendrick provides extremely valuable information on short-period changes in productivity growth rates for individual industries over time, and on the dispersion of productivity growth rates of a large sample of industries from their average value. In view of the reasonable stability of the productivity growth rate for the whole economy, the dispersion of changes for particular industry groups, and the fluctuation of industry group rates over time are very great. These facts illustrate how thorny a problem productivity poses for analyzing and forecasting economic growth. Because of the great variability over time of productivity growth in particular sectors, there is little gained by disaggregating national productivity growth figures, and thus we have not done so in studying the Canadian economy. Yet this leaves us without a causal explanation of the national productivity growth rate, immediately after we have stressed the magnitude of the contribution of productivity growth to the total rate of growth in United States real output.[20]

Productivity forecasting then must remain pretty much an exercise in blind extrapolation. Therefore, it is important, finally, to look at the change over time in the growth rate of productivity in the United States as a check on our interpretation of Canadian

[18] Kendrick, p. 251.

[19] Kendrick, pp. 251–253. It is true, of course, that periods of rapid substitution of capital for labor have typically been periods of rapid growth of output per man-hour.

[20] Kendrick, pp. 253–255. See also M. Abramovitz, "Resource and Output Trends in the United States since 1870," *AER*, 46:11–12 (May 1956).

experience. The careful students of United States productivity growth have all phrased their conclusions cautiously on this issue, and they are unanimous only in agreeing that the rate of growth of productivity has shown no tendency to decline. Writing a survey article and working mainly with Kuznets-type over-lapping decade figures, Abramovitz finds that the productivity of resources has "continued to grow at a steady, perhaps an accelerating, pace." [21] From the same sort of data Schmookler concludes that "little or no evidence was found to support the common belief that technical progress grows at an ever increasing rate." [22] Working with long series of annual data, however, Kendrick finds a break appearing around 1919 with the average annual percentage rate of change of total factor productivity standing at 1.1 per cent for the preceding two decades and 2.2 per cent for the succeeding three. But he also finds no tendency away from a constant growth rate after this shift at the time of World War I.[23] There is little evidence that United States technological advance is slowing down. On the other hand, recent data do not seem to indicate accelerating technological advance despite the entrenched position of research in the modern corporation.

FORECASTING CANADIAN PRODUCTIVITY

How should we estimate the future growth of Canadian productivity? Simply extrapolating the average growth rate of the past three decades is an excessively mechanical procedure ignoring much available information. More elaborate but still mechanical statistical techniques also have proved unacceptable.[24] Ruling out these possibilities leaves us with the task of *a priori* speculation on the basis of all available evidence.

Taking agriculture first, let us ask what factors would seem to

---

[21] Abramovitz, pp. 6–7.

[22] Schmookler, p. 230.

[23] Kendrick, p. 253.

[24] Logarithms of the series from Table 35 of GNP per member of the employed work force were related by multiple regression to time and to the percentage of the labor force employed, but these two variables explain only 32 per cent of the variation of the productivity series and the time trend only 7 per cent. By contrast, Kendrick has shown that in the United States these same two variables explain 97 per cent of the variation of real gross private product per man-hour, 1909–1950. See "National Productivity and Its Long-Term Projection," *Long-Range Economic Projection*, p. 85.

call for some forecast other than an extrapolation of the trends of the last two or three decades. On the one hand, a bit of optimism might seem justified. Although mechanization may not provide the annual productivity increases which it has accounted for in the years 1938–1952, it will surely account for some. Possibly of more importance will be the continued movements toward farms of more efficient size, more scientific use of fertilizer, increased irrigation and drainage, and perhaps most important of all a continued shift of agricultural production toward the high value farm commodities such as livestock, poultry, and dairy products demanded by a nation of increasingly urbanized consumers. Finally, generally high Canadian employment levels and the drawing power of higher earnings outside agriculture will assure a continuous draining of marginal labor from the farms and a shrinking of the agricultural work force as a percentage of the total work force. All these factors would contribute to justifying projection of a rate for the next decade greater than the 1.5 per cent per annum experienced in the past.

Cast up against this, however, are two factors which strongly imply that the historic rate should stand as a ceiling for any view of future productivity gains in agriculture. First, the considerable surpluses of United States wheat in storage and United States productive capacity for wheat guarantee little improvement in the terms of trade for Canada's major farm product barring drastic harvest failures. In either case, the prospect would be for reduced productivity gains, since deteriorating terms of trade for agriculture normally call a quick halt to productivity-raising investments, especially farm mechanization. Second, the historic growth rate for Canadian agricultural productivity is biased upward because harvests on the average have been much better in the later years than in the earlier ones for which statistics are available. The 1.5 per cent figure is then a slight overestimate of the long-term trend, a fact confirmed by looking at United States experience.[25] Allowing for all of these factors, our judgment would be that 1.5 per cent per man-year is a good guess for the rate of increase of agricultural productivity in Canada.

[25] J. W. Kendrick, "National Productivity and Its Long-Term Projection," pp. 90–91, gives a historic productivity growth rate per man-hour of 1.25 for United States agriculture and 1.9 for the rest of the economy.

What of the expected rate of increase in output per worker outside agriculture? The current feeling in Canada surely is that the 1.5 per cent annual increase of the 1926–1955 period will be exceeded in the following fifteen years. The decline in output per man-year in the early 1930's presumably will not be experienced again, at least not for the same reasons. Similarly the negative changes of the immediate postwar years will not recur if peace continues and if we encounter few of the violent changes in production techniques which marked the end of the war. Eliminating these negative changes from the 1926–1955 period would, of course, raise the average percentage considerably. On the other hand, during normal peacetime years we would not expect such sudden jumps in output per man as occurred in 1941 and 1942. During the 1935–1944 period the output of nonagricultural workers increased at an average rate of more than 5 per cent per year. Presumably this would be just as unlikely to prevail over the next decade as the average annual decrease in output per man of about 1.5 per cent per year which applied to the 1928–1934 period. Table 38 illustrates how greatly the average annual increase in output per worker varies with the period chosen.

By looking at the prosperous years which were relatively free of easily identifiable nonrecurring changes in output per man, either upward or downward, it is possible to approximate a sustainable annual rate of increase in output per man which one might expect to be realistic for the next decade. The average of the annual percentage increases for 1927–1929, 1937–1939, and 1948–1950 is 2.1 per cent. (Note that in 1929 the change was

Table 38. Average percentage rate of increase in output per man-year in nonagricultural employment in Canada and in the United States, for selected periods, 1929–1954.

Period	Canada	United States
1929–1939	0.76	0.81
1939–1946	3.83	2.41
1946–1950	−0.13	0.33
1950–1954	1.06	2.10
1929–1954	1.53	1.40
1935–1954	2.17	1.96

Source: Canadian rates from Table 36; United States rates computed from data in United States Department of Commerce, *Survey of Current Business, National Income Supplement, 1954.*

negative.) Dropping 1937 and 1938 because they were not definitely prosperous years would raise the average to 2.3 per cent.

Some light is also shed on the reasonableness of various possible forecasts by comparing the annual rate of increase in output per man-year for the nonagricultural sectors in various periods for the United States and for Canada. In Table 38 it is seen that the United States has not maintained an increase in nonagricultural output per man-year in excess of 2.5 per cent for any of the periods shown. Canada's 3.83 per cent annual rate of increase for the 1939–1946 period is of course atypical due to the war, and her 2.17 per cent annual increase for the 1935–1954 period is atypical because of the abnormally low productivity per man-year in the depression years. In view of these historical data, an annual increase of 2.5 per cent per year might be considered as a maximum sustainable annual increase in output per man-year in nonagricultural employment for the next decade with 2.0 per cent as a medium "best guess."

The 1926–1955 average annual increase of 1.5 per cent is probably a safe conservative minimum estimate. In part this is because of the high employment assumption. In addition the expanded role of industrial research promises a greater stream of technological improvements in capital equipment than before the war; in this regard the accelerated development of automatic controls and handling devices, popularly referred to as "automation," can be mentioned. The increased strength of organized labor would seem also to assure constant pressure for wage increases, which pressure in turn will force employers continually to substitute capital equipment for labor, thus increasing output per man. It is well to recall the United States experience of a high correlation between heavy investment and rapidly rising productivity per worker. The development of energy sources and the growing exploitation of mineral reserves would appear to harbinger higher productivity increases than was the case prior to 1950. (Whether or not the mineral resources continue to contribute to Canadian income as at present depends on their terms of trade in the world market and thereby on production costs in other regions, but Canada seems safe enough in this regard.)

Increases in productivity have been especially striking in manufacturing. In the ten years since the end of the war, the annual increase in output per man-hour has averaged about 2.5 per cent, but since 1951 the annual increase has averaged more than 6.5 per cent. Because of the reduction in the work week, the annual increase in output per man-year has been less than this. In evaluating the significance of these increases for the economy as a whole, it should be remembered that less than one-fourth of the work force is engaged in manufacturing.

To gain some perspective on the probable rate of increase in productivity we can look at other writers' estimates. Mr. J. E. Coyne, governor of the Bank of Canada, has suggested a straight 2 per cent per annum increase in productivity per man-year.[26] His justification for this rate is not given in any detail but he does note that this has been the average rate over the last twenty-five years. A second discussion of the probable rate of increase in productivity is presented by Van der Valk.[27] He is far more optimistic and assumes that over the "next few decades" productivity per man-year will rise at a rate of 3.5 per cent per year. He also mentions that the historical rate of increase has been only 2 per cent, but he feels that the future rate will be much higher because of the avoidance of depressions and the shifting of the work force from low-productivity agriculture to high-productivity industry. But historic productivity growth in prosperous periods does not support a forecast as high as 3.5 per cent, and the shift of labor out of agriculture is not a new development but on the contrary an old one which if anything will slow down in the future. Recently an avowedly optimistic estimate of productivity growth prospects in the nonagricultural sector of the economy has come from the Royal Commission on Canada's Economic Prospects.[28] Basing its estimate on the productivity growth rates experienced since World War II, the Commission staff foresees a productivity growth rate between 2.5 and 3.25 per cent per annum. They justify ignoring prewar experience because of the superior quality of the recent data and because they feel the postwar years reflect much more accurately the general economic conditions likely for the future. Both of these arguments carry some weight, but not sufficient to lend approval

[26] J. E. Coyne, "Some Possible Features of Economic Growth and Investment in Canada, 1955–1975," address at annual meeting of the Dominion Mortgage and Investment Association, May 5, 1955 (mimeo.), p. 4.

[27] H. M. H. A. van der Valk, *The Economic Future of Canada* (Toronto, 1954), pp. 176–177.

[28] Canada, RCCEP, *Preliminary Report* (Ottawa, 1956), pp. 9–10.

to the commission's estimate. First, there is no justification for completely disregarding earlier statistics unless some net bias is suspected, and the commission gives no reason for expecting one. Second, although the correlation between the employment level and the productivity growth rate is normally very high, some economists have raised the question of whether high employment is so conducive to rapid productivity gains when it is sustained over a long period of time. The years 1956 and 1929 seem to support these fears.

It is also helpful to glance at productivity growth projections for the United States. In the volume *America's Needs and Resources*[29] the annual rate of increase in output per *man-hour* for the 1950–1960 decade was predicted to be 2.3 per cent, very slightly higher than our medium estimates of 2.0 per cent in nonagricultural and 1.5 per cent in agricultural employment per *man-year*. The Paley Commission estimated that the annual increase in output per *man-hour* would be 2.5 per cent for the 1950–1975 period.[30]

These two estimates make our suggested rates of increase for Canadian productivity look fairly conservative, especially if one considers certain reasons why productivity in Canada might rise faster than in the United States over the next decade. First, as was noted in Chapter 2, there is some fairly sound evidence that in fact Canadian productivity has been growing faster in recent years.[31] Second, certain efficiencies resulting from increased population density may increase productivity per worker in Canada faster than in the United States. For example, it would seem that economies in transportation and domestic trade due to the country's "filling up" would be more likely in Canada than in the United States. Furthermore, as the domestic market expands, a few firms and industries may be able to operate with improved efficiency through taking advantage of economies of scale.[32]

---

[29] J. F. Dewhurst and Associates, *America's Needs and Resources: A New Survey* (New York, 1955), p. 42.

[30] United States President's Materials Policy Commission, *Resources for Freedom* (Washington, 1952), Vol. I, p. 7, and Vol. II, p. 112.

[31] See Sutton, pp. 196–201, and A. Maddison, "Productivity in an Expanding Economy," *EJ*, 62:584–594 (September 1952).

[32] For a general discussion of economies of scale and economic growth which carefully qualifies the possibilities of such gains, see T. Scitovsky, "Economies of Scale, Competition and European Integration," *AER*, 46:71–91 (March 1956), and E. Rothbarth, "Causes of the Superior Efficiency of U.S.A. Industry as Compared with British Industry," *EJ*, 56:383–390 (September 1946).

Finally, Canada may have a special advantage through improving terms of trade for her natural resources which would raise the value productivity of their extraction more than the rate of physical productivity growth.

However, there are enough debit items in the ledger to remove the taint of pessimism from our outlook for productivity growth. First, as was indicated in Chapter 2, gains to Canadian productivity through increasing economies of scale are likely to be significant only in a few industries. Generally, Canadian plants are not significantly smaller than their United States counterparts, and economies external to the plant are too nebulous to bear the weight of forecasting a much higher productivity growth rate for Canada than the United States. Second, a higher forecast than our "best guess" presumes that in the future Canada will regularly be able to achieve productivity gains equal to those in her best peacetime full-employment years of the past. This just seems too unlikely. We do not foresee the disappearance of minor recessions, and it is quite clear that even a mild business recession will frequently render a year's productivity gain very small or actually negative. And there have been too many unexplained instances of full employment years with disappointing productivity gains to allow certainty that such years will not appear occasionally in the future. For these reasons we will hold to the estimate of a 2.0 per cent annual increase in output per man-year in nonagricultural employment and a 1.5 per cent annual increase in output per man-year in agricultural employment.

THE FORECAST OF GROSS NATIONAL PRODUCT

Table 39 shows alternative gross national product estimates for 1970 based on different rates of annual increase of productivity in agriculture and nonagricultural industries. Several steps involved in preparing this table need to be indicated. First, it required a distribution of the labor force between agriculture and other sectors — a difficult problem, because that distribution is not independent of the total growth foreseen for gross national product although it depends much more on the level of population and the prospective average unemployment rate. However, an iterative procedure readily produced consistent estimates of gross national product and the farm-nonfarm split of the labor force. Second, the base output per worker for applying the

Table 39.   Alternative forecasts of Canadian gross national product in 1970
(billions of 1955 dollars).

Rate of agricultural productivity growth (percent)	Rate of productivity growth in nonagricultural industries (percent)		
	1.5	2.0	2.5
1.0	43.9	47.7	51.7
1.5	44.2	48.0	52.0
2.0	44.6	48.3	52.4

Source: See text, pp. 301–302.

productivity growth rates appearing in Table 39 was the average value for recent full employment years. This is consistent with the general prospect of growth with reasonably full employment. With this much settled, the rest of the calculation was routine. The estimated 1970 output per worker in the agricultural and nonagricultural sectors of the Canadian economy was multiplied by the number of workers in each sector and the results were summed.[33] Finally, since the output series for agriculture and nonagricultural industries represented national income originating from these sectors rather than gross national product, allowance was made for the very stable percentage by which these two aggregates normally differ.

If it be granted that in agriculture the annual productivity increase over the next decade will lie between 1.0 and 2.0 per cent, and the nonagricultural productivity increase between 1.5 and 2.5 per cent, the range of 1970 gross national product in 1955 dollars will be roughly from $44,000,000,000 to $52,000,000,000. Our "best guess" productivity growth figures of 1.5 per cent in agriculture and 2.0 per cent in the nonagricultural sectors imply a forecast of $48,000,000,000, an increase of roughly 80 per cent over 1955. Much of this increase is explained, of course, by the population increase rather than by the increase in output per worker. But personal disposable income per capita is expected to rise by about 40 per cent, representing a 40 per cent improvement

[33] Since we have followed the DBS practice of not including persons in the Canadian armed forces in the labor force, a small adjustment was made for military pay and allowances in the forecast GNP figures.

in the standard of living of the average Canadian due to productivity gains over a fifteen year period. We are saying, then, that there will be about one-third more people in Canada in 1970 than in 1955 and that the real output per person will be about 40 per cent greater.

It is evident from the range of GNP estimates given in Table 39 that the forecast is much more sensitive to errors in the productivity projections than to slips in the estimation of 1970 population and labor force. The GNP projections will suffer considerably more from an error in productivity projection than from an error in the birth rate projection merely because the 1970 work force has already been born and thus is known except for the minor errors which may have been introduced in forecasting immigration and mortality. Therefore the productivity experience of the years immediately ahead will have particular significance.

In Figure 9 our forecast of the Canadian GNP is placed against the historic experience of income growth in Canada, against other forecasts for the Canadian economy, and against similar data for the United States. Of the other forecasts of Canadian GNP the most interesting are those of the Royal Commission on Canada's Economic Prospects. The commission's best-guess estimate, based on a productivity growth rate outside of agriculture of 2.88 per cent and annual net immigration of 75,000, implies a GNP growth trend just slightly higher than our best guess. Their maximum estimate (based on productivity growth of 3.25 per cent, net immigration of 100,000) lies above the trend of our maximum estimate, and their minimum estimate (based on productivity growth of 2.5 per cent and net immigration of 50,000) lies between the trends of the low and medium estimates of the present study.[34] The commission staff is slightly more optimistic on both net immigration and expected productivity gains in the nonagricultural sectors of the economy. Indeed, their greater optimism would seem to imply greater differences in the forecasts than actually appear, and there may be partially offsetting differences in the assumptions the two sets of forecasts make about such factors as the rate of transfer of labor out of the agricultural sector. Figure 9 also shows two forecasts of a relatively more casual nature for 1975. Van der Valk's estimate is highly optimistic and lies above the trend of the high estimate for both the present study and that

[34] RCCEP, *Preliminary Report*, p. 10.

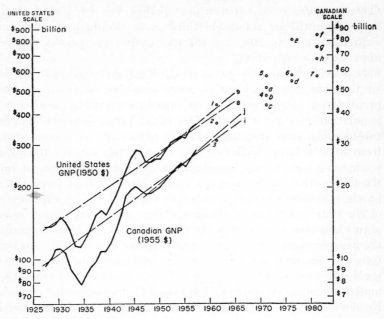

Fig. 9. Comparison of trends and projections of growth of United States and Canadian GNP.

United States GNP

1, 2, 3. High, medium, and low projections for 1960 by J. F. Dewhurst and Associates, *America's Needs and Resources, A New Survey* (New York, 1955), p. 46.

4. Dewhurst's medium estimate for 1960 extrapolated on the basis of 1946–1955 experience to 1970. This figure was used in the present study in estimating Canada's foreign trade prospects.

5, 6, 7. High, medium, and low projections for the decade centered on 1970 by President's Materials Policy Commission, *Resources for Freedom* (Washington, 1952), Vol. II, p. 112.

8. Trend line fitted visually to full-employment years for the United States economy (1926–1929, 1939–1941, 1946–1956).

9. Trend line fitted visually to postwar years 1946–1956.

Canadian GNP

a, b, c. High, medium, and low estimates calculated in the present study.

d. Estimate by J. E. Coyne, cited in *Brief Submitted by the Vancouver, New Westminster and District Trades and Labour Council to the RCCEP* (Vancouver, 1955), p. 2.

e. Estimate by H. M. H. A. van der Valk, *The Economic Future of Canada* (Toronto, 1954), p. 179.

f, g, h. High, medium, and low estimates by the RCCEP, *Preliminary Report* (Ottawa, 1956), p. 10.

of the Royal Commission on Canada's Economic Prospects. Coyne's estimate lies between the trends of the low and medium estimates of the present study.[35]

Figure 9 also contains trend lines fitted casually to the Canadian and United States data to facilitate comparison of the historic experience with the forecasts. Note that the long-run full employment trend lines for the two countries are almost exactly parallel, but the trend for Canada in the post-World War II years is perceptibly steeper than for the United States. United States forecasters, notably the President's Materials Policy Commission, have been notably pessimistic relative to the simple trends of economic growth in the United States, while Canadian forecasters (including the present study) have generally been optimistic by the measure of historical experience.

We state our 1970 GNP forecast in monetary units of 1955 purchasing power, so that we are essentially forecasting an index of the aggregate productive capacity and real income of the Canadian economy. It was argued in Chapter 1 that a slight upward drift in the price level is probably the most likely occurrence under our general assumptions, but that this fact needs no separate consideration in setting the forecast of physical changes. In interpreting this GNP projection it is equally important to remember the likelihood that the prices of some goods may change relative to the prices of others. For example, it is fairly likely that the prices of agricultural commodities will stand lower relative to nonagricultural goods in 1970 than now. Some allowance was made for this outlook in estimating the probable productivity growth rate in agriculture. The GNP projection is valuable in giving a picture of the general growth potential of the economy, but one can make specific sense of it only by looking at the changes likely to occur in particular parts of the Canadian economy. This is the task of the remaining chapters of this study.

---

[35] The RCCEP staff has compiled a large chart showing all of the GNP forecasts appearing in material submitted to the Commission. On the average these seem to run slightly to the optimistic side of the present study's forecasts.

---

i. Trend line fitted visually to full-employment years for the Canadian economy (1926–1929, 1939–1941, 1946–1956).

j. Trend line fitted visually to postwar years 1946–1956.

Personal Consumption Expenditures

Economists now know a good deal about consumption and changes in consumption in the short run. The importance of the consumption-income relation to the theory of employment has spurred dozens of studies in this area. It appears to one crusty British economist, Sir Dennis Robertson, that parameters are being added to the consumption function at the rate of one a week. When the forecaster requests information on long-run changes in consumption and consumption patterns, however, he meets a deathly silence. About the role of consumption in economic development there exist only a few skinny generalizations and only a little empirical work of any sort. With affairs in this awkward state, we have tried to proceed by applying the theory and facts of short-run consumption changes to forecasting the long run. The first of the following sections sets forth this procedure and the problems it involves. The second reviews the historical evidence on Canadian consumption patterns and the third develops a forecast of the size and composition of Canadian consumption in 1970.

CONSUMPTION PATTERNS AND THEIR CHANGES

Economists analyzing and forecasting short-run changes in consumption normally use two concepts — the consumption function and the income elasticity of expenditure on particular commodities. They thus break down the question of how consumers use their incomes into two subsidiary ones: how much of their incomes people do not save, and how they distribute this portion not saved among various sorts of consumer goods and services. This breakdown implies adoption of the hypothesis that saving by consumers is determined in special ways such that it cannot be treated as simply another "good" or another method of income disposal. Empirical evidence seems fairly clearly to support this practice.

Familiar ways of studying short-run changes in consumption suggest a simple approach to forecasting changes in the expenditures of a nation's consumers. Estimate the consumption function, relating the total volume of consumer expenditure to personal disposable income and whatever other variables are deemed relevant. Secure forecasts of these independent variables determining total consumption, and figure the volume of consumer expenditures they imply for the date of the forecast. Calculate income elasticities of consumer expenditure on any desired set of classes of consumer goods and services. Using the income forecast for the target year, figure the consumer expenditures implied by the income elasticities for each class of goods and services at such an income level. Check the total of these consumption categories against total consumption estimated from the consumption function; they may not agree for a variety of reasons.[1] Eliminate any disagreement between them by altering the estimates of particular classes of consumption expenditure until their total agrees with forecast total consumption. (This step can be done in many different ways.)[2]

Picking holes in this sort of general forecasting procedure is an easy task. But no particularly appetizing alternatives are available, and so it will be necessary to use it as a starting point. We shall, however, give fairly lengthy consideration to possible objections — first, two problems concerning the logical validity of the procedure, and second, several possible complaints about its economic relevance or realism.

One possible objection to this forecasting procedure on logical grounds is that it depends on least-squares estimation procedure and studies the consumption-income relation apart from the rest

[1] The more obvious and important of the reasons are (1) inclusion in the consumption functions of variables other than personal disposable income, so that variables affect the estimate of total consumption which do not enter the income elasticity calculations; (2) statistical biases affecting the computed consumption function or income elasticities; and (3) errors in the data from which these functions were calculated.

[2] This procedure seems to be roughly the same one used by J. F. Dewhurst and associates for securing an estimate of the United States 1960 consumption pattern from a vantage point in the early 1950's. They seem to have made rather casual use of the method, however. Their correlation of consumption items with personal disposable income was performed "graphically, not mathematically," and it is quite difficult to be certain what they have done by way of reconciling the total of separate consumer expenditure items with any forecast of aggregate consumption through a long-run consumption function. See *America's Needs and Resources, A New Survey* (New York, 1955), ch. iv and pp. 1003–1004.

of the economic system in which it is imbedded.[3] Some deep-seated doubts can arise here, for it is well known that the least-squares technique will deliver a biased estimate of structural economic relations under highly likely circumstances. This does not mean, however, that a biased estimating procedure will necessarily yield a biased economic forecast. The "bias" in the estimator results from the fact that not only does income affect consumption, but simultaneously other variables in the economy may affect or be affected by both of them. The bias in the least squares estimate of the consumption-income relation arises because it will reflect the working of these other relations as well as the direct consumption-income dependence.[4] But for forecasting purposes, unless the relations of consumption and income with the other variables are expected to change, they should be allowed to exert their "bias" on the calculation of the expected level of consumption.[5] More elaborate procedures were rejected on grounds of their lack of promise of improving the forecast and the heavy cost of developing them statistically.[6]

A second logical problem in the choice of a method for estimating consumption arises because alternate methods exist for deriving income elasticities of consumer expenditure. These may not yield the same results, so the forecaster should have some conviction that he employs the correct one. The choice lies between computing income elasticities from time series and from cross-sectional data. The former method involves regression of series of annual totals for different types of consumption expenditures

[3] Of course in order to use the competing limited-information estimating technique one need not calculate a model for the whole economy, only identify the form of the other equations sufficiently to draw up a list of all the predetermined variables in the system. But since in fact least-squares estimation has been used through this study, the issue can stand as stated in the text.

[4] For a lucid, classical formulation of this problem, see T. Haavelmo, "The Statistical Implications of a System of Simultaneous Equations," *Econometrica*, 11:1–12 (January 1943).

[5] See the discussion of the relative merits of the two estimating procedures in C. F. Christ, "Aggregate Econometric Models, A Review Article," *AER*, 46:397–398 (June 1956). L. R. Klein rigorously explores the problem discussed here in *A Textbook of Econometrics* (Evanston, Ill., 1953), pp. 249–264, but he offers rather little practical assistance to the worker with limited resources and poor data.

[6] This decision seems consistent with Robert Ferber's summary of the accumulated experience with consumption function estimation; see his *A Study of Aggregate Consumption Functions* (New York, 1953).

on personal disposable income; thus it deals with observations taken over time. The other method, using cross-sectional data, tries to get at the same result in a different way. Its raw data are not aggregate consumption expenditures over time but rather the consumption expenditures of families or individuals at different income levels at the same moment in time. The hypothesis on which this method rests is that the people who are a little richer next year will spend their incomes exactly the same way as people who are exactly that rich this year. This method, while it sounds much less direct than the time series method, has certain theoretical advantages. 1. Problems of price deflation are avoided. 2. A large income range is available since comprehensive budget studies usually involve a high income group 500 or 600 per cent above the lowest income class. 3. The theoretical problems of time series manipulation discussed above which cast doubt on the least-squares estimating procedure disappear.

Our old standby, time series regression, also has certain merits. 1. The theoretical problems of time series just mentioned create more difficulty for structural estimation than for forecasting. 2. More important, cross-section analysis does not take into account the change over time of socially accepted consumption patterns, a phenomenon discussed below. That is, when consumption standards are changing systematically it is not likely to be true that people earning $10,000 a year in 1970 will spend it in the same way as people who earned $10,000 in 1955. The weight of this consideration plus the weakness of the budget studies available for Canada were responsible for the decision to use time series as a basis for computing income elasticities. Elasticities were calculated from cross-sectional data, however, and are used below as a check on the former set.

The problems of consumption forecasting just discussed have nothing essential to do with the actual data on past and present consumption relations. They would arise even if we knew that consumers behave in some completely rational and systematic way subject to the effect of known influences. Our forecasting model assumes that consumers in the aggregate have stable preference patterns which have historically determined the total amount and pattern of personal consumption expenditures in connection with the level of disposable income and random variables. Furthermore, it assumes that this same stable preference pattern will go on operating in the future. We should identify the reasons why these assumptions may not be met in practice, not only to clarify the limits of the procedure but also for the more constructive purpose of bringing to bear some sociological observations on patterns of Canadian consumption which ultimately bolster our confidence in the forecasting method.

There are three basic ways in which the real world can fail to match the assumptions of the model — ways involving either happenings in the historic period on which we base our calculations or future events over the period between the present and the target year of the forecast. These sources of invalidity for the assumptions are changing relative prices, changing income distribution and changing consumer tastes.

The first of these, changing relative prices of various consumer goods, creates difficulty because the income elasticities described for the forecasting method are expenditure elasticities rather than quantity elasticities. This fact is dictated by the form consumption data take in Canada as well as in most other countries.[7] If the price of some basic necessity of life has risen sharply during the period of recorded statistics, people will probably have increased the share of total expenditure devoted to securing this necessity rather than do without. A calculated income elasticity would then forecast an increasing proportion of total income devoted to securing this commodity as income increased, yet if its price relative to other goods should cease to rise the opposite result might occur. By the same token, such a relative price change in the future could falsify a forecast based on past experience in which such a change was not encountered.

The second threat to the empirical assumptions of the forecasting method comes from changes in the distribution of income. For example, if all consumers or households had fixed preference patterns, any historic changes in the income distribution pattern would make an impression on the calculated aggregate consumption pattern except in extremely peculiar cases. Furthermore, the result would be a wrong forecast unless the income distribution kept changing in just the same way in the future. In the context

[7] One should not turn this proposition around and suppose that adequate quantity data could settle the whole problem. It could not unless all future shifts of relative prices could be foreseen and unless quality changes could somehow be resolved into quantity changes to avert the quantity measuring rod turning to rubber.

of long-range economic forecasting the problem of changing income distribution becomes more complex than in static economic usage, and we shall have to examine it carefully. The usual discussion of income distribution and consumption patterns turns on a connection between the *functional* distribution of income and the total pattern of consumer expenditures. In empirical work it is customary to employ wage and profit income as separate variables influencing the level of aggregate consumption, a separation which seems to have statistical significance in explaining short-run consumption changes in Canada. The underlying hypothesis is that the marginal propensity to consume of wage recipients is different from that of profit recipients, presumably because the latter typically have higher total personal incomes, whatever their functional origin.[8] Thus this customary attention to the functional distribution is a short-cut approach to taking account of the fact that personal income is not evenly distributed among consuming units and the fact that this distribution often varies slightly over time.

Implicitly or explicitly, the preceding view of income distribution assumes a fixed population of fixed ages, usually by means of visualizing the *simultaneous* existence of different personal income distributions, all other things held constant. But one of the most important aspects of income distribution for forecasting over the next decade is that the *age distribution* of the population will be changing because of changes in the population pyramid. People's consumption patterns are different at different times in their life-spans, even though their "tastes" in some philosophical sense may remain constant. Thus when the age composition of the population changes — and Canada's is going through striking changes — we would expect variations in aggregate consumption even with nothing else changing in the system. For example, the 18–24 age group and those over 65 will increase in the next decade relative to the age groups in between. It is exactly these two groups which normally have the lowest rate of saving.[9] Fortunately, it

[8] Kuznets has confirmed this supposition in showing that in the United States during 1919–1938 the top 1 per cent of income recipients gained 65 per cent of all dividend income but only 6.5 per cent of total employee compensation. See S. Kuznets, assisted by E. Jenks, *Shares of Upper Income Groups in Income and Savings* (New York, 1953), p. xxxvi.

[9] M. W. Smelker, "Problems of Estimating Spending and Saving in Long-Range Projection," in National Bureau of Economic Research, Conference on

is quite clear what the age distribution of the Canadian population will be in 1970, or at least what the absolute size of all groups over 15 years of age will be. Insofar as we know how age changes affect consumption, this can be taken into account in setting our forecasts.

The third threat to the empirical assumptions of the consumption forecasting model at first glance appears the most dangerous of all — changing consumer tastes. Some economists would argue that the volatility of consumer tastes warrants a throwing up of hands over the possibility of any dependable long-range forecasting. But empirical observation does not warrant extreme pessimism. First of all, we do not aim to estimate consumer expenditures in 1970 for any highly detailed list of commodities, only a set of roughly two dozen large categories. Many of these categories contain numerous goods which are close substitutes for one another. Following Alfred Marshall's famous dictum, "Natura non facit saltum," one would expect the great bulk of changes in tastes to affect only goods which are fairly closely related (that is, substitutable) anyhow. Thus only major changes in tastes are a real threat to the forecasting procedure outlined here.

Does the threat of changing tastes and the other menaces mentioned above render the forecasting model useless? Are income elasticities themselves too elastic for safe use? Certainly this question must be answered in the main by looking to see whether trends in Canadian consumption patterns have been stable over time or whether they have varied in systematic ways. But certain broader observations on the social aspects of consumption in modern North American society are relevant at this point.

Modern consumption patterns in wealthy countries bear only the slightest relation to human subsistence. The great bulk of purchases made by a modern Canadian are not made to insure his elemental physical survival. Rather, they serve to satisfy a variety of "needs" determined in part physically but even more by his society and culture — by the ways by which people in-

---

Research in Income and Wealth, *Long-Range Economic Projection, Studies in Income and Wealth, Volume Sixteen* (Princeton, N. J., 1954), p. 346. For a special study revealing significant differences in income elasticities for persons of different ages, see C. Zwick, "Demographic Variation: Its Impact on Consumer Behavior," *RES*, 39:451–456 (November 1957).

tegrate themselves into complex modern societies. These various needs can be "satisfied" by many different goods and services, and a rising standard of living basically means satisfying these needs with more and better goods.[10] Many shrewd observers have stressed the importance of these social aspects of consumer behavior. It has been argued that material abundance and a growing amount of leisure time have made consumption much more a social phenomenon than it was for our busier and perhaps more individualistic nineteenth-century ancestors.[11] What do these conditions imply for future changes in the level and composition of consumption? If consumption satisfied needs which were purely physical, we might expect that as income rose, saving would increase percentagewise. Surely man's physiological needs do not rise in proportion to his income! But viewing consumption as a social phenomenon, rapid increases in saving as consumer income rises are by no means a logical necessity; the percentage of income saved might just as well stay constant or even decrease. Moreover, we would expect a particular family's consumption level and composition to be a function not of its absolute income measured in dollars so much as its position in the income distribution scale. As all consumers try to imitate the relatively narrow range of socially approved consumption patterns, those with low incomes will always tend to run short at the month's end, those with high incomes tend to have enough left to show significant savings.[12] The consumption patterns of persons in the same cultural setting — say, English-speaking North Americans — are likely to be quite similar except where varying conditions of physical environment intervene. A final consequence of the social character of consumption is that new styles and qualities of consumer goods are likely to be disseminated rapidly into the budgets of all consumers — with a corresponding decline of popular suspicion of "new-fangled gadgets." With industrial research collaborating to produce a steady stream of new products, the consumption level to which people *aspire* is likely to rise very rapidly in future years. Hence the future rate of personal

[10] J. S. Duesenberry, *Income, Saving and the Theory of Consumer Behavior* (Cambridge, 1949), chs. ii–iii.

[11] Riesman, David, in collaboration with R. Denney and N. Glaser, *The Lonely Crowd; A Study of the Changing American Character* (New Haven, 1953).

[12] Duesenberry, ch. iv.

saving is by no means clearly destined to rise as consumers are tempted on to ever higher standards of living.

There are several points raised in this discussion of social patterns of consumption which are relevant to the accuracy of consumption forecasts based on projection of past experience. First of all, any changes in the total consumption pattern are likely to be continuous and gradual, because socially developed standards change only slowly. The consumer with sharply varying preferences tends to feel "out of step." Consumption is likely to increase most rapidly for those articles to which society attaches a high prestige value — fashionable women's clothing, new automobiles, and so forth. Consumption is likely to increase relatively rapidly in types of commodities which show large scope for product differentiation and "styling," for example, television sets compared to bathtubs. If average rates of innovation in different sorts of consumption goods persist into the future, if the prestige commodities of the past remain the prestige commodities of the next decade, if the rates of change of consumption patterns in the past have enough momentum not to be altered violently before 1970, forecasting the future size and distribution of consumption on the basis of past trends seems not to be an especially risky venture.

CONSUMPTION AND CANADIAN ECONOMIC DEVELOPMENT

Having recorded these general reflections on consumption forecasting, we can turn to the historic record of Canadian consumption patterns. The following pages will examine first the relation of aggregate Canadian consumption to personal disposable income in both the short and long runs, then the historic distribution of Canadian consumer expenditures by classes of goods and services.

Published research on the short-run consumption-income relation in Canada was summarized in Chapter 3. This work clearly shows that the strongest force determining any year's personal consumption expenditures is current personal disposable income. This relation is so strong that for the years 1926–1955 (omitting 1942–1945) undeflated personal disposable income explains 99.85 per cent of the variance of undeflated personal consumption.[13] Other variables also proved to be significant determinants of the

[13] Calculated in connection with the present study.

level of personal consumption — particularly the previous year's consumption and the distribution of income between wages and profits. Two questions arise about the possibility of using this information for purposes of long-range forecasting.

1. Are the short-run determinants of Canadian consumption other than personal disposable income likely to exert an independent influence on consumption a decade hence? One can erect strong arguments respectively on logical and empirical grounds for counting out both previous consumption and income distribution as determinants of current personal consumption. The previous year's consumption has a visible influence on current consumption only because income has been changing by unequal amounts. But in the long-range forecasting there is no hope of foreseeing year-to-year variations in rates of economic growth. Our intention is only to predict the location of the long-run trend for major economic variables of the Canadian economy in 1970. Hence there is no point in giving consideration to lagged consumption.[14] The effect of changes in distributive shares on the consumption function seems to call for no more attention. The stock-in-trade proposition among North American economists is that the labor share of national income has a remarkable long-run constancy. One recent examination of this belief has found it largely true for the United States, though the total labor income share seems to have risen a little during the last half-century. D. Gale Johnson finds a rise from 69 per cent for the years 1900–1909 to 75 per cent for 1940–1949.[15] The Canadian figures suggest that the increase there has been a little more rapid than

---

[14] This argument could be demonstrated algebraically. Consider the behavior of a hypothetical national income in the case where $Y_t = C_t + I_t$ and $C_t = a_1 Y_t + a_2 C_{t-1}$ and where we suppose that from time t on, investment assumes some fixed and unchanging value for all future periods. We can then write the value of Y in future time periods $t + 1$, $t + 2$, $t + 3$, and so forth, as functions of I and C_{t-1} only. In these successive periods, the influence of C_{t-1} upon Y steadily diminishes relative to that of I. That is, in each successive period the nest of coefficients relating Y to C_{t-1} approaches closer and closer to zero on the obvious assumption that a_1 and a_2 are both less than unity.

[15] D. G. Johnson, "The Functional Distribution of Income in the United States, 1850–1952," *RES*, 36:175–182 (May 1954). Johnson explains away this increase by claiming that the contribution of property to national output is becoming understated to a greater and greater degree because no income is imputed in national income accounts to government property. This is an interesting point but irrelevant for present purposes, since our concern is with forecasting national income (and its components) as conventionally defined.

in the United States. However, this trend still requires no attention in forecasting Canadian consumption unless we foresee a change in the rate of increase of the labor share compared to the past quarter-century. It does not seem possible to construct a persuasive argument to support such a change.

2. Is a consumption-income relation based on the years 1926–1955 an economically sensible forecasting device for a decade ahead? This question really raises two subsidiary ones — the obvious one about the meaning of the statistically fitted consumption function and a subsidiary one about the accuracy of Canadian income and consumption statistics. Let us dispose of the latter first. It is possible to make one test of the validity of Dominion Bureau of Statistics consumption figures because the Bank of Canada has constructed a series of annual estimates of personal saving which is entirely independent of the residual savings estimate made by the Bureau of Statistics. The Bank of Canada estimates are figured directly by estimating changes in consumer assets and liabilities, rather than as a residual after all other components of gross national product have been calculated.[16] As an experiment, it was assumed that the DBS estimates of personal saving are wrong by the amount of the difference between the DBS estimate of personal saving and the Bank of Canada's estimate. When the DBS consumption figures were amended by this difference and the relations between the disposable income series and the "new" and the "old" consumption series calculated, it turned out that this change improves the over-all correlation between personal consumption and personal disposable income slightly without changing the regression coefficient significantly. Apparently the DBS series cannot be shown to contain serious biases.

There is still the question of the basic economic sense of forecasting the historic consumption-income relation. The slope of consumption function computed on the basis of Canada's 1926–1955 experience implies that Canadians would have done no net personal saving at income levels prevailing in Canada not long before World War I. But in fact there was some personal saving

---

[16] Bank of Canada, *Statistical Summary, Financial Supplement 1955* (Ottawa, 1956), pp. 54–55; D. J. R. Humphreys, "Personal Saving in Canada: Direct Estimates 1939–1953," *Proceedings of the Business and Economic Statistics Section, American Statistical Association* (September 10–13, 1954), pp. 207–214.

in Canada in the years before World War I, and indeed it may have been as large percentagewise as in the 1920's. The computed consumption function thus cannot be projected backward to give a correct estimate of consumption for earlier years, and thus there is a serious possibility that it would underestimate consumption at the level of income likely to prevail a decade from now. Some consumption function workers have tried in various ways to extract a secular consumption function from year-to-year data by such devices as including only years at the top of the business cycle. Modigliani has published calculations of both a cyclical and a secular marginal propensity to consume for Canada. The values themselves, respectively 0.54 and 0.75, are not especially interesting because they refer only to the interwar period and use inferior earlier versions of the national income statistics. Nonetheless the order of difference between these two figures once again confirms the view that the simple-minded consumption-income relation will be biased downward.[17]

Another sort of common-sense question can be asked: if some great calamity suddenly reduced the real income of Canadians to the 1929 level, would Canadian consumption in a reasonably short time drop to the level the computed regression suggests? The answer is certainly negative, because the Canadian standard of living has risen greatly since 1929, and Canadians would be loath to give up this standard before exhausting their liquid savings and available credit. That is, our simple consumption function is not a correct short-run function either.[18]

Clearly it would be helpful to have information on long-run changes in the Canadian consumption-income relation covering more than the last thirty years. Unfortunately, such evidence on Canadian consumption, its composition, and its relation to income is woefully scarce. O. J. Firestone's work provides some broad impressions and definite numbers for a few earlier years. Buckley has estimates of gross saving back to the turn of the century, but not much information can be extracted from these about

[17] F. Modigliani, "Fluctuations in the Saving-Income Ratio: A Problem in Economic Forecasting," Conference on Research in Income and Wealth, *Studies in Income and Wealth, Volume Eleven* (New York, 1949), pp. 392–395.

[18] This contrast between long- and short-run consumption-income relations is stressed by J. S. Duesenberry, "Income-Consumption Relationships and Their Implications," in *Income, Employment and Public Policy, Essays in Honor of Alvin H. Hansen* (New York, 1948), pp. 54–81.

personal saving and hence personal consumption. This leaves us
with only the period of good national income estimates, 1926 on,
plus whatever can be inferred from the superior long-run consumption and saving data for the United States.

Firestone's study of Canadian economic growth gives enough
information for us to figure the compound annual growth rates for
total personal consumption since 1870. For the four broad periods
which Firestone uses these are: 1870–1890, 3.13 per cent; 1890–
1910, 3.65 per cent; 1910–1930, 2.26 per cent; 1930–1953, 3.46
per cent.[19] If there were corresponding estimates of personal disposable income, one could at least have some notion whether in
the long run Canadians have tended to consume a smaller fraction
of higher incomes. Unfortunately, only figures for gross national
product exist, and these are not much help since investment and
government expenditures have in general grown faster than
personal consumption since 1870.

Buckley has shown that from 1901 to 1930 Canada's net
national saving stayed reasonably constant as a percentage of
gross national product. Excluding the half-decade of World War
I, it stayed within the limits of 6.4 per cent and 7.8 per cent of
gross national product and showed no systematic change.[20] The
main components of net private domestic saving are personal saving and business retained earnings. Unfortunately there is no way
of knowing what has happened to their relative importance, and
thus Buckley's work offers no real help in identifying the long-run
consumption-income relation.

Since Canadian statistics are relatively poor for estimating
long-run consumption-income relations, the results of intensive
work on this problem in the United States are of interest. Simon
Kuznets was among the first to call attention to the remarkable
long-run constancy of the shares of capital formation and personal
consumption in national income. In 1942 he set forth a summary of his statistical findings covering much of the preceding
century along with what is still one of the best statements of the

---

[19] These figures are taken from O. J. Firestone, *Canada's Economic Development 1867–1953, With Special Reference to Changes in the Country's National
Product and National Wealth* (London, 1958), Table 15.

[20] Kenneth Buckley, *Capital Formation in Canada, 1896–1930* (Toronto,
1955), p. 64. Buckley's estimate of depreciation to be subtracted in estimating
net saving is the roughest sort; he places it at 10 per cent of gross national
product.

possible reasons for this constancy.[21] More recently an exhaustive study by R. W. Goldsmith shows that whether consumption as a percentage of income has changed over the past half-century depends on whether one counts consumers' durables as consumption (as in the present study) or as investment. In the latter case, the ratio of consumption to income in the United States has not changed significantly since the Civil War. In the more relevant former case (consumers' durables not counted as investment) the consumption ratio has undergone a very slight secular increase over the last fifty to one hundred years.[22] Because of the great similarity between the United States and Canadian growth patterns in other respects, it is quite unlikely that they differ in this one. Therefore it would take a sound argument to defend a total consumption forecast yielding a consumption-income ratio differing much from that prevailing in the more normal years of the last few decades.

To finish our survey of the historical record of Canadian consumption, let us look at the evidence on the distribution of expenditures among various classes of goods and services. The National Accounts going back to 1926 provide information on the year-to-year changes in the composition of Canadian consumption, and Firestone has unearthed some information on earlier years. Table 40 shows the distribution of Canadian consumption expenditures for selected years, and, to provide a basis for comparison, Table 41 offers the same information for the United States for as nearly comparable years as possible. Since the United States information is available in considerable detail, it was possible to combine categories to secure exact correspondence to those used in less detailed presentations for Canada.

Only the following trends can be read unambiguously from the Canadian data. Expenditures on shelter have certainly declined since early in the century, even if they have not fallen much since 1930. Expenditures on transportation and tobacco and alcohol have definitely increased, though the latter trend may have been reversed. Expenditures on food are well below the 1900 level as a percentage of total expenditure, but seem to have been rising

[21] S. Kuznets, *Uses of National Income in Peace and War* (New York, 1942), pp. 3–15 and *passim*.

[22] R. W. Goldsmith, *A Study of Saving in the United States* (Princeton, N. J., 1955), Vol. I., pp. 75–83.

Table 40. Long-run percentage distribution of Canadian consumption expenditures, by expenditure categories, selected years, 1900–1955.

Expenditure category	1900	1930	1939	1950	1952	1955
Food	31.0	25.4	23.5	25.3	25.6	24.1
Tobacco and alcohol	5.9	6.6	7.2	9.1	8.9	8.1
Clothing and personal furnishings	16.7	13.5	12.6	13.0	12.8	11.4
Shelter	13.6	16.5	16.1	11.4	12.2	13.6
Household operation	11.5	13.1	13.4	12.5	12.6	13.0
Transportation	4.6	8.9	10.0	12.3	11.8	12.4
Personal and medical care	4.9	6.5	6.6	6.1	6.3	6.6
Miscellaneous	11.8	9.5	10.6	10.3	9.8	10.8
Total[a]	100.0	100.0	100.0	100.0	100.0	100.0
Durable goods		7.3	7.5	11.2	11.1	11.2
Nondurable goods		56.2	56.6	60.2	58.2	56.1
Services: total		36.5	35.9	28.6	30.7	32.7
excluding shelter		20.0	19.8	17.2	18.5	19.0

[a] Columns may not add to 100 per cent because of rounding errors.

Sources: O. J. Firestone, *Canada's Economic Development 1867–1953, With Special Reference to Changes in the Country's National Product and National Wealth,* Table 17; DBS, *National Accounts, Income and Expenditure, 1950–1955,* Table 44.

Table 41.   Long-run percentage distribution of United States consumption expenditures, by expenditure categories, selected years, 1909–1952.

Expenditure category	1909	1921	1930	1939	1947	1950	1952
Food	25.57	24.94	24.95	23.53	28.83	27.30	29.21
Alcohol and tobacco	8.43	5.17	4.22	7.70	7.70	6.42	6.43
Clothing and personal furnishings	14.85	16.74	14.37	13.58	15.10	12.83	12.52
Shelter	19.31	17.36	15.18	13.25	8.82	10.39	11.01
Household operation	15.86	16.14	18.78	19.39	17.40	16.97	17.13
Transportation	5.17	8.62	9.06	9.57	9.37	12.10	10.99
Personal and medical care	3.31	3.40	4.76	5.02	4.72	4.89	4.98
Miscellaneous	7.50	7.63	8.68	7.96	8.06	9.10	7.73
Total	100.00	100.00	100.00	100.00	100.00	100.00	100.00

Source: J. F. Dewhurst and Associates, America's Needs and Resources, pp. 984–996.

since the 1930's. Looking at the breakdown into durables, non-durables, and services, durables have definitely and nondurables possibly increased over the last twenty-five years at the expense of all services, including shelter.

The United States pattern is very similar. The recent increase in expenditures on food is much clearer than for Canada, and the increase in tobacco and alcohol less clear. Expenditures on shelter have declined more, and expenditures on transportation risen more than in Canada. Apart from these differences, the post-World War II consumption patterns in the two countries are quite similar except for certain differences probably due to climate: Canadians regularly spend relatively more on clothing, shelter, and tobacco and alcohol than Americans; they economize much more on household operations.

Important developments are masked beneath this highly aggregated measure of changes in Canadian consumption. The food category conceals a steady decline of staple items and a rise of high-value foods and restaurant meals, just as in the tobacco and alcohol category spirits have fallen while tobacco has increased strongly. The household furnishings category has not varied much as a whole, but it contains a decline of clothing and footwear and a rise of such services as laundering and dry cleaning. The same is true of household operations, for which fuel costs and domestic service have become much less important, household appliances much more so. Shelter expenditures have declined, but it is quite possible that this trend will be reversed because of the rapid growth of "nonfamily households" and the end of the artificial force of rent controls in the preceding fifteen years.[23]

CANADIAN CONSUMPTION IN 1970

In the light of these reflections we can indicate the decisions actually made in setting the 1970 forecast of personal consumption. The order of march was first to establish upper and lower limits on total personal consumption, then to calculate the consumption total implied by use of income elasticity forecasts of separate expenditure categories (it falls between these limits). Finally, some qualitative adjustments were made in gingerly fashion to take account of certain ways in which we expect future

[23] Firestone, *Canada's Economic Development,* Part II, Section 4.

consumption patterns to deviate from an extrapolation of past experience.

Using a short-run consumption function based on 1926–1955 experience and the personal disposable income figure implied by our "best-guess" gross national product estimate, 1970 consumption (1955 prices) would be about $30,500,000,000 if the calculations are all based on constant-dollar figures, a trifle higher if based on current-dollar amounts. On the basis of the discussion above we can accept this as a lower boundary for 1970 personal consumption. We can set a comparable upper boundary by figuring the *average* propensity to consume for peacetime full-employment years during the period for which good national income statistics are available. When this average value is applied to the personal disposable income forecast, an upper boundary personal consumption forecast of $31,400,000,000 emerges. Another way to set the upper limit would be to calculate a consumption function based only on the prosperous peacetime years of the 1926–1955 period,[24] thereby deriving the *trend* of the normal average propensity to consume rather than its *mean* value. This alternate upper limit would be roughly $31,100,000,000.

Now let us turn to the problem of estimating particular categories of personal consumption expenditures, an alternate route to building a forecast of total personal consumption in 1970. Time series are available for the eight major classes of consumption shown in Table 42, and for several subclasses of most of these categories as well.[25] There are two difficulties in these time series which, though not crippling, must be recalled later in gauging the accuracy of the results. First, the expenditure figures are based on sales of retail outlets, weighted by the product composition of 1941 retail sales by type of outlet as recorded in the 1941 census of distribution. But since 1941 there has undoubtedly been some change in the product composition of sales by various types of retail outlets. For instance, since 1945 chain grocery stores have begun to carry many nonfood items. The second

[24] This approximates the usual method for deriving a secular consumption function from data consisting of a relatively small number of annual observations.

[25] For the years 1930–1950 (except 1931–1934 in some cases), data appear in Canada, DBS, *National Accounts, Income and Expenditure, 1926–1950* (Ottawa, 1951), pp. 74–75; data for 1951–1954 were supplied from unpublished material in DBS files.

Table 42. Forecasts by time-series regression of 1970 consumption in Canada by expenditure category.

Expenditure category	Percentage variation explained[a] (1)	Income elasticity[a] (2)	Consumption forecast (millions of 1955 dollars) (3)
Food	98.64	1.002	8,025
Tobacco and alcohol	95.89	1.292	3,206
Tobacco	90.55	1.081	1,095
Alcohol	97.37	1.429	2,109
Clothing and personal furnishings	94.27	0.911	3,959
Men's and boys' clothing	92.37	0.843	969
Women's and children's clothing	95.37	1.038	1,635
Footwear	87.18	0.772	466
Laundering and dry cleaning	98.43	1.354	290
Other	81.30	0.699	598
Shelter	76.19	—	3,030
Household operations	98.04	0.866	3,785
Fuel	95.44	0.806	830
Electricity	88.09	0.725	251
Gas	—	0.555	77
Telephone	84.29	0.934	268
Furniture	96.88	1.087	495
Other	96.00	0.868	1,864
Transportation	97.03	1.199	3,876
Streetcars, railway, etc.	85.80	0.808	743
New automobiles	80.68	1.831	1,470
Other user operated	—	—	1,663
Personal and medical care	97.61	0.876	1,868
Medical and dental care	93.99	0.757	457
Hospital care, medical ins.	91.10	1.020	601
Other	99.20	0.863	813
Miscellaneous	95.38	0.898	3,182
Motion pictures	71.26	1.323	364
Newspapers and magazines	95.99	0.583	115
Net expenditure abroad[b]	—	—	406
Other	93.12	0.619	2,298
Grand total	99.44	0.959	30,931
Durable goods	94.47	1.419	4,301
Nondurable goods	98.65	1.013	18,996
Services	95.12	0.625	7,625

[a] 1942–1945 excluded.
[b] Data inadequate; forecast is residual of miscellaneous category.
Source: See text.

problem is that a large part of total consumer expenditure has been included in rather ill-defined categories. Fortunately, there exists the more elaborate breakdown for the United States in the Twentieth Century Fund's study, *America's Needs and Resources,* which will later prove helpful in unraveling the Canadian data.

Each of the thirty-four available consumption time series was regressed on personal disposable income in six different ways: (1) undeflated; (2) undeflated, 1942–1945 excluded; (3) deflated to 1952 prices; (4) deflated to 1952 prices, 1942–1945 excluded; (5) deflated per capita; (6) deflated per capita, 1942–1945 excluded. Coefficients of the regression equation and the correlation coefficient were computed for each of these combinations. In general, the correlations were much higher for the series which excluded the war years, were usually higher for the total deflated than for the deflated per-capita figures, and often were a little higher for the undeflated series than for the deflated. Nonetheless, it was decided to use the deflated series because of the ambiguity of projecting an undeflated relation. Table 42 shows for each of the time series used the percentage of variation of the series about its average value "explained" by the movements of personal disposable income (column 1), the income elasticity derived from each regression equation (column 2), and finally the 1970 consumption forecast got by applying each regression equation to the forecast 1970 personal disposable income figure of $34,161,000,000 (1955 prices). The figures in column (3) do not, however, represent an entirely mechanical forecast. Previously in this chapter two reasons turned up why we should expect projections based upon regression on 1926–1954 data to be understated: (1) because of almost inevitable changes in the age composition of the population; (2) because if we had information on income-consumption relations before 1926, it would give our consumption function a steeper slope (and therefore forecast higher consumption). Because of this, 1970 consumption was adjusted upward in the categories for which it seemed most appropriate in light of postwar trends — shelter, transportation, the miscellaneous group, and (very slightly) household operations. The resulting total consumption is $30,931,000,000, compared to an unadjusted minimum figure of $30,500,000,000 and an unadjusted maximum of either $31,400,000,000 or $31,100,000,000.

The percentage distribution forecast for 1970 consumption by this adjusted projection of regressions on data for 1930–1954 agrees fairly well with the trends found by inspection of the longer-run data in Table 40. Food expenditures continue the upward trend of the last few decades (although they were down in

1955 because of the effect of extra heavy durables purchases). Tobacco and alcohol also rise, possibly too sharply in view of the consumers' reaction in the last few years to medical warnings about the dangers of cigarette smoking. Shelter continues to decline percentagewise and transportation to rise, though because of very heavy automobile purchases in recent years this increase is not marked.

A second check on the income elasticities shown in Table 42 can be made by comparing them with income elasticities derived from cross-sectional data as described above. For a sample survey of urban family expenditures in five major Canadian cities in 1953 the Dominion Bureau of Statistics provides a breakdown of family consumption expenditures by class for each bracket of family income. Each of these types of expenditure was regressed on average personal disposable income for each income bracket. Table 43 shows the income elasticities extracted by this procedure. In comparing these elasticities to those derived from time series, the absolute magnitudes are not so important as the ranks of the items in the two lists. The different consumer budget items are listed in Table 43 in the order of the income elasticities derived from the cross-section data. Clearly, the order of the two

Table 43.   Income elasticities derived from cross-sectional expenditure data and from time series data.

Expenditure classes[a]	Cross-sectional data (1)	Time-series data (2)
New automobiles	1.681	1.831
Clothing	1.103	0.911
Other (residual category)	0.789	0.898
Tobacco and alcohol	0.698	1.292
Personal care (exclusive of medical care)	0.689	0.863
Household operation	0.654	0.866
Housing, fuel, light and water	0.475	—[b]
Other transportation	0.450	0.808
Medical care	0.447	0.757
Food	0.327	1.002

[a] Ranked in descending order of elasticities in column (1).
[b] No comparable elasticity computed from time-series data.
Sources: column (1) — Computed from DBS, *City Family Expenditures 1953,* Reference Paper No. 64 (Ottawa, 1956), p. 40.
   column (2) — Table 42, column (2).

series is quite close except for two items — food and tobacco and alcohol. Specifically, in the time-series data we find food expenditures rising just about as fast as income; in cross-section data, people with higher incomes turn out to spend much less of their earnings on food. The explanation is that food purchases are the supreme example of a budget item for which consumption standards are purely a "convention" — a common social standard which changes over time. As food consumption standards continue to rise for Canadians in future years, the poor as well as the rich will raise their expenditures on food, but food expenditures will always be a much larger item in the budgets of the poor than of the rich. The other item for which the two series give different results is tobacco and alcohol. Here it seems that

Table 44. Income elasticities for Canada and the United States.

Expenditure category	United States (1)	Canada (2)
Food and nonalcoholic beverages	0.998	1.002
Alcoholic beverages	1.176	1.185
Tobacco	1.039	0.971
Clothing, accessories, and personal care	1.176	0.919
Shoes	0.969	0.843
Cleaning, repair, maintenance	1.280	(1.182)[a]
Personal care	0.803	0.792
Household and utilities		
Imputed rent	0.919	0.775
Fuel, ice, lighting supplies	1.085	0.916
Electricity	0.836	0.801
Gas	0.712	0.499
Household operation and equipment		
Furniture	1.019	1.034
Mechanical appliances	1.110	(0.947)[a]
Communication (utilities)	0.998	(1.035)[a]
Consumer transportation	0.874	1.112
New and net used cars	0.190	(1.499)[a]
Auto parts, repair, and maintenance	1.019 }	
Gas and oil	1.222 }	0.997
Public transportation	1.487	0.835
Medical care and insurance	1.126	0.955
Personnel	0.990	0.881
Insurance	2.509	1.050
Other	1.072	0.966

[a] Figures for which comparability is less certain.

Sources: column (1) — Computed from Dewhurst, pp. 89, 1005–1007.

column (2) — Income elasticities computed from current-dollar series, excluding 1942–1945.

the time-series income elasticity of 1.292 is too high. This is taken into account in the forecast finally derived from Table 42. Aside from these two items the cross-section analysis gives further support to the consumption forecast based on time-series data.

As a final check on the reasonableness of these projections, the Canadian income elasticities are compared with similar time-series elasticities computed for the United States by J. F. Dew-

Table 45.   Personal consumption in Canada by interindustry sector, values and percentages, 1949 and 1970.

	1949		1970	
Sector	Value (millions of 1949 dollars)	Percentage[a]	Value (millions of 1955 dollars)	Percentage[a]
Agriculture	965.1	8.8	1,155	3.7
Forestry	0	0	0	0
Fishing, hunting, trapping	11.3	0.1	25	0.1
Coal mining, crude petroleum, natural gas	148.2	1.4	125	0.4
Other mining and quarrying industries	0	0	0	0
Food, beverage, and tobacco industries	2,595.3	23.7	7,698	24.9
Clothing and household-goods industries	1,569.3	14.3	4,181	13.5
Forest-products industries	66.6	0.6	237	0.8
Metal-products industries	609.8	5.6	2,288	7.4
Electrical apparatus and supplies industry	187.5	1.7	948	3.1
Mineral-products industries	462.8	4.2	1,546	5.0
Miscellaneous manufacturing industries	291.4	2.7	872	2.8
Construction	0	0	0	0
Transportation, storage, trade	558.2	5.1	1,443	4.7
Communication, finance, insurance, real estate, public utility operation	1,488.0	13.6	4,303	13.9
Other service industries	1,644.2	15.0	4,420	14.3
Imports	669.8	6.1	1,690	5.5
Unallocated and indirect taxes	−304.3	−2.8	—	—
Total	10,963.2	100.0	30,931	100.0

[a] Does not add to 100 per cent because of rounding errors.
Source: 1949 data from interindustry table, DBS, *The Inter-Industry Flow of Goods and Services, Canada, 1949*, Reference Paper No. 72 (Ottawa, 1956), Table 1; 1970 data computed. See text, p. 329 and Table 42.

hurst. This comparison is made because of the conclusion drawn from Tables 40 and 41 that the rate and direction of change of consumption patterns in Canada and the United States are quite similar, despite certain relatively constant climatic and ethnic differences. Table 44 presents the comparison where the expenditure classes are equivalent, the figures in parentheses being those for which comparability is less certain. It should be remembered that the American income elasticities are not literally computed by regression methods; Dewhurst does not present his results in this form. However, the elasticities can be inferred from his projections from 1950 to 1960 by dividing the percentage increase in the particular consumption item by the percentage increase in disposable income. It is easy to see that the elasticities are quite close except for those listed under "consumer transportation," where Dewhurst's projections are influenced by what he assumed to be abnormalities of the base year 1950.

To get from the consumption estimates in Table 42 to a classification of consumer demand according to sectors of the interindustry table required some further estimation. First, each of the eight major classes of consumption expenditures appearing in Table 42 was decomposed and allocated among the seventeen sectors of the interindustry table. In some cases this was easy, in others (such as "household operation") it could be done only with the aid of detailed United States consumption figures to suggest the most likely distribution among subclasses. Adding these figures gave estimated total consumer purchases of the output of each interindustry sector *including* competing imports. But, since imports appear as a separate sector in the interindustry table, imports entering directly into consumption had to be estimated for 1970 and subtracted from the interindustry consumption totals. Estimating the allocation of imports among final demand sectors was done with information on 1970 imports appearing in Chapter 13, and on the amounts of 1949 imports for personal consumption classified according to the international trade commodity groups used by the Dominion Bureau of Statistics.[26]

Table 45 shows the complete estimate of 1970 personal consumption by interindustry sector, its percentage distribution, and the corresponding 1949 figures for purposes of comparison.

[26] Information supplied by J. A. Sawyer.

Investment Expenditures

Advanced industrial countries such as Canada must maintain a high level of investment to restore the capital stock used up in current production and to expand that stock in order to sustain a constantly rising standard of living. This means not just building new factories and machinery — the obvious source of tomorrow's larger stream of goods and services — but also expanding the "social capital" of housing and institutions, and the inventories of goods and materials which allow production and sales to proceed smoothly. Yet, historically speaking, capital formation has been a volatile component of national expenditures, displaying substantial swings in both composition and total amount. From this checkered history one must try to discover the "normal" relation between capital accumulation and Canadian economic development.

This chapter will discuss, first, possible methods of estimating 1970 investment within the framework of assumptions used in this study. Second, the historic pattern of capital accumulation will be searched for clues as to future developments. Finally, a series of projections will be presented and their allocation among sectors of the interindustry table derived.

WAYS OF FORECASTING INVESTMENT

A search of the economic literature reveals two plausible approaches to forecasting future investment, both of which are used in this study. One focuses on the capital *required* to produce the output expected in future years. The other tries to detect how much people will decide to invest if gross national product and other variables stand at specified levels.

The first approach examines the ratio between the size of a country's stock of productive capital and the net output of goods and services which that capital stock produces over a specified time period. Checking this relation between capital stock and output for successive periods, one can tell whether it has shown any regularity in its behavior. If the capital-output ratio, as this relation is called, behaves in some systematic way, we can clearly predict the required capital stock for some year in the future for which we have some independent estimate of the output flow. The first problem which crops up is how to measure the "capital" and "output" terms in this ratio. Gross national expenditure will not quite do as a measure of output, because part of gross domestic investment goes to renew the capital stock. What we want is a measure of the net increase in output after maintenance of the original physical capital stock is provided for, "net national product," which equals gross national expenditure *less* depreciation. This will be used as an output measure in this chapter, but the obvious caution must be inserted that the depreciation charges appearing on firms' books are a very poor measure of the physical deterioration of Canada's capital, and they certainly furnish a biased estimate of the current costs of capital renewal in periods of rapidly changing price levels.

Because of problems of valuation, measurement of a nation's capital stock at a point in time is a much trickier matter, a fact reflected in the collapse of the popularity of national wealth estimates. There is, however, another way of measuring the capital-output ratio which does not have to face the problem of valuing the accumulated capital stock. Instead of looking at the *total* capital stock and *total* net national product, we can examine over a period of several years the *increase* in net national product and the *increase* in the capital stock (which is identical with the total amount of net investment) associated with it. This way we measure the capital-output ratio at the margin and can predict by knowing the annual increase in output expected for some future year roughly how much investment is likely to take place that year to support the increase.[1]

The other approach to forecasting the level of investment is both less specific and more flexible than that just discussed. It tries to determine from the record of past economic activity what variables seem to be closely related via the demand side to the level of certain types of investment. Thus it might turn out that residential construction is closely related to the level of personal

[1] This method is described by William Fellner, "Long-Run Tendencies in Private Capital Formation: The Rate of Growth and Capital Coefficients," in Conference on Research in Income and Wealth, *Long-Range Economic Projection, Studies in Income and Wealth, Volume Sixteen* (Princeton, 1954), pp. 275–331.

Table 46. Five-year totals of investment components as percentages of Canadian gross national product in current and constant dollars, 1901–1955.

Period	Construction		Machinery and equipment	Change in inventories	Gross domestic investment	Net foreign[a] investment	Gross capital formation
	Residential	Nonresidential					
Current dollars							
1901–1905	4.1	9.2	7.0	3.9	24.2	− 5.3	18.9
1906–1910	5.8	12.9	7.2	3.1	29.0	− 9.2	19.7
1911–1915	4.9	13.3	7.8	3.0	29.0	−12.4	16.5
1916–1920	3.2	8.0	6.5	2.8	20.6	− 1.2	19.3
1921–1925	3.5	7.7	5.6	0.7	17.3	0.3	17.7
1926–1930	3.9	6.3	7.0	2.2	19.3	− 2.0	17.4
1931–1935	2.7	6.1	3.7	−1.3	11.3	− 0.4	10.9
1936–1940	3.1	5.6	6.2	1.9	16.8	3.0	19.8
1946–1950	4.2	7.6	7.5	1.8	21.2	0.8	22.0
1951–1955	4.5	10.2	8.4	1.8	24.8	− 1.6	23.3
Constant 1935–1939 dollars							
1901–1905	5.1	11.3	7.3	3.3	27.0	—	—
1906–1910	6.7	15.0	7.8	2.7	32.1	—	—
1911–1915	6.4	17.3	9.2	2.9	35.8	—	—
1916–1920	3.9	9.6	6.5	2.0	22.0	—	—
1921–1925	2.8	6.2	4.7	0.5	14.2	—	—
1926–1930	4.0	6.7	7.7	1.4	19.8	− 2.3	17.4
1931–1935	2.7	6.2	3.8	−0.9	11.8	1.4	13.1
1936–1940	3.0	5.7	6.1	2.7	17.6	3.2	20.8
1946–1950	3.3	7.3	7.7	1.9	20.1	0.7	20.8
1951–1955	3.2	9.0	8.4	1.8	22.5	− 1.4	21.1

[a] No satisfactory way was found to reduce the net foreign balance to a constant-dollar series for the years before 1926; indeed the significance of such a deflation is obscure in any case.

Source: A full description of the sources appears as an appendix to this chapter.

income, the birth rate, or the rate of family formation. If we can find determinants such as these for all types of investment expenditure, *and* if we can independently forecast all these determinants for some future year, then we can estimate the level of total investment on the assumption that these relationships continue as in the past.

The following section presents the data required for making use of these forecasting methods in the form of a general review of the historic size and composition of the flow of investment in Canada.

INVESTMENT IN CANADA

The basic facts of capital formation in Canada over the last half-century are set forth in Table 46 and Figure 10. The former

Fig. 10. Five-year totals of major investment components as percentages of gross national product (current dollars).

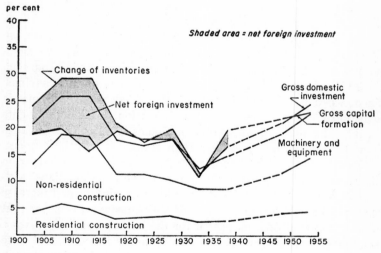

Source: Table 46.

shows major classes of investment — construction, machinery and equipment, inventory accumulation, and net foreign investment — as percentages of gross national product for five-year periods from 1901–1905 to 1951–1955. This is done for these series valued both in current dollars and in constant 1935–1939 dollars. Figure 10 presents graphically the percentages computed from current-dollar data. (The original data were constructed from various sources; since the description of method is fairly technical and of limited interest, it and the parent data appear as an appendix to this chapter — see pp. 355–358.)

A word is necessary on the accounting concepts used in Table 46 and Figure 10. Residential and nonresidential new and replacement construction, new machinery and equipment, and changes in inventories add up to "gross domestic investment," or the total of current gross additions to Canada's capital stock. This total, however, may not be exactly equal to total domestic savings. Part of this investment has at many times been financed by the savings of foreigners, termed net capital imports. That is, Canadians may borrow the savings of foreigners (who thereby acquire claims on Canadian assets) to finance the import or construction of capital goods which could not be as readily financed by Canadians. In the international balance of payments statistics this appears as a surplus of imports over exports on current account. Net foreign investment — by definition an increase in Canadians' net holdings of foreign assets — is then said to be negative, and when we "add" this negative figure to gross domestic investment we get a smaller number for domestic saving. Conversely, during some periods Canadians on balance have exported part of their savings. Then, when net foreign investment is added to gross domestic investment to get gross capital formation, which represents roughly the total of all forms of domestic Canadian savings, domestic savings appear larger than gross domestic investment.

Several facts of great importance are immediately obvious from Figure 10. Gross capital formation, representing Canadians' willingness to restrict current consumption to maintain and increase the capital stock, has been a remarkably constant 18–20 per cent of gross national product except for the chaotic years 1931–1935. The much greater fluctuations of gross domestic investment have mirrored the changing importance of net foreign investment. Thus, the great expansion of Canadian capital in the years 1901–1913 was the direct result of tremendous capital imports, imports of an importance percentagewise which dwarfs the capital inflows of the period 1951–1955 though they failed to attract the public clamor raised over the latter. Capital imports dropped off in the 1920's and became negative during the Great Depression (that is,

Canada reduced her foreign indebtedness), thus augmenting the decline in the domestic savings rate.[2]

Looking at the components of gross domestic investment, residential construction and net inventory accumulation have been remarkably stable fractions. Housing has followed a cycle of its own, but has never strayed outside the limits of 3 and 6 per cent of gross national product. Inventories were run down during the depressed years 1931–1935, but otherwise they have been a systematically declining percentage of gross national product — their decline being another reflection of the "filling up" of the Canadian economy and the improvement of transportation facilities. Nonresidential construction and machinery and equipment have been the volatile components of gross domestic investment. The former particularly is responsible for the increases in the relative share of investment in the uses of gross national product in the periods before World War I and after World War II.

Another aid in understanding the over-all picture of capital accumulation in Canada is a computation of the capital-output ratio discussed in the preceding section. The ratio of net domestic investment minus inventory changes to increase in net national product was calculated for the following five- and ten-year periods:

1911–1920	3.61
1921–1930	3.27
1931–1940	(1.32)
1941–1950	(1.22)
1946–1955	3.12
1951–1955	2.91

That is, in the years 1951–1955 an increase of $1 in Canada's net national product was associated on the average with net domestic investment of $2.91. Before 1911, no estimates of net national product can be made of sufficient reliability to estimate its growth. The numbers in parentheses, those for 1931–1940 and 1941–1950, are certainly nonsignificant. Both decades are overwhelmingly influenced first by depression and then by war. In the depression year 1931, output was far below industrial capacity. To that extent, the increase in output occurring by 1940 did not require new investment to expand productive capacity. Likewise,

[2] No prediction of 1970 capital imports is made in this chapter; further discussion appears in Chapter 13.

the 1940's ratio is not "normal" because throughout World War II productive capacity strained far beyond normal efficient usage; output was stretched and investment was shrunk, artificially reducing the ratio. The figures for the remaining years, however, merit some slight confidence. They do reveal a clear trend toward lower over-all capital requirements, or, to put it the other way around, a given amount of investment now apparently produces a larger increase in output than in the early years of the century. Checking the behavior of the capital-output ratio for the United States offers interesting corroborative evidence. It apparently has declined at least since the 1880's, and now seems to stand at about 2.5, compared to roughly 3.0 for Canada.[3]

A computation of the capital-output ratio and related statistics has been made by O. J. Firestone for Canadian manufacturing taken alone. (See Table 47.) Manufacturing, along with construc-

Table 47. Average annual percentage changes in various measures of development of Canadian manufacturing industries, by twenty-year periods, 1890–1950[a].

Item	1890–1910	1910–1930	1930–1950
Gross value of production	4.25	2.99	4.14
Value of fixed capital	6.94	4.01	0.03
Number of persons working	3.73	0.64	3.33
Value of production per person working	0.50	2.34	0.79
Value of fixed capital —			
per person working	3.09	3.35	−3.19
per $1000 output	2.57	0.99	−3.94

[a] All measures are in constant dollars.

Source: O. J. Firestone, *Canada's Economic Development, 1867–1953, With Special Reference to Changes in the Country's National Product and National Wealth,* Income and Wealth Series VII, Table 75.

tion, is often called the secondary sector of the economy, in contrast to the primary (agriculture and extractive industries) and tertiary (services and utilities) sectors. Firestone's figures show a healthy decline in the capital-output ratio for manufacturing in the years 1930–1950 and a modest rise in the preceding years 1910–1930. Presumably the coefficient began falling in some

[3] Fellner, pp. 306, 317.

year not far from 1930. This is reasonably consistent with the findings previously described for the economy as a whole.

Capital coefficients differ sharply from industry to industry. Thus in interpreting aggregate capital coefficients one must know something about the uses to which the investment flow has been put and how changes in its composition have interacted with changes in its total volume. Consequently, the following paragraphs will present a sketchy summary of the major changes over the last half-century in this stream of investment.[4]

Like so many other boom periods in Canada's history, the prosperity of the years 1901–1913 sprang from heavy investment and expansion of primary industry — this time prairie agriculture. Prairie farm investment predominated until at least 1905 when the strain on the existing capacity of Canada's service industries set off a wave of investment in tertiary industries, particularly railroads and prairie construction such as grain elevators.[5] This development explains the great burst of nonresidential construction shown in Table 46; and it was railroads and similar utilities which received the bulk of the foreign capital flowing into Canada in those years. Under the tariff protection of the "National Policy," manufacturing industry in eastern Canada was also stimulated by the prairie boom, but the relative importance of manufacturing in these years was much less than either in the late nineteenth century or in the 1920's.[6]

The great increase of Canada's population through immigration during the years 1901–1913 left its mark on the record of capital accumulation during these years. It may explain the fact that capital per worker in manufacturing rose at a slower rate during the years 1890–1910 than in the two-decade intervals which preceded and followed. For the economy as a whole, both output and the capital stock per capita grew much less rapidly than in the years before or after 1901–1913. The compound annual rate of growth of national income per capita for the years 1870–1900 was 1.7 per cent; for 1900–1920, 1.3 per cent; and for 1920–1952,

---

[4] See also Chapter 3 *supra*.

[5] Kenneth Buckley, *Capital Formation in Canada, 1896–1930* (Toronto, 1955), chs. i-iii.

[6] O. J. Firestone, *Canada's Economic Development, 1867–1953, With Special Reference to Changes in the Country's National Product and National Wealth* (London, 1958), Part II, Sec. 5.

1.9 per cent.[7] These facts testify to the initial difficulty faced by the economy in absorbing such a large stream of immigrants, just as the rapid expansion of the period from World War I to the end of the 1920's gives evidence of their great ultimate contribution.

Investment in the 1920's was less tightly dependent on export demand than in the early years of the decade, and expansion centered much more in the "secondary sector" (manufacturing and construction) than in the primary extractive or tertiary service segments. The most immediate stimulus behind this development was World War I. Defense requirements forced expansion particularly of Canadian iron and steel, shipbuilding and aircraft, and in general promoted the industrial diversification of the economy. Canadians began to refine much of the nonferrous metal ores they had previously exported.[8]

After 1925, detailed information becomes available on the allocation of investment to various types of users. As we saw in Chapter 3, a striking decline occurred from 1929 to midcentury in the relative importance of manufacturing, with a corresponding increase in the primary (especially agriculture) and tertiary (public investment, commerce, and finance) sectors. Utilities have declined in the tertiary sector and in 1929 were certainly down in importance relative to previous decades. In transportation, especially, the decline in the importance of railway investment after 1913 had not been offset by investment required in competing forms of transport.[9]

Investments in manufacturing industry and construction (especially residential), then, were the most dynamic factors in the 1920's. The real value of Canada's stock of residential buildings per family was higher in 1931 than in 1921, 1941, or 1951, as shown by the following values (1935–1939 dollars):

1921	$2232
1931	2412
1941	2341
1951	2342.[10]

[7] Computed from Firestone, Tables 19, 75.
[8] Firestone, Part II, Sec. 9.
[9] Buckley, *Capital Formation in Canada,* ch. iii.
[10] Computed from O. J. Firestone, *Residential Real Estate in Canada* (Toronto, 1951), p. 99; Canada, DBS, *National Accounts, Income and Expenditures, 1950–1955;* figures for number of families taken from Census of Canada data appearing in *Canada Year Book* (various years).

Residential construction activity for most industrial countries including Canada seems to show a cycle of about fifteen to seventeen years duration quite separate from (though not independent of) the general business cycle. For Canada a peak in this construction cycle clearly came in 1929, explaining the relatively large stock of housing existing in 1931.[11] Turning to manufacturing, evidence shows that, while constant dollar manufacturing output increased about two-thirds between 1920 and 1929, gross value of capital employed more than doubled. In Canada, as in the United States during this decade, capital was extensively substituted for labor in manufacturing processes, as is shown by changes in the occupational distribution of the labor force between census years 1921 and 1931. "There were striking relative increases in the numbers gainfully occupied as unskilled workers, in the service industries (custom and repair, domestic, personal and professional services), in transportation, and in construction. Neither manufacturing nor agriculture kept pace with these industries." [12]

Canada's third great investment boom of the twentieth century, running from 1947 to the present, has been propelled by both of the prime forces which supported its two predecessors — strong foreign demand for Canadian primary products and the industrial diversification created by the all-out mobilization of World War II.

About two-thirds of the industrial war structure created during World War II was found to be adaptable to peacetime uses. Although peacetime reconversion, modernization and expansion involved large capital outlays and although supply shortages slowed down the implementation of the program, most of the work was completed by the end of 1947. Manufacturing industries were then geared to turn out an expanding volume of civilian capital and consumer goods. The process of reconversion came to an end in 1947, but further expansion and modernization of Canadian manufacturing plants continued.[13]

[11] Buckley, *Capital Formation in Canada*, p. 40; W. A. Mackintosh, *The Economic Background of Dominion-Provincial Relations*, RCDPR *Report*, Appendix 3 (Ottawa, 1939), p. 43.

[12] Mackintosh, p. 43. The same sorts of changes in employment patterns were occurring in the United States. R. A. Gordon has noted that manufacturing employed no more workers in 1929 than in 1919 [*Business Fluctuations* (New York, 1952), p. 369], and F. C. Mills has shown a net displacement of labor from manufacturing for the crucial years 1923–1929 [*Economic Tendencies in the United States* (New York, 1932), p. 531].

[13] Canada, Department of Trade and Commerce, *Private and Public Investment in Canada, 1926–1951* (Ottawa, 1951), p. 37.

Scarcely was this process under way when the Korean War gave a second fillip to Canada's aircraft, ship building, and electronics industries.

In general, the post-World War II manufacturing investment has been characterized as partly a "filling-in" and "rounding-out" process. Thus major investments by individual firms were usually undertaken for expansion vertically or horizontally into related fields of activity, increased domestic processing of Canadian raw materials, modernization of technology and equipment, decentralization of plants to lower-cost sites, and so on. They did not involve major changes in the economy's structure as did manufacturing investment in the late 1920's and earlier years, and indeed as late as 1951 Canadian manufacturing investment had not attained the peak physical volume reached in 1929.[14] The recent economic expansion has been as great as it has because of rapid investment in other sectors, particularly primary production.

THE FUTURE OF CANADIAN INVESTMENT

Following the methodology set forth in the first section of this chapter, two separate methods will be used to estimate total investment in 1970, and any major difference will be reconciled on the basis of judgment about the validity and accuracy of the two approaches. It was pointed out in the preceding section that the ratio for Canada by decades of net increases in the capital stock of durable goods to increases in net national product had declined from 3.61 in 1911–1920 to 3.12 for 1946–1955 (or 2.91 for 1951–1955). Income data are not good enough to allow presenting definite figures for years before 1911, but it seems quite clear that the capital-output ratio had been rising up to that time. This evidence agrees exactly with what investigators have found for the United States, where it appears that the ratio reached its peak between 1910 and 1920, measured either by the ratio of total capital to total income or by the ratio of increases in capital to increases in income.[15] Therefore, despite the difficulties of measuring the quantity of capital in existence, one feels

---

[14] *Private and Public Investment in Canada, 1926–1951,* pp. 39–42.

[15] Fellner, pp. 306, 317; Daniel Creamer, assisted by Martin Bernstein, *Capital and Output Trends in Manufacturing Industries, 1880–1948* (New York, 1954), ch. iii; Israel Borenstein, *Capital and Output Trends in Mining Industries, 1870–1948* (New York, 1954), pp. 6–7.

some confidence in this account of the over-all trends in the ratios.

Just what causes aggregate capital-output ratios to rise or fall is practically unknown, and the *possible* explanations are unpleasantly numerous. One cause frequently cited is technological change, which in advanced countries such as the United States and Canada constantly creates new machinery which will produce a given output at lower unit capital costs. But it must be noted that new technology is in principle no less likely to displace labor and make profitable the use of *more* capital per unit of output. Another cause for a declining coefficient would be economies of scale as the output of a firm or industry grows larger; but how many firms enjoy increasing returns, and how long they shall continue to do so, is nearly impossible to determine empirically. Yet another possibility is that a declining capital-output coefficient is explained by changes in the *composition* of total output, that is, because industries with low capital-output ratios have been growing faster than industries with high ratios, even if none of these industry ratios have changed. In United States manufacturing, at least, it has been proved that this is not the case.[16]

Uncertainty about the exact causes of movements of the capital-output ratio precludes any "scientific" finding about its future behavior. Something can be said, however, about its trends in the primary, secondary, and tertiary sectors of the economy taken separately. Primary sectors such as agriculture, mining, and forestry seldom undergo drastic technological change and are likely to face decreasing returns because of their immediate dependence on natural resources. It is not likely that the capital-output ratio for these industries will fall much in the next decade, especially when one considers the rapid expansion in prospect for petroleum and natural gas, both heavy users of capital relative to output.

Looking at the secondary portion of the economy, manufacturing and construction, convincing arguments exist both for and against a future decline of the capital-output ratio. On the one hand, the rapid development of a full complement of manufacturing industries in Canada since 1920 has certainly meant economies of scale for the sector as a whole, making their appearance,

[16] Creamer, ch. v.

for example, through the filling-in process described in the preceding section whereby firms which have acquired markets and technology are able to use these in expanding to related fields. On the other hand, one American economist highly versed in such matters has argued that the past thirty years' decline in the capital-output ratio for manufacturing is spurious for purposes of prediction, because of the historical accidents of, first, the depression of the 1930's, in which the capital stock actually declined, and the overstraining of capacity from World War II through the Korean War, which caused producers to maintain output at a level greater than normal relative to existing plant and equipment.[17] Taking into account both the force of technology and the vagaries of recent history, one would expect a slight continuation of the decline in capital-output ratios in secondary industries as the most likely development over the next decade.

In tertiary industries, public utilities and services, the probable behavior of the capital-output ratio is slightly clearer. It is in the public utility field that the great economies of scale will accrue as the Canadian economy continues to fill up in terms of population and resource utilization. Communications, transportation and power should all yield greater output with relatively small increases in capital. Personal and business services, using very little capital, will lower the coefficient as they become relatively more important.

On balance, then, one might expect a slight decline in Canada's over-all capital-output ratio from the value observed for the post-World War II decade. The decline of the coefficient from 1911–1920 to 1946–1955 was 13.3 per cent. A continued fall at the same rate would bring it from 3.12 down to 2.88, a figure not unreasonably low in view of the current value of about 2.5 for the United States. (At any point in time, higher levels are to be expected for Canada than for the United States because of the relatively great importance of such capital-intensive industries as agriculture, construction, and transportation.) This figure of 2.88 is very close to the value of 2.91 observed for the years 1951–1955, when the burst of investment made in the late 1940's previous to this period was having its full impact on the country's productive capacity. If we include the accumulation of inventories historically associated with output increases, the forecast

[17] Simon S. Kuznets, "Introduction" to Creamer, pp. 12–13.

capital-output ratio in 1970 would be 3.35, compared to 3.41 for the years 1951–1955.

Using this ratio, we can make a tentative forecast of total investment. The forecast 1970 gross national product of $48,000,-000,000 would correspond to a net national product (subtracting $5,000,000,000 depreciation) of $43,000,000,000. That net national product will be *increasing* in 1970 at a rate of 3.93 per cent per year, or by the amount of $1,690,000,000 per year. Multiplying this by the capital-output ratio of 3.35, we get net investment of $5,660,000,000; adding the $5,000,000,000 depreciation estimate, we get $10,660,000,000 gross capital formation. It should be noted that this figure does not include investment by government departments and therefore does not double-count any government investment forecast in Chapter 12 in the category "Government purchases of goods and services."

Having completed the projection using capital-output ratios, we can turn to the other method of forecasting long-range investment discussed above. That method simply involves seeking statistical correlations between investment components and other economic data on the assumption that a high correlation exposes a crucial factor which people somehow consider when they decide to undertake a particular sort of investment. The categories of investment we shall try to explain in this way are those appearing in Table 46 — residential construction, inventory accumulation, machinery and equipment, and nonresidential construction.

Without a complete structural model of the Canadian economy it has not been possible to develop statistical explanations of year-to-year changes in investment demand. Moreover, research on United States investment determinants strongly suggests that the determinants of year-to-year changes in the level of investment are by no means the same as the long-run determinants of its secular growth. For instance, investment in machinery and equipment in the short run depends on recent years' corporate profits, firms' liquidity position, and so forth. These variables will no doubt continue to determine changes in such investment from 1969 to 1970. But the general level of corporate profits and other such variables will in the years around 1970 themselves depend on more fundamental variables. To find these it was necessary to experiment further with the statistical model of

Canadian economic growth developed in Chapter 4, seeking explanatory variables for the long-run investment series developed
in an appendix to this chapter (see p. 356).

   In the statistical model of Chapter 4 we discovered that residential construction bears some relation to the current number
of births and little or no relation to immigration in the previous
half-decade. For forecasting purposes the construction-immigra-
tion relation is of little interest anyhow because of the decline
foreseen in the importance of immigration. Residential construction in the long run seems more closely correlated with two
other variables — the level of GNP and the rate of growth of
population. However, we also must take into account the well-
known long-run fluctuation of residential construction apart from
the general business cycle. Residential construction has a "cycle"
all its own, relatively independent of the general business cycle.
The average time elapsing from one peak to the next of this
widely recognized "construction cycle" is about fifteen to seventeen years, much longer than for the general business cycle over
the last century. Figure 11 shows the movements over time of
the five-year totals of constant-dollar construction investment —
both residential and nonresidential. The peaks and troughs observed in the annual series are marked by the letters "P" and "T"
respectively along the base of the figure. Both the residential
and nonresidential construction series clearly reflect two peaks
and two troughs; more can be found at regular intervals by
carrying the series back into the nineteenth century. The persistence of this cycle requires us to consider it in making a forecast
of construction investment for a target year such as 1970. Why
does the construction cycle take just fifteen to seventeen years to
run its course, and why should it continue to do so in the future? The answer to the first question is not known for certain;
the average durability of buildings seems to have something to do
with it, but chance factors of population movements are thought
by many economists to dominate instead. Fortunately, the second question can be answered independently: there are good
reasons for thinking that the construction cycle will continue to
operate over the time-span of our forecast. World War II not
only forced a moratorium on many sorts of construction, it also
created a great demand backlog for residential construction in
particular, in the form of a rapidly growing population with

enough liquid savings to afford better housing. This sort of back-log explains the bursts of construction in the late 1940's and in the years 1953–1956. Because of the amount of construction which has taken place, and because of the current decline in the

Fig. 11. "Construction cycle" in five-year totals of residential and non-residential construction investment, 1901–1970.

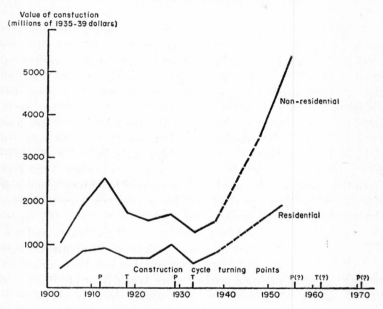

Construction cycle turning points:

Peak	Trough
1912	1918
1929	1933
1956–57 (?)	1961–62 (?)
1970–72 (?)	

Source: construction time series from Table 51; historic construction cycle turning points from Kenneth Buckley, *Capital Formation in Canada, 1896–1930,* Canadian Studies in Economics, No. 2 (Toronto, 1955), p. 40.

rate of family formation in Canada (due to the current coming of age of the stunted generation of the 1930's), it seems likely that the growth of construction investment will slack off for five to seven years until rapid changes in the age composition of the population and depreciation of old housing set it off again. Finally, if its historic periodicity continues to hold, the construction cycle will again be fairly near its peak in the year 1970.

Taking this into account, the forecast for 1970 residential construction derived from its long-run relation to gross national product and rate of population growth is increased slightly for 1970, making the 1970 prediction $1,992,000,000 dollars in 1955 prices.

Another investment component whose long-run determinants seem fairly clear is inventory accumulation. Historically, the stocks of goods held in the economy have on the average increased at a fairly steady rate relative to the growth of the total flow of those goods to final consumers (measured by gross national product). It is often said quite correctly that changes in inventory levels are very important in minor business recessions such as 1954. This is quite true, but nonetheless the long-run data in Table 46 show the remarkably steady behavior of inventories (except for periods such as 1931–1935) when looked at from the long-run point of view. The ratio of inventory accumulation to gross national product has shown some tendency to decline during the twentieth century, no doubt due to improved transportation, more efficient wholesale-retail distribution, and the filling-up of Canada's vast land area with people. In both constant and current dollars, inventory accumulation has been about 1.8 per cent of gross national product since World War II; it has not varied significantly from this percentage since World War I. Consequently, average annual inventory accumulation around 1970 will be forecast at 1.77 per cent of a gross national product of $48,000,000,000 in 1955 prices, or $859,000,000.

Except for the periods of World War II and the depressed years 1931–1935, constant-dollar figures for investment in machinery and equipment have shown an extremely close relation to the level of real gross national product. No other variable seems to add much to the explanation of demand for machinery and equipment. Since this segment of investment is not so much subject to very long-run influences, a direct relation to gross national product (implying a "marginal propensity to invest") seems a fairly sensible approach. On this basis, 1970 machinery and equipment investment will be $3,892,000,000.

The remaining investment component — nonresidential con-

Table 48. Percentage distribution of gross investment in Canada by economic sector,[a] selected prosperous years, 1926–1955.

	Agriculture, fishing, trapping	Forestry	Mining, quarrying, oil wells	Manufacturing	Construction	Transportation, storage, communication, public utilities	Trade	Finance, insurance, real estate	Service
1926	11.99	0.74	2.10	27.44	1.73	21.50	2.97	27.19	4.33
1927	12.32	0.63	1.90	29.61	1.58	21.50	2.85	24.34	5.27
1928	12.76	0.53	2.82	28.61	2.20	21.65	4.40	22.01	5.02
1929	9.77	0.53	3.46	28.12	2.48	25.86	5.11	20.08	4.59
1930	8.73	0.57	4.27	26.28	2.66	27.99	4.08	20.68	4.74
1937	12.21	0.77	5.10	21.63	1.85	28.13	4.33	28.13	4.17
1939	13.06	0.83	4.12	16.20	1.82	19.83	4.96	31.90	6.28
1940	12.22	0.73	3.55	33.49	1.47	16.01	4.28	25.31	2.93
1948	13.07	1.04	3.91	21.56	2.20	21.08	6.03	24.95	6.15
1949	14.12	0.88	4.11	18.06	1.85	22.84	6.50	26.08	5.56
1950	14.71	1.06	3.70	15.61	2.21	22.33	7.28	26.77	6.34
1951	13.52	1.52	4.75	20.81	1.73	23.57	6.17	22.31	5.62
1952	13.04	0.92	4.96	22.86	1.72	27.16	4.63	19.67	5.05
1953	11.28	0.70	5.31	20.02	1.88	24.92	6.82	23.53	5.54
1954	8.32	0.99	5.96	17.62	2.08	23.98	7.89	27.28	5.89
1955	8.08	1.19	6.37	17.93	3.30	20.72	6.24	30.02	6.14

[a] Investment by government departments is not included, but investment by government business enterprises appears in the appropriate sectors.

Source: Computed from National Accounts, Income and Expenditure 1926–1950 and 1950–1956, Table 25. Rows may not add to 100 per cent because of rounding errors.

struction, comprising factories, institutional construction, transportation systems, dams, and so forth — is the most difficult to explain. It is not closely related to gross national product in the long run. Contrary to Buckley's suggestion, it is totally unrelated to the level of Canadian exports. Unlike residential construction, it is not very well explained by population growth. To make some sort of estimate for nonresidential construction, the following (rather involved) procedure was developed.

1. The percentage distribution of gross investment among major sectors of the Canadian economy was studied for the relatively prosperous and normal years of the period 1926–1955. This information is shown in Table 48 broken down by those

Table 49. Estimation of 1970 gross investment in Canada by major economic sectors.

Sectors	Estimated distribution 1970 gross investment (per cent)	Current ratio machinery and equipment to total investment (per cent)	Estimated 1970 investment (millions of 1955 dollars)		
			Machinery and equipment	Total	Construction
	(1)	(2)	(3)	(4)	(5)
Agriculture, fishing, trapping	8.0	80.8	658	771	113
Forestry (primary woods operations)	1.5	43.9	71	145	74
Mining, quarrying, oil wells	8.0	32.2	248	771	523
Manufacturing	23.5	64.6	1,369	2,266	897
Construction	2.5	89.1	210	241	31
Transportation, storage, communication, public utility operation	21.0	40.0	771	2,026	1,255
Trade	6.0	43.7	252	578	326
Finance, insurance, real estate	23.5	1.6	38	2,265	2,227
Service	6.0	24.2	143	578	435
Subtotal	100.0		3,760	9,641	5,881
Government investment not classified as gross domestic investment in *National Accounts*			132	1,448	1,316
Total			3,892	11,089	7,197

Source: See text, pp. 348–349.

categories given in the *National Accounts*. Note that the category "Finance, insurance, and real estate" in this and in the following table includes residential construction, although we have just forecast this separately. Because it was more convenient to do so, it was carried clear through the following computations, keeping in mind the forecast of $1,992,000,000 already made.

2. Using information in Chapters 10 and 15 through 19 of this study on output and technology trends for these sectors, a rough distribution of 1970 investment was developed; it appears as column (1) of Table 49. Also, the average ratio in the past five years of investment in machinery and equipment to total gross investment for each of these sectors was computed; it appears in column (2) of Table 49.

3. Now the absolutely crucial assumption was made that the ratios in column (2) of Table 49 will be the same in 1970 as in the 1950's; historic trends do not dictate any clear likelihood of change, and the argument that the construction cycle will be in about the same phase in 1970 as now supports this assumption somewhat. Having made this assumption, we can derive by simple arithmetic the distribution of our forecast $3,892,000,000 machinery and equipment investment among the economy's sectors.

4. If the assumption of constant ratios is correct, then in 1970 investment in machinery and equipment will be 39 per cent of the total of this category *plus* total investment in construction. This means the total will be $9,641,000,000, and applying the estimated percentage distribution of this total from column (1) of Table 49 we get the figures in column (4). Finally, subtracting column (3) — machinery and equipment investment — from column (4) — total investment — we get total construction. Recall again that the previously forecast residential construction figure of $1,992,000,000 has been consciously included clear through the computation. Subtracting it out of the total for column (5) we get $3,889,000,000 investment in private non-residential construction. Adding estimated construction by government departments (not included as "gross domestic investment" in the *National Accounts*) of $1,316,000,000, as given in Chapter 12, we get total nonresidential construction of $5,205,-000,000.

Recapitulating, the 1970 investment pattern forecast, by seeking separately the determinants of construction, machinery and equipment, and inventory accumulation, is as follows.

Residential construction	$ 1,992,000,000
Nonresidential construction	3,889,000,000
Machinery and equipment	3,760,000,000
Inventory accumulation	859,000,000
Gross domestic investment	10,500,000,000
Construction by government departments	$ 1,316,000,000
Government purchases of machinery and equipment	132,000,000
Gross public and private domestic investment	$ 11,948,000,000

Within the limits of significance possible in a forecast such as this, the figure for gross domestic investment of $10,500,000,000 arrived at here does not differ significantly from that of $10,660,-000,000 forecast by use of the capital-output ratio. In view of the great uncertainties surrounding the latter, the $10,500,000,000 figure will be used for 1970 gross domestic investment, and the corresponding figure of $11,950,000,000 for public and private capital formation (including government investment not so classified in the *National Accounts*). This means gross public and private capital formation will stand at about the same percentage of gross national product in 1970 as during the past six years, and therefore higher than for most of the preceding half-century.

What does this investment forecast mean for the rate of economic growth and the level of employment? It seems wise, with this investment forecast in hand, to take a long look at the problems of sustaining a high level of employment and a high rate of capital formation and economic growth in an advanced industrial economy. For, as Professor Alvin Hansen has insisted, the experience of the post-World War II decade has in no way disproved the stagnation thesis developed during the 1930's, but rather raised the possibility that ambitious and well-conceived government policies can avert the dangers to growth and stability which that thesis identified — such factors as a declining rate of population growth, increasingly productive technology, and the end of the expansion stimulus of territorial growth.[18]

How do these matters relate to the present forecast? We have assumed a continued willingness of the Canadian government to use its fiscal and monetary powers to sustain a high level of employment and have contended that given this willingness a high average level of employment can be sustained which will constrain the business cycle to fluctuations milder than, say, the one of 1937–38. Against this background we have constructed our investment forecast, indicating investment levels which we believe will persist if government action sustains the level of employment and if private investors retain confidence in the continued use of such policies. Is all of this internally consistent? Is confidence in full-employment policies enough to guarantee what is certainly a high-investment economy over the next decade? Will the output of this rapidly expanding capital stock be taken off the market at prices which will validate and sustain investors expectations, without the use of really massive pump-priming?

The issue obviously cannot be laid to rest here. The forces identified by the Hansen stagnation thesis are not absent in the Canadian economy. A tendency for secular decline in the birth rate is clearly evident in the statistics, and our forecast holds that that decline will resume its course during the next decade. The great productivity of new technology, the fact that replacement investment normally involves a large increase in productive capacity — these forces so much discussed in the United States are equally present in Canada. The frontier, which nourished the Canadian economy in the early twentieth century, as it did the United States economy in the nineteenth, no longer calls forth massive capital formation. On the other side of the balance, we have identified numerous powerful investment incentives which are sure to continue in operation over the next decade. Even though it may again tend to fall, Canada's population growth rate is high by the standards of modern industrial countries. Its age composition is favorable to a high level of consumption expenditure. Exploitation of natural wealth will continue to furnish an

[18] A. H. Hansen, "Growth or Stagnation in the American Economy," *RES*, 36:409–414 (November 1954).

open frontier of investment opportunities akin to the frontier of old. And barring a drastic outbreak of peace, the world's demand for this natural wealth will continue unabated. The contention of this study is that these latter factors will suffice, at least for a decade, and that they will render the policy problem of reasonably full employment and sustained growth a manageable one.

An important factor which bolsters this conclusion has, however, not yet been explicitly mentioned. One force mitigating the stagnation-inducing factors would be a rise in the marginal capital-output ratio, which would reduce for any given level of net investment the growth in final demand necessary to validate the investors' expectations. We have forecast only a slight decline in the capital-output ratio over the next decade. But more important than this for present purposes is the likelihood that the capital-output ratio, taken over all public and private investment, is itself sensitive to the balance of forces tending toward stagnation or expansion and will, in the long run, respond to them in an equilibrating fashion. Investment which is highly productive in terms of immediate dollar value received, such as new automobile assembly plants, competes directly for society's resources with investments of less immediate and less measurable productivity, such as improved educational facilities, highways, basic scientific research, long-run resources development and conservation, and so forth. Slackened investment in "highly productive" investment in the narrowly defined sense of immediate cash returns opens the door for the "less productive" investment in the same narrow sense. Any change in these proportions is not an automatic development; the economy's decision-making units must be both willing and able (that is, effectively enough organized) to make such adjustments. Because of improved understanding by public officials of the economic impact of fiscal policy adjustments and public works, and by corporation managers and directors of the importance to the economy of long-run development and accumulation, it is possible to feel that such decisions can be made, and that modern industrial societies are at least in principle capable of turning their "economic maturity" from a burden to an asset.[19]

---

[19] For a theoretical treatment of these issues in terms of modern business cycle theory, compare N. Kaldor, "Mr. Hicks on the Trade Cycle," *EJ*, 61:841–845 (December 1951), and *idem.*, "The Relation of Economic Growth and Cyclical Fluctuations," *EJ*, 64:65–71 (March 1954).

1970 INVESTMENT BY INTERINDUSTRY SECTOR

As a final step, forecast 1970 investment expenditure must be allocated among the industries to which it will be paid, grouping them as in the interindustry table discussed in Chapter 14. This will be done separately for investment in durable goods (construction and machinery and equipment) and inventories.

The allocation of forecast durable goods demand is quite simple, because in our highly aggregated interindustry table almost all investment expenditures go to four sectors — construction, metal products, electrical apparatus and supplies, and imports. Furthermore, we know[20] what the breakdown was for 1949 of imports passing into investment by type and could thus tell for each interindustry sector exactly how much of the total value of that type of good passing into investment was produced within Canada and what portion was imported.

Table 50 shows the allocation of 1949 investment expenditures among the interindustry sectors in terms of both current 1949 prices and in terms of percentage of total gross domestic investment. Of the imports of goods and services, which were 16.9 per cent of total investment in 1949, 15.9 per cent were commodity imports. Of this 15.9 per cent, 0.8 per cent were imports competing with Canadian miscellaneous manufacturing, 2.8 per cent competed with electrical apparatus and supplies, and 11.5 per cent competed with Canadian metal products. Taken together, the last two Canadian industries supplied about 60 per cent of the total investment demand for their products.

Columns (3) and (4) of Table 50 present the allocation of 1970 forecast durables investment among interindustry sectors respectively in 1955 dollars and in percentages. The percentages were derived as follows: since total construction of $5,881,000,000 was forecast independently above, 61.5 per cent of the investment total could be immediately allocated to the construction industry. Small adjustments were made in the minor items, allowing for a slight decline percentagewise for investment purchases from agriculture; clothing and household goods; forest products; and transportation, storage, and trade; a slight increase was allowed for mineral products and miscellaneous manufactures. This leaves metal products, electrical apparatus and supplies, and the

[20] Information supplied by J. A. Sawyer, Dominion Bureau of Statistics.

Table 50. Distribution of 1970 Canadian investment forecast by interindustry sectors of investment goods origin.

| Selling sector | Investment sales | | | | 1970 net change in inventories (millions of 1955 dollars) |
	1949 (millions of 1949 dollars) (1)	1949 (percentage of total gross domestic investment) (2)	1970 (millions of 1955 dollars) (3)	1970 (percentage of total gross domestic investment) (4)	(5)
Agriculture	7.7	0.26	19	0.20	0
Forestry	—	—	—	—	45
Fishing, hunting, trapping	—	—	—	—	0
Coal mining, crude petroleum, natural gas	—	—	—	—	15
Other mining and quarrying industries	—	—	—	—	5
Food, beverage, and tobacco industries	32.0	1.08	96	1.00	135
Clothing and household goods industries	8.5	0.29	19	0.20	52
Forest products industries	561.9	18.93	1,755	18.20	43
Metal products industries					101
Electrical apparatus and supplies industry	122.9	4.14	524	5.43	25
Mineral products industries	0.6	0.02	5	0.05	42
Miscellaneous manufacturing industries	14.4	0.49	53	0.55	11
Construction	1,645.0	55.42	5,881	61.50	35
Transportation, storage, trade	19.7	0.66	58	0.60	340
Communication, finance, real estate, public utility operation	—	—	—	—	5
Other service industries	—	—	—	—	5
Imports	501.2	16.89	1,327	13.77	—
Total	2,968.0[a]	100.00[a]	9,641	100.00	859

imports which compete with them. A slight increase in market share for the Canadian industries is forecast — to 65 per cent for the two taken together. This allows us to compute the percentages which each of these three sources would provide of total investment purchases.

To estimate the industrial distribution of 1970 inventory investment, two methods were used. For the nonmanufacturing sectors, where, in general, good figures for inventory *stocks* are not available, the procedure used was simply to increase the average annual inventory investment figure for recent years by the roughly estimated percentage change of that sector's total output to 1970. For manufacturing, where satisfactory inventory stock figures exist, a slightly more complicated procedure was used. For the relatively normal prosperous year of 1953, the ratio of year-end inventories[21] to gross value added was computed for each of the manufacturing interindustry sectors. Then, from the interindustry table itself, the ratio of gross value added in 1949 to sales into the consumption and durable goods investment sectors was computed. Multiplying these two numbers together gives a ratio of inventory stocks to sales into consumption and investment. And weighting each of these new ratios by the total of consumption and investment sales already forecast for each of these sectors, we get an estimate of the normal value of 1970 inventory stocks for each sector. If all these are assumed to be increasing at the same rate (as a percentage of initial stock), then the remainder of the inventory investment forecast can be distributed among them. Column (5) of Table 50 shows the results. One peculiarity should be noted: agricultural inventory investment, not to be confused with "grain in commercial channels," is forecast at zero for 1970 because of the persistent secular decline in farm-held inventories of crops.

APPENDIX

Basic Data on Long-Run Canadian Investment, 1901–1955

Since this series of data on Canadian investment can be found in existing publications only in fragmentary form, we include a full description of sources and methods used to derive the series shown in the accompanying Appendix Table 51.

[21] DBS, *General Review of the Manufacturing Industries, 1953* (Ottawa, 1955), p. 51.

Table 51. Five-year totals of major investment components and gross national product of Canada, 1901–1955 (millions of dollars).

Period	New construction Residential (1)	Nonresidential (2)	Machinery and equipment (3)	Inventories (4)	Gross domestic investment (5)	Net foreign investment (6)	Gross capital formation (7)	Gross national product (8)
				Current dollars				
1901–1905	234	518	393	222	1,367	−301	1,066	5,650
1906–1910	493	1,095	607	262	2,457	−784	1,673	8,482
1911–1915	598	1,623	944	360	3,525	−1,515	2,010	12,178
1916–1920	675	1,670	1,368	589	4,302	−262	4,040	20,923
1921–1925	781	1,724	1,253	159	3,917	72	3,989	22,589
1926–1930	1,116	1,817	2,000	625	5,558	−563	4,995	28,758
1931–1935	552	1,243	754	−268	2,281	−78	2,203	20,258
1936–1940	859	1,547	1,729	541	4,676	828	5,504	27,868
1946–1950	3,223	5,759	5,718	1,392	16,092	632	16,724	76,072
1951–1955	5,405	12,211	10,087	2,185	29,888	−1,898	27,990	120,288
			Constant 1935–1939 dollars					
1901–1905	483	1,070	686	308	2,547			9,448
1906–1910	854	1,898	984	338	4,074			12,698
1911–1915	933	2,532	1,343	425	5,233			14,602
1916–1920	697	1,723	1,172	367	3,959			18,022
1921–1925	701	1,548	1,182	120	3,551			24,942
1926–1930	1,008	1,690	1,949	345	4,992	−592	4,400	25,268
1931–1935	568	1,307	795	−198	2,472	290	2,762	21,011
1936–1940	831	1,564	1,678	740	4,813	868	5,681	27,336
1946–1950	1,558	3,500	3,051	895	9,604	339	9,943	47,700
1951–1955	1,902	5,360	4,993	1,006	13,360	−809	12,551	59,431

Source: See text, pp. 377–8

1. *New residential construction.* For 1926–1955, the *National Accounts* current value figures were increased by the amount of government-constructed housing listed in Table 41 of the *1926–1950* volume and Table 54 of the *1950–1955* volume. For 1901–1925, figures in K. A. H. Buckley, "Capital Formation in Canada," *Problems of Capital Formation, Concepts, Measures and Controlling Factors, Studies in Income and Wealth, Volume Nineteen* (Princeton, 1957), p. 102, were increased by the ratio to Buckley's 1926–1930 figure of the *National Accounts'* 1926–1930 figure. The constant-dollar series for 1926–1955 are from *National Accounts, 1926–1950,* Table 3; *1950–1955,* Table 50. To deflate the government housing figure, the implicit price deflators for residential construction from Tables 4 and 51 respectively were used. To deflate the figures for earlier years, Buckley's index of construction prices on a base of 1913 was converted to 1935–1939 prices by linking it to DBS' residential construction implicit deflator by the common years 1926–1930.

2. *Nonresidential construction.* For 1926–1955 the same sources and methods were used as for residential construction. For 1901–1925, nonresidential construction was got by subtracting residential construction from Buckley's figures for total construction, and deflation was by the DBS nonresidential construction implicit deflator, linked by the common years 1926–1930 to Buckley's cost of construction index.

3. *Machinery and equipment.* K. A. H. Buckley argues ("Capital Formation," pp. 109–115) that the *National Accounts'* machinery and equipment figures for the interwar period have a systematic bias in the trend. They are taken from *Private and Public Investment in Canada 1926–1951,* which attempted to estimate such expenditures by direct survey of investing firms rather than by the flow-of-materials method used by Buckley for the years 1901–1930 and also for the years 1926–1941 in Table 6a of the volume *Public Investment and Capital Formation.* However, Anthony D. Scott has pointed out that there is little discrepancy once a large typographical error is removed from the figures in *Private and Public Investment.* This was done, and its figures were used for 1926–1940. Buckley's own figures for 1901–1925 become comparable when increased 3.5 per cent to allow for a difference in commodity classification. For the post-World War II years, the *National Accounts* figures for machinery and equipment were used, increased by direct government purchases of machinery and equipment shown in *Private and Public Investment,* Table 9, and *National Accounts 1950–1955,* Table 54. To get the deflated series, *National Accounts* deflated series were used for 1946–1955, with the direct government purchases deflated by the machinery and equipment implicit price deflator, which was also used to deflate the 1926–1940 figures from *Public Investment and Capital Formation.* To get a comparable price index prior to 1926, a series was constructed from information given by O. J. Firestone, *Canada's Economic Development, 1867–1953,* Tables 29 and 30; it is given there for isolated years, and was assumed to move between benchmarks in proportion to the wholesale price index.

4. *Inventory accumulation.* Buckley's inventory figures were used for

1901–1925, and after that the *National Accounts* figures, made comparable by subtracting the inventory valuation adjustment figures given in the *National Accounts 1926–1950*, pp. 28–29, *1950–1955*, p. 17. Deflated figures 1926–1955 were taken from the *National Accounts;* before that, deflation was by the wholesale price index.

5. *Gross domestic investment* is the sum of columns (1) through (4).

6. *Net foreign investment* is the difference between exports and imports of goods and services shown in the *National Accounts* for the years 1926–1955; for 1901–1925 the figures are given in Buckley. *Capital Formation in Canada, 1896–1930*, p. 134. The deflated series was got by subtracting the *National Accounts'* deflated imports figures from deflated exports figures. No deflated series was attempted for the earlier years.

7. *Gross capital formation* is the sum of columns (5) and (6).

8. *Gross national product* for 1926–1955 is taken from *National Accounts;* for earlier years from estimates given in Buckley, *Capital Formation*, p. 135. The deflated series 1926–1955 was also taken from the *National Accounts,* and the deflator for the earlier years was constructed from Firestone's implicit deflators. These figures for isolated years were assumed to move proportionally to the wholesale price index.

Public Finance in 1970

In theory there are few, if any, economic variables more difficult to predict than government expenditure. In practice, estimates of future government budgets may well be no more inaccurate than other economic forecasts.

The logical case against long-range projection of public expenditures is clear. Economic forecasting is based on formulation of relations among such variables as income, expenditure, prices, and investment, followed by the specification of exact mathematical connection among the variables deduced from past behavior. Economic projections generally assume that the interrelation of the variables will be the same in the future as in the past, or at least that changes in these interrelations will follow some past trend of change. However, these assumptions are not valid for public finance. Government expenditures change from year to year as a result of policy changes — decisions to increase or decrease spending on defense, education, roads, health, and welfare. No mathematical system of prediction can include variations due to future policy shifts. As a simplified example, one might conclude from historical evidence that the government budget is a fixed percentage of gross national product. He could then arrive at an estimate of future government expenditures by projecting future GNP. (The following projections are actually based on a modification of this approach.) Suppose we predict that next year will bring unemployment and a lower national income; we could then predict a decline in public spending. But it is entirely possible for government to combat depression by increased expenditures on public works, unemployment relief, and so forth, with a resulting increase in its total spending. The prediction would be wrong not only about amount, but even about direction of change.

The way of the forecaster may be somewhat smoother than implied above. First, a study of peacetime public finance in Western democracies over the past twenty years indicates that net combined expenditure by all levels of government range uniformly between 18 and 30 per cent of the annual value of GNP.

This imposes limits, albeit broad ones, on the range of the prediction.

Second, the long-range projections customarily specify peacetime prosperity; serious fluctuations are simply assumed away by identifying the projection with "a typical prosperous year" 15, 25, or 50 years from now.

Third, in many countries including Canada the economic role of government is much better defined and subject to more general agreement than fifteen or twenty years ago. Compared to the 1930's, there appears to be much less likelihood of major shifts in government economic policy resulting from changes in political power. For example, in the United States the Republican victory in 1952 was expected to result in a reduction of government expenditures. Actually, average combined United States federal, state, and local expenditures in the years 1953–1955 were higher than the 1951–52 totals. Federal expenditures taken separately also rose slightly.

Considering both the nature of the fundamental assumptions of the present study (no war, no major depression) and the apparent stabilization of government's role in the economy, the projections which follow may be somewhat less rash than theory would indicate. At the same time, it must be emphasized that this is stability relative only to the fluctuations which theoretical considerations might suggest. Since 1934, government expenditures in Canada (excluding 1939–1945) have been subject to somewhat wider annual fluctuations and considerably greater long-run variability than GNP. From 1934 to 1954, after correcting for changes in the price level, GNP increased roughly 300 per cent while all government expenditures increased 350 per cent and dominion expenditures 500 per cent. From 1946 to 1949, GNP rose 9 per cent, while public spending fell over 20 per cent.

It seems reasonable to conclude that the following forecasts are more reliable than initial observation would suggest, but subject to a wider percentage margin of error than estimates of GNP, consumption, and imports. The subsequent discussion should be read in light of these considerations.

RESOURCE ALLOCATION AND PUBLIC FINANCE

Any society makes, through centralized or decentralized decisions, a conscious choice about how it will spend its income. In essence, national expenditure, public or private, on goods and services represents the outcome of a system of priorities. Deciding what to produce and buy, either for a household or an economy, is a process of compromise, in which a fixed amount of resources (purchasing power) is allocated among various objectives. Increasing the amount spent for any activity means reducing expenditures on others. The process of choice in a full employment economy means that every benefit from increased availability of certain services is at least partly offset by the sacrifice of others.

The significance of the resource allocation process for public finance is clear. First, there is the problem of choice between private and government spending. In a predominantly private-enterprise economy, we may assume that there will be a continuing tendency for most of gross national product to be spent by firms and households for private purposes. Assuming full employment, every dollar increase in government expenditure means a roughly equal decrease in private purchasing power.[1]

This means that there will be in a private enterprise economy a continuing pressure against increases in government expenditures, except as proposed increases are for purposes which have overwhelming political support. From the point of view of economic forecasting, this means that sharp increases in per cent of GNP going to public finance are unlikely, barring emergency conditions.

The second aspect of resource allocation relevant to government finance is the apportionment of expenditures within the government sector, both among federal, provincial, and local governments and among competing activities — highways, education, defense, health, and welfare. Each program has its advocates — those who fight against any reduction in veterans' payments, refuse disposal, and rural free delivery. The attempt to increase any single activity at the expense of others implies conflict. In

---

[1] If the government simply taxes one group in the economy, and pays the proceeds out as income to someone else, as in the case of family allowances, then the result is to shift purchasing power not from private persons to government, but rather from one group to another within the private sector. However, if this shift of private purchasing power is an aspect of government policy, the statement above is true. In the case of Canada's family allowances, for example, the government decides that people with large families should have relatively more purchasing power at the expense of the celibate.

a society of diverse interest groups, major changes will tend to be infrequent, and when they occur will ordinarily reflect either emergency or a broad consensus developing over a period of years.[2]

This does not mean that change in scope and emphasis of government programs is rare. For example, Canadian government expenditures on health and welfare increased 60 per cent between 1947 and 1953, while total government expenditures increased less than 45 per cent. Expenditures per capita on education increased over 40 per cent during the period, while sanitation expenses doubled. However, after allowing for sharp fluctuations in defense expenditure, there is relative short-run stability in the portion of government budgets devoted to various activities; even changes in emphasis tend to be gradual.

The conflict of objectives within a framework of limited government financial resources therefore acts to stabilize the ways of using these funds and thus to lessen the margin of error in long range projections of government expenditures. Furthermore, sharp expenditure changes, such as those noted above, often reflect not changing government policies but fixed policies facing (predictably) changing social needs.

FRAMEWORK AND SUMMARY OF PROJECTIONS

Besides the general assumptions for this study listed in Chapter 1, the projections of government expenditures rest on the special assumptions of: (1) no major change in the present functions of federal, provincial, or local governments, or the allocation of functions among them except for the implementation of the national health insurance program; (2) national defense expenditures stable at roughly $1,500,000,000 annually, reflecting both an increase in the cost of modern weapons and a decrease in armed forces manpower; (3) a balanced federal budget.[3] In addi-

[2] It was argued above (Chapter 7) that in a relatively wealthy and diversified economy such as Canada's the pressure group support necessary to pass any major increase in the scope of government activities is less likely to coalesce than in an economy less far along in its development. Also note the argument that a wealthy society enjoying nearly full employment and secular inflation tends systematically to slight the economic functions normally fulfilled by government; this is developed by J. K. Galbraith in *The Affluent Society* (Boston, 1958).

[3] Unless otherwise specified, all constant-dollar values in this chapter are stated in 1952 prices. Before the remainder of this study was changed to a

tion, it is well to keep in mind the general assumption that peacetime prosperity can be maintained without massive government pump-priming. If a major depression were in progress in 1970, expenditures on health and welfare, public works, and unemployment relief might be considerably higher than foreseen here.

In 1953, 27.3 per cent of Canadian GNP was devoted to government expenditures; 67 per cent of the total was federal expenses ($4,400,000,000 in 1952 prices), 18 per cent provincial ($1,300,000,000) and 15 per cent municipal ($1,000,000,000). Adjusting for direct federal payments to the provinces, net provincial-municipal expenditures were reduced from $2,300,000,000 to $1,900,000,000, and the federal expenditures rose to about 70 per cent of the combined net total.

The 1970 medium projections call for net government expenditures of $10,800,000,000 — 23.5 per cent of a gross national product of $46,000,000,000 in 1952 prices. Provincial-municipal expenditures net of transfers from the federal government remain at 33 per cent of all public expenditures, that is, $3,600,000,000 compared to a federal budget set at $7,200,000,000. (In all but the final section of this chapter we are concerned with public finance in general, not just government purchases of goods and services. Thus all figures are inclusive of transfer payments unless otherwise specified.)

The following sections give details of the long-run relation between GNP and government expenditures and of trends in federal, provincial and municipal finance. Three trends stand out in the resulting forecast of government finance. The big increases will come in education, highway construction, and health and welfare expenditures. Federal debt payments, agricultural program expenditures, and payments to veterans will decline.

METHOD OF PROJECTION: GOVERNMENT FINANCE AND GNP

One can use several different methods for long-run projection of total government expenditures. One method is to use past per

---

1955 price basis, elaborate procedures were used to deflate historic government expenditures to the earlier year's price level. It has not been feasible to perform this operation again, except in the special calculations of forecast government expenditures on goods and services summarized in Table 63. In the following pages, wherever a forecast figure is stated as a percentage of 1970 GNP, the reader should remember that this pertains not to the $48,000,000,000 figure appearing elsewhere but to this figure reduced to 1952 prices by use of the DBS implicit deflators.

capita spending rates, as modified by proposed policy changes in various fields. Another approach is to extrapolate current trends into the future, either by approximation or by statistical techniques. This method is unsatisfactory because it assumes implicitly that government expenditure is not affected by policy changes or by the state of the economy as a whole. Yet we need some simple gross method of this sort. The bulk of this chapter will be devoted to a detailed estimation of separate expenditure categories by *ad hoc* methods, and some such check is needed for the reasonableness of the resulting figure for total government expenditures.

The method that probably provides the smallest margin of error for long-range projection is linking government expenditures to gross national product. The relation has been moderately stable in the past few decades, varying from 20 to 27 per cent of GNP after deducting extraordinary defense expenditures (defined as those in excess of $1,500,000,000). In the years since 1952, ordinary government expenditures have been almost exactly 26 per cent of GNP in every year but the recession year of 1954.[4] Under the assumptions of this study, it seems unlikely that by 1970 public finance will absorb over 26 to 27 per cent of GNP for two reasons: (1) the relative increase in social welfare, education, and highway costs will be compensated for by a relative decline in defense and debt charges; (2) at the level of GNP projected for 1970, large absolute increases in public services can be financed without increasing the ratio of government expenditures to GNP. But, while the assumptions of this study preclude substantial relative increases in spending, the historical patterns of economic growth show that increasing wealth has often been associated with increasing demand for public services. The upper limit to government spending mentioned above implies that the role of government in 1970 will not exceed the present proportion of the total. No definite lower limit can be set, but a reasonable one would certainly exceed the present absolute volume of gov-

[4] Many writers, of course, have tried to draw conclusions about the future role of government in the economy from a study of much longer-run trends. But, as O. J. Firestone has pointed out, such a long gallop down the corridors of history can lead to serious misinterpretation of short-run trends; see his *Canada's Economic Development, 1867–1953, With Special Reference to Changes in the Country's National Product and National Wealth* (London, 1958), part II, Sec. 6.

ernment expenditures. The analysis of subsequent sections indicates a slight relative reduction in government purchasing power to perhaps 23.5 per cent of GNP.

Within the public finance sector, there is a fairly stable split among federal, provincial, and municipal expenditures. In postwar years federal expenditures have ranged from 60 to 70 per cent of all public budgets, with a marked upward trend in recent years. If payments to provinces are deducted from the federal budget, then federal expenditures, after adjusting the military budget, range from 57 to 66 per cent of all public finance.

Will the federal budget continue the long-term trend and increase relative to provincial and municipal expenditures? The projection implies stability or even slight decline in the ratio of the federal budget to all public finance, after deducting tax rental payments from federal totals. The reasons for this conclusion are straightforward.

1. Canada is becoming increasingly urban. Urbanization means increasing costs per capita of municipal finance.

2. There will be substantial budgetary emphasis on education, highways, public health, and other provincial-municipal fields of responsibility.

3. The trend of the postwar series of tax-rental disputes and armistices indicates that dominion concessions will put an increasing supply of funds at the disposal of the provinces. The 1957–1961 agreements step up the rate of payment compared to their predecessors and contain very large potential increases through the stabilization grants clause. On the other hand, the uncertainties of participation by Ontario and Quebec leave the matter very much in doubt how great the increase will be by 1970.

Of the 34 to 43 per cent of all public finance spent by municipal and provincial governments, there has been an irregular trend for an increasing proportion to be spent by municipal governments. Provincial governments still spend over half of the combined provincial-municipal total. However, in 1953–1956, provincial governments were spending only 52 to 55 per cent of the provincial-municipal total compared to about 60 per cent a few years earlier.

Projection of the probable 1970 relation between provincial and municipal expenditures is difficult. The growth of cities with typical increases in per capita cost of city government must be balanced against the rising trends in provincial expenditure on health, education (including subsidies to local school boards), and highways. Since some of the increase in provincial costs will take the form of grants to municipalities, it is likely that the relative shift will be toward increased importance of municipal expenditure (see Table 56), but the shift will probably be slight. The provincial-municipal ratio could vary from 55/45 to 45/55, with 50/50 as the compromise estimate indicated by the trends.

In summary, we can anticipate, allowing a reasonable margin for error, that 22 to 27 per cent of GNP will be devoted to public expenditure in 1970. The program estimates made independently in the following section bear out this crude approximation, totaling about 24 per cent (medium projection). Within the public finance category about 65 per cent (60 per cent if grants to provinces are deducted) will be federal expenditure, with the balance evenly divided between provincial and municipal expense.

PROJECTIONS OF FEDERAL PUBLIC FINANCE

This section, starting from the assumptions listed above, formulates projections of federal expenditures for 1970, analyzing each major activity separately.[5] Three more assumptions are added for the discussion of federal finance.

1. Provincial subsidy and tax rental will take 9 to 11 per cent of the federal budget if all provinces participate.

2. If unemployment rises, federal expenditures will increase relative to other levels of government and to gross national product.

3. Federal revenues will be composed of: personal and corporate income tax — 50 to 60 per cent of total revenue; sales tax and customs duties — 30 to 40 per cent; miscellaneous receipts — 10 per cent. Federal taxation will therefore continue to take 13 to 15 per cent of GNP annually.

Three projections have been made under these assumptions, varying from a low projection of 12 per cent of GNP to a high of 18 per cent, with the medium projection (15.6 per cent) regarded as most probable. (See Table 52.) The high projection

---

[5] A useful source of information and analysis of the federal budget is Canadian Tax Foundation, *The National Finances, An Analysis of the Programme of Revenues and Expenditures of the Government of Canada, 1957–58* (Toronto, 1957).

Table 52. Projected Canadian federal expenditures, 1970
(millions of 1952 dollars).

Expenditure category	Projection		
	Low	Medium	High
National defense	1,500	2,000	2,000
Agriculture	115	115	400
Health and welfare	1,437	2,309	2,376
Public works	85	110	170
Resource development	100	125	200
Transportation	237	252	340
Unemployment insurance	84	137	200
Veterans	240	240	240
Public debt charges	500	500	550
Provincial subsidy and tax rental	550	550	750
General government	798	835	1,200
Total	5,646	7,173	8,426

Source: Based on projected GNP. See text, pp. 366–375.

assumes that some government countercyclical policy will be necessary to assure prosperity.

The projections were reached as follows:

National defense. We merely assume $1,500,000,000 as a low and $2,000,000,000 as a medium and high estimate. There can be no satisfactory detailed defense of this or any other guess of the cost of armed forces a decade from now. This particular assumption implies a continued state of world tension without actual warfare but also without international agreement or confidence. Thus the medium estimate foresees continued expenditure at present absolute levels with a corresponding decline as a percentage of GNP. If we assume instead a sharp reduction to $1,500,-000,000 in defense costs around 1970, the impact on a $46,000,-000,000 economy and even on a $6,500,000,000 federal budget would be much less than a similar reduction today. If the world situation were to require as much defense expenditure relative to GNP in 1970 as in 1954, the armed forces budget would approach $3,000,000,000. However, considering the cost of new weapons, $4,000,000,000 might represent a closer approximation to the levels of preparedness implied by current defense budgets. The continuation of defense budgets of 6 to 8 per cent of GNP ($3,000,000,000 to $4,000,000,000) means an international politi-

Table 53. Percentage composition of Canadian federal budget, by
expenditure category, selected years, 1939–1970.

Expenditure category	1939	1947	1950	1953	1970
National defense	19.1	8.7	25.1	42.2	22.8
Agriculture	7.7	3.6	4.6	2.4	1.8
Health and welfare	5.4	11.4	14.2	9.6	31.9
Public works	2.2	0.8	1.4	1.5	1.8
Resources development	2.5	0.8	1.5	1.4	1.9
Transport	12.8	2.8	5.1	3.6	3.8
Unemployment insurance	3.6	1.2	1.7	1.4	2.1
Veterans	7.3	11.7	6.8	5.3	3.7
Public debt	19.6	16.0	13.9	11.0	7.6
Provincial payments	5.6	5.3	3.9	7.6	10.7
General government	13.2	37.4	22.1	12.6	12.1

Source: 1939–1953, computed from DBS, Public Accounts of Canada; and 1970,
based on medium projection in Table 52. Totals may not add to 100 per cent because of rounding errors.

cal system balanced ever on the verge without either deviating
into war or arriving at some detente that will permit a decline in
armaments. The effect of such a situation on these projections
would be continuing inflationary pressures in the economy and a
larger percentage of GNP devoted to federal finance — somewhere from 19 to 22 per cent, compared with 13 to 19 per cent
in these projections and 16 to 18 per cent currently. Federal taxation, especially income taxation, would weigh more heavily. Public debt expenditures would be swollen, while expenditures on
agriculture and unemployment relief would be reduced at all
levels of government.

Agriculture. During the depression from 4 to 8 per cent of all
federal expenditures went to agriculture, reflecting relief programs for prairie farmers and grain price support operations.
Since 1945, agricultural income has by and large been left to free
market determination, with government intervening principally
as the marketing channel for wheat and certain other internationally traded commodities (pork and dairy products). Certain
relatively small-scale subsidies enter into current agricultural
programs,[6] bringing the total cost of federal farm programs to

[6] The subsidies include feed freight assistance for western grain, hog pre-
miums, and losses incurred under the postwar price guarantee system for certain
crops that the government of Canada sold under contract to the United
Kingdom.

somewhat over $100,000,000 annually in recent years, or 2 to 4 per cent of the federal budget. (See Table 53 for the recent and forecast percentage composition of the federal budget.)

The future of government aid to agriculture is an issue of politics and economics. In recent years, as noted above, agriculture has been of declining importance in the federal budget. At the same time farm income declined steadily from 1951 to 1954, and in 1956 was only 84 per cent of the 1951–52 average. Some of the decline is compensated by the postwar shift of people to other occupations, but there was still a fall of farm income per worker from $2424 in 1951 to an estimated $1550 per annum in 1955. Another problem for Canadian agriculture is created by United States farm policy. If the United States continues its current policy of price support and dumping grain and dairy products through two-price systems and local currency deals, Canadian farm prices are likely to suffer, with prairie agriculture the principal victim. For federal finance, the problem is whether the relatively unfavorable prospects for Canadian staple export crops will lead to large-scale government support programs. The answer to this question is hardly clear, but the constellation of political forces seems unfavorable from the farmer's view, considering the declining role of agriculture in the economy. The low and medium projections assume a continuation of the present trend of declining expenditure per capita on agriculture (from $11.50 in 1948 to $7.80 in 1954). The high projection assumes a program of subsidy or price support for prairie agriculture designed to raise farm income per capita to 1953 levels.

Health and welfare. This is the area where greatest absolute and relative expansion of federal spending can be forecast. Federal expenditures on health and welfare have increased steadily since 1947 from $45 per capita in that year to over $80 per capita in 1954, or from $569,000,000 to $1,200,000,000 in total. The principal components are family allowances, old age security payments, old age assistance, veterans payments, unemployment insurance contributions, and general health grants. The amounts spent for all of these purposes, except veterans payments and unemployment insurance, both discussed in later paragraphs, will necessarily tend to increase with the growth of population. In addition, the medium and high projections call for national health insurance costing $40 per capita annually, the groundwork for which was recently laid in the Hospital Insurance and Diagnostic Services Act of 1957.

The projections of federal health and welfare expenditures were computed as follows. *Low:* family allowance at the per capita rate of $75.70 per child per year estimated for 1958, with 6.8 million children covered; old age assistance maintained at the current rate of $552 per year to all persons over 70 and to persons 65–69 in financial need (20 per cent of the age group); health grants maintained at the present rate of $2.00 per capita; miscellaneous (blindness allowance, general expenditures) maintained at present levels of $2.00 per capita; hospital insurance and diagnostic services for the total population at the cost per capita estimated for 1956, $11.42. *Medium:* first four factors same as low estimate above; a more extensive health insurance program costing $40 per capita per year. The estimate is based on Ontario's estimates of the cost of the provincial program. *High:* family allowances as above; old age assistance at $600 a year to all persons over 70 and all persons 65–69 who can show needs; health grants raised 25 per cent as an anticyclical device; miscellaneous as above; health insurance as in medium estimate above.

Public works. These have been relatively steady at about 1.2 to 1.5 per cent of the budget in postwar years ($3–4 per capita). The low projection assumes per capita constancy, the medium projection a 20 per cent rise, and the high projection a doubling of expenditure as a countercyclical device. The increase from present levels in the medium projection reflects the assumption that, at higher levels of income, expansion of public buildings, national park improvements, and so forth, are likely to be more in demand.

Resource development. This item is projected on the same basis as public works. The principal problem here is estimating the relative roles of private and public expenditures in surveying, conservation, and development of natural resources, particularly in the North. Current expenditures on these activities — fisheries, mines, northern territories, and national parks — are about the same magnitude as public works. Expenditures on mineral development are increasing most rapidly. It is likely that these projections are too conservative. However, the entire category has not exceeded 2.4 per cent of the federal budget in the past twenty years, and there is no reason to expect a major relative increase, although a moderate one is likely.

Transport. Historically the major item here has been railroads, notably over the past thirty years the Canadian National Railways deficit, which absorbed up to 11 per cent of federal budgets during the 1930's. The postwar era has seen substantial decline in this particular charge, as well as a decline in the relative importance of transport expenditures generally from 17 per cent of federal expenditure in 1939 to about 3.5 per cent in 1951–1955. In constant 1952 dollars, the annual expenditure has been roughly constant at about $150,000,000 annually. Within the transport sector, expenditures on air transport have increased most sharply, with increases also registered for canal and marine transport, while the railway deficit has contracted recently.

Road expenditures being in general the affair of local governments, federal participation is limited to work in national parks and contributions to the Trans-Canada Highway.

The most difficult issues raised in projecting transport expenditures to 1970 are: (1) will there be a substantial CNR deficit? (2) how rapidly will air transport and the federal services assisting it expand? (3) will the federal government enter the highway construction field? (4) what role will Ottawa play in northern area transport development? The CNR deficit is of course a child both of railroad cost-revenue trends and a variety of political pressures. Neither can be analyzed fully here, but it can be noted that rapid resource development in Canada's northern areas favors the CNR revenue position, while political forces will continue to make it undesirable for the government corporation to show either a significant profit or a large loss. The latter possibility is also limited by the 1952 CNR capital revision making a significant portion of its interest payable only when earned. Hence the low and medium projections assume a negligible CNR deficit. The current-costs portion of government air transport expenditures has grown at least in part proportionally to the rapid postwar rise of commercial aviation. A slightly dampened continuation of this trend is foreseen, and roughly the same can be said for water transport. The low and medium projections also assume no federal highway contribution and no major federal expenditures for northern development. The result is an expenditure pattern of $252,000,000, or $12 per capita, slightly more than current levels. The high projection sees a CNR deficit at 1949–50 levels and some federal contribution to road building activities as an antidepression measure, raising the government transportation program to somewhat over $300,000,000.[7]

Unemployment insurance. This projection covers only federal contributions to the fund. The medium projection calls for an increase of 78 per cent above current federal contribution to the fund, reflecting a 42 per cent increase in work force and an annual 2 per cent compounded nonagricultural productivity increase. The low projection simply *assumes* that the government contribution will fall behind the productivity increase rates. There is some difficulty in this projection because it implies the development of an unemployment insurance fund of massive proportions, with employer, employee, and government contributions far in excess of payments to the unemployed. The high projection implies substantial income maintenance through unemployment insurance.

Veterans. Pensions, veterans allowances, and medical benefits and miscellaneous veterans welfare costs appear to be fairly stable at about $240,000,000 since 1951. The projections assume no change in this bill by 1970, since any pressure for increased payments will be compensated by the declining number of veterans.[8] The result is a decline in cost from $16 per head to $11.50.

Debt service. This projection is predetermined for the low and medium projections by the balanced-budget assumptions. The high projection assumes some countercyclical deficit financing and therefore a slightly higher debt service charge. In any case, there will be a substantial fall in the per capita cost.

Provincial subsidy. The bill for fiscal 1957–58 under the new agreements is estimated at $345,000,000. This is about the same as under the 1952–1956 tax rental agreements due to several offsetting changes. On the one hand, rates of payment to the provinces have been stepped up in several ways; on the other hand, Ontario now collects a corporation income tax instead of renting

[7] Chapter 7 (*supra*) describes the great sensitivity which the railway deficit has historically shown to changes in the level of employment.

[8] For useful evidence on the past time pattern of veterans' benefits payments, see Canadian Tax Foundation, *The National Finances, 1957–58*, pp. 98–102.

Table 54. Canadian federal government expenditures, 1954
and estimated 1970 (dollars per capita).

Expenditure category	1954	1970
National defense	133.69	95.24
Agriculture	7.81	5.47
Health and welfare	61.01	104.76
Public works	5.01	5.24
Resources development	4.83	5.95
Transport	11.79	12.00
Unemployment insurance	4.17	6.52
Veterans	16.34	11.43
Public debt	33.94	23.81
Provincial payments	23.13	33.33
General government	38.85	39.76
	340.57	343.51

Source: 1954, computed from DBS, *Public Accounts of Canada;* and 1970, based on medium projection in Table 52.

this revenue source, thus lopping an estimated $132,000,000 from the total.[9] We assume that the same basic arrangements will hold in 1970 as today. Then, given 1955 tax rates and the estimated 1970 GNP, the amount would come to $550,000,000. The high projection allows for $200,000,000 in federal stabilization payments to the provinces.

General government. This miscellaneous category of administrative functions is assumed to be proportional to population rather than gross national product, implying that much of it is overhead cost which will incur relatively small increases because of income increases. Therefore the low and medium projections call for unchanged per capita levels. The high projection assumes additional countercyclical projects.

The medium projection bears out the assumptions of increased importance of welfare, health, and income maintenance payments. The major increases in public works and road costs are assumed to fall on provinces and local government. Private capital is given the principal responsibility for resource development. Although the income maintenance payments projected are high (about $3,200,000,000), they remain at 7 per cent of GNP, as in the 1953–1955 period. This may indicate that the current old age and family allowance programs impose a rather heavy redistribu-

[9] Canadian Tax Foundation, *The National Finances, 1957–58*, p. 113.

Table 55.   Projected Canadian government expenditures, 1970
(millions of 1952 dollars).

Expenditure category	Amount	
Federal government		
National defense	2,000	
Agriculture	115	
Health and welfare	2,309	
Public works	110	
Resource development	125	
Transportation	252	
Unemployment insurance	137	
Veterans	240	
Public debt charges	500	
Provincial subsidy and tax rental	550	
General government	835	
Total		7,173
Provincial-municipal governments		
Education	1,110	
Natural resources	168	
Sanitation	126	
Public debt	399	
Protection of persons	336	
Transportation	925	
Health and welfare	735	
General government	378	
Total		4,177
Gross government expenditures		11,350
Less intergovernmental transfers		550
Net government expenditures		10,800

Source: Medium projection in Tables 52 and 57.

tive burden on the national economy, one that will not increase relatively at 1970 levels of GNP. However, the long-run redistributive trend initiated about 1935 is projected to continue with increased provincial payments and the health insurance program.

If the medium projection of a federal expenditure to GNP ratio of 15.8 per cent were valid, it would represent a slight decline from the 16.5 to 17.5 per cent levels of current budgets. This supports the more general reasoning developed above. Table 54 shows the trend of per capita federal expenditures. Table 55

Table 56.   Canadian gross provincial and municipal government
expenditures, annually, 1946–1954.

Year	Provincial expenditures Total (millions of 1952 dollars)	Per capita (1952 dollars)	Municipal expenditures Total (millions of 1952 dollars)	Per capita (1952 dollars)
1946	763	62.11	653	53.09
1947	928	74.09	687	54.73
1948	943	73.54	632	49.30
1949	1,073	79.98	686	50.97
1950	1,140	83.18	777	56.67
1951	1,184	84.49	890	63.54
1952	1,320	91.49	861	59.70
1953	1,351	91.44	1,098	74.26
1954ᵃ	1,471	96.78	1,100	72.36

ᵃ Expenditures for 1954 are estimated.
Source: Compiled from DBS, *Statistics of Provincial Finance, Statistics of Municipal Finance* (Ottawa, 1946–1954).

shows total 1970 total expenditures for federal, provincial, and municipal governments.

PROJECTION OF MUNICIPAL AND PROVINCIAL PUBLIC FINANCE

Postwar Canadian provincial and municipal expenditures show a rising trend in both total and per capita terms. Table 56 gives the information in constant dollar terms.

In recent years the largest items of expenditure in provincial-municipal government budgets have been streets and highways, health and welfare, and education. These three categories have comprised about 65 to 70 per cent of municipal-provincial expenses. For provincial governments, general government, debt charges, and natural resources have accounted for an additional 25 per cent, while in the municipal governments, general government, debt charges, and protection of persons require 35 per cent of budgeted funds.

In projecting combined municipal-provincial expenditures to 1970, the following assumptions are made. (1) Education, health and welfare, and highways will continue to take 65 per cent of combined expenditures. (2) Municipal expenditures will show increases per capita as urbanization continues.

Table 57. Projected gross municipal and provincial expenditures in Canada, 1970 (millions of 1952 dollars).

Expenditure category	Amount
Health and welfare	735
Education	1,110
Natural resources	168
Sanitation	126
Public debt	399
Transportation	925
Protection of persons	336
General government	378
Total	4,177

Source: See text, pp. 375–383.

The projected expenditures for 1970 are shown in Table 57. The estimates were reached in the following ways. (1) Debt — estimated at current levels of $19.00 per capita. (2) Sanitation, protection of persons and natural resources — current trends projected to 1970, with sanitation costs rising from $4.38 to $6 per capita, protection of persons from $13.68 to $16 and natural resources from $6.97 to $8. (3) General government — municipal expenses projected at current trend, provincial estimated at current level. (4) Health and welfare — unemployment insurance contributions expected to grow in proportion to total wage payments with fund expenditures based on an assumed 3 per cent average rate of unemployment; welfare services, grants, and miscellaneous activities held at constant rates per capita; provincial hospital and medical care reduced 50 per cent due to displacement by the federal program; municipal health and welfare expenditures projected in accord with the 1947–1953 per capita rate trend. (5) Education and transportation calculations are discussed in detail below.

Table 58 shows the current levels of expenditure per capita which were used as a basis for the projections. The forecast total, when reduced by the projected federal tax rental and subsidy payments, comes to 7.9 per cent of GNP, or 0.6 per cent below the estimate based on GNP trends alone. The estimates of Table 57 are presumably more reliable in the aggregate than by separate activities, for the trend over the past fifteen years has been

Table 58. Combined municipal and provincial expenditures per capita in Canada 1947-1953 and 1970 projection (1952 dollars).

Expenditure category	1947	1948	1949	1950	1951	1952	1953	1970
Education	27.86	25.59	27.68	30.35	33.70	31.54	38.19	52.86
Transportation and public works	30.65	29.80	29.30	28.92	32.77	33.84	37.37	44.05
Health and welfare	20.04	19.51	24.24	25.85	25.40	25.13	27.51	35.00
Public debt	15.68	14.40	15.60	17.33	18.58	21.04	19.39	19.00
Sanitation	2.12	1.85	1.96	2.18	2.86	2.37	4.38	6.00
General government	16.47	16.29	17.53	16.21	16.82	18.97	18.11	18.00
Protection of persons	9.25	8.76	9.25	10.67	12.41	11.77	13.68	16.00
Natural resources	6.55	6.62	6.18	5.92	6.20	6.51	6.97	8.00

Source: 1947–1953, DBS, Statistics of Provincial Finance, Statistics of Municipal Finance (Ottawa, 1946–54); 1970, Table 57.

much steadier as an aggregate percentage of GNP than as sector by sector percentages.

Analysis of government expenditures on highway and street construction

The postwar period has been marked by the increasing relative importance of the motor vehicle in both the private and public sectors of the economy. From 1945 to 1954, automobile registration increased by 140 per cent from 1,500,000 to 3,600,000.[10] During the same period, provincial and municipal expenditures on highways rose by 380 per cent and 226 per cent respectively. Highway expenditures have grown more prominent in provincial and municipal public finance. They now absorb 18 and 30 per cent respectively of municipal and provincial expenditures, compared to 9 and 25 per cent before World War II.

Municipal highway and street expenditures have increased from a prewar average of 9 per cent of total expenditures to a 1949–1953 average of 16 per cent. Provincial highway expenditures in the prewar years averaged about 25 per cent of total outlay. The 1951–1955 average is 29.2 per cent. The rise of the automotive era in Canada is also demonstrated by the statistical indications that the rate of growth of automobile use is outstripping the population growth rate. This applies both to passenger and commercial vehicles with the latter increasing relative to the former. Substantial expenditure on highways has resulted in an 82 per cent increase in surfaced highway mileage since the war. However, road construction has not kept pace with the increased registration, and the number of registered vehicles per mile has continued to increase. (See Table 59.) Up to a point this trend is desirable, as it imposes less of an overhead burden per vehicle. The heavier usage of roads is a form of economy of scale as the nation grows.

The trend to increased congestion persists in the face of increasing expenditures on highways. The $36.00 per capita level of 1954 is about 10 per cent higher than comparable public road expenditures per capital in the United States. In both countries, expenditures per vehicle have fallen in recent years with Cana-

---

[10] Canadian Tax Foundation, *Tax and Traffic* (Toronto, 1955); *Financial Post,* May 28, 1955.

Table 59.   Miles of surfaced and paved roads in Canada and vehicle-mileage ratio, 1937–1953.

Year	Miles (thousands)			Number of registered vehicles per mile of road
	Surfaced	Paved	Total	
1937	95	10	105	12.4
1939	101	14	115	12.2
1945	115	17	132	11.3
1946	122	18	140	11.4
1947	127	19	146	12.3
1948	129	21	150	13.3
1949	139	23	162	14.2
1950	142	25	167	15.6
1951	149	26	175	16.6
1952	152	29	181	17.7
1953	160	31	191	17.9

Source: Canadian Tax Foundation, *Taxes and Traffic* (Toronto, 1955).

dian expenditures per vehicle ranging from 20 to 50 per cent higher than in the United States.

The relatively greater public expenditure on roads in Canada reflects the special problems of Canadian highway finance. In the first place, except for the urban areas of a few large cities, notably Toronto, Victoria, Montreal, and Vancouver, the rate of car ownership is substantially less than in the United States, with an average in 1953 of one motor vehicle for each 4.3 persons compared to United States levels of one vehicle per 2.9 persons in the same year.[11] Per capita income is at least one-fourth lower in Canada than in the United States, although road maintenance costs are considerably higher due to climatic differences.

Projecting public expenditures on highways forward to 1970 requires a number of simplifying assumptions. The projection rests on the following assumptions.

1. There will be an increase in the number of motor vehicles per capita until by 1970 there will be an average of one passenger car per family (3.7 persons), as in the United States today.

2. Commercial vehicles will remain at about 25 per cent of total vehicular registrations.

3. The average number of vehicles per surfaced highway mile

[11] *Statistical Abstract of the United States, 1954*, pp. 13, 564.

will continue to increase at the rate of 1 per cent per year (same as United States rate 1940–1954).

4. Constant-dollar expenditures per capita will rise no faster than productivity (2 per cent annually). Several major factors support this final assumption and indicate no greatly increased rate of public expenditure on highways. First, government expenditures are already around 25 per cent of gross national product, and the competition of expenditure needs for health, social welfare, and educational programs make any large relative increase in highway building unlikely. In the same vein, the level of public expenditure per capita or per vehicle is already high in Canada compared to other countries, and any increase greater than the productivity growth rate foreseen for the bulk of the economy would imply a higher relative burden per capita than is warranted in a projection based on prior experience. Finally, technical problems make difficult any greatly expanded road building activity. The construction season is short; trained civil engineers are in chronic short supply and will be for years to come, assuming continued general construction activity at a high level.

Given these considerations, we can project Canadian highway and street expenditures ahead to 1970, under conditions of steadily increasing demand for roads. The basic projection can be approached in three ways. Using constant per capita figures, the 1970 expenditure would be $756,000,000. Using per vehicle data, a steady decline to $110 per vehicle would afford an $852,000,000 expenditure. The former relation is used as a base, however, because it has remained most stable in constant-dollar terms since 1947. The third method, percentage of GNP, can be used, as throughout this study, to check on the basic method of projection. Highway and street expenditures since 1947 have been very stable at 2.2 per cent of GNP, varying between 2.0 and 2.4 per cent. This highly stable relation can be used to compare with the per capita projection. If we add to the basic per capita projection a compounded 2 per cent productivity increase from 1955 to 1970, the projected expenditure is almost $1,100,000,000. This compares with $966,000,000 for an estimate based on projecting the current percentage of GNP. For projective estimates, the lower figure is preferable because of the technical difficulties facing large-scale road construction. Therefore, the tentative 1970 projection for government expenditures on highways and

Table 60. Proportion of children in Canada aged 5–17 enrolled in provincially controlled schools, selected years 1931–1970.

Year	Number of children enrolled (thousands)	Population aged 5–17 (thousands)	Per cent enrolled
1931	2,200	2,727	78.9
1941	2,128	2,706	78.6
1951	2,390	3,054	78.2
1952	2,502	3,150	79.4
1953	2,644	3,277	80.2
1960[a]	3,726	4,572	81.5
1965[a]	4,119	4,993	82.5
1970[a]	4,417	5,322	83.0

[a] Numbers for 1960, 1965, and 1970 are estimated.

Source: Canada Year Book, 1954; Canadian Teachers Federation, *Educationa Finance in Canada* (Ottawa, 1954).

streets is $900,000,000 to $950,000,000, with a point estimate of $925,000,000.

Municipal and provincial expenditures on education

In 1953, enrollment in provincially controlled public schools totalled 2,650,000, an increase of 500,000 in seven years.[12] This represents about 80 per cent of all persons in the 5–17 age groups, a figure that has remained relatively stable over the years. (See Table 60.)

The projections assume that 83 per cent of all school age children will be in attendance by 1970. The slight increase from 1952–53 levels in the projections assumes both continued prosperity and a return to more "normal" age distribution in the 5–17 age group. Figures for 1952–53 include a high proportion of five-year-olds, reflecting unusually high birth rates in 1947–48. In many provinces, a large proportion of five-year-olds do not attend public school.

What will be the fiscal impact of such an increase in public school enrollment? The postwar years have been marked by steadily rising expenditures per capita and per enrolled pupil. The fraction of municipal budgets devoted to financing education rose 17 per cent from 1946 to 1953. The principal questions arising in

[12] Canadian Teachers Federation, *Status of Educational Finance* (Ottawa, 1954).

projecting 1970 levels of educational finance, assuming a pupil-teacher ratio of 30 to 1 or less, are the size of the student population, the adequacy of the present capital plant, and the teachers' wage level. This study assumes a school attendance of 4,400,-000. This figure is obviously far beyond the present capacity of the school system, in which 13 per cent of the students in 1953–54 were occupying classrooms with over forty children each.

The actual estimation of new school construction and replacement needs is most difficult because of population shifts from province to province, city to city, farm to city, as well as from central city to suburb. However, under simplifying assumptions, some estimate is possible of school construction and replacement requirements over the next decade.

If we take the requirement for new construction as one new room for every thirty additional pupils and project both the increase in student population and the anticipated rural-urban shift, plus a 2 per cent annual replacement expenditure, the projection shown in Table 61 can be established.

The projection indicates that by 1970 the peak of the postwar population boom will have been passed, with school construction expenditures leveling off to a steady $145,000,000 rate per annum. From this we may tentatively conclude that any substantial increases in school expenditures in 1970 will come from increases in salaries, maintenance, and supplies rather than from construction.

In the years 1949–1953, an average of $130,000,000 (constant dollars) or about 20 per cent of all government expenditure on

Table 61.   Estimated school population and school construction requirements in Canada, 1953–1970.

Period	Average number of students (thousands)	Construction (millions of 1952 dollars)		
		New	Replacement	Total
1949–1953	2,395	88.2	42.2	130.4
1955–1960	3,344	141.9	56.3	198.2
1961–1965	3,961	81.2	66.7	147.9
1966–1970	4,298	66.7	73.4	140.5

Source: Numbers of students based on population projection from Chapter 8; for construction data, see text, p. 382.

Table 62. Projected average annual public expenditures for education in Canada, 1955–1970 (millions of 1952 dollars).

Period	Capital	Noncapital	Total
1955–1960	198.2	594.0	792.2
1961–1965	147.9	775.3	923.2
1966–1970	140.5	915.5	1,056.0

Source: Table 61 and p. 383.

schools went for school construction. The balance, an average of $375,000,000 annually (1949–1953) in constant dollars went for teachers' salaries, supplies, equipment, and maintenance, according to the Canadian Teachers Federation. Since there were on the average 85,000 teachers during the period, the expenditure per teacher was $4410 in constant dollars. Since there is no readily accessible source for a breakdown of school expenditures by object, the 1970 projection is arrived at as follows. The 1949–1953 expenditure per teacher is projected, increasing the number of teachers by one for each 26.5 pupils (1950–1954 average). To this figure is added a compound 1.78 per cent annual cost increase per teacher. This figure assumes that noncapital school expenditures will increase at the same rate as productivity.

The results of the projections of combined capital and noncapital expenditure are given in Table 62. The $1,056,000,000 average total expenditure for 1966–1970 implies educational expenditure in 1970 of about $1,100,000,000, about 2.4 per cent of the projected GNP compared to 2.24 per cent in 1953.

ALLOCATION OF FORECAST GOVERNMENT EXPENDITURE

Government purchases of goods and services, including the services of civil servants, are one part of "final demand" in the interindustry table. Consequently, the forecast of total government expenditure by function must be converted into a forecast of purchases of goods and services classified by the sectors of the interindustry table.

This process involved three steps. First, all items not consisting directly of purchases of currently produced goods and services were netted out of total 1949 government expenditure. The former included, to quote the Dominion Bureau of Statistics, "subsidies, transfer payments to individuals and private non-com-

Table 63.   Distribution of Canadian government purchases among
interindustry sectors, 1949 and estimated 1970.

Sector[a]	1949 (millions of 1949 dollars)	1970 (millions of 1955 dollars)
Agriculture	32.0	78.2
Clothing and household goods industries	2.6	6.5
Metal products industries	37.1	123.8
Electrical apparatus and supplies industry	7.0	26.1
Miscellaneous manufacturing industries	7.8	19.6
Construction	469.7	1316.4
Transport, storage, and trade	2.7	6.5
Communication, finance, insurance, public utility operation, real estate	8.0	45.6
Other service industries	1561.3	4894.3
Total	2128.0	6517.0

[a] Purchases from sectors not listed are insignificant.

Source: 1949 expenditures are from DBS, *The Inter-Industry Flow of Goods and Services, Canada, 1949,* Reference Paper No. 72 (Ottawa, 1956), Table 1; 1970 estimates are based on Table 55.

mercial institutions, transfers to other governments, losses of government-owned enterprises, provisions for debt retirement, reserves, write-downs and other bookkeeping adjustments, and purchases of land and used capital assets." [13] Then the percentage which purchases of goods and services constituted of total expenditure was computed for each functional category of expenditure. Second, these percentages were applied to the functional estimates of 1970 government expenditure in Table 55, making adjustments where changes in the character of particular types of expenditure are foreseen and converting to 1955 prices. One example of such an adjustment would be within health and welfare expenditures by the federal government, which under expanded health programs will consist more of administrative services in 1970 than in 1949. Third, the percentage distributions by function of government purchases of goods and services for 1949 and 1970 were compared to see how they would alter the total pattern

[13] DBS, *The Inter-Industry Flow of Goods and Service, Canada, 1949,* Reference Paper No. 72 (Ottawa, 1956), p. 46.

of government purchasing. The main changes indicated were the following.

1. Health insurance and related measures will increase relatively the demand on the service sector for administrative personnel.

2. Defense expenditures rise over the 1949 level (although the 1970 forecast is lower than more recent years) will affect construction, metal products and services (military pay and allowances).

3. The relative rise in expenditures on transportation, mainly at the provincial-municipal level, means relatively stronger demand for construction and other manufacturing sectors.

4. The increase in education's share of total government purchases of goods and services in the early 1960's will favor construction very strongly. But by 1970 the composition of this category will have shifted toward demand for personnel services.

Making largely qualitative judgments on the basis of these forecast changes, the 1970 government demand for goods and services was estimated as shown in Table 63. The 1949 actual government demand is presented for purposes of comparison.

13

Canada's Foreign Trade in 1970

The main purpose of this chapter is to forecast the structure of Canada's international trade in 1970. Forecasts for nearly all major imports and many exports are reviewed in other chapters, so that massive detail will not be required. Yet trade is so important to the Canadian economy that any general survey of its prospects must devote some space to discussing the problems raised by this intense participation in the world economy. Consequently, the following sections discuss trends in the structure of Canada's import and export trade and future mechanism of adjustment of the Canadian balance of payments. Because of the historic variability of her export earnings, because of her mounting obligations to make interest and dividend payments abroad, and because of the crucial role imports play in maintaining the Canadian standard of living, these trends must be searched for the possibility of future crises in the Canadian trade and payments situation.

Table 64. Leading Canadian exports, ranked by value, 1926 and 1952.

Rank	1926	1952
1	Wheat	Wheat
2	Newsprint	Newsprint
3	Wheat flour	Planks and boards
4	Planks and boards	Wood pulp
5	Wood pulp	Aluminum, primary and semifabricated
6	Barley	Nickel, primary and semifabricated
7	Fur skins, undressed	Barley
8	Whiskey	Wheat flour
9	Farm implements	Copper, primary and semifabricated
10	Copper, primary and semi-fabricated	Zinc, primary and semifabricated
11	Pulpwood	Farm implements
12	Lead, primary and semi-fabricated	Asbestos, unmanufactured

Source: DBS, *Canada Year Book, 1954*, p. 985.

THE STRUCTURE OF CANADA'S TRADE

As the well-known staple theory of Canadian economic growth shows, the demands of the world economy for Canadian resource-based products have been the main determinants of Canadian growth.[1] With no integrated domestic market during much of her history, the story of her spurts of rapid growth has been the story of the development of her major exports. Table 64, listing the leading Canadian exports by value for 1926 and 1952, shows to what a great extent these staples dominate Canadian export trade. Furthermore, a complicated pattern of developments under-lies each change in this ordering — international changes in demand, technology, resource availability, trade regulations, and the like.

Table 65. Canadian exports by degree of manufacture, as percentages of total value, selected years, 1900–1950.

Year		Raw materials	Partially manufactured	Fully manufactured
Fiscal	1900	41.5	17.7	40.8
	1910	51.2	16.1	32.7
	1914	63.2	10.1	32.7
	1926	47.1	14.4	38.5
	1937	38.2	22.5	39.3
Calendar	1946	26.1	22.1	51.8
	1950	28.1	31.3	40.7

Source: D. W. Slater, "Changes in the Structure of Canada's International Trade," *CJEPS*, 21:5 (February 1955).

It is this ever-changing picture of resource development which dominates Canada's trade. Contrast it to the steady trend toward a higher degree of manufacture which marks the composition of United States exports over the last half century. Table 65 shows Canada's fully manufactured exports making up almost exactly the same percentage of total exports now as in 1900 (having dipped in the intervening years due to the great grain boom). Even this result is deceptive because newsprint, Canada's second export, is fully manufactured but has very low value added by manufacture. There is a clear trend in Table 65 toward increasing importance of partially manufactured goods, due to the rise of minerals and nonferrous metals exports.

[1] See Chapters 2, 5, and 6.

Because she is both economically advanced and internationally specialized, Canada's total trade per capita is nearly the highest in the world. Measured in 1948 dollars, her 1937 total trade per capital was $316. In 1947 it was $478; in 1953, $510.[2] The relative importance of exports to the economy, however, may have declined some in the last three decades. Unadjusted current-dollar exports were 24 per cent of gross national product in 1926 and 21.5 per cent in 1926–1929. But by 1950 they were down to 17.3 per cent and to just over 16 per cent in 1955.[3] As earlier discussion showed, the proof is still not clear that the dependence of Canada on her export trade has declined in any ultimate sense. Smart money would not bet on this trend. In any case, Canada's exports are still more than twice as large a share of national product as the exports of the United States.

A substantial volume of research confirms two reasons why Canada's prosperity and growth have depended on a large volume of trade.[4] First, Canada's natural resources, especially those developed in the twentieth century, can be profitably exploited only on a large scale. Many are located in the interior or northern regions, necessitating high initial costs for exploration and development. These can be incurred only when foreign markets are in prospect. Hence the rapid and massive expansion of mining activities during the interwar period, while the rest of the economy saw a decade of moderate growth followed by a decade of stagnation, tended to increase the economy's orientation toward world markets. Second, Canada is quite favorably located for shipping to the world's major markets. Many Canadian producers find themselves closer to American population centers than to the majority of Canadian markets. And the two great waterways of the Great Lakes–St. Lawrence system and Hudson Bay make cheap water transport available. Given access on favorable terms to the world market and the chance to develop a large volume trade in staples, she has been able to use her factors of production so much more efficiently than if she produced only for the

---

[2] Canada, DBS, *Review of Foreign Trade — Calendar Year 1953*, p. 10.
[3] "Structural and Directional Changes in Foreign Trade," Canadian Bank of Commerce, *Commercial Letter* (May 1956), p. 3.
[4] A cursory glance at the work of O. D. Skelton, H. A. Innis, or A. W. Currie will confirm this.

Table 66.   Percentage distribution of Canadian exports and imports by
commodity classification, 1869–1915 (1900 prices).

Commodity group	1869–1875	1876–1885	1886–1895	1896–1905	1906–1915
	Exports				
Agricultural products	12.3	23.0	21.0	21.5	32.4
Animals and animal products	24.1	34.5	39.2	38.5	23.9
Fibres and textiles	0.9	0.7	0.9	1.2	1.7
Wood and paper	38.7	30.5	27.4	19.1	15.6
Iron and steel	1.2	1.4	0.7	2.3	4.8
Nonferrous metals	1.8	1.5	1.4	10.1	13.8
Nonmetallic minerals	2.9	2.0	3.4	3.3	3.2
Chemicals	0	0	0.3	0.6	1.3
Miscellaneous	18.1	6.4	5.7	3.4	3.3
	Imports				
Agricultural products	27.0	23.7	22.2	20.6	16.6
Animals and animal products	7.5	9.1	8.4	8.2	7.8
Fibres and textiles	26.5	28.7	26.0	21.7	17.4
Wood and paper	0	4.9	4.7	5.1	5.8
Iron and steel	12.8	12.4	12.6	16.9	21.4
Nonferrous metals	1.1	1.9	3.4	4.7	6.0
Nonmetallic minerals	5.0	7.4	11.3	10.8	13.2
Chemicals	2.3	2.4	3.3	3.1	2.8
Miscellaneous	17.8	9.5	8.1	8.9	9.0

Source: K. W. Taylor and H. Michell, *Statistical Contributions to Canadian Economic History* (Toronto, 1931), Vol. II, pp. 4–5.

domestic market that any concerted effort to achieve autonomy would be expensive indeed.[5]

Against this background, let us examine the historic changes in the commodity composition of Canada's trade. Tables 66 and 67 together show the changes in the composition of Canadian exports and imports from Confederation up to the present. From 1869 to 1920, the most striking change in exports is the rise of agricultural and vegetable products due to the opening up of the wheat economy. At the same time, animal products, which had constituted nearly 40 per cent of Canada's exports, fell off as British demand for bacon, cheese, and the like was transferred to Denmark, Australia, and New Zealand, and as Canada's domestic

[5] See statement in Canadian Pulp and Paper Association, *Submission to the RCCEP* (Montreal, 1956), p. 90.

Table 67.   Percentage distribution of Canadian exports and imports by commodity classification, selected years, 1920–1954 (current dollars).

Commodity group	1920	1929	1939	1948	1952	1953	1954
Exports							
Agricultural products	40.5	11.7	23.8	20.9	27.5	26.6	20.7
Animals and animal products	15.8	17.0	14.3	14.1	5.5	6.1	7.0
Fibres and textiles	1.6	1.0	1.6	1.5	0.7	0.6	0.5
Wood, wood products, and paper	24.0	47.0	26.2	31.0	31.8	31.5	35.5
Iron and its products	6.5	2.2	6.8	9.2	9.5	8.7	7.7
Nonferrous metals	3.9	12.7	19.8	12.9	16.4	16.6	18.3
Nonmetallic minerals	3.4	3.6	3.2	3.1	3.3	3.6	3.8
Chemicals and allied products	1.7	2.2	2.6	2.6	2.9	3.3	4.2
Miscellaneous	2.7	2.5	1.8	4.7	2.4	3.0	2.4
Imports							
Agricultural products	20.9	12.0	17.0	13.3	12.1	11.1	13.2
Animals and animal products	5.0	4.9	4.4	3.2	2.1	2.0	2.1
Fibres and textiles	19.7	9.4	13.4	13.3	8.9	8.8	8.1
Wood, wood products, and paper	4.6	5.8	4.5	2.8	3.4	3.7	4.1
Iron and its products	19.8	36.5	24.4	29.7	34.9	35.0	32.3
Nonferrous metals	4.5	7.2	5.6	5.9	7.4	8.3	8.7
Nonmetallic minerals	16.6	15.6	17.7	23.0	15.9	15.0	14.6
Chemicals and allied products	3.1	3.0	5.8	4.5	4.7	5.1	5.4
Miscellaneous	5.9	5.6	7.2	4.4	10.6	11.0	11.5

Source: DBS, *Canada Year Book, 1932, 1942, 1951;* DBS, *Review of Foreign Trade — Calendar Year 1953, 1954.*

demand grew faster than available supply. The wood products group was rising by 1920 as the fast-growing pulp and paper industry offset the declining importance of lumber. The nonferrous metals group throughout the period had provided few exports except when major gold discoveries occurred. However, the upward trend for iron and iron products, chemicals, and textiles reflected the growth of Canadian manufacturing over the long run and the stimulus of World War I in particular.

Changes to 1920 on the import side reveal Canada's growing self-sufficiency in food and textiles, her rapidly increasing requirements for imports of investment goods and other manufactures of ferrous and nonferrous metals, and great growth in the demand for petroleum.

From 1920 to the present, the trend toward agricultural self-sufficiency in Canada continued. Agricultural products and animals and animal products declined sharply as a share of both exports and imports. To a fairly large extent the decline in agricultural exports as a percentage of total export value is the result of a decline in the price of grain relative to other things. Animal products exports would have declined much more except for the rapid rise of fish exports. Tariff protection of textile industries both in Canada and elsewhere has cut fibres and textiles as a share of both imports and exports. The dramatic increases in Canadian exports have been in nonferrous metals, wood and its products, and iron and steel products, representing the most dynamic sectors of the Canadian economy in those years. The big increases on the side of imports were in iron and iron products, nonferrous metals, and chemicals and allied products. These changes reflect mainly the increase of spending on imported consumer durables and industrial materials and equipment. The Canadian chemical and steel industries increased their share of the home market during this period, but the growth of the market was fast enough to make a diminished market share for these imports bulk larger in import cargos.[6]

As Canada gains greater and greater prominence among the world's trading nations, the question naturally arises whether she has significant monopoly power in any export markets or monopsony power against the sellers of her imports. The monopsony possibility is easily ruled out. Canada is not a purchaser of a major percentage of world exports of any important commodity. On the export side, Canada is a competitive seller of all her exports except pulp and newsprint, nickel, and asbestos. Slater concludes from his research that, in addition, "Canada has some effect, quite a limited one, on the world prices of wheat, copper, lead, and zinc."[7]

The commodity composition of Canada's trade, of course, bears a close relation to the "country composition" of her trading partners. The facts of overwhelming importance here are two: First, Canada has always carried on the bulk of her trade with the United States and the United Kingdom. Second, for both her exports and her imports, the typical bundle of commodities traded varies considerably depending on which of these two countries

---

[6] On this whole pattern of development, see David W. Slater, "Changes in the Structure of Canada's International Trade," *CJEPS*, 21:5 (February 1955), and Canadian Bank of Commerce, *Commercial Letter* (May 1956). Slater's extensive study, *Canada's Imports* (Ottawa, 1957), became available after the completion of the present chapter.

[7] Slater, p. 9, note 7.

Table 68.   Percentage of Canadian trade with United States and
United Kingdom, selected periods, 1901–1956.

Period	Exports to —		Imports from —	
	U.S.	U.K.	U.S.	U.K.
1901–1905	35	55	59	25
1926–1929	38	32	67	16
1936–1939	36	40	62	18
1946–1949	44	25	72	10
1950–1954	59	16	71	10
1955	60	18	73	8
1956[a]	61	17	76	8

[a] First quarter.
Source: "Structural and Directional Changes in Foreign Trade," Canadian Bank
of Commerce *Commercial Letter* (May 1956), p. 2.

buys or sells it.[8] This is why any study trying to analyze and
forecast Canada's trade structure must give close attention to
trends in the destination of Canada's export cargos.

In the early years following confederation, Canada traded extensively with the United States. But, by 1900, United States
trade had dropped off because of Canada's failure to reach a
commercial agreement with that country and, more important,
because economic development in the United States and Canada
was clearly of a competing sort during these years, causing Canada to find her main markets abroad in Great Britain. Table 68
shows how the share of these two countries in Canada's total
imports and exports has changed since the turn of the century.
There the striking trend toward greater trade with the United
States appears, interrupted only by Imperial Preference and the
economic collapse of the United States in the 1930's. Also clear is
Canada's regular tendency to run a current account deficit with
the United States and a surplus with the United Kingdom. A third
important fact shown in the table is that, although Canada has
throughout the twentieth century bought a steady 80 to 85 per
cent of her imports from these two traders, she has diversified her
export markets so that the United States and United Kingdom together now take less than 80 per cent of Canada's exports.

[8] See, for instance, the RCDPR *Report,* Vol. I; for an attempt to measure the
total impact of the differences between the composition of Canadian exports to
the United States and United Kingdom, see R. E. Caves, "The Inter-Industry
Structure of the Canadian Economy," *CJEPS,* 23:326–327 (August 1957).

The greater share of Canada's trade with the United States is not just the result of the rapid growth of that country. Canada has increased her share of the United States import market from 11 per cent in 1926–1929 to 23 per cent in 1953, and she has furnished to the United States 26 per cent of her total export markets in 1953, in contrast to 15 per cent in 1925–1929.[9] Despite persistent tariff barriers between the two countries, the complementarity of their development since 1900 has strongly asserted itself. On the one hand, the quality of Canada's natural resources and her efficiency in certain types of manufactures have found her ready markets at her southern border. On the other, Canadian desires for specialized machinery and equipment and taste for mass-produced American consumer goods have stimulated the trade flow in the opposite direction.

The strength of this trend bodes ill for Canada's current desires for a declaration of economic independence from the United States. Prime Minister Diefenbaker's proposal that Canada reallocate 15 per cent of her trade away from America to Britain will no doubt return to haunt him in his declining years. Such a shift could be accomplished only by a full customs union with Britain and much higher tariffs against the United States, and this shift would necessitate a corresponding sacrifice of real income which Canadians have no desire to accept. American manufacturers have a huge advantage over United Kingdom rivals wherever differentiated goods are involved, because Canadian consumers have grown up on American tastes and Canadian industry is built upon United States technology. Moreover, Britain's exports to and imports from Canada are mostly goods whose markets are growing very slowly (that is, goods with low income elasticities). Even if Britain keeps her present share of Canada's trade *in every commodity,* her share of Canada's total trade will continue to drop.[10]

PROSPECTS FOR CANADIAN EXPORTS AND IMPORTS

It seems clear from this examination of long-run trends in Canadian trade that the two questions of whom Canada trades

[9] R. G. C. Smith, "The Changing Pattern of U.S. Foreign Trade," *Foreign Trade,* 102:2–4 (October 16, 1954).

[10] This last is a significant problem in Britain's over-all long-run trade situation. See H. Tyszynski, "World Trade in Manufactured Commodities, 1899–1950," *Manchester School,* 19:286–297 (September 1951).

with and *what* she trades are inseparable. One is faced with the nearly absurd problem of forecasting them jointly for more than a decade into the future. There is, however, the saving fact that some fairly definite information is available on what determines the level of world trade as a whole. The historical characteristic of world trade used in this study to permit a projection is the dependence of the total volume of world trade on the level of income (or output, or some related variable) of the advanced industrial countries. W. Arthur Lewis has argued that the growth of advanced countries' demand for raw materials is the dynamic factor governing the world demand for industrial products, and that this relation may be observable even after the crash of 1929 (though since that convulsion a given level of manufactures output has supported a smaller volume of primary products trade).[11] Likewise, the statistical work of Polak and Neisser and Modigliani shows the imports of "primaries countries" as dependent on their manufactures output. Polak, in fact, puts at the center of his system a "reflection ratio" which supposedly shows the relation between an increase in a country's exports and the induced increase in imports, and he asserts that these reflection ratios are stable enough to support a prediction.[12]

The gist of all this is that future world trade in primary products will clearly continue to depend upon the growth potential (population, resources, technology) of the advanced industrial countries. In the specific case of Canada, doing 80 per cent of her trading with the United States and the United Kingdom, attention can be centered on the future demands of these two industrial nations with reasonable certainty that trade with the rest of the world will not develop at violently different rates. That is, the changes in Canada's exports to *all* countries including the United

---

[11] W. A. Lewis, *Economic Survey 1919–1939* (London, 1949), chs. 12, 13; Lewis, "World Production, Prices and Trade, 1870–1960," *Manchester School,* 20:105–138 (May 1952).

[12] J. J. Polak, *An International Economic System* (Chicago 1953), pp. 123–126; Polak, "Conceptual Problems Involved in Projections of the International Sector of Gross National Product," in Conference on Research in Income and Wealth, *Long-Range Economic Projection* (Princeton, 1954), pp. 377–418; H. Neisser and F. Modigliani, *National Incomes and International Trade* (Urbana, 1953), esp. chs. ii, iv; see also W. Beckerman, "The World Trade Multiplier and the Stability of World Trade, 1938 to 1953," *Econometrica,* 24:239–252 (July 1956).

States and United Kingdom are likely to relate closely to changes in the level of income in those two countries.

Because of this dependence, it is desirable to have some idea about the level of gross national product in 1970 for the United States and United Kingdom. For the former we have the recent projections to 1960 by J. Frederick Dewhurst and Associates. These still promise to be reasonably accurate although a bit conservative. Their "medium" projection is that the United States national income will increase by 29 per cent from 1950 to 1960 to $370,000,000,000 in constant 1950 dollars. Projecting this same rate of increase to 1970 we get a gross national product of $477,000,000,000 (this would correspond to a national income of $406,000,000,000).[13] The total percentage increase over the twenty-year period is about 69 per cent, and the annual compound growth rate about 2.6 per cent. No really careful estimate of the probable rate of growth of gross national product seems to exist for the United Kingdom. One at least suggestive of the probable magnitude of that growth is the United States Paley Commission's forecast that British GNP would increase 62 per cent between 1950 and 1975, corresponding to an annual rate slightly under 2 per cent.[14] The most recent glance into the future made by the Organization for European Economic Cooperation conveys about the same impression. Between 1950 and 1955 the annual compound increase in gross national product per man-hour in Britain was 1.7 per cent, well below most other European countries. The O.E.E.C. foresees a slight rise in this figure for the period 1956–1960 due to heavy industrial investment in recent years and the possible adverse effects of balance of payments crises in the early 1950's.[15] Nonetheless, the increase in productivity growth could scarcely put the annual compound rate of gross national product increase above 2 per cent.

How is Canada's trade likely to be divided between the United States and United Kingdom in future years? The determinants of this split for the last twenty-five years have been

[13] J. F. Dewhurst and Associates, *America's Needs and Resources, A New Survey* (New York, 1955), ch. ii.

[14] United States, President's Materials Policy Commission, *Resources for Freedom* (Washington, 1952), Vol. II, p. 131.

[15] Organization for European Economic Cooperation, *Europe Today and in 1960, Eighth Report of the O.E.E.C.* (Paris, 1957), Vol. II, ch. 2.

"abnormal" from the point of view of this study — first, Imperial Preference in the 1930's, then World War II and its aftermath causing abnormal exports to Britain, then most recently the "dollar shortage" and systematic European discrimination against dollar area exports, throwing the balance the other way and sharply cutting Canada's overseas market for transportation equipment and other manufactures.[16] Clearly, there are two possibilities that cut against one another: (1) relaxation of the dollar shortage and ending of European exchange restrictions against the dollar area would increase Canada's exports to the Commonwealth; (2) generally freer world trade would encourage the secular tendency for Canada to trade more extensively with the United States. Developments in 1954 reflected both these tendencies. Relaxed United Kingdom restrictions increased sales of Canada's efficiently produced chemicals and wood and paper products. But in grain sales Canada continued to lose position to France, Argentina, and Australia in the United Kingdom market, in addition to the disruption caused by United States grain gifts abroad.[17]

Strong forces support a secular increase in Canada's trade with the United States. First, the United States is turning more and more to Canada as a source of industrial raw materials — not just of the woodpulp and nonferrous metals already important, but also for growing exports of Canadian iron ore, petroleum, and natural gas. This role of materials supplier is reflected in the fact that only 44 per cent of Canada's exports to the United States are fully manufactured (much of this is newsprint), whereas 84 per cent of Canada's imports from the United States are "chiefly manufactured" goods. Even so, heavy exchange of manufactures between the two countries is not out of the question. Industrial countries in the past have shown tendencies to a highly specialized division of labor and heavy exchange of manufactures (for example, United Kingdom and Germany before World War I); this sort of thing already exists between Canada and the United States in farm machinery due to elimination of tariff

[16] Great Britain, Board of Trade, "Canada, Economic and Commercial Conditions," *Overseas Economic Surveys* (London, 1950), Vol. II, p. 96.

[17] R. P. Bower, "What Canada Is Selling to Britain," *Foreign Trade*, 102:4-5 (13 November 1954).

barriers. It might well increase.[18] The whole matter is summed up well by Professor Mackintosh:

It is scarcely to be expected that Empire markets will revive as sheltered markets for Canadian exports. Indeed protection of local industry is likely to raise higher barriers. In so far as we can continue to export manufactures to these markets we must be able to compete with the United States and United Kingdom products. In so far as we seek alternative markets in the United States, Latin America, the Far East, and the Middle East, we must be able to meet open competition.[19]

The future allocation of Canada's foreign trade will, of course, be affected by the outcome of plans for a European common market and associated free trade area. Unfortunately, the political and economic outcome of these proposals is quite dubious at this writing. The best bet is that the six continental "Messina powers" will go through with their plans for a common market and common atomic energy pool. Inspired by the experience of the European Coal and Steel Community, these nations are firmly convinced of the long-run merits of a large market unhindered by tariff barriers. Less certain is the ultimate decision of the United Kingdom and the remaining O.E.E.C. countries on forming an associated free trade area — a common market without a common tariff against the outside world. Britain is obviously on the spot. The European common market would seriously cut total markets for her manufactured exports if she stays out. But she cannot enter and continue tariff preferences for Commonwealth exporters (including Canada). Hence, the proposed compromise on a free trade area for Britain and the peripheral O.E.E.C. nations. In trade negotiations with Canada during October 1957, the British explicitly proposed an extended free trade area including Canada and possibly other Commonwealth countries. To reduce a lengthy and difficult evaluation to one word, this stretching of the free trade area proposal would be impossible. Even negotiations on the European free trade area have now broken down.

[18] H. Marshall, "Canada — Northern Neighbor," *JASA*, 50:1–15 (March 1955).
[19] W. A. Mackintosh, "Export Markets Overseas," in *Canada's Economy in a Changing World*, ed. J. D. Gibson (Toronto, 1948), p. 149.

If we grant that Canada will not belong to any European regional tariff preference systems which may emerge, then it is fairly clear that they will be a further force tending to cut Canada's trade ties with Europe. Such regional arrangements could affect the network of world trade in two basic ways — rearranging it through changing the pattern of tariff schedules, and augmenting it through a faster rate of growth in European real income. Since the latter force is very unlikely to be important, and since the composition of Canada's trade renders it quite insensitive to the former, the total impact on the Canadian economy will in any case be slight. The fundamental economic forces tending to increase trade with the United States and the Western Hemisphere generally will go on working.[20]

Our immediate purpose is to set forth the estimates of Canadian imports and exports developed in light of these basic considerations. In Table 69 they are presented, classed by the sectors of the interindustry table described in Chapter 14.[21] For most of these classes no detailed discussion will be given in this chapter. It appears in the chapters covering the corresponding domestic

[20] Sources helpful in foreseeing the effects of European regional arrangements on Canada are C. G. F. Simkin, "Commonwealth Countries and the Common Market," *New Commonwealth,* 33:302–315 (April 1, 1957), and R. C. McIvor, "Canadian Foreign Trade and the European Common Market," *International Journal,* 13:1–11 (Winter 1957–58).

[21] One adjustment of the figures in the table is necessary before the export figures can be plugged into the interindustry table. In preparing its interindustry table for 1949, the Dominion Bureau of Statistics has divided the "freight and shipping" revenue category in the balance of trade statistics into two parts. The first part represents earnings accruing to Canadians for transporting export goods from point of production to port. The other part covers Canadians' earnings for transporting exports beyond port of embarkation, or transporting the output of other countries. These parts are handled in different ways in the interindustry table and must be projected separately. Factory-to-port transportation earnings follow the volume of Canadian exports quite closely and can be forecast on this basis. The St. Lawrence Seaway will, however, put more Canadian-furnished transport services into the other class. Consequently, a transfer of about 8 per cent of the forecast total was made to the port-to-recipient class. Canadian earnings in the latter class stem mostly from two sorts of services — handling United States rail shipments between Buffalo and Detroit, and Great Lakes shipping. The first source will not grow rapidly in future years, but the latter definitely will. For shipping beyond Canadian ports, 1970 earnings should be about $215,000,000. Earnings for factory-to-port shipping of $280,000,000 will bring the total to $495,000,000. Canadian payments to foreigners for shipping services, which enter the balance of payments on the imports side, are closely correlated with the physical volume of commodity import. Projecting this relation gives for 1970 an amount of $407,000,000.

Table 69. Canadian exports and imports, forecast for 1970[a] (millions of 1955 dollars).

Sector and commodity	Exports	Imports
Agriculture		
Wheat, wheat flour	567 }	30
Other grain	43 }	
Fresh fruits, vegetables	18	165
Live animals	10	5
Raw wool	2	90
Raw cotton	0	37
Meat	30	12
Other	0	33
Total	670	372
Forestry		
Pulpwood	31	—
Other manufactured wood (logs, poles, and so forth)	17	—
Total	48	33
Fishing, hunting, and trapping	97	10
Coal mining, crude petroleum, and natural gas		
Coal	3	162
Crude petroleum	192	150
Natural gas	96	0
Total	291	312
Other mining and quarrying industries		
Nickel	357	0
Copper	163	0
Lead	76	0
Zinc	113	0
Silver	32	0
Gold	158	0
Iron ore	298	0
Tungsten	10	0
Uranium	285	0
Asbestos	288	0
Miscellaneous minerals[b]	30	32
Structural minerals	4	70
Aluminum	646	75
Other	40	42
Total	2,500	219
Food, beverages, and tobacco	500	500

Sector and commodity	Exports	Imports
Clothing and household goods		
Textiles and products	13	420
Furniture	0	0
Leather products	2	17
Jewelry and silverware	0	25
Total	15	462
Forest products		
Lumber	338	22
Newsprint	1,003	42
Other paper	50	0
Woodpulp	529	10
Wood products	50	37
Total	1,970	112
Metal products		
Iron and steel products	524	2,886
Nonferrous metal products	30	30
Total	554	2,916
Electrical apparatus and supplies	54	552
Mineral products		
Nonmetallic mineral products	15	135
Coal products	5	19
Petroleum products	0	180
Chemicals and allied products	300	290
Total	320	624
Miscellaneous manufacturing		
Rubber products	0	90
Printing and publishing	10	110
Miscellaneous	342	798
Total	352	998
Construction	0	0
Transportation, storage, trade	495	407
Public utility operation, and so forth	10	16
Other service industries	5	5
(Tourist services)	410	590
Grand total	8,292	8,128

[a] Totals and subtotals may not reconcile precisely because of rounding errors.
[b] Except structural.
Source: See text, pp. 400–402.

sectors — Chapter 16 for minerals, Chapter 17 for forest and fisheries products, and Chapter 18 for manufactures.

In general, specific export classes were projected by looking at the following things: (1) prospective rate of growth of income and demand in the countries which are the best customers for each export; (2) trends in Canadian exportable supply — that is, the excess of Canadian productive capacity over probable domestic consumption; and (3) potential output of producers competing with Canada in the export of each commodity. The material above indicated how the first of these was handled. For each export, or group of exports, the growth of Canada's major overseas markets has been estimated from the economic growth rates of the relevant areas and rough estimates of the income elasticity of demand where such an estimate was feasible.

Figuring the size and significance of trends in Canada's exportable surplus of particular commodities over domestic consumption involves nasty practical problems and also some nice quandaries at the theoretical level. On the practical side, it is hard to tell which industries have highly elastic long-run supply functions (or cost functions). In these cases, supply will adjust to demand, and thereby the supply side of the picture disappears. In cases where diminishing returns seem in prospect even after the current rate of technological change is allowed for, so that the historic supply function will not be perfectly elastic, actual exports cannot be forecast without reference to the domestic demand foreseen in 1970. Calculations of this sort have necessarily been very crude, but, because of the importance in Canada's trade of industries closely tied to limited natural resources, ignoring the force of diminishing returns and resource exhaustion would be an obvious mistake. The notion of "exportable surplus" conceals a theoretical problem which is seldom recognized by most of its users, both practical and academic. Why should the amount of a product available for export be identified with a surplus over domestic demand any more than available domestic supply should be seen as a surplus remaining after export shipments are made? Why not treat these two portions of total demand for a product as coordinate? The usual answer, that greater transportation costs usually put the foreign buyer at a disadvantage, has the drawback of being factually incorrect in many cases. A more likely answer is that producers (especially producers of differentiated products) often seem to view their foreign markets as marginal business appended to the base of their domestic operations; and they do so with some justification because of the much greater chances for political assistance in their behalf to maintain the stability and soundness of the domestic markets.[22] If exporters view foreign markets as marginal for this reason, the economic forecaster would be unwise to do otherwise.

The third consideration shaping the export forecasts was Canada's potential competition in foreign markets from home producers or other exporters. Here all sorts of data clamor for attention. The problem is particularly acute because the heavy trade restrictions of the last three decades make it almost impossible to sort out long-run and short-run factors. For example, comparing Canada's trade with "third countries" other than the United States and United Kingdom in 1937–38 with that trade in 1954–55, one finds that the constant-dollar flow of highly manufactured exports has hardly increased at all. In some areas, such as Australia and New Zealand, this has been due to the use of import restrictions and growth of domestic production. In others, such as Latin America, import control plus competition from such nations as Germany and the United States has been important.[23] In all cases, there has been the effect of heavy foreign demand for Canada's primary products, which has priced Canadian manufactures out of many markets through its effect on Canada's foreign exchange rate and internal cost levels. The procedure followed in constructing the estimates in Table 69 has been to take some account of growing competition furnished to Canadian exporters by home market producers. But not much could be done about including the effects in changes in the competitive position of other exporters, except for presuming in a general way that the anticipated strong demand for Canadian exports of many primary products will impair the competitiveness of other would-be exporters. More detailed study of trends in

[22] British writers harp with such persistence on the problems of building an export trade without a large home-market base that one ultimately doubts that they are entirely kidding themselves; see, for example, J. M. Jackson, "British Exports and the Scale of Production," *Manchester School*, 22:90–112 (January 1954). An interesting general discussion which subsumes the problem reviewed here appears in Gunnar Myrdal's *An International Economy, Problems and Prospects* (New York, 1956), chs. 3, 4.

[23] A convenient statistical picture of these changes appears in "Canada's Exports to Third Countries," *Foreign Trade*, 107:6–9 (May 11, 1957).

foreign competition has, of course, been both necessary and possible for a few commodities, such as wheat, copper, and newsprint.[24]

PROSPECTS FOR THE BALANCE OF PAYMENTS

The estimates of 1970 Canadian exports and imports of goods and services cannot rest on long-run trends of income and substitution effects alone. They must be such that they could be part of a stable over-all pattern of international transactions. That is, they must be consistent with equilibrium in the balance of payments. The totals of the export and import columns of Table 69 are respectively $8,292,000,000 and $8,128,000,000, leaving an export surplus of $164,000,000. These totals represent all the items normally counted in Canada's current account except interest and dividend payments and a miscellaneous group made up mainly of government grants and loans. What do these figures mean for balance of payments stability?

One way to test the chances for long-run stability in the Canadian balance of payments would be to try forecasting all the items included in it, such as interest and dividends and all capital account transactions, as well as trade in goods and services. This would be so dubious an operation, however, that more can be gained by noting the ways adjustments *normally* occur in the Canadian balance of payments. This will make possible some qualitative guesses about how present happenings throughout the Canadian economy will be mirrored in balance of payments adjustments in future years.

Classic textbook explanations of the Canadian balance of payments mechanism always stress the role of short-term capital movements, such as changes in foreign holdings of Canadian currency, in the foreign assets of the chartered banks, and in "leads and lags in commercial payments." Only in the last few years has it been realized that the really important adjustment mechanism of the Canadian international sector, especially over the moderately long run, operates through the long-term capital accounts and the level of Canadian domestic investment.

It works like this. In periods of very rapid Canadian economic growth, especially when Canada is growing faster than her main trading partners, the United States and United Kingdom, her

[24] Some helpful information appears in Slater, pp. 10–18.

imports are likely to be growing faster than her exports.[25] The main reason is that such a boom in Canada is accompanied by a very high level of investment, and Canada has always leaned heavily on foreign suppliers for machinery and equipment. The current account becomes passive. But this same high profitability of investment attracts foreign capital, both direct and portfolio. A surplus on long-term capital account covers the current account deficit, and balance in the supply and demand for Canadian currency as an international payments medium is nicely maintained. One reason this mechanism works so precisely is that the persons or firms making capital imports into Canada are frequently the same ones making extra imports of producers' goods, so that the two sets of decisions are very closely coordinated.

In a period when Canada's development has slowed down or is running slower than that of her trading partners, the current account tends to become active (exports exceeding imports). Foreign demand for Canada's exports grows faster than Canada's demand for imports. High dividend and interest payments abroad create a strong demand for foreign exchange. More important, the capital installed in a previous period of heavy capital imports starts to have its effect. Enlarged capacity of the export industries raises the outflow of goods and allows them to raise their share of the domestic market, cutting the need for imports. At such times Canadian savings find not such a ready market at home and are often used to buy Canadian securities or shares held by foreigners. That is, some of the foreign capital previously invested in Canada is repatriated. Again this tends to make the capital account passive (or at least less active than would otherwise have been the case), counteracting the active current account.[26]

This is not all the mechanism of adjustment of the balance of payments. Other major aspects come to mind when one con-

[25] This process and its relation to changes in Canada's national income were discussed in Chapter 3.

[26] More or less complete accounts of this mechanism are found in G. M. Meier, "Economic Development and the Transfer Mechanism: Canada, 1895–1913," *CJEPS*, 19:1–19 (February 1953); V. W. Malach, "The Mechanism of Adjustment in Canada's Balance of Payments, 1921–9," *CJEPS*, 18:303–321 (August 1952); P. M. Cornell, "Flexible Exchange Rates: The Canadian Case," unpublished Ph.D. dissertation (Harvard University, 1956), pp. 120–125 and *passim*.

siders what would happen over a short period of time if the
Canadian dollar were to go at a discount *vis-à-vis* the United
States dollar (as, under the regime of flexible exchange rates, it
is free to do). First, the classic short-term capital movements
come into play. Canadians, finding it expensive to make payments
to United States citizens, try to defer such payments; on the
other hand, the latter find it an opportune time to settle their
debts with Canadians. United States investors find outstanding
Canadian securities a good short-term investment, so long as
confidence remains in the long-run soundness of the Canadian
economy. Second, in the consumption of goods and services, the
prices of imports tend to rise relative to the prices of the Canadian
goods with which they compete, and total spending on imports
may decline. Conversely, Canadian goods become a better buy
abroad, and spending on them may increase. Third — and here is
the point frequently neglected in discussion of these matters —
a large number of manufacturing firms have plants with similar
types of capacity in both Canada and the United States, and
others without actual operations in both countries have close
relations with suppliers in both. If the Canadian dollar goes at a
discount, an international firm will be able to lower its manufacturing costs by producing in Canada more of the components
of the product it markets in Canada; indeed, it finds it profitable
(if its productive capacity allows) to export to the United States
components formerly imported into Canada. Likewise, independent manufacturers in Canada find it more profitable to shop
domestically for supplies formerly imported, if the latter must
be paid for in dollars purchased at a premium.[27] The example of
"parts" and "components" is used advisedly; the existence of
tariffs always limits the importance of switching operations of
this type, but Canadian tariffs are low or nonexistent for parts in
many cases where the finished product is heavily protected.

All three of these mechanisms tend to hold the Canadian dollar
around long-run parity with the United States dollar. (They
tend, of course, to work in the opposite direction when the
Canadian dollar is at a premium.) The first of these, short-run
capital movements, can for the most part operate in one direction
only for a short period of time. The latter two, although they

[27] Evidence of this turned up in a number of Submissions to the RCCEP. See
Chapter 17.

can take place quickly, are essentially long-run adjustments in that they permanently change trading relationships. One often hears skepticism about the second — variations in final demand as a source of exchange rate adjustment — and admittedly it will not work favorably for adjustment unless the elasticities of demand for imports are fairly high in the short run. The third mechanism, substitution in production, is probably surer in its action, although it has not been possible to construct empirical proof of this.

This panoply of adjustment mechanisms seems likely to persist into the future. Canada's growing complement of manufacturing industries competing with imported manufactures creates a larger cushion. It may not please the managers of such firms to know that they bear the brunt of short-run international adjustments, but the Canadian balance of payments is nonetheless strengthened by their presence. Popular thought holds firmly that the natural place of the Canadian dollar is at par with the United States dollar. This conviction is itself a source of strength, and these short-run mechanisms are strong enough to sustain it.

What of the long-run adjustments discussed earlier in this section, involving capital imports and growth of Canada's capital stock? The argument presented in this and other chapters holds that at some time in the next decade or so the effect of current heavy capital formation will be to expand export availability of many primary products and some manufactures and furnish stiffer competition for manufactured imports, thus tending to turn the current account deficit around as suggested in the description of past experience. Table 70 shows in particular the distribution of the flow of direct investments to Canada from the United States. Of the total for the years 1946 to 1953 of $1,598,-000,000 gross inflow, only $139,000,000 has gone to transportation and finance, sectors which serve primarily the domestic market. The remainder has gone to extractive industries or manufacturing, there to have the effects discussed on Canada's current account balance. The export and import totals presented above nicely confirm this conjecture. On the export side, nonferrous metals, newsprint, and petroleum become much more prominent as a share of total exports than in 1949. And on the import side, many types of consumer goods, especially soft goods, are less in evidence in the import lists foreseen for 1970.

Table 70. Net flow of direct investments from United States to Canada, 1946–1953 (millions of dollars).

Type of investment	1946	1947	1948	1949	1950	1951	1952	1953	Total
Extractive industries	2	14	28	69	128	177	227	259	904
Manufacturing industry[a]	46	45	49	42	89	114	85	85	555
Transportation	—	—	—	—	18	10	51[b]	17[b]	96
Finance	15	7	2	3	8	8	—	—	43
Gross investment	63	66	79	114	243	309	363	361	1598
Return of capital	25	8	18	30	43	39	44	31	238
Net U.S. capital inflow	38	58	61	84	200	270	319	330	1360
Reinvested profits	129	97	178	187	114	167	127	158	1157
Other	-43	-35	20	17	17	34	161	8	179
Net increase of book value of direct investments	124	120	259	288	331	471	607	496	2696
Net Canadian investment in U.S.[c]	-5	6	13	13	46	-5	-47	-43	-22
Net direct capital flow from U.S. to Canada	119	126	272	301	377	466	560	453	2674

[a] Includes miscellaneous investments.
[b] Included with manufacturing industry.
[c] Negative sign means net flow of Canadian capital to United States.
Source: R. A. Radford, "Canada's Capital Inflow, 1946–53," International Monetary Fund Staff Papers, 4:226–231 (February 1955).

These developments furnish most of the explanation for the export surplus of $164,000,000 projected for 1970 in the previous section. What does this surplus mean for balance of payments equilibrium? Recall that we have not yet taken into account international payments of interest and dividends, an item in which Canada has incurred deficits in most postwar years of at least this amount. When this item is included, certainly no major surplus on total current account need be expected. Indeed, many Canadians fear that heavy dividend outpayments might create a painful deficit. There is no way of telling what these dividend payments will be in 1970. We cannot make a reasonable guess about how much longer heavy capital imports from the United States will continue. We do not know how much of their earnings United States direct investors will withdraw. We do not know how much repatriation of foreign-held securities Canadians will undertake. And, last, we cannot estimate how much Canadians themselves will invest abroad in future years and what size inflow of interest and dividends their securities will earn.

But, within the limits of accuracy of this forecast of exports and imports, it is highly plausible that net dividend and interest payments abroad should roughly offset the favorable balance on goods and services. Whatever problems United States direct investment in Canada creates in terms of foreign control of Canada's natural resource development, it does not force Canada to burden her balance of payments by agreeing to fixed interest charges, as she would for importing the same quantity of capital solely by selling bonds abroad. Dividend remittances are heavy only if Canada is prosperous. And she is prosperous only when exports are strong. This "theoretical" reason affords much support for the conjecture that dividend payments will not upset the balance of payments apple-cart, and that the current account in 1970 is quite likely to be in balance on the net.

Will long-term international capital movements be important in 1970? There is really no way of telling. On the one hand, sustained economic growth within Canada might still be attracting the attention of foreign investors. On the other, the maturation of Canada's own capital market and heavy domestic saving might make Canada herself a major foreign investor by that time. It is easy to forget that even now Canada's gross holding of external assets are roughly half as large as her gross liabilities to other countries. All signs point, at any rate, to effective adjustment in Canada's international sphere.

I4

The Interindustry Table

Table 71 presents an interindustry table for Canada for the year 1970. It summarizes nearly all of the projections developed throughout this report and, besides, forecasts the technical structure of production for the whole Canadian economy. The first of the following sections describes this table and tells how it was assembled. The second tells how it can be used to test the over-all consistency of the projections of this report. And the third explores what new information the table itself can provide about the future structure of the Canadian economy.

SOURCES AND INTERPRETATION OF THE INTERINDUSTRY TABLE

Like the familiar national income accounts, the interindustry table is a system for recording a nation's economic activity for a given period of time. It shows nearly everything normally included in the national accounts and much more besides. In the interindustry accounts all production of goods and services in Canada has been divided into sixteen classes or "sectors," the names of which appear both along the side and across the top of Table 71. These represent the same condensation of the 1949 forty-two-sector table as that employed in Chapter 4.[1]

The final demand columns 19 through 23 — personal consumption, gross investment except inventories, change in inventories, government purchases of goods and services, and exports — are taken from Chapter 10 through 13 of this study where they were originally estimated.[2]

[1] The parent document is Canada, DBS, *The Inter-Industry Flow of Goods and Services, Canada, 1949,* Reference Paper No. 72 (Ottawa, 1956); see also J. A. Sawyer, "The Measurement of Inter-Industry Relationship in Canada," *CJEPS,* 21:480–497 (November 1955). Much of the work of this study was done before publication of Reference Paper No. 72, and the authors are heavily indebted to Mr. Sawyer for making available numerous preliminary estimates.

[2] Some minor adjustments have been performed on the numbers actually appearing in those chapters — adjustments having only procedural importance. In the consumption column, reallocation have been made to allow for two things: (1) a correction of the handling of exports and imports of tourist services; (2) reclassification of certain purchases of services to the industries producing the product serviced. In the export column, commodity exports have been increased by the amount of transport costs from point of production to port.

A word should be said about the logic of handling international trade in the interindustry table. Exports are a "final demand" for goods in the same way as consumption — both remove a portion of the total supply of goods and services available within the economic system. Imports increase this total supply and consequently appear as row 17 in the table, just as if they were a domestic industry. Thus imports which pass directly into final uses are shown as purchased from the "import sector," while imports which are bought by various Canadian industries for further processing appear as inputs into the purchasing sectors. To present imports this way, it was necessary to reallocate the full import forecast of Table 69, where imports are classed by the domestic sector with which they *compete* rather than the one which they *supply*.

One very important trait of the interindustry table is that all flows of goods are valued at purchasers' prices. Thus the forecast figures of $7,748,000,000 for purchases of clothing and household goods for personal consumption is what we foresee as the actual dollar expenditures of consumers on these items. The retail and wholesale gross margins, warehousing costs, and, most important, transportation costs involved in getting these goods to final purchasers appear as an *input* of the sector labeled "Transportation, storage, and trade" into the clothing and household goods industry. The total value of these services appears in the transportation, storage, and trade row (row 14) in the seventh cell — $1,363,000,000. Thus the amount which the transportation, storage, and trade sector sells directly to final consumers is not the total value of the goods it handles, but only of the services it sells directly to the public, such as railroad passenger travel.

A few other special characteristics of the table require mention. The titles of most of the sectors accurately depict the industries included, but one major exception is the inclusion of a number of repair and service industries in the manufacturing sector producing the product they service. Thus automotive garages are included in "metal products industries," radio repairing in "electrical apparatus and supplies," and so forth. Some industries have side lines of dissimilar products which are nonetheless included in the main group, for example, the value of timber cut from farm woodlots is included in the agricultural sector rather than in forestry. In some cases, however, the more desirable practice has

Table 71. Interindustry flow of goods and services, Canada, 1970ª (millions of 1955 dollars).

	1. Agriculture	2. Forestry	3. Fishing, hunting, trapping	4. Coal, crude petroleum, gas	5. Other mining and quarrying	6. Food, beverage, tobacco	7. Clothing and household goods	8. Forest products	9. Metal products	10. Electrical apparatus and supplies	11. Mineral products	12. Miscellaneous manufactures
1. Agriculture	95	18	0	0	1	3,083	42	61	0	0	90	0
2. Forestry	1	0	0	0	0	0	0	979	1	0	0	0
3. Fishing, hunting, trapping	0	0	3	0	0	183	7	0	0	0	0	0
4. Coal, crude petroleum, gas	0	0	0	3	51	13	6	27	13	0	260	1
5. Other mining and quarrying	2	0	0	0	45	1	26	14	295	30	63	5
6. Food, beverage, tobacco	424	0	0	0	0	1,001	25	1	0	0	43	1
7. Clothing, household goods	42	4	10	0	3	33	1,191	30	14	32	7	94
8. Forest products	10	1	3	0	50	230	95	556	95	32	80	272
9. Metal products	86	71	10	50	134	235	72	110	1,782	266	112	25
10. Electric apparatus, supplies	0	0	0	0	27	13	10	34	144	128	29	6
11. Mineral products	407	44	16	8	122	234	60	118	281	43	447	133
12. Misc. manufacturing	33	0	6	3	8	46	38	12	128	17	30	114
13. Construction	62	15	0	16	43	30	18	35	65	9	24	8
14. Transport, storage, trade	675	12	34	457	240	1,491	1,363	645	1,743	574	1,096	446
15. Communication, etc.	396	7	4	33	155	191	68	179	164	33	130	61
16. Other service industries	1	0	0	2	16	229	56	50	97	41	121	63
17. Imports	48	1	4	2	181	679	595	157	1,084	290	337	211
18. Unallocated	50	194	26	16	202	334	190	294	664	195	237	239
19. Total intermediate input	2,332	367	116	574	1,278	8,026	3,862	3,302	6,630	1,690	3,106	1,679
20. Total primary input	3,435	747	213	468	1,918	2,961	2,688	1,850	4,091	1,152	2,875	1,292
21. Total input	5,767	1,114	329	1,042	3,196	10,987	6,550	5,152	10,721	2,842	5,981	2,971

ª Horizontal totals may not add exactly because of rounding errors. The figure "0" indicates amounts less than $500,000.
b The peculiar entry of − $410,000,000 in the personal consumption column is an offset for estimated 1970 expenditures of foreign tourists

	13.	14.	15.	16.	17.	18.	19.	20.	21.	22.	23.	24.	25.
	Construction	Transportation, storage, trade	Communication, Finance, etc.	Other services	Unallocated	Total intermediate output	Personal consumption	Gross investment	Change in inventories	Government purchases	Exports	Total final output	Total output
1. Agriculture	0	29	12	147	274	3,854	1,165	19	0	78	652	1,914	5,767
2. Forestry	36	0	0	0	0	1,017	0	0	45	0	54	99	1,114
3. Fishing, hunting, trapping	0	1	0	6	0	200	25	9	0	0	105	130	329
4. Coal, crude petroleum, gas	5	66	122	20	15	602	125	0	15	0	301	441	1,042
5. Other mining, quarrying	87	4	0	3	21	600	0	0	5	0	2,590	2,595	3,196
6. Food, beverage, tobacco	0	71	0	896	112	2,574	7,748	0	135	0	530	8,413	10,937
7. Clothing, household goods	8	83	29	86	320	2,046	4,331	96	52	7	18	4,504	6,550
8. Forest products	941	153	26	61	208	2,813	237	19	43	0	2,040	2,339	5,152
9. Metal products	1,663	394	43	310	382	5,745	2,463	1,755	101	124	533	4,976	10,721
10. Electric apparatus, supplies	522	146	58	33	36	1,186	1,023	524	25	26	58	1,656	2,842
11. Mineral products	1,099	417	177	273	130	4,009	1,596	5	42	0	329	1,972	5,981
12. Misc. manufacturing	65	292	93	673	95	1,651	872	53	11	20	364	1,320	2,971
13. Construction	8	446	681	548	0	2,008	0	5,881	35	1,186	0	7,102	9,110
14. Transport, storage, trade	76	258	90	226	526	9,952	1,543	58	340	6	264	2,211	12,167
15. Communication, etc.	154	887	884	521	269	4,136	4,303	0	5	46	10	4,364	8,500
16. Other service industries	93	252	150	307	0	1,478	4,410	0	5	5,025	5	9,445	10,921
17. Imports	308	299	15	98	801	5,110	1,690	1,327	0	0	0	3,017	8,128
18. Unallocated	506	11	401	55	0	3,614	−410[b]	0	0	0	410	0	3,612
19. Total intermediate input	5,571	3,809	2,785	4,263	3,189	—	—	—	—	—	—	—	48,381[c]
20. Total primary input	3,537	8,358	5,715	6,658	423	—	—	—	—	—	—	—	—
21. Total input	9,108	12,167	8,500	10,921	3,612	—	31,121	9,737	859	6,518	8,263	56,498	—

[c] This figure should equal the total of the final demand columns minus imports. Actually the latter total — $56,498,000,000 minus $8,128,000,000 — falls short by $11,000,000, a measure of the rounding errors present in the table.
Source: See text.

been followed of including in a given sector all *activities* of that type, rather than just all *establishments* primarily engaged in that activity. An important example is the construction sector (row and column 13), which takes into account not just construction contractors but the operations of all firms which use their own employees on construction projects. Some 1949 inputs and outputs could not be allocated by the Dominion Bureau of Statistics to any industrial sector; these are responsible for the "unallocated" row and column in Table 71.

The process by which the Canadian interindustry table for 1949 sired our forecast of the 1970 interindustry structure was a fairly complicated one. Our goal was to work backwards from the forecasts of final demand developed in the four preceding chapters to the total output required from each sector to supply this final demand, and then to record the interindustry transactions necessary to yield such a set of total outputs. The first step was to condense the Bureau of Statistics 1949 table to the sixteen-sector version desired for this study and to derive the matrix of structural coefficients, which relates each sector's individual inputs to its total output. From this structural matrix one can calculate the final demand implied by any total output pattern for the economy. But our desire was to work in the opposite direction — from an estimate of the level of final demand to the required total outputs. Hence, the inverse of this 1949 structural matrix was calculated.[3]

Now the intended use of this inverse was for forecasting certain features of the Canadian economy in 1970. But the inverse represents a measurement of the Canadian economy in 1949, a measurement made under some special assumptions. It is necessary to ask whether the 1949 inverse coefficients could be expected to remain stable over time, and, if not, whether any discernible laws might govern their rates of change. Both theory and fact shed considerable light on these questions. Changes in these coefficients could theoretically stem from four causes: (1) changes in technology; (2) changes in the relative prices of inputs; (3) changes in the scale of production; (4) changes in the commodity composition of a sector's output.[4] Changing tech-

[3] More exactly, the inverse of the corresponding Leontief matrix, or $(I - A)^{-1}$ where A is the matrix of structural coefficients.

[4] U.S., Mutual Security Agency, Special Mission to Italy for Economic Co-

nology of production alters the combination of inputs used in some productive process, whether it involves creating an entirely new product or just cutting the cost of producing an existing one. Changing relative prices of the different factors of production alter our "coefficients" because the latter are expressed in value terms; if all inputs used by a firm are kept constant in *physical* terms when wages — the price of labor — rise, the other (non-labor) coefficients will all drop and the share of total costs paid to labor will rise. Changing levels of total production of some commodity may change the input coefficients because a larger scale of operations frequently allows use of different technique. Finally, since the output of each sector in our highly condensed interindustry table is really a collection of different goods and services, changes in the composition of this bundle will change input coefficients even if all "technical" conditions and factor prices stay constant.

Fortunately, enough use has been made of interindustry methodology to allow one to guess the threat these sources of possible change pose to its use for long-range forecasting. The last-mentioned source of change of the coefficients — variations in a sector's product-mix — has been explored by trying different aggregations on actual interindustry tables and observing their effect on the predictions generated. For reasons not wholly clear yet, these effects on the predictions are surprisingly small.[5] Assessing the actual size of changes of the other sorts can come only from looking at the behavior of observed coefficients over time. No check is possible on the Canadian economy itself, since an interindustry table exists only for the year 1949. For the United States, however, interindustry studies of varying degrees of refinement go back to 1919, and sundry evidence exists for other countries. An Australian study showed the major interindustry transactions bear quite stable relations to total output of the purchasing sector. And several studies of interindustry coefficients for individual industries have shown that they are subject to

---

operation, *The Growth and Structure of the Italian Economy* (Rome, 1953), pp. 15–20.

[5] T. M. Whitin and O. Morgenstern, untitled note in Conference on Research in Income and Wealth, *Input-Output Analysis: An Appraisal, Studies in Income and Wealth, Volume Eighteen* (Princeton, 1955), pp. 128–135.

short-run variations due to the business cycle, but remain fairly stable in the long run.[6]

A test was run on the United States data to discover how much the structural coefficients — the set of figures giving "dollars' worth of input per dollar's worth of total output" — varied on the average over decade intervals. Between 1929 and 1939 these average changes were quite large. The average input coefficient from the petroleum and natural gas industry into all other industries rose 66 per cent, while that of lumber and paper fell 29 per cent. All other average changes for United States sectors fell within this range.[7] Such rates of change as 66 per cent in a decade look quite frightening, but some hope appears when one notes which sectors enjoyed increased importance as inputs into other industries and which ones declined. The changes which took place by 1939 were surely just about what one would have expected looking forward from 1929. It certainly would have been clear to a person making predictions in 1929 that petroleum, electricity, nonferrous metals, and nonmetallic minerals were growing relatively more important as industrial inputs, and that agriculture and lumber were declining. That the trends in these coefficients for the United States in the interwar period so nearly approximated the input substitutions known to be occurring is quite encouraging. If a United States forecaster in 1929 had correctly predicted the 1939 final demand, and if he had made these obvious adjustments in the 1929 interindustry coefficients and then calculated the 1939 total outputs, he would probably not have been wrong by more than 10 per cent for any major sector.

Hence, an attempt was made at forecasting changes in the Canadian coefficients to 1970, using three different sorts of evidence. Historic trends in the coefficients of the United States interindustry tables for 1919, 1929, and 1939 were studied. Differences between the coefficients of the Canadian economy in 1949 and the United States in 1947[8] were examined (where the in-

[6] B. Cameron, "The Production Function in Leontief Models," *Review of Economic Studies*, 20:62–69 (1952–53); A. Phillips, "The Variation of Technical Coefficients in the Antifriction Bearing Industry," *Econometrica*, 23:432–441 (October 1955).

[7] W. W. Leontief, "Structural Change," in *Studies in the Structure of the American Economy* (New York, 1953), pp. 17–52. All of the following comments refer to coefficients of a highly condensed thirteen-sector table.

[8] Comparable tables for the United States 1919, 1929, and 1939 appear in Leontief, pp. 24–26; for 1947, see W. D. Evans and M. Hoffenberg, "The Inter-

Table 72.   Total 1970 output required in Canada to meet demand, estimated by actual production coefficients for 1949 and by forecast for 1970 (millions of 1955 dollars).

	Total output required in 1970		Percentage by which 1949 estimate exceeds 1970 estimate
Sector	using 1949 coefficients	using 1970 coefficients	
2. Forestry	1,298	1,114	16.5
8. Forest products industries	5,510	5,152	6.9
14. Transportation, storage, trade	12,740	12,167	4.7
4. Coal mining, crude petroleum, natural gas	1,083	1,042	3.9
1. Agriculture	5,991	5,767	3.9
13. Construction	9,189	9,110	0.9
7. Clothing and household goods industries	6,552	6,550	0.0
3. Fishing, hunting, trapping	329	329	0.0
16. Other service industries	10,919	10,921	0.0
18. Unallocated	3,610	3,612	−0.1
6. Food, beverage, and tobacco industries	10,943	10,987	−0.4
5. Other mining and quarrying industries	3,185	3,196	−0.4
12. Miscellaneous manufacturing industries	2,951	2,971	−0.7
9. Metal products industries	10,476	10,721	−2.3
11. Mineral products industries	5,740	5,981	−4.0
15. Communication, finance, insurance, real estate, public utility operation	8,143	8,500	−4.2
10. Electrical apparatus and supplies industry	2,601	2,842	−8.5

Source: See text, p. 416.

dustry groupings were comparable) on the hypothesis that the latter might suggest structural trends which would be visible in the Canadian economy as it grows more industrialized. The third source was general knowledge about current trends in the relative importance of various intermediate goods, including the material on future imports collected for Chapter 13. Examples of changes predictable in this way are larger inputs of electric power into agriculture, petroleum into transportation, mineral products into construction, smaller inputs of lumber into construction, coal into

industry Relations Study for 1947," *RES*, 34:97–142 (May 1952), especially Table 5, following p. 142.

transportation, and so forth — all interpreted as changing percentages of total output of the purchasing sector. Table 72 shows the total effect of these changes. It indicates what total outputs would be necessary to produce our forecast 1970 bill of final demand under two sets of circumstances: (1) the same interindustry coefficients hold for 1970 as for 1949; (2) production coefficients change as forecast by 1970. The third column of the table shows the percentage (plus or minus) by which total output would have to be increased to supply the same final demand were the 1949 coefficients to hold in 1970 instead of the set actually forecast. The interindustry sectors are ranked in the order of these percentages.

The changes we foresee in the interindustry coefficients will in this sense make the greatest saving in forestry and forest products and will place relatively heavier demands upon electrical apparatus and supplies and the communication, finance, insurance, real estate, and public utilities sector. The transportation, storage, and trade sector also will have decreased importance in the technical structure of production.

CONSISTENCY OF PROJECTIONS

This section adds few substantive facts to our outlook for the Canadian economy in 1970, but it was important to the research underlying this outlook. The justification for presenting estimates covering the *whole* of the Canadian economy is that we can place some confidence in our estimates for particular sectors only if we can check their consistency with the changes our outlook implies for the rest of the economy. Research on the aggregative aspects of the Canadian economy has been designed throughout to allow as much cross-checking as possible.

Not all of this checking is done through the interindustry table, although this is one of the main uses of interindustry analysis in government statistical collection as well as in economic forecasting.[9] But this chapter is as convenient a place as any to take a general review of the consistency of the estimates in all chapters of this study.

The first check has to do with gross national product and its components. In the *National Accounts,* gross national product (or gross national expenditure) is subject to two separate break-

[9] Sawyer, pp. 480–481.

downs. One breakdown divides this measure of the total flow of final goods and services according to the uses to which it is put — consumption plus gross domestic investment plus government purchases of goods and services plus exports *minus* imports (because imports have been counted in the other categories, although they are not "domestically produced"). The other divides it according to the incomes paid out to the factors of production which create this flow of goods and services. At any step in the productive process these factor payments are called "value added," and so gross national product equals the sum of the "value added" by all economic sectors.

In Chapter 9 of this volume, gross national product was estimated roughly at $48,000,000,000 in 1955 dollars on the basis of labor force and productivity trends. In Chapters 10 through 13 the final demand sectors — consumption, investment, and so forth — were estimated from a wide variety of sources of information. As recorded in Table 71, these final demand sectors add to an implied gross national product as follows:

Personal consumption	$31,121,000,000
Gross investment (excl. inventories)	9,737,000,000
Inventory change	859,000,000
Gov't. purchases of goods, services	6,518,000,000
Exports *minus* imports	135,000,000
	48,370,000,000

The excess of this total over the rounded figure of $48,000,000,-000, less than 1 per cent, is not serious in light of the range of possible error in these projections. Insofar as this excess of the final demand total implies an error in the projections, that error is probably in the consumption sector. As will be seen below, there is some evidence that demand for certain basic consumers' goods has been overestimated. The closeness of the gross national product total derived from productivity and labor force to the sum of the final demand sectors may give comfort in one major way. The latter total represents, in a sense, total decisions to spend on currently produced goods and services. If the final demand-estimated gross national product greatly exceeded or fell short of national capacity output estimated from productivity trends, that is, if the flow of money expenditures grew much faster or slower than did the potential flow of goods and services, this might mean a structural tendency for the price level slowly to rise or fall

Table 73. Output measures for Canada from interindustry table compared with independent estimates from industry studies.

Sector	Output measures (millions of 1955 dollars)		Percentage (2) is of (1) (3)
	Interindustry table (1)	Independent studies (2)	
A. Comparisons of *total output at producers' prices*			
Fishing, hunting, trapping[a]	286	250	87.5
Coal mining, crude petroleum, natural gas	534	2068	387.3
Other mining and quarrying industries	2956	2472	83.6
Food, beverage, and tobacco industries	9496	7000	73.7
Clothing and household goods industries	5187	3412	65.8
Forest products industries	4506	4142	91.9
Metal products industries	8978	9560	106.5
Electrical apparatus and supplies industry	2268	1802	79.5
Mineral products industries	4884	4620	94.6
Miscellaneous manufacturing industries	2526	2210	87.5
Construction	9034	9495	105.1
B. Comparisons of *net value added*			
Transportation, storage, trade	8358	7977[b]	95.4
Other service industries	6658	6401	97.6

[a] The independent estimate from Chapter 17 covers only fishing, but since hunting and trapping is extremely small, the independent estimate revised to include it would just about equal the interindustry table figure.

[b] Chapter 19 gives the figure $8,577,000,000 for transportation, storage, trade, and communication, and no careful forecast of communication has been made independently. It should be roughly $600,000,000 in 1970, giving rise to the figure $7,977,000,000 for an independent estimate for transportation, storage, and trade.

Source: (1) Based on Table 71; (2) See Chapters 16–19.

apart from changes in national monetary policy or any other factors affecting the price level. (Of course, such a discrepancy also might mean an error in our estimation of the trends. This is the more likely, if less interesting, possibility.) Since the GNP estimates by the two methods are so nearly in agreement, no trend is foreseen either toward chronic unemployment problems or secular "demand-pull" inflation.

A second check on the consistency of projections in this report uses the interindustry table directly. The last column of Table 71, the total outputs by interindustry sector, can be compared to many of the total outputs forecast in the individual industry studies of Chapters 15 through 19. The comparison appears in Table 73. These independent output forecasts become comparable when the total outputs of the interindustry table are converted from the prices purchasers pay to the prices producers receive (that is, when distribution costs are removed). This has been done to the figures in Column (1). Column (2) shows the independent estimates from succeeding chapters, and column (3) converts them to percentages of the interindustry table total outputs. For the services sectors this kind of comparison could not be used. The forecasts in Chapter 19 are on the basis of value added, rather than value of service which is expressed in the interindustry table. (For trade, this latter would be equivalent to the gross margin of all distribution facilities.) However, row 20 in Table 71, the "primary input" row of the interindustry table, gives the "value added" for all interindustry sectors, so the two "value added" figures can be compared. For sector 15 — communication, finance, insurance, real estate, and public utility operation — no comparison is possible because the interindustry sector includes imputed rent on all housing, a datum not estimated elsewhere in this study. No comparison is possible for forestry either, because gross output is estimated only in physical terms for primary woods operations in Chapter 17.

The only stupendous discrepancy between the two sets of estimates is in sector 4, coal mining, crude petroleum, and natural gas. Unquestionably the estimate deriving from the interindustry table is too low, because the year 1949 which the original interindustry table covers passed before the prairie boom in petroleum and natural gas was well under way, and the revision of the coefficients made to allow for this was grossly inadequate. The information in Chapter 16 on fuels should be taken as correct on this sector. If the interindustry table were revised to take this into account, the following are the major changes which would have to be made: (1) the coefficients for the coal mining, crude petroleum, natural gas *row* would all have to be raised markedly; (2) the fraction primary input constitutes of total input would be cut slightly for most sectors (because the greater availability of fuels will allow producers to substitute *energy* for *labor* in

Table 74. Labor requirements in Canada by industry, and estimated total labor force[a], in 1970.

Sector	Requirements[b]
Agriculture	708,000
Forestry	154,500
Fishing, hunting, trapping	50,000
Coal mining, crude petroleum, natural gas	20,600
Other mining and quarrying industries	161,800
Food, beverage, and tobacco industries	265,000
Clothing and household goods industries	418,500
Forest products industries	236,500
Metal products industries	558,700
Electrical apparatus and supplies industry	56,000
Mineral products industries	135,700
Miscellaneous manufacturing industries	181,000
Construction	877,100
Transportation, storage, trade	2,028,000
Communications, finance, insurance, real estate, public utility operation	433,000
Other service industries	1,571,000
Total	7,855,4co
Labor force forecast from Chapter 9	7,230,000

[a] In the 1949 interindustry table all wage payments were allocated to the industries listed here; consequently, no "unallocated" labor category is needed.

[b] All sectors but agriculture in terms of average employment.

Source: For requirements, see Chapters 15–19. For estimated total labor force, see Table 34.

production); (3) the input coefficients into the coal mining, crude petroleum, and natural gas *column* probably would require drastic changes, especially from the hard goods industries, because of the much greater mechanization of the total fuels sector as coal mining declines in importance.

Another serious discrepancy between the interindustry table and the independent industries studies appears for the two big consumer goods sectors — food, beverages, and tobacco, and clothing and household goods. The independent estimates are much too low. The differences came about because of the final demand projections embodied in the interindustry table. On the basis of recent signs of rapidly rising consumer demand for these products in both Canada and the United States, a trend toward greater prominence of these categories in consumers' budgets was forecast. This does not agree with longer-run trends in the domestic disappearance of these categories when plotted against personal disposable income, as in the independent estimates. It is not possible to settle which interpretation is right. Many American economists are convinced that product innovation is definitely shifting consumer budgets in the long run toward these goods, yet the statistical evidence does not yet prove this unambiguously. The issue must remain in doubt.

Otherwise, the independent estimates of total output agree relatively well with those coming from the interindustry table, and no further discussion of them will be presented.

A third reconciliation remains — that of the total labor force forecast in Chapter 9 against the labor requirements forecast for each separate industry in Chapters 15 through 19. Table 74 summarizes employment requirements by interindustry sector. On the face of it, the labor force requirements estimated sector by sector seriously exceed the estimated total 1970 labor force. If both the estimated total labor force (derived from the population projection) and the requirements for each industry (based on that industry's output and productivity trends) are correct, this would mean that our whole gross national product estimate is too high. It is, however, fairly certain that this is not the case. Two major factors bias upward the labor requirements by sector. First, although most of the sectors are properly computed on the basis of average employment (as is the total labor force estimate), the agricultural labor force of 708,000 includes a large number of people — perhaps between 200,000 and 300,000 — who work part of the time in other industries, especially forestry and construction, and are partly double-counted in those occupations. The same may be true for construction if noncontractors using their own labor for construction do not correspondingly subtract it from labor force reported for their main activity. A second bias upward in the labor requirements results from estimated rates of productivity growth by industry being too low. Particularly suspect in this regard are trade, construction, forest products, and a number of subcategories of the manufacturing sectors. It should be noted that the productivity growth estimates for each industry were independently reached by studying the poor and sketchy information available. No attempt was made to bring the weighted average of the productivity growth rates into equality with the aggregate productivity growth rate forecast for the nonagricultural portion of the Canadian economy. If we were to revise the whole set of estimates to insure complete internal consistency, this would be the most proper simple way to balance prospective supply of and demand for labor. It would still be far from ideal, though; some of our industry productivity estimates are put forth with considerably more certainty than others. Amending them by an across-the-board increase would be undesirable.

In view of these considerations it does not seem that the gap between labor force and total industry labor requirements seriously threatens to call the gross national product forecast into question. If Canadian labor markets in fact stay tight in future years, low-wage, low-productivity industries such as trade, services, food, and clothing will be hard pressed to attract additional labor. In such a case they might draw more heavily on the marginal elements of the labor force, which in the past have proved very elastic in response to changes in the number of jobs available. These industries would be under pressure to innovate (that is, raise labor productivity). Failing either of these developments, they would have to expand their operations less rapidly than otherwise. This problem of reconciling employment in the tertiary sector with the general outlook for income and employment is taken up from another point of view in Chapter 19.

CANADA'S ECONOMIC STRUCTURE IN 1970

Besides providing a framework for a set of comprehensive checks on the consistency of our predictions, the interindustry table for 1970 can be compared to its 1949 ancestor to measure the growth of various parts of the economy. It can also be manipulated to show how that economic structure will differ if 1970 final demand varies from our forecast.

Table 75 shows the 1949 total output of each sector of the Canadian economy and the 1970 total output which we calculated to be necessary to supply final demand.[10] The third column of the table shows the amount of the difference between the 1949 and 1970 figures, and the fourth column shows what percentage this change is of the 1949 output. The increases, of course, are much larger than those mentioned in other chapters of this report,

---

[10] Recall again that these figures are not in producers' prices, as in the Dominion Bureau of Statistics' *Census of Industry,* but in prices paid by purchasers.

Table 75. Size and composition of growth of total output in Canada by industry, 1949-1970.

Sector	Total output (millions of dollars)			Percentage increase		
	1949[a] (1)	1970[b] (2)	Amount of increase (3)	Total (4)	Due to intermediate demand[e] (5)	Due to final demand[e] (6)
Agriculture	3,103	5,767	2,664	85.9	76.5	9.4
Forestry	450	1,114	664	147.6	128.9	18.7
Fishing, hunting, trapping	131	329	198	151.1	96.9	54.2
Coal mining, crude petroleum, natural gas	367	1,042	675	184.0	104.2	79.8
Other mining and quarrying industries	814	3,196	2,382	341.7	99.5	242.2
Food, beverage and tobacco industries	3,949	10,987	7,038	178.2	41.0	137.2
Clothing and household goods industries	2,450	6,550	4,100	167.3	53.0	114.3
Forest products industries	2,008	5,152	3,144	156.6	87.7	68.9
Metal products industries	3,418	10,721	7,303	213.7	115.4	98.3
Electrical apparatus and supplies industry	641	2,842	2,201	343.3	138.7	204.6
Mineral products industries	1,931	5,981	4,050	209.7	139.5	70.2
Miscellaneous manufacturing industries	893	2,971	2,078	232.6	122.2	110.4
Construction	2,845	9,110	6,265	220.2	44.9	175.3
Transportation, storage, trade	4,492	12,167	7,675	170.9	138.2	32.7
Communication, finance, insurance, real estate, public utility operation	2,829	8,500	5,671	200.5	99.3	101.2
Other service industries	3,709	10,921	7,212	194.4	26.2	168.2
Unallocated	1,300	3,612	2,312	177.8	185.9	−8.1

[e] For a discussion of the assumptions necessary when subtracting column (1) from column (2), see text, p. 424 footnote 11.

[a] Millions of 1949 dollars.

[b] Millions of 1955 dollars.

[c] For the basis of the partitioning between columns (5) and (6), see text, pp. 424-425.

Source: Table 71 and DBS, The Inter-Industry Flow of Goods and Services, Canada, 1949, Reference Paper No. 72 (Ottawa, 1956), Table I.

where the base year from which changes are measured is usually 1954 or 1955.[11] Once again, Canada's growth industries stand out. "Other mining and quarrying," containing nonferrous metals extraction, minerals such as asbestos, and aluminum smelting, will rise nearly three and one-half times by 1970 from the 1949 bench mark. Sector 4, the fuels sector, will nearly triple even in the underestimated forecast of the interindustry table. The forest products industry will grow to one and one-half times its 1949 size on the basis of pulp and paper expansion and despite the relative stability of lumber. Rates of growth in sectors serving mainly the domestic market mirror the rising demands of a high-investment economy. Electrical apparatus and supplies will grow more than three times, while metal products, mineral products, miscellaneous manufactures, and construction will more than double. The growth of these manufacturing and export sectors will promote a near-doubling of the services sectors — the communications and utilities and the "other services" (containing largely government and institutions but also numerous business and community services). The food, clothing, and transportation and trade sectors, bellwethers of the domestic economy, will grow roughly 175 per cent between 1949 and 1970.

The last two columns of Table 75 allocate the percentage growth of total output of each sector to two separate sources. Part of the increase in total output will result from growing final demand; column (6) of the table shows the part of the total percentage growth due to this. The rest will go to serve heavier requirements for the output of each sector as an intermediate good in producing other outputs. Column (5) shows this portion of the total percentage growth. Some sectors will expand much more because of intermediate demand for their product than because of direct

---

[11] In interpreting Tables 75 and 76 it is very important to remember that they compare outputs measured in 1949 dollars with outputs measured in 1955 dollars. Needless to say, it would have been highly desirable to have a price index for each sector to convert its value in 1949 prices to 1955 prices; unfortunately, no such information exists for Canada. Thus the absolute magnitudes of the changes and absolute values of the corresponding percentages are relatively meaningless, as they bundle together both price and quantity changes. One can still compare the percentages with one another if the intersectoral terms of trade shifts in the Canadian economy 1949–1955 were small relative to the real output changes foreseen 1949–1970. This is certainly the case, so that at least the impure of heart can draw rough conclusions from the relative size of these percentages.

Table 76. Growth of total output and of final demand in Canada by interindustry sector, 1949 to 1970, expressed as percentages.

Sector	Per cent of increase	
	Total output (1)	Final demand (2)
1. Agriculture	85.9	18.0
2. Forestry	147.6	578.1[a]
3. Fishing, hunting, trapping	151.1	119.5
4. Coal mining, crude petroleum, natural gas	184.0	197.4
5. Other mining and quarrying industries	341.7	316.7
6. Food, beverage and tobacco industries	178.2	180.9
7. Clothing and household goods industries	167.3	164.4
8. Forest products industries	156.6	144.8
9. Metal products industries	213.7	208.2
10. Electrical apparatus and supplies industry	343.3	381.8
11. Mineral products industries	209.7	219.7
12. Miscellaneous manufacturing industries	232.6	295.3
13. Construction	220.2	235.8
14. Transportation, storage, trade	170.9	198.8
15. Finance, insurance, real estate, public utility operation	200.5	190.8
16. Other service industries	194.4	194.5

[a] This increase appears abnormally large because inventories were sharply reduced in 1949, the base year for the comparison.

Source: (1) taken from Table 75, column (4); (2) computed from Table 71, column (24), and Canada, DBS, *The Inter-Industry Flow of Goods and Services, Canada, 1949*, Reference Paper No. 72 (Ottawa, 1956), Table I.

demand from consumers. Agriculture and forestry are obvious examples of sectors which sell their output not to final consumers but to processors. Less obvious is the fact revealed by the interindustry table that the growth of the metal products and mineral products sectors will be due more to rising intermediate demand than to demand by final users of their products.

Table 76 further illustrates this fact that the growth of final demand for a sector's output and the growth of that total output may be quite unequal. Indeed, they are approximately the same for only five of the sixteen sectors listed. Electrical apparatus and miscellaneous manufactures depend mainly on growth of final demand for their expansion, while the primary sectors grow mostly in response to intermediate demand in the domestic market.

Some changes in individual cells of the interindustry table showing intermediate demand are worth noting, especially where

Table 77. Changes in total Canadian outputs required by high consumption or ultra-high investment in 1970.

Sector	Absolute increase in total output for high consumption (millions of 1955 dollars) (1)	Percentage increase in total output for high consumption (2)	Rank by absolute change (3)	Rank by percentage change (4)
Food, beverage, and tobacco industries	298	2.7	1	1
Communication, finance, insurance, real estate, public utility operations	165	2.0	2	4
Clothing and household goods industries	157	2.4	3	2
Other service industries	149	1.4	4	6
Transportation, storage, trade	77	0.6	5	9
Miscellaneous manufacturing industries	31	1.0	6	7
Agriculture	21	2.1	7	3
Coal mining, crude petroleum, natural gas	7	0.6	8	8
Fishing, hunting, trapping	6	1.8	9	5
Mineral products industries	−2	—	10	10
Forestry	−12	−1.1	11	14
Other mining and quarrying industries	−13	−0.4	12	11
Unallocated	−31	−0.9	13	12
Forest products industries	−51	−1.0	14	13
Electrical apparatus and supplies industry	−58	−2.0	15	15
Metal products industries	−235	−2.3	16	16
Construction	−580	−6.4	17	17

Source: (1) calculated from Table 71 by reducing the investment forecast for 1970 by one billion dollars and increasing consumption by the same amount; (2) computed from column (1) and Table 71.

major technological change has been foreseen. For instance, between 1949 and 1970, inputs of metal products into the fuels sector (coal mining, crude petroleum, and natural gas) will increase nearly ten-fold, as will inputs of electrical apparatus and supplies into the transportation, storage, and trade sector. At the other end, inputs of the coal mining and crude petroleum sector into transportation, storage, and trade will increase only 20 per cent (diesel fuel is a product of the mineral products sector) and inputs of transportation, storage, and trade into agriculture will rise a mere 30 per cent.

Throughout this volume, most forecasts have been stated as a single number rather than a *range* of possible outcomes. The reason for this was explained in Chapter 1. Some experimentation is possible with the interindustry table, however, for we can vary the forecast of final demand and check the resulting changes in the predicted set of total outputs for the interindustry sectors. For instance, in Chapter 11, in discussing investment in Canada, we noted that our forecast is for a high-investment economy. We might wonder what changes in the outputs of the various sectors would occur if consumption should claim a larger portion of gross national product. Or, alternatively, we might wonder how the economy would look if investment were even higher than forecast. Table 77 gives a partial answer to these questions. Suppose that our investment forecast were reduced by one billion dollars (each sector dropping proportionally) while consumption increased to one billion more than forecast. Table 77 ranks the interindustry sectors both according to which total outputs would increase the most *percentagewise* because of this change, and by order of the *absolute* amount (measured in 1970 dollars) of the hypothetical increases. The absolute ranking in particular shows that it is consumer goods and services' industries which would benefit, construction and investment goods products which would suffer in a high consumption economy. Table 77, like a railroad time table, can be read up as well as down. If we do this, and change the signs on all numbers so that minuses becomes pluses and vice versa, we have a table showing which industries would be more prominent in an ultra-high investment economy, such as might result from a boom period or heavy defense spending. Heavier demands would be made

Table 78. Changes in total Canadian outputs required by a low-export or high-export economy in 1970.

Sector	Absolute increase in total output for low exports (millions of 1955 dollars) (1)	Percentage increase in total output for low exports (2)	Rank by absolute change (3)	Rank by percentage change (4)
Food, beverage, and tobacco industries	219	2.0	1	2
Clothing and household goods industries	165	2.5	2	1
Other service industries	150	1.4	3	4
Communication, finance, insurance, real estate, public utility operation	139	1.6	4	3
Electrical apparatus and supplies industry	26	0.9	5	5
Transportation, storage, trade	18	0.1	6	7
Agriculture	16	0.6	7	6
Construction	13	0.1	8	8
Mineral products industries	7	0.1	9	9
Metal products industries	5	—	10	10
Miscellaneous manufacturing industries	−5	−0.2	11	11
Fishing, hunting, trapping	−8	−2.4	12	13
Unallocated	−25	−0.7	13	12
Coal mining, crude petroleum, natural gas	−36	−3.6	14	14
Forestry	−57	−5.1	15	15
Forest products industries	−265	−5.2	16	16
Other mining and quarrying industries	−318	−10.0	17	17

Source: (1) calculated from Table 71 by reducing the exports forecast for 1970 by one billion dollars and increasing consumption by the same amount; (2) computed from column (1) and Table 71.

upon construction, the investment goods industries, and forestry and forest products.

Another important characteristic of the final demand forecast of this report is the role of high exports in sustaining the growth of the whole economy. With the interindustry information, we can show how the pattern of total outputs would change if growth should depend upon expansion of the domestic economy supplying high consumption demands, rather than upon strong export demand. Suppose our total export forecast were reduced by one billion dollars (spread proportionally over all sectors) and personal consumption were similarly increased a billion dollars. (In this case, as in the preceding one, *total* final demand is assumed unchanged.) Table 78 shows the change this would produce in total output by interindustry sector, ranked in terms both of percentage and absolute changes. The top part of each list looks similar to the previous case. The consumption goods and domestic services sectors would bulk relatively more important. Five sectors which count on both the domestic and foreign markets for their sales would be relatively unaffected. The dramatic evidence of Canada's dependence on exports appears in the sharp declines Canada's primary sectors would suffer. "Other mining and quarrying" would recede 10 per cent, despite the fact that *total* final demand is being assumed constant in these calculations. Table 78, like its predecessor, can be read up as well as down. Doing this, we can see how the opposite type of transfer of final demand from consumption to exports would dramatically expand all of Canada's primary producing sectors.

Obviously, many other alternative final demand patterns could be thought up and tested this way. These two suffice to give an idea how the total outputs of the various sectors of the Canadian economy would behave under different sorts of general patterns of economic development. Another kind of useful information which interindustry analysis will supply is exact measures of how expansion of final demand for one sector's product will in turn affect that sector's demand for the output of another sector. The answer to any question of this sort is supplied by the coefficients of the inverse matrix. While we shall not present the entire inverse of the revised 1970 structural matrix,[12] Table 79

[12] For the inverse of the 1949 DBS table, see R. E. Caves, "The Inter-Industry Structure of the Canadian Economy," *CJEPS*, 23:330 (August 1957).

Table 79. Intermediate demand for each interindustry sector in Canada (millions of dollars).

Sector (1)	Highest intermediate demand (2)	Second highest intermediate demand (3)
Agriculture	Food, beverages (33)	Other services (5)
Forestry	Forest products (22)	Construction (3)
Fishing, hunting, trapping	Food, beverages (2)	Other services (0.2)
Coal mining, crude petroleum, natural gas	Mineral products (5)	Other mining (2)
Other mining and quarrying industries	Metal products (4)	Construction (2)
Food, beverage, and tobacco industries	Other services (10)	Agriculture (9)
Clothing and household goods industries	Miscellaneous mfg. (6)	Fishing, hunting (5)
Forest products industries	Construction (14)	Miscellaneous mfg. (12)
Metal products industries	Construction (26)	Electrical apparatus (15)
Electrical apparatus and supplies industry	Construction (7)	Metal products (2)
Mineral products industries	Construction (16)	Agriculture (10)
Miscellaneous manufacturing industries	Other services (7)	Transport, storage (3)
Construction	Real estate, etc. (10)	Transport, storage (6)
Transportation, storage, trade	Coal, petroleum (50)	Clothing, household (30)
Communication, finance, insurance, real estate, public utility operation	Agriculture (11)	Transport, storage (10)
Other service industries	Forestry (19)	Forest products (12)

Source: See text for method of calculation.

contains some of the most interesting facts it has to offer. We can interpret Table 79 as follows: if final demand for *some* interindustry sector is to increase by $100,000,000, *intermediate* demand for the output of the sector listed in column (1) will increase the most if that sector is the one listed in column (2), and the next most if it is the one listed in column (3). Thus, if final demand for some sector other than agriculture is to rise by $100,000,000, the intermediate demand for agricultural output will increase most if that sector is food, beverages, and tobacco ($33,000,000), next most if that sector is other services ($5,000,-000). This result for agriculture is rather obvious of course — restaurants are included in "other services." But in many cases, this is not so. The sensitivity of the mineral products industry and the communication, finance group to increases in agricultural output would not be expected *a priori*.

What are some of the more striking conclusions which follow from interindustry analysis? It has clearly supported the general outlook of this report. It has illustrated the dependence of Canada's primary production on export markets and of her domestic hard goods industries on the level of domestic investment. It has confirmed the status of these sets of industries as Canada's main growth prospects. It has shown how technological change may affect the Canadian economy in future years, with rising productivity and excellent supplies of energy sources preventing labor supply limitations from throwing up a serious barrier to rapid growth. It has illustrated the uses of interindustry analysis both as a predictive device itself and as a check on other predictive methods.

15

The Primary Industries: Agriculture[1]

What will be the demand for the products of Canada's farms in 1970? Will Canadian agriculture be readily able to meet this demand, and more? Or will the exodus of factors of production from agriculture have come to a stop and new land be brought into production? Which farming regions will flourish? Which will have to make changes from their present normal output patterns? The present chapter considers these aspects of the demand-supply balance in Canadian agriculture in 1970. It considers both aggregate demand and supply for farm produce and also the prospects for particular products or product groups — wheat, feed grains, hay and forage (including pasture), beef, pork, dairy products, poultry products, potatoes, fruits, vegetables, and tobacco.

DOMESTIC DEMAND FOR FARM PRODUCTS

Enough studies have been made of the determinants of the demand for agricultural output that the methodology is fairly standard. Aggregate demand is determined by the number of persons to be supplied, their purchasing power, and their propensity to spend their incomes for farm products. The demand for particular products, if one seeks accurate forecasts, becomes more complicated. It depends on the same variables as aggregate demand plus the numerous forces affecting consumer choice between various substitutable farm products.

Forecasts of the major determinants of aggregate demand are available from other portions of this study. The 1970 Canadian population projected in Chapter 8 is roughly 21,000,000, a 50 per cent increase over the 14,000,000 Canadians enumerated in the 1951 Census. More precisely, the projected increase from mid-1955

[1] The basic forecasts of Canada's agricultural sector in 1970 appearing in this chapter were originally prepared by Professor David L. MacFarlane of Macdonald College, McGill University, and Professor John D. Black and Mr. John A. Pincus of Harvard University. The present chapter constitutes our revision of a paper by Professors MacFarlane and Black, *The Development of Canadian Agriculture to 1970* (Montreal: Macdonald College, McGill University, 1958).

to mid-1970 is from 15,637,000 to 20,984,000 a growth of 34 per cent. The national income estimates of Chapter 9 imply a disposable income per capita in 1970 of about $1,625, compared to an actual figure of $1,170 in 1955. This increase is about 39 per cent.

How much of the 39 per cent increase in personal disposable income per capita will be spent on food and other farm products? It is a widely accepted view that these expenditures rise much more slowly than personal disposable income. All studies show that high income families spend a smaller portion of their incomes on the necessities of life than low income families. Also it is generally true that as the income of the average family rises a smaller portion of its income goes to providing such necessities. Certain statistics calculated for the United States bear out these generalizations. United States food consumption per capita excluding marketing services had been rising before 1950 at a rate of 0.2 per cent for each 1.0 per cent rise in disposable income per capita.[2] The same rate for the period 1955–1970 would give a 6.5 per cent increase per capita at the rate of income growth foreseen for the United States by the Paley Commission. Applied over a fifteen-year period to the faster growth rate estimated for Canada in the present study, it would indicate a 7.8 per cent increase in food consumption per capita over a fifteen-year period.

Given the extent of the Canadian data, the best strategy is not to calculate directly a figure for Canada corresponding to the general income elasticity of 0.2 for food in the United States. We can, however, test the appropriateness of this measure to the Canadian economy by examining the income elasticities for specific food products calculated for the present study. These computations, appearing in Table 80, were based on 1926–1954 data with the war years 1941–1945 omitted. All data were in the form of annual real per capita figures. The food items listed in the table cover just two-thirds of the Canadian family food budget. If we use the income-elasticity coefficients from the table and weight them by the weights these food categories take in the DBS Consumer Price Index, we get a weighted average income elasticity for these foods of 0.32. The major food items omitted from Table 80 are fresh fruits and vegetables and canned and frozen

[2] U.S. President's Materials Policy Commission, *Resources for Freedom* (Washington, 1952), Vol. V, p. 63.

Table 80.   Income elasticities of demand for selected
Canadian farm products.

Product	Income elasticity
Beef and veal	0.80
Pork	0.60
Poultry	0.84
Eggs	0.35
Cheese	0.59
Fluid milk	0.25
Butter	−0.14
Wheat	−0.15

Source: Based on 1926–1954 data excluding the war years of 1941–1945.

foods, which tend to have an income elasticity at retail higher than 0.5. If these had gone into the weighted average, it certainly would have been around 0.4, representing the income elasticity of demand for all foods at retail. Since the income responsiveness for farm products is usually found to be a little over one-half of that for food at retail, we conclude that the income elasticity of demand for food at the farm level in Canada lies between 0.20 and 0.25, probably closer to the former figure. Applied to the 39 per cent increase foreseen in personal disposable income per capita, Canadian demand for food at the farm level should increase a little over 8 per cent between 1955 and 1970. In conjunction with a 34 per cent increase in population this would give a 45 per cent increase in the total domestic consumption of farm products in 1970.

All of these results are consistent with the more recent United States studies. Rex F. Daly has estimated an income elasticity between 0.20 and 0.25 for the United States on the basis of the Agricultural Marketing Service's index of per capita food consumption. Since this index includes some marketing and processing services, he suggests that his results imply an elasticity of 0.15 at the farm level.[3] This, of course, is less than the figure given above for Canada, but some of Daly's other results easily explain the difference. Daly notes that "some evidence suggests that income elasticities tend to decline at . . . higher income levels and may decline as incomes rise over time." He cites results

[3] Rex F. Daly, "The Long-Run Demand for Farm Products," *Agricultural Economics Research,* 8:78 (July 1956). This article brings together the results of many earlier studies.

giving an elasticity of 0.15 for consumer units in the income range \$2500–\$4000, but an elasticity as high as 0.3 for consumer units receiving \$750–\$1250.[4] Now income per person and per family in Canada is clearly lower than that in the United States, perhaps 30 per cent lower.[5] One would expect the elasticity of food consumption per capita to be higher in Canada, and 0.20 to 0.25 thus seems to be a highly acceptable rough figure.

This increase in the amount of food produced per person of course does not imply increased gluttony among Canadians. The increase is not in calorie intake,[6] but rather in a shift of consumption to more expensive foods — meats, dairy products, eggs, fruits, and vegetables — and away from cereals and potatoes. Nor does this increase reflect the probable trend in the portion of consumer income to be spent on food in the future. The elasticity of demand for food processing services, especially restaurant meals, is very high, which explains why the percentage of United States disposable income spent on food has been about the same since 1940.

We now turn to the problem of forecasting the domestic consumption of major farm products and product groups in 1970. The main resources available for the task are the income elasticities of Table 80 and the population and personal disposable income forecasts previously developed for this study. However, a considerable body of evidence on United States patterns will be drawn upon.[7] Not much argument seems necessary to justify the borrowing of demand elasticities calculated from United States data. Chapter 10 has already shown the similarity between income elasticities in the two countries for major classes of consumer expenditures. Indeed, anyone familiar with the great cultural

[4] Daly, p. 78.

[5] Compare John H. Young, "Comparative Economic Development: Canada and the United States," *AER*, 45:86 (May 1955).

[6] Calorie intake if anything will continue to reflect dietary adjustments toward more sedentary occupations. For a description of this process, see L. E. Drayton, "Food Consumption Trends, Standards and Consumer Preferences," *CJAE*, 5:15–19 (Number 2, 1957).

[7] The Paley Commission report (*Resources for Freedom*, Vol. V, p. 64) contains projections of United States consumption per capita in 1975 of eight product groups and twenty individual products. Since its publication, two other investigations have sought to review and update these projections, the study by Daly previously cited and John D. Black and James T. Bonnen, *A Balanced United States Agricultural in 1965*, National Planning Association Special Report No. 42 (New York, 1956).

similarities between the two countries would probably concede the point without resort to a desk calculator.

Wheat

A simple continuation of the 1925–1955 trend away from wheat in United States diets, when combined with seed and feed uses, would give a 15 per cent reduction in consumption per capita by 1970. But the Canadian situation is clearly different. Human consumption per capita is almost 16 per cent higher in Canada, reflecting largely the lower income level previously noted. However, the rate of decline in consumption per capita for human use (1935–1939 to 1952–1954) has been similar, 18 per cent for Canada and 20 per cent for the United States. The income elasticity for wheat (−0.15) calculated in connection with the present project agrees fairly well with Daly's coefficient for the United States of −0.20. There appears no reason for doubting that the decline will continue for the next decade.

Another difference in the Canadian situation lies in the fact that, far from showing any reduction, the use of wheat for livestock feed has increased. The increase since the 1935–1939 period is about 50 per cent. Farmers have learned the value of wheat for feed, thus overcoming fear of its use. Equally important has been the recent difficulty in marketing wheat as cash grain. (The former trend will be considered in the section of this chapter on feed grains.)

It seems reasonable to take the position of Daly, who assumes a slight flattening out in the rate of decline of human consumption of wheat per capita, arriving at a 10.6 per cent reduction for a twenty-two-year period. This would be about 7 per cent for fifteen years. For 1955, the Canadian estimated consumption per head was 145 pounds of wheat flour or 203 pounds, grain equivalent. Combining the projected decline in consumption per capita with the expected population increase, we anticipate an increase in consumption of 25 per cent. In aggregate terms, the estimated human consumption of wheat, which was 52,000,000 bushels in 1955, is projected at 65,000,000 for 1970.

Because of the sharp rise in the use of wheat for feed, extrapolation from long historical series is not warranted. Over the five crop years 1950–51 to 1954–55, the average amount of wheat used for feed has been 67,000,000 bushels. (See Table 81.) The

Table 81.   Grains used for feed in Canada, 1950–51 to 1954–55.

Crop year	Wheat	Oats	Barley	Corn[a]	Rye	Flaxseed[a]	Tame hay[b]
			(million bushels)				(million tons)
1950–1951	55	300	85	22	5.1	3.2	19.5
1951–1952	77	372	118	22	3.9	3.8	19.1
1952–1953	62	336	108	26	5.2	4.7	19.7
1953–1954	65	325	108	28	6.6	3.3	19.5
1954–1955	74	295	120	28	3.6	3.4	19.9

[a] Quantity crushed during calendar year.
[b] Quantity produced plus imports.
Source: Canada, DBS, *Quarterly Bulletin of Agricultural Statistics;* Canada, DBS, *The Grain Trade of Canada;* Canada, DBS, *Trade of Canada.*

prospect of prices of wheat somewhat lower than those of the past decade would suggest increasing use of wheat for feed. The shifting use pattern and lack of clear-cut trends leaves us without a satisfactory basis for projecting the use of wheat for feed. Hence we make the conservative and simple assumption that the use of wheat for feed will increase in proportion to the increase in the quantity of meat produced between now and 1970. This would mean the use of 98,000,000 bushels of wheat for feed in 1970, and total domestic wheat consumption would account for 163,000,000 bushels.

Feed grains and hay forage

The livestock feed economy of Canada is built around barley, oats, wheat, hay, forage, and pasture. Table 81 shows the size and pattern of the domestic feed economy in terms of domestic disappearance of feed for each of five recent years.

Projection of the domestic demand for feeds requires having in hand estimates of the prospective domestic demand for livestock products — a matter considered below. However, we may refer to these projections now. The indicated increases in demand for the major livestock products are as follows, expressed as percentage increases over 1955–1970: beef and veal, 55; pork, 50; poultry meat, 58; dairy products, 29; eggs, 47. These increases in turn indicate a demand for 16,300,000 tons of feed grains, compared to 11,100,000 tons in 1955.[8] This computation, which gives

[8] In making this estimate a Canadian Federation of Agriculture distribution of feed grains requirements for each livestock product in 1954 was used as a guide. An allowance of grain for horses was also made.

a 47 per cent increase in the demand for feed gains to meet domestic demand for livestock products in 1970, does not allow for any improvement in the efficiency with which feeds will be used. Thus, an adjustment is required. Black and Bonnen have calculated, considering the major classes of livestock together, that by 1965 only ninety-three units of feed will be needed to produce the volume one hundred units produced in 1955.[9] Extending this rate of increase in efficiency to 1970, we would find 10 per cent less feed required to produce one unit of livestock products. Applying this efficiency factor to determine the feed required to secure the projected increase in livestock products, we conclude that only 14,600,000 tons of feed grain rather than 16,300,000 tons would be required. Thus, the demand for feed grains would increase only 32 per cent from 1955 to 1970. If it is assumed that this increase applies equally to all of the grains, then the 1970 requirements would be: wheat, 98,000,000 bushels; oats, 389,000,-000 bushels; barley, 158,000,000 bushels; corn, 38,000,000 bushels; rye, 5,000,000 bushels; flaxseed, 4,000,000 bushels; tame hay, 26,000,000 tons.[10]

Domestic requirements of coarse grains for food and industrial uses in 1955 were 5,000,000 bushels for oats, 200,000 bushels of barley, and 300,000 bushels of rye. These are projected at 7,000,-000 bushels for oats, 300,000 for barley, and 400,000 for rye. In these projections the quantities were assumed to increase in proportion to population, following Daly's method of assuming no change in consumption per capita.[11]

Beef and veal

Due to the rapid growth foreseen for real income per capita in Canada and the high income elasticity for beef, consumption per capita is expected to increase considerably. The income elasticity for beef calculated for the present study is 0.40 at the farm level. Applying this to the 39 per cent increase anticipated in income per capita from 1955 to 1970 gives an increase of 16 per cent in beef consumption per capita. Forecasting the actual amount of

[9] Black and Bonnen, p. 17.
[10] In this study the demand for tame hay has been assumed to increase by the same proportion as grains. This may tend slightly to overstate the demand for hay.
[11] Daly, p. 84.

Table 82. Total consumption of meats in Canada, yearly average for 1935–1939 and annually 1953–1955 (millions of pounds).

Kind of meat	1935–1939	1953	1954	1955
Beef and veal	721	1,076	1,249	1,260
Pork	440	813	815	904
Lamb and mutton	62	35	38	43
Poultry	194	389	437	432

Source: Canada, DBS, *Quarterly Bulletin of Agricultural Statistics,* 49:54–55 (January-March 1956).

beef consumption in 1970 is complicated because of production cycles in the historic data which recently have been about ten years long. The year 1956, with beef cattle numbered at the highest level and farm prices down to around $16 and $17 per hundredweight, may have been the peak of the present cycle. A projection to 1970 would place that year close to the bottom of the cycle, while in 1955, our base year, consumption of beef plus veal was well above the trend line at 81 pounds per capita (seventy-two for beef alone). The 1955 trend value for beef alone was 66 pounds per capita,[12] and we will base our projection on this trend. Thus the 1970 trend value for beef consumption is expected to be 76 pounds per capita. Combining this increase attributable to rising incomes with an expected 34 per cent increase in population, the aggregate demand for beef in 1970 is expected to exceed the 1955 trend level by about 55 per cent.

In order to place the projections of meat consumption in a more meaningful framework, Table 82 sets forth the quantities of the major meats consumed in Canada in each of the years 1953–1955, with a 1935–1939 comparison. (Comparable data are not available for the intervening years.) These will serve as a basis for later analysis of meat production.

Pork

The situation in the United States provides some guidance for projecting consumption per capita of pork products. Consumption per capita rose only slightly over the long period 1925–1940, but it has grown considerably since the year 1940. Canadian con-

[12] The Canadian Federation of Agriculture estimates a "normal" 1955 consumption figure of 65 pounds. Compare their *Brief to the RCCEP,* p. 23.

sumption data extend back only to 1935.[13] During the 1935–1939 period, consumption was 40 pounds per capita. It rose sharply during the war period, reaching 64 pounds per capita in 1943 and 1944. Since that period, consumption reached 58 pounds in 1955, 8 pounds per capita under that of the United States for the same year.

Over the past two hog cycles, Canadian consumption has averaged 58 pounds per capita. This level in relation to consumption over the previous fifteen years furnishes one guide for making a projection. Another guide is the low Canadian total meat consumption (146 pounds in 1955 compared to 161 pounds in the United States); this has significance if one grants the probability that the Canadian pattern is moving toward the American. A third guide is the income elasticity for pork products. The statistical study carried out in connection with this project yielded 0.60 per cent positive response in consumption at retail levels to each 1.0 per cent increase in disposable income. Considering the marketing margin on these products the income elasticity at farm level would be about 0.30. This is a reasonable measure. It is distinctly higher than Daly's 0.20, but this difference is accounted for by comparative income patterns and the leaner quality of Canadian pork which makes it more readily competitive with beef. With incomes rising, consumption per capita will increase about 12 per cent and total pork consumption will rise 50 per cent by 1970.

The foregoing analysis has avoided consideration of the interrelations between pork and beef and effects of the livestock cycle. Actually the low point of the beef cycle is expected in 1970. The effect of this is that actual beef supplies may be more than 100,000,000 pounds less than the projected trend. This "deficit" will be made up by comparable increases in other meats, particularly pork and poultry.[14] Thus the effect of experiencing a low point on the beef cycle will not affect our feed grain analysis materially. The grain not used for beef will be fed to other livestock.

[13] These can be found in Canada, DBS, *Quarterly Bulletin of Agricultural Statistics* (various issues).

[14] This implies or assumes price relations for these products which would bring forth the additional supply.

Poultry meat

Canada has a high consumption rate for poultry meat — 22.5 pounds of hens and chickens and 6.1 pounds of other poultry in 1954, compared to 21 and 5 pounds for these categories in the United States in 1955. There has been a trend toward increased consumption since 1935. However, farm prices have fluctuated erratically with the result that poultry numbers and meat production have varied considerably. A satisfactory guide to changes in consumption per capita in relation to income changes is the income elasticity measure at the retail level prepared for this project. Considering the marketing margin on this product, the elasticity would be about 0.45 at the farm level. This would, in turn, account for an 18 per cent increase in consumption per capita, which along with a 34 per cent increase in population would give a 58 per cent increase in the domestic demand for poultry meat. This result is generally in agreement with the report of the Paley Commission, and it projects a higher rate of growth than the Daly study. This conclusion is reasonable in terms of Canadian consumption habits and income patterns.

Dairy products

Because of the variety of uses of milk, it is difficult to make a single projection of milk consumption to 1970 without estimating the demand for the various products of milk. The consumption level of fluid milk and cream has been fairly constant at a little more than 400 pounds per capita since 1948. This is a substantial reduction from the World War II peak of 464 pounds (1945) coming when fluid milk consumption was subsidized, but compares to the 1935–1941 average of 402 pounds. Drayton finds no clear-cut trend in Canadian fluid milk consumption over the last thirty years, although consumption of other dairy products reveals definite trends.[15] The income elasticity for fluid milk computed for the present study is 0.25 at retail, implying an elasticity a little higher than 0.10 at the farm. A recent study prepared at Macdonald College gives a lower figure at retail of 0.17, corresponding to 0.08 at the farm.

Turning to the United States information, we find Black and

[15] Drayton, p. 17.

Bonnen projecting no increase in milk and cream consumption per capita by 1965.[16] However, Daly's recent study estimates the income elasticity of fluid milk and cream demand at the farm level at 0.12,[17] exactly in agreement with the present investigation. If this measure of response to income change is combined with the projected 39 per cent increase in disposable income per capita, there would be a 4 per cent increase in fluid milk and cream consumption by 1970. Incorporating the 34 per cent rise in population foreseen, the total increase comes out to be 39 per cent. Fluid milk consumption accounts for 30 per cent of total milk production.

Butter prospects are less optimistic if the present price structure is maintained. The long run trend in butter consumption shows a steady decline from a prewar average of about 31 pounds per capita to less than 21 pounds per capita in 1955. However, one should remember that the substitution of margarine for butter has largely run its course. With the introduction of margarine in 1949, butter consumption per capita fell almost immediately by nearly 18 per cent. In subsequent years, the use of margarine has increased at the average rate of 2.3 per cent annually. Margarine appears to have been displacing shortening and other fats about as much as it has butter.

The statistical study of the income elasticity for butter yielded a measure of —0.14. This would indicate a decline of 5 per cent, or 1 pound per capita, by 1970. However, since margarine is relatively high-priced in Canada compared with the United States, prices are likely to come more closely into line and lead to a further decline in butter consumption. This is placed at an additional 2 pounds per capita. Thus consumption of 18 pounds per capita is projected for 1970. With a population of 21,000,000 in that year total butter consumption would be 378,000,000 pounds compared to about 320,000,000 pounds in 1955.

Combining the results for the various dairy products we have considered and making arbitrary estimates for the 20 per cent of milk uses not discussed results in a projected required output of milk in 1970 of 22,400,000,000 pounds. In 1955, production was 17,300,000,000 pounds.

[16] Black and Bonnen, p. 23.
[17] Daly, p. 80, Table 2.

Eggs

There was a fairly steady growth of egg consumption in Canada from 1935–1939 until 1947, with consumption rising from 246 to 289 eggs per capita. Since that date there has been little increase in consumption, which was 293 eggs per capita in 1955. This level is far below the corresponding United States figure of 366. Thus the evidence is conflicting, but the response of egg consumption to increasing income in Canada is apparently small. The statistical study of the present investigation yielded an elasticity of .35 at retail, which would be about 0.25 at the farm level. This is in fairly close agreement with Daly's work.[18] The elasticity estimate applied to the projected 39 per cent increase in income would indicate a 10 per cent increase in consumption per capita due to income change. Total demand for eggs, then should rise by about 47 per cent. This approach involving income elasticity yields a result lying between a simple extrapolation from 1935 and one from 1947.

Potatoes

Consumption of potatoes per capita fell from 200 pounds in the 1935–1939 period to a level of 150 pounds by 1952–1954. This compares with a decline from 144 pounds in 1925–1929 to 101 pounds in 1955 in the United States. Daly estimates an income elasticity for potatoes of −0.25. Applying this to Canada, consumption per capita would decline by 1970 by 10 per cent to 135 pounds, considering the 39 per cent rise in disposable income per capita. However, in the aggregate there would be an increase of 21 per cent in the total consumption of potatoes due to the 34 per cent increase in population.

Tobacco

The demand for tobacco in Canada is measured by the withdrawal of the product for manufacture. In the 1954–55 crop year ending September 30 these withdrawals were: flue-cured, 95,000,-000 pounds; cigar, 6,000,000 pounds; dark, 1,000,000 pounds; burley, 6,000,000 pounds. The total 108,000,000 pounds indicates

---

[18] Daly's figure (p. 80) is 0.15. On Canadian patterns, compare Drayton, pp. 17, 20.

Table 83.   Rates of growth of consumption in Canada, minor agricultural
products, 1955–1970.

| Product | Percentage increase in consumption, 1955 to 1970 | |
	Per capita	Total
Fresh vegetables	9.5	47
Processed vegetables	16.5	56
Apples	− 2.4	31
Lamb and mutton	15.0	54
Citrus fruits	30.0	74
Other fruits (excluding apples)	4.5	40
Sugar	1.0	36
Cotton	− 6.3	26

Source: Percentages calculated from forecasts described in text and historic
data from Canada, DBS, *Quarterly Bulletin of Agricultural Statistics* (various issues)

a consumption level of 7 pounds per capita. This compares with
12 pounds in the United States.

For a number of reasons a fairly substantial increase in tobacco consumption seems likely for Canada. First, the difference
between Canadian and American rates of consumption seems
largely due to income differences, implying a movement of Canadian consumption toward the higher United States figure. Second,
while Canadian population will grow 34 per cent between 1955
and 1970, population of smoking age will grow much faster (43
per cent) because of the abnormally large portion of children in
the population at the earlier date. Third, cigarette consumption
seems to have recovered from the initial shock of medical warnings and has continued its growth in both Canada and the United
States, and neither government seems prone to act to protect its
citizens. Daly's estimate yields a 19 per cent increase in consumption per capita over the twenty-two-year period from 1953
to 1975.[19] Canadian evidence seems to warrant forecasting this
same increase over a fifteen-year period. Allowing for population
growth, total 1970 tobacco consumption will be 54 per cent over
the 1955 level.

Miscellaneous products

Under this heading we list several minor food products grown
in Canada and several imported agricultural commodities. Rates

[19] Daly, p. 84.

of increase in consumption per capita in all cases are those utilized in *Resources for Freedom,* the report of the United States President's Materials Policy Commission. The percentage changes in per capita and total consumption of these commodities foreseen for the 1955–1970 period appear in Table 83. Not included in the table are several Canadian nonfood farm products about which considerable uncertainty exists. During the period 1953–1955, forest products, flax, and furs contributed respectively $84,000,000; $26,000,000; and $13,000,000 to cash farm income. Furs would seem most responsive to income changes, having an income elasticity of perhaps 1 at the farm level. The influence of "style" and synthetic furs on this demand, however, renders any projection most uncertain. Farm-produced forest products go chiefly into newsprint production, which also has a high response to income changes. Lumping these nonfood farm products into a single group, and including tobacco consumption to get a figure covering all the major nonfood commodities produced on Canadian farms, we can estimate a 20 to 30 per cent increase in consumption per capita between 1955 and 1970, implying a 60 to 75 per cent increase in total consumption.

Total domestic demand

We can recapitulate these projections of domestic demand for Canadian farm products by calculating a weighted figure for the whole group. For nonfood products a total increase of 60 to 75 per cent has just been indicated. The increase for the range of farm products used as food is likely to be around 45 per cent. Finally, combining these figures by a reasonable weighting procedure, we estimate a 46 per cent increase in the domestic demand for products of agricultural origin.

EXPORT DEMAND FOR FARM PRODUCTS

The export demand for farm products of a country is difficult to project at any time. It is particularly difficult for a country such as Canada and a time such as the present. Most of Canada's agricultural exports compete directly in world markets with the products of numerous other countries. Furthermore, both exporting and importing countries attempt to sway the working of market forces by comprehensive agricultural programs. How long and how earnestly they will combat the principle of comparative

advantage is even more difficult to foretell than what will happen
to the pattern of comparative advantage itself.

Wheat

Forecasting Canada's major agricultural export encounters all
of the difficulties just mentioned. All of the countries which offer
major markets for Canada's wheat are striving to come nearer to
domestic self-sufficiency through various domestic support
schemes. In 1954 the International Wheat Council collected
figures on the prices at which domestic wheat was supported by
major European countries. These ranged, in terms of United
States dollars per bushel, from a low of $2.21 for Sweden to $4.04
for Finland. The figure for the United Kingdom was a relatively
modest $2.31. Actions by other exporters have no less significance
for Canadian wheat sales abroad. The evidence is fairly clear that
United States surplus wheat disposal schemes have recently
taken noticeable cuts out of normal Canadian wheat markets.
The International Wheat Agreement has sought to bring some
order out of this chaos, though with only modest success. These
arrangements, which aim to bring some stability to prices and
market shares, covered only about half of world wheat trade
under the 1953–54 to 1955–56 agreement; only 35 to 40 per cent
is covered by the current 1956–57 to 1959–60 pact. Exporting
countries accounting for 90 per cent of all wheat exports are now
signatories of the agreement, but it is questionable how much
effective moral suasion this can exert against disposal methods
inconsistent with the agreement.

The normal geographic distribution of Canada's wheat exports
is critically important to assessing their future. The main market
for Canadian wheat is the United Kingdom, which normally
takes one-third to one-half of Canada's exports and secures from
Canada 60 to 80 per cent of her total imports.[20] This market
exists not out of Commonwealth loyalties but because the British
milling and baking trade requires and is geared to use Canadian
wheat. The bread of the United Kingdom is very different from
that consumed in North America and is a type which requires the
special high protein qualities of Canadian wheat. Thus Canadian
wheat is largely noncompetitive with that of the other major ex-

---

[20] For information on the distribution of Canada's grain exports in recent
years, see Canada, DBS, *The Grain Trade of Canada, 1954–55,* pp. 93–95.

porters, although the Canadians fear that this situation may not be permanent. Canada has less firm but still substantial markets on the Continent in Belgium, the Netherlands, Switzerland, and West Germany. These and other European countries come closer to being self-sufficient in wheat, and Canadian wheat has much less of the advantages of a differentiated product.

Since Canada's exports of wheat go and will continue to go predominantly to the United Kingdom and western European countries, it is necessary to make projections of the population and income changes which may control wheat consumption in these countries in 1970. The 1955 population of European countries which represent Canada's most important present and potential market was 310,000,000.[21] This population is projected to be 360,000,000 in 1970.[22] While disposable income per capita is likely to increase by 25 to 30 per cent between 1955 and 1970, this will have little or no effect on the consumption of wheat. The leveling off or even slight decline in consumption per capita which began on this continent two or three decades ago is beginning to show up in European countries. Thus it seems reasonable to conclude that consumption per capita may do no better than to hold present levels. The implied zero response to income changes compares with −0.15 for Canada and −0.20 for the United States. Thus the total demand for wheat in western European countries will increase between 1955 and 1970 only in proportion to population, or by 16 per cent. On the basis of these estimates, it seems reasonable to expect that aggregate disappearance (production plus net imports) in Canada's European market will rise to 1,940,000,-000 bushels in 1970 from an average of 1,647,000,000 bushels in 1950–51 to 1954–55.

Determining the level of imports requires an appraisal of potential production in these countries. In the first half of the 1950's, production held an average level of 1,203,000,000 bushels and net imports, 444,000,000 bushels. Considering the relative advantage of producing livestock rather than grains in Europe, we project stable acreage in these countries at the level of recent

[21] United Kingdom, France, West Germany, Italy, Switzerland, Spain, Portugal, Netherlands, Belgium and Luxembourg, Norway, Denmark, Sweden, Ireland, Yugoslavia, Austria, Greece, and Finland.
[22] Based on estimates in United Nations, Department of Economic and Social Affairs, *The Determinants and Consequences of Population Trends* (New York, 1953), p. 153.

years. However, on the basis of recent observation it is reasonable to expect an increase in yields of 2 or 3 bushels per acre over the period 1955–1970. An extra 2.5 bushels per acre would bring production to a level of 1,341,000,000 bushels in 1970 and indicate a net import of 569,000,000 bushels in that year.

Over the past five years Canada has provided 42 per cent of the net imports of Europe. The only factor which might justify forecasting an increase in this proportion is the prospect that the United States might gradually reduce her exports to a level of 100,000,000 bushels. And here the long-run prospects are scarcely bright enough to warrant optimism.[23] True, achievement of the goal of the soil bank program would reduce American wheat acreage to between 40,000,000 and 43,000,000 acres. This reduced production, after meeting domestic needs, would leave about 100,-000,000 bushels for export.[24] Relatively more efficient producers, such as Canada and Australia, could then claim an increased share of the world market. However, on top of doubts about the soil bank goals being achieved, one must place the possibility of further United States moves toward a two-price system creating further disruption of international trade channels. Long-run prospects for diminished United States participation in world wheat trade are not clearly better. Black and Bonnen conclude that by 1965 American agricultural production generally will still continue to run ahead of demand, and that wheat production in particular will exceed demand unless major price declines oc-

[23] On the other hand, it is almost impossible to imagine Canada's wheat producers' being dislodged from any really large part of their present market. All authorities seems to agree that Canada's comparative advantage is substantial and may be increasing relative to other wheat producers due to rapid industrialization in Australia and to Argentina's tendency to switch more toward beef. Furthermore, Canadian wheat farmers take considerable prodding to be displaced from this staple; when prairie agriculture was in fact reoriented during World War II it returned to wheat specialization immediately after the war. See Wm. Mackenzie, "Possible Trends in the Demand for Canadian Farm Products," *CJAE*, 3:7 (Number 1, 1955); G. E. Britnell, "Perspective on Change in the Prairie Economy," *CJEPS*, 19:438–439 (November 1953); and Chapter 6 of the present study.

[24] This is based on an official U.S. Department of Agriculture report, *The Wheat Situation*, August 1956, p. 23. Beyond the possibility that the program's goal will not be reached, there is the question whether the Department of Agriculture's output estimates take full account of the fact that, with the reduced acreage, more wheat would be grown on summer fallow with considerably higher yields.

cur or substantial efforts to reduce production succeed.[25] Thus even the high probability of less favorable weather in the next decade than in the 1950's does not warrant forecasting any retreat of the United States farmer from the world wheat market. Thus no increase in the Canadian share of the European market can be foreseen. If Canada continues to hold 42 per cent of the European wheat trade, she would export 239,000,000 bushels to Europe in 1970, compared with an annual average of 188,000,000 bushels in the 1950–51 to 1954–55 period.[26]

The prospective import situation for non-European countries is difficult to project. There is a scarcity of knowledge about these countries, particularly about their potential bread grain and rice production in 1970.[27] Perhaps the best procedure is to project Canadian exports to these countries at two-thirds of the average of the period 1950–51 to 1954–55. This would be 72,000,000 bushels. This ratio is used to take account of the fact that exports in two of the five years were unusually high and clearly out of a normal range.

Thus the total export demand for Canadian wheat is projected at 311,000,000 bushels compared with an average of 298,000,000 in the years 1950–51 to 1954–55. This period has been used rather than 1955 alone to introduce a measure of stability into widely fluctuating quantities. Along with the domestic demand projected earlier at 163,000,000 bushels, this would indicate a market for 474,000,000 bushels of Canadian wheat in 1970.

Barley and oats

Over five recent crop years, Canada's barley exports have ranged between 64,000,000 and 122,000,000 bushels. Oats exports ran around 70,000,000 bushels before dropping to almost nothing in 1955–56. Barley exports accounted for 35 per cent of domestic production, oats exports 11 per cent of the total Canadian crop.[28] Exports of both grains have been quite unstable over time except in a few markets where Canadian grain has a quality advantage over its competitors, such as the American brewing market for

[25] Black and Bonnen, pp. 15–16, 27–28.
[26] Compare W. M. Drummond and Wm. MacKenzie, *Progress and Prospects of Canadian Agriculture* (Ottawa, 1957), pp. 49–52.
[27] See, however, the discussion by Drummond and MacKenzie, pp. 42–49.
[28] DBS, *The Grain Trade of Canada* (various issues).

barley and the American market for oats to be converted into oatmeal or rolled oats. Canadian barley is used as a feed grain in the European market, but it has a very slender hold. Good years for exports there have recently depended on such accidental factors as the absence of foreign exchange crises and reduced availability of Argentine corn. The United States market for oats as a feed grain is equally uncertain, although they enjoy a preference in the New England region. United States import quotas might eliminate this market at any time.[29]

With an overall increase of 32 per cent in livestock feeds to meet the projected Canadian consumption, this alone will place some pressure on production resources. Such an increase would absorb nearly twice the amounts of feed grains presently exported. However, it is a reasonable assumption that Canada may continue to hold a portion of her specialized malting barley and rolled oats export markets. It would seem prudent to project Canadian exports of oats and barley at about one-third of their recent levels, or at about 16,000,000 bushels for oats and 29,000,-000 bushels for barley. This takes account of three important factors: (1) exports over five recent years have reflected an unusually favorable period so far as yields are concerned; (2) the prospect for a gradual increase in acreage and long-term average yields; and (3) as the United States moves toward freer farm prices, United States agriculture will likely substitute coarse grains for some corn, thus reducing import needs for the former. The implication of this projection for land and other factors of production will be considered later.

Livestock and meat

In several recent years Canada was a net importer of beef even though the beef cycle was upward bound. This would suggest that Canada may be clearly out of the beef export market by 1970 except for sporadic shipments to the United States. Such a prospect is supported by the fact that the projected increase in the demand for beef in Canada is 55 per cent.

Exports of pork and pork products over the past five years have ranged from a low of 31,000,000 pounds in 1952 to a high of 75,000,000 in both 1953 and 1955. This export level accounts for somewhat less than 10 per cent of Canadian pork production,

[29] Drummond and MacKenzie, pp. 53–56.

in contrast to 40 per cent in 1935–1939. However, fresh pork exports to the United States have been increasing in the past two or three years and account for almost all of Canada's fresh pork exports.

Considering that (1) Canada is a deficit country in beef, (2) exports of pork products account for less than 10 per cent of Canadian production, and (3) the projections of domestic demand set forth earlier in this study indicate a 55 per cent increase in beef and a 50 per cent increase in pork by 1970 over 1955, we project very modest exports of livestock and livestock products for 1970. The chances of a European market for pork products growing permanently substantial seem poor, and the United States market cannot be counted on because of the likelihood that the efficient United States industry will be able to match the present Canadian product advantage in lean hog production.[30]

Other agricultural exports

During World War II Canada produced for export large quantities of cheese, concentrated milk, and milk powders. However, these have dropped sharply in recent years. Canada is not an efficient dairy producer, and neither government nor farm sector is much interested in expanding the export market. Even considering the fall in Canadian butter consumption per capita, Canadian dairy products exports will be trivial by 1970. The 1 or 2 per cent of Canadian egg production exported to specialized United States and Latin American markets may be maintained, but 1970 prospects seem most likely to imply no *net* Canadian egg exports.

In recent years exports of potatoes have varied from 2,000,000 to 5,000,000 bushels out of commercial production which has ranged from 50,000,000 to 70,000,000 bushels. About half of the exports have been of certified seed, the balance being table stock. This is one of Canada's chronically ill agricultural industries, due to the effects of the negative income response for potatoes and import curbs imposed by the United States. A substantial acreage reduction has been made over the past two decades. While some success may attend the strong efforts being made to hold and expand the market for certified seed, there is little prospect that potato exports in 1970 will be a significant source of income or

[30] Compare Drummond and MacKenzie, pp. 56–58.

require more than a negligible proportion of Canada's agricultural resources.

Canada's apple industry, which was built traditionally on the basis of exports of the fresh fruit to the United Kingdom, now has passed through two decades of very difficult adjustment. This was required by the virtual closing of the British market with the onset of the war. It has not reopened. The adjustment has been made with some measure of success. This change, however, stressing as it does the production of a high quality dessert apple, results in a very expensive product. Hence it is doubtful that exports will be more than negligible in 1970. In recent years they have run from 2,000,000 to 3,000,000 bushels out of a production which has ranged from 12,000,000 to 18,000,000 bushels.

Export summary

Total Canadian exports of farm products over the years 1951–1955 were: 1951, $759,000,000; 1952, $1,185,000,000; 1953, $1,104,-000,000; 1954, $810,000,000; 1955, $743,000,000. Wheat and wheat flour accounted for 60 per cent of these exports. Other grains represented another 18 per cent. The foregoing analysis of export demand implies a substantial export of wheat and small exports of oats and barley in 1970. Other exports are projected for 1970 at modest levels, in large part on the ground that domestic demand will absorb nearly all of the livestock products and that crop exports, for example, apples, potatoes, flaxseed, grass seeds, show little prospect of being much larger absolutely in 1970 than at the present time. The value of the projected exports of wheat, oats, and barley (1955 prices) would be $610,000,000. This compares with $426,000,000 in 1955 and an average of $427,000,000 in the five-year period 1951–1955. If wheat prices should decline by 1970, these estimates will overstate the value of exports and, in thinking of the balance of payments prospects for Canada in 1970, one should remember the rather strong likelihood that the prices of these export staples will have fallen relative to the average price of imported goods.

TOTAL OUTPUT AND FACTOR REQUIREMENTS

We can now consider the total output of various Canadian farm products likely to be demanded in 1970 and the adequacy of the land and labor employed by Canadian agriculture for producing

Table 84. Canadian production of major farm products, 1955 compared with 1970.

Product	Unit	1955 Actual	1970 Projected
Wheat	million bushels	397[a]	493
Oats	million bushels	329[a]	440
Barley	million bushels	202[a]	203
Beef and veal	million pounds	1,310	2,031
Pork	million pounds	1,020	1,530
Poultry meat	million pounds	406	641
Milk	million pounds	17,289	22,303
Eggs	million dozens	383	563
Tobacco	million pounds	150[b]	231

[a] 1951–1955 acreage with normal yield.

[b] 1951–1955 average.

Source: Canada, DBS, *Quarterly Bulletin of Agricultural Statistics* (various issues) oJr 1955 data, 1970 projections consolidated from estimates described in text.

them. Table 84 collects our projected outputs for products which give rise to more than 90 per cent of the cash farm income of Canadian agriculture. Outputs for the year 1955 are included, or average or normalized outputs for crops subject to large fluctuations.

A rough index of the required increase in production by 1970 is provided if we convert these output figures to cash sales in terms of 1955 prices. The actual cash farm income of Canadian agriculture in 1955 was $2,386,000,000. In order to take account of abnormal yields of small grains and of the current difficulties of prairie farmers in marketing grains, the incomes from crops were normalized. The result is that, with 1955 prices, normalized acreages and yields, cash farm income would have been $2,375,-000,000. Using the weighting given by the various commodity components of Table 84 for 1970, a cash income of $3,286,000,000 is implied for that year. This is a 38 per cent increase, corresponding to a compound annual growth rate of 2.25 per cent. It provides a general guide to the extent of the increase in physical output required by 1970. As indicated, livestock products constitute the great bulk of the required increase in production.

Will the amount of land under cultivation in Canada have to be expanded to meet these rising requirements for agricultural products? Or will the Canadian farm sector in 1970 have more than adequate capacity for the demands to be made of it, thereby implying problems of "overproduction" and falling farm prices?

Before turning to the probable changes in regional patterns of agricultural production, we can examine the prospective adequacy for 1970 output of farm land currently used for each major farm product. The present acreage seems more than adequate to produce the extra 47,000,000 bushels of wheat required in 1970. Canada has experienced a general upward trend in yields per acre over the past fifteen years that has been unrelated to weather conditions. It has been due to more timely planting and harvesting, better use of fallow, use of rust-resistant varieties of wheat, chemical weed sprays, and better conservation of soil moisture. Black and Bonnen project a yield increase of about three bushels per acre in fifteen years for the United States, perhaps half the gain which could be won if known technology were fully applied.[31] An unpublished study which considers the probable impact in various regions of the Canadian prairies of improved use of fertilizer, crop rotation, and other cultural practices makes the Black-Bonnen projection look reasonable for Canada as well. If this is the case, Canada's 1970 wheat requirements could be met with one million less acres than were under wheat cultivation in 1955.

With the large increase in demand anticipated for meat, it is interesting to consider together the increased requirements for coarse grains, hay, and pasture. Again the question is whether productivity will increase as fast as demand, permitting the land presently used for such purposes to suffice in the future. In the feed-livestock sector of the farm economy, productivity increases can come through both increased efficiency in feed production and increased output of livestock per unit of feed. An allowance for a 10 per cent increase in feeding efficiency has already been made in estimating domestic feed requirements in 1970. Significant increases in the yield of the various feeds per acre are also in prospect. Yields of oats and barley should improve at about the same rate as yields of wheat. For the whole period 1955–1970 corn yields per acre should improve 25 per cent, and better harvesting and storage methods should help augment the yield of hay by the same percentage while improving its quality. Comparing the prospective growth rates for demand and productivity,

[31] Black and Bonnen, p. 15.

we find that an extra one and one-half million acres will be needed for oats production and half of that amount for corn production. The other crops can be produced on their present acreages. Expanded livestock production also means much greater pasture requirements, but here the possibilities of greater productivity from applying known technology are very great.[32] The extra requirements could be met by existing acreage.

The picture for potatoes, fruits, and vegetables is rather uncertain. Output increases will be large for most of the members of this category except potatoes, and yield gains will probably be small. If this is the case, there will be some encroachment on general farming lands in central Canada and British Columbia which may be significant, especially considering the urban encroachment now going on in the same areas. The extra land requirements can be set at 200,000 acres.

Combining these net changes in land requirements for major products, we find that an extra 1,400,000 acres will be needed by 1970. This amount is trivial beside the land now considered suitable for agricultural settlement. Estimates of this amount vary a great deal, but all of them leave us with the same conclusion. Drummond and MacKenzie place 6,000,000 acres in this category.[33] Hudson cites estimates by Hurd classing 14,000,000 acres as potentially available for settlement in eastern Canada alone.[34] This latter estimate does not even include land which has been abandoned to rough pasture and which might be reclaimed. What stands out most clearly from all this is that the economic means of securing the more than one-third increase required in Canadian agricultural production is mainly the more intensive use of existing agricultural land, although extensive expansion will entail little difficulty.

The portion of the Canadian labor force working in agriculture has been falling at a breath-taking pace in recent years. This figure was 18.4 per cent in 1951, only 15.3 per cent in 1955. It is not surprising that, along with this, farm wages in Ontario quadrupled between 1940 and 1955.[35] D. J. Daly has shown by interregional comparisons the extent to which the exodus is due to

---

[32] *Resources for Freedom,* Vol. V, p. 68.

[33] Drummond and MacKenzie, ch. iii and p. 97.

[34] S. C. Hudson, "Speculation on Agricultural Production in Eastern Canada During the Next Fifty Years," *CJAE,* 3:10–11 (Number 1, 1955).

[35] Drummond and MacKenzie, pp. 101, 199.

rapidly rising nonagricultural incomes and abundant jobs outside of agriculture.[36]

Before asking whether this trend will continue, it is wise to examine two interrelated features of the changing farm scene —
increasing mechanization and increasing size of farms. In areas
where farms remain primarily in cash grain, mechanization will
cause the 160-acre and 320-acre farms to be combined with other
farms to make them large enough to use power machinery efficiently. The report of the Royal Commission on Agriculture and
Rural Life of Saskatchewan points out that the number of quar-
ter- and half-section farms in that province declined by 40 per
cent between 1936 and 1951.[37] The swing is still under way. Indeed, the results of the 1956 Census have shown it to be even
more rapid than had been previously believed.[38]

Mechanization of Canada's farm sector has largely come in the
years since World War II. The great contrast between the farm
prosperity of the postwar years with the poverty and near-starva-
tion of the prewar period has meant a massive re-equipment of
this capital-poor sector of the economy in less than two decades.
There is still room for more mechanization, but the rate will not
be as rapid as previous years have experienced.[39]

Mechanization and increasing farm size of course are interrelated changes, and their effects appear jointly on the size of
the farm work force. The movement toward fewer and larger
farms and more mechanized farms is well under way in Ontario
and is even making a start in Quebec. The rapid spread of industrialization and the growth of cities is contributing to the movement there by providing plentiful off-farm employment for the
sons and daughters, and even for some of the farmers themselves.[40] As Chapter 6 has shown, the same is true for the prairie
provinces, particularly Alberta. An important element in the
prairie agriculture situation is the fact that livestock enterprises
can be added to or enlarged on grain farms with little or no addi-

---

[36] D. J. Daly, "Aspects of the Decline in Employment in Canadian Agriculture," *CJAE*, 3:21–24 (Number 2, 1955).

[37] Royal Commission on Agriculture and Rural Life, *Report No. 7, Movement
of Farm People* (Regina, 1956), p. 86, Table 28.

[38] Drummond and MacKenzie, p. 99 and Table 44A.

[39] D. J. Daly, p. 29; Drummond and MacKenzie, pp. 21–23.

[40] Drummond and MacKenzie have noted the very rapid exodus of unpaid
family workers in the postwar period (pp. 24–25).

tion to the labor force, since most of the extra work is done at times when labor is otherwise largely idle. It is important to point out that when a cash-grain farm is converted into a feed-livestock farm its output is increased because the grain is put through a second production process, and the farm thus converted becomes larger without adding more acres. Once again, however, farm size and the chances of expanding livestock production are interrelated. The Saskatchewan Royal Commission report points out that many of the present livestock and feed-livestock farms have too few acres and head of livestock to mechanize efficiently.[41] Market pressures will bring further consolidation and further efficiency in the use of the labor force.

The United States experience has considerable meaning for Canada. In the northeastern United States, as many as one-third of the farmers in many counties work off their farms one hundred days or more annually, and one-third of the labor force living on farms in the United States in 1950 was not employed in agriculture. The same trend toward part- or full-time nonfarm employment will certainly characterize eastern Canada's farm labor force in the coming years. Total output of the farms of the United States increased 30 per cent between 1940 and 1955, while the farm labor force according to the Census Bureau figures was declining 37 per cent. John D. Black in his presidential address to the American Economic Association projected a further decline of 20 per cent in the number of farms in the United States by 1975, and of 24 per cent in the farm labor force. In this same period agricultural output will increase by at least another 26 per cent.[42] The United States and Canada have another thing in common that is pertinent to the future of the farm labor force. Both have a large region of low-income farming — the South in the United States and Quebec and the Maritimes in Canada. It is in the South that the number of farms has been declining most rapidly in the United States. This is true of the Maritimes although not of Canada's other low-income area, Quebec.[43]

Canada can be expected to follow a somewhat similar pattern

[41] Royal Commission on Agriculture and Rural Life, *Report No. 7,* p. 124.
[42] John D. Black, "Agriculture in the Nation's Economy," *AER,* 46:8–18 (March 1956).
[43] Compare Drummond and MacKenzie, chs. vii, viii.

of change in farm size and number of farms to that of the United States. However, it is necessary to take account of the fact that a smaller annual increase in required output is expected for the United States. In applying this to Canada, therefore, it is concluded that to meet the 38 per cent increase in farm output required by 1970 there will be about a 15 per cent decline in the number of farms and a decline of some 20 per cent in the farm labor force. The decline of the farm labor force between 1941 and 1951 in Canada was 31 per cent (an annual rate of decline of 2.7 per cent compounded) while output increased by 42 per cent (an annual rate of 3.6 per cent compounded). The problem in 1970 will not be one of meeting the farm labor requirements but one of having the reduced force available in those areas capable of fully utilizing its services.

REGIONAL POTENTIALS

In this section we will describe the prospective changes in the character of agricultural production in Canada's four major regions, emphasizing prospective shifts in the regional percentage distribution of production and their relation to factor supplies.

Atlantic provinces

During the past four decades there has been a rapid and steady decline in the acreages of cropland in the Atlantic provinces; nor do our projections for the area envision a reversal of this trend. The index of agricultural output for the three Maritime provinces in 1955 was only 120 on a 1935–1939 base, compared with 133 for central Canada.[44] The most important reasons for the slow increase in output in this period are (1) the decline in exports of apples due to the loss of the British market, and (2) the slow growth of population and lagging industrial development. The important potato crop also suffered from a decline in consumption per capita in central Canada, the principal outlet, and from restrictions on exports to the United States.

The Atlantic provinces will have a much slower population growth in the next decade than central Canada, and indeed are most likely to decline very slightly between 1955 and 1970, while central Canada increases by nearly one-half. Thus growth of the

---

[44] Canada, DBS, *Quarterly Bulletin of Agricultural Statistics*, 50:105 (April-June 1957).

domestic market will provide almost no encouragement to Atlantic agriculture except for a slight rise in local demand for foods of livestock origin. The Maritime region is now on a slight import basis for dairy products and a substantial one for beef. Thus there is a fairly good prospect that the region will become more self-sufficient in food and particularly that beef production will expand.[45] Yields per acre of hay and pasture can easily be increased, and the main problem is one of securing a substantial increase in farm size.

The most evident change in the agriculture of this region is the concentration of farming operations in the few areas of productive land, for example, the Annapolis Valley, the St. John River Valley, Prince Edward Island, and an area through central and northern Nova Scotia. On the basis of projected population and demand it is expected that the output of the region will rise by about 15 per cent between 1955 and 1970. However, this result could be affected by the possible reduction in freight assistance on feed grains. (The subsidy in 1953 was $12.82 per ton to Nova Scotia, over half the freight cost from the Lakehead.) An important factor in the situation is also the transport cost of potatoes from Prince Edward Island and New Brunswick to the big cities in Quebec and Ontario.

Central Canada

How will the increased output which will be demanded from central Canada's agriculture be provided? Considerable land is classed as available for agricultural settlement, but it is not highly productive and the expense of clearing it would be relatively great.[46] Furthermore, in the 1941–1951 decade the area in occupied land in Quebec and Ontario decreased by 8 per cent during a period of rapid output expansion, leading one to expect that further production increases will come from land already in cultivation.

The prospects for use of improved technology are important for weighing the future of central Canada's agriculture. Yields of hay and the carrying capacity of pasture land could be doubled, the latter by reseeding, fertilizing, and proper management. Grain yields could be increased, but not by so much; yields of

[45] Drummond and MacKenzie, pp. 157–160.
[46] Hudson, p. 10; Drummond and MacKenzie, pp. 66–67.

fruits, vegetables, and potatoes will increase little. If known technology were fully applied by 1970, there would be no problem transferring sufficient land from hay and pasture to fruits and vegetables to meet the region's prospective requirements. If technological improvement goes on at the more modest historic rate, there may be a slight pinch on the existing agricultural land supply of eastern Canada, with rising land and food prices and pressure for new land settlement. The actual course of events will probably lie somewhere between.[47]

Another source of uncertainty about the agricultural future of central Canada lies in the Feed Freight Assistance Programme, which subsidizes the movement of feed from the prairies to central Canada. Prior to this program nearly one-half of Canada's hogs were raised in the prairie region. But the proportion in some recent years has fallen to less than one-third. The prairies have a clear advantage in livestock production, and, although prairie farmers resist this activity when incomes from wheat sales are satisfactory, reduction or removal of feed freight assistance would noticeably shift hog production back toward the prairies. Regardless of such a policy change, pressure on eastern Canada's farm resources, including opportunities for nonfarm employment, will tend to shift a larger portion of livestock production to the prairies.

Combining all of these considerations, we can see that, even though Ontario and Quebec have the capacity to produce economically all the indigenous products required in 1970, substantial changes will have to occur in the farming of the region. The types of changes are those which have been occurring for two to three decades, particularly in the war and postwar years. Most important perhaps is the decline in the number of farms and, accompanying it, a still greater reduction in the farm labor force. These changes, along with a substantial increase in machinery investment per farm and per acre of cropland, are effecting a critically important economic reorganization of the farm industry. The number of farms declined 11 per cent in Ontario in the last intercensal decade, 1941–1951, and 7 per cent in Quebec. The labor force in agriculture in Ontario declined by 25 per cent in the decade of the 1940's and by a further 15 per cent to June

[47] Compare Hudson, pp. 10–11.

1956; in Quebec, the proportions were 25 per cent in the decade of the 1940's and a further decrease of 30 per cent by June 1956. During this period there was a reduction of cropland in Ontario — 7 per cent in the 1940's. In Quebec, the decline in this period was 6 per cent, occurring in the face of a fairly vigorous "colonization" scheme. Farm machinery investment per acre of improved land rose from $11 to $35. During this period the number of tractors used on the smaller areas of farm land increased from 35,000 to 105,000 in a single decade. While the rate of increase of mechanization of Quebec farms in the last census decade was remarkably high, this would seem to reflect the backwardness of the area at the beginning more than any high degree of mechanization achieved in this period. Tractors, for instance, which increased from 6,000 to 32,000 in the decade, were still found on only one farm in every five in 1951.[48]

In setting forth the need for further changes in the direction of larger farms, a reduced labor force, and larger machinery investment per farm and per acre, it should be recognized that the more productive and advanced agricultural areas in both provinces have made considerable progress in mechanizing and in adjusting the labor force to this situation. Thus the major adjustments over the next decade require finding a means for further increasing the size of farms by combining units, particularly in the more productive areas, and dealing with, or comfortably neglecting, the large areas of low-income agriculture, particularly in the province of Quebec. There is assurance of further progress in the productive farm areas, and it will be accompanied by strengthening of the economic position of farming in these areas. Because of the remarkable decline in the labor force in Quebec since 1951, we have an indication that the traditional pattern of large families and of maintaining a large underemployed labor force on farms is being broken. Only the next census can show from which areas the speed of migration is fastest. Yet it seems safe to conclude that the low-income areas are being affected as much as the productive farm regions.[49]

---

[48] This statistical information appears in *Census of Canada, 1951,* Vol. VI, and *Census of Canada, 1956,* Bulletins 2–5, 2–6, 2–11.

[49] Compare Daly, *passim,* and Drummond and MacKenzie, pp. 190–196, 226–242.

Prairie provinces

From the discussion in the preceding section of the general adequacy of Canadian farm land to 1970's requirements, it is clear that the prairies will be more than adequate to the demand for wheat and coarse grains. This becomes doubly clear if we note the productivity gains which the report of the Paley Commission has indicated as possible on the basis of known technology. These so-called "A-estimates" for the United States, 1950–1975, indicate possible yield increases per acre of 50 per cent for wheat, 70 per cent for oats, 40 per cent for barley, 70 per cent for hay and pasture, and 35 per cent for range land.[50]

The main question with respect to the prairies is how and when the major shift toward livestock production will come, as it ultimately must.[51] This question leads us to certain subsidiary problems: (1) the short-run effects of feed freight assistance and relative production costs of livestock in eastern and western Canada; (2) the prairie provinces' probable share of major nongrain farm products in 1970; and (3) the probable patterns of change in the various soil belts of the prairies.

To what extent will feed grains produced in the prairie provinces be fed in this region instead of being shipped to central Canada, the Maritimes, and British Columbia? Public policy will determine this in considerable measure as it decides whether the Feed Freight Assistance Act is to continue to function as at present or whether the levels of assistance are to be reduced or abolished. One move to reduce this assistance has already been made. In terms of the total national economy, and outside of war conditions, it would seem best in the long run to feed the livestock on the farms where the grain is produced and ship the dressed meat. But unemployment or underemployment in the farming areas of some parts of eastern Canada may warrant doing the feeding in considerable part in the East until readjustments can be made. Still, subsidies to smooth out these readjustments should not become permanent supports of economic

---

[50] *Resources for Freedom,* Vol. V, pp. 66–68. Compare also Drummond and MacKenzie (p. 265) for possible gains from greater use of fertilizer in the prairie provinces.

[51] Drummond and MacKenzie's study prepared for the Gordon Commission notes that: "The domestic demand for meats is likely to require a level of meat production by 1980 over twice that of the average of the 1951–55 period. Most of the increase in production must come from the Prairie Provinces" (p. 268).

inefficiency. Another factor in the problem is that parts of eastern Canada may have comparative advantages over the prairies in producing hay and roughage but still need more supplementary grain than can be produced economically in these regions. Nevertheless these areas should in the long run pay the transport costs of shipping this grain from the West.

By 1970 how far will the emphasis in the Canadian livestock economy have shifted to western Canada? In 1955 the prairie provinces accounted for the production of 59 per cent of the cattle marketed and 46 per cent of the hogs. Both of these proportions are somewhat higher than the average over the past decade, due to increases in prairie production resulting from difficulties in marketing grains. However, (1) with the resources over more than half of the prairies suited to livestock production, (2) with the vast quantities of feed grain grown in the area, (3) with the inevitable declining relative importance of wheat, and (4) with the need for diversification of agriculture to add to the income of grain farms and to give greater employment to the family labor supply, it is expected that by 1970 the prairie area will produce two-thirds of the cattle and 55 per cent of the hogs. Removal of feed freight assistance would raise the proportion of hogs produced in the prairies to 60 per cent.

Prairie farmers produced just one-third of Canada's poultry meat and 28 per cent of the eggs in 1955. Since overcoming production hazards in cold climates is expensive, and since poultry meat and egg production are increasingly market-oriented, it is expected that these proportions will not change significantly. Thus in 1970 the prairies' production of poultry meat would be 213,000,000 pounds and of eggs 158,000,000 dozen.

Farmers in this region produced 22 per cent of the national output of milk in 1955. Slightly more than one-half of this went to butter production. As the dairy industry of central Canada moves toward a greater emphasis on fluid milk production, the prairies are expected to produce even a greater share of Canada's butter. Thus they are likely to account for about 25 per cent of the total milk output in 1970, or 5,600,000,000 pounds compared to 3,800,000,000 in 1955.

The ultimate transformation of prairie agriculture implied by Canadians' high income elasticity of demand for meat and negative elasticity for wheat will not be particularly visible until near or after 1970. In the nearer future some of the most arid parts of southeastern Alberta and southwestern Saskatchewan still in farms will go into grazing land, and the carrying capacity of grazing lands generally will be increased. More intensive use of irrigated land in the brown soil zone will include fattening beef cattle as a supplementary enterprise, along with increases in the output of fodder and specialty crops. Supplementary feeding of cattle and hogs will grow more common on the large wheat farms of the dark brown soil zone. Ultimately the shift toward livestock implies a reduction of summer fallow practices and increased intensity of land use, along with a crop shift from wheat toward coarse grains. But that is far in the future and probably will occur only in response to visible changes in relative prices.[52]

British Columbia

The largest factor in the agricultural prospect for British Columbia is the rapid population increase expected by 1970. Population is projected at 2,449,000 compared to a 1955 figure of 1,305,000. British Columbia will share fully in, or even exceed, the yield and livestock efficiency increases projected for the rest of the country. Considering the importance of hay and pasture crops in that province, this increase is estimated at 20 per cent. Expansion of her agriculture will be both intensive and extensive, with some new land called into use in the central mixed farming area and a considerable expansion around the Peace River. It is interesting that the provincial government estimates include very little expansion in the British Columbia portion of the Peace River territory, for the strength of demand suggests a considerable part of this land may be brought into agriculture by 1970. However, it is not prudent to suggest that more than one-fourth of the total farm output in 1970 will be produced on land not now in agriculture. Such an increase, along with the greater output from a more intensive use of present land, should permit a total increase of about 45 per cent or somewhat less than 3 per cent annually. Even with this large increase, British Columbia, already a deficit area for grains, meats, and dairy products, will fall considerably further behind in terms of meeting her own

---

[52] Drummond and MacKenzie, pp. 268–272; Sol Sinclair, "Agricultural Production Possibilities in the Year 2000 — Western Canada," *CJAE*, 3:15–24 (Number 1, 1955).

food needs. Fortunately, Alberta, with a productive agriculture, is a surplus producer of exactly the products British Columbia requires. Favored by climate and with land resources varying from dyked delta land and rich intermountain valleys to range and wheat land, British Columbia should be able to meet all its 1970 needs for dairy products (except butter and cheese) and eggs and for the fresh fruits and vegetables presently grown in the area. The mounting food deficit of the province will continue to be in feed grains, meats, butter, and cheese.

In making the changes projected, British Columbia agriculture, which has suffered a decline of 50 per cent in its labor force since the end of the war, will be confronted with an extremely great difficulty in getting the necessary labor and thus with very high wages. The result will be much more rapid progress toward capital intensive agriculture than elsewhere in Canada.

Summary of regional studies

The purpose of this statement is to bring together the regional projections made above and to fill the gaps that may exist. The normalized farm income of Canada for 1955, calculated earlier, was $2,375,000,000. If we add to that the value of farm products used in the home in that year, $405,000,000, the net income of

Table 85. Regional distribution of Canadian agricultural output and labor force, 1955 and 1970.

Region	1955	1970
Output (millions of 1955 dollars)		
Atlantic provinces	157	175
Central Canada	1,392	1,804
Prairie provinces	1,109	1,434
British Columbia	122	170
Total	2,780	3,683
Labor force (thousands)		
Atlantic provinces	47	27
Central Canada	436	361
Prairie provinces	368	290
British Columbia	30	30
Total	885	708

Source: Canada Year Book, 1957; Canada, DBS, *The Labour Force.* For method of developing 1970 estimates, see text.

agriculture was $2,780,000,000. The regional distribution is that presented in Table 85.

In making the projection, that portion of normalized farm output which leaves the farm (cash farm income) is increased by 38 per cent over the country as a whole. That part which is consumed on the farm is assumed to remain unchanged to 1970. This takes account of both a 15 per cent reduction in the number of farms by 1970 and a corresponding increase in the value of perquisites per farm. The result of these two projections makes up a national total of $3,683,000,000 for 1970.

The regional breakdown is consistent with the analysis provided earlier. Fifteen and 45 per cent increases in value of output are indicated for the Atlantic provinces and British Columbia respectively. Again following the analysis set forth earlier, we conclude that the increase in farm output for the prairies will be somewhat higher than for central Canada. The rates actually used were 35 per cent in the case of central Canada and 43 per cent for the prairie provinces. Because farm products consumed in the household are assumed to remain constant over the fifteen-year period, the output of Canadian agriculture to meet market and farm household needs would have to increase not by 38 per cent but by 32 per cent. It is scarcely necessary to repeat that this is well within the resources and capacity of the industry.

The other aspect of agriculture which it is desirable to examine on a regional basis is the labor force. The farm labor force on June 1, 1955, is shown on a regional basis in Table 85. The projections of the 1970 work force take account of the resource and demand aspects of the outlook described earlier. With a 20 per cent decline in the national farm labor force, the assumed proportionate reductions by region are: Maritimes, 43 per cent; central Canada, 17 per cent; prairie provinces, 21 per cent; and British Columbia, unchanged.

16

The Primary Industries: Minerals

The lonely, bearded prospector has been replaced by the team of geologists and the burro and his pack by the plane and its load of aerial prospecting gear, but the excitement is the same excitement of a century ago. The raw romance of Cariboo, Klondike, and Cobalt was but flirtation beside the more lucrative and calculated love affairs at Leduc, Flin Flon, and Knob Lake. Mineral development advanced at such an accelerated pace after World War II that it caught the imagination of everyone concerned with the country's economic future. Yet in 1955 and 1956 less than 4 per cent of the national income originated in "Mining, Quarrying and Oil Wells," which proportion seems minuscule beside the publicity this sector has attracted in recent years. There are several reasons for this. Certain minerals are becoming the nation's new export staples and promise to provide the country with an increasing proportion of its foreign exchange earnings. Furthermore, mineral development is attracting investment funds, expenditure of which has provided buoyancy to the economy. The fact that a substantial portion of these investment funds is from outside the country is also causing considerable concern. And of course the small proportion of national income originating in the sector gives no indication of the repercussions felt in other sectors of the economy. The processing of the minerals involves some investment and employment, as does the transportation of the goods and the business of supplying these industries with their various requirements. One means of putting mineral production in better perspective is to point out that, whereas in 1926 copper was the only mineral among Canada's ten leading export commodities, in 1956 aluminum, nickel, copper, iron ore, and asbestos were all among the ten leading exports.[1]

The postwar upsurge of mineral development in Canada can

---

[1] It is misleading, perhaps, to classify aluminum as an extractive industry since no bauxite is mined in the country. The raw material is brought to Canada's hydroelectric power to be processed into aluminum.

be readily understood by comparing the increases in mineral prices with those of other goods since before the war. Whereas the wholesale price index in 1956, the peak year for many of the metal prices, stood at 225.6 (1935–1939 = 100), the index for copper and its products had risen to 385.9 (its peak for any one month was 426.5 in early 1956), lead to 323.4, zinc to 320.5, and pig iron rose all through 1956 to reach 295.3 in 1957. Between 1949 and 1955 the gross national product increased about 32 per cent in real terms and the physical volume of manufacturing output by about 25 per cent; mineral production, on the other hand, increased by 80 per cent over the same period. In 1956 again the index of physical production in mining rose more than either the GNP or the index of manufacturing production, the percentage increases being 13 per cent as compared with 7 per cent and 6 per cent. Thus the growth of the mineral output of Canada has indeed been striking and the high world prices for minerals which prevailed through 1956 influenced greatly the nature of Canadian economic growth. We must now examine the prospects for the future development of the mineral industries in Canada.

THE METHODOLOGY OF MINERAL PROJECTIONS

Predicting the probable level of output for each of the major minerals is more difficult than projecting most other magnitudes in the Canadian economy because mineral production is so dependent on conditions external to the economy. Since the bulk of Canada's minerals is sold on the world market, the country's mineral output depends upon (1) the world demand for the individual minerals, (2) trade and exchange restrictions which may prohibit buyers from importing from the cheapest sources, and (3) the cost of production at sources of supply which compete with Canada relative to Canadian production costs.

We have already spelled out in Chapter 1 our assumption that economic activity in the industrial countries of the world will remain at a high level throughout the projection period with but brief interruptions. It has also been assumed that in general international trade restrictions will be eased slightly over the long pull.

As for the third set of determinants of demand for Canadian minerals, namely, Canadian production costs relative to production costs at competing sources of supply, we will assume that within the period of projection there will be no discoveries of new mineral deposits so large or so inexpensive to exploit as to displace Canadian sources to any serious extent. This assumption can be justified on several counts. First of all, the recent history of mineral exploration and development in Canada would seem to support the general belief that the pre-Cambrian shield is truly rich in mineral deposits. Secondly, the pre-Cambrian shield is so vast, covering all of Labrador, most of Quebec, Ontario, and the Northwest Territories, as well as sizeable portions of Manitoba and Saskatchewan, that a very minor part has been explored for minerals as yet. Third, the development of aerial exploration has so reduced exploration costs as virtually to assure continued discovery of reserves until 1970, barring a complete collapse of world prices. Fourth, Canada's mineral deposits in the shield appear more accessible than those of the other unexploited areas of the world. With a transportation system more highly developed than most of the areas of other countries thought to hold workable deposits, Canada may be in a unique position among the world's mineral producers. (The relative accessibility of possible deposits in the Cordilleran Belt is a moot point.) Fifth, the capital and technological knowledge requisite to mineral development are much more readily available to Canada than to under-developed low-income countries, which must attract foreign capital and management and yet cannot promise that profits may be repatriated. Finally, the higher wage costs in Canada would not seem to put the country at a serious disadvantage with the other mineral producers of the world. The period 1946–1953 saw man-year productivity increase in the mineral industry at the rate of nearly 5.5 per cent per annum, lending partial support to the notion that Canadian producers can mechanize sufficiently to pay high wages and still produce at world prices.[2] All these factors, especially the technical knowledge, the availability of capital, and the accessibility, would appear to assure that Canada will continue to be a leading mineral producer.

Ideally, the problem of determining the output of the various Canadian minerals in 1970 could be solved by a massive study

[2] Some of the annual increases in productivity in the entire industry reflect shifts in the composition of output toward those minerals where productivity is higher, rather than increases with respect to each individual mineral. The extent of this distortion can be noted when the individual minerals are examined.

of the supply and demand conditions for each mineral for each country where any supply or demand originates. It might be possible to estimate the elasticity of supply for each supplying country, then construct for each country demand functions, including not only the price of the given mineral but of substitutes as independent variables, and by means of a general equilibrium model then to estimate the quantity of each mineral to be supplied by each country. Such a study would be a book in itself, and this is not that book. We must be content with a far less sophisticated approach.

As a rule, the forecast of output for each mineral begins with an examination of the recent history of the output and reserves of that mineral so that the determinants of supply can be inferred. If the mineral is sold largely into the export market, the next step is to estimate free world production by 1970. At this point the report of the President's Materials Policy Commission is used extensively because of the free world supply and demand projections which it contains.[3] Some of these estimates were adjusted in light of developments since the report was published. Canada's share of the free world production was then examined to learn what factors seemed to be shaping this proportion. With the country's share estimated for 1970, the domestic disappearance was projected, giving as a residual the amount available for export. For some minerals the procedure was simpler either because production is for the domestic market only or because the United States takes such a large amount that free world production need not be studied. These estimating procedures seemed serviceable if not exactly *avant garde.*

A final section of the chapter forecasts the employment requirements for each of the mineral industries. We do not bare all methodological details of each industry's forecast, but generally speaking the historical increases in man-year productivity were extrapolated to 1970. In many cases the year-to-year changes in physical productivity per worker have fluctuated over a wide range in the period for which data are available. Some of these fluctuations have been due to short work weeks, as during the depression. Others have been due to miscellaneous factors such as substantial capital improvements which have been bunched

[3] U.S. President's Materials Policy Commission, *Resources for Freedom* (Washington, 1952), 5 vols.

in certain years and which have pushed productivity up very quickly. This latter type of fluctuation can be particularly troublesome in a mineral industry consisting of but few firms, for then the policies of a single firm can have a significant impact on the productivity data for the industry as a whole. We have attempted to work in terms of long-term movements in productivity per worker even though these estimates are subject to considerable error in some industries.

The proportion of this chapter devoted to the energy minerals in general and to coal in particular may seem grossly out of keeping with the relative importance of this group of minerals. We defend this imbalance, however, on three grounds: (1) the mix of the country's energy sources is changing rapidly; (2) the oil and gas development has such a short history and is proceeding at such a rapid pace that it poses especially troublesome forecasting problems; and (3) coal is the only mineral for which an actual decline in output is anticipated and this fuel has been so important as a source of employment in Nova Scotia and Alberta that it justifies special attention.

THE OUTLOOK FOR COAL, OIL AND NATURAL GAS

The relative importance of the various minerals has changed markedly since the end of the war, as is indicated in Table 86.

Table 86.   Canadian production of the ten most important minerals, listed in order of value, 1949 and 1955.

1949		1955	
Mineral	Value (millions of 1949 dollars)	Mineral	Value (millions of 1955 dollars)
Gold	148.4	Crude petroleum	303.6
Coal	110.9	Copper	239.4
Copper	104.7	Nickel	216.4
Nickel	99.2	Gold	157.3
Zinc	76.4	Zinc	116.4
Crude petroleum	61.1	Iron ore	113.4
Lead	50.5	Asbestos	98.7
Asbestos	39.8	Coal	92.2
Cement	32.9	Sand and gravel	65.8
Silver	13.1	Cement	64.4

Source: 1949 data, Canada, DBS, *Canada Year Book, 1954*, pp. 1270–71; 1955 data, Canada, DBS, *Weekly Bulletin*, Jan. 6, 1956.

The jump in rank of crude petroleum from 1949 to 1955 is most striking. Coal production is down, even in absolute terms, because of the new competition from oil and natural gas. Since the oil industry has been the glamour boy of Canadian economic development since the end of the war, it might seem to warrant separate and special treatment. But the future of oil so intimately affects the future of coal and natural gas that these three fuels can most profitably be discussed together.

The oil industry is most important of the three in the sense that the future of coal and the future of natural gas are largely dependent on the future of oil rather than vice versa. The extent to which coal will be displaced by oil may be a bit more dependent on developments in the oil industry than developments in the coal industry. Natural gas, to the extent that it is a by-product of oil, will also be tied to petroleum production to some degree.

The level of output of each of these fuels in 1970 will be determined by several factors: (1) the level of gross national product in 1970; (2) the increase in energy consumption likely to be required to produce a given increase in the gross national product; (3) the future production cost and world price of each of the fuels and the transportation costs to market; (4) the technological changes affecting the efficiency of utilization of the individual fuels; (5) the extent to which substitution among fuels takes place in response to changes in relative prices of the fuels; and (6) the level of export demand for Canadian fuels.

The demand for energy

The gross national product in 1970 has already been estimated at $48,000,000,000 in 1955 dollars. How much energy is the country likely to consume in the process of producing such a quantity of goods and services? The data available on total energy consumption annually since 1926 indicate that in the peacetime years every $1,000,000,000 increase in the GNP (in constant 1955 dollars) required an increase in energy consumption of about 100 trillion [100×10^{12}] Btu's. Furthermore, this relation between energy consumption and the national product is a surprisingly good one. If the war years 1941–1945 are omitted, during which time energy conservation distorted the energy-GNP relation, the correlation is 0.984.[4] Thus it is with considerable confidence that

---

[4] This covers the period 1926–1952. The data are from C. L. O'Brian, *Coal*

one can state that the 1970 energy consumption in Canada will be on the order of 4600 trillion [4.6×10^{15}] Btu's, if the gross national product is $48,000,000,000.

Oil

Canada has been producing some petroleum since the late 1870's, but not until the discovery of the Leduc field in Alberta in 1947 did the country become one of the world's significant oil-producing countries. From the beginning of the war until 1947, imports were accounting for an increasing proportion of the total consumption, being about four and five times as great as domestic output. Imports have leveled off since the development of the Alberta fields and exports have skyrocketed with production, which has been increasing at a startling average rate of more than 40 per cent per year, 1947–1955, the increase in some years exceeding 50 per cent.[5] From a level of about 8,000,000 barrels in 1947, production had risen to about 130,000,000 barrels in 1955.

Although domestic production in 1955 equalled about two-thirds of the domestic consumption, imports nevertheless also accounted for about two-thirds of domestic consumption. This anomaly exists because until the pipeline is extended to Toronto and Montreal it is cheaper for the big eastern Canadian market to buy its crude oil from abroad than from Alberta. Hence oil is exported in the West and imported in the East. Whether this trade pattern will continue until 1970 will be discussed briefly later.

How large is petroleum production likely to be by 1970? Output is now limited not by production costs so much as by marketing problems of various sorts. But, since these marketing problems may be cleared up within the next few years, a consideration of the 1970 level of output does require an examination of production costs.

---

and Energy in Canada Since the War (reprints of five articles from *Canadian Mining and Metallurgical Bulletin,* 1950–1954), p. 32. The explained variance is so close to 100 per cent as to make one suspect that the published time series data were estimated in part from a relation to the GNP. Mr. O'Brian has assured the writer that this was not the case, however, and that the energy consumption data were built up from data on the individual fuels. Generally in this chapter the O'Brian data are used as background because they are more complete than the data in Canada, DBS, *Energy Sources in Canada, Commodity Accounts for 1948 and 1952,* Reference Paper No. 69 (Ottawa, 1956).

[5] This production is in terms of producers' shipments; see Canada, DBS, *Canadian Statistical Review, 1957 Supplement,* Table 22.

Production costs will be in part a function of the availability of reserves. If reserves are plentiful, exploration costs relative to pure production costs will be lower because of greater accessibility, shallower wells, and a lower dry hole ratio. There is no question that Canadian oil reserves will remain huge, relative to current production, until 1970 at least. This is not to say, however, that any precise statements about the absolute quantity of reserves can be set down. Most of the estimated oil reserves are for "proved" reserves: "that part of discovered oil which can be recovered by known methods and at present levels of costs and prices." [6] But reserve estimates now available grossly underestimate actual reserves. Reserve estimates are based on drilling, and oil companies drill in the hope of producing. Therefore reserves and production increase together since both result from drilling.

In the United States, over the past 30 years the reserves have been about 12 or 13 times annual production.[7] In Canada the ratio is about 26 to 1.[8] Although the amount of undiscovered reserves which exist in areas not yet drilled obviously cannot be estimated, there are about one-half million square miles of actual and potential oil-producing territory in Alberta, Saskatchewan, Manitoba, and British Columbia; only one well is drilled for every eighty square miles. Several writers predict that this territory will eventually rival Texas as a producer of gas and oil.[9]

Canada's ample reserves result in a low dry hole ratio. In the United States about 20 per cent more wells must be drilled to find a given number of producer wells than is the case in Canada.[10] Furthermore, the average well depth is greater in the United States than in Canada. In 1955 the average depth of all on-shore wells drilled in the United States during the year was a bit more than 4000 feet while in Canada the average depth was just over 3700 feet.[11]

[6] National Petroleum Council, *Petroleum Productive Capacity* (1952), p. 5.

[7] U.S. President's Materials Policy Commission, Vol. III, p. 5.

[8] *1955 World Petroleum Report* (Dallas, 1955), p. 34.

[9] See, for example, H. G. Cochrane, "The Natural Gas Story," *Canadian Business,* 29:14 (March 1956).

[10] Government of Saskatchewan, *Prospects for Economic Growth in Saskatchewan, a Submission to the RCCEP by the Government of Saskatchewan* (Regina, 1955), p. 106.

[11] J. E. Pogue and K. E. Hill, *Future Growth and Financial Requirements of the World Petroleum Industry* (New York, 1956), p. 20; and *1955 World Petroleum Report,* p. 34.

Thus the available evidence indicates that Canada will continue to have favorable oil production costs as compared with the United States. The more critical problem concerns the marketing of the product. In 1953 the Maritimes and Quebec received over 40 per cent of all crude refined in Canada and this oil all came from foreign sources. The Inter-Provincial Pipeline brings Alberta crude to Sarnia but pipeline costs are now such that it is not certain that pipeline crude could compete in Toronto and Montreal with crude brought in by tanker. Water transportation costs for oil are about one-third of pipeline costs for similar distances. Consequently Venezuelan oil can usually be laid down in Montreal for a price low enough to discourage pipeline construction to Montreal from the West. Whether the line will be extended to Montreal within the next few years is a hotly debated question, but by 1970 such a pipeline would be a distinct possibility.[12]

The geographical extent of the market for the prairies' crude petroleum in 1970 is uncertain largely because such a substantial proportion of the oil supplied to North America is produced and therefore priced by a few integrated companies whose crude oil operations have the earmarks of a disciplined cartel.[13] Consequently, whether the Montreal market will be supplied by the prairie provinces or by foreign sources may depend largely on the pricing and marketing policies of the companies who control production in both supply areas. But at least two factors will help determine policy on this matter. The Montreal refineries are engineered to process the lower grade imported crude rather than the oil from the west. In addition, the prairies are virtually certain to become important suppliers of crude to California by 1970. So the entrance of western oil into eastern Canada might be retarded because of these two factors.

If the oligopolistic pricing system were to be broken up by 1970, which seems quite unlikely, world oil prices would surely fall. Since production costs in the various oil fields of the world

---

[12] The Imperial Oil Company in its submission to the RCCEP, *Prospects for Canada's Oil Industry, 1955–1980* (Toronto, 1956), indicated that it expects western crudes to be marketed in Montreal within a few years.

[13] The operations of the companies involved are described in U.S., Federal Trade Commission, *The International Petroleum Cartel,* staff report submitted to the Subcommittee on Monopoly of the Select Committee on Small Business, United States Senate, 83d Cong., 2d sess. (Washington, 1952); see especially pp. 32–33.

are apparently impossible to obtain, one cannot say which petroleum markets would then be served by which sources of supply.[14] But at the moment the probability of the pricing system being seriously altered by 1970 seems sufficiently remote to rule out this contingency.

With this quick review of the supply conditions behind us, we will turn to a discussion of the natural gas and coal outlook in order to determine the probable strength of these two fuels which compete with oil. We can then return to the oil projection.

Natural gas

Natural gas production in Canada has increased with crude oil production but at a considerably slower rate; in the late 1920's there was almost no oil being produced in Canada, but there was a significant amount of natural gas being produced in New Brunswick, Ontario, and Alberta. As a result the rate of increase in output since 1929 is substantially greater in the case of oil.[15] Gas was first produced in significant quantity in 1913, when the output was 20,500,000,000 feet. By contrast, 1955 production was just over 150,000,000,000 cubic feet. And the geographical origin of production had moved westward, for the early production was concentrated in the East whereas in 1955 over 90 per cent of the Canadian gas came from Alberta and Saskatchewan.

The difficulties of marketing natural gas have been even greater than those involved in marketing petroleum. In both industries transportation presents a major obstacle, but natural gas producers must cope with the added problem of developing a market. The demand for refined petroleum products already exists in all parts of Canada, but this is not true of natural gas. This point is of some importance to us, for it means that development of the industry is likely to be slower than would be true if Canadian gas had but to displace imported natural gas. It is nearly true to say that the existence of a market is a prerequisite for construction of a pipeline and vice versa.

In Alberta the provincial government created yet another obstacle to development when for a while it refused to allow exports

---

[14] See Harvey O'Connor, *The Empire of Oil* (New York, 1955), pp. 299-300.

[15] The 1955 crude petroleum output was more than 100 times the 1929 output whereas natural gas production in 1955 was not 6 times as great as the 1929 output.

of gas from the province. Since much of the natural gas is a by-product of oil production, however, the rapid accumulation of gas reserves caused a retreat from this position and natural gas may now be exported from the province. Two new pipelines will carry the gas out of the fields. The Trans-Canada pipeline runs eastward from the Princess gas field southeast of Calgary and will eventually be extended to Montreal. The Westcoast Transmission pipeline serves Vancouver and the Washington and Oregon market from the Peace River gas field in northeastern British Columbia.

Given at least a partial solution of the transmission problem, to which we will return, one must look next at the reserve. As with oil reserves, estimates of gas reserves are extremely uncertain and generally understated because the reserves in undrilled areas are not known. Natural gas actually under cap (ready to market) totaled about 12 trillion [12×10^{12}] cubic feet in 1956 and the total reserves in Western Canada were estimated at 22 to 25 trillion feet.[16] At the 1955 rate of consumption of natural gas in Canada these reserves would provide about 150 years' supply. This statement is misleading since gas was not yet available to many consumers in Canada in 1955, but nevertheless it is clear that reserves will be ample for domestic consumption plus some export through 1970.

What rate of increase in natural gas consumption can be anticipated in Canada? One means of estimating this is to look at the history of natural gas development in the United States. There from 1929 to 1955 the per capita increase in consumption was on the order of 4.75 per cent per annum. In the latter year per capita consumption in the United States stood at more than 56,000 cubic feet compared with but 9,700 cubic feet in Canada. It would seem quite certain that, given the higher costs of competing fuels in Canada, gas consumption will surely grow much more rapidly than was true in the United States. In several industries gas would probably find a ready market as soon as change in equipment and processes could be implemented. Cement, primary iron and steel, metallurgy of various sorts, food processing, and numerous fabricating industries will probably convert to gas as it becomes available. Furthermore, certain new industries in the petrochemical field are likely to develop near the new sources of gas supply. Finally, the advantages of gas as a household fuel are apparent.

[16] Cochrane, p. 14.

These promising markets for natural gas provide ample grounds for expecting domestic gas consumption in Canada to rise at nearly twice the historic United States rate. We will put the domestic consumption estimate for 1970 at 700,000,000,000 cubic feet (compared with 150,000,000,000 in 1955). This is an annual increase of about 8.5 per cent per capita. Even though this rate may seem astronomical when compared with the United States experience, per capita natural gas consumption in 1970 would be only a little more than 33,000 cubic feet compared with the 1955 United States figure of 56,000 cubic feet.

Is Canadian per capita consumption likely to pull up even closer to the United States figure by 1970? Perhaps, but at least two considerations need to be underscored here. First, it takes time to conduct all the negotiating and the physical construction work necessary to complete a pipeline of the sort necessary to reach eastern markets from the prairies. The long and notoriously turbulent history of the Trans-Canada line makes this fairly clear, although it is true that building a second, parallel line would come off far more smoothly than did the construction of the first. But delay in the development of natural gas consumption can result not only from the various financial, regulatory and physical problems of trunk pipeline construction, but also from the difficulties of developing a market quickly. New equipment must be planned and installed by prospective final users, distribution companies must be set up and distribution lines built. Secondly, the question of pricing policy must be raised. If the various contracts signed are designed to yield, say, eleven cents per thousand cubic feet at the field, the market will not be penetrated as quickly as if the contracts were drawn up at lower prices averaging out to, say, eight cents per Mcf. Since much of the natural gas is a by-product of crude petroleum, its marginal cost of production is zero or very nearly so. If the pressure of reserves is great enough, contracts may be let to yield very low net-backs. On the other hand it is not inconceivable that prices might be initially higher than the long-run equilibrium rather than lower, until it is clear just how low the price must be to achieve capacity operation of the transmission lines.

With these problems in mind, it seems not unrealistic to use the 700,000,000,000 cubic feet domestic consumption estimate. This figure can be put in perspective by noting that the Trans-

Canada pipeline could move at capacity about 200,000,000,000 cubic feet per year and Westcoast Transmission about 150,000,-000,000 cubic feet, including exports.

The export prospects are particularly cloudy. Not only must the supply and demand conditions be forecast; public policy toward the international sale of energy must also be considered and in this realm especially the uncertainty is very great. The provincial government of Alberta is not likely to be a barrier, although licenses to export gas from the province are required and presumably the government could decide to restrict export to other provinces and to the United States at any time. But national policy, too, is a question. It is apparent that the Canadian government must assure itself that the country's future energy needs are not being jeopardized by exports before sizeable shipments to the United States will be permitted. Because natural gas is an irreplaceable natural resource, any gas exported now is that much less for the country to consume at some later date. If the country's time horizon for this kind of decision were infinity and its rate of time preference zero (as might befit a nation though it would be most unnatural, not to say presumptuous, for the individual), it might refuse to export any gas whatsoever. Even the most casual observer of Canadian affairs, however, would grant that these are not the values assigned to the two parameters. Perhaps this is due to the individual's reluctance to grant that he should be no more concerned about what happens to the nation during his lifetime than afterward. At any rate, it would probably be conceded that the man in the street in Canada shows more concern for his own than for his grandchildren's welfare on this question of exports of natural gas, especially if the individual has a financial interest in natural gas production. The final decision will obviously permit exports of some magnitude.

But public policy south of the border is also problematical. The Federal Power Commission can prohibit imports of natural gas into the United States if it wishes. Judging from the recent performance of the FPC and the general tendency for the United States to encourage by means of tariffs and import restrictions the exhaustion of its exhaustible resources to maintain the country's defensive strength, we can surely expect continual delaying tactics on the part of this agency.

Exports of 200,000,000,000 cubic feet per year was already

contracted for by mid-1956.[17] In view of the growing concern for conservation of energy which seems to mark Canada today, we will put the export projection for 1970 at 300,000,000,000 cubic feet. This projection may well prove quite conservative, depending on the policy decisions of the regulatory bodies on both sides of the international boundary.

Domestic production must then reach 1,000,000,000,000 cubic feet by 1970 in order to meet domestic demand of 700,000,000,000 cubic feet plus the export demand of 300,000,000,000.[18] Such a prognostication seems consistent with recent experience, for production was increasing at a rate of 15 per cent per year over the 1950–1955 period even without the big pipelines. In order to reach 1,000,000,000,000 cubic feet by 1970, domestic production must grow at only 13 per cent per year. Such a large rate of increase would seem unrealistic were it not for several supporting arguments: (1) over the 1940–1955 period the average rate of increase was 9 per cent despite the probable retardation in the rate of growth caused by the war; (2) natural gas discoveries are in large part a function of oil discoveries, so gas reserves are likely to increase with oil production, which is expected to continue its rapid climb; (3) natural gas is of particular use in metallurgical work, so the future of natural gas is in part tied to the bright prospects for the metals; (4) since gas production is in part a function of oil production and since gas storage is likely to be a problem, "dump" gas at very low prices for industrial use is a certainty, the only doubt being whether the dump gas will represent a large proportion of total gas output. Especially for

[17] See *Financial Post,* September 10 and October 15, 1955; and June 30, 1956.

[18] This forecast was drawn up before the appearance of the volume by John Davis, *Canadian Energy Prospects* (Hull, 1957), a study prepared for the RCCEP. His forecast of domestic consumption of 75,000 cubic feet per capita by 1980 comes surprisingly close to our estimate of roughly 33,000 cubic feet per capita by 1970 if a constant rate of increase 1955–1980 is applied (p. 176). His export projection of 1,000,000,000,000 cubic feet in 1980 (p. 177) implies exports of about 360,000,000,000 cubic feet in 1970 (as compared with our 300,000,000,000) if one interpolates by applying a constant rate of increase in exports from the (estimated) 100,000,000,000 cubic feet in 1957 to 1,000,000,-000,000 cubic feet in 1980. Even though Davis examined the United States demand for Canadian gas far more carefully than we have done, the uncertainty about the export projection caused him nonetheless to state that in his study that "it has been assumed, *quite arbitrarily,*" that exports will amount to 1,000,000,000,000 cubic feet in 1980 (p. 177, italics ours).

these reasons, an annual rate of increase of 13 per cent to 1970 does not seem unduly optimistic.

Coal

The problem of predicting the level of Canadian coal production in 1970 is the problem of estimating the extent to which domestic coal will be displaced by alternative fuels, including imported coal.

The country's coal reserves are ample, estimated at between 90,000,000,000 and 100,000,000,000 tons. In 1954 and 1955 domestic disappearance of coal was less than 35,000,000 tons per year, implying that the reserves could supply the domestic market for 2500 years. Thus, even after adjusting the reserves downward to take into account the unrecoverable proportion, the available coal supplies are enormous.

But these huge supplies are far from the major markets. Canada's coal is concentrated in Alberta, Saskatchewan, British Columbia, and Nova Scotia, while the central provinces where the demand is concentrated produce almost no coal. As a result of the distance between her supplies and her markets, Canada is now importing more than half of her coal requirements despite her coal reserves. Almost all of this comes from the central United States. The opening of the St. Lawrence Seaway may increase this proportion since the cheaper United States coal will be able to move down the St. Lawrence, encroaching further on the market for coal from the Maritimes.[19]

The provincial distribution of production since 1925 is shown in Figure 12. The drop in coal production in Alberta and British Columbia is explained by the dieselization of the mountain divisions of the railroads and by the substitution of oil and gas for coal in many industrial uses in the area. Nova Scotian coal is feeling the pressure from imported crude oil. New Brunswick coal production has been rising because of the increase in the proportion of strip mining, but the province's reserves can support only twenty years of production.[20] Saskatchewan, on the other hand, produces a low grade coal primarily from strip mines.

[19] Dominion Steel and Coal Corporation, *Preliminary Submission to RCCEP* (1955), p. 8.

[20] Government of the Province of New Brunswick, *The New Brunswick Economy, Past, Present and Future Prospects* (Fredericton, 1955), p. 41.

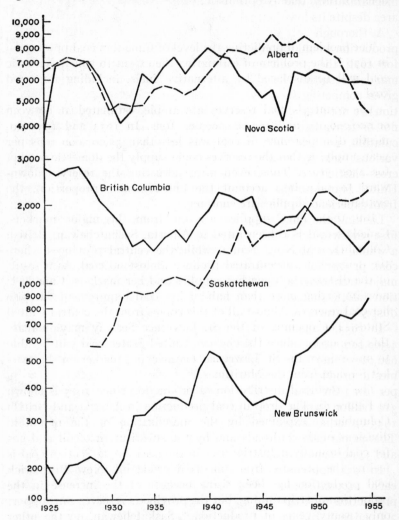

Fig. 12. *Coal production, by province, 1926–1955 (thousands of tons).*

Source: DBS, *Mineral Production of Canada, 1956;* DBS, *The Coal Mining Industry* (various years).

Production costs are so low, because of the high degree of mechanization, that coal is the cheapest source of energy in the area despite its low thermal value.

A thorough job of predicting the future of Canadian coal production would involve estimating the cross-elasticity of demand for coal, the percentage change in the quantity of coal demanded resulting from a 1 per cent change in the price of a given competing fuel. But the data requisite to such a computation are not available in Canada as yet. The competing fuels have not been available long enough in enough areas to make the calculation, nor are data on the prices and consumption of the various fuels by area in satisfactory shape. No studies of the cross-elasticity of demand for coal seem to be available in the United States, so that we cannot even lean on conclusions drawn from experience in the latter country.

Lacking the data for a more sophisticated approach, we will first review quickly the changes in the coal market in Canada as a whole, then proceed to a province-by-province summary of the coal production outlook, concluding with a discussion of the major technological developments in coal production and utilization which should be recognized as possibly improving the industry's future.

In 1955, Canada's coal output was 14,800,000 tons, of which 4,500,000 were subbituminous or lignite. Exports amounted to 600,000 tons, but the imports, 18,300,000 tons, exceeded domestic production. Using a conversion factor of 21,000,000 Btu's per ton, the domestically produced coal accounted for about 310 trillion [310×10^{12}] Btu's of energy, 12 per cent of the total 1955 Canadian energy demand of 2600 trillion [2.6×10^{15}] Btu's. This 12 per cent share in 1955 compares with 17 per cent in 1952 and 31 per cent in 1940.[21]

In 1952, households, the railroads, and "other industrial buyers" each accounted for about one-fourth of the market. Coke production took another 15 per cent and central electric stations 2.5 per cent. But each of these buyers is shifting away from coal, as is shown in Table 87. Although the "solid fuel" category includes wood and therefore overstates the shift of domestic users away from coal, the pattern for the other buyers of coal is clear enough. Over the 1940–1952 period covered, coal lost another 10

[21] O'Brian, p. 32.

Table 87. Percentage of Canadian energy consumption furnished by alternative fuels to types of consumer, 1940 and 1952.

Fuel	Domestic and heating purposes		Industrial purposes		Thermal electric power generation		Transportation		Total, including exports[a]	
	1940	1952	1940	1952	1940	1952	1940	1952	1940	1952
Oil	7.8	32.7	9.6	16.3	13.5	15.5	45.1	63.7	22.4	39.1
Natural gas	5.8	7.8	1.9	2.4	4.6	15.4	—	—	2.3	3.6
Hydro-electricity	3.4	7.7	19.4	21.9	—	—	0.4	0.2	7.5	9.2
Solid fuel	83.0	51.8	69.1	59.4	81.9	69.1	54.5	36.1	67.8	48.1
	100.0	100.0	100.0	100.0	100.0	100.0	100.0	100.0	100.0	100.0

[a] Exports in 1952 equaled 2 per cent of domestic consumption.
Source: C. L. O'Brian, *Coal and Energy in Canada since the War* (reprints of five articles from *Canadian Mining and Metallurgical Bulletin*, 1950–1954), pp. 39, 40, 42, 43.

Table 88. Costs and revenues in Canadian coal mines per net ton of marketable coal produced, and tons produced per manday, 1954.

	Unit	Nova Scotia	New Brunswick	Saskat-chewan	Alberta prairie	Alberta foothills	Alberta mountain	British Columbia and Yukon	Canada
Total cost f.o.b. cars, inclusive of depreciation, depletion, and interest charges	dollars	8.75	7.55	1.56	4.48	6.32	6.29	6.50	6.35
Distribution costs	per	1.14	.22	.19	.19	.22	.13	.36	.57
Total costs	net	9.89	7.77	1.75	4.67	6.54	6.42	6.86	6.92
Coal revenues	ton	9.53	7.78	1.99	4.80	5.97	6.48	7.06	6.84
Production (tons per manday)		2.31	3.17	24.93	6.21	3.88	4.75	4.16	3.64

Source: Nova Scotia Light and Power Company, Limited, *Brief Presented to the Royal Commission on Canada's Economic Prospects by Nova Scotia Light and Power Company, Limited, with Respect to the Availability and Cost of Electric Power in Nova Scotia and Its Relationship to Industry* (1955); Appendix D, Sheet 2. (Processed).

per cent of the industrial market, almost 13 per cent of the thermal electric power market, and 18 per cent of the transportation market. The last is, of course, a reflection of the railroads' dieselization program. These losses in market shares were incurred while the market for energy was expanding so rapidly, however, that coal consumption in absolute terms continued to rise. In 1940 coal consumption was at 35,300,000 tons while in 1952 over 40,000,000 tons were consumed, this being down from the 1948 peak of 49,500,000 tons.

The marked shift of household consumption away from solid fuel in Table 87 is noteworthy. Considering that natural gas had not yet become available to the populous market of central Canada, coal's loss of this market is progressing at an impressive rate.

We can move on to the problem of the coal industry's production prospects in the various provinces. Nova Scotia and New Brunswick most certainly will see their coal output decline unless the industry is more heavily subsidized. Especially in Nova Scotia the coal is extremely expensive to mine, largely because the roadways are long (running as much as five miles out under the ocean), seams pitch and are gassy, and roofs and pavements are weak. The striking differences between coal cost at the mine in the Maritimes and in the western provinces is shown in Table 88. It has been said by the major Maritime producer that no presently conceivable degree of mechanization of Maritime coal mining can lower prices sufficiently to compete with the residual oil from crude oil imported into eastern Canada.[22] The submission of the government of Nova Scotia hopefully mentions the shortage of feasible hydro sites in central Canada and the possible development of the coal-fired gas turbine locomotive as sources of future demand for coal, but the weight of opinion seems to be that central Canada will continue to use United States coal (barring substantial increases in tariffs or subsidies to Maritime coal) supplemented sometime after 1970 by atomic power plants.

The Maritimes in 1955 produced about 6,500,000 tons of coal compared with 8,500,000 tons produced in 1940. Within the next few years they seem likely to lose most of the 1,900,000 ton market represented by Quebec and eastern Ontario in 1955, leav-

[22] Dominion Steel and Coal Corporation, p. 11.

ing a market of something less than 5,000,000 tons.[23] The possible loss of the local power companies' trade would cause a loss of another 500,000 tons.[24] Dieselization of the railroads will reduce demand by another 400,000 tons, lowering total demand to the range of 4,000,000 tons. Some foreign demand is conceivable but only with a subvention. It appears, then, that a 4,000,000 ton estimate for combined Nova Scotia and New Brunswick coal output for 1970 is not too pessimistic. If this is divided as in 1954 between the two provinces, Nova Scotia will be producing about 3,500,000 tons and New Brunswick 500,000.

Central Canada's use of Canadian coal is expected virtually to disappear by 1970. In 1953 over 70 per cent of her needs were met by United States coal. Considering the certainty of the greater penetration of the central provinces by oil and natural gas as well as United States coal, it does seem clear that little Canadian coal will be shipped to the central provinces in 1970 unless substantial production or transportation subsidies are instituted. Given present well-head and transmission cost estimates for natural gas and oil, the relative cost of one million Btu's of energy from natural gas, coal and fuel oil, respectively, in Montreal will be roughly $0.65, $0.45 and $0.30. Coal is so costly in central Canada that Ontario is looking to nuclear power for some of its future power needs.[25] But little of such development is expected prior to 1970.

As for the prairies, the prospects for coal production in Alberta and Saskatchewan are vastly different. Saskatchewan coal costs only 25 to 40 per cent as much as Alberta coal because the former is strip mined, which permits very high output per man, as Table 88 shows. The low thermal value of the Saskatchewan lignite results in a high transportation cost per million Btu's and consequently it is displaced by Alberta coal from all markets more than about 140 miles from Estevan, the center of the strip mining area. But within this area the Saskatchewan lignite will provide the fuel for power generation. It is anticipated that

[23] See Dominion Steel and Coal Corporation, pp. 11–13.
[24] See Nova Scotia Light and Power Company, *Brief Submitted to RCCEP with Respect to the Availability and Cost of Electric Power in Nova Scotia and Its Relationship to Industry* (1955), p. 7 (processed).
[25] Province of Ontario, Department of Economics, *Submission of Ontario to the RCCEP* (1956), p. 18.

considerable losses of the household heating market and smaller losses in the industrial market by 1970 will result in a slight decline in the rate of increase in Saskatchewan's coal production. Lignite production just about doubled between 1940 and 1955, rising from 1,100,000 tons to something over 2,000,000 tons. This growth has been due primarily to the area's increasing demand for steam power, but in addition the lignite output gained at the expense of bituminous coal use in the area. Output could conceivably double again, to 4,000,000 tons by 1970, but considering the expected losses in market share a probable output of 3,000,000 tons seems more realistic. This outlook is supported by the submission of the government of Saskatchewan to the Gordon Commission, in which it is estimated that coal will disappear from domestic use after 1965, from locomotive use after 1970, and from industrial use sometime after 1985, leaving a 1970 consumption of 3,200,000 tons.

An examination of the Alberta coal industry is complicated by the fact that the province's coal reserves are of several different types and are produced and sold under different supply and demand conditions. Viewed in the aggregate the coal production outlook in Alberta is indeed bleak, since output, after having climbed from a 1931 low of about 4,500,000 tons to a peak of more than 8,500,000 in 1946 and 1949, has now fallen by almost 50 per cent back down to the depression low.

Unfortunately data on the amount of Alberta coal going to various end-uses are not available in detail. But information in Alberta's submission to the Royal Commission on Canada's Economic Prospects and in Dominion Coal Board sources makes it possible to classify Alberta's coal into groups defined on the basis of geographical origin. The primary uses for each group are indicated in Alberta's submission, so the demand for each group can be projected in a rough way.[26] We assume (1) that the railroads' demands for Alberta coal will be negligible by 1970, (2) that other coal sales with the exception of those of strip-mined coal will fall by roughly 50 per cent by 1970 due to competition from oil and gas, and (3) that the output of strip-mined coal will continue to rise so that the 1970 output is double the 1954 rate. The sum of these estimates puts Alberta's 1970 output at a bit

[26] See Province of Alberta, Department of Economic Affairs, *Alberta's Economic Prospects* (Edmonton, 1955), pp. 86, 87, 100.

over 3,000,000 tons. But suppose we settle on a more optimistic figure of 3,500,000 tons compared with the 1955 output of a 4,500,-000. If the output of strip-mined coal fails to increase as suggested above, output could drop to the neighborhood of 2,500,000 tons.

The coal outlook in British Columbia is at least as bleak as in Alberta. Coal must compete not only with oil and gas but with hydro power as well. Only about one-tenth of the province's potential hydro power is utilized now.[27] In its submission to the Gordon Commission, the provincial government estimated that British Columbia's coal consumption would drop from about 1,700,000 tons in 1953 to 1,000,000 in 1975. This was assuming that coal's share of the energy market would drop from 18 per cent to 2.1 per cent and that energy consumption per capita would be 2.9 times as great in 1975 as in 1953.[28] This latter estimate is not supported in the submission and seems incredibly high since in the last quarter century energy consumption per capita in all of Canada increased by only 53 per cent. Using the population estimate and the rate of fall in coal's share of the energy market assumed by the provincial submission but assuming that energy consumption per capita in British Columbia will be similar to that for the rest of Canada, coal consumption in the province will be about 1,400,000 tons in 1970. This is just about equal to the 1955 output for the province. In 1955, however, as in previous years, some of British Columbia's coal requirements were met with Alberta coal. The proportion seems not to be known; if we assume that one-third of the province's coal normally comes from Alberta, our 1970 estimate for coal *production* in British Columbia is about 1,000,000 tons annually.

These projections by province point to a 1970 output of 11,500,-000 tons, a drop of 22 per cent. This is in the face of an increase of about 80 per cent in the nation's total energy requirements. Canadian coal's share of the total energy provided is expected to drop, then, from about 12 per cent in 1955 to about 5 per cent in 1970.

A crude check on this 11,500,000-ton projection can be worked out by estimating the 1970 purchases of coal by each of the major types of consumer, using national rather than provincial

[27] Government of the Province of British Columbia, *Submission the RCCEP by the Government of the Province of British Columbia* (Victoria, 1955), p. 16.
[28] Government of the Province of British Columbia, p. 16.

data since the latter are not available.[29] The population estimate of Chapter 8 implies about 5,100,000 households in 1970, which indicates a demand for about 245 trillion [245×10^{12}] Btu's of energy from coal for domestic use. This assumes that the average household will require about 240 million Btu's of fuel annually, as at present, and that 20 per cent of the households will burn coal.[30] When natural gas is available to populous Central Canada, conversion to gas may render this 20 per cent figure too high.

In the last few years roughly ten million tons a year have been used in transportation. In 1970 it is likely that a negligible amount will be so used since dieselization should be largely completed by that time. Industrial energy consumption has been increasing by 1 per cent for each 1 per cent increase in the GNP. If this relation continues to hold and if coal's share of this industrial energy market continues to shrink as it did from 1940 to 1952, about 560 trillion [560×10^{12}] Btu's will be used by industry in 1970 in the form of coal.

The remaining major coal users are the thermal power stations. In recent years they have accounted for only 3 or 4 per cent of all coal consumption in Canada but that proportion is certain to increase at least for the next decade or so. Since 1940, energy consumed by thermal power plants has increased more than twice as rapidly as the GNP. This relation seems likely to hold until 1970, especially since Ontario will be turning increasingly to thermal plants. At this rate, the 1970 GNP of $48,000,000,000 will require 90 trillion [90×10^{12}] Btu's of energy from thermal power plants. About 69 per cent of the energy consumed by these plants in 1952 was from coal compared with 82 per cent

[29] Were it not for the prospect of a marked increase in the use of natural gas, it would be feasible to predict coal consumption by regressing per capita coal consumption on the price of coal relative to the price of fuel oil and per capita income on the premise that coal consumption per capita has been affected by the price of fuel oil and by the variables which move with per capita income. (The relative price of coal was taken as the coal price index divided by the price index of petroleum products, which is unsatisfactory as a price index of fuel oil but no alternative price series is published.) These two variables, however, explained only about 70 per cent of the variation in coal consumption over the 1926–1952 period and so would not be usable for prediction even if new fuel substitutes were not in prospect.

[30] The 20 per cent figure is estimated from the trend in the proportion of households with coal and coke heating equipment. See O'Brian, pp. 39, 53, and Canada, DBS, *Household Facilities and Equipment,* September, 1955.

in 1940. If this share drops to 60 per cent by 1970 because of continuing encroachments of oil in this market, 63 trillion [63 $\times$ 10^{12}] Btu's will be required of coal for thermal power stations.

Total coal consumption in 1970 by this method gives a total of about 41,000,000 tons or 860 trillion [860 $\times$ 10^{12}] Btu's: 240 trillion for domestic use, 560 trillion for industrial use, and 63 trillion in power plants. In 1955 about 58 per cent of the country's coal requirements were imported, but in 1970 the percentage will certainly be considerably higher. United States coal displaces Canadian coal in Ontario and to some extent in Quebec. The Seaway will mean greater Quebec markets for United States coal, and the great increase in coal consumption by thermal power plants, mentioned just above, will be concentrated in Ontario where hydro power sites are now scarce and where industrial growth is going to be rapid. So in central Canada coal demand will grow, but it is here that imported, rather than domestic, coal is likely to be used. The situation can be summed up by saying that the markets which use domestic coal are those most likely to shrink, whereas those calling for imported coal are those most likely to grow.

Barring significant increases in subventions, then, it is quite conceivable that the proportion of coal consumption represented by imported coal may increase from its present level of roughly 60 per cent to at least 65 per cent by 1970. If this occurs, Canadian mines will be providing a little less than 300 trillion [300 $\times$ 10^{12}] Btu's, or about 6.5 per cent of Canada's energy requirements. This amounts to about 14,000,000 tons. The estimate built up from projections by province gave an expected 11,500,000 tons (about 240 trillion Btu's) or roughly 5 per cent of the total energy requirements. These two estimates of 11,500,000 and 14,000,000 tons compare with the 1955 production of 14,800,000 tons. The higher estimate involves mildly optimistic assumption of the proportion of the industrial and household markets which coal can retain, and the lower estimate is probably weakest on the estimated demand from thermal power plants. We will settle on a 13,000,000 ton estimate. If 65 per cent of total coal consumption is met by foreign coal, about 28,000,000 tons will be imported.

In the early 1960's, however, consumption of domestic plus

Table 89.   Annual coal production in Canada, 1954, 1960–1965, and 1970,
by province (millions of tons).

Province	1954 actual	1960–1965 estimated	1970 estimated
Nova Scotia	5.8	4.8	4.2
New Brunswick	0.8	0.6	0.5
Saskatchewan	2.1	2.9	3.3
Alberta	4.9	4.2	3.9
British Columbia	1.3	1.2	1.1
	14.9	13.7	13.0

Source: 1954, DBS, *Canadian Statistical Review;* 1960–1965 and 1970, see text.

imported coal will almost certainly fall below the 1970 projection
of 41,000,000 tons as substitution away from coal continues. Then
a gradual increase in coal consumption up to the 41,000,000-ton
level by 1970 is likely as hydro sites become scarce and as the
country's growth continues to demand large energy inputs. However, the marked drop in coal consumption is likely to occur
primarily in central Canada, and consequently the imports, rather
than domestic production, are likely to undergo this sharp dip
and partial recovery before 1970. The fact that in 1951–52 the
railroads took 4,300,000 tons of Canadian production and that
this market will have largely disappeared by 1965 supports this
assumption that domestic output will decline more rapidly before
1965 than after.

Table 89 gives an estimate of the provincial distribution of coal
production in 1960–1965 and in 1970 as well as actual production
in 1954. The provincial distribution was derived by assuming in
1970 that the total of 13,000,000 tons would be distributed among
the provinces proportionally as the 11,500,000 tons of the 1970
projection worked out above by examining the cost and market
prospects for each of the provinces.

This projection of 13,000,000 tons production in 1970 is considerably lower than the estimates of the man who probably is the
best-known authority on the Canadian coal industry, Mr. C. L.
O'Brian of the Dominion Coal Board. He estimated in April 1954
that in 1965 the country will need some 45,000,000 tons of coal.[31]
Retaining our assumption that only 35 per cent of this will come

[31] O'Brian, p. 56.

from Canadian mines, the demand will be for about 16,000,000 tons of Canadian coal in 1965, or about 21,000,000 in 1970, a rate of output more than 50 per cent greater than that arrived at above.[32] The high figure is not due to a high population projected but rather to what is proving to be a rosy view of coal's share of the market. On the other hand the estimate of Canadian production in the present study is quite consistent with Davis's study for the Gordon Commission. He has projected the 1965 production at 10,800,000 tons and the 1980 production at between 16,000,000 and 24,500,000 tons. These imply a 1970 range of 12,500,000 to 15,400,000 tons.[33]

The coal industry in the United States in recent years has shown a new vitality which one might conceivably look for in Canada in the near future. But an examination of the United States experience shows that fortunate location relative to water transportation has been a major influence, as has the consolidation of companies to improve financial strength, the signing of long-term sales contracts to cut selling costs and increase borrowing ability, and the accelerating of mechanization. Although the Canadian mines may mechanize, consolidate, and sign long-term sales contracts, they can scarcely improve their location. For this reason especially it seems likely that the Canadian coal industry will not hold its share of the energy market until 1970. The possibility of the development of new by-products and the expansion of demand in the West for metallurgical coke may be underrated here, but we will hold to our 13,000,000 ton projection for Canadian production.

Some time long after 1970 the country's oil and gas reserves may become scarce. It is the relative abundance of coal which leads industry spokesmen to state with such certainty that coal's future is assured because oil and gas reserves are limited. But in view of current advances in atomic power, it becomes doubtful whether coal will ever regain its old importance. It seems generally

---

[32] The 21,000,000 tons in 1970 is derived from the 16,000,000 ton 1965 estimate on the basis of O'Brian, Table XXII, p. 48. He there predicts a 60 per cent increase in coal consumption between 1965 and 1975. Half of this percentage increase applied to the 16,000,000 ton 1965 estimate gives approximately 21,000,000 tons as an implied 1970 estimate.

[33] Davis, p. 97. The author states that he built up the projections from provincial supply and demand estimates, but since those estimates were not published we cannot check them against our own projections in detail.

granted that nuclear power will provide electricity within the next ten years in the high power-cost areas of the world.[34] But one does not need to be particularly bullish about atomic power to appreciate that within a generation it may well be coal's most powerful competition.

Coal, oil, and natural gas: conclusions

How much oil, gas, and hydroelectric power will be required to fulfill Canada's energy needs beyond those met by coal? In some areas hydroelectric power will continue to provide the new power source, but sites are becoming scarce in other provinces. Nova Scotia has developed about 85 per cent of her potential and Ontario has exploited about one-half of the possible sites.[35] The other provinces have plenty of sites still available but the distance from markets in many cases is too great at present to make them economical. Thus Ontario has very few remaining spots where plants could be feasible, and consequently the province is already turning to steam plants and looking to atomic energy to provide new power within the next ten to fifteen years. British Columbia is at the other extreme with ample water power yet undeveloped. Quebec also appears to have ample water power resources not touched as yet. Since 1954 the proportion of the country's energy requirements met by water power has fluctuated between 7 and 9 per cent. In view of the low relative cost of water power and the growth of mineral production in the less accessible country where the power sites have not yet been touched, the 9 per cent figure is probably reasonable for application to 1970. This would mean about 415 trillion $[415 \times 10^{12}]$ Btu's would be provided by hydroelectric power as compared with about 270 trillion Btu's from the 28,000,000 tons of imported coal. From estimates in submissions to the Gordon Commission and from newspaper reports of expansion plans, a province-by-province estimate of hydroelectric production by central electric stations was constructed. These estimates totalled 375 trillion Btu's rather than 415 trillion. But central electric stations data exclude power plants of industrial firms producing power for their own

[34] See U.S. Bureau of Mines, *Minerals Facts and Problems,* Bulletin No. 556 (Washington, 1956), p. 950.

[35] Huet Massue, *Highlights of Electric Power in Canada* (Montreal, 1955), p. 7 (processed).

consumption. Such firms in 1953 accounted for about 10 per cent of the total installed hydro capacity in Canada.

The estimated 1970 domestic consumption of natural gas would provide 700 trillion Btu's of energy, or 15.2 per cent of the total energy demand. This share compares with 3.1 per cent in 1952 and 4.5 per cent in 1955. (In the United States, natural gas supplied 23 per cent of the country's energy as against 12 per cent before the war.)

The 700 trillion Btu's from gas, 415 trillion from hydropower, 260 trillion from Canadian coal, and 490 trillion from imported coal leaves a balance of 2735 trillion $[2.735 \times 10^{15}]$ to be provided by oil. This 2735 trillion Btu's, the equivalent of about 475,000,000 barrels, can be checked by looking at the per capita consumption data. The projection implies that in 1970 oil consumption per capita will be about 130,000,000 Btu's per capita compared with 74,000,000 Btu's in 1955, an increase of 4 per cent per annum. From 1926–1929 to 1952–1955 consumption per capita increased much faster, about 5.5 per cent per year, but we would expect the annual increase to fall a bit in the future. Certainly there is no new use of petroleum of the magnitude of the automotive industry in view, so the oil industry cannot expect consumption to maintain the historic rate of increase. Nonetheless the per capita figure will still rise more rapidly than will the total energy consumed per capita, which has been climbing at about 1.5 per cent per year.

The 1970 export demand for Canadian oil is a most uncertain estimate. The west coast of the United States would seem to be the most likely export market, yet for some refineries there Canadian crude is second choice to Middle Eastern crude. Canadian producers will certainly increase their share of the west coast market considerably but it is not clear how far they will go toward displacing other crudes there. In Minnesota, Wisconsin, and Michigan, Canadian crude is already being refined. As with the west coast market, Canadian producers could move in more extensively in this part of the United States if they were willing to accept lower net-back prices. To what extent this will happen is, of course, extremely difficult to say. If drilling and development costs fall in Canada, producers there may be willing to accept lower well-head prices; but if these costs remain high, expansion may be considerably slower.

Under the circumstances, perhaps the most appropriate means

of forecasting Canadian petroleum production is to assume merely that Canadian output will follow the growth pattern of the United States industry. Such a naïve procedure has a better basis than is at first apparent. The living standards of the people in the two countries are sufficiently alike to make the cases parallel insofar as final consumer demand is concerned. The location of the fields relative to markets is similar in a very rough way, although the more general availability of water transportation for crude oil in the United States is in marked contrast with Canada. Wage rates and equipment costs in Canada approximate very roughly those in the United States industry. And finally, oil must compete in Canada with the same fuels as was the case historically in the United States. In many ways the two countries' petroleum industries differ significantly, needless to say. But in view of the difficulties of evaluating the probabilities of the various export markets developing substantially, we will choose to rely more than we like on the parallel with the United States industry.

Accordingly an output of about 500,000,000 barrels is forecast for 1970. This would leave the country with net exports of 25,000,000 barrels. Gross exports must be considerably in excess of this 25,000,000 barrels, however, since oil will be imported in the eastern part of the country and exported from the prairies.

This 500,000,000-barrel estimate calls for an increase of 400 per cent in the output over 1954's level of roughly 100,000,000 barrels. Other estimates are consistent with this expectation. The Imperial Oil Company expects the 1980 output to lie between 720,000,000 and 1,080,000,000 barrels,[36] Shell Oil predicts 370,-000,000 barrels by 1965,[37] and British-American Oil estimated 460,000,000 barrels in 1970 and 760,000,000 barrels in 1980.[38] Davis's lowest 1970 estimate is about 500,000,000 barrels.[39]

The expected changes in shares of the energy market between 1952 and 1970 are summarized in Table 90. The shifts in market shares may seem improbably large but by 1955 the magnitude of the expected changes was already becoming apparent. Only 710 trillion [710×10^{12}] Btu's of coal were consumed in 1955; thus

[36] Imperial Oil Company, p. 4.
[37] Shell Oil Company of Canada, Ltd., *Petroleum in Canada's Economy, A Submission to the RCCEP* (Toronto, 1956), p. 4.
[38] British American Oil Company, Ltd., *A Submission to the RCCEP* (Toronto, 1956), Exhibit I.
[39] Davis, p. 141.

Table 90.   Energy consumed in Canada, 1952 and 1970,
by source of energy.

Energy source	1952 Actual		1970 Estimated	
	MMMM Btu's	Percentage	MMMM Btu's	Percentage
Coal	1,014	48.5[a]	750	16.3
Oil	826	39.4	2,735	59.5
Hydro-electricity	190	9.0	415	9.0
Natural gas	68	3.1	700	15.2
Total	2,098	100.0	4,600	100.0

[a] These percentages differ slightly from those in Canada, DBS, *Energy Sources in Canada Commodity Accounts for 1948 and 1952*, Reference Paper No. 69 (Ottawa, 1956), p. 16. Data there, concerned with mineral fuels only, indicate 1952 consumption (available supply) to have been distributed as follows: coal, 53.8 percent; oil, 41.3 per cent; and natural gas, 4.9 per cent. The mineral fuels consumption of the present table are distributed thus: coal, 53.3 per cent; oil, 43.3 per cent; and natural gas, 3.5 per cent.

Source: 1952, C. L. O'Brian, *Coal and Energy in Canada Since the War* (1950–1954), p. 44; 1970 estimates are from text.

coal's share of the 1955 energy market had already dropped from 48.5 per cent in 1952 to 27.3 per cent. Oil consumption was up to 1120 trillion [1.12×10^{15}] Btu's, or 43.1 per cent of the energy market, and natural gas was up to 4.5 per cent. In view of the development in the first three years of the eighteen-year span covered in Table 90, the 1970 projections do appear justifiable.

Table 91 presents the expected production, imports, and exports of the three mineral fuels. The margin of error is probably greatest for the natural gas projection. The production could easily exceed the one trillion [1×10^{12}] cubic feet by 20 per cent, the added output being sold both on the domestic market and into

Table 91.   Canadian production, imports, and exports of coal, oil, and natural gas, estimated for 1970.

Product	Production	Imports	Exports
Coal (millions of tons)	13	25	—[a]
Oil (millions of barrels)	500	50	75
Natural gas (billion cu. ft.)	1,000	0	300

[a] Less than 500,000 tons.
Source: See text.

the export market. The export estimate of 300,000,000,000 cubic feet is probably more conservative than the domestic consumption estimate of 700,000,000,000, however. The oil import estimate assumes that eastern Canada will import 50,000,000 barrels from abroad, this being about one-third of the area's probable requirements. The net export estimate seems more certain than either gross imports or gross exports, however.

NICKEL AND COPPER

The metallic minerals are next to be considered, followed by the nonmetallics (divided into two categories, asbestos and other nonmetallics) and a final group, clay products and structural materials.

Nickel and copper mining are logically considered together because all but a very small fraction of the nickel in Canada is found with copper and about half of the copper production is from nickel-copper ores. The two materials are now second and third in importance among the minerals in Canada by value of production. For the last decade or more, about 80 per cent of the free world's nickel has come from Canada, and the current production is about 160,000 tons per year. The known reserves of over 6,000,000 tons metallic content could support this rate of output for more than thirty-five years. New and promising bodies of ore have been developed within recent years near Lynn Lake, Manitoba; and in the Yukon the Hudson's Bay Mining and Smelting Company has increased its known nickel ore reserves. There would seem to be no supply limitation to Canadian nickel production operating before 1970. The nickel reserves are concentrated in Ontario's Sudbury Basin where there appear to be nearly 5,500,000 tons of nickel reserves within a radius of twenty miles of Sudbury.

Copper reserves are not as ample as those of nickel, but the known reserves could support production to 1970 at the 1955 rate of output. As is so frequently the case, however, the ratio of reserves to current production gives a distorted view of potential production. It is more indicative that in the eighteen months beginning January 1, 1954, copper ore reserves in Canada increased by about 30 per cent; this increase was in response to the 30 per cent price increase over approximately the same

Table 92. Distribution of copper ore reserves among Canadian provinces, 1953 and 1955 (thousands of tons).

Province	1953 Actual	1955 Estimated
British Columbia	2,948	17,948
Quebec	31,843	107,843
Newfoundland	0	8,000
Ontario	296,112	311,112
Manitoba	31,083	31,083
	361,986	475,986

Source: Canada, DBS, *Nickel-Copper Mining, Smelting and Refining Industry,* 1953; E. A. R. Germain, "Copper Mining Prospects in Canada," *Commercial and Financial Chronicle,* Sept. 29, 1955, p. 5 ff.

period.[40] This experience with copper supports the argument set forth earlier, namely, that the Canadian shield holds sizeable reserves of minerals as yet untapped and continual strong world demand for these minerals will bring them forth.

The effect of the new findings on the provincial distribution of reserves is approximated in Table 92.

With the decline in copper prices in 1956–57 the search for new copper reserves was relaxed as the firms concentrated rather on developing the known reserves and beginning production. (Some firms halted production to await more favorable prices.) Thus production may outstrip additions to reserves in some years over the next decade or so, but such a development need not necessarily invalidate the expectations outlined here. The point is that Canadian copper appears to be so plentiful that known reserves are very elastic with rises in the world price.

Copper production and nickel production have followed roughly the same growth curves, with copper production averaging roughly twice as great a tonnage as nickel production. In the 1920's, however, copper production expanded considerably more rapidly than nickel production, presumably because of the expanded use of electricity and electrical products during that decade. Since the early years of World War II, nickel production has been

[40] Computed from estimates reviewed in E. A. R. Germain, "Copper Mining Prospects in Canada," *Commercial and Financial Chronicle,* September 29, 1955, p. 5 ff.

somewhat more buoyant than copper production, probably because nickel has been brought into use in more defense items, whereas copper is being displaced in some uses by substitutes. Nickel production hit a peak of 144,000 tons during the war, compared with but 32,000 tons in 1931. Production fell off to 96,000 tons in 1946, but since has risen to a level of about 175,000 tons in 1955. Copper production reached 322,000 per year during the war and fell off to 183,000 tons after the war and is now at the 325,000-ton level.

The bulk of the copper and nickel production goes into the world market. In 1954, over 98 per cent of the nickel production was exported (two-thirds of it to the United States) and almost 70 per cent of the copper output was sold abroad. Because of the importance of the export market, world demand (and especially the United States demand) and competing sources of supply will determine the level of copper and nickel production for the next decade.

The President's Materials Policy Commission (the Paley Commission) predicted that the free world's demand for nickel would approximately double between 1950 and 1975, rising from 130,000 tons to 264,000 tons, implying an annual rate of increase of about 2.75 per cent.[41] The actual rate of increase in free world output for the 1950–1954 period has been just over 10 per cent per year, the 1954 free world production having already reached 195,000 tons. Were this to continue, by 1975 the free world production would be 900,000 tons instead of the Paley Commission projection of 264,000 tons.

The 10 per cent annual rate of growth in free world production in the 1950–1954 period undoubtedly cannot be maintained steadily for the coming years even assuming that high level employment will be maintained during the period. The gross national products of the major industrial countries are expected to rise at rates between 2 and 5 per cent per annum and it has been argued that the demand for nickel can be expected to increase accordingly. The Paley Commission anticipated that United States nickel demand, which in recent years has accounted for about 70 per cent of world demand, would increase proportionally with the gross national product.[42]

[41] U.S. President's Materials Policy Commission, Vol. II, pp. 125 and 135.
[42] U.S. President's Materials Policy Commission, Vol. II, pp. 125 and 135.

Technological advances in metallurgy and high defense requirements have meant that the uses for nickel have been rising rapidly. It is essential to products with expanding markets, such as high-temperature alloys, stainless steel, nonferrous alloys, electro-plated goods, and chemical products of various sorts. Thus, even if the total output of goods in major countries grows more slowly than the output of services and thus more slowly than the GNP, the demand for nickel is still very likely to keep up with the growth of the GNP.

The United States demand for nickel since the end of the war provides an uncertain base for projecting the needs for Canada's largest nickel customer. The Korean War accelerated civilian uses as well as the country's consumption of nickel for defense purposes. In addition, the United States stockpile program for strategic materials appears to have absorbed sizeable proportions in some years. Although data on stockpile acquisitions are not available it is possible to construct some estimates which, when deducted from total United States imports of nickel, yield an estimate of actual consumption of nickel in the United States.[43] These estimates show an increase of some 26 per cent for United States consumption between 1948 and 1955, or about 3.5 per cent per year. If we assume that short nickel supplies have discouraged the development of new nickel uses and that the rate of growth in nickel consumption will be nearer to, say, 4 or 5 per cent per annum, United States nickel needs (assuming no stock-piling) will rise from 235,000,000 pounds in 1955 to between 425,-000,000 and 490,000,000 pounds by 1970. Assuming that by 1970 the United States is taking but 65 per cent of the world supply (due to the nickel demand of other countries increasing more rapidly than that of the United States) the free world demand would total between 650,000,000 and 750,000,000 pounds. If Canada is still meeting 80 per cent of the world's needs, as now appears most likely, she will be selling 525,000,000 to 600,000,000 pounds per year. In view of the fact that past experience indicates that conservative estimates of consumption of the key metals have been much too low, the higher of these two estimates will be retained.

[43] The estimates of stockpile acquisitions were constructed from U.S. Department of Commerce, *A Review of Nickel in the United States, 1946 to 1956* (Washington, 1955), pp. 16, 18, 21 and 22. Also see *The New York Times,* March 14, 1956, p. 46.

An alternative means of estimating probable Canadian nickel output can be based on the estimated United States nickel consumption for 1960. The nickel industry has estimated United States nondefense requirements in 1960 to be 300,000,000 pounds.[44] Assuming that defense requirements will add another 30,000,000 to 50,000,000 pounds, that demand will grow at 5 per cent per year for the next ten years, that the United States will be taking about 65 per cent of the world supply and that Canada will supply 80 per cent of the latter, Canadian output will range between 650,000,000 and 700,000,000 pounds.

The final, and simplest, projection method presumes merely that Canadian output to 1970 will increase at 4 to 5 per cent per year, keeping pace with the growth of the major nickel-consuming countries. This would put Canadian nickel output at between 600,000,000 and 700,000,000 pounds.

In sum, then, the three projection methods give estimates of Canadian nickel output of 600,000,000, 650,000,000–700,000,000 and 600,000,000–700,000,000 pounds, respectively. For the purposes of the remainder of this work, the 650,000,000-pound estimate will be used. This is 325,000 tons, just 85 per cent greater than the 1955 output of 175,000,000 tons.

The regression of domestic consumption of nickel on Canadian GNP indicates that the 1970 domestic disappearance will be about 5,000 tons if the GNP reaches $48,000,000,000 dollars by that year. This would leave about 320,000 tons for export, compared with 174,000 tons in 1955, an increase of about 85 per cent.

The Paley Commission estimated that the copper demand of the free world countries would increase from 2,600,000 tons in 1950 to 3,900,000 tons in 1975, equivalent to an annual rate of 1.6 per cent.[45] The actual increase in free world production from 1950 to 1954 was 1.5 per cent per year, implying a total free world copper consumption by 1970 of just under 3,500,000 tons. The Paley report anticipated that United States mine production would fall from the 909,000 tons of 1950 to 800,000 tons by 1975. This expectation still appears justified in spite of United States output having fluctuated around 925,000 tons for the last four years; the life of the present open pit operations in the United

[44] U.S. Department of Commerce, p. 16.
[45] U.S. President's Materials Policy Commission, Vol. II, pp. 118 and 133.

States seems to be limited to from ten to twenty years under current conditions.[46]

If the United States can produce 800,000 tons of copper in 1970, the rest of the free world must produce the remaining 2,800,000 tons which are expected to be demanded. In 1954, Canada's share of the free world (exclusive of the United States) production was 16 per cent after having fluctuated between 9.3 and 11.6 per cent over the preceding five years. The very great increase in copper reserves in Canada in 1954–55 would seem to promise that Canada can retain this share and perhaps increase it slightly. If we expect that the very large copper reserves in Chile and Peru, which combined now yield about half again as much copper as Canada's mines, are not exploited to the utmost because of inaccessibility, political instability in the two countries, and so forth, the output of these two countries may not infringe on Canada's share of the world market. Using 17 per cent as an estimate of Canada's share in 1970 gives an expected annual output of 480,000 tons, nearly 50 per cent greater than the 1955 output.

The change in the nature of Canada's copper exports has been particularly interesting. Since 1926, copper production has nearly quintupled, rising from 66,000 tons to 325,000 tons in 1955.[47] Domestic disappearance of copper, on the other hand, in 1955 was about eleven times the 1926 figure, having climbed from 10,000 tons in 1926 to 110,000 tons in 1955. In other words in 1926 only about 15 per cent of production was consumed domestically but in 1955 almost 33 per cent was used by the domestic market. This domestic consumption seems to be correlated more with the GNP than with any other likely variables, but still only 82 per cent of the fluctuations in domestic consumption of copper 1926–1955 (excluding war years) is explained by the GNP. Using this rather weak relation to project the 1970 domestic copper consumption gives a figure of 275,000 tons, a little over 55 per cent of the total expected production of 480,000 tons. But this increase in the proportion of copper consumed at home, although consistent with historical experience, is a mistaken application of correlation

[46] U.S., Bureau of Mines, p. 234.

[47] "Copper" here includes the copper in ore, ingots, bars, billets, rods, strips, sheets, and tubing but not in goods of any higher degree of manufacture.

analysis. It is quite clear that this very rapid increase in domestic copper production which has marked the past thirty years is not going to continue until 1970. The ideal measure of domestic consumption of copper would include not only copper produced and consumed in Canada but also the copper content of all imported goods. If such a measure were available, copper consumption per capita might be worked out and correlated with income with some confidence. But we do not know how much copper was imported in the form of manufactured goods. Since 1926 the country's own electrical goods industry has grown rapidly and consequently copper which formerly was imported in various manufactured goods is now manufactured at home. The very rapid increase in copper produced and consumed domestically reflects not only an increase in copper consumption per capita but also a considerable increase in the proportion of copper consumption met with domestic raw copper rather than with imported copper goods.

That this argument is valid is demonstrated by the comparison of copper consumption per capita for the United States and Canada for 1929–1953, the longest time span for which sufficient data for both countries are available. During this period apparent consumption of new copper in the United States rose from 14.6 pounds per capita to only 18.0 pounds per capita, about 0.5 per cent per year.[48] Presumably in 1929 as well as in 1953 a very small proportion of total copper consumed in the United States was imported in the form of manufactured goods. In Canada, on the other hand, raw copper consumption increased from 1.3 pounds per capita in 1929 to 8.8 pounds per capita, equal to an annual rate of increase of more than 8 per cent. By 1955, domestic consumption in Canada had risen to 14.1 pounds per capita. This rapid rate of increase in Canada's use of its own copper probably can best be interpreted as a shift away from the importation of copper goods toward domestic production of such manufactures.

It was noted above that correlating domestic copper consumption with the GNP leads to an estimate of 275,000 tons consumption in 1970. But this would be equal to a per capita disappearance in 1970 of 26.4 pounds compared with the present

[48] U.S., Bureau of Mines, p. 221.

per capita consumption of 18.0 pounds in the United States and 14.1 pounds in Canada. Since copper consumption has been increasing so slowly in the United States, the jump to 26.4 pounds per capita seems definitely beyond reason. In view of the great rate at which Canadian industry seems to be taking over the production of the country's copper goods, the most feasible projection of copper consumption might be based on the presumption that by 1970 copper consumption in Canada will be the same as in the United States and that in the United States the long-run rate of increase of 0.5 per cent per year in per capita consumption will continue. This procedure yields 19.6 pounds per capita as the 1970 figure for both the United States and Canada. The 1970 population therefore will require 206,000 tons of copper, leaving 272,000 tons available for export.

GOLD

Canada is the world's third largest producer of gold, ranking behind the Union of South Africa (12,000,000 ounces in 1953) and Russia (9,500,000 ounces estimated 1952 production). Canada's 4,300,000 ounces production in 1954 compares with a peak production of 5,300,000 ounces in 1941 and a postwar low of 2,700,000 ounces produced in 1945. Ontario accounts for more than one-half of the current production, reflecting that the pre-Cambrian shield is the country's primary source of the metal. Production in the Northwest Territories, however, is growing more rapidly than in any of the provinces, the Northwest Territories having climbed from seventh place in 1946 to third place in 1953, outstripping in the latter year all the provinces except Ontario and Quebec.

Although gold production increased six-fold between World War I and World War II and then rose again at nearly the same annual rate from the 1945 low to 1950, the current and prospective cost-price relations would seem to forestall such a rate of increase being resumed in the next decade or so. Rising wages and exploration costs are bumping against the nearly inflexible gold price to indicate limited growth for the industry. In British Columbia, the Northwest Territories, and in some Ontario locations, new reserves are being uncovered, but "the success stories aren't quite enough to encourage further development of the many gold properties of established promise." [49] Gold exploration in the Northwest Territories had virtually stopped in 1956.

In projecting gold production to 1970 the probable level of the price of gold must first be established. Since we are assuming a high level of employment in the industrial countries it would be inconsistent to anticipate a gold price increase arising out of depression conditions. Raising the price of gold was rather widely discussed immediately after World War II and also more recently as a means of increasing the value of the dwindling gold reserves of the countries of western Europe. The United States, however, has not given even the faintest support to the sentiment for a price increase. Barring, then, serious depression and a sudden urge to help the Union of South Africa, Russia, and Canada, it would appear unduly optimistic for the gold producers to anticipate a price increase by 1970.

We will not, of course, entertain the possibility that the managed currencies of the world should be cut loose from gold since the ethos of the world financial community seems quite unlikely to permit such a move. If in the event of severe economic upheaval this should happen, however, the price of gold could conceivably fall. Stephen Leacock has noted that, after all, gold has very little use value except for "false teeth, coffin handles," and the like.

The prospects for lowering operating costs do not appear bright enough to warrant projecting any sizeable increase in the rate of gold production before 1970. Wage costs represent about two-thirds of total costs. In 1955 they were about 25 per cent lower than Sudbury wages and nearly 15 per cent below the prevailing wage in Toronto industry. Surely real wage increases will be necessary if workers are to be retained in the industry. The resulting cost-price squeeze will be fatal for many of the current producers. [50]

Yet for other producers the prospects are quite favorable. Some of the ore bodies are still very large and some are even getting richer as the mine is run deeper. The astounding growth of production from the Northwest Territories is a reminder that the pre-Cambrian shield is scarcely touched as yet. And of course even

[49] *Financial Post,* March 5, 1955, p. 62.
[50] Committee of Inquiry into the Economics of the Gold Mining Industry, *Gold Mining in Ontario* (Toronto, 1955).

if all the gold mines were to close down, some gold would still be produced as a by-product of other minerals.

Assuming that new ore finds will offset production lost from closed mines, the 1970 gold production for the country is estimated at 5,000,000 ounces, 11 per cent above the 1955 output but still about 300,000 ounces below the postwar peak production.

LEAD, ZINC AND SILVER

The price and production history of lead and zinc in Canada since the end of the war has provided some interesting evidence on the lagged supply response to price increases of these two metals and the irreversibility of established supply. Lead production after the war moved along at the 155,000–175,000 ton level through 1952 with no apparent trend either upward or downward. This stability persisted despite a huge increase in prices from the wartime level. The price jumped from about 7 cents per pound in 1946 to 14 cents in 1947 and 18 cents in 1948. After a dip the price was pulled up by the Korean affair to 18.4 cents in 1951, from which level it dropped with the return of more normal demand conditions. Not until 1952, however, was the supply response to the high 1947–1951 price evident. The search for new ore bodies during that period helped push production upward beginning in 1952. The peak production of about 220,000 tons was recorded in 1954 but by this time the lead price was about 27 per cent below the 1951 high. Since 1954 the lead output has fallen but in 1956 was still above the 1947–1951 level.

Zinc production has risen much faster than lead production since the 1920's. For the entire period 1925–1955 the rate of increase was about 6 per cent per annum and for the 1947–1954 period the rate was about 7.5 per cent per year. In 1956 zinc production stood at 420,000 tons, about 23 per cent above 1951, even though the price in 1956 was about 25 per cent *below* the 1951 level. Thus for zinc as for lead there is evidence that once production is brought in by high prices, it continues despite substantial price declines; that is, the supply function is not reversible. One would expect this to be the case with mining, in which the exploration and development costs are high and the marginal costs of production frequently relatively low.

The increase in Canadian production of lead and zinc in the face of the marked price drop since 1951 is especially significant when compared with the short-run supply elasticities prevailing in the other major producing countries. Over the 1951–1954 period the production of lead in the United States, Canada's largest customer for lead, dropped from 390,000 tons to 320,000 tons. United States zinc production dropped over the same period from 681,000 tons to 465,000 tons. It would seem, therefore, that United States lead and zinc producers are more frequently marginal than Canadian producers. Australian production of lead and zinc has increased by about the same proportion as Canada's. Mexico, the fourth large base metal producer, actually produced less lead in 1954 than in any of the years 1949 through 1952, thus implying an elastic lead supply due to a significant proportion of marginal mines. Mexican zinc output, on the other hand, has increased about 25 per cent since 1951, but her rate of increase since the end of the war has not kept pace with that of Canada.

The favorable prospects for Canadian lead and zinc producers relative to those in the United States are upheld in the Paley report. It is stated there that the United States lead producers could be expected to maintain their 1950 rate of output for only about a half dozen years, and that the 1975 rate would be between 200,000 and 300,000 tons, compared with the 1950 output of 430,000 tons.[51] Since the United States output fell to 340,000 tons in 1953 and to 320,000 in 1954, the Paley projection in this respect seems justified.

The Paley Commission considered United States zinc producers to be somewhat more favorably situated than the lead producers. It was expected that the zinc industry would be able to maintain a rate of production of 600,000 to 700,000 tons per year through 1975 at the 1950 zinc price (about 15 cents).[52] But since then the Australian and Canadian output (and to some extent the Mexican production) has been raised and the price is down to 12 and 13 cents. Presumably in response to the lower price, United States production fell to 465,000 tons in 1954.

Thus the recent production trends and the available information on United States reserves imply that Canada's lead and zinc resources are now and will probably remain cheaper to find and to exploit than those in the United States and Mexico. In view of the continuing exploratory activity in Canada and some of the

[51] U.S. President's Materials Policy Commission, Vol. II, p. 41.
[52] U.S. President's Materials Policy Commission, Vol. II, p. 47.

recent finds (especially the new five million ton find of 4 per cent lead and 7 per cent zinc at Pine Point), Canada's growth as a major base metals producer is apparently assured.

In its projections of world demand for new lead, the Paley Commission estimated an increase of 53 per cent in the United States demand from 1950 to 1975 and an increase of 78 per cent for the rest of the free world. The percentage is relatively lower for the United States primarily because of the expected rise in the recovery ratio. Such rates of increase would involve free world mine production rising from 1,628,000 tons in 1950 to 2,700,000 tons in 1975, or 2 per cent per year. The actual rate of increase of free world production of new lead for the 1950–1955 period was more than 3 per cent per year.

To project Canadian lead production, we must estimate not only the probable rate of increase in the free world's production of new lead to 1970 but also make some estimate of the share of that increase which Canada is likely to provide.

The relatively slow rate of growth in lead production in the world in the 1920's and 1930's has been attributed to substitution which has already run its course. Unlike copper, for example, the prospects for continued substitution away from lead are considered rather limited. Hence the growth in lead consumption to 1970 may well proceed faster than before World War II. Offsetting this partly will be the increase in the supply of secondary lead. From 1950 to 1952 alone the ratio of secondary lead production to total lead consumption in the United States rose from 35 per cent to 43 per cent, although the latter percentage was undoubtedly higher than the trend value will prove to be because of the high price of lead in 1951 and early in 1952. If we raise the Paley Commission's estimated annual increase of 2 per cent to a 2.5 or 3.0 per cent rate of increase, 1954–1970, free world production in the latter year will be between 2,750,000 and 3,000,000 tons as compared with the 1954 output of 1,860,000 tons.

Canada's share of free world mine production of lead since the war has varied from 10 per cent in 1950 and 1951 to as high as 14 per cent in 1948. In 1953 and 1954 the percentages were 11.0 and 11.8 respectively. If we assume that United States and Mexican lead production will remain relatively stable while Canada and Australia increase their output, a 13 to 15 per cent share of the market may provide the most plausible assumption for the 1970 target year. Such a share would mean an output of about 400,000 tons in Canada, an increase of 83 per cent over the 1954 output of 219,000 tons.

Since 1949 and 1950, Canada's domestic consumption has increased from 55,000 tons to 68,000 tons. At this rate, the 1970 domestic consumption will be about 148,000 tons, or 37 per cent of her output, compared with the 31 per cent of her output currently consumed at home. The 1949–1954 rate of increase in domestic consumption of 5 per cent may be a bit higher, however, than can continue permanently. If Canada uses lead on the average in the same ways as the United States, about one-third of the lead consumed goes into storage batteries, another 11 per cent into construction, 11 per cent into cable covering and 10 per cent into oil refining and gasoline. Therefore the 1950–1954 rate of increase of domestic lead consumption in Canada may reflect in part the high level of construction activity and of automobile output.[53] Adjusting for these abnormalities implies a 4 per cent rate of increase to 1970 and a domestic consumption figure of 128,000 tons rather than 148,000 tons. If we say, then, that total Canadian production of lead will be about 400,000 tons and domestic consumption about 130,000 tons, 270,000 tons remain for export, an increase of 8 per cent over the 1954 level of lead exports.

With respect to the free world demand for zinc, the Paley Commission expected an increase in mine production from the 1950 level of 1,931,000 tons to 3,200,000 tons in 1975. At this rate, free world mine production would have been about 2,090,000 tons in 1954. The actual 1954 production figure was almost 2,500,-000 tons. In other words, the commission projected a 60 per cent increase for the twenty-five-year period (less than 2 per cent per year), yet a 20 per cent increase had already been achieved within four years.

Zinc is used primarily in galvanizing, die castings, pigments and salts, brass and bronze, and rolled zinc. The Paley Commission study assumed that in die-casting and in brass and bronze, substitutes, especially aluminum, would cause little in-

---

[53] Domestic consumption of lead for the last thirty years has not moved with the GNP nor with any of its major components. This erratic behavior may be caused by inventory fluctuations, which might have been large because lead is found with zinc.

crease in zinc demand in these uses. Magnesium is expected to replace rolled zinc in dry cells and engraving plates. The big increase is expected in the demand for zinc for galvanizing. The 1950–1953 data on zinc consumption in the United States indicate that the use of zinc in brass products was accounting for a growing, rather than a shrinking, proportion of total United States zinc consumption. Over that three-year period total zinc consumption rose by about 2 per cent while consumption of zinc in brass products increased 28 per cent.[54] This is a very short period on which to base estimates of longer-term changes; but it may possibly indicate that at the low zinc prices prevailing in 1952 the substitution of aluminum for zinc was slowed. If zinc prices continue below their 1950–51 levels, the full substitution expected by the Paley Commission may not materialize.

Assuming, then, that the relative price of zinc will rise above the unusually low 1952–53 levels and that substitution of other metals for zinc will proceed, one can argue that the 4 per cent rate of increase in free world zinc production which has marked the 1950–1954 period will not continue. Settling on a 2 per cent rate of increase (fractionally higher than the Paley rate) as most probable for the 1954–1970 period gives an estimated free world output of about 3,400,000 tons compared with the 1954 output of 2,500,000 tons.

Canada's share of world zinc production has remained quite stable at 15 and 16 per cent since the end of the war, despite falling United States output. Apparently the other zinc producers have shared about equally in that part of the market formerly held by United States producers. Mexican zinc production jumped 25 per cent between 1951 and 1952, indicating a very elastic supply (at least during times of rising prices, though perhaps not during times of falling prices), quite unlike Mexican lead production. If we suppose Canada to be able to hold her share of the market at 16 per cent, she will be producing about 540,000 tons, an increase of 45 per cent over the 1954 level of 376,500 tons. Such an increase can be easily accomplished, especially if the Consolidated Mining and Smelting operation at Pine Point gets into production by 1970. A mining rate of 10,000 tons per day has been mentioned; since the ore is reportedly 4 per cent lead and 7.4 per cent zinc, annual production of about 250,000

---

[54] U.S., Bureau of Mines, p. 995.

tons of zinc is possible. The question is whether this rate will be achieved by 1970.[55] If it is, the present projection of 540,000 tons of zinc will prove much too low.

Domestic consumption of refined zinc has fluctuated over a wide range since the end of the war. Consumption fell from 55,600 tons in 1945 to 45,600 tons in 1949. It then bounced back up to 61,000 tons in 1951 and since then has been in the neighborhood of 50,000 tons per year. No very clear-cut growth pattern or correlation is indicated. If 1948 and 1949 are taken as more or less normal years and compared with 1952–1954, it is seen that an increase of about 18 per cent in the gross national product (in real terms) is associated with an 8 per cent increase in domestic zinc consumption. Using this as the best available indication of the probable trend in domestic consumption and anticipating an increase of 80 to 100 per cent in the gross national product between 1952–1954 and 1970 leads to an estimated domestic consumption figure of about 70,000 tons. Such a level of domestic use when total output is 540,000 tons would leave 470,000 tons for export, an increase of about 20 per cent over the 1954 level.

Silver ranks seventh among Canada's metallic minerals by value of output. In 1954 nearly $26,000,000 worth of silver was produced but this amounted only to 3.2 per cent of total production of metallic minerals. It is interesting that in spite of silver's being such a small contributor to total metal mining, Canada is the third largest silver producer in the free world, ranking behind Mexico and the United States.

Canadian silver is found in many ores, but about 70 per cent of the production comes from silver-lead-zinc mines. The remainder is found in copper-gold-silver ores, silver-cobalt ores, nickel-copper ores, and with gold. Even in the case of silver-lead-zinc mines, however, silver accounts for less than 5 per cent of the total output. Thus silver is produced only as a by-product of other metals, primarily lead and zinc. This is important for our purposes because it signifies that economically silver has little or no life of its own in that silver production depends primarily on the supply and demand for other metals.

Since almost three-fourths of silver production comes from silver-lead-zinc ores, we will expect silver production to move

[55] See *Financial Post*, March 5, 1955, p. 42; also *Financial Post Survey of Mines*, 1956 (Toronto, 1956), p. 75.

primarily with these two other base metals as it has in the past. The expected 1954–1970 rates of increase in lead and zinc production in Canada, weighted by the average of their 1954 and 1970 production, is just under 3.2 per cent per annum. On the assumption that the ores which contribute the other 30 per cent of the silver production will not vary enough from this rate of increase to inject a large error into the total silver production estimate, we will use this 3.2 per cent as the expected rate of increase in total silver production. At this rate, production will increase from the 1955 level of 27,700,000 fine ounces to 44,200,-000 ounces in 1970. In terms of current prices this is an increase from $23,500,000 to $37,600,000 by 1970.

The most promising method for estimating what proportion of this total output will be exported is to assume that the proportion will remain at the 1952–1954 level of about 85 per cent. Domestic silver consumption has fluctuated greatly and seems not to be correlated with the GNP or with disposable personal income in spite of the fact that about one-third of the domestic consumption of silver goes into sterling silver and other silver alloys and another 30 per cent is used in silver nitrate. Before the war exports accounted for 85 to 95 per cent of production, but in the immediate postwar years this proportion dropped to almost 70 per cent before climbing again to the 85 per cent range.

If 85 per cent of domestic production is exported in 1970, Canada will earn about $32,000,000 in foreign exchange from silver in 1970. Imports are expected to be negligible, as they have been for several years.

IRON ORE

The development of iron ore mining in Canada has been spectacular. Prior to 1939 no iron ore was mined as such in the entire country. The discovery of Steep Rock, Michipicoten, and more recently Knob Lake has sent output skyrocketing from a mere 120,000 tons in 1939 to 16,500,000 tons in 1955. Yet, in 1955, shipments were made from Knob Lake only during the later months of the year. Iron ore production in Canada provides clear-cut evidence of the growing pressure on Canada to produce the mineral requirements of the heavily industrialized countries. The United States especially is looking to the north for iron as her own high grade deposits are depleted.

It has been estimated that Canada's iron ore reserves total about 4,400,000,000 tons of 50 per cent iron content or more. This compares with about 20,000,000,000 tons of such ore estimated for Brazil and for India and between 10,000,000,000 and 15,000,-000,000 tons of 35–50 per cent ore for Cuba, France, and the Union of South Africa. The United States has only about 2,000,-000,000 tons of high grade ore left and Venezuela, with about 1,000,000,000 tons, is the only other potential supply source of consequence in this hemisphere.[56] Thus Canada's reserves are ample and a considerable proportion of them are located close to water and rail transportation so that they are particularly attractive to United States mills looking for new sources of supply.

In addition to the 4,400,000,000 tons of high-grade ore, Canada has unknown quantities of low-grade ore. The proved reserve at Knob Lake is 400,000,000 tons of 50 per cent ore but there are additional unproved amounts of high- and low-grade deposits. The operating company needed at least 400,000,000 tons of proved reserves to warrant development of the site and consequently it has not sought out all the available deposits yet. The great attraction of the Knob Lake ore is that it is suitable for direct shipment, that is, its iron content is high enough (50–60 per cent) to make concentration of the ore unnecessary. The Bell Island reserves in Newfoundland have been estimated at between 1,000,000,000 and 10,000,000,000 tons, a more precise estimate being impossible because reserves cannot be determined much ahead of mining. This ore, too, is more than 50 per cent iron, but its phosphorous content is so high as to make it unsuitable for the Bessemer converter.[57] The Dominion Steel and Coal Company, owner of the Bell Island operation, has furnaces designed to handle this ore but the exports go to Europe rather than to the United States because of the phosphorous content.

As the search for high-grade ore has pressed forward since the end of the war, various large bodies of low-grade deposits have been discovered. In contrast with the direct shipment ores, these

[56] U.S. President's Materials Policy Commission, Vol. II, p. 148. This estimate for Canada compares with a U.S. Bureau of Mines estimate of 4,600,000,000 tons of 50 per cent ore (*Mineral Facts and Problems*, p. 382) and a United Nations estimate of 2,200,000,000 tons (United Nations, *World Iron Ore Resources and Their Utilization*, p. 66.)
[57] Government of the Province of Newfoundland, *Submission by the Government of the Province of Newfoundland to the RCCEP* (n. p. 1955), p. 45.

low-grade bodies can be exploited only if beneficiation (concentration) plants are built at or near the mine site. Canada's reserves of these low-grade ores appear to be enormous. Not only are there substantial quantities near the high-grade deposits, but the Ungava Bay and Belcher Island deposits apparently amount to billions of tons. Thus Canada's high-grade deposits of iron ore are enormous and the low-grade deposits, many of which will not become economically feasible to develop for several years, assure her position as a major iron ore producer for several decades.

Since the accessible supplies of Canadian ore are so adequate, the probable 1970 rate of output will be dependent primarily on the demand conditions in the iron ore market. Only about one-third of the current production is going into the domestic market and the increases in ore production in the future are likely to be caused primarily by expanding exports. Thus the foreign demand for iron ore will be of particular importance in the 1970 projection.

The domestic consumption of iron ore in 1970 is relatively simple to forecast. Since iron ore is the raw material for steel and since steel is used in so many different products, one would expect the consumption of iron ore to move closely with the GNP. An even closer relation might be expected between iron ore consumption and gross domestic investment, however, because of the heavy steel content of investment goods and the well-known fact that steel production fluctuates sharply over the business cycle.

In Canada this proves to be the case. Over 90 per cent of the variation in iron ore consumption, 1926–1954, was explained by variations in gross private domestic investment if the war years are excluded. If gross domestic investment expenditures in 1970 total $11,000,000,000 (see Chapter 11), domestic iron ore consumption will total about 12,700,000 tons, almost two and three-quarters times the 1954 domestic consumption figure. Although there has been gradual substitution of lighter metals for iron and steel over the past two or three decades, the deviations of the actual iron ore consumption from the computed values from the regression equation do not vary systematically, indicating that the regression equation reflects this gradual substitution over time. Using the regression equation to arrive at the 12,700,000-ton estimate for 1970 assumes that steel is such a basic raw material that it is unlikely to be displaced by substitute materials more rapidly over the next decade or so than over the past thirty years. The 12,700,000-ton estimate will be used in the belief that this assumption is valid.

As with so many of the minerals, the export demand for iron ore in 1970 is a bit more difficult to project than the domestic demand largely because satisfactory data on world production and consumption and the variables determining world output are unavailable. The Paley Commission estimated that between 1950 and 1975 the iron ore consumption of the free world excluding the United States would increase at slightly more than 2 per cent per year.[58] From 1950 to 1953 the iron ore consumption of the free world excluding the United States actually increased by more than 12 per cent per year. Such a rate of increase is obviously greater than any long-run normal increase. It seems more defensible to argue that 1950 consumption was unusually low, due to delayed reconstruction of basic industry rather than that 1953 was unusually high relative to the path of future growth. Therefore the Paley rate of increase will be figured from the 1953 iron ore consumption rather than from 1950. This method gives a 1970 estimated iron ore consumption figure of about 240,000,000 tons for the free world excluding the United States, compared with 162,000,000 tons in 1953, an increase of 48 per cent.

If the United States GNP continues to rise at 3 per cent per annum, the 1970 consumption of iron ore implied by the Paley report relation of ore consumption to GNP would be 205,000,000 compared with the 240,000,000 tons for the rest of the world. This projection of United States demand is supported by the expected rate of increase in United States steel mill capacity.[59] In 1953 the United States accounted for almost exactly half of the total free world consumption, so the projection anticipates that the United States share will fall from 50 per cent to about 45 per cent.

How much of this 445,000,000 tons total free world demand will be satisfied by Canada? A detailed projection of United States iron ore requirements published by the United States Bureau of Mines sheds some light on the probable level of Canadian

[58] U.S. President's Materials Policy Commission, Vol. II, p. 132.

[59] See *Financial Post*, March 3, 1956, p. 41.

ore exports in 1970.[60] The Bureau of Mines estimated that in 1970 Canada would supply the United States with 38,000,000 tons, or 21 per cent, of its total ore requirements of 183,000,000 tons. The latter figure is granted to be conservative and is surely too low in view of the United States steel industry's expansion plans. The 21 per cent figure, however, seems plausible. The Bureau estimates that by 1970 the United States will be importing 31 per cent of its requirements as compared with 15 per cent in 1955, since the United States reserves of high grade ores are rather low. Venezuela is expected to account for the bulk of the United States imports from countries other than Canada. Applying this 21 per cent ratio to the United States demand of 205,-000,000 tons gives an estimated 43,000,000 tons for 1970 Canadian exports to the United States. Adding the 12,700,000 tons domestic demand gives a total of about 56,000,000 tons of Canadian production for 1970. If we assume that eastern Canada's exports to the United Kingdom and British Columbia's exports to Japan remain at their present levels as non-North American buyers turn away from the dollar area as a source of iron ore, Canada will be exporting about 4,000,000 tons to countries other than the United States, bringing the market for Canadian ore up to 60,000,000 tons.[61]

Sixty million tons output is about eight times the 1954 output and about three and one-half times the 1955 output and may now seem astronomically high. But men of the industry in Canada have indicated that the Bureau of Mines' 38,000,000 ton estimate of 1970 exports to the United States will be reached "a lot earlier" than 1970.[62] The Knob Lake area is expected to be producing some 20,000,000 tons annually as soon as the Seaway opens and the Steep Rock and Michipicoten deposits are likely to be shipping another 12,500,000 tons per year by 1960.[63]

Thus in the early 1960's Ontario plus the Knob Lake area will be producing about 32,500,000 tons annually. Assuming that British Columbia and Newfoundland do no more than hold to their recent peaks of 1,000,000 and 3,800,000 tons respectively gives a

[60] U.S. Bureau of Mines, p. 394.

[61] Japan is buying the entire iron ore production of British Columbia but is reported to object to the content of sulphur, phosphate, and other impurities. See *Financial Post*, June 9, 1956, p. 9 of supplement on Japan.

[62] *Financial Post*, March 3, 1956, p. 41.

[63] See *Canadian Year Book, 1955*, p. 480.

total Canadian ore production of 37,300,000 tons by the early 1960's. Since in 1955 ore production was but 16,500,000 tons, a rate of increase of about 12 per cent per annum is expected for the next seven or eight years. In order to reach 60,000,000 tons output by 1970, this rate of increase could drop to about 7 per cent over the 1963–1970 period. Such a pattern in the development of Canadian iron ore production seems entirely feasible.

We will assume that the increase in output will be provided primarily by the Ontario and Knob Lake deposits rather than by those in British Columbia and Newfoundland, although the Newfoundland output is likely to expand slightly with the growth of the domestic market. British Columbia seems not to have the reserves required to support a basic steel industry and the export market is uncertain.

The 43,000,000-ton estimate of Canadian exports to the United States is both a gross and net export figure. In 1954, Canadian blast furnaces consumed almost four times as much imported as domestic ore, importing almost 3,000,000 tons of ore while over 6,000,000 were exported. With the completion of the Seaway, it is expected that domestic ore will be used exclusively by Canadian steel mills.

MISCELLANEOUS METAL MINING

Many of the metals which have not yet been discussed, such as bismuth, antimony, cadmium, selenium, and tellurium are by-products of lead, zinc, and copper mining. It can be expected that their output, therefore, will move with the output of the major metals with which they are found, on the presumption that price relations will not change so drastically by 1970 that the ores will be mined for what is now the by-product rather than for the main product.

Unfortunately, however, the DBS annual publication, *The Miscellaneous Metal Mining Industry* is drawn up in such a way as to make it impossible to determine which of the twenty-five metals discussed are by-products of other metals and which are mined as such. Prior to 1955, iron mines were included in the miscellaneous metal mining industry but the iron ore production data are available and can be netted out. The make-up of the value of the output of this industry after deducting iron ore is uncertain, however. Since antimony, bismuth, cadmium, indium, selenium, tellurium, and tin are largely produced in Canada as by-products of other metals, the residual production appears to be comprised largely of tungsten and molybdenum and, since 1954, uranium. Prior to 1954, uranium production data were not published. Magnesium production data have been available only since 1947.

Because the historical data are so inadequate for the industry, we will simply examine the 1954 value of output and proceed from there to construct the forecast. In that year the industry's gross value of product was $83,400,000. This included $49,700,000 worth of iron which, when deducted, leaves $33,700,000. But in 1954 the value of uranium and pitchblende products was $26,-000,000 and presumably all of this should be considered output of the miscellaneous metal mining industry since uranium is seldom a by-product of other mining. If we can operate on this assumption, only $7,700,000 of the industry output was represented by all the other metals. Tungsten seems to have contributed about $5,000,000 to this total in 1954. Projecting the miscellaneous metal mining industry (net of iron) is primarily, then, a job of projecting uranium and tungsten production.

There is little doubt that Canada has vast uranium reserves and will be the free world's major source of the metal by 1960.[64] The United States reserves currently known will be dwindling by 1962, it is reported, and the country will be looking increasingly to Canada to supply its needs. But just what the free world's needs for uranium will be by 1970, or what production is likely to be, is particularly obscure because of the enforced reticence of the industry. Fortunately the few known facts can be used to construct at least an estimate for 1962 Canadian production. Production amounted to $26,000,000 in 1955 and $45,700,000 in 1956. Contracts with Canadian mines signed as of July 1956 called for $1,000,000,000 worth of output to be delivered before the end of 1962. The United States government has not made clear its post-1962 policy except to set a price for United States producers of $8 per pound from 1962 to 1966, and it is inferred that some contracts will be signed for post-1962 production

[64] The following discussion is based primarily on Bureau of Mines, pp. 947–951; and *Financial Post*, July 28, 1956, p. 43.

within the next two or three years. Meanwhile the United Kingdom and some western European powers have given Canadian producers some hope for a market continuing beyond 1962.

However, large scale use of atomic energy for power production is not anticipated until after 1970 and consequently some dip in production between 1962 and the late 1970's is a distinct possibility. At present the industry is expected to expand to an annual production rate of $250,000,000 to $300,000,000 by 1960. Production in the 1960's will depend on the rate of advance in the atomic energy utilization and on the demand for defense and stockpile needs. If it is anticipated that defense needs will level off a bit in the early 1960's after the current build-up of supplies of uranium, government purchases in the 1960's cannot be counted on to expand significantly. At the moment the most likely path of growth for uranium production in Canada seems to be a rise to a $300,000,000 output by the early 1960's and stable production until after 1970, followed by a rise in the later 1970's as atomic power comes into wider use. On the basis of the very flimsy evidence at hand, then, we will estimate Canadian uranium production in 1970 at $300,000,000 dollars, about twelve times the 1955 rate of output but less than seven times the 1956 output of $46,000,000.

The lack of data on the nature of the contracts means that the estimate of exports must be quite unreliable. But since Canada seems likely to be the free world's major uranium producer in 1970, surely at least 90 per cent of the production will be shipped abroad. We will assume that, as in the case of tungsten, 95 per cent, or $285,000,000 worth, will be exported in 1970.

Since tungsten is used primarily as a hardening agent for steel and since it is particularly useful in alloy steels which must withstand very high temperatures, the probable increase in the rate of consumption in the United States will be high. The Paley Commission estimated that United States demand for tungsten would increase from 6,000,000 pounds in 1950 to 15,000,000 pounds in 1975, equivalent to an annual rate of increase of something more than 3 per cent.[65] The actual United States consumption of tungsten has fluctuated so since 1950 that no light is shed on the accuracy of the Paley projection. United States consumption jumped from 6,600,000 pounds in 1950 to 11,400,000 in 1951,

[65] U.S. President's Materials Policy Commission, Vol. II, p. 26.

8,600,000 in 1952, and 7,700,000 in 1953. If 1950 and 1953 prove
to be on the long-term trend line, the annual rate of increase will
be almost 4 per cent per year.

Before World War II, China was the source of about one-
fourth of the world's production of tungsten. The loss of this
source of supply has accelerated the search for other deposits. It
is expected that the United States will draw increasingly from
Canada, but the extent to which Canadian production will be substituted for imports from Bolivia and Spain is extremely difficult
to say. We will estimate that Canada's rate of output will increase at 5 per cent per year, presuming that the current development of tungsten deposits will continue as the United States demand for the metal continues to outrun its own supplies.[66] The
Paley report supports such an estimated rate of increase to the
extent of noting that in the future Canadian output is expected
to contribute substantially to the world total.[67] At this rate of
increase, tungsten production in 1970 will amount to about $10,-
500,000, or 3,900,000 pounds metallic content, an increase of 80
per cent over 1954. About 95 per cent of the tungsten is exported
currently. If Canadian production of specialty steels increases as
the economy grows, her tungsten consumption will increase. If
domestic consumption increased, then, with production, exports of
tungsten will be $10,000,000 annually.

Besides tungsten and uranium, we are including silver-cobalt
mines in the miscellaneous category although DBS classifies them
separately. Since silver-cobalt mines in 1954 produced less than
1 per cent of the total value of metallic minerals and only about
0.4 per cent of the total value of all minerals, this group does not
warrant careful analysis. It is assumed that the 60 per cent increase in silver output mentioned earlier will apply to these
mines, raising the gross value of output from the $5,900,000 level
of 1954 to $8,500,000 in 1970.

NONFERROUS SMELTING AND REFINING

The gross value of output of the nonferrous smelting and refining industry might be projected to 1970 by correlating output
with the output of the nonferrous metallic minerals. The correlation would be high since the most important component of the

---

[66] *Canada Year Book, 1955,* p. 477.
[67] U.S. President's Materials Policy Commission, Vol. II, p. 29.

gross value of output of this industry is the value of the mineral ores charged to smelters. To get at a less specious correlation the net value (value added, roughly) might be correlated with the output of nonferrous metallic minerals. However, an important component of the nonferrous smelting and refining industry, namely the primary aluminum industry, is not based on Canadian ores and so should be handled separately.

Since net value of product for primary aluminum is not available historically, gross value of output data had to be used in constructing the nonferrous smelting and refining projection. The historic relation between the gross value of output in nonferrous smelting and refining, aluminum excluded, and nonferrous metallic mineral production points to a gross value of output of nonferrous smelting and refining, aluminum excluded, of about $1,600,000 in 1970 (1955 prices).

The primary aluminum production estimate was prepared separately from the rest of the nonferrous smelting and refining industry. Since at least 85 per cent of Canadian production of primary aluminum has been exported, one must look first at the free world requirements and then work back to probable Canadian production. Free world production has shown a very stable annual percentage growth rate if the war years are omitted. This relation if projected to 1970 indicates a free world production of about 8,500,000 tons as compared with about 2,900,000 in 1955 and 700,000 tons in 1939. The projection of the past growth rate presumes that the uses to which aluminum will be put will continue to expand until the target year. It may be quite optimistic to say that the leveling off of the growth rate will not occur until after 1970, yet an examination of the possibilities for displacing other metals with aluminum seems to warrant such optimism. The expansion of aluminum consumption in construction, electrical transmission and equipment, pipe manufacture, packaging, and transportation equipment is likely to be particularly great. The anticipated increased demand for aluminum for automobile production deserves special mention. In 1956 the United States automobile manufacturers used about 35 pounds of aluminum per car. This figure is expected to rise to 75 pounds by 1960 and 200 pounds by 1980 as the automobile firms seek to reduce the weight of the car as well as its cost.[68] If the United States auto-

[68] Aluminum Company of Canada, Ltd., *Submission to the RCCEP* (Montreal, 1956), pp. 25–26.

mobile and truck industry were to produce 9,000,000 units in 1970 as compared with the 6,900,000 units produced in 1956, and if 140 pounds of aluminum were used in each unit, that one industry would demand about 514,000 tons more aluminum in 1970 than in 1956. If the possibilities for expanding aluminum consumption in the tropical countries, where it is ideally suited for construction, are considered alongside the potentials in the industrialized countries, the prospects for a continued rapid rate of growth in free world production of aluminum seem quite bright.

What role will Canada play in this picture? She has no bauxite reserves but she does have hydro power. The production function and factor costs in primary aluminum production are such as to cause the industry to locate near power sources rather than near the ore. The possibility that Canada will retain her share of free world production would seem to be quite good considering her hydro power resources, especially when compared with United States hydro sites. A constant market share of free world production of primary aluminum would mean 1970 production of about 2,000,000 tons. At 21 cents per pound, the gross value of production would be $840,000,000.

The 2,000,000-ton figure is fully consistent with the Canadian experience. In 1955 Canadian production was 608,000 tons and announced plans by 1956 were indicating 1960 capacity of over 1,000,000 tons. The industry's production doubled between 1947 and 1955; it may not be too optimistic to expect it to double again between 1960 and 1970.

To estimate the probable level of domestic disappearance and exports of primary aluminum in 1970 it is simplest to work with domestic disappearance per capita. But it is difficult to make an appropriate allowance for the effect of the very rapid growth of Canada's aircraft industry on this figure. For example, domestic disappearance per capita rose from a bit under 2 pounds in 1939 to more than 10 pounds in 1954, a rate of increase which would put the 1970 per capita figure at 65 pounds! This 12 per cent rate seems definitely higher than any foreseeable long-run trend. Using the 1929–1955 per capita data would give a rate of 8 per cent per capita per year. The Aluminum Company of Canada, Ltd., expects per capita consumption to increase from 1955 to 1980 at a rate of about 5 per cent per year.[69] This seems a

[69] Aluminum Company of Canada, Ltd., p. 34.

little conservative in view of the historic experience, and so we have used a 6 per cent rate of increase in per capita consumption. This indicates domestic consumption of about 283,000 tons in 1970.

By separating aluminum smelting from other nonferrous smelting and refining in this way, the 1970 estimate of gross value of output for the entire industry is $2,440,000,000 — $840,000,000 of this being aluminum production.

ASBESTOS

The remaining minerals fall into two groups: nonmetallics and structural materials. In 1954 the gross value of output of the nonmetallic minerals was just over $130,000,000 and asbestos alone accounted for just two-thirds of that total. For this reason we will discuss briefly the prospects for asbestos production and then proceed to discuss the remaining nonmetallics as a group.

Canada in 1953 produced about 70 per cent of the free world's asbestos, and over 95 per cent of Canada's production came from the mines in eastern Quebec. British Columbia and Ontario are now producing small amounts of asbestos as well. Exports have accounted for between 95 and 97 per cent of output almost every year in the last three decades. Since the end of the war, the domestic market has taken more than 5 per cent of the output only in 1946 and 1949 when the proportion rose to 7 per cent.

On a tonnage basis, Canada provides the United States with about 95 per cent of its asbestos imports and the United States takes between 60 and 70 per cent of the total Canadian production. Another 8 to 10 per cent of the output goes to the United Kingdom. In spite of the fact that only about two-thirds of the exports go to the United States, the correlation between Canada's total absestos exports and the United States GNP is very high, the variations in the latter accounting for 97 per cent of the variations in Canada's asbestos exports over the 1929–1955 period if the war years are excluded. Asbestos is used in so many products (brake linings, asbestos-cement pipes, insulation of many varieties, and so forth) that one would expect a good correlation between a country's consumption and the GNP, but here we see that asbestos exports to countries other than the United States are highly correlated with the United States GNP. This probably reflects close relations between other countries' asbestos consumption and their gross national products, taken along with the close correlation between GNP changes in the major industrial countries.

Canada's position as the world's leading asbestos producer seems secure for the next couple of decades at least. Reserves are so great that if all exploration were to stop now, production could increase gradually for another forty years before depleting the reserves.[70] Also there appears to be no serious threat of the substitution of other materials for asbestos. Since we anticipate that the national incomes of the industrial nations will go on fluctuating together, we can expect this rather odd correlation between total Canadian exports of asbestos and the United States GNP to continue. If the United States GNP reaches the expected $600,000,000,000 in 1970, Canadian asbestos exports should reach 1,675,000 tons, a 67 per cent increase over the 1955 level of 1,002,-000 tons and a 94 per cent increase over 1954.

Domestic consumption of asbestos must be estimated by subtracting the total exports from producers' shipments. The resulting time series moves in a highly random manner, perhaps because there is no means of adjusting for inventory changes. In 1934, for example, exports exceeded producers' shipments by some 200 tons, indicating some exporting from inventory by firms other than asbestos producers. At any rate this erratic time series is correlated with the GNP only in the roughest way. Since domestic consumption is such a small proportion of the total, a rather crude estimate can be used without causing any substantial error in the estimated total industry output. We will therefore assume that domestic consumption will take 5 per cent of total production in 1970. This percentage is fractionally higher than the average for the 1926–1955 period.

If the export demand is 1,675,000 tons and if domestic consumption accounts for 5 per cent of total production, the industry will be producing between 1,750,000 and 1,800,000 tons by 1970. The increased output may be shared proportionally by the three provinces now producing asbestos except that Newfoundland will be contributing a small amount to national production because

[70] A. L. Penhale, *Memorandum to the RCCEP on the Subject of the Canadian Asbestos Industry* (Montreal, 1956), p. 17.

of a new development and British Columbia may see her output increase a bit more than proportionally because of the faster rate of growth of the area's economy.[71]

An industry spokesman presented to the Gordon Commission projections for 1965 and 1980 which, when interpolated, give a 1970 output of just under 1,700,000 tons.[72] We will therefore use as a point estimate the lower figure in the production range mentioned above, 1,750,000 tons.

OTHER NONMETALLIC MINERALS

Our classification scheme includes in this category all nonmetallic minerals except fuels, structural materials, and asbestos. Specifically, the minerals in the classification are feldspar, quartz and nepheline syenite, gypsum, iron oxides, mica, peat, salt, talc and soapstone, and miscellaneous nonmetals. Since these minerals in 1954 accounted for less than 2.5 per cent of all mineral production and only 3 per cent of the nonfuel mineral production, the projection need not be as carefully constructed as for the other mineral industries.

These products are of such a variety that when taken as a group their output is more likely to move with the gross national product than with any other single variable. Satisfactory production data are available only back through 1935. The variations in the GNP explain 95 per cent of the variation in the output of this group of minerals over the last twenty years if the war years are excluded and, consequently, we will base the projection of output on the expected increase in the GNP. This is a bit risky, however, since about 30 per cent of the production was exported and since competition from imports is great; in 1954, imports amounted to about 50 per cent of total production. Consequently, tying the output of the industry to the GNP to derive a 1970 estimate implies that the correlation with the GNP over the last twenty years provides an accurate measure of the changing importance of imports and exports over the next twenty years. Rather than examine the history and prospects for the foreign trade in each of these commodities we will use the relation of production to the GNP as our guide for the 1970 estimate even though this is very questionable procedure.

---

[71] *Canada Year Book, 1955,* p. 487.
[72] Penhale, Table 5.

The estimating equation based on this relation of industry production to GNP gives an expected output of $65,000,000 in 1955 prices in 1970 if the GNP is $48,000,000,000. In addition to the 1970 output of presently produced minerals, however, a new and very large potash development in Saskatchewan will be operating by 1970. The expected rate of output when the mine is in operation will be valued approximately at $10,000,000 per year. This brings the total 1970 other nonmetallic minerals projection up to $75,000,000. If the 1954 relation of imports and of exports to industry output still applies in 1970, imports will amount to $32,000,000 and $30,000,000 will be exported.

CLAY PRODUCTS AND OTHER STRUCTURAL MATERIALS

This final category in the mineral industry includes only clay products, cement, lime, sand and gravel, and stone. In 1954, cement accounted for about the same proportion of the total as did sand and gravel, roughly 29 per cent. Stone accounted for 19 per cent, clay products 15 per cent and lime about 7 per cent. It is interesting but not surprising that these shares have remained quite stable over the years.

The output of this segment of the minerals industry is quite easy to forecast because all the components are used primarily in construction. Indeed, the new and repair and maintenance construction expenditures explain 99 per cent of the variation in the output of this industry over the 1926–1951 period, war years excluded.[73] Since these products are relatively expensive to ship and are produced in many parts of Canada (and the United States), there is little movement in international trade.

With such a tight correlation between production of structural materials and total construction, projecting the former comes down to the problem of projecting the latter. This has been done in Chapter 11, where total public and private construction is estimated at $7,200,000,000 in 1970. Substituting into the estimating equation, which expresses output of the clay products and structural materials minerals industry as a function of total construction expenditures, yields an estimate of just under $300,000,000 worth of production for this industry in 1970.

---

[73] The data on new and repair and maintenance construction expenditures were taken from Department of Trade and Commerce, *Private and Public Investment in Canada, 1926–1951* (Ottawa, 1951), p. 151.

EMPLOYMENT IN MINING IN 1970

The employment forecast for the minerals industry must be worked out not only in order to see what proportion of the work force will be attached to this industry but also to see what the geographical distribution of that work force will be. In this section we will merely summarize the employment forecasts for each of the components of the industry; in the section which follows the geographical distribution of production will be discussed.

A word of caution must be injected here. Employment in mining is not only a function of output but also of the rate of exploration and development. Therefore one frequently finds that output per worker fluctuates widely over time in various minerals not because output per worker in the mine is varying so but because the proportion of workers engaged in exploration and development is fluctuating. In some instance, too, the work force may be occupied to a considerable extent in making capital improvements at the mine and their presence can make productivity figures behave peculiarly. These are two attributes which are more or less unique to mining and which make the employment projections a bit shaky. We can only fall back on the forecaster's prayer that he is neither consistently high nor consistently low in what we hope are "intelligent" guesses.

The fuels

In the postwar years the output per man-year in coal mining was rising at about 2.25 per cent annually. Because productivity per worker varies so from province to province and because the provinces' shares of coal production are expected to change, productivity and work force requirements were developed on a province-by-province basis. The 1970 employment estimate is 9600 workers as compared with 18,000 in 1954. The marked decline is caused in part by the expected fall in coal production (from 14,900,000 tons in 1954 to 13,000,000 in 1970), but more important is the shift toward the capital-intensive strip mining, where output per worker is especially high.

In the case of oil, employment in exploration and development is large relative to total employment in the industry. Since the data do not permit relating of employment to both drilling activity and output, the forecast is based only on the latter. Considering the nature of the unique relation between employment and output, the 10 per cent annual increase in output per worker which was experienced over the 1941–1954 period was the basis for the 1970 estimate. By this method, employment in crude oil should be about 5300 in 1970.

Since 1950, natural gas employment has increased by 4.55 persons for every 1,000,000,000 cubic feet increase in gas production. In order to produce the 800,000,000,000 cubic feet projected for 1970, 5700 employees will be required if this relation of employment to production continues. Two forces will be at work to change this relation, however. The production of the gas now under cap in the West can be achieved with relatively little labor input and consequently the labor requirements per unit of increase in gas production can be expected to fall. Counteracting this, however, is the probability that because of the discovery of new gas fields, particularly Peace River, a higher proportion of the natural gas production will come from gas wells rather than from wells producing both oil and gas. It was mentioned above that workers producing natural gas are counted as employment in oil in the case of wells producing both oil and gas. The 5700 estimate for employment in natural gas will be too low, therefore, if the proportion of natural gas coming from oil-gas wells falls. In the hope that these two forces will offset each other, the 5700 employment figure will be used as the point estimate.

Nickel and copper

Recent irregularities in the quantity of nickel and copper production per employee in the nickel-copper mining, smelting, and refining industry as reported by DBS make satisfactory predictions of the probable labor requirements of the industry almost impossible. The figure for tons of nickel plus copper (metal content) per man-year produced by the nickel-copper mining, smelting and refining industry actually fell slightly from 1950 to 1954, when it was 14.4 tons per man-year. The likely explanation is that the industry in these four years concentrated more on exploration and development than on production. Also International Nickel was converting from open pit and underground operations to all underground operations and it may well be that a sizeable proportion of their work force was engaged in this construction work rather than in mining as such. If we assume that a return to a normal ratio of workers actually mining to all other mine employees would raise the output to 16 tons per man-year and then apply the historic 3.75 per cent annual increase in productivity per worker in mining, the 1970 output of nickel-copper metal content from nickel-copper mines would be 28.8 tons per man-year. (This assumes a continued shortening of the work week at the 1926–1954 rate.) Nickel production of 325,000 tons in 1970 would then require 21,200 men, the same number as in 1954. That is to say that the expected increase in industry output would equal the expected productivity increase of the present work force.

Copper-gold-silver

Employment in copper-gold-silver mines is expected to fall from the 1954 level of 7800 to about 6000 because the expected increase in productivity per worker more than offsets the relatively small percentage increase in the output of this industry. Although output per worker in this group has actually fallen in recent years, we will presume this to have been due to the exploration and development work and not a reflection of productivity in the strict sense. The 6000 employment estimate presumes output will rise at 3.0 per cent per man year compared with the historic 3.75 per cent for the mineral industries as a whole.

Gold

We presume that the gold ores are likely to become more lean over the years, slowing the increase in output per man. A 3 per cent annual increase over 1954 would give a 1970 work force of 13,500 as compared with 18,800 in 1954.

Silver-lead-zinc

It appears that the pounds of lead and zinc content of ores shipped from Canadian mines has increased at about 2.5 per cent per year per employee since 1949. At this rate the number of employees in the silver-lead-zinc industry by 1970 will be about 6500 compared with 5400 in 1949 and 6400 in 1954. This assumes that the projected lead output dictates the output of these mines and that the zinc requirements will be partially met by the output of the copper-gold-silver mines.

Iron ore

The short history of iron ore production in Canada poses special problems in projecting employment. Applying a 4.0 per cent annual increase to the 1954 output per worker (the historic increase being about 3.75 for all mining) gives an estimate of 20,000 persons in iron mining in 1970.

Miscellaneous metal mining

The probable error in the employment projection for this industry must be especially large, chiefly because of the same difficulties encountered in the output projections. By making historically founded assumptions about (1) the proportion of gross value of product paid to employees, (2) the annual average earnings, and (3) the annual increase in income per worker, the projected employment comes to about 18,000 workers. This may well be an exaggerated figure but we will hold to it.

Silver-cobalt

Only 800 persons were employed in silver-cobalt mines in 1954 and, at the historic 3.75 per cent per annum increase in productivity in mineral production, the 1970 output can be produced by a work force of the present size. Since this class of mining is so small, it is included with miscellaneous mining in Table 93.

Nonferrous smelting and refining

The estimated 1970 employment in primary aluminum production is put at 50,000, compared with 20,000 in 1955. This allows for a productivity increase per worker of less than 2 per cent per year, somewhat more than the historic rate of increase in this industry. In the rest of nonferrous smelting and refining, productivity per employee has been nearly stable since the 1930's and consequently employment is expected to move upward proportionally as output.

Asbestos

A review of productivity in this branch of mining points to a 2.0 per cent annual increase in output per man-year for the period

Table 93. Production, by regions, and number employed in the fuels and mining industries of Canada, 1954 and 1970.[a]

Product	Year	Production						Number employed
		Canada	Atlantic provinces	Quebec	Ontario	Prairie provinces	B.C., N.W.T., and Yukon	Canada (thousands)
Fuels								
Coal (millions of tons)	1954	14.9	6.6	—	—	7.0	1.3	18.1
	1970	13.0	4.7	—	—	7.2	1.1	9.6
% change		− 8	− 22			+ 3	− 15	− 48
Natural gas (billion cu. ft.)	1954	120.7	0.2	—	10.0	110.5	.03	2.9
	1970	700.0	0.2	—	10.0	689.3	.5	5.7
% change		+480	0		0	+525	+1670	+97
Petroleum (millions of barrels)	1954	96.1	0.01	—	0.4	95.2	0.4	3.9
	1970	500.0	0.01	—	0.4	499.1	0.4	5.3
% change		+420	0		0	+425	0	+36
Metal mining (millions of 1955 dollars)								
Nickel-copper mines	1954	94.5	—	—	92.7	1.8	—	21.2
	1970	190.9	—	—	172.9	18.0	—	21.2
% change		+102			+87[b]	+900		0
Copper-gold-silver mines[b]	1954	105.9	2.9	51.9	—	31.7	19.4	7.8
	1970	127.1	3.2	69.9	—	33.0	21.0	6.0
% change		+ 20	+ 10	+ 35		+ 4	+ 4	23
Silver-lead-zinc mines	1954	136.3	15.9	16.1	0.6	9.4	94.3	6.4
	1970	201.7	60.0	16.5	.8	9.6	114.8	6.5
% change		+ 48	+277	+ 2		+ 2	22	2
Gold mines	1954	130.7	0.3	26.9	78.4	4.3	20.8	18.8
	1970	148.1	0.3	29.6	86.2	4.2	27.8	13.0
% change		+ 13	0	+ 10	+ 10	− 2	35	31
Iron mines	1954	49.7	21.7	3.8	20.4	—	3.7	5.0
	1970	403.0	24.0	201.3	170.3	—	7.4	20.0
% change		+711	+ 10.5	+5190	+735		+ 100	+300

Table 93. Continued.

Product	Year	Production						Number employed
		Canada	Atlantic provinces	Quebec	Ontario	Prairie provinces	B.C., N.W.T., and Yukon	Canada (thousands)
Miscellaneous metal mines[e]	1954	39.0	.2	.8	.9	11.8	25.2	2.3
	1970	319.0	.3	32.4	32.6	83.3	170.4	19.1
% change		+719	+ 50	+3950	+3520	+605	+ 575	+730
Nonferrous smelting and refining (net value of production)	1954	407.3	—	68.9	263.4	31.0	44.0	26.0
	1970	1000.0	—	200.0	520.0	80.0	200.0	64.0
% change		+146		+ 190	+ 98	+158	+ 355	+146
Total metal mining	1954	963.4	41.0	168.4	456.4	90.0	207.4	77.5
	1970	2386.8	87.8	549.7	982.8	228.1	541.4	148.8
% change		+148	+114	+ 226	+ 115	+153	+ 161	+ 92
Nonmetal mining (millions of 1955 dollars)								
Asbestos	1954	86.4	—	79.9	3.6	—	2.9	6.6
	1970	163.3	—	147.8	6.8	—	8.7	7.5
% change		+ 89		+ 85	85		+ 200	+ 14
Other nonmetal mining	1954	35.7	10.3	9.7	7.7	4.0	4.0	4.3
	1970	75.0	18.8	17.6	14.0	17.3	7.3	5.5
% change		+110	+ 82	+ 82	82	+333	+ 82	+ 28
Total nonmetal mining	1954	122.1	10.3	89.6	11.3	4.0	6.9	10.9
	1970	238.3	18.8	165.4	20.8	17.3	16.0	13.0
% change		+ 95	+ 83	+ 85	+ 84	+132	+ 132	+ 19
Clay products and structural materials (millions of 1955 dollars)								
	1954	208.9	17.8	62.0	84.9	27.8	16.4	16.1
	1970	300.0	22.5	90.0	120.0	42.0	25.5	13.0
% change		+ 44	+ 26	+ 45	+ 41	+ 51	+ 55	− 19

[a] 1970 figures are estimates.

[b] Copper-gold-silver mine output is distributed proportionally as copper output for 1954 except that Ontario's entire copper production apparently is from nickel-copper mines and so it is classified with the latter group of mines.

[e] Includes silver-cobalt mines.

Source: 1954, see DBS, *General Review of the Mining Industry;* 1970, see text.

1951–1970 as most defensible. This indicates an output of 240 tons per man-year and a work force of 7500 persons.

Other nonmetallic minerals

The productivity per worker in this industry has been rising very rapidly, almost 4 per cent per year, since 1939. Given the 1970 output estimate, projecting this annual productivity increase gives an employment estimate of 5500 compared with 4300 in 1954.

Output per employee in the clay products and structural materials industry has been increasing at almost 5 per cent per year since 1939. If this rate continues, less than 12,000 workers will be required in the industry in 1970. Since few industries have maintained such a rate of increase for such an extended period of time, this employment estimate may prove too low. Consequently we will inch it up to 13,000 as a point estimate.

GEOGRAPHICAL DISTRIBUTION OF PRODUCTION

In some instances the geographical distribution of mineral production given in Table 93 follows directly from the discussion of 1970 output. In other cases, for example, gold, the distribution was estimated by extending recent production trends in the various regions. In still other cases, not only production trends but also information on new reserves and exploration and development activity were taken into account. Consider silver-lead-zinc, for example, to which the Pine Point lead and zinc find will probably be contributing by 1970, perhaps more than Table 93 shows.

The metal mining industries in Table 93 require some additional explanation. Since most metals are found in combination with other metals and since so much of the DBS data are in terms of class of mine rather than type of metal, it seemed preferable to recast the mineral production estimates in terms of mine types for Table 93. This recasting procedure can be illustrated with nickel and copper. Since nickel comes only from nickel-copper mines, it was assumed that the copper production from these ores would increase proportionally as the nickel output. About 94 per cent of the copper other than that found with nickel is produced in copper-gold-silver mines. In these mines copper contributed for the group about 70 per cent of the value of output in 1954 so we assume that copper, rather than gold or silver, is likely to dictate the rate of output of these mines. About a 20 per cent increase in the output of this class of mine is necessary to meet the 1970 copper projection. Since the major copper finds of recent years appear to be most promising in Quebec, the expected increase in production is greater than 20 per cent for Quebec and less for the other copper-producing areas of Canada.

These regional forecasts are, of course, subject to a substantial margin of error for obvious reasons and should not be pressed very far. But some approximation of the regional distribution was necessary so that the distribution of the work force and hence the population could be worked out in Chapter 20.

SUMMARY

Table 94 is a condensation of Table 93 except that the former presents the data for the entire industry in value terms whereas Table 93 presents the fuels in physical units. The striking conclusion of Table 94 is that the output of the minerals industry is expected to triple by 1970.

Natural gas and petroleum are expected to increase the most in relative terms, but metal mining will show the greatest absolute increase in output.

This tripling of mineral output may seem astonishing for just a fifteen-year period, yet some of the individual minerals which

Table 94. Value of mineral and metal production in Canada, by industry, 1954 and 1970 (millions of 1955 dollars).

Industry	1954 Actual	1970 Estimated	Percentage change
Coal	96.6	84.2	−13
Gas	12.5	724.0	+480
Crude petroleum	243.9	1,260.0	+421
Metal mining	963.4	2,389.8	+148
Non-metal mining	122.1	238.3	+95
Clay products and structural materials	208.9	300.0	+44
	1,647.4	4,996.3	

Source: See Table 93 and text.

have been discussed may well increase more than projected. Copper, zinc, and nickel are three which might prove to grow considerably more than has been expected here. Natural gas and petroleum may not increase quite as much as Table 94 indicates, but even if these two 1970 estimates were to prove as much as 25 per cent too high, total mineral production in 1970 would be only 2.8 times as great as in 1954 rather than 3 times as great.

It is difficult to believe, then, that on balance the minerals industry will expand substantially less than 200 per cent between 1954 and 1970. As one looks at the minerals one by one, it is crystal clear that the industrial countries of the world and particularly the United States will be drawing on Canada for more of their minerals. Therefore Canadian output will not just increase as fast as the population of the United States and Canada, and not only as fast as the GNP of the two countries, but even faster than this because of the shift in the source of supply. In other words, Canada will be providing a growing proportion of a growing total mineral demand. Viewed in these terms, an increase of 200 per cent does not seem unreasonable, if the assumption of reasonably full employment in the industrial countries is granted.

Since the Canadian GNP is expected to increase by some 80 per cent over 1954–1970, an increase of 200 per cent in the gross value of mineral production signifies that mineral production will represent a growing proportion of the national income.[74] The growth of Canada, then, will continue to be marked by rapid growth of mineral production. Primary production rather than secondary production will apparently continue to set the pace of Canadian development. The manufacturing sector will most certainly grow in absolute terms, but it will not grow sufficiently to turn Canada into a significantly more self-sufficient country exporting manufactured goods rather than primary products. The shift away from raw materials exports toward semi-

[74] A 200 per cent increase in gross value of production may be accompanied by an increase in "value added" of more or less than 200 per cent. Since the sum of the "value added" (total sales less purchases from other firms) for all firms is the GNP, to be completely accurate we should talk here of value added in mineral production rather than gross value of output. But value added is a much higher proportion of gross value in mineral production than in most other industries so the distortion is not great.

manufactured goods may continue, but the probability of a significant shift toward exports of fully manufactured goods seems remote. The countries buying Canada's primary products are not likely to reduce their tariff barriers on manufactured goods sufficiently to allow the entire manufacturing process to take place in Canada prior to export. But the raw materials may be processed to a greater extent than is now the case.

Although Chapter 20 deals specifically with the provincial distribution of industry and of population, the general pattern of change in the location of mineral production can be seen in Table 93. Fuels production in the Atlantic provinces will decline with the fall in coal production. Because of the prospects for oil and natural gas, the prairies and British Columbia, the Northwest Territories, and the Yukon will see their production increase. In metal mining, the Atlantic provinces again seem likely to increase their output considerably more slowly than the national average. Quebec's very large increase may be too large relative to Ontario; Quebec's production increase is so large primarily because the bulk of the increase in iron and in copper production is expected in this province and her power may cause a relative shift of smelting and refining toward Quebec. The prairies and British Columbia are expected to increase their metal mining somewhat faster than the national average. Nonmetal mining is expected to increase more rapidly in the West than in central and eastern Canada because of the potash and asbestos development.

In sum, the Atlantic provinces will probably not share in the growth of mineral production to the same degree as the other provinces. Quebec seems likely to experience the greatest growth in metal mining, with the prairies, of course, providing the huge increase in fuels production.

17
The Primary Industries:
Forestry and Fisheries

Analysis of the economic future of Canada's forest and fisheries industries, as for other parts closely related to the nation's natural resource base, must encompass both the "demand" and "supply" factors influencing the level of activity in this sector. Besides, to see how the fisheries, forestry, and forest products industries will fit into the over-all Canadian economy in 1970, we must survey the location of these activities and the size of the labor force necessary to sustain them. This chapter, consequently, considers the demand for forest and fisheries products, the availability of their natural resources, their employment and labor force requirements, and, finally, trends in the location of these industries.

First, this chapter reviews the prospects of a group of Canadian industries performing the first two manufacturing processes in the conversion of living timber into directly usable commodities. The forestry or woods operations industry harvests wood and converts it into logs and bolts and pulpwood primarily for sale to the forest products industries (lumber, pulp and paper, and "wood-using industries") which transform them into such important products as lumber, newsprint, other papers, and so forth. Thus the woods operations industry produces logs and bolts for the lumber industry and pulpwood for the paper and pulp industry; it also produces fuelwood for sale directly to final consumers. The wood-using industries purchase lumber from the lumber industry for further processing, with the exception of the plywood and veneer, which are classed as procuring their raw material direct from the forestry sector.

DEMAND FOR WOOD PRODUCTS

This section examines demand prospects for two of the sectors identified above, the lumber industry and "wood-using industries" producing such goods as veneer, hardwood flooring, sashes and doors, boxes and baskets, cooperage, and furniture. The lumber industry is responsible for at least half of the gross value of products of these two groups, and hence will receive the most extensive analysis.

Canada's construction industry takes roughly three-quarters of her domestically consumed lumber. The remainder is used in shipping and in manufacturing miscellaneous products. Clearly at any time the level of construction and the general level of commercial activity will strongly affect the demand for lumber. Unfortunately for the ease of forecasting future demand, an additional major variable enters — the steady trend to substitute other products for lumber in almost all of its major uses. Since before World War II, the use of lumber for such building staples as lath and shingles has declined, while the use of competing materials has risen rapidly.[1] Two factors are at work here. First, technological change in recent decades has unearthed new building materials more satisfactory or cheaper than wood or both. Second, the price of lumber has risen steadily relative to other materials so that even without the discovery of new materials there would have been a definite trend toward the substitution away from lumber.

As a basis for projection, lumber consumption in constant dollars had to be related to the level of activity in the lumber-using sectors mentioned above, and to the substitution trends just discussed.[2] Specifically, the relation was computed between per capita lumber consumption (constant dollars) as dependent variable and per capita constant dollar construction (residential plus nonresidential construction) and a time trend as independent variables. Ideally, a ratio of the prices of lumber to the prices of its substitutes would have been used instead of time to test the force of the substitution effect. But such a price series would be hard to obtain and would have little predictive value. The years included in the computation were 1926–1941 and 1946–1953. Time trend and the level of construction activity serve only

[1] See, for example, Canadian Lumbermen's Association, *Brief Presented to the RCCEP* (mimeo., n.p., 1956), Appendix.

[2] Strictly speaking, the measure used here is not consumption of lumber but "domestic disappearance" — production plus imports minus exports; it will differ from lumber consumption in any given year to the extent that inventories change during the period. This difference is seldom a cause of difficulty in long-run forecasting.

moderately well to explain the movement of lumber disappearance,[3] but duly tempered with qualitative judgment this equation can be used for prediction.

To make this prediction of course requires a forecast of private construction per capita in 1970. This was got by relating real per capita private construction to real gross national product per capita for the years 1926–1953, excluding 1942–1945. These calculations, along with the assumptions made to take account of long-run fluctuations in the volume of residential construction, were described in Chapter 11. The estimate developed there for residential construction, $1,992,000,000 for Canada as a whole in 1955 dollars, implies construction per capita for a population just under 21,000,000 of about $95.

It was possible to check the reasonableness of this calculation by using a more complex procedure involving separate forecasts of the number and the average unit value of dwelling units to be built annually in 1970. The number of dwelling units was forecast by a method which has been applied to Canada by Jacques Henripin.[4] He forecasts the number of dwelling units required on the basis of the number of households in existence. Thus he assumes that all married couples, widows, and widowers will demand separate housing facilities (as defined by the census), but unmarried persons will not. This seems a reasonable compromise assumption. Present rates of celibacy are assumed to persist for each specific age-sex group. In fact, the number of dwelling units at the present time is much less than the number of family units calculated by this method, so Henripin makes definite assumptions about the rate at which this deficiency will be cut down. Replacement requirements for old dwelling units are figured by assuming an average life of 80 years. Average value of new dwelling units in 1970 was estimated roughly on the basis of the historic relation between constant-dollar average value of new dwelling units and constant-dollar disposable personal income per capita. Upon making the further assumption that the value of new and repair construction moves proportionally, it was possible to derive a figure for gross residential con-

---

[3] Of the variation of the lumber series around its mean value, only 71 per cent is due to the independent variables, per capita construction and time trend.
[4] J. Henripin, "Les besoins futurs de nouveaux logements au Canada, jusqu'à 1971," LE, 32:191–209 (juillet-septembre 1956).

Table 95. Canadian lumber exports to the United States and the
United Kingdom, 1937, 1939, 1951, 1953 (million feet board measure).

Species	1937		1939		1951		1953	
	U.S.	U.K.	U.S.	U.K.	U.S.	U.K.	U.S.	U.K.
Birch	38	75	40	46	66	6	56	3
Cedar	31	21	41	37	166	3	213	6
Douglas fir	107	473	102	671	536	488	766	245
Hemlock	19	72	44	106	219	305	330	214
Pine	75	49	104	36	146	22	136	21
Spruce	251	322	283	280	943	69	877	104
Total planks and boards	537	1027	625	1189	2167	895	2450	596

Source: DBS, *Trade of Canada, 1939,* Vol. II; *Trade of Canada, 1953,* Vol. II.

struction quite close to the forecast of $1,992,000,000 given above.

Going back to the relation of lumber consumption to private construction, we now have the evidence necessary to estimate lumber demand. That equation forecasts total domestic demand for lumber in 1955 dollars of $341,200,000, compared to a quantity sold in 1952 of $309,900,000 (again in 1955 prices). This represents a 10.1 per cent increase, which compares well with the increase of 5.9 per cent forecast for United States lumber demand over the same period in the elaborate study prepared by Stanford Research Institute for the Weyerhaeuser Timber Company.[5]

Canada's lumber industry not only supplies the domestic market but also sends nearly half of its output to foreign markets, one-third going to the United States alone. The highly important changes in the pattern of Canadian lumber exports in the last two decades are shown in Table 95. For generations preceding World War II the British market had been Canada's most important overseas outlet. There she competed with European timber producers by offering specialty species and large dimension material of white pine, yellow birch, and Douglas fir.[6] The dislocation of trade caused by World War II took a heavy toll in this market. Not only has Britain's ability to buy been impaired,

[5] Stanford Research Institute, *America's Demand for Wood, 1929–1975* (Palo Alto, 1954), Table 37.
[6] Canadian Lumbermen's Association, p. 20.

but the tree species most successful in the British market are just those which are relatively most scarce in Canada. Furthermore, increased demand levels in North America have tended to make demand run ahead of supply within that area, reducing the incentive for producers to seek markets abroad. Thus Canadian lumber exports to the United States in 1953 were 322 per cent greater in physical volume than in 1939, while exports to the United Kingdom were down 46 per cent. There seems to be nothing temporary about this situation. Increased European demands will be met by Finland, Sweden, and possibly the Soviet Union, while relatively short supplies will guarantee a low level of exports to outside areas.[7]

In forecasting Canada's overseas exports, the difficulty lies in deciding whether this increasing isolation of the North American and European markets has stabilized itself, or whether it will continue further to cut into Canada's overseas exports. Several product groups likely to enjoy a rather stable demand have not declined significantly since shortly after the end of World War II, and so the guess can be made that further falls in total physical volume are unlikely, and that the 1970 exports of Canadian lumber to these overseas markets will be about the same as in the years 1950–1953. In 1955 prices this would be $93,300,000.

Demand for Canadian lumber in the much more important United States market depends on trends to 1970 of the United States demand for and availability of lumber. Most studies agree that in the United States as in Canada the cost of producing lumber relative to competing products will continue to rise due to increased costs of logging more remote areas, absence of economies of scale in mill operations, rising distribution costs, a low rate of productivity growth, and so on. Although in the 1970's growth of timber of all kinds will probably balance the total drain through cutting, it is not at all certain that this will be true for saw timber.[8] More information on this matter so fundamental to the future of Canadian lumber exports is available in the United States Forest Service's elaborate Timber Resource Re-

[7] Stanford Research Institute, p. 24; Canadian Lumbermen's Association, p. 20.

[8] U.S. President's Materials Policy Commission, *Resources for Freedom* (Washington, 1952), Vol. I, pp. 37–38.

view. Assuming past wood price trends to continue in the future and examining major wood products one by one, the Forest Service concludes that between 1952 and 1975 total demand for wood will increase by 17 per cent, demand for industrial wood by 25 per cent, while fuelwood demand will decline by 25 per cent.[9] This means an increase from 12,245,000,000 to 14,291,000,000 cubic feet, an estimate which agrees exactly with that of the Materials Policy Commission and closely with that of the Stanford Research Institute on all wood uses except fuelwood. Assuming some net lumber imports, the Service calculates the growth of saw timber in 1975 necessary to supply this demand ("needed growth") and also the growth foreseeable on the basis of present forest resources ("projected growth"). In line with the Materials Policy Commission's findings, it concludes that total United States timber growth will be sufficient, but that it is not clear that this growth will be ideally distributed according to the location of demand. Eastern (mainly southern) softwoods will be relatively short, as will western stands, according to the figures. However, the latter shortage "has little significance because so much of the western commercial forest land is occupied by old-growth timber with relatively little net growth." [10] From this two things are clear: (1) softwoods, especially for lumber use, are likely to grow relatively scarcer in the United States by 1970; (2) eastern (that is, southern) stands in particular are likely to be inadequate, shifting a greater portion of the supply burden onto western forests. The Stanford study, reaching the same conclusion, remarks that this renders likely an increase in United States dependence on Canadian exports, especially from British Columbia.[11]

About 91 per cent of all United States lumber imports come from Canada. And in making its computation of needed growth of United States timber reserves, the Forest Service made the "conservative" estimate that the volume of all Canadian wood products imported into the United States would rise by 8.7 per

[9] U.S. Department of Agriculture, Forest Service, "Chapter 1: Timber Resources for America's Future" (preliminary draft from *Timber Resource Review*), (Washington, 1956), pp. 26–31. In fact *two* demand estimates are developed in this document, the one quoted and a higher one which assumes no further substitution of other materials for wood.

[10] *Timber Resource Review*, pp. 109–112.

[11] Stanford Research Institute, pp. 22–24.

cent. This would just a little less than maintain Canada's present 5 per cent share of the United States lumber market. In fact it is likely that Canada can at least maintain her share; an increase in Canadian exports of lumber to the United States of 10 per cent between 1952 and 1970 is forecast. In value terms, this means $244,600,000 in 1955 prices, compared to $222,400,000 as the annual average in current prices for 1952–53 exports. The main product groups included are logs, railroad ties, planks and boards, square timber, shingles, and spoolwood; pulpwood, normally treated with this group, will be discussed and estimated along with newsprint and woodpulp.

Besides lumber, the forest products sector of the Canadian economy includes a miscellaneous group of "wood-using industries," producing such goods as boxes, barrels, furniture, veneer, plywood, and excelsior. Systematic projection for these industries is not feasible. In the postwar years, every increase of 1 per cent in gross national product has been accompanied, on the average, by a 1.277 per cent increase in production of this group of products (all measurements in constant dollars). This result — surprising since some industries in the group are certainly declining relatively in the economy — stems mainly from the rapid growth of plywood and veneer, both in domestic usage and as exports. The Stanford Research Institute estimates for the United States an increase in demand 1952–1970 of 100 per cent for softwood plywood and veneer and of 30 per cent for the hardwood varieties. For Canada the potential growth percentage-wise is probably greater than this. British Columbia's softwood plywood industry can supply expanding domestic demands, but creation of much of an export market for it would require, among other things, a change in United States tariff policy. Hardwood plywood, on the contrary, is already strong in foreign markets, though it will probably not grow significantly in the future because of the inroads of "birch die-back" disease on Canadian white and yellow birch supplies. One buoyant segment is the furniture industry, whose output normally grows slightly faster than GNP. It is probably safe to assume that physical output of the wood-using industries group will rise to 1970 as rapidly as GNP; this would imply a 1970 output valued (1955 prices) at $1,182,600,000.

DEMAND FOR PAPER PRODUCTS

Since the collapse of United States tariffs facing Canadian newsprint before World War I, the Canadian newsprint industry has come to provide the paper on which half of the world's newspapers are printed. A classic case of the resource-based export industry, it has provided Canada both with purchasing power in world markets and a strong stimulus to the development of other industries. Canada's efficiency in this sort of production has carried over to production of a group of related pulp and paper products, the demand for which will be discussed separately from newsprint itself.

In 1954, the Canadian newsprint industry sold 7 per cent of its output to Canadian publishers and placed 93 per cent on the world market. Newsprint constitutes one-third of Canada's exports to the United States. Canadians look forward to a similarly prosperous future for this industry. Yet among American customers, suffering from the newsprint shortages of the postwar years, the question is regularly raised of what source of newsprint will replace anticipated *declines* in Canadian exports. In this section the potential demand for Canadian newsprint is surveyed on the assumption that current price relations continue; only when the over-all adequacy of Canada's forest resources to future demands upon them is reviewed can we definitely pass upon Canada's ability to supply these amounts.

Fortunately, there exists ready-made an excellent study of world demand for Canadian pulp and paper products in the submission to the Royal Commission on Canada's Economic Prospects of the Canadian Pulp and Paper Association.[12] Even where the findings of this document are not accepted in all details, the complete information it presents makes simple the task of constructing alternative estimates. For Canada's domestic demand for newsprint the CPPA (Canadian Pulp and Paper Association) employs three separate techniques of projection. One is a simple projection of the historic trend in per capita consumption; the second works on the assumption that the relation between per capita newsprint consumption and GNP is the same in Canada as in the United States. The third projects

[12] Canadian Pulp and Paper Association (Montreal, 1956).

Table 96. Various long-term projections of United States newsprint requirements (thousands of tons).

Year	Projection					
	(1)	(2)	(3)	(4)	(5)	(6)
1955	6600	—	—	—	—	—
1960	7200	—	6700	7500	—	7150
1965	7850	—	7300	—	—	7975
1970	8650	8700	7900	—	—	—
1975	9500	8700	8600	—	9300	—
1980	10450	8700	—	—	—	—

(1) Canadian Pulp and Paper Association.
(2) United States President's Materials Policy Commission.
(3) Stanford Research Institute, *America's Demand for Wood, 1929–1975.*
(4) American Newspaper Publishers Association, *News-Print Now and In the Next Decade.*
(5) United States Forest Service, "Timber Resource Review."
(6) Intelligence Unit of The Economist, London, *Paper for Printing and Writing, Tentative Forecasts of Demand in 1955, 1960 and 1965.*
Source: Canadian Pulp and Paper Association, *Submission to the RCCEP* (Montreal, 1956), p. 33.

the past relation between Canadian per capita newsprint consumption and per capita gross national product. The CPPA takes the third and slightly highest of the three, and that one is also accepted in this forecast. However, per capita income in 1970 as estimated in Chapter 9 is higher than the CPPA's estimate — a 33 per cent increase over 1955 by 1970 instead of a 24 per cent increase. This implies 1970 domestic newsprint consumption of 744,000 tons rather than 692,000.[13]

Extensive information exists to aid in forecasting United States demand for newsprint, and indeed a number of careful forecasts already exist, most notably that of the CPPA.[14] Total United States newsprint consumption obviously can be thought of as having two dimensions — total newspaper circulation and average number of pages per copy. But, according to the CPPA, a forecaster would err if he projected separately total circulation and the number of pages per copy (determined mainly by advertising expenditures) and multiplied the results. This is because the rapid increase in average newspaper size in recent years has been accompanied by a decline in circulation per United States adult, suggesting that the average newspaper reader will cut the total

[13] CPPA, p. 34–40.
[14] Pp. 21–34.

Table 97.   Outlook for overseas newsprint demand, by regions, 1955–1970 (thousands of tons).

Region	1955	1960	1965	1970
Europe	3361	3950	4500	5000
South America	459	580	750	1000
Asia	909	1200	1550	1950
U.S.S.R.	600	760	1050	1400
Africa	115	150	195	245
Other North America	150	210	265	330
Oceania	350	400	475	500
Total	5944	7250	8785	10425

Source: Canadian Pulp and Paper Association, *Submission to the RCCEP* (Montreal, 1956), p. 42.

number of papers purchased when the number of pages in each paper rises noticeably. Taking this into account, the CPPA gets the forecast of United States newsprint consumption shown in Table 96, along with several other important estimates of future United States consumption. The reasonableness of the CPPA estimate and the basic United States forecasts upon which it rests allow its acceptance for this study.

The forecast used by the CPPA for total newsprint demand elsewhere in the world is based on a study for UNESCO made by *The Economist* of consumption trends projected to 1965.[15] This is extended on a trend basis to 1970 and later years, and indicates a 75 per cent increase by 1970 over the still war-depressed consumption level of 1955. The projection method used in the UNESCO study based on per capita newsprint consumption trends is for all practical purposes the same as that resorted to for the United States by the CPPA. Consequently, if any "conventional ceiling" on newspaper size in other advanced countries had already appeared, it would have showed in a declining growth rate for per capita consumption. In fact this does not seem to be the case, nor does it seem likely that any other countries will experience this in statistically significant form in the next decade. Thus the apparent optimism of the estimated growth of overseas demand in Table 97 seems justified

[15] Intelligence Unit of The Economist, London, *Paper for Printing and Writing, Tentative Forecasts of Demand in 1955, 1960 and 1965* (Paris, 1954).

Table 98.   United States newsprint supply by sources, historic and projected, 1920–1970.

Year	Thousands of tons from —				Percentages from —		
	Canada	U.S.A.	Europe	Total	Canada	U.S.A.	Europe
1920	679	1,466	51	2,196	31	67	2
1930	2,145	1,272	134	3,552	60	36	4
1939	2,281	942	310	3,534	65	26	9
1950	4,748	1,002	171	5,921	81	16	3
1955	5,025	1,270	125	6,420	78	20	2
1960	5,250	1,850	100	7,200	73	26	1
1965	5,710	2,040	100	7,850	73	26	1
1970	6,380	2,168	100	8,650	74	25	1

Source: Canadian Pulp and Paper Association, *Submission to the RCCEP* (Montreal, 1956), pp. 43, 48.

— negatively on the consideration just discussed, and positively by the great differences existing now in per capita newsprint consumption among countries at different stages of development. Persistence of relatively stable world conditions will surely mean large percentagewise increases in newsprint consumption per capita in future years.

Totaling the demand forecasts for Canada, United States, and other areas, we find a forecast increase of world demand from 13,000,000 tons in 1955 to 19,800,000 tons in 1970. How much of this enlarged market will be supplied from Canadian woodlands? Quite clearly they will retain the domestic market. But their future in the United States and other markets is subject to copious and conflicting evidence.

Table 98 shows both the historic and projected patterns of newsprint supply to the United States market. It reveals the steady gain in Canada's share of this giant market until the past five years, as well as the near-complete disappearance of European producers in the postwar years. The really important question is how United States producers will fare in their home market. The main site of expansion in recent years, and the most likely source of increased output in coming years is the United States South.[16] The resurgence of the American industry came

[16] CPPA, p. 44; United States Senate, Committee on Banking and Currency, 84th Cong. 2d sess., *Newsprint Production and Supply* (Washington, 1956), p. 5; V. E. Johnson, "Statement to the R.C. on C.E.P.," (processed, n.d.), pp. 8–10; Stanford Research Institute, p. 25.

with technological developments permitting newsprint production from resinous, fast-growing softwoods. Briefly, the South's advantages lie in lower wood costs, proximity to large and growing markets, power costs no higher than Canadian hydro, and cheaper transportation. It is estimated that manufacturing costs are 20 per cent lower than those in Canada. But certain disadvantages exist and may grow in importance. One is a lack of large quantities of pure water. Also, Southern wood is well suited to many other uses (for example, kraft paper) and hence may rise in price (though not necessarily faster than the Canadian resource). Recent years have seen rapid growth of United States capacity due both to these factors and to the encouragement of accelerated amortization, though this expansion shows signs of ceasing around 1960.

Does Canada face continued long-run displacement from United States newsprint markets? Given no major technological changes, it does not seem that United States capacity can achieve a markedly greater market share than is foreseeable in the next few years without facing seriously rising costs. Canadian producers have expressed fears that hardwood pulp or bagasse (sugar cane) will displace Canadian pulpwood in the production of newsprint. Neither development now seems much of a threat. Overcoming the technical problems in the use of bagasse in the near future is unlikely.[17] The use of hardwood is definitely advancing, but it will probably prove as much of an advantage to paper mills in eastern Canada as to those in northeastern United States. Hardwood cannot be transported by river, but for those mills forced to bring softwood pulpwood by road or rail from a distance it may be cost-reducing by allowing the utilization of nearby hardwood timber stands passed up in earlier days. In summary, the rise of United States producers' market share is not likely to continue at its present pace into the 1960's. Hence the CPPA submission takes a reasonable view when it assumes that in 1970 Canadian exporters will have the same market share as can be foreseen when presently planned investment in both countries is completed. This argument underlies the forecast in Table 98, which shows 1970 Canadian exports to the United States at a level of 6,380,000 tons, compared to 5,025,000 in 1955.

Making the same sort of required-Canadian-imports analysis

[17] Committee on Banking and Currency, p. 5.

for the rest of the world is an awesome task, but it has been attempted quite carefully by the CPPA on the basis of information published by the United Nations and related agencies. In the absence of omens of any other result, it is assumed that the United States will continue to export the same percentage of its domestic production (roughly 12 per cent) as at present, due to its entrenched position in portions of the Latin American market. Having forecast United States production, this leaves demand for Canadian newsprint as a residual. The CPPA forecast for exports other than to the United States may be questioned on at least three grounds. First, as already noted, it is quite sanguine on future non-North American demand. Second, it perhaps underrates the chances that certain rapidly industrializing countries will increase their own pulp and paper output and consequently approach self-sufficiency.[18] Third, in view of the rapid growth foreseen in the United States domestic market, it predicts quite a high level of United States exports. However, these biases are strongly self-canceling. Overseas newsprint production is not likely to grow rapidly unless world income and hence demand for newsprint also grows rapidly. Any overestimation of world demand will create an overestimate of Canadian exports, but an overestimate of United States exports produces the opposite bias in estimating Canadian exports. Hence this objection can be dropped en bloc. Totaling the estimated demand for Canadian newsprint in Canada, the United States, and other areas, we reach the following figures (in tons):

1960	7,100,000
1965	8,300,000
1970	9,750,000

Prospective demands for other Canadian paper products, again taken from CPPA, are shown in Table 99. Some slight modifications were made to bring the bases of estimation into conformity with the rest of the projections in the present study. The method used in most cases was to examine trends in per capita Canadian consumption and in the share of production exported and share of consumption imported. As a general matter, the firms producing this group of commodities seem to suffer from the small size of

[18] See, for example, C. S. Bissett, "Argentine Imports Hit by Dollar Shortage," *Foreign Trade*, 109:23–25 (January 4, 1958).

Table 99.   Computation of demand for other Canadian paper products, 1960 and 1970 (thousands of tons).

Product	Year	Production	Exports	Imports	Consumption
Book and writing	1960	325	49	13	289
paper	1970	444	74	18	388
Paper and build-	1960	1,425	139	0	1,286
ing board	1970	2,095	189	0	1,906
Wrapping paper	1960	317	25	3	295
	1970	418	35	3	386
Tissue and sani-	1960	119	0	0	119
tary papers	1970	161	0	0	161

Source: Canadian Pulp and Paper Association, *Submission to the RCCEP* (Montreal, 1956), pp. 54–71.

the domestic markets and the tariff barriers surrounding foreign markets, as their fixed costs are clearly higher per unit of output than for United States mills.[19] They themselves will probably remain adequately protected in the Canadian market, so that developments in the international sector are likely to be few. The value of 1970 production is estimated at $510,000,000, consumption at $465,000,000 in 1955 prices for this group of products.

Canadian woodpulp, besides yielding paper products in domestic factories, may also be exported to foreign users or converted domestically into other products such as rayon. As is the case with newsprint, the major United States market reveals continuing inadequacy of domestic production and increasing demand for imports.[20] Studies by the Organization for European Economic Cooperation and other agencies likewise indicate a continued rise in European demand. Canada's share of the United States market has increased abnormally in the World War II and postwar period, and the CPPA is willing to concede that it will decline slightly to about 90 per cent by 1980. If this figure is also used for the intervening years 1960, 1965, and 1970, then exports to the United States can be forecast as they appear

[19] CPPA, pp. 54–58.
[20] Stanford Research Institute, pp. 56–58.

Table 100. Forecast of volume and value of exports of Canadian woodpulp and pulpwood, 1960, 1965, 1970.

	1960	1965	1970
Woodpulp exports			
Volume (millions of tons)			
United States import demand[a]	2.8	3.2	3.6
Canadian exports to the United States	2.5	2.9	3.2
Canadian exports to other countries[b]	0.61	0.73	0.86
Value (millions of 1955 dollars)			
Canadian exports to the United States	325.9	378.0	417.1
Canadian exports to other countries	79.5	95.2	112.1
Dissolving pulps	11.0	12.4	15.1
Total	416.4	485.6	535.3
Pulpwood exports			
Volume (millions of roughwood cords)	1.4	1.3	1.3
Value (millions of 1955 dollars)	33.0	30.6	30.6

[a] Stanford Research Institute, *America's Demand for Wood, 1929–1975* (Palo Alto, 1954), p. 58.

[b] Canadian Pulp and Paper Association, *Submission to the RCCEP* (Montreal 1956), pp. 72–74.

Source: Forecasts developed by methods described in text, except as footnoted above.

in Table 100. Also included in this table are demand estimates for dissolving pulps on the domestic market and European demand for all pulps. Finally, Table 100 shows the forecast of a slight decline for Canadian pulpwood exports. These are likely to decline because of growth of Canadian processing facilities. But this trend should not be overstressed because these exports, comprising border trade in New Brunswick and Ontario, rest more on location than on price factors. Moreover, they are sensitive to variation in the United States dollar exchange rate, tending to rise sharply when the Canadian dollar is at a discount.

Table 101 contains a recapitulation of forecasts of value of total production and exports for major classes of forest products. The value of production total cannot be used for aggregation purposes because it double-counts the purchases of lumber by the wood products industries, by an amount probably in the neighborhood of $350,000,000. There is, however, no other double-counting in the total production column and none in the export column.

Table 101. Summary of demand forecast for major classes of Canadian forest products in 1970, by value, and timber requirements to meet demand.

Product	Production (millions of 1955 dollars)	Exports	Timber requirements (million cu. ft.)[a]
Lumber	656.6[b]	337.9	1,532
Wood products	1,182.6	50.0	170[c]
Paper products	1,596.1	1,053.3	1,741
Newsprint	1,086.3	1,002.8	d
Book and writing paper	115.1	19.2	d
Paper board and building board	256.7	24.0	d
Wrapping paper	87.2	7.3	d
Tissue and sanitary	26.9	—	d
Other paper	23.9	—	d
Woodpulp	535.3	520.2	d
Pulpwood exports	30.6	30.6	142
Fuelwood	43.4	—	700
Total	4,044.6	1,992.0	4,285
Wastage allowance			600[e]
Total drain on timber inventory			4,885

[a] For conversion factors not concerning woodpulp and paper, see Canada, Department of Resources and Development, Forestry Branch — Economics Section, *Forest and Forest Products Statistics* (Ottawa, 1952), p. 6; Stanford Research Institute, *America's Demand for Wood, 1929–1975* (Palo Alto, 1954), *passim.*

[b] This figure is less than the total of $679,100,000 for exports plus domestic consumption reached in the text by $22,500,000, a nominal allowance for imports.

[c] Most of the wood consumed by the wood products industries is purchased from the lumber industry. This figure represents mostly veneer and plywood logs.

[d] Included in "paper products" total; for conversion factors used in figuring this total, see Canadian Pulp and Paper Association, *Submission to the RCCEP* (Montreal, 1956), p. 81.

[e] This figure, a slight reduction from that for recent years on the assumption of better control over disease and forest fire, rests on the same arbitrary basis as the Forest Service's annual estimates at present.

CANADA'S TIMBER RESERVES

Table 101 also shows the drain on Canadian woodlands which would be associated with this level of activity in the forest product industries. In principle, in order to check whether it will be feasible for the economy to supply this volume of products, one should examine the timber inventory and its growth rate against the prospective drain. This has in fact been attempted for the United States by the Forest Service of the U. S. Department of Agriculture.[21] Canadian statistics, however, will not bear the weight of such examination.[22] Forest inventory figures are based on numbers submitted by the provincial governments. In no province are forest lands more than two-thirds surveyed, and in most cases the estimate is a much cruder approximation (especially Quebec). Nothing systematic is known about growth rates of Canadian timber. "Appraisals of growth against drain have been local only, and served to do no more than indicate at the times they were made an over-all ability to meet requirements. Any appraisal of net increment potentials must be made in general terms and by arbitrary estimates based on inadequate statistics. Complete and concrete figures are simply not available." [23]

As a prologue to making this sort of appraisal, it should be recalled that the demand estimates made above assume that the price of wood relative to the price of competing materials will continue to rise in the future at roughly the same rate as in the past. This allows for two basic characteristics of forestry as an industry: (1) the absence of a relatively continuous trend toward increasing labor productivity; (2) the inevitably increasing costs of exploiting less accessible or lower quality timber. Consequently, when we ask whether supply will be adequate to meet the forecast demand, we really desire to know whether this supply will be forthcoming if price rises no faster on the average than over the last quarter-century.

Stated in these terms, it is clear that Canada will face no *over-all* shortage of timber resources in the next decade. U. S. Forest Service computations of a rough sort suggest annual growth of Canadian saw-timber exceeds annual cut by one-fourth.[24] Such estimates are relatively meaningless when Canada has large stands of virgin timber which add little net annual growth. Only now is Canada coming to the point where sustained-yield forestry becomes an economic necessity and such calculations can meaningfully be made. In 1954, Canada had 577,361 square miles of forest land classed as "accessible productive,"

---

[21] *Timber Resource Review,* chs. i, vii.

[22] H. L. Keenleyside, *The Place of the Forest Industry in the Canadian Economy* (Vancouver, 1950), p. 7.

[23] CPPA, pp. 82–83; information furnished by Economics Section, Canadian Forest Service.

[24] *Timber Resource Review,* p. 16.

or productive and exploitable under current economic conditions; only 324,819 square miles were "occupied" for exploitation, either as Crown lands under timber license or in private holdings and woodlots.[25] On the average, gross annual depletion for the decade 1942–1951 was 1.3 per cent on the accessible productive woodland, but 2.9 per cent on the occupied portion. And by 1952 it was up to 3.5 per cent on the occupied portion. In the words of the *Canada Year Book*, "These rates are indicative of the fact that in many localities severe over-cutting is taking place, whereas the annual growth is not being used on the less accessible portions of the productive forest." [26] This is clearly a logical necessity when the annual growth as a percentage of inventory is never high in Canada's slow-growing forests, and will be zero for stands of mature virgin timber. Thus resources are ample for future demands and most authorities do not foresee in the next two decades any necessity for serious efforts to make more forests accessible to exploitation, but economic forces will bring increasing pressure for more careful management of Canada's timber resources.

The growing acceptance in Canada of the idea that forests should be "farmed" as a renewable natural resource of course will help to maintain adequate timber stocks. All the spokesmen for the forest industries (at least in submissions to the Royal Commission on Canada's Economic Prospects) concede the necessity of this procedure, and the chances seem good that precept will become practice. Small beginnings are being made, and provincial legislation seems likely to take a hand if commercial interests are slow in acting. Legislation requiring reforestation seems likely in Ontario and is on the books although not in extensive use in British Columbia.

All this discussion about the adequacy of over-all timber resources does not deny shortages of particular types of wood or the possibility of local timber famines. Shortages of particular types of material (such as birch and white pine) have been taken into account in the demand projections, and they will again make their appearance in the discussion of future changes in location. It should be stressed that for most purposes there is high substitutability among at least some different tree species. Red pine

[25] Canadian Lumbermen's Association, Appendix Tables I, II.
[26] *Canada Year Book, 1955*, p. 446.

is currently being adapted to many of the traditional uses of white pine, and jack and lodgepole pine are finding many new employments.

Important enough for separate discussion is the adequacy of future supplies of wood for pulping. The CPPA feels that forest areas *currently* owned or leased for pulpwood production can yield the increase forecast for future years. They foresee the increase over present cutting coming from fuller use, slightly improved care of forests against fire and disease, use of new species, use of sawmill waste (now advanced in British Columbia), reduction of fuelwood demand, and a slight increase in occupied lands.[27] Thus it seems clear that only minimal governmental interference will be required to assure adequate supplies of this crucial resource.

LOCATION OF FORESTRY AND FOREST PRODUCTS, 1970

A number of trends appear in the percentage distribution among Canada's provinces of the net value of the output of all forest industries, gross primary forest production, and gross output of pulp and paper. British Columbia's share of primary forest production has fluctuated erratically, but her share of both total net value and of pulp and paper production has clearly been rising. Though less important in absolute terms, Alberta has been increasing her share at an even more rapid rate. In the East, Quebec's share in all cases has stayed just about constant while Ontario's has declined at all stages of production, although less rapidly in pulp and paper than in forest industries as a whole. The Maritimes' share in general is down slightly from two decades earlier; the rise in the "other provinces" group in pulp and paper is due almost entirely to the inclusion of Newfoundland after 1949.

Many factors of *a priori* importance will influence the working of these trends in the future.

1. *Timber reserves location.* In the United States, only the extraordinarily rapid growth of southern pine prevents a large shift of lumber production to the West. Canada lacks such rapid-growth areas and will certainly depend much more heavily for lumber on such areas as coastal and central British Columbia; all

[27] CPPA, pp. 81–88; Canadian Pulp and Paper Association, Western Division, *A Brief to the Royal Commission on Forestry* (Vancouver, 1955), pp. 23, 25; Johnson, pp. 4–5.

other areas will decline relatively, and possibly even absolutely by 1970. For pulp and paper, reserves will be much less of a problem because declining eastern supplies are offset by technology allowing use of new species.

2. *Sources of power.* There seems to be considerable uneasiness in the pulp and paper industry over the adequacy of future hydro resources in eastern Canada. It seems very likely that Alberta natural gas will attract some pulp and paper to that province, and the northern areas of all the prairie provinces may gain due to possessing undeveloped hydro sites. Other parts of the forestry industry are not affected by these matters.[28]

3. *Markets.* The relatively rapid increases in prospect for European and other overseas demand for newsprint favor the possibility of developments in Newfoundland and its Labrador section, and, conceivably, the old Maritime provinces. The increasing inability of lumber to sustain long overland transport costs will limit the decline of lumber and wood products in the eastern provinces.

4. *Technology.* Technological change in forest operations and wood products is quite rare. As already mentioned, hardwood pulping will sustain pulp and paper operations in eastern Canada. But, on the other hand, the great economic success of using sawmill waste in pulp and paper operations in British Columbia will in the future tend to pull pulp and paper operations toward the location of major lumber activity.[29]

5. *St. Lawrence Seaway.* Its effects on forest products will probably be relatively slight. The competitive position of eastern Canada's (here including Manitoba) pulp and paper industry in northeastern and midwestern United States markets will be improved, and Manitoba and Ontario lumber may move more extensively toward United States east coast markets. Lumber production in Alberta and British Columbia will not be affected.

Taking account of all these things, the distribution of 1970 pulp and paper production might be roughly as follows: Quebec, 40 per cent; Ontario, 27 per cent; British Columbia, 16 per cent; other provinces, 17 per cent (due mainly to expansion in Alberta and possibly Newfoundland).

[28] *Financial Post,* January 27, 1956, pp. 11, 24.
[29] "B. C. Lumbermen Woo Buyers Overseas," *Financial Post,* June 9, 1956, p. 14; Canadian Pulp and Paper Association, Western Division, p. 23.

Table 102. Number of persons employed in Canadian forest industries, 1953 and 1970, with forecasts of rates of productivity growth.

| Industry | Labor force | | Annual rate of productivity growth (percent) (3) |
	1953 (1)	1970 (2)	
Woods operations	135,981	154,500	0.00
Lumber industry	60,933	61,600	0.88
Wood-using industries	73,377	121,500	0.66
Pulp and paper industry	58,194	73,850	1.81
Total	328,485	391,450	

Source: (1) actual data from various DBS Census of Industry volumes on these sectors and Canadian Pulp and Paper Association, Submission to the RCCEP (Montreal, 1956), pp. 103–107; (2) calculated from columns (1) and (3); (3) sources of estimates discussed in text.

For lumber and wood products the main problem is deciding how great will be the shift toward Alberta and British Columbia. The submission of the latter province to the Royal Commission contains a forecast which in light of our over-all demand estimates would mean a decline in lumber production in the rest of Canada taken together.[30] This does not seem likely. Consequently the following chances, 1953–1970, in the provincial shares of lumber production by volume are forecast: Maritimes, down from 9 to 6 per cent; Quebec, 16 to 11 per cent; Ontario, 11 to 7 per cent; prairie provinces, 8 to 10 per cent; British Columbia, 55 to 65 per cent.

EMPLOYMENT IN THE FOREST INDUSTRIES

Having forecast total demand for products of Canada's forest resources, and possessing some knowledge of the increase in the real cost of supplying them, it is possible to estimate what portion of the 1970 labor force will be occupied in this segment of the Canadian economy. All that is required is an estimate of the 1970 physical productivity per man-year in the various sorts of forest products production. One major hitch will be discussed later: historical data on employment are in the form of man-years,

[30] Government of the Province of British Columbia, Submission to the RCCEP by the Government of the Province of British Columbia (Victoria, 1955), p. 11.

which in such a seasonal industry as logging will be much less than the total number of persons actually employed during the year — the relevent datum for finding the prospective distribution of the labor force.

Table 102 shows actual 1953 and estimated 1970 employment in four separate portions of the forestry industries, plus the assumed annual rate of change of productivity from the 1951–1953 average. The reason for the surprisingly small increase in labor requirements is that the portion of the forest products sector facing the most rapidly rising demand, pulp and paper and wood-using industries, is exactly the one in which productivity rises relatively rapidly.

The rate of productivity growth in pulp and paper is adapted from figures given by the CPPA on a man-hour basis, converted to a man-year basis on the assumption that the length of the standard work week in the industry drops from 40 hours to 38 hours by 1970.[31] The resulting rate of growth of man-year productivity of 1.81 per cent compares well with other Canadian industries when one counts in the *a priori* likelihood that pulp and paper production would be subject to diminishing returns as total output increases. For the wood-using industries and for lumber production, historic man-year productivity series were derived by dividing a deflated gross output series by the Dominion Bureau of Statistics' series on total employment in these sectors. The behavior of the resulting productivity index is very erratic and leaves one suspicious of the quality of the underlying data. In the wood-using industries, man-year productivity fluctuated randomly between $2500 and $2850 (1935–1939 prices) in the years 1926–1951. Then it suddenly rose in 1952 to $2963 and in 1953 to $3123. Since certain sectors of this industry group are subject to more mechanization than at present, some increase in productivity is likely. Consequently a rate of less than 1 per cent annually is forecast.

In the lumber industry, the situation is similar but even more puzzling. Man-year productivity, after staying roughly constant for two decades, dropped precipitously in 1949 and has not yet regained its old level. We have not determined whether a change in the procedure for reporting employment might have caused this, but some such influence seems likely. At any rate, a slight

[31] CPPA, pp. 104–105.

rate of annual increase of man-year productivity was forecast. Similar data problems invalidate any effort to establish a productivity series for woods operations; the best that can be said is that roughly constant productivity is occasionally disturbed by an innovation such as the power saw. Since this sort of change is not likely more than to offset decreasing returns through exploitation of less accessible and lower quality timber, no increase in productivity is forecast.

Employment figures in this chapter are presented in the form of the Dominion Bureau of Statistics' measure of man-years. But, since it is desired to reconcile the labor force requirements estimated for all industries separately with the total available 1970 labor force, this can be done by developing the relation between man-years worked and the maximum number of seasonal production workers as determined from monthly averages. This statistic is still subject to a wide margin of error, but it is conceptually correct at least for this purpose.

FISHERIES PRODUCTION

The fisheries of Canada take the prize for slowest rate of growth of any of the major Canadian industries, with output rising only slightly more than 0.5 per cent annually since 1926. The history of the industry's output is reflected in Figure 13.

Fig. 13. Quantity of seafish landings, 1926–1956 (millions of pounds).

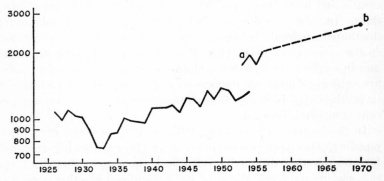

a Includes Newfoundland.
b Estimated 1970 catch.
Source: DBS, *Canadian Statistical Review, 1955 Supplement; Canada Year Book, 1956.*

Table 103. Quantity of fish landed in Canada[a] and value of products by regions and for selected species, 1954.

	Quantity (millions of pounds)	Percentage	Value (thousands of dollars)	Percentage
Atlantic Coast				
Cod	658	32	28,172	16
Herring	185	9	4,692	3
Haddock	118	6	7,764	5
Lobster	47	2	21,287	12
Rosefish	49	2	1,812	1
Sardines	33	2	5,501	3
All other	253	12	17,443	10
Total	1,342	65	86,671	50
Pacific Coast				
Herring	361	18	7,340	4
Halibut	25	1	5,965	3
Salmon	179	9	50,284	29
All other	35	2	5,567	3
Total	600	29	69,156	40
Inland	116	6	18,572	11
Grand total	2,059	100	174,399	100

[a] Includes Newfoundland. Totals may not sum due to rounding errors.
Source: Canada, DBS, *Fisheries Statistics, 1954,* Table 1; and Government of the Province of Newfoundland, *Submission to the RCCEP* (n. p., 1955), p. 63.

Fresh water fish production is omitted from the figure but it has seldom exceeded 5 per cent of total fish landings. This slow rate of growth is explained not by inadequate fishery resources but rather by loss of some foreign markets and loss of manpower to industries which can provide a more attractive level of living.

In Table 103 the distribution of the catch by area and by major species is given. Notice that the cod catch on the east coast is so large relative to the value that the Atlantic accounts for 65 per cent of the weight landed but only 50 per cent of the value of fisheries products. On the Atlantic the lobster catch is second in importance in value although the weight landed is less than for herring and haddock. On the Pacific of course the salmon catch is of overwhelming importance in value terms although it is a poor second to herring in weight.

The projection of the fisheries industry output requires consideration of the prospect for domestic consumption, for exports, and for the fisheries resources. For the most part the resources of the Atlantic fishing grounds, which accounted in 1954 for just about half of the value of fisheries production in Canada, are plentiful.[32] Lobster fishing has been pursued so heavily in recent years on the Atlantic coast that restrictions on gear and the length of the season have had to be instituted in order to avoid depletion, and the Atlantic salmon catch has showed a steady decline in recent years. With these two exceptions, there seems to be no supply problem on the east coast. Indeed, the gradual rise in the temperature of the Atlantic is actually increasing the supply of fish within reach of the Atlantic provinces.

On the Pacific coast, the salmon catch normally amounts to about 70 per cent of the total catch by value. The prospects for continued salmon production on a sustained yield basis have appeared quite good because the controls necessary to prevent depletion are well established and seem to be operating successfully. However the production from year to year does fluctuate considerably because of variations in stream levels and stream flow. Recently the question has been raised whether there might be some long-term influences operating to reduce salmon stocks.[33] So little is known about the true causes of the small runs in 1956 and 1957 that it is difficult to evaluate the significance of this experience for the long pull. There is the constant threat that hydroelectric dams and industrial establishments along the rivers will reduce the salmon run but to date it appears that the various practices and devices employed to prevent this have been at least reasonably successful.[34] Presumably such arrangements can be worked out in the future as well as they have been in the past and the salmon industry can continue to grow at least for the next decade. Eventually, however, it is entirely possible that British Columbia may have to choose between salmon and power

[32] This discussion is based primarily on Fisheries Council of Canada, *Submission to the RCCEP* (Ottawa, 1956); Newfoundland Fisheries Development Authority, *Submission to the RCCEP* (n.p., 1956); and the *Canada Year Book, 1955*.

[33] "Why Salmon Are Disappearing," *Financial Post*, November 16, 1957, p. 39.

[34] See "B. C. Fish vs Power Battle Takes Its Case to Ottawa," *Financial Post*, October 12, 1957, p. 8.

perhaps even on the Fraser as the available power sites come to be exploited. That painful day, however, is beyond our ken.

About 65 per cent of the country's catch, by value, is exported, approximately 70 per cent of the exports going to the United States and another 10 per cent to the United Kingdom.[35] This pattern of trade is quite in contrast with the last half of the 1920's, when less than 40 per cent of the exports were to the United States. Exports of fisheries products have illustrated the shift in Canada's foreign trade from east-west to north-south. The exports to the United States have increased steadily for the past twenty-five years and show no signs of diminishing; consequently the magnitude of the foreign demand for the products of Canadian fisheries in 1970 will depend largely on the size of the United States demand.

Per capita fish consumption in the United States has been remarkably stable for the past twenty years at 10.5 to 11 pounds. Apparently as incomes increase people simply do not increase their consumption of fish. As for the proportion of United States consumption provided by Canada, the Canadian exports to the United States have risen steadily from 1.30 pounds per capita in 1929 to 1.47 pounds in 1935–1939, 1.88 pounds in 1947–1949, and 2.02 pounds in 1955. At this rate by 1970 Canada will be supplying United States consumption needs in the amount of 2.53 pounds per capita.[36]

Exports of fish products to the rest of the world have fallen relative to shipments to the United States but the movements in these exports since 1926 have been affected by various unsystematic factors which make any kind of extrapolation a most uncertain procedure. Because of the year-to-year fluctuations in the size of the catch, it is best to view the changes in exports to other countries in terms of five-year averages. In the second half of the 1920's, Canada was exporting slightly more than 260,000,-000 pounds annually to countries other than the United States. This fell to 150,000,000 pounds annually in the five years prior to World War II, rose to 195,000,000 in 1946–1950, and in the last five years this group of exports has slid off a bit to 188,000,-

[35] Fisheries Council of Canada, p. 8.
[36] This is based on an arithmetic increase (0.036 pounds per capita per year) rather than a geometric increase because the former fits the 1935–1939 to 1955 experience much better than the latter.

ooo. During the 1930's, competition from low-cost producers was apparently the primary cause of the reduction. After World War II the European countries' purchases were reduced for at least two reasons. Currency difficulties forced the Mediterranean countries, who in the past have been major buyers of cod, to enforce import quotas and to shift their purchases to Iceland and Norway, particularly. In addition, the purchasing countries expanded their own fishing fleets. As a result, Canadian cod is moving increasingly into Caribbean and South American markets rather than European markets. But the shift in cod exports has been accompanied by a steady decline in the total cod shipments to about one-half the level of the years immediately following World War I. Since the population of what are now the major markets for Canadian cod will be increasing, it is possible that the decline in cod exports might stop within a few years.

The production of frozen ground-fish, meanwhile, has increased very rapidly since before World War II because of the development of the frozen fish industry in the United States. It is this growth which has offset the decline in cod production and resulted in the very modest increase in the output of the Canadian fisheries.[37]

From the above discussion it follows that the growth of the Canadian fisheries will depend in part on the rate of growth of the United States and the South American markets, assuming no tendency for the trade with Europe to return to its pre-World War II importance. But a second factor, at least as important as the first, is the rate at which productivity per man can be raised. Modernization of fishing equipment and processing plants is imperative if the fisheries are to expand output even as fast as their possible markets. This is necessary not only because the competition from foreign fleets is substantial but also because the infamously low productivity of the Maritimes fisherman must be raised if his income is going to rise sufficiently to keep him (or his son) from leaving the industry. It is significant that between 1946 and 1953 the number of persons employed in

[37] Unfortunately the data on exports of frozen fish are obscured because the exports statistics do not consistently distinguish between fresh and frozen fish. The production of frozen ground-fish in Newfoundland, however, has increased from less than 800,000 pounds in 1939 to over 53,000,000 pounds in 1954. (Government of the Province of Newfoundland, *Submission of the Government of the Province of Newfoundland to the RCCEP* [n.p., 1955], p. 75.)

Table 104. Gross value of output of Canadian fisheries industry, 1954 and 1970 (millions of dollars).

Species	1954 Actual	1970 Estimated
Cod	27.4	27.4
Salmon:		
Domestic consumption	18.0	26.7
Exports to United States	12.0	14.9
Exports to other countries	19.8	23.5
Other:		
Domestic consumption	23.1	34.4
Exports to United States	65.8	113.4
Exports to other countries	8.1	9.5
Total	174.2	249.8

Source: 1954 data from Canada, DBS, *Trade of Canada, 1954,* Vol. II; and Fisheries Council of Canada, *Submission to the RCCEP* (Ottawa, 1956); see text for methods of estimating 1970 data.

fishing and in the processing of fish has declined by about 15 per cent.[38] This exodus is understandable in view of the estimated annual net income of about $500 per fisherman in the Maritimes.[39]

There is some apparently well founded hope that the productivity per man can be increased substantially within the next few years. In the case of cod, productivity per man has been held down because the time required for drying the fish limited the time which could be spent fishing. One fresh-frozen and salt-fish plant is now experimenting with taking the fish in the round state, rather than gutted, filleting them and placing the fillets in chilled brine for artificial drying in the slow winter months. If this experiment proves successful, the individual fisherman could fish for several months rather than just a few weeks and his income could be greatly increased. The possibilities of increasing production by shifting toward herring, haddock, and lobster and by using fishing methods recently developed by the Federal

[38] From 87,891 to 74,979 excluding Newfoundland, where another 14,000 men left the industry after 1945. See Government of the Province of Newfoundland, p. 77.

[39] For a discussion of the productivity problem as well as the industry's more general problems in Newfoundland, see H. B. Mayo, "The Economic Problem of the Newfoundland Fisheries," *CJEPS,* 17:482–493 (November 1951).

Department of Fisheries and the Fisheries Research Board of Canada hold some promise. But the probable rate of adoption of these techniques by a capital-poor industry is very uncertain.

In Table 104 the 1970 projected level of output for the fisheries industry is compared with that for 1954. The level of cod production is left unchanged, on the ground that the loss of European markets will be offset by the growth of the Caribbean and South American purchases due to population increases. The domestic consumption of both salmon and other fish is expected to increase about 10 per cent faster than the population. Between 1944 and 1954, per capita consumption of fish in Canada rose from 9.8 pounds to 13.8 pounds.[40] This great increase has been attributed to improved refrigeration and distribution as well as the development of frozen packaged fish. Since there are several reasons why per capita consumption of fish in Canada might be greater than in the United States, it is assumed that it will rise another 10 per cent, to the 15-pound range, in spite of the fact that consumption in the United States has leveled off at 11 pounds per capita.

The projection of salmon exports to the United States assumes that the supply problems mentioned earlier will not cause serious trouble over the next decade and that because of competition from United States and Alaskan fleets the British Columbia salmon producers will only be able to increase their sales to the United States proportionally as the United States population increases.[41] The exports of other fish to the United States, however, are expected to rise considerably more than are salmon exports. This presumes that the fish population continues to move northward, giving Canadian fisheries an advantage; that therefore the United States will continue to buy more fish from Canada as its own fleets come to operate under a growing geographical and operating cost handicap; that no tariff barriers will be erected to stop this movement; and that the fish per capita provided the United States by Canada will continue to rise as it has for three decades to 2.53 pounds per capita.

The exports to other countries are expected to rise at 1 per cent

[40] Fisheries Council of Canada, p. 30.
[41] The expected United States population increase is to 204,000,000 in 1970. This is the latest estimate found in federal publications. See U.S. Bureau of Mines, *Mineral Facts and Problems* (Washington, 1956); p. 8.

per year. This is a slow rate of increase indeed, but the developments of recent years do not support a greater rate of increase.[42] Even this 1 per cent rate may be too high.

The projected output of $250,000,000 represents an expected annual rate of increase of about 2.25 per cent per year. It should be emphasized once more that this rate of increase depends primarily on continued access to the United States market and substantially increased productivity per man so that earnings might be great enough to retain the work force. If either or both of these conditions fail to hold, the industry may shrink not only in terms of manpower but in terms of output as well.

Imports have not yet been mentioned. They have fluctuated between 10 and 15 per cent of production for the last twenty-five years. We will estimate the 1970 imports of fishery products at 12.5 per cent of production, or $31,000,000.

The employment requirements of the fisheries in 1970 are particularly difficult to project because of the inadequacies of the available historical data and the uncertainties as to output per man and the relative attractiveness of other industries to the people now engaged in the fisheries. The catch per man in primary fishing has been rising at the rate of a little more than 1 per cent per year since the latter half of the 1920's. As a long-run rate of increase, however, this figure may be optimistic, considering the fact that catch per man each year during 1926–1929 was higher than any of the years of the 1930's. In other words, the entire increase in output per man was achieved during and after the war. To what extent this is explained by technological developments rather than mere reduction in disguised unemployment is difficult to say. It is conceivable that the 1940–1954 increase in catch per man simply lifted the industry to a new plateau and that the rate of increase will now be much lower than during the war and postwar years. As a compromise we will assume that the rate of increase will be the same as that achieved from 1926–1930 to 1950–1954, about 1.125 per cent.[43] This would require a work force in primary fishing of about

---

[42] Compare T. R. Kinsella, "How Fisheries Fared in '55," *Foreign Trade*, 105:3–4 (March 17, 1956).

[43] Since the data, understandably, do not show catch per man by species, it is impossible to know to what extent the increase in the catch per man may be due to any changes in the distribution of the catch among different species.

30,000 persons, an increase of about 20 per cent over 1953–54.[44]

In fish processing establishments, productivity per man has had about the same history as in primary fishing except that the postwar jump has been even greater. If one contrasts 1950–1954 with 1926–1930, an annual rate of increase in output per man of about 4 per cent appears. But, again, nearly all of this increase has been accounted for by the postwar developments in processing, for the annual rate of increase to the late 1930's, was scarcely 0.25 per cent. If we say that output per person is likely to increase at about 1 per cent per year 1954–1970 on the grounds that the postwar rate of increase will not hold for the long pull, about 17,300 persons will be occupied in the fish processing industry in 1970, assuming that the processing expands no more rapidly than the output of the fisheries industries combined. However, it is the object of developmental work in the fisheries to increase the degree of processing performed in Canada, for the domestic as well as for the export product. And historically the ratio of employment in processing to employment in primary fishing has been rising gradually. It may not be too optimistic to put the employment estimate for 1970 for primary fishing plus processing at 50,000 with 30,000 workers in primary fishing and another 20,000 in the processing plants. But it must be stressed again that this is a rougher estimate than many of our employment projections for several reasons. The data on employment do not permit a measure of output per man by species of fish; disguised unemployment is impossible to measure; the supply conditions, especially with regard to salmon, may be uncertain; export markets depend not only on ultimate consumer demand but also on the policies of foreign governments with respect to tariffs and subsidization of fishing fleets; and the degree of processing is also determined in part by the nature of foreign tariffs.

As for the geographical distribution of production and the work force, it is expected that the west coast fisheries will be produc-

---

[44] This is not comparable with the 79,700 figure reported in Canada, DBS, *Fisheries Statistics 1954,* as the number of fishermen in Canada in 1954. The *Fisheries Statistics* figures include some persons who were primarily engaged in other industries, apparently, for the DBS Reference Paper No. 58, *The Labour Force, November, 1945–January, 1955,* shows about 24,000 persons in fishing and trapping in 1954 and 26,000 in 1953. To avoid double counting, we need to use the latter concept.

ing 35 per cent of the output, or $87,000,000 worth. This extrapolation presumes that total west coast production will increase proportionally as salmon products output. This leaves $163,000,000 for the rest of the country, divided between fresh water and Atlantic areas as in 1954, $26,000,000 and $137,000,000. Productivity in the west coast fisheries is considerably higher than in the rest of the country: in 1954, British Columbia accounted for twice as great a percentage of the output as of the work force. Thus in 1970 the west coast fisheries can be expected to employ a work force of about 8000 persons. If the rest of the work force is distributed proportionally as in 1954, Quebec will employ another 6500, Ontario 2000, the prairies 6200, and the remaining 27,300 will be in the Atlantic provinces.

18
The Manufacturing Industries

At the risk of considerable embarrassment over the results, it was decided in the early stages of this project to attempt to project the components of the Canadian economy by two different methods, the one serving as a check on the other. Long-range economic forecasting, it can be argued, is difficult enough without seeking out problems in reconciliation. We trust, however, that the internal check is one of the virtues of this study and that the corpus of economic forecasting is solid enough to survive such a check.

Having completed the projection of the primary industries, we will proceed in this chapter to summarize the projections of the individual manufacturing industries. The forecasts of the present chapter were prepared before the 1970 interindustry table was completed, so there was no possibility that the projections of the manufacturing industry groups could be shaped even subconsciously to agree with the results of Chapter 14. As we have already stated in that chapter, we did not force a complete reconciliation between the individual industry forecasts and the forecasts produced in the interindustry table since such agreement would be palpably false. We consider the differences between the two sets of forecasts to be of more interest than the similarities, for they reveal the probable errors in the 1970 picture we are drawing.

One reason the differences between the two sets of forecasts are no larger is that the projections of this chapter cannot be completely independent of the aggregates produced in Chapters 8 through 14. We have had to take the population, gross national product, personal disposable income, and investment forecasts from those chapters as given in order to draw up most of the manufacturing industry estimates. So the "independence" of the forecasts in this chapter is not to be exaggerated. However they are independent of each other in the sense that they have been drawn up generally with little consideration for the interdependence of industries, the interdependence which the inter-industry table is designed to handle.

The methodology of this chapter is straightforward. In most instances it has been possible to construct time series of domestic disappearance and then examine the historic determinants of that magnitude. Next, export and import levels were studied to see whether the reasons for future changes in the flow of international trade in the product could be clarified. This latter step calls for prayerful artistry on the part of the economic forecaster since trade policy is as much a political as an economic matter. Even the correlation analysis requires considerable judgment. Ideally, one would prefer to construct for each industry a time series of deflated value of output, domestic disappearance, imports, and exports for the years since World War I and then seek out the variables which best explain the behavior of these time series. The data for many of the manufacturing industries do not permit this, however, and in many cases it was necessary to base the forecast only on the post-depression, prewar years of 1937–1939 plus the 1946–1954 period.[1]

Fortunately the industry submissions to the Royal Commission on Canada's Economic Prospects were just being presented at the time these forecasts were being prepared and so in many instances we could check our results against the industry's own expectations. Whether or not we have let those submissions temper the projections has depended not only on the apparent care expended on construction of the industry estimate but also on such questions as whether the industry forecast might have been shaped into conformity with a policy recommendation to the commission. In general, the presentations by firms and trade groups have been of great assistance in uncovering aspects of the industry's operations in Canada which might otherwise have escaped our attention.

The sum of the output projections for 1970 is compared with the output of the sector in 1954 to see whether the implied rate of growth appears consistent with the discussion in Chapter 2 concerning the relative importance of manufacturing in the Canadian economy. Then in a final section of this chapter the

[1] Unless it is indicated otherwise, the industry projections are based on these years only.

regional distribution of output and employment is discussed. As each industry's 1970 output was forecast, the regional distribution in 1939, 1950, and 1954 was examined to determine whether the gradual westward shift was in evidence and to what degree. The causes of this shift were considered and from this background an estimated distribution of output was prepared for 1970. The last two tables in this chapter summarize the regional distribution material.

The estimates of regional distribution of output and employment had to be constructed as a prerequisite to a final estimate of the distribution of population in Canada. The estimate was prepared on an industry-by-industry basis despite the regional data for past years being weak, in some instances, because of the disclosure rule. The small number of firms in some industries in Canada not only causes trouble if one works with provincial data for past years but also introduces into the projections an element of uncertainty which would not be present in a larger economy. In Canada the decision of one firm to expand output in one region rather than in another can affect the regional distribution of the industry significantly. We can here rely only on the defense, ancient as it is weak, that when aggregating the industries the errors hopefully will offset one another in some degree.

PROJECTIONS OF THE MANUFACTURING INDUSTRIES

Food, beverages, and tobacco products

In 1954 this industry group accounted for a greater gross value of output, a greater net value added, and a greater number of employees than any other group in Canadian manufacturing, even greater than wood products or iron and steel products. In 1954, approximately 16 per cent of the income originating in manufacturing came from this sector. But the relative importance of food, beverages, and tobacco has been shrinking slightly; in 1929, 22.5 per cent of the gross value of manufacturing output was in this industry but by 1954 the percentage had dropped to 20.2 per cent. This decline gives some support to an argument presented later in this chapter, namely that as an area grows, the food products manufacturing industry is one of the first to appear in the manufacturing sector while the industries in which there are substantial economies of scale develop later in the growth process. But we will see that, over the next few years, foods, beverages, and allied products will expand a bit more rapidly than the GNP. The "up-grading" of consumer food purchases which has marked the postwar years is primarily responsible for these bright growth prospects.

Correlation of domestic disappearance of food, beverages, and tobacco manufactures with personal disposable income for 1937–1939 and the postwar years shows that the latter accounts for over 90 per cent of the variance of the former. On the basis of this relation, which is not as good as one might wish, domestic disappearance of food, beverages, and tobacco products in 1970 will be between $6,500,000,000 and $7,000,000,000, probably closer to the latter.[2] This is nearly double the 1954 consumption of $3,700,000,000. The proportion of domestic requirements which have been imported has fluctuated between 6.5 per cent and 8.5 per cent since before the war and there is no trend in evidence. This seems wholly logical: the foods which Canada imports simply cannot be produced there, and the growth of the domestic market does not attract sugar plantations as it might attract steel fabricators. Eventually we might expect some slight increase in the proportion of domestic requirements imported as higher incomes cause greater-than-proportional increases in the demand for such foods as citrus fruits, but since a high proportion of food imports are of staples (for example, sugar, tea, and coffee), such an increase is likely to be small if it appears at all.

Exports as a percentage of total production have declined since before the war but the decline has not been of a sort that points clearly to a 1970 estimate. In 1937–1939, exports average 14.0 per cent of production, but since 1949 the percentage has ranged between 10.3 and 11.0 per cent (except for 1950–51, Korean War years, when the percentages went to 11.2 and 11.7) without showing any definite trend. The bulk of the decline in percentage of production exported has been in meat and dairy products. Canadians appear to be consuming a greater proportion of their output of these items as the population grows and as incomes increase.[3]

---

[2] The 1970 projections in this chapter are all in terms of 1955 prices.

[3] A portion of the decline must be attributed to the United States embargo imposed because of hoof-and-mouth disease.

If, in 1970, imports of food, beverages, and tobacco products provide for 7.5 per cent of the domestic requirements and if exports take 8 per cent of production (this assumes that exports as a percentage of output will continue to drop off gradually), then the industry will be producing about $7,000,000,000 worth of goods annually, imports will be a shade more than $500,000,000, and exports will be about the same as imports. Since exports are of relatively little importance, the export percentage might range between 7 and 9 per cent of production without throwing the production forecast off by more than $100,000,000.

Clothing and household goods

In this group of industries are included clothing, textile products, furniture, leather products, and jewelry and silverware. We will combine the first two and examine them together but the others will be studied individually.

Only half of the year-to-year variation in the domestic disappearance of textile products per capita is explained by personal disposable income per capita. But the deviations of the observed from the calculated values are systematic for the postwar years, showing a kind of "clothing cycle" in 1946–1952. Purchases in 1946–1949 were abnormally high because former servicemen and consumers generally were rebuilding their wardrobes after the war. Then for a year or two expenditures were abnormally low, apparently because of low replacement demand. The domestic disappearance in 1952 and 1953 seems to have been a return to normal, with 1954 being low because of the recession.

Because of the unique postwar clothing cycle, the 1970 estimate of domestic disappearance of textile products is based on the prewar years and 1950, 1952, and 1953, which seem to be years relatively free of short-run abnormalities. This procedure gives a domestic disappearance of $135 per capita in 1970 or a little more than $2,800,000,000 in the aggregate.

Imports immediately before the war were accounting for 15–18 per cent of domestic disappearance of textile products. By 1952–1954, however, this percentage had fallen to the bottom of this range, 15 per cent, implying that Canada is coming to rely slightly less on imports for its domestic requirements. We must square such a conclusion, however, with the textile industry's loud complaints that imports are providing *more* rather than *less* of the Canadian requirements and that the domestic producers are being annihilated.[4] The Primary Textiles Institute presents data in terms of linear yards of fabric which show that in 1935–1939 only 28 per cent of the domestic requirements were met by imports whereas since 1951 about 40 per cent have been met by imports. When the data are presented in terms of value rather than physical quantity, however, the increase in the ratio of imports to consumption is not as great, rising only from 22 per cent in 1939 to 26 per cent in 1953.[5]

In terms of value, then, Canada's primary textile requirements are being met increasingly by imports while her *total* textile products requirements are being met increasingly by domestic production. Besides primary textiles (yarns and fabrics) the textile products industry as we have defined it here includes clothing and a residual "other" category has been growing much more rapidly than the other two. In 1939 less than 7 per cent of Canadian textile products production was in this category whereas by 1953 the proportion had more than doubled. The drop in *total* textile products consumption represented by imports, then, is caused largely by the growth of the importance of this third sector, in which imports are minor.

Canadian textile producers are likely to be pinched by rising wages over the long pull. Textile production is labor intensive, and productivity has been rising more slowly than in the country's export industries. These two factors mean not only that the wage bill is a large part of total production costs but also that wage increases are likely to pull ahead of productivity increases. Competition from imports may well be a growing problem. But, on the other hand, consumption can be expected to shift toward those products of which a lower proportion are imported. On these grounds we will expect the ratio of imports to

---

[4] See Primary Textiles Institute, *Submission to the RCCEP on behalf of the Canadian Primary Textile Industry* (Toronto and Montreal, 1956), p. 15; also Solomon Barkin, Textile Workers' Union of America, *Statement to the RCCEP* (n.d., processed), pp. 15–16.

[5] Because of certain difficulties encountered in classifying trade data consistently with production data, the change in this percentage over the fourteen-year period is more reliable than the percentage itself in either year. There is some question about precisely what products are considered "primary" textiles. The important point is that these percentages are based on the same classification scheme for the two years in question, but one or two minor categories may have been omitted in both years or included in both years erroneously.

domestic consumption to hold to the 15 per cent level. This percentage will be affected by such factors as tariff changes, technological changes in Canadian textile production, and immigration policy, so the estimate is rather uncertain.

Exports as a percentage of production have fallen from 3.4 per cent in 1937–1939 to 1.4 per cent in 1952–1954. In view of the probability of rising real wages in Canada due to the general prosperity which is expected, it may not be unrealistic to assume that Canada's exports will drop still more. They might drop to zero, but there is some prospect of an export market for specialized winter clothing.[6] We will work with a nominal 0.5 per cent estimate of the proportion of production which will be exported in 1970.

Domestic disappearance of textile products of $2,800,000,000, exports of 0.5 per cent of production and imports of $420,000,000 (15 per cent of domestic requirements) gives a total production of a bit less than $2,400,000,000 for the industry for 1970 in terms of 1955 prices.

So as to show the margin of error that may be involved if the import projection is off, domestic production was recomputed assuming that the imported percentage would increase from 15 to 20 per cent and assuming that it would fall to 10 per cent. The first alternative gives a domestic production estimate of $2,240,-000,000, compared with $2,400,000,000 above. The second alternative yields a production figure of $2,530,000,000. So the margin of error in the production forecast caused by this probable error in the import projection is less than 7 per cent.

The case of furniture is quite simple. About 90 per cent of the changes in domestic disappearance are explained by personal disposable income. Given the expected 1970 personal disposable income, the domestic disappearance of furniture will be about $525,000,000. Exports have taken less than 0.5 per cent of production since the end of the war and even within this small percentage a decline, to 0.1 per cent in 1953 and 1954, has appeared. The proportion of domestic requirements provided by imports has also been declining, from 3.6 per cent in 1937–1939 to about 2 per cent in 1953 and 1954. Both imports and exports, then, seem to be approaching the vanishing point and we can expect furniture

[6] See Barkin, p. 3.

production to equal furniture consumption by 1970, foreign trade in this item being negligible by that time.

The leather products projection must be as uncertain as the furniture forecast was certain. When domestic disappearance of leather products per capita is plotted against personal disposable income per capita, the postwar behavior of the observations seem to be similar to those for textile products. However, the data for 1950, 1952, and 1953 do not provide the basis for a compromise projection as in the earlier instance since the observations for those years are so scattered and since 1952 and 1953 show such a very slight increase over the prewar years. It would be justifiable to eliminate 1946 and 1947 because consumption was unusually high due to the postwar build-up of consumer inventories. The slope of the regression line would be reduced considerably but the fit would still be rather poor.

In order to resolve the difficulty, the projected income elasticity estimate for footwear of 0.772 (see Chapter 10, p. 324) was used. This step renders the leather products forecast less independent of the interindustry table than are the other industry projections but there seemed to be no attractive alternative. The percentage increase in income and the percentage increase in leather products consumption were computed from the average 1951–1953 income and the average 1951–1953 leather products consumption. The 1970 estimate by this procedure is $20.20 per capita as compared with $15 per capita, the average for 1951–1953. The $20 per capita projection is consistent with the postwar experience if 1946 and 1947 are omitted. For the entire leather products industry domestic disappearance is expected to rise from the $204,000,000 of 1954 to about $425,000,000 in 1970.

Imports and exports are both relatively unimportant. Imports account only for about 3.9 per cent of domestic disappearance (average for 1952–1954) and only 1.2 per cent of production is exported. The 1937–1939 imported percentage was a bit lower than in 1952–1954, 3.1 per cent, but the post-war years saw imports of less than 2.7 per cent of domestic requirements in three years so the import forecast must be based on an erratic record. The projection will use a 4.0 per cent import share, fractionally higher than 1952–1954 but actually lower than 1953–54.

Exports as a proportion of production have fallen slightly,

from 1.8 per cent in 1937–1939 to 1.2 per cent in 1952–1954. The fluctuations in the export percentage are not as wide as in the case of imports and the decline in the proportion exported seems quite definite. We will assume that the exported percentage will decline 0.6 per cent over the 1955–1970 period as it did over the fifteen years previous, to 0.6 per cent.

This combination of domestic disappearance, imports, and exports resolves into the following amounts for 1970: production, $410,000,000; imports, $17,000,000; and exports, $2,500,000.

Jewelry and silverware production in 1954 amounted to just over $47,000,000, less than 2.5 per cent of the output of the entire clothing and household goods sector with which we are dealing. The correlation of domestic disappearance with personal disposable income is a bit less than is desirable for very firm projection, but by dropping 1946 a fairly solid forecast for 1970 can be constructed. Per capita consumption rose, 1939 to 1953, by $0.495 for every $100 increase in income. This basis gives per capita 1970 disappearance of $5.20 and an aggregate for the country of $109,200,000.

Exports have been negligible but imports as a percentage of domestic disappearance have increased from 17 per cent in 1937–1939 to 19.8 per cent in 1952–1954. In anticipation of rising imports, particularly from Europe, we will assume another 3 per cent increase for the period ending in 1970. Thus, of the domestic market demand for $109,000,000, about $25,000,000 will be imported and the remaining $84,000,000 will be produced at home. This domestic production is an increase of nearly 80 per cent over the 1954 level.

Forest products

The production, imports, and exports data for forest products were computed in the course of Chapter 17, dealing with forestry and fisheries. The derivation of the estimates has been presented there in such detail that a summary will suffice at this point. Since furniture production, imports, and exports have been included in the clothing and household goods sector, they will not be included in the tables which follow.

In Table 105 the expected changes in production are of particular interest. By far the greatest increase is expected in paper and paper products, followed by newsprint. Since the regional

Table 105. Production, exports, imports, and domestic disappearance in forest products manufacturing industries of Canada (millions of dollars).[a]

Industry	Production			Exports	Imports	Domestic disappearance
	1954	1970	% incr.	1970	1970	1970
Lumber	580.7	656.6	13	337.9	22.5	341.2
Wood-using (excl. furniture)	429.8	658.0	53	50.0	37.0	645.0
Paper	230.4	509.9	121	50.5	5.3	464.7
Newsprint	657.5	1086.3	65	1002.8	37.0	120.5
Woodpulp	353.7	535.3	52	520.2	10.0	25.1
Paper-using	386.4	695.5	80	0	10.0	705.5
Total	2638.5	4141.6	58	1961.4	121.8	2302.0

[a] 1954 data in 1954 dollars; 1970 data in 1955 dollars.

Source: 1954 figures computed from data in Canada, DBS, *Trade of Canada,* various years, and *Census of Manufactures,* various issues; for 1970 data, see Chapter 17.

shift is so great for this industry, the forecast is given in detail in Table 106. There the expected distribution of production in 1970 is compared with that of 1954. All the provinces are expected to lose some of their relative share of production to the West, where production is expected to increase by very large percentages primarily because of the availability of the timber supply and power. The rationale for the shift in location is contained in Chapter 17.

Metal products

This group of manufacturing industries will be divided into two parts for purposes of this discussion: iron and steel products (including primary iron and steel, agricultural implements, transportation equipment and other iron and steel products) and non-ferrous metal products.

Using as before the years 1937–1939 and 1946–1954 as the basis for projection, domestic disappearance of iron and steel products is very well correlated with gross public and private investment, nearly 96 per cent of the variance in the former being explained by the investment series. Judging from this, the 1970 projection of $11,100,000,000 domestic disappearance of iron and steel products can be viewed as quite a firm estimate.

Table 106. Geographical distribution of the forest products manufacturing industries of Canada, 1954 and 1970.

Industry	Atlantic provinces		Quebec		Ontario		Prairie provinces		B.C., Yukon, and N.W.T.		Total	
	1954	1970	1954	1970	1954	1970	1954	1970	1954	1970	1954	1970
Percentage distribution												
Lumber	8.3	7.0	16.5	11.0	13.7	7.0	5.6	10.0	55.8	65.0	100.0	100
Wood-using	7.5	6.5	24.6	24.0	28.5	26.0	11.4	12.0	27.9	31.5	100.0	100
Paper, newsprint, woodpulp	15.0[a]	13.0	42.9	40.0	29.4	27.0	—[a]	4.0	12.7	16.0	100.0	100
Paper-using	1.1	1.0	30.6	31.0	54.9	55.0	5.6	5.0	7.8	8.0	100.0	100
Value distribution (1954 in millions of 1954 dollars; 1970 in millions of 1955 dollars)												
Lumber[b]	48.2	46.0	96.0	72.2	79.6	46.0	32.6	65.7	324.2	426.8	580.7	656
Wood-using[b]	32.1	42.8	105.9	157.9	122.7	171.1	49.0	79.0	120.1	207.3	429.8	658
Paper, newsprint, woodpulp[b]	186.5[a]	277.1	532.3	852.4	365.0	575.5	—[a]	85.3	157.8	341.0	1241.6	2131
Paper-using[b]	4.1	7.0	118.8	215.6	213.2	382.5	22.1	34.8	28.4	55.6	388.6	695

[a] Given only for Atlantic and Prairie provinces combined.
[b] 1953 rather than 1954.
Source: 1954 figures, computed from data in Canada, DBS, *Trade of Canada*, various years, and *Census of Manufactures*, various issues; for 1970 data, see Chapter 17.

Table 107. Production, imports, exports, and domestic disappearance of selected iron and steel products, in Canada, 1939 and 1954.

Industry	1939 (millions of current dollars)					1954ᵃ (millions of current dollars)				
	Production	Imports	Exports	Domestic disappearance	Percentage imported	Production	Imports	Exports	Domestic disappearance	Percentage imported
Motor vehicles and parts[a,b]	107	41	26	122	34	1143	319	75	1387	23
Farm implements	16	21	7	30	70	119	143	77	185	77
Other machinery	48	43	11	80	54	324	380	37	667	57
Primary iron and steel	76	33	9	100	33	384	99	17	466	21
Engines and boilers	9	8	—	17	47	88	92	24	156	29
Aircraft and parts[a]	13	6	—	19	32	399	112	40	471	24

[a] Motor vehicles and parts and aircraft and parts data are for 1939 and 1953 rather than 1939 and 1954.
[b] Excludes automobile engine imports and exports, which are included in "engines and boilers."
Source: Canada, DBS, Trade of Canada, 1939, 1953, and 1954; and The Manufacturing Industries of Canada, 1939, 1953, and 1954.

A bit of light is shed on the earlier discussion of the probable growth of the manufacturing sector by looking at the proportion of domestic disappearance which is imported. For the years 1937–1939 and 1946–1954 this ratio has been remarkably stable, never rising above 29.5 per cent (in 1947) nor falling below 24.9 per cent (in 1938). With the exception of 1947, the ratio since 1946 has not varied by more than 1 per cent from the postwar average of 26.8 per cent.

The ratio of imports to domestic disappearance for major categories has not remained stable, however, in all cases. In Table 107 an attempt has been made to construct domestic disappearance estimates for six of the more important of the iron and steel products. (These six accounted for about one-half of the total domestic disappearance of *all* iron and steel products in 1939 and about three-fourths in 1954.) The domestic disappearance percentages are only approximate because of the numerous differences between the commodity classes used in the DBS international trade data and those used in the production data. Even if this source of error is taken into account, certain conclusions can be drawn from Table 107. In the case of motor vehicles, aircraft and parts, and primary steel, Canada is coming to rely less on imports than before the war. Total imports of farm implements, however, have increased a bit relative to total domestic disappearance. But notice that farm implement exports have risen from 45 to 65 per cent of production as a result of the elimination of tariffs on these items by the United States and Canada after World War II. The "other machinery" category shows an increase in the ratio to domestic disappearance, but it is such a small increase that the change may fall within the range of error rising from the classification problem. Engines and boilers show a more definite increase, but here there may be a sizable error. Combining engines and boilers with motor vehicles and parts and with aircraft and parts shows that the ratio of imports to domestic disappearance for the sum of the three groups has declined from 35 per cent in 1939 to 27 per cent in 1954.[7]

For the entire group of industries shown in Table 107 the imported ratio has dropped from 42 per cent in 1939 to 34 per cent in 1954. We can conclude that for these important and basic in-

---

[7] Data for 1953 rather than for 1954 were used in Table 107 for motor vehicles and aircraft because of certain difficulties with the trade data.

dustries, then, the country is becoming more nearly self-sufficient. But for *all* iron and steel products, we noted above that the proportion of consumption imported had remained surprisingly stable at about 27 per cent. Therefore at least some of the iron and steel products *not* included in Table 107 must have been supplied from imports rather than domestic production to a greater extent in 1954 than in 1939, otherwise the imported ratio for the entire iron and steel products group would have fallen. Scanning the import data reveals scattered categories which have increased massively since 1939. Although imports of all iron and steel products were 6.3 times as great (undeflated dollars) in 1954 as in 1939, imports of tubes, pipes, and fittings were $59,700,000 in 1954 as against only $2,300,000 in 1939, showing the effect of oil and natural gas development; tools and hand implements were up to $23,600,000 as against $2,400,000 in 1939; imports of valves rose from $500,000 to $7,900,000; and so on. The building boom plus the mineral development boom has apparently been primarily responsible for the larger-than-average increase in imports.

This list of items provides a clue to what industries within the iron and steel products group are likely to grow next in Canada. Certainly present and prospective manufacturers keep an eye on these imports since they serve as a crude index of the size of the market which a new domestic producer might supply. The new pipe mills which have recently been built or which are expanding production provide an example of industrial development based on the production of import-competing goods.

Can we forecast that the ratio of imports to domestic disappearance will hold to the historic 27 per cent level? The major groups in Table 107 show the fall in the percentage of domestic consumption coming from imports. But they still show a higher-than-average ratio of imports to domestic disappearance, 34 per cent. Furthermore, it seems to be granted that for a long while Canada will import a very large proportion of certain specialized products. For example, some of the new processing plants require structural shapes which Canadian rolling mills are not wide enough to handle. Some types of specialized machinery cannot now be produced economically for the Canadian market and certainly this condition will continue in some degree. In the 1949–1954 period domestic production accounted for only 1 per cent of the textile equipment sold in Canada; 2 per cent of the printing and publishing machinery; 16 per cent of the metal working machinery; and 25 per cent of the industrial engines.[8] But the equipment required by the larger industries is more commonly produced in Canada; 75 per cent of the pulp and paper machinery, 45 per cent of the logging and sawmill machinery, and 44 per cent of the mining machinery (excluding oil and gas well drilling equipment) was produced domestically during this period.[9] However, the Machinery and Equipment Manufacturers Association argued before the Gordon Commission that, with the exception of water wheels and turbines, woodworking machinery, and mining machinery, Canadian machinery manufacturers had a smaller share of the domestic market in 1953 and 1954 than in the previous four years.[10] This may indicate that the competition from United States producers is especially great when the latter are not operating at full capacity on domestic orders. Further, investment expenditures fluctuate over such a wide range that Canadian manufacturers of capital equipment have difficulty keeping up with orders when investment expenditures are at unusually high levels. Such a situation leads to larger imports of these goods.

Thus it appears that the motor vehicles, aircraft, and primary iron and steel will be supplied increasingly from domestic production but many types of machinery and specialized equipment will continue to be imported in substantial proportion. Among the primary iron and steel products this will be especially true for structural steel and for hot rolled sheets, which were imported in recent years to a greater extent, relative to total consumption, than any other major type of primary steel. Primary steel consumption on the west coast is especially likely to be met in significant measure (nearly 50 per cent) by imports.[11] Tariff revisions on some steel products could reduce the imported percentage for some categories. But, since primary iron and steel consti-

[8] See Machinery and Equipment Manufacturers Association of Canada, *Representations to the RCCEP* (n.d., n.p., processed), p. 4. These data presumably are no more reliable than those of Table 107 because of the classification problem.
[9] Machinery and Equipment Manufacturers Association of Canada, p. 4.
[10] *Ibid.*
[11] See J. P. Lounsbury and Frank Pelletier, "Canada's Steel Imports and Their Regional Significance," *Foreign Trade*, August 4, 1956, pp. 8–9; and Bank of Nova Scotia, "Canada's Primary Steel Industry," *Monthly Review*, July, 1956.

tutes less than 15 per cent of the entire iron and steel products category, changes in the tariffs on primary steel might not affect the group estimates significantly.

Countering these arguments that the imported ratio will remain at the historic level is the point that Canadian imports of machinery and equipment seem to be particularly sensitive to the level of investment in basic industry. The type of equipment required for refineries and many types of manufacturing plants must be imported in substantial amounts. Therefore the level of imports of iron and steel products may be expected to drop fractionally below the levels reached during the investment boom of the early 1950's. We will project the import percentage at very slightly less than the historical average, namely 26.0 per cent rather than 27 per cent.

Exports of iron and steel products took 11 per cent of domestic production in 1937–1939 but this percentage has been falling steadily since the end of the war, reaching a low of 5.7 per cent in 1954. The future of this percentage depends so largely on whether United States tariffs are reduced in the spirit of the General Agreement on Tariffs and Trade and whether other foreign countries, particularly those in Latin America, are able to pursue their industrial development programs that a forecast must have a substantial margin of error. The percentage also depends, of course, on whether the domestic demand is likely to tax domestic production facilities, as in 1955–56. If a reduction of the pressure on domestic production facilities is anticipated by 1970 and if the search for export markets is intensified, it is quite conceivable that the Canadian iron and steel products producers might be able to hold their exports at the present levels. Exports of this class of products to Latin America especially seem likely to increase substantially, not only because Canada has always found sizable export markets in Latin America but also because the Latin American market is widely granted to be the most rapidly growing market in the world. With this probable development in mind, plus the probable further integration of United States and Canadian manufacturing operations by firms owning plants in both countries, we will put the 1970 export ratio at 6 per cent of production, roughly the 1954 level.

Exports of 6 per cent of production and imports of 26 per cent of domestic disappearance lead to a production estimate for 1970 of $8,738,000,000 if domestic requirements of $11,100,000,000 are to be met. The export estimate is quite uncertain, but if the range of the export ratio is 2 per cent on either side of the 6 per cent forecast, the domestic production estimate falls between $8,550,-000,000 and $8,825,000,000. So the range of error in the export projection does not seriously distort the projection. The median projection of production, $8,738,000,000, is an increase of 130 per cent over the 1954 output (translated into 1955 prices).

Within the iron and steel products group as it is here defined the two largest categories are primary iron and steel and motor vehicles. We can summarize the outlook for these two industries. Domestic disappearance of primary iron and steel is poorly correlated with gross public and private investment for the years 1937–1939 and 1946–1954 but only because of the aberration generated by the Korean affair and its aftermath. If 1951–1954 are ignored, the relation between the two sets of data points to primary iron and steel consumption of about $1,400,000,000 in 1970, given the expected gross public and private investment estimate of $11,900,000,000 for that year. The 1950–1954 experience proves, however, that, although this $1,400,000,000 may be a reliable estimate for the "normal" relation between the two variables, an abnormality of the magnitude of the Korean War, or even of the 1938 recession, can cause a rather serious deviation of the actual from the projected value.

Canada has become less dependent on imports for her primary iron and steel. Table 107 showed that the proportion of consumption imported has fallen from 33 to 21 per cent since 1939. The proportion of production exported has also fallen, from 11.8 per cent in 1939 to 4.4 per cent in 1954. Probably imports will fall a bit less rapidly over time because of the likelihood of there being some irreducible minimum of requirements (for specialized items) which must be imported, so we will put the imported proportion at 10 per cent for 1970. If exports fall to 2 per cent of production, domestic production must be about $1,285,000,000 in 1970 in order to provide for domestic requirements of $1,400,-000,000. This $1,285,000,000 output is 3.3 times the 1954 output but only about 2.4 times the 1955 output. In terms of steel ingot equivalent tonnage and capacity, we are expecting output to increase from the 1954 level of 3,200,000 tons to about 10,500,000 tons in 1970. The 1955 productive capacity in basic steel was about 5,000,000 tons per year.

This primary steel projection is a bit higher than the projections submitted to the Gordon Commission by Algoma Steel and by Steel Company of Canada. Their implied production estimates for 1970 are 9,500,000 and 8,800,000 tons.[12] But the discrepancy is largely explained by the different assumptions about the magnitude of imports. These two companies talk of imports of 15 and 17 per cent compared with the 10 per cent of the present study. But, even after this discrepancy is removed, the 10,500,000 ton projection is still a bit high. This is explained primarily by the high level of investment expenditures expected in 1970 in this study. In the two submissions the trend of consumption per capita was merely extended, which seems a less desirable approach than that applied here.

As for motor vehicles, the second major component of iron and steel products which we wish to examine separately, a careful and complete analysis would involve a model similar to that used to project population. New passenger car purchases gives the birth rate, scrappage is the death rate, and there is an age distribution and some net immigration to worry about.[13] But such an approach was too time-consuming for the purposes of this study and so a far simpler approach will be used. New car purchases cannot be expressed as a function of income because of the wild behavior

[12] Computed by interpolation from the estimates for 1957 and for 1980 presented in the submissions. See David Holbrook, Algoma Steel Corporation, *Statement before the RCCEP* (Toronto, 1956, processed), p. 5; and Steel Company of Canada, Ltd., *Brief Presented to the RCCEP* (n.p., 1956, processed), p. 22.

[13] The most famous study of the demand for automobiles expressed sales in the United States as a function of income, an index of automobile prices, the current stock of cars, maximum ownership (a function of income, durability, and the number of families) and "replacement pressure," which was in turn dependent on income, price, and the theoretical scrapping rate. See C. F. Roos and Victor von Szeliski, "Factors Governing Changes in Domestic Automobile Demand," in *The Dynamics of Automobile Demand* (New York, 1939), quoted and summarized in Joel Dean, *Managerial Economics* (New York, 1951), pp. 220–229. A more recent study has developed a simpler model in which new car sales in the United States are taken as a function merely of the stock of cars, the length of life of the average car (which is taken as a datum rather than as a variable as in the Roos and Szeliski article), and the rate at which the stock has been increasing over time. See Hans Brems, "Long-Run Automobile Demand," *Journal of Marketing*, 20:379–384 (April 1956).

of car sales relative to income since the end of the war. A far more reliable relation would seem to be that between income and the car population, since, to the extent that scrapping of old cars can be retarded, we would not expect the stock of cars to rise as violently relative to income at the end of the war as did new car sales. Given a projected car population, dividing by the expected average life will give the production estimate.[14]

Disposable income per capita explains 90 per cent of the variance in automobile registrations per thousand population for the years 1929–1941 and 1949–1954. The projected personal disposable income per capita in 1970 gives a car population of 221 per thousand population compared with 177 in 1954. The 21,000,-000 population estimate thus suggests a car population of 4,650,-000 by 1970 or more than one car for every 4.5 persons, compared with one for every 5.4 persons in 1955. If the average retirement age is ten years, the annual sales of passenger cars will be about 465,000 units compared with an estimated 375,000 in 1955 and 320,000 in 1954.[15]

Imports in 1954 provided about 12 per cent of the consumption, and less than 2 per cent of the production was exported. If by 1970 Canada is self-sufficient with respect to her automobile production except for, say, 5 per cent of her requirements, production will have to increase by about 55 per cent over 1954's production of 287,000.

An alternative projection is available in the submission of the Ford Motor Company of Canada presented to the Gordon Commission.[16] Compared with our projection of a passenger car popu-

[14] Actually it will give only the replacement demand but not the demand for the new cars which represent the net increase in the car population. But the uncertainty about the probable life is so great that we can ignore the latter component of new car demand.

[15] The average retirement age in the United States for selected years has been estimated as follows:

1925	6.5	1941	10.2
1930	7.0	1952	14.3
1935	8.3	1953	13.8

(See Automobile Manufacturers Association, *Automobile Facts and Figures 1955,* quoted in Brems.) If these figures are reliable, they show the increase in average durability since 1925 but the 1952 is undoubtedly higher than the trend value because of the war, as the 1953 figure suggests. Brems thinks that a 10 year average retirement age is probably the "lowest the industry can possibly hope for."

[16] Ford Motor Company of Canada, *The Role of the Automobile in Canada's Next Quarter-Century,* Submission to the RCCEP (Toronto, 1956), p. 10.

lation of 4,650,000 by 1970, Ford expects a population of 5,320,-000 in 1970 (about one car for every four persons) and a production of just over 600,000 cars annually. The population projection not only seems optimistic but the annual production seems particularly optimistic because it implies an average life of less than nine years. Perhaps the estimate reflects every good car salesman's hope that the whole world will some day be a Los Angeles. It is stressed that the postwar baby crop will be reaching driving age and marrying age in the 1960's and consequently a bulge in the growth of automobile production can be expected at that time. In other words, a greater-than-average proportion of the 1970 output of automobiles will go to increase the car population rather than merely to replace discarded cars. Taking the Ford projection into account, our estimate of 465,000 passenger cars annually may prove conservative, indeed.

The nonferrous metal products group as defined here includes aluminum products, brass and copper products, white metal alloys, and miscellaneous nonferrous metal products. The DBS classification entitled nonferrous metal products includes not only these categories but also jewelry and silverware and nonferrous smelting and refining. The former category, which is quite small, was handled under our clothing and household goods rubric. The latter, which is far more important, has been considered in the chapter on minerals production.

Since it is impossible satisfactorily to classify imports and exports of the nonferrous metal products on the same basis as the production data published by DBS, domestic production of these items, rather than domestic disappearance, was correlated with the GNP.[17] Fortunately this correlation is very high (98 per cent explained variance) so the projected production of $822,000,-000 in 1970 (in 1955 prices) based on this relation is on rather solid ground. In 1954 the output was but $330,000,000 (in 1955 prices — $295,000,000 in 1954 prices). So an increase of 150 per cent is expected, considerably more than the increase of 80 per cent expected in the GNP. This conclusion is consistent with a point to be made later in this chapter, namely, that it is in the metal products fields that we would expect to find very substan-

[17] A substantial proportion of the brass and copper products, for example, are probably included in the electrical apparatus trade data.

tial increases in output in a rather small but growing market such as Canada's.

Exports are expected to offset imports, each being at a level of about $39,000,000. The export figure is at what seems to be the current level. The position of the Canadian producers in the export market in this industry is not particularly strong because, as in electrical apparatus and supplies, United States producers can export at lower prices the mass-produced goods, and the United Kingdom and Germany in particular can export at lower prices the goods with high labor input. So no change from the current export figure is anticipated. The imports are expected to remain roughly at their present ratio to domestic disappearance since the prospects for increased imports in absolute terms are quite strong.[18]

Electrical apparatus and supplies

The history of the electrical apparatus and supplies industry is difficult to analyze because although imports have provided between 15 and 25 per cent of the domestic consumption, they are very hard to identify in the foreign trade statistics. There is no import category entitled "electrical apparatus and supplies" and electrical goods appear to be scattered throughout such categories as "machinery (except agricultural)," automobile parts, "tool and hand implements," "copper and manufactures of," and so on. Fortunately, however, in 1955 a careful report on the Canadian electrical manufacturing industry was completed by three able Canadian economists headed by Professor F. A. Knox.[19] The report employs estimates of imports and exports from detailed foreign trade data made available by the Dominion Bureau of Statistics, and consequently it was decided to lean heavily on the Knox report for the purposes of the present study.

However there are a few disadvantages to using the Knox paper. First of all, the Knox definition of the industry is a bit broader than that of DBS; the 1953 output of the industry by Knox definition is about 12 per cent greater than reported by

---

[18] See Canadian Manufacturers' Association, *Representations to the RCCEP* (n.p., 1955), pp. 14–18.
[19] F. A. Knox, C. L. Barber, and D. W. Slater, *The Canadian Electrical Manufacturing Industry: An Economic Analysis* (Toronto, 1955).

DBS. Thus the Knox data and the DBS data are not comparable and one must use one to the exclusion of the other. Furthermore, the Knox report is based only on the postwar years plus 1926 and 1937. In spite of these two drawbacks, it was decided that the painstaking task of constructing our own detailed production, imports, and exports time series was not warranted for this study.

Domestic disappearance of electrical apparatus and supplies is correlated closely with the gross national product. The domestic disappearance corresponding to the 1970 GNP of $48,000,000,000 is $2,300,000,000.[20] This is the equivalent of $108 per capita disappearance as compared with $69 per capita disappearance in 1952 and $86 in 1953 (all in 1955 dollars). Disappearance per capita in 1947 in the United States was $81 in 1955 prices. Our estimate seems reasonable quite aside from the evidence provided by the regression line.

The future of imports and exports of electrical apparatus and supplies is extremely difficult to deal with because there are no clear-cut trends in either case, partially because of changes in tariff policies. The industry's competition from imports has been considerably greater in recent years than at any time since 1929. This increase in the imported ratio is not due to a shift in demand toward those goods which have historically been imported but rather to the increase in the imported ratio on certain important items. Import competition has increased in recent years particularly in refrigeration equipment, generators, motors, switchgear, transformers, and instruments and meters.

As in the case of metal products, the future of the imported percentage will be determined by tariff policies and by the rate at which the Canadian market becomes large enough to support producers of certain specific products. The industry complains that it feels competition mostly from the United States in appliances and other goods which are mass-produced whereas imports from the United Kingdom, which enter under preferential tariffs, are particularly important in the fields of communications

[20] The 1953 observation was eliminated from the regression estimate because the jump in domestic disappearance from 1952 to 1953 seemed to be due primarily to very substantial increases in imports of radios, television sets, and other appliances. It was reasoned that many of these appliances, particularly the television sets, were bought in abnormal amounts in 1953. If this one year were not eliminated, projected domestic disappearance would be closer to $2,400,000,000 rather than $2,300,000,000.

equipment and heavy apparatus.[21] Several reasons are cited for this increased import competition: the devaluation of sterling, the West German policy of holding down wages and prices, tariff concessions negotiated under the General Agreement on Tariffs and Trade, and the premium on the Canadian dollar. Since, with the possible exception of the last-mentioned cause, none of these reasons seem temporary, the future trend of the imported proportion of domestic disappearance will depend primarily on the tariff structure and on the success of the industry in selling in sufficient volume to lower production costs and hence prices. The prospects in these two fields are so uncertain that the most sensible projection seems to be the 24 per cent ratio of 1953.

The proportion of output exported rose in 1951 and 1952 but this increase was due to world shortages of electrical equipment caused by the Korean outbreak and to a substantial export to Brazil on the account of the Brazilian Traction Company. As a "best guess" for the 1970 exported ratio we will use 3.0 per cent on the grounds that although this is lower than any other year in the Knox study except 1950, it is justified on the grounds that exchange rate conditions will continue to make it difficult for Canadian manufacturers to sell abroad. To the extent that production increases in absolute terms, of course, this allows for an increase in exports in value terms.

If imports and exports prove to equal the expected percentages in 1970 (imports equaling 24 per cent of domestic disappearance and exports equaling 3 per cent of production), domestic production must equal $1,800,000,000 in order to provide the domestic requirements of $2,300,000,000.

The margin of error on this $1,800,000,000 production estimate may be large because of the gross uncertainty about imports and in some measure exports. But production will likely be between $1,600,000,000 and $2,100,000,000. The lower figure makes the very bleakest assumptions: exports at zero and imports at 30 per cent of domestic requirements, well above even the 1929 figure. The upper limit to the range, $2,100,000,000, assumes that imports might possibly drop to 15 per cent of requirements and exports might rise to 6 per cent of production.

---

[21] Canadian Electrical Manufacturers Association, *The Canadian Electrical Manufacturing Industry in Transition* (brief presented to the RCCEP, 1955, processed), pp. 42–43.

In order to keep our manufacturing sectors consistent with each other, it is now necessary to translate the above projections based on the Knox report categories into the terms of the DBS manufacturing classification. The above forecast points to a 1970 industry output just 80 per cent greater than the 1953 production. The electrical apparatus and supplies industry as defined by DBS produced just over $1,000,000,000 worth of output in 1953 (in 1955 prices). An 80 per cent increase indicates a 1970 output of $1,800,000,000.

Nonmetallic mineral and allied products

This rather cumbersome title will be employed to cover three industries, namely, nonmetallic mineral products, chemical and allied products, and products of petroleum and coal. It must be stressed that here we are concerned with the products manufactured from minerals rather than with the minerals themselves. In 1954 this group of industries accounted for over 13 per cent of the gross value of all manufactures and about 8 per cent of the employees in manufacturing. The 1970 prospects will be considered for each of the three industries individually.

About three-fourths of the ouput of the nonmetallic minerals products industry consists of cement and cement products, glass products, abrasives, and clay products. The remaining items are such things as asbestos and allied products, lime, salt, brick, and stone.

Projection of the output of this industry to 1970 is relatively simple for several reasons. First of all, the high proportion of building materials in the industry output causes production to move with construction activity. Second, the products are so costly to transport relative to value that the imports and exports are negligible. Hence there is no problem of predicting foreign demand. Finally, the prospects of substitution of other materials for those produced by the industry seem to be quite limited.

The gross value of nonmetallic minerals products output is very well correlated with expenditures on new construction plus repair and maintenance construction, 99 per cent of the variance in the former being explained in 1926–1951 (war years excepted). (This regression had to be computed from the two time series in current rather than constant dollars because no satisfactory price index for this industry's products is available.) The estimating equation indicates a 1970 output of about $904,000,000 for the nonmetallic mineral products industry if total new and repair and maintenance construction is $9,750,000,000 as forecast in Chapter 11. Since the correlation of the time series is so good and since there is little reason to expect any significant substitution away from these products, this result can be accepted. In any case, relying on the estimating equation for the 1970 projection presumes not that substitution will be absent but rather that it will take place at the same rate as it has over the period on which the estimating equation is based.

The movements in imports and exports of these items suggest that for 1970 the export projection should be about $15,000,000 and imports about $135,000,000. Notice how small these amounts are relative to the $9,750,000,000 expected production. An error of several hundred per cent in the international trade estimates would be necessary to change the production estimate by as much as 5 per cent. Given these estimates, domestic disappearance of nonmetallic mineral products will come to about $1,024,000,000.

Because petroleum products and coal products are so dissimilar and because the output of each is affected by different factors, they must be treated separately. The domestic disappearance of coal products moves very closely with the GNP, the relation explaining 95 per cent of the variance.[22]

A 1970 GNP of $48,000,000,000 will be associated with coal products consumption of about $109,000,000 in 1955 prices, about 60 per cent above the 1954 consumption. Imports averaged about 10 per cent of domestic disappearance before the war but in the postwar years the ratio has generally exceeded 10 per cent, reaching a peak of 18 per cent in 1948. After 1950, however, imports began declining steadily until in 1954 they were just above the prewar level. We will project on the basis of the 10 per cent imported ratio since the evidence seems to indicate that this is the "normal" relation.

In the case of exports, both before the war and in 1953–54, exports averaged about 3 per cent of production, so this percentage will be used for the projection. Taking imports at 10 per cent of domestic requirements, exports at 3 per cent of domestic production, and domestic requirements at $190,000,000 and solving

---

[22] Based on 1935–1939 and 1946–1954.

for production gives $176,000,000, the expected 1970 domestic output. In contrast, the 1954 production was $117,000,000.

In the case of petroleum products the domestic disappearance is correlated just as neatly with the GNP as in the case of coal products. Domestic disappearance in 1970 should be about $1,780,000,000. A negligible proportion of domestic production of refinery products has been exported in the past; and there seems no reason to expect this situation to change since it is far more economical to ship crude than refined products. But imports have risen as a proportion of domestic disappearance since before the war from about 9 per cent to 16–17 per cent in the last few years. This high level is not likely to be maintained, however, for it has been caused by a disproportionate growth in the demand for the middle distillates (diesel fuel and light fuel oils primarily). Canadian refiners could not meet the domestic demand for middle distillates without producing more gasoline than they could dispose of. Consequently, imports of this class of product have increased substantially. With the completion of dieselization by the railroads, especially, the demand for the middle distillates should grow at a reduced rate and within a few years after 1960 the demand for gasoline should catch up, making it possible for a greater proportion of the demand for middle distillates to be met from domestic refineries.[23] We will estimate that the proportion of domestic requirements imported will fall to 10 per cent. This leads to a 1970 production estimate of $1,600,000,000 — 2.3 times the 1953 production.[24]

The chemical and allied products industry produces a multitude of dissimilar products. In 1953 the major subindustries, ranked in order of gross value of output, were acids, alkalies, and salts; paints and varnishes; medicinals and pharmaceuticals; soaps, washing compounds, and cleaning preparations; fertilizers;

[23] See Imperial Oil Ltd., *Prospects for Canada's Oil Industry, 1955–1980* (n.p. 1956), p. 12.

[24] The 1954 gross value of output of petroleum products was $92,000,000, according to Canada, DBS, *Preliminary Statement of Manufactures, 1954*, but this figure is not comparable with the 1953 output, according to a footnote. Since the data for a reconciliation of the two are not given, we must here compare the 1970 output with the 1953 figure of $695,000,000; $700,000,000 in 1955 prices.

vegetable oils; and primary plastics. These seven groups accounted for two-thirds of the industry output.

Because of the great variety of products the output of chemical and allied products would be expected to move with the GNP and indeed this is the case. Using data for 1926–1941 and 1946–1954, 98 per cent of the variance in domestic disappearance is explained by the gross national product. The 1970 domestic disappearance estimated on the basis of this relation is $1,930,000,-000, slightly more than double the 1954 consumption.

In the last few years about 18 per cent of Canadian production has been exported, more than half of it going to the United States. Because this proportion has varied so greatly in the past few years, total Canadian exports were correlated with the United States GNP in an attempt to find some sort of stable relation. Only 75 per cent of the variance is thus explained, but the deviations of the observed from the estimated values follow a rather systematic pattern. Dropping the very early 1930's would give projected Canadian chemical and allied product exports of about $240,000,000 if the United States GNP reaches the expected level of $510,000,000,000 in 1970 (in 1955 dollars) rather than the approximate $220,000,000 which the original estimating equation gives. This $240,000,000 export figure is probably too low, however. The export market prospects for primary plastics and fertilizers and for other chemical products are bright if one looks at the non-United States export market as well as the United States market. This is especially true for certain products which are likely to be produced in British Columbia in order to take advantage of cheap power as well as the area's domestic market requirements. Consequently we will put the export estimate up to $300,000,000. This amounts to about 15 per cent of domestic consumption, the proportion which DuPont considers likely for the next few decades.[25]

Imports relative to domestic disappearance have fallen off very slightly from 22.5 per cent before the war to 21 per cent after the war. In normal years this percentage has remained surprisingly stable. We would expect imports by 1970 to supply just 20 per cent of the domestic disappearance if this relation were to continue, but the advent of natural gas and crude petroleum on a

---

[25] H. H. Lank, DuPont Company of Canada, Ltd., *Submission to the RCCEP Covering the Growth of the Canadian Chemical Industry* (n.p., 1956), p. 5.

really large scale in the West seems to hold promise of accelerated development in the chemical field. It would seem justifiable, then, too expect a faster reduction in this imported percentage than the past record would support. If we lower the 1970 imported percentage to 15 rather than 20, then domestic production must be about $1,940,000,000 in order to supply 85 per cent of the domestic output plus $300,000,000 worth of exports. This output is slightly more than double the 1954 production level. It is probably on the conservative side because the chemical industry seems to be entering a new phase, particularly with the greater availability of the petrochemical raw materials.

DuPont Company of Canada expects the domestic demand for chemical products to be about 20 per cent higher than the $1,930,000,000 estimated in this study even though their estimate of the 1970 GNP is fairly close to ours.[26] Since the DuPont estimate seems to have been carefully done, our $1,930,000,000 domestic disappearance estimate should clearly be considered as a minimum figure. It is perhaps more appropriate to say that 1970 consumption will probably be two to two and one-half times as great as 1954 output.

There is probably no substantial error in the production estimate which can be attributed to errors in the export projection. If exports were as much as twice the $300,000,000 projected, domestic production would have to increase by only 15 per cent over the $1,940,000,000 set forth above.

Miscellaneous manufactures

In this group of industries are included not only the "Miscellaneous manufacturing" industry as defined by DBS but the rubber products industry and printing and publishing and allied industries.

The rubber products output seems quite simple to project, for all the relations have been either stable or changing in a consistent manner. Over 92 per cent of the variance of the rubber products is explained by the GNP for the 1937–1939, 1946–1954 period. The domestic disappearance for 1970 is forecast as $750,-000,000, roughly two and one-half times the 1954 level.[27] Imports

---

[26] Lank, p. 4, and Appendix II, p. 3.

[27] The Rubber Association of Canada, projecting total demand for rubber products by first projecting tire demand and then projecting the ratio of all

have been increasing quite steadily from an average level of 6.9 per cent of domestic disappearance in 1937–1939 to an average of 10.2 per cent in 1952–1954. Since the trade data show this increase in imports to be due to a wide variety of items rather than any single type of rubber product, the increase in the proportion of consumption imported seems to be broadly based, so we will expect the imported proportion to continue increasing but at a slower rate than has been the case since before the war. Therefore the 1970 import ratio will be put at 12 per cent.

Exports have been declining steadily from over 20 per cent prior to the war to an average of 4.4 per cent for 1952–1954. Projecting exports to zero by 1970, imports to 12 per cent of domestic requirements, and domestic requirements to $750,000,000 gives domestic production of $660,000,000, about 2.2 times the 1954 rate of output.

As for printing and publishing, production has moved reasonably in line with the gross national product.[28] Employing this relation for the projection yields a 1970 estimated output of just under $950,000,000, a 65 per cent increase over 1954. Exports amount to a tiny fraction of production and are set at $10,000,000 in 1970, a 50 per cent increase over 1954 but still only 1 per cent of production. In the absence of any evidence to the contrary, the relation of imports to domestic disappearance is expected to remain stable.

The DBS classification "miscellaneous industries," the third and final group in our miscellaneous industries category, consists of tag ends. The five largest industries included are scientific and professional equipment; plastics products; electric, neon, and other signs; brooms, brushes, and mops; and sporting goods. Of the industries studied in this project it is the smallest except for leather goods, which was included in the clothing and household goods group.

The margin of error in any forecast of this group is very wide indeed primarily because it is extremely difficult to construct any sort of time series of production and trade data which are sure to be based on a classification scheme consistent over time.

---

other rubber products demand to tire demand, arrived at an implied demand of about $725,000,000 for 1970. See Rubber Association of Canada, *Past, Present and Future Problems of the Rubber Industry in Canada* (Toronto, n.d., processed), p. 51.

[28] Nearly 90 per cent of the variance is explained by GNP.

The nature of the DBS production data make it appear that various and sundry firms' output have been put into this group and then removed in later years and put into separate classifications. The domestic disappearance of this group of industries correlated better with the GNP than with any other likely time series, but even then only 64 per cent of the variance could be explained. Weak as this crutch is, there seems to be no alternative but to use it. The projection of domestic disappearance based on this poor relation is $1,140,000,000 in 1970, contrasted with $637,-000,000 in 1954 (all in terms of 1955 prices). The percentage increase, then, is 79 per cent, almost exactly the same percentage increase as is expected for the GNP. So the magnitude of the 1970 projection seems reasonable enough even though there is a large probable error.

As we might expect of such a conglomeration of industries, imports and exports have behaved rather wildly. Imports as a percentage of domestic disappearance shot up to 89 and 94 per cent in 1946 and 1947 when goods were scarce relative to purchasing power. In 1937–1939 they averaged 68.5 per cent and none of the three years' percentages were more than 1.5 per cent off this average. In 1952–1954 the average was 77 per cent, the range being 74.5 per cent to 78.2 per cent. The increase in 1946 and 1947 points to a very high import elasticity of demand for the commodities included in this category. As a shot in the dark, we we will estimate the 1970 imported percentage at 70 per cent of domestic disappearance, a decline back toward the prewar ratio. The main argument for this reversal of the trend in the ratio is that these miscellaneous industries for the most part are small-scale industries. As the current boom in Canada relaxes a bit, one would expect capital to find its way into this sort of firm increasingly.

Exports, on the other hand, accounted for about 43 per cent of domestic production on the average in 1937–1939 as well as 1952–1954, although the fluctuation was considerable over the peacetime years between 1937 and 1954. Therefore this percentage will be used for the projection.

Applying the assumed export and import ratios and the domestic disappearance of $1,140,000,000 for 1970 gives an expected production of $600,000,000, exports of $258,000,000, and imports of $798,000,000. The production for 1970 will be nearly two and

Table 108. Production of Canadian manufacturing industries, 1954 and estimated 1970, by major industry group, ranked by relative and by absolute increase in output.

Industries in order of relative increase	Production		Increase 1954 to 1970			Rank by increase	
	1954	1970	Actual	Relative [a]		Percentage	Absolute
	(millions of 1955 dollars)						
Metal products	4,115	9,560	5,445	1.32		1	1
Nonmetallic minerals and allied products	2,363	4,620	2,257	.96		2	3
Miscellaneous manufactures	1,137	2,210	1,073	.94		3	6
Food, beverages, and tobacco products	3,750	7,000	3,250	.87		4	2
Clothing and household goods	1,886	3,412	1,526	.81		5	4
Electrical apparatus and supplies	1,010	1,802	792	.78		6	7
Forest products	2,639	4,142	1,503	.57		7	5
Total	16,900	32,746	15,846	.94			

[a] Decimal fraction by which 1970 exceeds 1954.

Source: For 1954, DBS, Manufacturing Industries of Canada, 1954; for 1970 estimated, see text.

Table 109. Production of Canadian manufacturing industries, 1954 and estimated 1970, by minor industry group, ranked by relative and by absolute increase in output.

Industries in order of relative increase	Production (millions of 1955 dollars)		Increase 1954 to 1970		Rank by increase	
	1954	1970	Actual	Relative[a]	Percentage	Absolute
Nonferrous metal products	330	822	492	1.49	1	8
Other miscellaneous manufactures	254	600	346	1.36	2	12
Iron and steel products	3,785	8,738	4,953	1.31	3	1
Furniture	233	525	292	1.25	4	13
Rubber products	304	660	356	1.17	5	11
Nonmetallic mineral products	424	904	480	1.13	6	9
Chemical and allied products	924	1,940	1,016	1.10	7	3
Leather products	204	410	206	1.01	8	15
Food, beverages, and tobacco products	3,750	7,000	3,250	.87	9	2
Electrical apparatus and supplies	1,010	1,802	792	.78	10	5
Petroleum products	899	1,600	701	.78	11	7
Paper products	1,628	2,827	1,199	.74	12	6
Textile products, including clothing	1,396	2,393	997	.71	13	4
Printing and publishing	579	950	371	.64	14	10
Jewelry and silverware	53	84	31	.58	15	18
Other wood-using products	430	658	228	.53	16	18
Coal products	116	176	60	.52	17	16
Lumber	581	657	76	.13	18	17
Total	16,900	32,746	15,846	.94		

[a] Decimal fraction by which 1970 exceeds 1954.

Source: For 1954, DBS, Manufacturing Industries of Canada, 1954; for 1970 estimated, see text.

one-half times the 1954 output, largely because of the expected reduction in the imported share of domestic disappearance.

Summary

One means of recapitulating the projections of this chapter is to array the industries by the expected rate of growth to 1970. The data are so grouped in Tables 108 and 109. The former presents the output estimates in terms of the manufacturing sectors of the interindustry table. The latter shows the same data in more detail, giving the output of the subindustries within the big interindustry table categories. Thus the metal products industry does not appear in Table 109 but rather its two components, iron and steel products and nonferrous metal products, are shown.[29]

The metal products industry and nonmetallic mineral products (chemicals, products of petroleum and coal, cement, glass, asbestos, and so forth) head the list in Table 108 when the industries are ranked in order of the percentage increase in output. Food and beverages are likely to grow at a slower rate, but the volume is so large that in the last column of Table 108 they outrank nonmetallic mineral and allied products in terms of the absolute increases. The miscellaneous industries category shows a large percentage growth but a much smaller absolute growth relative to the other manufacturing sectors.

But we can be more precise than this by looking at Table 109. Nonferrous metal products and iron and steel products, the latter category including transportation equipment, still head the list.[30] But furniture, buried in "forest products" in Table 108, promises to grow so much more rapidly than the other components of forest products that it ranks fourth in the detailed list. Similarly, rubber products, a component of the miscellaneous manufactures sector, are expected to increase much more rapidly than the gross national product.[31]

[29] Since food, beverages, and tobacco products and electrical apparatus and supplies were not broken down into subindustries, they appear in both tables.

[30] The "other miscellaneous manufactures" 1970 estimate is so uncertain that it should be ignored here. It was noted earlier that the unsystematic behavior of the variables involved in forecasting demand, imports, and exports were so unstable that a large margin of error is present in this industry's estimate. The projections for rubber products and printing and publishing, the other two subindustries in the miscellaneous manufactures sector, are much more reliable.

[31] We have not attempted to reconcile our projections with those prepared by

Looking at the absolute increases expected, foods and beverages and chemical and allied products appear among the top five, as well as textile products and electrical apparatus and supplies.

The interindustry table of Chapter 14 has revealed that Table 108 may underestimate the probable growth in foods and beverages and in clothing and household goods. The growth prospects for electrical apparatus and supplies may also be understated by Table 108. Among the minor industries as listed in Table 109, the projected increase in chemical and allied products seems most likely to be understated.

These projections of the individual industries show that in 1970 the manufacturing industries will be producing output valued at 90 per cent more than the 1954 output, in constant dollars. Since the gross national product is expected to increase by about 80 per cent, we are implying that the manufacturing sector will be somewhat greater relative to the other sectors in 1970 than in 1954. In Chapter 2 the factors determining the relative size of the manufacturing sector in Canada were discussed. It was pointed out that not only does the country have the very basic prerequisites to industrialization, namely good supplies of skilled labor and capital plus social and political stability, but also some additional attributes favorable to domestic manufacturing. The Canadian market is still small enough so that growth brings economies of scale to some manufacturing industries. Manufacturers in close touch with the Canadian consumer are in a much better position to produce for the local market and to differentiate the product in a profitable way than is the more distant producer. Some of the industries are sheltered simply by distance. Finally, the immense resource base eases supply conditions for several different types of manufacturers. The conclu-

---

Fullerton and Hampson for the Gordon Commission because the report became available only when this manuscript was going through its final editing. (See D. H. Fullerton and H. A. Hampson, *Canadian Secondary Manufacturing Industry* [Hull, 1957].) A table similar to our Table 109 can be prepared from their Table J (p. 202) except that their data compare 1980 output with 1953 output and they include only secondary manufacturing. These two factors may explain some of the differences in the rankings of the industries when they are arrayed in descending order of expected percentage increase in output. The greatest disparity is found in products of petroleum and coal, which the RCCEP report indicates will grow more than any other industry. Since Fullerton and Hampson were not able to indicate in detail how they arrived at their projection, we can do little but note this difference in passing.

Table 110. Percentage distribution in Canada of value added or national income originating[a], by industry, selected years, 1870–1955.

Year	Primary industries					Secondary industries			Tertiary industries				Total industry	Adjustment[b]	Grand total[c]
	Agriculture	Fishing and trapping	Mining	Forest operations	Total primary	Manufacturing	Construction	Total secondary	Public utilities	Government	Other service industries	Total tertiary			
1870	33.3	1.1	0.9	9.6	44.9	19.0	3.0	22.0	—	—	—	20.9	87.8	12.2	100.0
1880	32.0	1.9	1.0	8.6	43.5	18.9	3.8	22.7	—	—	—	22.4	88.6	11.4	100.0
1890	27.0	1.6	1.4	6.6	36.6	23.5	4.6	28.1	—	—	—	26.7	91.4	8.6	100.0
1900	26.7	1.6	3.3	4.9	36.5	20.8	4.2	25.0	—	—	—	29.4	90.9	9.1	100.0
1910	22.8	0.9	2.6	3.9	30.2	22.7	5.1	27.8	—	—	—	33.6	91.6	8.4	100.0
1920	19.4	0.9	2.5	3.8	26.6	24.2	5.5	29.7	—	—	—	35.3	91.6	8.4	100.0
1929	12.1	0.6	3.9	1.7	18.3	24.5	6.1	30.6	12.8	8.0	35.8	56.6	105.5	−5.5	100.0
1930	11.3	0.4	3.5	1.4	16.6	22.6	5.6	28.2	12.7	9.6	39.6	61.9	106.7	−6.7	100.0
1933	7.6	0.3	4.7	1.3	13.9	22.8	2.8	25.6	14.1	15.1	40.5	69.7	109.2	−9.2	100.0
1939	11.7	0.3	6.8	1.6	20.4	26.6	3.4	30.0	11.6	10.5	33.1	55.2	105.6	−5.6	100.0
1945	11.8	0.6	2.8	1.6	16.8	27.5	3.5	31.0	11.0	18.0	24.9	53.9	101.7	−1.7	100.0
1950	11.7	0.5	3.9	1.8	17.9	30.7	5.6	36.3	10.2	8.1	30.1	48.4	102.6	−2.6	100.0
1951	13.4	0.5	4.0	2.2	20.1	30.1	5.0	35.1	10.2	8.2	28.4	46.8	102.0	−2.0	100.0
1952	11.4	0.4	3.6	2.0	17.4	29.4	5.6	35.0	10.7	9.0	29.4	49.1	101.5	−1.5	100.0
1953	9.9	0.3	3.2	1.7	15.1	29.7	6.4	36.1	10.8	9.5	29.8	50.1	101.3	−1.3	100.0
1954	7.3	0.3	3.4	1.9	12.9	28.8	6.6	35.4	10.9	10.7	31.5	53.1	101.4	−1.4	100.0
1955	7.8	0.3	3.8	1.9	13.8	28.7	7.0	35.7	10.7	10.6	30.7	52.0	101.5	−1.5	100.0

[a] For 1870 to 1920 inclusive, the figures represent value added by each industry. For 1929 to 1953, the data pertain to income originating in industry as given in the National Accounts.

[b] Adjustment item comprises rent, indirect taxes, less subsidies, plus net income for 1870 to 1920 inclusive, and national income of nonresidents for 1929 to 1953.

[c] Covers gross national product for 1870 to 1920 inclusive, and net national income at factor cost for 1929 to 1953.

Source: O. J. Firestone, *Canada's Economic Development, 1867–1953, with Special Reference to Changes in the Country's National Product and National Wealth* (London, 1958), Table 68; DBS, *National Accounts, Income and Expenditure, 1950–1955*, Table 20.

sion of that discussion was that the factors which had operated to increase the share of national income originating in the manufacturing sector were likely to continue as in the past, although perhaps not as powerfully.

The increased importance of the manufacturing sector appears to be consistent with the long-run trends in the national income data. Table 110 shows the growth in the relative importance of manufacturing since 1870. If the ratio of national income originating to gross value of product remains fixed over the 1954–1970 period, our projections for the manufacturing sector suggest that in that year the manufacturing sector would account for 30.4 per cent of the national income, compared with 28.9 per cent in 1954 and a postwar peak of 30.7 per cent in 1950. So a very slight increase in the relative importance of manufacturing is expected.

THE REGIONAL DISTRIBUTION OF MANUFACTURING

We turn now to the geographical distribution of the manufacturing industries in Canada in 1970. As the individual industry projections were prepared, the percentage distribution of the industry's output among the four regions for 1939, 1950, and 1954 was studied in order to see how the industry had been shifting over the years. This historical information plus some basic notions about the determinants of the location of manufacturing provided the framework for the 1970 estimated geographical distribution of output.

Some general propositions about the location of manufacturing in Canada were first developed to provide a firmer basis for the location projections. The distinction between materials- oriented industries and market-oriented industries is so well known that we will not discuss it here in detail.[32] The case of production at the "in-between" point, generally a transfer point where neither markets nor materials are found, is also familiar. Such points provide favorable locations for manufacturers because materials can be collected there cheaply and product can be shipped out at costs which give minimum transfer costs for the collection of fuel and raw materials and the disbursement of the product. Much of the manufacturing at Hamilton, Ontario, illustrates this case.

[32] See E. M. Hoover, *The Location of Economic Activity* (New York, 1948), ch. iii.

Table III. Percentage distribution of gross value of products of Canadian manufactuiing industries, by regions for selected years, 1917–1954.

Region	1917	1920	1929	1939	1949[a]	1954[a]
Atlantic	7.95	7.01	4.18	4.40	4.52	4.15
Quebec	27.16	28.41	28.55	30.10	30.36	30.64
Ontario	51.64	50.29	52.03	50.24	48.91	48.73
Prairies	7.60	8.07	8.54	8.13	8.51	8.06
British Columbia, Yukon, and Northwest Territory	5.65	6.21	6.71	7.14	7.70	8.42

[a] Includes Newfoundland.

Source: DBS, *The Manufacturing Industries of Canada, 1953, Section G, Geographical Distribution;* and *Preliminary Statement of Manufactures, 1954.*

With this three-way classification of industries in mind, we can readily understand the locational patterns of several types of manufacturing. Many industries in the food and beverage group are market-oriented, for example, bread bakeries and carbonated beverage plants, and can be expected to shift with the population. Primary iron and steel, on the other hand, is among the industries tied to its raw materials, and population shifts will not affect the geographic location of production unless new raw materials are found.

The growth of Canadian manufacturing in the various provinces reflects these determinants of location. In Table III the percentage distribution of the value of manufactures among geographical areas is given for selected years since the end of World War I. The decline of the Atlantic provinces is immediately apparent. In 1917 they accounted for almost 8 per cent of Canada's manufacturing output but in 1954 this had fallen to just over 4 per cent. Quebec's share has risen slightly, but all the increase was prior to 1939; for the last fifteen years her share has increased but almost imperceptibly. Ontario has slipped off the least bit while the prairies have about retained their share since 1920. The large increase, of course, has been recorded for British Columbia. Expressed in its simplest terms, the explanation of the shift in manufacturing is clear enough: the Atlantic provinces have faced an increasing locational disadvantage with respect to the markets and materials sources for the goods in which they originally had a marked comparative advantage. The timber, mineral, and power resources of the west coast, on the other hand, have attracted resource-based industries.

The question of central concern here is: how far will the shift in the center of gravity of Canadian manufacturing proceed? Keeping the staple theory in mind, we would expect those areas with the greatest probable potential for further resource development to experience the greatest expansion in manufacturing. But the amount of manufacturing which a staple can generate, directly or indirectly, depends on the nature of the staple, as has been stressed in Chapter 2 and Chapter 6.

Also, in Chapter 6 we saw that part of the basis for the huge postwar expansion of manufacturing in British Columbia was the forest products industry, which provides a large number of jobs in processing relative to the number in primary production. Since the forestry-based industries of that province are in a strong long-run competitive position and since the mineral and power production prospects are so very bright, we can expect manufacturing in British Columbia to continue growing at a somewhat greater rate than in the rest of the country. By contrast, the manufacturing sector in the Atlantic provinces has been growing less rapidly than in the rest of the country. There the growth prospects for the processing of staples are not quite so bright. But the more outstanding features of the Atlantic provinces' economy is that the industries which are declining or expanding but slowly in terms of output, such as forestry, agriculture, and fishing, are labor intensive or at least absorb a high proportion of the work force. In Chapter 5 we noted the 50 per cent decline in the number of persons in agriculture in Nova Scotia between 1911 and 1951 and the 40 per cent fall in the number in that sector in New Brunswick. When this sort of change is going on, that is, when a large (in terms of percentage of the work force) or labor-intensive sector is declining, the manufacturing sector can grow at a rapid rate merely by drawing off the excess workers in the depressed areas. In the Atlantic provinces in 1951 the census showed some evidence of substantial disguised unemployment in the tertiary sector. Employment in the manufacturing sector might expand considerably, then, just by drawing people out of the tertiary sector although the total work force was growing very slowly. This slow growth of the work force is a factor which in itself limits the employment multiplier. The local market would not expand as rapidly in terms of the number of consumers as it would in the absence of the disguised unemployment

Table 112. Percentage of gross value of Canadian products produced by smallest 50 per cent of plants, ranked by value of output, 1951.

Product	Percentage of gross value
Clothing (textile and fur)	9.3
Leather products	5.3
Miscellaneous manufacturing	5.0
Wood products	3.9
Printing, publishing, and allied products	3.7
Food and beverages	2.6
Paper products	2.5
Nonmetallic mineral products	2.4
Chemicals and allied products	2.3
Products of petroleum and coal	2.2
Textile products (except clothing)	2.2
Electrical apparatus and supplies	2.1
Iron and steel products	2.0
Rubber goods	1.5
Nonferrous metal products	0.7
Tobacco and tobacco products	0.5
Transportation equipment	0.3

Source: Canada, DBS, *General Review of Manufacturing Industries of Canada, 1951*, Table 46.

and the new income created by new manufacturing is in part replacing the declining income in other sectors and so is not all net gain. Thus a new factory with a $100,000 annual payroll in the Atlantic provinces will not have quite the expansionary effect as would the same plant in British Columbia.

British Columbia, then, seems likely to increase its share of all manufacturing output further. We can go beyond this, though, and determine the types of firms most likely to move into British Columbia next. In Table 112 the seventeen industry groups as classified by DBS are arranged in ascending order of concentration. The meaning of this must be made clear. For each of the seventeen industries, the proportion of industry output produced by the smallest 50 per cent of the plants was computed.[33] Table 112 indicates that in the clothing industry the smallest 50 per cent of the firms accounted for 9.3 per cent of the gross value of output of the total clothing industry. Production in this industry was far less concentrated than in, say, the transportation equipment industry in which the smallest 50 per cent of the plants

[33] The criterion of size was gross value of output.

Table 113. Manufacturing industries of the Pacific coast states, 1953, ranked in ascending order of growth in value added since 1929, and manufacturing industries of Canada, ranked in ascending order of concentration, 1951.

Pacific coast states		Canada	
Rank — Industry	Ratio of value added in 1953 to value added in 1929	Rank — Industry	
1. Products of petroleum and coal	1.2	1. Clothing (textile and fur)	
2. Furniture and finished lumber products	1.7	2. Wood products	
3. Lumber and timber basic products	2.6	3. Printing, publishing and allied products	
4. Food and kindred products	2.6	4. Food and beverages	
5. Apparel and other finished products from fabrics	2.8	5. Paper products	
6. Stone, clay and glass products	3.3	6. Nonmetallic mineral products	
7. Rubber products	3.4	7. Chemical and allied products	
8. Chemical and allied products	3.6	8. Products of petroleum and coal	
9. Metals and metal products[a]	4.0	9. Textile products (except clothing)	
10. Printing, publishing and allied industries	5.5	10. Electrical apparatus and supplies	
11. Paper and allied products	5.6	11. Iron and steel products	
12. Textile-mill products and other fiber manufactures	6.5	12. Rubber goods	
13. Transportation equipment	10.6	13. Nonferrous metal products	
14. Electrical machinery	11.7	14. Transportation equipment	
15. Machinery except electrical	13.4		

[a] Includes iron and its products plus nonferrous metals and their products in 1929; these industries were re-grouped in 1953 into "primary metals" and "metal products." Hence the single industry, "metals and metal products," is used here.

Source: United States Bureau of the Census, Fifteenth Census of the United States, Manufactures, 1929, Vol. II, Table 12; United States Bureau of the Census, Annual Survey of Manufactures, 1953, Table 4; and DBS, General Review of Manufacturing Industries of Canada, 1951, Table 46.

produced only 0.3 per cent of the output. This crude measure of concentration provides a rough index of the economies of scale or of market orientation or both. That is to say, the fact that the clothing industry is less highly concentrated than the other industries in the list indicates either that the production cost economies enjoyed in large plants must be less than in other industries, or that the advantages of being located close to markets are so great that it pays to establish a small plant accessible to the market rather than a large plant more distant from the market.

The industries toward the top of the list in Table 112 can be expected to move with the population, then, except to the extent that they may be resource-based. So in the west coast industrial complex which is developing we would expect to find the industries toward the bottom of the list to be the late-comers.

Support for this argument is found by examining the nature of the growth of the manufacturing industries on the west coast of the United States. In Table 113 the ratio of value added in 1953 to value added in 1929 (in constant dollars) is shown for each of the fifteen industry groups in the Pacific coast states. The right-hand column is the list of Canadian industries in Table 112.[34] The comparison of these two lists must not be pushed too far because the United States and Canadian classification schemes are not quite identical, but the main drift of the comparison is quite illuminating. If we are justified in our conclusion that the industries toward the top of the list in Table 112 are the most likely to be the late-comers into a developing region, then we would expect the late-comers into the Pacific coast states to show a considerably greater growth between 1929 and 1953 than would be the case for those industries which were there even when the market was relatively small.

The correspondence between the two lists is striking. The "products of petroleum and coal" industry grew the least in the Pacific coast states in spite of the fact that the Canadian list implies that considerable scale economies operate in this industry. The explanation is, of course, that products of petroleum and coal, being resource-based, were already of considerable sig-

---

[34] Miscellaneous manufacturing, leather products, and tobacco products have been omitted because the latter two were too small to be listed separately in the *Census of Manufactures* for the Pacific Coast states and the uncertainty about the content of the former ruled its exclusion.

nificance in California in 1929. Notice that wood products (resource-based) and food products and apparel are all within the
top five industries in both lists. The nonmetallic mineral products
industry, directly comparable with the United States category
"stone, clay and glass products," holds the same rank as its
United States counterpart.

The United States and Canadian industries are least comparable when we get down to metals and metal products and machinery and equipment industries. But it suffices to note that on
the Pacific states' list, metals and metal products, transportation
equipment and machinery (electrical and nonelectrical) are all in
the bottom half of the list. Similarly, at the bottom of the Canadian list we see electrical apparatus and supplies, iron and steel
products, nonferrous metal products, and transportation equipment.

In sum, this little excursion into location theory and its application to the west coast has supported the hypothesis that the
metal and metal products industries can be expected to grow
rapidly in British Columbia as the market grows in size. At first,
these industries will produce primarily for the construction industry and for the various resource-based industries such as pulp
and paper. But eventually more consumer goods producers in
the metal products industry will go in. Meanwhile, particularly
rapid growth can be expected, of course, in those industries which
are based on the newly developed resources, such as natural gas.
In accordance with our hypothesis, the consumer goods industries
which are market-oriented, such as clothing, can be expected to
grow only with the area's total personal income.

With the above work as a frame of reference, the regional
distribution of output and employment for the manufacturing
industries was developed. In projecting the employment requirements, the productivity per person employed in each industry
was computed for the late prewar years and for the postwar years
in order to see what the rate of increase in productivity in the
given industry had been historically. This rate of increase was
projected to 1970 in each case because none of the historic
rates appeared either too high or too low to be maintained over
the period for which we are projecting.

The estimated 1970 regional distribution of output of the
manufacturing industries is shown in Table 114 and the distribu-

Table 114. · Regional distribution of gross value of product in Canadian manufacturing industries, 1954 and estimated 1970 (millions of 1955 dollars).

Industry	Year	Atlantic provinces	Quebec	Ontario	Prairie provinces	B.C., Yukon, N.W.T.	Canada
Food, beverages, and tobacco	1954	244	1,958	1,503	615	330	3,750
	1970	420	2,030	2,730	1,120	700	7,000
Clothing and household goods	1954	19	984	745	90	48	1,886
	1970	28	1,819	1,281	174	110	3,412
Forest products	1954	271	853	781	104	631	2,640
	1970	373	1,298	1,175	265	1,031	4,142
Metal products	1954	129	839	2,835	172	140	4,115
	1970	175	1,970	6,687	319	409	9,560
Electrical apparatus and supplies	1954	0	242	745	12	11	1,010
	1970	0	432	1,316	25	29	1,802
Nonmetallic minerals and allied products	1954	74	765	1,083	305	136	2,363
	1970	100	1,442	2,143	619	316	4,620
Miscellaneous manufactures	1954	27	282	721	66	41	1,137
	1970	47	553	1,431	105	74	2,210
Total	1954	764	5,023	8,413	1,364	1,337	16,900
	1970	1,143	9,544	16,763	2,627	2,669	32,746
Percentage distribution	1954	4.5	29.7	49.8	8.1	7.9	100.0
	1970	3.5	29.1	51.2	8.0	8.2	100.0

Source: See text.

Table 115. Regional distribution of employment in Canadian manufacturing industries, 1954 and estimated 1970.

Industry	Year	Atlantic provinces	Quebec	Ontario	Prairie provinces	B.C., Yukon, N.W.T.	Canada
Food, beverages, and tobacco	1954	12,300	53,300	75,800	31,000	16,600	189,000
	1970	15,900	76,800	103,400	42,400	26,500	265,000
Clothing and household goods	1954	2,600	135,700	101,100	12,200	6,500	258,100
	1970	3,500	226,600	153,900	21,200	13,300	418,500
Forest products	1954	17,000	55,800	51,800	11,200	56,200	192,000
	1970	19,700	64,600	59,100	18,800	76,400	238,600
Metal products	1954	10,400	65,800	223,800	13,800	11,200	325,000
	1970	10,600	113,700	390,900	19,100	24,400	558,700
Electrical apparatus and supplies	1954	—	18,500	56,800	900	800	72,000
	1970	—	13,400	40,900	800	900	56,000
Nonmetallic minerals and allied products	1954	2,700	32,200	53,200	9,700	5,800	103,600
	1970	2,700	39,900	70,400	13,200	9,500	135,700
Miscellaneous manufactures	1954	3,200	30,800	73,300	7,800	4,800	119,900
	1970	4,600	48,000	112,200	9,700	6,500	181,000
Total	1954	48,200	392,100	635,800	86,600	101,900	1,264,600
	1970	57,000	583,000	930,800	125,200	157,500	1,853,500
Percentage distribution	1954	3.8	31.0	50.3	6.9	8.0	100.0
	1970	3.1	31.4	50.2	6.8	8.5	100.0

Source: See text.

tion of employment in Table 115. The distribution of all manufacturing, it can be seen, is expected to shift slightly to the west, with Quebec and the Atlantic provinces losing some of their share while the other provinces increase theirs. But the change is not in significant amounts except for the Atlantic provinces, whose share is expected to fall considerably.

It is unnecessary to go into the detailed explanation of the regional growth of each of the manufacturing industries. However, a word about the petrochemical industry is probably appropriate because it would seem to provide the basis for extensive industrialization of the prairie provinces, given the vast oil and natural gas resources there. The location of the petrochemical industry was studied in considerable detail because of this question. Some petrochemicals are now being produced in Alberta, for example, polyethylene and cellulose acetate and certain ammonia and sulfur compounds. The pulp and paper industry as well as the chemical refining of the base metals provides a local market for some of these products. For some others, such as the synthetic resins, the high value relative to transportation costs may permit production near the source of materials. But the bulk of the petrochemical production will probably continue to develop in the Sarnia-Quebec strip, where most of the raw materials in the oil and gas fields are also available at the end of the pipeline or at the refinery, much closer to markets.[35] Therefore we do not expect a large shift in the industry toward the prairies.

The most important single conclusion one can draw from Tables 114 and 115 is that manufacturing in Canada will continue to grow mostly in those areas where it is already growing. Central Canada will retain its dominant position in manufacturing. Power, fuel, raw materials, the economies of scale, and the economies of agglomeration have dictated this regional concentration of manufacturing in the past. The same forces will be at work in 1970, reinforced by the St. Lawrence Seaway as an improved transportation artery. There will be significant developments in British Columbia and in the prairie provinces, but the core of Canadian industry will still be the St. Lawrence Valley.

[35] For a discussion of this problem, see Walter Isard and Eugene W. Schooler, *Location Factors in the Petrochemical Industry,* U.S. Department of Commerce (Washington, 1955).

19
The Service Industries

Previous chapters have dealt with agriculture, forestry and fisheries, minerals and manufacturing. The construction outlook was discussed in connection with the investment forecast. Now we turn to the remaining portion of Canadian industry, the "tertiary" or services sector including transportation and storage, trade, communications, public utilities, finance, insurance, real estate, personal and business services, and finally government service.[1] The statistical record of these sectors' past behavior is notoriously thin. The problems of measuring the gross output of a service and the cost of enumerating the many small establishments producing the typical service deter most statistical diggers. Our forecasts must be correspondingly uncertain.

TERTIARY PRODUCTION AND ECONOMIC GROWTH

Between 1870 and 1920 the share of service industries in total value added in the Canadian economy rose from 20.9 per cent to 35.3 per cent. The share of the work force in tertiary production climbed from 17.0 per cent to 36.9 per cent. By 1953, 46.2 per cent of all Canadians worked in the tertiary sector.[2]

It is tempting to attribute this increase in the role of tertiary production to the increase in income per capita, for services would seem to have a high income elasticity. As a community becomes wealthier, the demand for goods increases but the demand for services might be expected to rise at a more rapid rate. A high income community is generally thought to spend more than a poor community on medical services; education; recreation;

---

[1] The classification system we have been forced to use consists of five groups: transportation, storage and communications; trade; public utilities; finance, insurance and real estate; and other services, including personal, business, and government services. Government services here exclude all government corporations, which are included in the industrial sectors into which their operations most logically fall. For stylistic convenience we will refer to these industries synonymously as the "service industries" and the "tertiary sector."

[2] O. J. Firestone, *Canada's Economic Development, 1867–1953, With Special Reference to Changes in the Country's National Product and National Wealth* (London, 1958), Tables 66, 68.

personal services such as those provided by hotels, laundries, beauty parlors, and similar establishments; and government services.[3] Evidence for the last twenty-five years in both Canada and the United States raises the possibility, however, that the rise in tertiary production for personal consumption may be slowing down. In 1929, 56.6 per cent of Canada's national income originated in service industries. That figure has not since been exceeded in a prosperous year, and in the last decade it has wavered around 50 per cent. The income elasticity of demand for services calculated in Chapter 10 took a value of less than unity, reflecting this same failure of the service sector to grow in proportion to the rest of the economy.[4] Just about the same thing has been happening in the United States. Kuznet's figures show that between 1869–1878 and 1919–1928 consumer outlays on services rose fifteenfold in current dollars while total consumer outlays rose just over elevenfold. In 1929 the share of services in the expenditures of United States consumers stood at 40.1 per cent. After a rise during the depression it shrank to less than 30 per cent in 1947, recovered only to 36.5 per cent in 1954.[5]

Thus statistical evidence on consumer expenditures for the last quarter-century offers distinctly shaky support for what Colin Clark calls "Petty's law" — the proposition that as income per capita rises in an economy the share of employment in the tertiary sector also rises. The long-term growth of the tertiary sector, however, may be caused by forces other than increases in

[3] For partial support of this, see George J. Stigler, *Trends in Employment in the Service Industries* (Princeton, 1956), pp. 85 and 103; also United States Department of Labor, *Family Income, Expenditures and Savings in Ten Cities* (Washington, 1952); and United States, National Resources Board, *Family Expenditures in the United States* (Washington, 1941).

[4] Stigler has described in lurid detail the dangers of drawing conclusions about the relative growth of the services sector from calculations based on historic consumer expenditures and budget studies. The correspondence between consumer budget categories and the activities of particular service industries is weak at the very best. Income elasticities of demand for services calculated from cross-sectional studies in the United States have usually shown values greater than unity, but these have normally been lower in more recent studies. And furthermore, they have proved very bad predictors. See Stigler, pp. 26–27, 40–41.

[5] See Robert Ferber, "Consumer Expenditures for Services," *Journal of Marketing,* 21:24–30 (July 1956), and Carolyn G. Bernhard, "Growth of the Consumer Service Market," *Survey of Current Business,* 36:15–24 (May 1956).

income. In an economy growing in size but not in income per capita, the portion of the work force engaged in tertiary production might still increase. This is because growth in the size of the market permits firms and workers to specialize in various services which formerly were performed by people identified with other sectors. One community may be too small to support an employment agency, a theater, a beauty parlor, but a larger community may support such enterprises even if income per capita is the same in the two areas. If the market is small, the farmer will sell his produce directly to the consumer. With the growth of the economy, it eventually becomes efficient for full-time middlemen to enter between the farmer and the ultimate consumer.[6]

Thus the expansion of the tertiary sector is due not only to increases in income but to increases in the size of the market quite independent of changes in income. But still other pressures for the growth of the tertiary sector can be identified. George J. Stigler has pointed out that urbanization by itself will increase the demand for services. The family which moves to the city must now purchase from retail establishments many things it formerly got through its own labors. Furthermore it can avail itself of such services as restaurant meals which it could not previously buy. Its preferences may shift toward such services as those of dry-cleaning establishments which serve needs less urgently felt in the agricultural sector.[7] Stigler also argues that various changes in the character of the population will produce the same effect. For example, a higher portion of married women in the labor force will mean a greater demand for the services of beauty parlors and restaurants.[8]

Technological change is another force which may be increasing the role of the tertiary sector in the economy. Many new products and processes increase the capital-to-labor ratio in the household as well as in factory production.[9] As the community's

[6] For an excellent formal discussion of this point, see Harvey Leibenstein, *Economic Backwardness and Economic Growth, Studies in the Theory of Economic Development* (New York, 1957), ch. vii.

[7] Stigler, pp. 83–86 and 162–163.

[8] Stigler, pp. 86–88 and 163.

[9] Of course, increased capitalization of production is not wholly independent of increases in income as a cause of a larger share of tertiary activity, since raising the capital-labor ratio increases productivity per worker and hence per capita.

stock of capital equipment increases, a whole complex of firms arises to service and to sell this equipment. Industrial capital equipment requires various types of maintenance firms and dealers.[10] A similar need for appliance repair establishments and garages is painfully clear to the average citizen.

Thus we can readily conclude that a variety of economic forces can be cited which tend to push an increasing portion of the labor force into the service industries in the modern economy.

EMPLOYMENT AND INCOME ORIGINATING IN THE TERTIARY INDUSTRIES

Ideally the level of output of the tertiary industries should be projected by the same methods as the primary and secondary industries, that is, by studying the determinants of the gross value of output. But information on the tertiary industries is so meager that another approach must be used. The Dominion Bureau of Statistics does not cover the tertiary industries in the same detail as it does manufacturing, mining, and agriculture. Some data are presented in the decennial Census of Canada but the coverage is far from complete for our purposes.

Because the gross value of output data for these industries are inadequate, we must examine instead the figures for the national income originating there. These are published in the national accounts. The gross value of output of, say, retail trade is the revenue from sales. The income originating in retail trade by contrast is the revenue from sales *less* all payments to other firms. It consists mainly of the wages paid and net profit received by retail firms and can be thought of as the payment to the labor and capital (including land) engaged in the enterprise. Since the national income figures profess to cover the entire economy, doubts about the extent of the coverage are not nearly as serious as with the scattered and admittedly incomplete gross value of product data.

In view of the argument that the proportion of national income originating in tertiary production increases in the course of economic development, it would seem feasible to project each of the individual tertiary industries by projecting each individual industry's share of national income originating. But the proportion

[10] Stigler, ch. vii, presents empirical evidence of this trend in the United States.

Fig. 14. Percentage of national income originating in tertiary industries, 1926–1956.

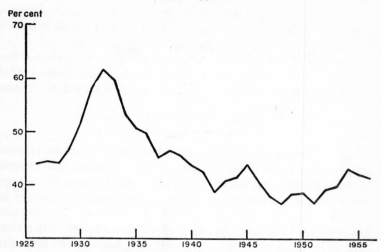

Source: computed from DBS, *National Accounts, Income and Expenditure, 1926–1950, 1950–1956.*

of national income originating in tertiary production has not followed any consistent pattern since national income statistics have been collected, as Figure 14 shows. And the ratio of the income originating in the individual sectors to the national income has fluctuated violently, in some cases, over the period (1926–1955) for which reliable annual data are available. Income originating in business and personal services, for example, fell from a peak of nearly 15 per cent in 1931 to less than 9 per cent in 1940 and a low of 6.5 per cent during World War II. Since the end of the war it has been rising gradually but still is not above 9 per cent. The same peak-trough-recovery cycle is present in the case of finance, insurance, and real estate. Ferber's study has shown the same sort of disorderly results for the United States. He found no clear-cut patterns in the behavior of individual service industries over time, and no systematic relation between the cyclical and secular behavior of consumer expenditures on the various classes of services.[11]

Because of the difficulties of telling the future of the service

[11] Ferber, pp. 30–35.

industries by use of any measure of gross output or income originating, we have resorted to forecasting employment in the tertiary sector. This is a happier approach on several grounds. First, as we shall see below, there does seem to exist a stable relation between services employment and other variables. Second, in reconciling the size of the services sector with our forecasts for the rest of the economy we need an employment figure rather than a figure for either gross output or value added.[12] A figure for income originating in each sector will be estimated, but less significance should be attached to it.

Despite the wobbly behavior of the share of national income originating in services, a highly stable relation exists between employment in the separate components of the services sector and gross national product. This relation permits a projection of employment in each industry, for in none of the five components of the services sector does GNP explain less than 94 per cent of the variance of the employment series. In two cases 97 per cent of the variance is explained.[13] One's first reaction is to be somewhat nervous about using *employment-income* relations as a basis for projecting the *labor force* in the service industries. An industry's employment and labor force will show the same elasticity with respect to national income growth over time only if the percentage unemployed in that industry remains about constant. Thus the fact that unemployment was higher on the average in the first part of the period covered by our data than in the last part implies an upward bias in the employment-income

[12] Figures for value added in the service industries emerge automatically from the 1970 interindustry table, but we have found no way of getting an independent estimate of value added for services or any other business sector.

[13] Such a large explained variance in this case raised the fear that DBS had estimated the employment figures in some of the service industries by some method itself dependent on gross national product. However, this is apparently not the case. Annual estimates of persons employed for noncensus years were reached by employment indices resting on various employment survey data. Of the index used to estimate intercensal service employment, the bureau says: "The Service index was compiled from data on hotels, restaurants and laundry and dry-cleaning plants obtained in connection with the monthly employment survey supplanted by information on employment in educational institutions obtained from the Education Statistics Diversion of the Bureau, data on employment in hospitals, sanatoria, and other health service institutions obtained from the Institutions Section of the Bureau and employment in Dominion Government departments from the Public Finance Division of the Bureau." See Canada, DBS, *Canadian Labour Force Estimates, 1931–1950* (Ottawa, 1951), p. 13.

relation when it is used as a tool for predicting the labor force. Of course, the much lower variability of employment in the tertiary sector than in the rest of the economy makes the bias much less significant than it would be for industries with highly volatile employment levels. Nonetheless, we can use employment-income relations for forecasting purposes only if some independent checks validate the results.

We have been able to make such independent checks by referring to census data on the labor force for both Canada and the United States. From this information we could calculate ratios between the growth rates of the labor force in various tertiary industries and the growth rate of the total labor force. These could be computed for Canada 1941–1951 and for the United States 1920–1950 and 1940–1950. (Employment classifications in earlier Canadian censuses are not comparable.) The results clearly validate the forecasts developed from employment-income relations for all segments of the tertiary sector but the large "services" segment. Here both the United States and Canadian census data imply a growth rate about 84 per cent greater than that of total employment, while the employment-income trend in this segment seems to call for a higher one. Consequently the more conservative figure based on census data has been used.

Table 116.   Number of persons employed and income originating in tertiary industries in Canada, 1955 and estimated 1970.

Industry	Number employed			Income originating		
	(thousands)		Percentage increase	(billions of 1955 dollars)		Percentage Increase[a]
	1955	1970		1955	1970	
Transportation, storage, and communication	405	688	70	1.7	3.4	93
Public utilities	54	93	72	0.5	1.1	136
Trade	773	1,340	73	2.8	5.2	82
Finance, insurance, and real estate	190	340	79	1.8	3.3	79
Services (including government)	963	1,571	64	3.9	6.4	64

[a] Calculated from unrounded income-originating figures.
Source: See text.

It would be unwise to preśent these employment estimates baldly without some discussion of productivity trends in the services sector. To incorporate this we include projections of national income originating in each segment of the services sector. These projections reflect prospective productivity growth rates for all factors (including labor) used in an industry, and they can be estimated from the forecast of work force growth and some of the historic data on income originating per worker. The results are laid out in Table 116. They call for a few words about procedural details and then a discussion of the meaning of the estimates. Figures on income originating per worker can be calculated as far back as 1926, but the severe abnormalities of the subsequent thirty years have forced us to use only three short portions of the period — 1926–1930, 1937–1939 and 1952–1954.[14] Largely from these historical data the probable income originating per worker was estimated for 1970. Multiplying 1970 employment in each industry by the expected income originating per worker gave the estimated 1970 income originating for each of the five subdivisions of the tertiary sector of the economy.

A special problem appears in calculating income originating for the public utilities sector. Although a series for employment in utilities goes back to 1926, the *National Accounts* combine this sector's contribution to national income with that of transportation, storage, and communication prior to 1951. Consequently, 1970 employment could be estimated independently for the two industries, but the growth of income originating in public utilities could be observed only for the period 1951–1955. During 1951–1955 the rate of increase in income originating per person employed in each of the two industries was substantial, 5.5 per cent per annum in public utilities and 2.5 per cent in transportation, storage, and trade. Projecting to 1970 for each industry these rates of increase in income originating per worker, then multiplying by the employment in each industry gave for 1970 an estimate of $4,300,000,000 income originating in transportation, storage, and communication and $1,800,000,000 arising in public utilities for a sum of $6,100,000,000. As a check on this estimate, employment in the two sectors *combined* was correlated with the

[14] An exception was finance, insurance, and real estate, for which employment data are available only since 1939.

GNP and projected at 1.75 per cent, the rate at which income originating per worker rose between 1926 and 1955.[15] This projection yielded an estimated $4,500,000,000 income originating in the two sectors combined, almost 27 per cent less than the estimated $6,100,000,000 arrived at by the first procedure. The cause of the discrepancy, of course, lies in the fact that the first projection presumes income originating per worker to rise at 2.5 per cent in one industry and 5.5 per cent in the other, these being the 1951–1955 rates; whereas the second procedure is based on only a 1.75 per cent increase in value added per worker, which has been the long-run rate of increase.

Which estimate should we take? Let us refer to United States experience for guidance. The long-run rate of productivity growth in American electric and gas utilities (1902–1942) has been 4.4 per cent annually, lower than the 5.5 per cent figure exhibited recently by all segments of the Canadian utilities industry. The productivity experience of American railroads (1899–1939) matches rather closely the long-term growth rate of income originating per worker in the Canadian industries group which combines utilities with transportation, storage, and communication — 1.8 per cent average annual growth of output per worker compared to 1.75 per cent average annual growth of real income originating.[16] Thus, judging by United States experience the long-run productivity growth prospects for the Canadian sectors are certainly well below the experience of recent years. The only portion which has historically shown any such long-run productivity gains is electric and gas utilities. And it is often noted that these two industries have come remarkably close to maximum theoretical efficiency in some of their operations, and so certainly are not likely to show greater productivity growth rates in the future than in the past. Thus on balance the low estimate of productivity growth prospects for these sectors seems most appropriate. Thus we accept the $4,500,000,000 figure for 1970 income originating in public utilities, transportation, storage, and communication taken together. We can sort out the implied productivity growth figures for public utilities and for the other

---

[15] The portion of the variance of the employment series explained by GNP in this instance was 95 per cent.

[16] See Jacob Martin Gould, *Output and Productivity in the Electric and Gas Utilities, 1899–1942* (New York, 1946), p. 137.

industries of the group separately if we assume that the former sector will continue to show productivity gains 2.2 times as great as the latter, as has been the case in recent years. Given the employment increases in the two sectors individually, and given the 1970 combined income originating of $4,500,000,000, the 1970 transportation, storage, and communication income originating will be $3,400,000,000, and that in public utilities will be $1,100,000,000. The implied rates of increase in income originating per person must be 0.88 per cent in the case of transportation, storage and communication, slightly more than 1.9 per cent in public utilities.

The increase in total income originating in trade is only slightly greater than the increase expected in the employment in that sector, denoting a very small increase in income originating per worker. The explanation for this small increase bears on the history of productivity in trade. In 1937–1939, income originating per worker in wholesale and retail trade was at the same level as in 1926–1930. During these two periods the figure fluctuated only between $2760 and $2900 (1955 prices) except for one year when it dropped to $2690. But, by 1952, income originating per worker had jumped to over $3600 and has fluctuated narrowly around this figure since. However, no trend is apparent; the development of supermarkets and probably the pull of better jobs in other industries have operated to reduce employment in this area relative to the volume of business handled. Arguing that this rise in productivity probably will not continue but rather will again remain relatively stable, we will project but a 5 per cent increase in income originating per worker in trade for the entire 1954–1970 period. It is because of this small increase that only an 82 per cent increase in total income originating is anticipated in trade in the face of a 72 per cent increase in employment. The productivity experience of the United States lends historical support to this projection. Harold Barger has estimated the average annual growth rate of output per man-hour (1869–1949) as 1.0 per cent.[17] Obviously even this modest gain would not have been won without the major distributive innovations of recent years, such as supermarkets and chain stores. These no doubt explain the upward shift of productivity in

---

[17] Harold Barger, *Distribution's Place in the American Economy since 1869* (Princeton, 1955), ch. iii.

Canadian distributive trade in recent years. They have not worked themselves out completely, but no doubt their major contribution has been felt. Thus it seems reasonable to expect that the growth of physical productivity in the Canadian trade sector over the next decade will average less than the long-run historic figure for the United States.

In the remaining two sectors — finance, insurance, and real estate and other services — total income originating is shown as increasing only by as much as employment. Neither of these sectors shows any evidence of any upward trend in income originating per worker, nor are the prospects particularly good. Mechanization will probably bring some improvement in productivity in banking and insurance through the installation of electronic tabulating and calculating equipment. Likewise, random improvements will no doubt occur in some of the service trades. Nonetheless, the prospects for measurable aggregate gains in productivity are negligible. The technology of haircutting has remained static for a good many years, and the prospect of a major change is as unlikely as it is terrifying. This situation is typical of many activities included in these sectors.

WAGES, PRODUCTIVITY, AND TERTIARY GROWTH

Large portions of the tertiary sector show productivity growth well below the national average. Trade, finance, and services show little or no productivity increases and account for over one-third of the work force. To bolster the projections given above, we must examine the determinants of productivity in these sectors and the likelihood that they will continue their low-productivity ways. The 1955 income originating per worker in each of the five tertiary industries was as follows: transportation, storage, and communications, $4,100; public utilities, $8,200; trade, $3,600; finance, insurance, and real estate, $9,200; services, including government, $4,000. Income originating per worker in public utilities is so high because this is a highly capitalistic industry and consequently the figure includes a very substantial amount of income to owners of the capital invested relative to the wages paid to workers. Transportation, storage, and communication are less capital intensive and the income originating per worker is lower. Productivity per worker in these two industries has been increasing over time because the nature of the industries makes possible the substitution of capital for labor, which is generally the key to rising productivity, and also because a number of technological improvements have occurred. In the case of trade the fact that income originating per worker is low is itself testimony to low capital intensity and concomitant freedom of entry; nearly all the income originating goes to pay wages and proprietors' salaries. The rather limited possibilities for greater capital intensity in trade explain in part the low productivity increases which this sector has evidenced over time. In services, income originating is low and unchanging for reasons similar to those applicable to trade. In finance, insurance, and real estate, income originating per person employed is high not because of a high capital-to-labor ratio but because the dummy item "imputed rent of owner-occupied dwellings" involves no direct employment. Thus the average figure for value added per worker in this segment of the economy intrinsically has little meaning.

Why has income originating per worker in trade risen so little over the last thirty years? And why does it appear not to have increased at all in services or in finance, insurance and real estate? [18] It is possible, of course, that the data are not showing satisfactorily just what is going on in these sectors. It is extremely difficult to conduct a satisfactory census of service and trade establishments merely because they are so very numerous. It is quite possible that the estimates of income originating in the late 1920's were based on inadequate coverage. As coverage of an industry improves, it is the smaller and less successful firms which are added to the survey. As these marginal firms, with their low income originating per capita, are added to the coverage they keep the average income originating per worker in the whole sector from appearing to increase. A second possible explanation for the poor historic productivity record of the service sector is that on purely chance grounds the technological revolution of our time has failed to touch it substantially during the last thirty years. A third possible explanation of the poor productivity record of the tertiary sector may lie in the fact

---

[18] In all countries for which data are available over some length of time, productivity in tertiary production has been generally observed to rise more slowly than in manufacturing. See Colin Clark, *The Conditions of Economic Progress* (London, 1951), pp. 314 ff.

that high unemployment has plagued the Canadian economy in a large share of the years covered by the statistical record. In periods of slack economic activity, entry of workers into the secondary and part of the primary sectors of the economy becomes closed. Large portions of the tertiary sector (plus agriculture and some other nontertiary activities) become the catch-basin of the temporarily surplus labor force. This could obviously explain a short-run deterioration of productivity and could probably explain a long-run failure of productivity to rise much because of the adverse impact of what afflicted tradesmen call "cut-throat competition."

The significance common to all of these possible explanations of low productivity growth in tertiary activities, of course, is that if they are valid it might be wrong to extrapolate this poor performance into the future. It would be wrong to foresee such a slow growth of productivity; it would also be wrong to foresee such a *rapid* growth of employment, since with greater productivity improvement the same requirements could be served with a smaller labor force.[19] Do any of the three factors listed suffice to explain the productivity experience of the past? Or, alternatively, can we accept the view implied by the forecasting technique used above that low productivity growth is an inherent trait of the tertiary sector?

That the poor productivity record of tertiary production is a statistical mirage is possible, but most unlikely. The story is so much the same from country to country. The evidence for some service sectors in the United States goes back many years, making it quite unlikely that statistical biases could explain such persistently observed results.

This same United States long-run experience leaves little room for arguing that low service productivity growth is a temporary thing. Common-sense observation also goes a long way toward convincing one that static technology and thus static productivity has been common to many service industries.

The third possible explanation of poor performance in the services sector — the impact of easy entry and under-full employment in the economy at large — is more complicated and

---

[19] To conserve space, we leave it to the reader to elaborate this crude formulation in terms of income elasticities and price cross-elasticities of demand, factor supply elasticities, and the like.

requires extensive discussion. The Canadian economy has run at nearly full blast for more than a decade since World War II. Our forecasts imply for the 1960's not quite such continuous full employment, but nonetheless fewer unemployed than most historic periods can boast. The forecasts summarized in Table 116 imply that the tertiary sector will continue to increase its share of the labor force, yet at the same time continue to make slower progress in productivity and thus in wage-paying capacity. Can these things happen at the same time in a full employment economy? This question in turn raises a trio of questions about the dynamics of wage and income structure. Are income differentials per worker between industries stable over time? How are they affected by divergent productivity trends? Does full employment put substantial pressure on the labor supply available to low-paying trades, including many industries contained in the services sector?

Available Canadian statistics give few answers to these questions, and ready-made research none at all. However, interesting if not conclusive answers turn up in some existing studies of wage structure in the United States and Great Britain.[20] First of all, long-term evidence for the United States suggests that inter-industry wage differences are extremely stable over time. One study of annual earnings in eighty-four United States industries produced extremely high rank correlation coefficients over as much as half a century. The correlation coefficient between these industries' rankings by average annual wages in 1899 and 1947 was 0.73. The changes which do occur in the ranking have been very gradual and seem surprisingly immune to disturbance by short-term events. Even major wars and depressions seem to produce temporary distortions rather than permanent changes.[21] Given this great stability in wage structure, it comes as no great

[20] Our concern in this chapter is with forecasting income originating per worker, which is of course something different from average annual wages. For instance, an industry facing a rising long-term interest rate might substitute intermediate goods extensively for capital, lowering income originating per worker while wage payments per worker remained unchanged or even rose. Nonetheless, intuitively it seems unlikely that these sums would move in opposite directions very often. Thus the evidence on wage structure seems largely relevant to a query about the structure of income originating per worker.

[21] Donald E. Cullen, "The Interindustry Wage Structure, 1899–1950," *AER*, 46:353–369 (June 1956), especially pp. 358–359.

surprise that economists seeking the determinants of wage structure changes have raised a rather thin crop. Some distinctly shaky evidence suggests that low productivity growth and slow growth of wages tend to go together, an industry's ability to pay having more to do with its wages bill than the general forces of seller competition in the labor market. Garbarino has argued that "a substantial degree of secular relationship between changes in productivity and earnings existed during the 1919–1940 period as a whole and for most of its parts." The correlation coefficient is 0.77 between lists of thirty industries ranked by the wage and by the productivity changes they showed between 1923 and 1940.[22] World War II seems to have destroyed this regularity in the United States wage structure, and in any case the rank correlation coefficients vary alarmingly when one makes slight changes in the bench-mark years used for comparison.[23] Still, it seems that wage differentials neither vary much over time nor change in ways sharply inconsistent with productivity changes. Another study has examined the impact of wartime full employment conditions on the dispersion of wage rates among industries to see how much of a squeeze a surfeit of jobs available puts on low-wage industries. In both the United Kingdom and the United States the coefficient of variation for average wage rates in twenty-eight industries fell by one-fifth or more between the pre- and post-World War II years. The same study seems to suggest on balance that this narrowing of the dispersion of wage rates did not change the ranking of low-wage trades.[24] One wishes more evidence existed on the impact of sustained prosperity on wage structure and on the ability of low-wage industries to expand rapidly,[25] but one can

[22] Joseph W. Garbarino, "The Productivity-Wage Relationship," *Industrial and Labor Relations Review,* 7:605–612 (July 1954).

[23] Compare Garbarino, p. 610; Frederic Meyers and Roger L. Bowlby, "The Interindustry Wage Structure and Productivity," *Industrial and Labor Relations Review,* 7:93–102 (October 1953) ; and Richard Perlman, "Value Productivity and the Interindustry Wage Structure," *Industrial and Labor Relations Review,* 10:27 (October 1956).

[24] Pamela Haddy and N. Arnold Tolles, "British and American Changes in Interindustry Wage Structure under Full Employment," *RES,* 39:408–414 (November 1957).

[25] Wage structure studies are not very conclusive about the regularity with which a rapidly expanding industry faces rising wage costs. See Cullen, p. 366 and references cited in his n. 21.

feel fairly confident that it takes a major war or a major change in the position of one industry in the economy to crack the stability of the existing wage structure.

The conclusions reached on this lengthy detour seem to give considerable support to our forecasts of future changes in Canada's tertiary sector. If these findings on American and British wage structure will survive transplanting to Canadian soil, they imply that the low-wage tertiary sector of the Canadian economy can continue its long-run pattern of a slow increase in its share of total employment even with continued slow growth of productivity and hence slower growth of income per worker than in other sectors of the economy. They imply that this can go on during a decade of unemployment rates somewhat lower than the historic long-term average. One final bit of evidence, taken this time from our own population projections, helps to bolster this forecast for the service industries. Consider the work force participation rates forecast in Chapter 9. They prophesy a society in which the average family's main breadwinner enters his life's occupation later than at present and retires earlier, and in which the wife or other secondary workers much more frequently hold regular jobs. In short, just the sort of labor force elements used by numerous segments of the service industries will grow relative to the sort demanded more heavily in the secondary and primary sectors of the economy. Of course, this will improve the chances of the tertiary sector showing the behavior forecast for it above.[26]

We are left with the somewhat tense conclusion that our historically based service industry projections are reasonable. But at the same time the chances seem greater that we will have erred in the direction of overestimating employment growth and underestimating productivity growth than in the opposite direction. One certainty is that the size of the tertiary sector is relatively flexible in the short run. It often acts as the residual user of the labor force after the relatively fixed requirements of

---

[26] Observers of United States employment trends, which are further along this same path than is the Canadian pattern, have noted not only that relatively more women will be entering the labor force but also that they are entering industries with more cyclically stable employment. Perhaps this suggests a long-run trend toward a Dogpatch type of society sustained by matriarchal labor with the males at least periodically reverting to a subsistence hunting-and-fishing role.

many portions of the primary and secondary sectors have been met. Thus, if any of these other sectors show growth rates differing sharply from those forecast in previous chapters (assuming our labor force growth rate to be correct), the tertiary sector will be sure to feel the pressure. More specifically, the excess of total jobs available in 1970 over work force available foreseen in the cross-checks of Chapter 14 implies that the growth of the tertiary labor force may be bent from its historic trend. Thus the tertiary employment forecast above should certainly be thought of as a maximum forecast in the context of this study as a whole, although it is a "best guess" forecast on the basis of trends considered in the present chapter. In the following chapter, we shall find that it becomes feasible to estimate a minimum total size for tertiary employment on the assumption that the work force in this sector is strictly a residual.

20

Regional Distribution
of Economic Activity

The regional distribution of production and employment has been on the periphery of the discussion in each of the last five chapters. It remains to assemble the geographic shifts forecast for each branch of economic activity to see what sorts of shifts are implied for regional totals of employment, population, income, and investment. In addition, certain problems in the regional distribution estimates and in the forces shaping regional growth in Canada will be summarized.

REGIONAL DISTRIBUTION OF PRODUCTION

In Table 117 the gross value of output of the major primary and secondary sectors of the economy is shown for 1954 and for 1970. The most notable increase is in mining in the prairies caused by the oil and natural gas production. Gross value of output of this sector in the prairies is expected to be more than five times the 1954 level. Scanning the ratios of 1970 to 1954 production, the growth in the prairies and in British Columbia is unmistakably clear. The much slower rate of growth in the Atlantic provinces is equally apparent.

Looking at the industry totals, the tripling of mining production is easily the most outstanding increase shown. But the gross value of construction activity is expected to double by 1970, and manufacturing output is likely to increase by about 90 per cent. Forestry is not expected to grow significantly in the aggregate, but in the prairies the increase in output is probably going to be about 100 per cent.

Since the figures of Table 117 are in terms of gross value of output, adding them to get a "total output" figure would involve a great deal of double counting. Therefore it would be illegitimate to try to sum the industry output figures by region. But a measure of the growth can be worked up by computing the employment requirements of each of the sectors, by region.

Table 117. Regional distribution of output of primary and secondary industries in Canada, 1954 and estimated 1970 (millions of 1955 dollars).

Region	Agriculture		Forestry		Mining[a]		Manufacturing		Construction		Fishing	
	1955	1970	1954	1970	1954	1970	1954	1970	1954	1970	1954	1970
Atlantic provinces	144	164 (1.14)[b]	48.2	46.0 (.95)	127.4	175.5 (1.38)	827	1,176 (1.42)	339	624 (1.84)	75.2	146.1 (1.94)
Quebec	527	654 (1.24)	96.0	72.2 (.75)	607.1	1,483.1 (2.44)	5,094	9,452 (1.86)	1,195	2,730 (2.28)		
Ontario	869	1,137 (1.31)	79.6	46.0 (.58)	738.9	1,504.7 (2.04)	8,329	16,464 (1.98)	1,751	3,549 (2.03)	16.0	16.9 (1.06)
Prairie provinces	1,088	1,538 (1.46)	32.6	65.7 (2.02)	417.1	2,318.9 (5.56)	1,342	2,605 (1.94)	1,093	1,628 (1.49)		
B.C., Yukon & N.W.T.	124	176 (1.42)	324.2	426.8 (1.32)	272.0	986.1 (3.63)	1,375	2,663 (1.94)	464	1,219 (2.63)	71.4	87.0 (1.22)
Canada	2,752	3,669 (1.33)	580.7[c]	656.6[c] (1.13)	2,162.5	6,468.3 (2.99)	16,967	32,360 (1.91)	4,842	9,750 (2.01)	162.6	250.0 (1.54)

[a] Includes nonferrous smelting and refining and consequently does not agree with Table 94.

[b] Numbers in parentheses are ratios of 1970 figure to 1954.

[c] Does not sum due to rounding.

Source: See text.

Table 118. Regional distribution of employment in Canada, 1954 and 1970 (thousands).

Sector	Atlantic provinces 1954	Atlantic provinces 1970	Quebec 1954	Quebec 1970	Ontario 1954	Ontario 1970	Prairie provinces 1954	Prairie provinces 1970	British Columbia, Yukon, N.W.T. 1954	British Columbia, Yukon, N.W.T. 1970	Canada 1954	Canada 1970
Agriculture	50.2	29.0 (0.58)a	214.5	172.0 (0.80)	250.6	192.0 (0.77)	339.5	261.0 (0.77)	22.8	26.0 (1.14)	879.3	680.0 (0.77)
Forestry	18.1	6.5 (0.36)	44.9	40.6 (0.90)	26.1	36.9 (1.41)	12.5	9.4 (0.75)	34.4	61.1 (1.78)	136.0	154.5 (1.14)
Fishingb	34.7	27.3 (0.79)	8.0	6.5 (0.81)	3.8	2.0 (0.53)	11.1	6.2 (0.56)	15.8	8.0 (0.50)	73.4	50.0 (0.68)
Mining	19.1	17.2 (0.90)	33.8	66.1 (1.96)	44.9	51.9 (1.16)	16.5	40.7 (2.47)	15.2	41.8 (2.75)	129.4	217.7 (1.68)
Construction	45.7	56.1 (1.23)	133.6	245.6 (1.84)	180.9	319.3 (1.77)	108.0	146.5 (1.36)	44.7	109.6 (2.45)	512.9	877.1 (1.71)
Manufacturing	48.2	57.0 (1.18)	392.1	583.0 (1.49)	635.8	930.8 (1.46)	86.6	125.2 (1.45)	101.9	157.5 (1.55)	1,264.6	1,853.5 (1.47)
Subtotal		195.9		1,090.2		1,506.8		595.1		444.8		3,832.8
First approximation												
Tertiary labor force		233.8		867.1		1,109.2		367.8		394.4		2,972.2
Total labor force		429.6		1,957.3		2,616.0		962.9		839.2		6,805.0
Tertiary % of total labor force		54.4		44.3		42.4		38.2		47.0		
Second approximation												
Tertiary labor force		267.1		991.1		1,267.8		420.4		450.8		3,397.2
Total labor force		463.0		2,081.3		2,774.6		1,015.5		895.6		7,230.0
Tertiary % of total labor force		57.7		47.6		45.7		41.4		50.3		47.0

a Numbers in parentheses are ratios of 1970 figure to 1954 (or 1953).
b Current figures are for 1953, not 1954.
Source: See text, p. 635.

The work force requirements by region and by industrial sector have been summarized in Table 118. The procedure underlying this calculation requires some explanation. The employment in 1970 in each of the primary and secondary sectors was taken from the previous chapters dealing with the sector in question. From work force data published by the Dominion Bureau of Statistics it was possible to compute for each region the ratio of the work force engaged in tertiary activities to the work force engaged in primary and secondary production. Applying this ratio to the primary and secondary total already forecast yielded a first approximation of the total work force for each region. Summing the employment by region gave a total work force figure which fell short of the work force projection of Chapter 9 by about 425,000 persons. It was assumed that the ratio of tertiary employment to all other employment was most likely to be in error as a forecast and so the 425,000 underestimate was distributed proportionally among the various regions.

This method provides us with an estimate of employment in the tertiary sector in 1970 of 3,397,200, the alternate estimate to the figure of 4,032,000 put forth in Chapter 19. The method used in that chapter was to assume the employment in each tertiary category related to changes in gross national product in the same way in the future as in the past. Here, by contrast, we have assumed that *in each region* the ratio of tertiary to other employment will remain about the same over the next decade as in recent years. The word "about" is used advisedly, because when we redistributed the 425,000 surplus left after the "first approximation" we assumed that the tertiary employment fraction would *grow* at the same rate in each region.

From the 1970 work force distribution it was possible to proceed to the population distribution by making an assumption about each region's ratio of total population to the work force. For all of Canada this ratio is expected to increase from 2.79 in 1954 to 2.92 in 1970.[1] It was assumed that in 1970 the relation between each region's 1954 population-work force ratio and that for the country would hold in 1970. From this information, then, the population distribution of 1970 was computed.

---

[1] See Chapters 8 and 9.

Table 119. Regional distribution of population and manufacturing in Canada, 1954 and 1970.

Year	Unit	Atlantic provinces	Quebec	Ontario	Prairie provinces	British Columbia[a]	Canada[b]
		Population					
1954	thousands	1,723	4,388	5,046	2,745	1,293	15,195
	percent	11.33	28.88	33.21	18.07	8.51	100.00
1970[c]	thousands	2,182	6,085	7,135	3,651	1,931	20,984
	percent	10.4	29.0	34.0	17.4	9.2	100.0
1970[d]	thousands	1,618	6,085	7,407	3,129	2,756	20,984
	percent	7.7	29.0	35.3	14.9	13.1	100.0
		Manufacturing					
1954	percent	4.87	30.02	49.09	7.91	8.10	100.0
1970	percent	3.63	29.21	50.88	8.05	8.23	100.0

[a] Includes Yukon and Northwest Territories.
[b] May not sum because of rounding errors.
[c] First approximation.
[d] Revised estimate.
Source: See text, pp. 635–638.

THE POPULATION DISTRIBUTION

The results are shown in Table 119. The second line, showing the "first approximation" of the 1970 population distribution, requires some explanation. To prepare some of the regional projections of individual manufacturing industries in Chapter 18 it was necessary to have in hand a proximate 1970 regional population estimate. This estimate of population was especially useful in considering the probable distribution of the market-oriented industries. This "first approximation" of the 1970 distribution was drawn up by assuming that the westward shift of population would continue but at a slightly slower rate than in recent years. The circularity of this methodology is clear enough but should not be exaggerated since none of the primary industries and only some of the secondary industries are market-oriented. Because of the obvious circularity, we tried to be conservative in estimating the westward drift of population when drawing up the first approximation.

The differences between the first approximation and the revised estimate in Table 119 are illuminating indeed. The errors in the first approximation are caused by estimating incorrectly not the direction of the population movements but the magnitude of the shifts. The Atlantic provinces will apparently lose considerably more than the first approximation indicates, and British Columbia especially will grow considerably more.

Because the first approximation was used in deciding how fast certain industries would shift westward, the underestimate of the population shift means that the movement of industry westward may also be underestimated to some degree. Therefore the large increase in the population of British Columbia shown in Table 119 is possibly understated. It must be kept in mind, however, that the revised estimate assumes that Canadians in the long run are quite willing to move in response to economic incentives. During World War II, Canadians showed a willingness to change their dwelling places ample to warrant such an assumption. But the stimulus for such action in the next decade will doubtless be less acute. In general, such large movements of population (an absolute decrease for the Atlantic region, small increase for the prairies, more than doubling for British Columbia) will take place only because of great opportunity in the growing areas and some actual distress in the declining ones. The preceding chapters leave no doubt about the former condition. And, on the dark side, it is not unlikely that "actual distress" will appear in some quarters. The pressure for consolidation of undersized farms in the Maritimes and the slender chances of rapid productivity increases in the east coast fisheries give ample forewarning of this. The prairie wheat economy is likely to see relatively hard times, and the population of Saskatchewan might even decline. The picture is less clear for the Atlantic provinces if only because aggressive efforts in the common cause might possibly allow them to avert a population decline. The only major activity in that region having good prospects is forestry, and that alone will not offset relative declines in the other sectors. In summary, these conditions support the second approximation to the 1970 population distribution. But against the technical character of the forecast which causes it to seem to understate the change must be placed the factor of economic inertia, which may cause the change to be overstated.

Table 119 gives the estimated percentage distribution of employment in manufacturing as well as the distribution of population for 1954 and 1970. The similarity in the distribution of manufacturing employment in the two years stands out in contrast with the change in the distribution of population. The realignment of manufacturing employment is insignificant except that the Atlantic provinces will lose a good bit of their share, this loss being picked up by the prairies and British Columbia. British Columbia's population growth will be so rapid because what we have called primary and tertiary industries will be the main driving forces. While her secondary (manufacturing and construction) sector will grow rapidly in the next decade, it is far from being the sole stimulus to rapid expansion. Ontario will remain the center of gravity of Canadian manufacturing, her long-standing advantages in this regard reinforced slightly by the St. Lawrence Seaway. Indeed, one of the most important long-run effects of the Seaway will be the perpetuation of this imbalance between the location of Canadian consumers and Canadian producers of manufactured goods.

Table 120. Relative provincial levels and growth rates of Canadian income per capita.

	Canada	Atlantic[a] provinces	Quebec	Ontario	Prairie provinces	British Columbia[b]
Average per capita personal income						
1926–1955 (dollars)	649.5	442.2	557.1	785.5	607.9	764.3
Ratio of each area to national total (percent)						
1926–1955	100.0	68.1	86.8	120.9	93.6	117.7
1951–1955	100.0	64.9	85.5	119.7	99.9	117.2
Average annual growth rate (percent)						
1926–1955[c]	5.10	5.00	4.88	5.01	5.79	4.84
1946–1955[d]	5.28	3.30	5.85	5.57	4.75	6.13
Ratio of area to national growth						
1946–1955 (percent)	100.0	62.5	110.8	105.5	90.0	116.1

[a] Newfoundland first included in 1949.
[b] Includes Yukon and Northwest Territories.
[c] Growth rate computed by regression.
[d] Growth rate computed by taking log of difference between first and last item of series.

Source: See text, p. 340.

REGIONAL DISTRIBUTION OF INCOME AND INVESTMENT

If Canadian personal income per capita did not differ significantly from province to province, the distribution of income received in 1970 would be the same as that of population (shown in Table 119). But, as is well known, personal income does vary sharply from one region of Canada to another. And these regional differentials, both in Canada and the United States, have been quite stable over time.

Table 120 provides some information on these matters. Line (1) shows average personal income per capita (in current dollars). Averaged over a period of changing prices, these figures have less significance than those in line (2), which shows the percentage each region's average income per capita was of the national average for two periods — 1926–1955 and 1951–1955. The striking thing about these two sets of percentages is how closely they resemble each other. In the past half-decade the Atlantic provinces have slipped slightly (though this was due largely to the inclusion of Newfoundland in 1949), and the prairies have done better than usual because of several excellent harvests. But otherwise these differences have been very stable, with Ontario and British Columbia well above the national average, the prairies, Quebec, and the Atlantic provinces below it in that order. Line (3) of Table 120 compares not the regional levels of per capita personal income but the regional *rates of growth* 1926–1955 and 1946–1955. If the ratios among regional income levels were constant over time, then necessarily average incomes in all regions would be growing at the same rate. This is nearly the case, for the 1926–1955 growth rates cluster closely around an annual compound rate of 5 per cent. (The figure 5.79 per cent for the prairie provinces is biased upward because of the abnormal depression of the early 1930's, and the abnormal prosperity of the early 1950's.) When we look at regional growth rates in the postwar years 1946–1955, it appears that the wealthier areas (in per capita terms) are increasing their margin of superiority. (Line [4] shows the rate of growth for each area as a percentage of the national growth rate 1946–1955.) Personal incomes have been growing very rapidly in Ontario and British Columbia, less rapidly in the prairies and the Atlantic provinces.

Table 121. Regional distribution of $36,800,000,000 personal income in Canada, forecast for 1970.

	Atlantic provinces	Quebec	Ontario	Prairie provinces	British Columbia [a]	Canada
(1) Forecast population distribution (percent)	7.71	28.95	35.30	14.91	13.13	100.00
(2) Forecast regional personal income per capita relative to national (percent)	65	88	117	97	119	100
(3) Forecast distribution of total personal income (percent)	4.9	25.1	40.4	14.3	15.3	100.0
(4) Distribution of personal income (billions of 1955 dollars)	1.80	9.24	14.87	5.26	5.63	36.8

[a] Includes Yukon and Northwest Territories.
Source: See text, p. 642.

An exception is Quebec, which has in general shown rapid economic advance since the end of World War II.

This information on levels and trends of per capita personal income can be used to develop a regional forecast of total personal income, with the aid of Table 119's evidence on the 1970 distribution of population. This historic stability of relative levels of income per capita militates against forecasting any sharp changes over the next decade. There is no particular reason for the Atlantic provinces to improve their position, although natural resource development in Newfoundland and New Brunswick will probably prevent a further decline. Quebec's rapid growth in recent years will probably improve her position slightly relative to the national average, while Ontario may slip a bit because of already having achieved much greater economic maturity than the rest of the country. In the prairies the decline in farm income and population in future years will be partly offset by resource-based development. British Columbia's favorable position will improve further.

These developments underlie the forecast appearing in line (2) of Table 121, which takes the form of predicted ratios of regional personal income per capita to the national average for 1970. To predict total personal income, these ratios were multiplied by the regional population shares for 1970 appearing in line (1). The results, reduced to a percentage basis, appear in line (3), and the corresponding regional distribution of a national personal income total of $36,800,000,000 is given in line (4).

DBS data permit constructing an estimate of regional distribution in 1970 of gross public and private investment. Table 122 contains the results of a projection of the distribution of gross investment and total new and repair construction (repair construction is not included in investment). The basic estimate for 1970 distribution of gross public and private investment was produced in the same way as the personal income estimate of Table 121. Figures for investment per capita by region disclose a fairly stable pattern over the past decade for the ratios of investment per capita in each region to the national per capita figure. Adjustments were made for probable changes in this pattern in the next decade (investment per capita will be lower in the prairies, slightly higher in Quebec and British Columbia relative to the national average). These forecast ratios were com-

Table 122. Regional distribution of investment in Canada, 1970.

Unit	Atlantic provinces	Quebec	Ontario	Prairie provinces	British Columbia[a]	Canada
Gross public and private investment						
millions of dollars	501	3,226	4,517	1,625	2,079	11,948
percent	4.2	27.0	37.8	13.6	17.4	100.0
Total new and repair construction						
millions of dollars	526	2,730	3,500	1,531	1,463	9,750
percent	5.4	28.0	35.9	15.7	15.0	100.0

[a] Includse Yukon and Northwest Territories.
Source: See text, pp. 642–643.

bined with the estimated population distribution to find the 1970 distribution of *total* public and private investment. The forecast distribution of new and repair construction was produced by assuming that this would bear the same relation to the distribution of gross investment as it did in the postwar years.

TRENDS AND FACTORS IN LOCATION OF ECONOMY ACTIVITY

The generalization that manufacturing will move westward less rapidly than population seems certain in light of the over-all findings of this study. The number of reasons supporting it is impressively large. First, as indicated earlier in this chapter, the boom in British Columbia will be mainly in primary and tertiary activity, so that the growth of manufacturing in the West, though rapid, will not keep pace with other forms of economic activity. Many forms of production involve such large economies of scale that the Pacific coast market will not support them for many years. The existence of a ready-made industrial complex like Ontario-Quebec always exerts a strong pull on new firms and industries, if only because it offers a pre-existing skilled labor supply and auxiliary services close at hand. But in addition new advantages are accruing to that area steadily. Oil and gas pipelines and the long-range planning of Ontario Hydro will continue to make that quarter Canada's best industrial location from the point of view of energy sources. Expanding output of a host of industrial raw materials in the northern part of these two provinces will encourage processing industries. Vast American markets are next door for those firms which can surmount tariff barriers. And finally, the Seaway can be used to cut costs in transporting some products. The rail transport pattern of manufactures moving west and primary products and semimanufactures moving east will, if anything, become more pronounced.

It must be conceded that important variables determining the pace of central Canada's economic development are within the control of individuals and small producer groups, such as the prairie well-head price of crude oil and natural gas, and the Knob Lake price of iron ore. Pricing decisions by the persons controlling these resources must be watched carefully to maintain an up-to-date picture of the prospects for development in Ontario and Quebec.

But the prospects for the development of the other regions are likely to be influenced even more by the decisions of a few individuals or by the discovery of one or two significant ore bodies. In a small regional economy the errors in forecasts are likely to be considerably greater than for the larger economic unit. This means that the estimate of total population, say, in a region is probably more accurate than the estimate of employment or output in any sector within that region.

Canada's population will become more and more urbanized in the next decade. This pertains to all large cities in Canada except some in the Maritime provinces, and to many smaller metropolitan centers in the more rapidly growing areas. Any "suburbanization" of nonresource-based economic activity will be merely movement out of congested quarters and not a flight into remote hamlets and villages. It has not been possible in this study to investigate the development patterns of the major Canadian metropolitan centers individually, but ample data exist for such an exercise.

Certain "problem areas" will exist for Canada in the coming years. One of these is the whole northern section of the pre-Cambrian shield. A great deal of imagination as well as investment will be required to exploit even some of the mineral reserves already discovered, to say nothing of those riches yet unknown. Technological advances such as the beneficiation of low-grade ores and possibly the pipeline transmission of ores in suspension must be continually implemented in order to keep the mineral frontier advancing.

The Atlantic provinces and at least part of the prairie economy present another kind of problem. They may develop the appearance of "depressed areas" relative to the rest of the economy. The prairie region as a whole is likely to suffer spells of agricultural depression periodically because the prospects are not bright for world grain prices or for the volumes of grain which other countries will allow to be imported. In all of the prairie provinces manufacturing and natural resource development have made such strides in the last fifteen years that the area is gradually escaping the perils of the "one-crop economy." But agricultural depression would definitely have secondary effects on other economic activities in the prairies. Manitoba and Saskatchewan will probably prove more vulnerable in this respect than Alberta, despite the fact that Manitoba will benefit some from the Seaway.

The Atlantic provinces are in many ways in a worse position than the prairies. Population has grown in all four of them in the past decade, but continued growth for all four over the next decade is not foreseen. (The "second approximation" forecast of 1,618,000 is below the 1,761,000 estimated for 1955; if the Atlantic provinces should have all of their present population in 1970, it would represent 8.4 per cent of the national total rather than the 7.7 per cent given in Table 119.) From the point of view of economic development, the cards are stacked against the region. The historic aspects of this were reviewed in Chapter 5. Except for forestry, the natural resource base is greatly inferior to that of Canada's other regions, and the Atlantic provinces' locational disadvantage with respect to central Canadian markets simply cannot be overcome. Not even expanded defense production of World War II helped the area much; the main activity along this line was construction, which leaves little or no residue of productive capacity suited for a civilian economy. The argument is frequently seen that plentiful labor will draw industry toward the Atlantic provinces in future years, by analogy to the experience of the United States South in the postwar years. The South, however, can offer cheap and accessible power, plentiful raw materials for the types of production carried on there, and no serious locational disadvantages with respect to markets; a case might be made for Quebec as an industrial site by this analogy, but the Atlantic provinces possess none of these qualifications. Within the area, Nova Scotia and Prince Edward Island will probably suffer much more than New Brunswick and Newfoundland, and Newfoundland will probably show net population growth for some time.

Is it not likely that unforeseeable discoveries of mineral resources will prove these regional population projections quite wrong? Probably not, because of the capital-intensive nature of most mineral production. It is the growth of labor-intensive primary production which pulls people about. Forestry, fishing, and agriculture have been the primary industries which have shaped Canada's population distribution. Mining, on the other hand, involves relatively few workers per dollar of output and, as the mining frontier moves northward, the employment multiplier of the typical new mining town will become smaller and smaller. The population distribution, then, will probably not be altered significantly by the colorful developments which may distinguish Canada's future as they have its past.

Bibliography

Books and Pamphlets

Adler, John H., Eugene R. Schlesinger, and Evelyn van Westerborg. *The Pattern of United States Import Trade Since 1923: Some New Index Series and Their Application.* New York: Federal Reserve Bank of New York, 1952.

Aluminum Company of Canada, Ltd. *Submission to the RCCEP.* Montreal, 1956. (Processed.)

American Petroleum Institute. *Petroleum Facts and Figures.* New York, 1953.

Annett, Douglas R. *British Preference in Canadian Commercial Policy.* (Canadian Institute of International Affairs, Studies in International Affairs No. 8.) Toronto: Ryerson Press, 1948.

Aubrey, Henry G. *United States Imports and World Trade.* Oxford: At the Clarendon Press, 1957.

Bancroft, Hubert Howe. *History of British Columbia, 1792–1887.* San Francisco: The History Co., 1887.

Barger, Harold. *Distribution's Place in the American Economy Since 1869.* (National Bureau of Economic Research, No. 58, General Series.) Princeton: Princeton University Press for National Bureau of Economic Research, 1955.

Barkin, Solomon. *Statement to the RCCEP.* N. p.: Textile Workers' Union of America, n.d. (Processed.)

Bates, Stuart. *Financial History of Canadian Governments: A Study Prepared for the RCDPR.* Ottawa: King's Printer, 1939.

Black, John D., and James T. Bonnen. *A Balanced United States Agriculture in 1965.* (National Planning Association, Special Report No. 42.) Washington: National Planning Association, 1956. (Processed.)

Bladen, Vincent W. *Introduction to Political Economy.* Toronto: University of Toronto Press, 1946.

Borenstein, Israel. *Capital and Output Trends in Mining Industries, 1870–1948.* (National Bureau of Economic Research, Studies in Capital Formation and Financing, Occasional Paper 45.) New York: National Bureau of Economic Research, 1954.

British American Oil Company, Limited. *A Submission to the RCCEP.* Toronto, 1956. (Processed.)

Britnell, G. E. *The Wheat Economy.* Toronto: University of Toronto Press, 1939.

Brown, George W. (ed.). *Canada.* (The United Nations Series, Robert J. Kerner, General Editor.) Berkeley and Los Angeles: University of California Press, 1950.

Buck, A. E. *Financing Canadian Government.* Chicago: Public Administration Service, 1949.

Buckley, Kenneth. *Capital Formation in Canada, 1896–1930.* (Canadian Studies in Economies, No. 2.) Toronto: University of Toronto Press, 1955.

Cairncross, A. K. *Home and Foreign Investment, 1870–1913, Studies in Capital Accumulation.* Cambridge, England: Cambridge University Press, 1953.

Canadian Economic Research Associates. *The Future Population of Canada 1955–1975.* Toronto, 1955. (Processed.)

Canadian Electrical Manufacturers Association. *The Canadian Electrical Manufacturing Industry in Transition.* (Brief submitted to the RCCEP.) N. p., 1955. (Processed.)

Canadian Lumbermen's Association. *Brief Presented to the RCCEP.* N. p., 1956. (Processed.)

Canadian Manufacturers' Association. *Representations to the RCCEP.* N. p., 1955.

Canadian Petroleum Association. *A Submission to the RCCEP with Respect to the Potential Development of the Oil and Gas Industry in Canada.* N. p., 1955. (Processed.)

Canadian Pulp and Paper Association. *Submission to the RCCEP.* Montreal, 1956.

Canadian Pulp and Paper Association, Western Division. *A Brief to the Royal Commission on Forestry.* Vancouver: Canadian Pulp and Paper Association, 1955.

Canadian Tax Foundation. *The National Finances, An Analysis of the Programme of Revenues and Expenditures of the Government of Canada, 1957–58.* Toronto: Canadian Tax Foundation, 1957.

———. *Taxes and Traffic, A Study of Highway Financing.* (Canadian Tax Papers, No. 8.) Toronto: Canadian Tax Foundation, 1955.

Cartwright, Steven. *Population: Canada's Problem.* (Canadian Institute of International Affairs.) Toronto: Ryerson Press, 1954.

Chapin, Miriam. *Atlantic Canada.* New York: Oxford University Press, 1956.

Charles, Enid. *The Changing Size of the Family.* (Census of Canada, 1941, Census Monograph No. 1.) Ottawa: King's Printer, 1948.

Clark, Colin. *The Conditions of Economic Progress.* 2nd ed. London: Macmillan Co., 1951.

———. *The Economics of 1960.* London: Macmillan Co., 1942.

Coats, R. H., and M. C. Maclean. *The American-Born in Canada, A Statistical Interpretation.* ("The Relations of Canada and the United States," a series of studies prepared under the direction of the Carnegie Endowment for International Peace, Division of Economics and History, James T. Shotwell, Director.) Toronto: Ryerson Press for the Carnegie Endowment for International Peace, Division of Economics and History, 1943.

Colm, Gerhard (ed.). *The Employment Act Past and Future, A Tenth Anniversary Symposium.* Washington: National Planning Association, 1956.

Conference on Research in Income and Wealth. *Studies in Income and*

Wealth, Volume Eleven. New York: National Bureau of Economic Research, 1949.

———. *Long-Range Economic Projection, Studies in Income and Wealth, Volume Sixteen.* Princeton: Princeton University Press for National Bureau of Economic Research, 1954.

———. *Short-Term Economic Forecasting, Studies in Income and Wealth, Volume Seventeen.* Princeton: Princeton University Press for National Bureau of Economic Research, 1955.

———. *Input-Output Analysis: An Appraisal, Studies in Income and Wealth, Volume Eighteen.* Princeton: Princeton University Press for National Bureau of Economic Research, 1955.

———. *Problems of Capital Formation, Concepts, Measures and Controlling Forces, Studies in Income and Wealth, Volume Nineteen.* Princeton: Princeton University Press for National Bureau of Economic Research, 1957.

Corbett, David C. *Canada's Immigration Policy.* Toronto: University of Toronto Press, 1957.

Corry, J. A. *Difficulties of Divided Jurisdiction.* (RCDPR *Report,* Appendix 7.) Ottawa: King's Printer, 1939.

———. *The Growth of Government Activities Since Confederation, A Study Prepared for the RCDPR.* Ottawa: King's Printer, 1939.

Creamer, Daniel, assisted by Martin Bernstein. *Capital and Output Trends in Manufacturing Industries, 1880–1948.* (National Bureau of Economic Research, Studies in Capital Formation and Financing, Occasional Paper 41.) New York: National Bureau of Economic Research, 1954.

Creighton, D. G. *British North America at Confederation.* (RCDPR *Report,* Appendix 2.) Ottawa: King's Printer, 1939.

———. *The Commercial Empire of the St. Lawrence, 1760–1850.* ("The Relations of Canada and the United States," a series of studies prepared under the direction of the Carnegie Endowment for International Peace, Division of Economics and History, James T. Shotwell, Director.) Toronto: Ryerson Press for Carnegie Endowment for International Peace, Division of Economics and History, 1937.

Currie, A. W. *Canadian Economic Development.* Toronto: Thomas Nelson and Sons, 1942.

———. *Economics of Canadian Transportation.* Toronto: University of Toronto Press, 1954.

Dales, John H. *Hydroelectricity and Industrial Development, Quebec, 1898–1940.* Cambridge: Harvard University Press, 1957.

Davis, John. *Canada's Energy Prospects.* Hull, Que.: Queen's Printer, 1957.

Dawson, R. McGregor. *The Government of Canada.* (Canadian Government Series, No. 2.) Toronto: University of Toronto Press, 1952.

Dewhurst, J. Frederic, and Associates. *America's Needs and Resources, A New Survey.* New York: Twentieth Century Fund, 1955.

Dominion Steel and Coal Corporation. *Preliminary Submission to the RCCEP on Behalf of the Dominion Steel and Coal Corporation in*

Respect of its Operations in Nova Scotia. Halifax, 1955. (Processed.)

Dresch, Francis W. *Productivity in Manufacturing in the Post War Period in Canada, Western Europe and the United States.* Palo Alto, Calif.: Stanford Research Institute, 1953.

Duesenberry, James S. *Income, Saving, and the Theory of Consumer Behavior.* (Harvard Economic Studies, Volume 87.) Cambridge: Harvard University Press, 1949.

Drummond, W. M., and W. Mackenzie. *Progress and Prospects of Canadian Agriculture.* (Study Prepared for the RCCEP.) Ottawa: Queen's Printer, 1957.

Durand, John D. *The Labor Force in the United States, 1890–1960.* New York: Social Science Research Council, 1948.

Easterbrook, W. T., and Hugh G. J. Aitken. *Canadian Economic History.* Toronto: Macmillan Co., 1956.

Facts and Factors in Economic History, Articles by Former Students of E. F. Gay. Cambridge: Harvard University Press, 1933.

Ferber, Robert. *A Study of Aggregate Consumption Functions.* (National Bureau of Economic Research, Technical Paper 8.) New York: National Bureau of Economic Research, 1953.

Field, Frederick William. *Capital Investments in Canada, Some Facts and Figures Respecting One of the Most Attractive Investment Fields in the World.* Montreal: Monetary Times of Canada, 1912.

Firestone, O. J. *Canada's Economic Development, 1867–1953, With Special Reference to Changes in the Country's National Product and National Wealth.* (Income & Wealth Series VII.) London: Bowes and Bowes, 1958.

——. *Residential Real Estate in Canada.* Toronto: University of Toronto Press, 1951.

Fisheries Council of Canada. *Submission to the RCCEP.* Ottawa, 1956. (Processed.)

Ford Motor Company of Canada. *The Role of the Automobile in Canada's Next Quarter-Century.* (Submission to the RCCEP.) Toronto, 1956.

Fullerton, D. H., and H. A. Hampson. *Canadian Secondary Manufacturing Industry.* Hull, Que.: Queen's Printer, 1957.

Gibson, J. D. (ed.). *Canada's Economy in a Changing World.* Toronto: Macmillan Co., 1948.

Gilmour, G. P. (ed). *Canada's Tomorrow, Papers and Discussion, Canada's Tomorrow Conference, Quebec City, November 1953.* Toronto: Macmillan Co., 1954.

Glazebrook, G. P. de T. *A History of Canadian Transportation.* ("The Relations of Canada and the United States," a series of studies prepared under the direction of the Carnegie Endowment for International Peace, Division of Economics and History, James T. Shotwell, Director.) Toronto: Ryerson Press for the Carnegie Endowment for International Peace, Division of Economics and History, 1938.

Goldsmith, Raymond W., *et al. A Study of Saving in the United States.* 3 vols. Princeton: Princeton University Press, 1955–56.

Goss, J. H. *Presentation to the RCCEP*. Toronto: Canadian General Electric Company, 1956. (Processed.)

Gouin, L. M., and Brooke Claxton. *Legislative Expedients Adopted by the Dominion and the Provinces*. (RCDPR *Report*, Appendix 8.) Ottawa: King's Printer, 1939.

Gould, Jacob Martin. *Output and Productivity in the Electric and Gas Utilities, 1899–1942*. (Publications of the National Bureau of Economic Research, Inc., No. 47.) New York: National Bureau of Economic Research, 1946.

Guthrie, John A. *The Newsprint Paper Industry: An Economic Analysis*. (Harvard Economic Studies, Vol. 68.) Cambridge: Harvard University Press, 1941.

Hansen, Alvin H. *The American Economy*. ("Economic Handbook Series.") New York: McGraw-Hill Book Co., 1957.

Henripin, J. *La population canadienne au debut du XVIIIᵉ siècle: nuptialité, fécondité, mortalité infantile*. (Institut National d'Etudes Démographiques, Travaux et Documents, Cahier Nᵒ 22.) Paris: Presses Universitaires de France, 1954.

Holbrook, David. *Statement before the RCCEP*. Toronto: Algoma Steel Corporation, 1956. (Processed.)

Hoover, Edgar M. *Location Theory and the Shoe and Leather Industries*. (Harvard Economic Studies, Vol. 55.) Cambridge: Harvard University Press, 1937.

————. *The Location of Economic Activity*. ("Economic Handbook Series.") New York: McGraw-Hill Book Co., 1948.

Hoselitz, B. F. (ed.). *Progress of Underdeveloped Areas*. Chicago: University of Chicago Press, 1952.

Howay, F. W., W. N. Sage, and H. F. Angus. *British Columbia and the United States: the North Pacific Slope from Fur Trade to Aviation*. ("The Relations of Canada and the United States," a series of studies prepared under the direction of the Carnegie Endowment for International Peace, Division of Economics and History, James T. Shotwell, Director.) Toronto: Ryerson Press for Carnegie Endowment for International Peace, Division of Economics and History, 1942.

Hughes, E. C. *French Canada in Transition*. Chicago: University of Chicago Press, 1943.

Imperial Oil, Limited. *Prospects for Canada's Oil Industry, 1955–1980*. Toronto, 1956.

Innis, Harold A. *The Cod Fisheries, the History of an International Economy*. ("The Relations of Canada and the United States," a series of studies prepared under the direction of the Carnegie Endowment for International Peace, Division of Economics and History, James T. Shotwell, Director.) Toronto: Ryerson Press for Carnegie Endowment for International Peace, Division of Economics and History, 1946.

————. *Essays in Canadian Economic History*. Toronto: University of Toronto Press, 1956.

———— (ed.). *Essays in Political Economy in Honour of E. J. Urwick*. Toronto: University of Toronto Press, 1938.

———— (ed.). *Essays in Transportation in Honour of W. T. Jackman.* Toronto: University of Toronto Press, 1941.

————. *Problems of Staple Production in Canada.* Toronto: Ryerson Press, 1933.

————. *Settlement and the Mining Frontier.* ("Canadian Frontiers of Settlement," ed. W. A. Mackintosh and W. L. G. Joerg, Vol. 9, Part II.) Toronto: Macmillan Co., 1936.

Innis, H. A., and A. R. M. Lower. *Selected Documents in Canadian Economic History, 1783–1885.* Toronto: University of Toronto Press, 1933.

Innis, H. A. and A. F. W. Plumptre (eds.). *The Canadian Economy and Its Problems, Papers and Proceedings of Study Groups of Members of the Canadian Institute of International Affairs, 1933–1934.* Toronto: Canadian Institute of International Affairs, 1934.

Isaac, J. *British Post-War Migration.* (National Institute of Economic and Social Research, Occasional Papers XVII.) Cambridge: Cambridge University Press, 1954.

Isard, Walter, and E. W. Schooler. *Location Factors in the Petrochemical Industry.* (U.S. Department of Commerce.) Washington: Government Printing Office, 1955.

Jackson, Gilbert, and Associates. *Exports and National Income.* (Memorandum for Postwar Planners, No. 5.) N. p., 1945.

Jerome, Harry. *Migration and Business Cycles.* (Publications of the National Bureau of Economic Research, Inc., No. 9.) New York: National Bureau of Economic Research, 1926.

Jones, Robert Leslie *History of Agriculture in Ontario, 1613–1880.* (University of Toronto Studies, History and Economic Series, Vol. 11.) Toronto: University of Toronto Press, 1946.

Keenleyside, Hugh L. *Canadian Immigration Policy.* (University of British Columbia Lecture Series, No. 3.) Vancouver: University of British Columbia Press, 1948.

————. *The Place of the Forest Industry in the Canadian Economy.* (University of British Columbia Lecture Series, No. 6.) Vancouver: University of British Columbia Press, 1950.

Knox, F. A. *Dominion Monetary Policy, 1929–34.* ("A Study Prepared for the RCDPR.") Ottawa: King's Printer, 1939.

Knox, F. A., C. L. Barber and D. W. Slater. *The Canadian Electrical Manufacturing Industry: An Economic Analysis.* Toronto: Canadian Electrical Manufacturers Association, 1955.

Kuznets, Simon, assisted by Elizabeth Jenks. *Shares of Upper Income Groups in Income and Savings.* (Publications of the National Bureau of Economic Research, No. 55.) New York: National Bureau of Economic Research, 1953.

————. *Uses of National Income in Peace and War.* (Occasional Paper No. 6.) New York: National Bureau of Economic Research, 1942.

Langlois, Georges. *Histoire de la population canadienne-française.* ("Documents historiques.") Montreal: Editions Albert Lévesque, 1934.

Lank, H. H., Du Pont Company of Canada, Ltd. *A Submission to the*

RCCEP Covering the Growth Potentialities of the Canadian Chemical Industry. N. p., 1956. (Processed.)

Leontief, Wassily W., *et al. Studies in the Structure of the American Economy.* New York: Oxford University Press, 1953.

Lewis, W. Arthur. *Economic Survey, 1919–1939.* London: Allen and Unwin, 1949.

Lower, A. R. M. *Colony to Nation: A History of Canada.* Toronto: Longmans, Green and Co., 1946.

――――. *The North American Assault on the Canadian Forest: A History of the Lumber Trade Between Canada and the United States.* With W. A. Carrothers, *Forest Industries of British Columbia,* and S. A. Saunders, *Forest Industries in the Maritime Provinces.* ("The Relations of Canada and the United States," a series of studies prepared under the direction of the Carnegie Endowment for International Peace, Division of Economics and History, James T. Shotwell, Director.) New Haven: Yale University Press for Carnegie Endowment for International Peace, Division of Economics and History, 1938.

Lower, A. R. M., and Harold A. Innis. *Settlement and the Forest and Mining Frontiers.* ("Canadian Frontiers of Settlement," W. A. Mackintosh and W. L. G. Joerg, eds., Vol. IX.) Toronto: Macmillan Co., 1936.

MacDonald, Norman. *Canada, 1763–1841: Immigration and Settlement; the Administration of the Imperial Land Regulations.* London: Longmans, Green and Co., 1939.

MacDougall, Donald. *The World Dollar Problem.* London: Macmillan Co., 1957.

MacGibbon, D. A. *The Canadian Grain Trade, 1931–1951.* Toronto: University of Toronto Press, 1952.

Machinery and Equipment Manufacturers Association of Canada. *Representations to the RCCEP.* N. p., n. d. (Processed.)

MacKay, Robert Alexander (ed.). *Newfoundland: Economic, Diplomatic, and Strategic Studies.* Toronto: Oxford University Press, 1946.

Mackintosh, W. A. *The Economic Background of Dominion-Provincial Relations,* A Study Prepared for the Royal Commission on Dominion-Provincial Relations. (RCDPR *Report,* Appendix 3.) Ottawa: King's Printer, 1939.

――――. *Prairie Settlement: The Geographical Setting.* ("Canadian Frontiers of Settlement," W. A. Mackintosh and W. L. G. Joerg, eds., Vol. I.) Toronto: Macmillan Co., 1934.

MacLean, M. C. *Analysis of the Stages in the Growth of Population in Canada.* Ottawa: King's Printer, 1935.

Main, O. W. *The Canadian Nickel Industry, A Study in Market Control and Public Policy.* (*Canadian Studies in Economics,* No. 4.) Toronto: University of Toronto Press, 1955.

Malach, V. W. *International Cycles and Canada's Balance of Payments, 1921–1933.* Canadian Studies in Economics, No. 1.) Toronto: University of Toronto Press, 1954.

Malenbaum, Wilfred. *The World Wheat Economy, 1885–1939.* (Harvard Economic Studies, Vol. 92.) Cambridge: Harvard University Press, 1953.

Marcus, Edward. *Canada and the International Business Cycle, 1927–1939.* New York: Bookman Associates, 1954.

Marshall, Herbert, Frank A. Southard, Jr., and Kenneth Taylor. *Canadian-American Industry: A Study in International Investment.* With an excursus on the Canadian balance of payments by F. A. Knox. ("The Relations of Canada and the United States," a series of studies prepared under the direction of the Carnegie Endowment for International Peace, Division of Economics and History, James T. Shotwell, Director.) New Haven: Yale University Press for the Carnegie Endowment for World Peace, Division of Economics and History, 1936.

Mason, Edward S., *et al. Productive Uses of Nuclear Energy.* Washington: National Planning Association, 1955.

Massue, Huet. *Highlights of Electric Power in Canada.* Montreal: Shawinigan Water and Power Co., 1955. (Processed.)

Maxwell, J. A. *Federal Subsidies to the Provincial Governments in Canada.* (Harvard Economic Studies, Vol. 56.) Cambridge: Harvard University Press, 1937.

——. *Recent Developments in Dominion-Provincial Fiscal Relations in Canada.* (National Bureau of Economic Research, Occasional Paper 25.) New York: National Bureau of Economic Research, 1948.

Meyer, John R., and Edwin Kuh. *The Investment Decision: An Empirical Study.* (Harvard Economic Studies, Vol. 102.) Cambridge: Harvard University Press, 1957.

Mills, Frederick C. *Economic Tendencies in the United States: Aspects of Pre-War and Post-War Change.* (Publications of the National Bureau of Economic Research, Inc., No. 21.) New York: National Bureau of Economic Research, 1932.

Moore, A. Milton, and J. Harvey Perry. *Financing Canadian Federation, The Federal-Provincial Tax Agreements.* (Canadian Tax Papers, No. 6.) Toronto: Canadian Tax Foundation, 1953.

Moore, E. S. *American Influence in Canadian Mining.* (Political Economy Series, No. 9.) Toronto: University of Toronto Press, 1941.

Morse, N. H. *Further Observations on the Economy of Nova Scotia.* Halifax: Nova Scotia Research Foundation, n. d.

Morton, Arthur S. *A History of the Canadian West to 1870–71.* Toronto: Thos. Nelson and Sons, 1939.

Myrdal, Gunnar. *An International Economy, Problems and Prospects.* New York: Harper & Bros., 1956.

National Petroleum Council. *Petroleum Productive Capacity.* Washington, 1952.

Neisser, Hans, and Franco Modigliani. *National Incomes and International Trade.* Urbana: University of Illinois Press, 1953.

Newfoundland Fisheries Development Authority. *Submission to the RCCEP.* N. p., 1956. (Processed.)

Nordegg, Martin. *The Fuel Problem in Canada*. Toronto: Macmillan Co., 1930.

Nova Scotia Light and Power Company, Limited. *Brief Presented to the RCCEP by Nova Scotia Light and Power Company, Limited, with Respect to the Availability and Cost of Electric Power in Nova Scotia and Its Relation to Industry*. Ottawa, 1955. (Processed.)

O'Brian, C. L. *Coal and Energy in Canada Since the War*. (Reprints of five articles from *Canadian Mining and Metallurgical Bulletin*, 1950–1954.) N. p., 1954.

Parnes, Herbert S. *Research on Labor Mobility*. (Social Science Research Council, Bulletin 65.) New York: Social Science Research Council, 1954.

Patterson, Gilbert. *Land Settlement in Upper Canada, 1783–1840*. (16th Report of the Department of Archives for the Province of Ontario, 1920.) Toronto, 1920.

Pearson, Lester B., *et al. Canada: Nation on the March*. Toronto: Clarke, Irwin and Co., 1953.

Penhale, A. L. *Memorandum to the RCCEP on the Subject of the Canadian Asbestos Industry*. Montreal: Canadian Institute of Mining and Metallurgy, 1956. (Processed.)

Perry, J. Harvey. *Taxes, Tariffs, and Subsidies, A History of Canadian Fiscal Development*. ("Sponsored by the Canadian Tax Foundation.") 2 vols. Toronto: University of Toronto Press, 1955.

Petrie, Joseph Richards. *The Taxation of Corporate Income in Canada*. Toronto: University of Toronto Press, 1952.

Pogue, Joseph E., Kenneth E. Hill, *et al. Future Growth and Financial Requirements of the World Petroleum Industry*. New York: Chase Manhattan Bank, 1956.

Polak, J. J. *An International Economic System*. Chicago: University of Chicago Press, 1953.

Pratt's Oil Price Handbook, 1954. New York: McGraw-Hill Book Co., 1954.

Primary Textiles Institute. *Submission to the RCCEP on Behalf of the Canadian Primary Textile Industry*. Toronto and Montreal, 1956. (Processed.)

Rosenbluth, G. *Concentration in Canadian Manufacturing Industries*. (National Bureau of Economic Research, No. 61, General Series.) Princeton: Princeton University Press, 1957.

Rubber Association of Canada. *Past, Present and Future Problems of the Rubber Industry in Canada*. Toronto, n. d. (Processed.)

Ruddick, J. A., R. M. Drummond, R. E. English, and J. E. Lattimer. *The Dairying Industry in Canada*. ("The Relations of Canada and the United States," a series of studies prepared under the direction of the Carnegie Endowment for International Peace, Division of Economics and History, James T. Shotwell, Director.) Toronto: Ryerson Press for Carnegie Endowment for International Peace, Division of Economics and History, 1937.

Saunders, S. A. *The Economic History of the Maritime Provinces, A Study Prepared for the RCDPR.* Ottawa: King's Printer, 1939.

———. *The Economic Welfare of the Maritime Provinces.* (Acadia University, Economic Publications, No. 1.) Wolfville: Acadia University Press, 1932.

Shell Oil Company of Canada, Ltd. *Petroleum in Canada's Economy, A Submission to the RCCEP.* Toronto, 1956.

Shortt, Adam, and Arthur G. Doughty (eds.). *Canada and Its Provinces, A History of the Canadian People and Their Institutions.* 23 vols. Toronto: Publishers Association of Canada, 1914–1917.

Spelt, J. *The Urban Development in South-Central Ontario.* (Sociaal Geografische Studies No. 2.) Assen, Netherlands: Van Gorcum, 1955.

Stanford Research Institute. *America's Demand for Wood, 1929–1975.* ("Prepared for Weyerhaeuser Timber Company.") Palo Alto: Stanford Research Institute, 1954.

Steel Company of Canada, Ltd. *Brief Presented to the RCCEP.* N. p., 1956. (Processed.)

Stigler, George J. *Trends in Employment in the Service Industries.* (National Bureau of Economic Research, General Series, No. 59.) Princeton: Princeton University Press for National Bureau of Economic Research, 1956.

Sufrin, Sidney C., and E. E. Palmer. *The New St. Lawrence Frontier, A Survey of the Economic Potential in the St. Lawrence Area of New York State.* (Maxwell School Series.) Syracuse: Syracuse University Press, 1957.

Taylor, Kenneth M., and H. Michell. *Statistical Contributions to Canadian Economic History.* 2 vols. Toronto: Macmillan Co., 1931.

Thomas, Brinley. *Migration and Economic Growth, A Study of Great Britain and the Atlantic Economy.* (National Institute of Economic and Social Research, Economic and Social Studies, XII.) Cambridge: Cambridge University Press, 1954.

Timlin, Mabel F. *Does Canada Need More People?* Toronto: Oxford University Press, 1951.

Trades and Labor Congress of Canada. *Labour Mobility, A Study Prepared for the RCCEP.* Ottawa: Queen's Printer, 1957.

Tucker, Gilbert Norman. *The Canadian Commercial Revolution, 1845–1851.* New Haven: Yale University Press, 1936.

Truesdell, Leon E. *The Canadian Born in the United States, An Analysis of the Statistics of the Canadian Elements in the Population of the United States, 1850 to 1930.* ("The Relations of Canada and the United States," a series of studies prepared under the direction of the Carnegie Endowment for International Peace, Division of Economics and History, James T. Shotwell, Director.) New Haven: Yale University Press for the Carnegie Endowment for International Peace, Division of Economics and History, 1943.

Valk, H. M. H. A. van der. *The Economic Future of Canada.* Toronto: McGraw-Hill Book Co., 1954.

Veyret, Paul. *La population du Canada.* (Publications de la Faculté des

Lettres de l'Université de Grénoble, VII.) Paris: Presses Universitaires de France, 1953.

Viner, Jacob. *Canada's Balance of International Indebtedness, 1900–1913.* (Harvard Economic Studies, Vol. 26.) Cambridge, Mass.: Harvard University Press, 1924.

Whelpton, P. K., and Clyde V. Kiser. *Social and Psychological Factors Affecting Fertility.* (Volume II, The Intensive Study: Purpose, Scope, Methods, and Partial Results. "Reprinted from *The Milbank Memorial Fund Quarterly.*") New York: Milbank Memorial Fund, 1949.

Wold, Herman, in association with Lars Juréen. *Demand Analysis, A Study in Econometrics.* New York: John Wiley and Sons, 1953.

Woytinsky, W. S., and E. S. Woytinsky. *World Population and Production, Trends and Outlook.* New York: Twentieth Century Fund, 1953.

Articles and Periodicals

Abramovitz, Moses. "Resource and Output Trends in the United States since 1870," *AER*, 46:5–23 (May 1956).

Aitken, Hugh G. J. "Note on the Capital Resources of Upper Canada," *CJEPS*, 18:525–532 (November 1952).

Allcut, E. A. "A Fuel Policy for Canada," *CJEPS*, 11:26–34 (February 1945).

Allen, Patrick. "La structure des emplois au Canada, 1941–1951," *LE*, 32:293–323 (juillet-septembre 1956).

Angus, H. F. "Future of Immigration into Canada," *CJEPS*, 12:379–386 (August 1946).

Bach, G. L., and Albert Ando. "The Redistributional Effects of Inflation," *RES*, 39:1–13 (February 1957).

Baldwin, Robert E. "Patterns of Development in Newly Settled Regions," *Manchester School*, 24:161–179 (May 1954).

Bank of Nova Scotia. *Monthly Review.* 1953–1957.

Barber, C. L. "Canada's Post-War Monetary Policy, 1945–1954," *CJEPS*, 23:349–362 (August 1957).

———. "Canadian Tariff Policy," *CJEPS*, 21:513–530 (November 1955).

———. "Inventory Fluctuations in Canada, 1918–1950," *CJEPS*, 18:372–378 (August 1952).

Beckerman, W. "The World Trade Multiplier and the Stability of World Trade, 1938 to 1953," *Econometrica*, 24:239–252 (July 1956).

Bernhard, Carolyn G. "Growth of the Consumer Service Market," *Survey of Current Business*, 36:15–24 (May 1956).

Billewicz, W. Z. "The Import Content of British Exports," *Economica*, 20:162–169 (May 1953).

Bing, R. A. "Petroleum in Canada's Balance of International Payments," *Southern Economic Journal*, 19:234–248 (October 1952).

Black, John D. "Agriculture in the Nation's Economy," *AER*, 46:1–43 (March 1956).

Bladen, Vincent W. "The Size of the Establishment in Canadian and American Industry," *Contributions to Canadian Economics* [University of Toronto Studies, History and Economics], 1:56–68 (1928).

Blyth, C. D., and E. B. Carty. "Non-Resident Ownership of Canadian Industry," *CJEPS*, 22:449–460 (November 1956).

Break, George F. "Income Taxes and Incentives to Work: An Empirical Study," *AER*, 47:529–549 (September 1957).

Brems, Hans. "Long-Run Automobile Demand," *Journal of Marketing*, 20:379–384 (April 1956).

Breul, F. R. "The Genesis of Family Allowances in Canada," *Social Service Review*, 27:269–280 (September 1953).

Britnell, G. E. "Perspective on Change in the Prairie Economy," *CJEPS*, 19:437–454 (November 1953).

Brown, T. M. "Habit Persistence and Lags in Consumer Behavior," *Econometrica*, 20:355–371 (July 1952).

Bryce, R. B. "The Effect on Canada of Industrial Fluctuations in the United States," *CJEPS*, 5:373–386 (August 1939).

———. "Federal Provincial Tax Arrangements," *Report of Proceedings of the Tenth Annual Tax Conference, 1956*. Toronto: Canadian Tax Foundation, 1957. pp. 299–307.

Buckley, K. A. H. "Economic Growth in Canada," *Financial Research and the Problems of the Day*. Thirty-seventh Annual Report of the National Bureau of Economic Research (May 1957), pp. 80–81.

———. "Urban Building and Real Estate Fluctuations in Canada," *CJEPS*, 18:41–62 (February 1952).

Cameron, Burgess. "The Production Function in Leontief Models," *Review of Economic Studies*, 20:62–69 (1952–53).

Canadian Bank of Commerce. *Commercial Letter*. 1954–1956.

"Canadian White Paper on Employment and Income," *Federal Reserve Bulletin*, 31:536–549 (June 1945).

Carrothers, W. A. "The Barter Terms of Trade between British Columbia and Eastern Canada," *CJEPS*, 1:568–577 (November 1935).

Caves, Richard E. "The Inter-Industry Structure of the Canadian Economy," *CJEPS*, 23:313–330 (August 1957).

Chambers, E. J. "The 1937–8 Recession in Canada," *CJEPS*, 21:293–308 (August 1955).

Chang, Tse-Chun. "A Note on Exports and National Income in Canada," *CJEPS*, 13:276–279 (May 1947).

Charles, E. "Differential Fertility in Canada, 1931," *CJEPS*, 9:175–218 (May 1943).

———. "Nuptiality and Fertility in Canada—A Study Based on Canadian Marriage Statistics," *Canada Year Book, 1942*. Ottawa: King's Printer, 1943. pp. 102–117.

Christ, Carl F. "Aggregate Econometric Models, A Review Article," *AER*, 46:385–408 (June 1956).

Clark, S. D. "The Religious Sect in Canadian Economic Development," *CJEPS*, 12:439–453 (November 1946).

Coats, R. H. (ed.). "Features of Present-Day Canada," *The Annals of the American Academy of Political and Social Science*, 253:1–266 (September 1947).

————. "Statistics Comes of Age," *CJEPS*, 2:269–287 (August 1936).

Cochrane, H. G. "The Natural Gas Story," *Canadian Business*, 29:12–22 (March 1956).

Corbett, D. C. "Immigration and Economic Development," *CJEPS*, 17:360–368 (August 1951).

————. "Immigration and Politics," *International Journal*, 6:207–216 (Summer 1951).

Creighton, D. G. "Economic Background of the Rebellions of Eighteen Thirty-seven," *CJEPS*, 3:322–334 (August 1937).

Cullen, Donald E. "The Interindustry Wage Structure, 1899–1950," *AER*, 46:353–369 (June 1956).

Currie, A. W. "Freight Rates and Regionalism," *CJEPS*, 14:427–440 (November 1948).

Dales, John H. "Fuel, Power and Industrial Development in Central Canada," *AER*, 43:181–198 (May 1953).

Daly, D. J. "Aspects of the Decline in Employment in Canadian Agriculture," *CJAE*, 3:19–31 (Number 2, 1955).

Daly, M. C. "An Approximation to a Geographical Multiplier," *EJ*, 50:248–258 (June-September 1940).

Daly, Rex F. "The Long-Run Demand for Farm Products," *Agricultural Economics Research*, 8:73–91 (July 1956).

Deutsch, J. J. "War Finance and the Canadian Economy, 1914–1920," *CJEPS*, 6:525–542 (November 1940).

de Vegh, Imre. "Imports and Income in the United States and Canada," *RES*, 23:130–146 (August 1941).

Drayton, L. E. "Food Consumption Trends, Standards and Consumer Preferences," *CJAE*, 5:15–25 (Number 2, 1957).

Due, Jean Mann. "Consumer Knowledge of Installment Credit Charges," *Journal of Marketing*, 20:162–166 (October 1955).

————. "Consumption Levels in Canada and the United States," *CJEPS*, 21:174–182 (May 1955).

Duesenberry, James S. "Income-Consumption Relationships and Their Implications," in *Income, Employment and Public Policy, Essays in Honor of Alvin H. Hansen*. New York: W. W. Norton and Co., 1948. pp. 54–81.

Dumareau, Pierre, "L'aspect et l'avenir demographiques du Canada français," *LE*, 28:5–26 (avril-juin 1952).

Easterbrook, W. T. "Uncertainty and Economic Change," *Journal of Economic History*, 14:346–360 (Autumn 1954).

Eastman, H. C. "Recent Canadian Economic Policy: Some Alternatives," *CJEPS*, 18:135–145 (May 1952).

Evans, W. Duane, and Marvin Hoffenberg. "The Inter-industry Relations Study for 1947," *RES*, 34:97–142 (May 1952).

Ferber, Robert. "Consumer Expenditures for Services," *Journal of Marketing*, 21:24–35 (July 1956).

————. "The Role of Planning in Consumer Purchases of Durable Goods," *AER*, 44:854–874 (December 1954).

Fergusson, D. A. "The Industrial Development Bank of Canada," *Journal of Business of the University of Chicago,* 21:214–229 (October 1948). *Financial Post.* 1955–1957.

Fisher, J. L. "The Role of Natural Resources," in *Economic Development, Principles and Patterns.* (H. F. Williamson and J. A. Buttrick, eds.) New York: Prentice-Hall, Inc., 1954.

Fowke, V. C. "The National Policy — Old and New," *CJEPS,* 18:271–286 (August 1952).

Garbarino, Joseph W. "The Productivity-Wage Relationship," *Industrial and Labor Relations Review,* 7:605–612 (July 1954).

Gérin-Lajoie, P. "Looking to a New Era in Federal-Provincial Relations," *Canadian Tax Journal,* 5:62–68 (January-February 1957).

Gibson, J. D. "The Changing Influence of the United States on the Canadian Economy," *CJEPS,* 22:421–436 (November 1956).

———. "Postwar Economic Development and Policy in Canada," *CJEPS,* 20:439–455 (November 1954).

Gillies, J. "Some Financial Aspects of the Canadian Government Housing Program: History and Prospective Developments," *Journal of Finance,* 8:22–33 (March 1953).

Gordon, R. A. "Population Growth, Housing and the Capital Coefficient," *AER,* 46:307–322 (June 1956).

Grauman, J. V. "Effects of Population Trends upon Age Structure, With Application to the Americas," *Estadistica,* 14:271–287 (June 1956).

Grey, R. "Federal Aid — A Critique," *Canadian Tax Journal,* 2:111–115 (March-April 1954).

Haddy, Pamela, and N. Arnold Tolles. "British and American Changes in Interindustry Wage Structure under Full Employment," *RES,* 39:408–414 (November 1957).

Hansen, Alvin H. "Growth or Stagnation in the American Economy," *RES,* 36:409–414 (November 1954).

Harberger, A. C. "A Structural Approach to the Problem of Import Demand," *AER,* 43:148–160 (May 1953).

Hartland, Penelope E. "Factors in Economic Growth in Canada," *Journal of Economic History,* 15:13–22 (No. 1, 1955).

Harvey, Pierre. "Conjoncture et structures: les perspectives spatiales du plein-emploi au Canada," *LE,* 32:383–404 (octobre-decembre 1956).

Heath, J. B. "British-Canadian Manufacturing Productivity," *EJ,* 67:665–691 (December 1957).

Heaton, Herbert. "Other Wests Than Ours," *The Tasks of Economic History,* 6:50–62 (1946).

Henripin, Jacques. "Les besoins futurs de nouveaux logements au Canada, jusqu'à 1971," *LE,* 32:191–209 (juillet-septembre 1956).

———. "Observations sur la situation demographique des Canadiens français," *LE* 31:559–580 (janvier-mars 1957).

Hildebrand, G. H., and A. Mace, Jr. "The Employment Multiplier in an Expanding Industrial Market: Los Angeles County, 1940–47," *RES,* 32:241–249 (August 1950).

Hood, W. C. "Empirical Studies in Demand," *CJEPS*, 21:309–327 (August 1955).

Hood, W. C., and O. W. Main. "The Role of Canadian Life Insurance Companies in the Post-War Capital Market," *CJEPS*, 22:467–480 (November 1956).

Hoover, Edgar M. "Some Institutional Factors in Business Investment Decisions," *AER*, 44:201–213 (May 1954).

Hoover, Edgar M., and Joseph L. Fisher. "Research in Regional Economic Growth," in *Problems in the Study of Economic Growth*. (Ed. Universities-National Bureau Committee on Economic Research.) New York: National Bureau of Economic Research, 1949. (Processed.)

Hudson, S. C. "Speculation on Agricultural Production in Eastern Canada During the Next Fifty Years." *CJAE*, 3:9–14 (Number 1, 1955).

Humphreys, D. J. R. "Personal Saving in Canada: Direct Estimates, 1939–1953," *Proceedings of the Business and Economic Statistics Section, American Statistical Association*. (Meeting held at Montreal, September 10–13, 1954.) pp. 207–214.

Hurd, W. Burton. "The Decline in the Canadian Birth-Rate," *CJEPS*, 3:40–57 (February 1937).

――――. "Population Movements in Canada, 1921–1931," *Proceedings of the Canadian Political Science Association*, 6:220–237 (1934).

――――. "Some Implications of Prospective Population Changes in Canada," *CJEPS*, 5:492–503 (November 1939).

Hurd, W. Burton, and J. C. Cameron. "Population Movements in Canada 1921–1931: Some Further Considerations," *CJEPS*. 1:222–245 (May 1935).

Hurwicz, Leonid. "Prediction and Least Squares," *Statistical Inference in Dynamic Economic Models*. (Cowles Commission for Research in Economics, Monograph No. 10, T. C. Koopmans, ed.) New York: John Wiley and Sons, 1950. pp. 266–300.

Ingram, James C. "Growth in Capacity and Canada's Balance of Payments," *AER*, 47:93–104 (March 1957).

Isard, Walter, and William M. Capron. "The Future Locational Pattern of Iron and Steel Production in the United States," *JPE*, 57:118–133 (April 1949).

Isard, Walter, and Robert E. Kuenne. "The Impact of Steel upon the Greater New York-Philadelphia Industrial Region: A Study in Agglomeration Projection," *RES*, 35:289–301 (November 1953).

Jackson, J. M. "British Exports and the Scale of Production," *Manchester School*, 22:90–112 (January 1954).

Johnson, D. Gale. "The Functional Distribution of Income in the United States, 1850–1952," *RES*, 36:175–182 (May 1954).

Johnson, Harry G. "Canada — A Lost Opportunity?" *Three Banks Review*, June 1954, pp. 3–21.

――――. "Canada's Economic Prospects," *CJEPS*, 24:104–110 (February 1958).

Kendrick, John W. "Productivity Trends: Capital and Labor," *RES*, 38:248–257 (August 1956).

Kent, T. W. "The American Boom in Canada," *Lloyds Bank Review*, N.S. No. 43 (January 1957), pp. 17–33.

Kerr, Donald. "The Physical Basis of Agriculture in British Columbia," *Economic Geography*, 28:229–239 (July 1952).

Keyfitz, Nathan. "The Growth of the Canadian Population," *Population Studies*, 4:47–63 (June 1950).

Kilduff, Vera Reynolds. "Economic Factors in the Development of Canadian-American Trade," *Southern Economic Journal*, 8:201–217 (October 1941).

Klein, L. R., and J. B. Lansing. "Decisions to Purchase Consumer Durable Goods," *Journal of Marketing*, 20:109–132 (October 1955).

LeNeveu, A. H., and Kasahara, Y. "Demographic Trends in Canada, 1941–1956, and Some of Their Implications," *CJEPS*, 24:9–20 (February 1958).

Leontief, Wassily. "Factor Proportions and the Structure of American Trade: Further Theoretical and Empirical Analysis," *RES*, 38:386–407 (November 1956).

Lewis, W. Arthur. "World Production, Prices and Trade, 1870–1960," *Manchester School*, 20:105–138 (May 1952).

McDiarmid, O. J. "Some Aspects of the Canadian Automobile Industry," *CJEPS*, 6:258–274 (May 1940).

Macdonnell, J. M. "Parliament and the Purse: Current Procedures and Problems," *Queens Quarterly*, 63:528–539 (Winter 1957).

MacGregor, D. C. "Manufacturer's Expenses, Net Production, and Rigid Costs in Canada," *RES*, 27:60–73 (May 1945).

———. "The Problem of Public Debt in Canada," *CJEPS*, 2:167–194 (May 1936).

McIvor, R. Craig. "Canadian Foreign Trade and the European Common Market," *International Journal*, 13:1–11 (Winter 1957–58).

Mackenzie, William. "Possible Trends in the Demand for Canadian Farm Products," *CJAE*, 3:1–8 (Number 1, 1955).

Mackintosh, W. A. "Canada's Economic Prospects," *Canadian Chartered Accountant*, 70:220–225 (March 1957).

———. "The Canadian Economy and Its Competitors," *Foreign Affairs*, 34:117–127 (October 1955).

———. "Innis on Canadian Economic Development," *JPE*, 61:185–195 (June 1953).

———. "Some Aspects of a Pioneer Economy," *CJEPS*, 2:457–463 (November 1936).

McLeod, H. "Mineral Production Up Again," *Canadian Mining Journal*, 76:54–64 (February 1955).

Maddison, A. "Productivity in Canada, the United Kingdom, and the United States," *OEP*, 4:235–242 (October 1952).

———. "Productivity in Canadian Manufacturing, 1935–1948," *CJEPS*, 19:222–225 (May 1953).

———. "Productivity in an Expanding Economy," *EJ*, 62:584–594 (September 1952).

Malach, V. W. "Elasticity of Demand for Canadian Exports," *RES,* 39: 23–30 (February 1957).

———. "External Determinants of the Canadian Upswing, 1921–29," *CJEPS,* 17:50–64 (February 1951).

———. "Internal Determinants of the Canadian Upswing, 1921–29," *CJEPS,* 16:184–198 (May 1950).

———. "The International Business Cycle and Canada, 1927–39," *CJEPS,* 21:88–100 (February 1955).

———. "The Mechanism of Adjustment in Canada's Balance of Payments, 1921–29," *CJEPS,* 18:303–321 (August 1952).

Marcus, Edward. "A Comment on the 1937–8 Recession in Canada," *CJEPS,* 22:249–250 (May 1956).

———. "The Cyclical Adjustment Pattern of an 'Open Economy': Canada, 1927–1939." *EJ,* 62:305–317 (June 1952).

———. "The Effectiveness of Canadian Fiscal Policy," *Journal of Finance,* 7:559–579 (December 1952).

Marshall, Herbert. "Canada — Northern Neighbor," *JASA,* 50:1–15 (March 1955).

Maxwell, J. A. "Canadian Dominion-Provincial Relations," *QJE,* 55:584–610 (August 1941).

Mayo, H. B. "The Economic Problem of the Newfoundland Fisheries," *CJEPS,* 17:482–493 (November 1951).

Maywald, Karel. "National Savings and Changing Employment in Canada, 1926–54," *CJEPS,* 22:174–182 (May 1956).

Meier, Gerald M. "Economic Development and the Transfer Mechanism: Canada, 1895–1913," *CJEPS,* 19:1–19 (February 1953).

Meyers, Frederic, and Roger L. Bowlby. "The Interindustry Wage Structure and Productivity," *Industrial and Labor Relations Review,* 7:93–102 (October 1953).

Mills, Frederick C. "The Role of Productivity in Economic Growth," *AER,* 42:545–557 (May 1952).

Miner, Horace. "The French-Canadian Family Cycle," *American Sociological Review,* 3:700–708 (October 1938).

Moore, A Milton. "What Alternative to the Tax Rental Agreements?", *Canadian Tax Journal,* 2:281–289 (September-October 1954).

Moore, Frederick T., and James W. Petersen. "Regional Analysis: An Interindustry Model of Utah," *RES,* 37:368–383 (November 1955).

Munzer, E. "Exports and National Income in Canada," *CJEPS,* 11:35–47 (February 1945).

Musolf, Lloyd D. "Canadian Public Enterprise: A Character Study," *American Political Science Review,* 50:405–421 (June 1956).

Neufeld, E. P. "Canada's Economy Now," *The Banker,* 107:430–437 (July 1957).

North, Douglass C. "Location Theory and Regional Economic Growth," *JPE,* 63:243–258 (June 1955).

"Ontario Gold Mining Committee Interim Report, March, 1955," *Canadian Mining Journal,* 76:66–67 (May 1955).

Pennie, T. E. "The Influence of Distribution Costs and Direct Investments on British Exports to Canada," *OEP*, 8:229–245 (October 1956).

Pentland, H. C. "Physical Productivity in Canada, 1935–52," *EJ*, 64:399–404 (June 1954).

———. "The Role of Capital in Canadian Economic Development before 1875," *CJEPS*, 16:457–474 (November 1950).

Perlman, Richard. "Value Productivity and the Interindustry Wage Structure," *Industrial and Labor Relations Review*, 10:26–39 (October 1956).

Petrie, J. R. "The Impact of the Sterling-Dollar Crisis on the Maritime Economy," *CJEPS*, 16:347–352 (August 1950).

Phillips, Almarin. "The Variation of Technical Coefficients in the Antifriction Bearing Industry," *Econometrica*, 23:432–441 (October 1955).

Phillips, Roger. "The Big Uranium Hunt," *Canadian Business*, 27:61–62 (October 1954).

Plumptre, A. F. W. "The Nature of Political and Economic Development in the British Dominions," *CJEPS*, 3:489–507 (November 1937).

———. "Newfoundland, Economic and Political. I. The Amulree Report (1933): A Review," *CJEPS*, 3:58–70 (February 1937).

Poapst, James V. "Life Insurance Savings in Canada," *CJEPS*, 19:202–209 (May 1953).

———. "The National Housing Act, 1954," *CJEPS*, 22:234–243 (May 1956).

Prest, A. R. "National Income of the United Kingdom, 1870–1946," *EJ*, 58:31–62 (March 1948).

Radford, R. A. "Canada's Capital Inflow, 1946–53," *International Monetary Fund Staff Papers*, 4:217–257 (February 1955).

Rosenbluth, G. "Changes in Canadian Sensitivity to United States Business Fluctuations," *CJEPS*, 23:480–503 (November 1957).

———."Changing Structural Factors in Canada's Cyclical Sensitivity, 1903–54," *CJEPS*, 24:21–43 (February 1958).

———. "Industrial Concentration in Canada and the United States," *CJEPS*, 20:332–346 (August 1954).

Rothbarth, E. "Causes of the Superior Efficiency of U.S.A. Industry as Compared with British Industry," *EJ*, 56:383–390 (September 1946).

Rowat, D. C. "Recent Developments in Canadian Federalism," *CJEPS*, 18:1–16 (February 1952).

Ryder, Norman B. "Components of Canadian Population Growth," *Population Index*, 20:71–80 (April 1954).

Saunders, S. A. "The Reciprocity Treaty of 1854; a Regional Study," *CJEPS*, 2:41–53 (February 1936).

Sawyer, John A. "The Measurement of Inter-Industry Relationships in Canada," *CJEPS*, 21:480–497 (November 1955).

Schmookler, Jacob. "The Changing Efficiency of the American Economy: 1869–1938," *RES*, 34:214–231 (August 1952).

Scitovsky, Tibor. "Economies of Scale, Competition and European Integration," *AER*, 46:71–91 (March 1956).

Scott, F. R. "Constitutional Adaptations to Changing Functions of Government," *CJEPS*, 11:329–341 (August 1945).

———. "The Constitutional Background of Taxation Agreements," *McGill Law Journal*, 2:1–10 (Autumn 1955).

———. "The Privy Council and Mr. Bennett's 'New Deal' Legislation," *CJEPS*, 3:234–241 (May 1937).

Siebert, Fred V. "50th Anniversary Review of Mineral Development in the Prairie Provinces," *Canadian Mining Journal*, 76:49–53 (August 1955).

Simkin, C. G. F. "Commonwealth Countries and the Common Market," *New Commonwealth*, 33:302–315 (April 1, 1957).

Sinclair, Sol. "Agricultural Production Possibilities in the Year 2000 — Western Canada," *CJAE*, 3:15–24 (Number 1, 1955).

Slater, David W. "Changes in the Structure of Canada's International Trade," *CJEPS*, 21:1–20 (February 1955).

Slichter, Sumner H. "On the Side of Inflation," *Harvard Business Review*, 35:15–36, 162–170 (September-October 1957).

Smith, J. M. "Newsprint in World Affairs," *Behind the Headlines*, 13:1–18 (November 1953).

Sutton, G. D. "Productivity in Canada," *CJEPS*, 19:185–201 (May 1953).

Tatham, Laura. "Titanium in Canada," *Canadian Business*, 27:26 (October 1954).

Taylor, K. W. "Economic Implications of the Report of the Royal Commission on Price Spreads," *CJEPS*, 1:510–517 (August 1935).

Timlin, Mabel F. "Economic Theory and Immigration Policy," *CJEPS*, 16:375–382 (August 1950).

Tyszynski, H. "World Trade in Manufactured Commodities, 1899–1950," *Manchester School*, 19:272–304 (September 1951).

Urquhart, M. C. "Public Investment in Canada," *CJEPS*, 11:535–553 (November 1945).

Usher, T. H. "An Appraisal of the Canadian Family Allowance System," *Review of Social Economy*, 9:124–136 (September 1951).

Valavanis-Vail, Stefan. "An Econometric Model of Growth, U.S.A. 1869–1953," *AER*, 45:208–221 (May 1955).

Waines, W. J. "Dominion-Provincial Financial Arrangements: An Examination of Objectives," *CJEPS*, 19:304–315 (August 1953).

Walton, Edward A. "The Vulnerability of the Canadian Economy," *CJEPS*, 20:10–18 (February 1954).

Wansbrough, V. C. "Implications of Canadian Iron Ore Production," *CJEPS*, 16:334–339 (August 1950).

Watts, G. S. "The Canadian Balance of International Payments, 1950–2, and the Mechanism of Adjustments," *CJEPS*, 20:19–26 (February 1954).

———. "Some Longer-Term Factors in the Canadian Balance of International Payments," *CJEPS*, 16:12–21 (February 1950).

Wolfbein, S. L., and A. J. Jaffe. "Demographic Factors in Labor Force Growth," *American Sociological Review*, 11:392–396 (August 1946).

Wolfe, J. N. "Tax Rentals and Provincial Autonomy," *Canadian Tax Journal*, 2:359–362 (November-December 1954).

Young, John H. "Comparative Economic Development: Canada and the United States," *AER*, 45:80–93 (May 1955).

Younge, Eva R. "Population Movements and the Assimilation of Alien Groups in Canada," *CJEPS*, 10:372–380 (August 1944).

Zay, N. "Analyse statistique du travail de la femme mariée dans la province de Québec," *LE*, 32:488–501 (octobre-decembre 1956).

Zwick, Charles. "Demographic Variation: Its Impact on Consumer Behavior," *RES*, 39:451–456 (November 1957).

Government Documents[1]

Alberta, Government of the Province of. *Estimates of Revnue and Amounts to be Voted for the Public Service of Alberta for the Fiscal Year April 1st, 1955, to March 31st, 1956*. Edmonton, 1955.

Alberta, Province of, Department of Economic Affairs. *Alberta's Economic Prospects*. Edmonton, 1955.

British Columbia, Government of the Province of. *Submission to the RCCEP by the Government of the Province of British Columbia*. Victoria, 1955. (Processed.)

British Columbia, Province of, Department of Industrial Development, Trade and Commerce, Bureau of Economics and Statistics. *British Columbia Facts and Statistics*. Vol. X. Victoria, 1956.

British Columbia, Province of, Department of Mines. *Annual Report of the Minister of Mines, 1951*. Victoria, 1952.

British Columbia, Province of, Economic Council. *Statistics of Industry in British Columbia, 1871–1934*. Victoria, 1935.

British Columbia, Province of, Economic Council, Research Department. *The Trade of British Columbia with Other Canadian Provinces and with Foreign Countries, Calendar Year 1935*. Victoria, 1937.

Canada, Bank of Canada. *Statistical Summary, Financial Supplement 1955*.

———. *Statistical Summary, Financial Supplement 1956*.

Canada, Board of Inquiry into the Cost of Living in Canada. *Report of the Board*. 2 vols. Ottawa: King's Printer, 1915.

Canada, Department of Finance and Report of the Auditor General. *Public Accounts of Canada for the Fiscal Year Ended March 31, 1946–1954*.

Canada, Department of Reconstruction and Supply. *Encouragement to Industrial Expansion in Canada, Operation of Special Depreciation Provisions, November 10, 1944-March 31, 1949* (1948). (Processed.)

Canada, Department of Reconstruction and Supply. *Location and Effects of Wartime Industrial Expansion in Canada, 1939–1944* (1954). (Processed.)

Canada, Department of Resources and Development, Forestry Branch — Economic Section. *Forest and Forest Products Statistics* (1952).

---

[1] To conserve space, we have refrained from listing a vast number of regular publications of the Department of Trade and Commerce of the Government of Canada, particularly those of its statistical agency, the Dominion Bureau of Statistics.

Canada, Department of Trade and Commerce, Economic Research Branch. *Investment and Inflation* (1949).

Canada, Department of Trade and Commerce. *Private and Public Investment in Canada, 1926–1951* (1951).

Canada, DBS. *Canadian Labour Force Estimates, 1931–1950.* Reference Paper No. 23 (1951).

Canada, DBS. *Chronological Record of Canadian Mining Events from 1604 to 1947 and Historical Tables of Mineral Production of Canada* (1948).

Canada, DBS. *City Family Expenditures, 1953.* Reference Paper No. 64 (1956).

Canada, DBS. *Energy Consumption in the Manufacturing and Mining Industries of Canada, Selected Years 1926–1953.* Reference Paper No. 73 (1957).

Canada, DBS. *Energy Sources in Canada, Commodity Accounts for 1948 and 1952.* Reference Paper No. 69 (1956).

Canada, DBS. *Energy Sources in Canada — Commodity Statements for 1926, 1929, 1933 and 1939.* Reference Paper No. 74 (1957).

Canada, DBS. *The Inter-Industry Flow of Goods and Services, Canada, 1949.* Reference Paper No. 72 (1956).

Canada, DBS. *The Labour Force, November, 1945-January, 1955.* Reference Paper No. 58 (1955).

Canada, RCCEP. *Preliminary Report,* December 1956.

Canada, RCDPR. *Report.* 3 vols. (1940).

Great Britain, Board of Trade. *Canada, Economic and Commercial Conditions.* ("Overseas Economic Surveys") 1950, 1957.

League of Nations, Economic, Financial, and Transit Department. *Industrialization and Foreign Trade.* New York: League of Nations, 1945.

Manitoba, Government of the Province of. *Prospects for Development in Manitoba, A Submission Presented to the RCCEP.* Winnipeg, 1955.

New Brunswick, Government of the Province of. *The New Brunswick Economy, Past, Present and Future Prospects: A Brief Presented by the Government of the Province of New Brunswick to the RCCEP.* Fredericton, 1955.

Newfoundland, Government of the Province of. *Submission by the Government of the Province of Newfoundland to the RCCEP.* N. p., 1955. (Processed.)

Nova Scotia, Government of the Province of. *Submission by the Government of the Province of Nova Scotia to the RCCEP.* N. p., 1955. (Processed.)

Nova Scotia, Province of, Chief Commissioner of Mines. *Report of the Chief Commissioner of Mines for the Province of Nova Scotia for the Year 1867.* Halifax, 1868.

Ontario, Government of the Province of. *Economic Survey of Ontario, 1955.* N. p., 1956. (Processed.)

Ontario, Province of, Department of Economics. *Submission of Ontario to the RCCEP.* N. p., 1956.

Ontario, Province of, Department of Mines. *Report on the Mining and Metallurgical Industries of Canada, 1907–08.* Toronto, 1909.

Organization for European Economic Cooperation. *Europe Today and in 1960, Eighth Report of the O.E.E.C.* 2 vols. Paris, 1957.

Prince Edward Island, Government of the Province of. *Submission of the Government of Prince Edward Island to the RCCEP.* N. p., 1955. (Processed.)

Quebec, Province of. *Report of the Minister of Lands and Forests of the Province of Quebec, 1908.* Quebec, 1909.

Quebec, Province of, Department of Trade and Commerce. *La Province de Québec, Industrial Expansion.* Montreal, 1952.

Saskatchewan, Government of the Province of. *Prospects for Economic Growth in Saskatchewan, A Submission to the RCCEP by the Government of Saskatchewan.* Regina, 1955.

Saskatchewan, Province of, Royal Commission on Agriculture and Rural Life. *Report No. 7, Movement of Farm People.* Regina, 1956.

U.N. Department of Economic and Social Affairs, Statistical Office of the United Nations. *Demographic Yearbook, 1948.*

U.N. Department of Economic and Social Affairs. *The Determinants and Consequences of Population Trends* (1953).

U.N. Food and Agriculture Organization. *A Reconsideration of the Economics of the International Wheat Agreement.* (Commodity Policy Studies No. 1.) Rome: FAO, 1952.

U.N. Food and Agriculture Organization, Canadian Interdepartmental FAO Committee. *Agriculture, Fisheries, Forestry and Nutrition in Canada 1947.* (Annual Progress and Program Report to the Food and Agriculture Organization of the United Nations.) N. p., 1947.

U.S. Bureau of Mines. *The Asbestos Industry.* Bulletin No. 552 (1955).
———. *Mineral Facts and Problems.* Bulletin No. 556 (1956).

U.S. Department of Agriculture, Forest Service. "Chapter 1: Timber Resources for America's Future." Preliminary draft from *Timber Resource Review* (1956).

U.S. Department of Commerce. *A Review of Nickel in the United States, 1946 to 1956* (1955).
———. *Statistical Abstract of the United States, 1957.*

U.S. Department of Commerce, Bureau of the Census. *Current Population Reports.* Series P-25, No. 78 (September 1953).

U.S. Department of Labor. *Family Income, Expenditures and Saving in Ten Cities.* Bulletin No. 1065 (1952).

U.S. Executive Office of the President, Office of Defense Mobilization. *Stockpile Report to the Congress* (1955).

U.S. Federal Trade Commission. *The International Petroleum Cartel.* Staff report submitted to the Subcommittee on Monopoly of the Select Committee on Small Business, United States Senate, 83d. Congress, 2d. Session, 1952.

U.S. Mutual Security Agency, Special Mission to Italy for Economic Cooperation. *The Growth and Structure of the Italian Economy* (1953).

U.S. National Resources Board. *Family Expenditures in the United States* (1941).

U.S. President's Materials Policy Commission. *Resources for Freedom.* 5 vols. (1952).

U.S. Senate, Committee on Banking and Currency. *Newsprint Production and Supply.* ("Preliminary Report and Supplements.") 84th Cong., 2d sess., 1956.

Unpublished Material

Cornell, Peter M. "Flexible Exchange Rates: the Canadian Case." Unpublished Ph.D. dissertation, Harvard University, 1956.

Eldon, W. D. R. "American Influence in the Canadian Iron and Steel Industry." Unpublished Ph.D. dissertation, Harvard University, 1952.

English, H. E. "The Role of International Trade in Canadian Economic Development since the 1920's." Unpublished Ph.D. dissertation, University of California, 1957.

Islam, Nurul. "Studies in Foreign Capital and Economic Development." Unpublished Ph.D. dissertation, Harvard University, 1955.

Steinthorsen, Dallas H. "Problems in Input-Output Analysis of the Canadian Economy." Unpublished Ph.D. dissertation, Harvard University, 1954.

Index

Abramowitz, M., 295
Age structure. *See* Population
Aitken, H. G. J., 33
Alberta. *See* Prairie Provinces
Agriculture: employment, 161–163; forecasting, 432–466; labor force, 43, 162–163, 288–290, 296–297; productivity, 453–466; public finance, 368–369; regional distribution, 161–163, 172–173, 202–205, 222, 225, 458–468
Agricultural machinery industry, 43, 432–436, 441–443, 446
Agricultural products: consumption, 437–438, 443–445; exports, 34, 446, 449–452; investment, 43, 95–96. *See also* Agriculture; Dairy Products; Farm products
Aluminum and aluminum industry: employment, 531; forecasting, 531; production, 522–524, 531. *See also* Nonferrous metals products industry
Ando, A., 17
Asbestos: employment, 531, 534; forecasting, 524–526, 531–534; mining, 531, 534; production, 524–526. *See also* Nonferrous minerals
Atlantic Provinces: agriculture, 161–163; agricultural production, 458–459; defined, 144–145; economy, 147–155, 156–160, 164–165, 175–181; income, 166–167; labor force, 162–163; population, 161–162
Automotive and automotive parts industry, 69, 71, 587–589

Bach, G. L., 17
Balance of payments, 106, 109–110, 127–129, 402–407
Barger, H., 624
Bates, S., 240
Beverage industry. *See* Food, beverages and tobacco products industry
Black, J. D., 438, 441–442, 448, 454
Bladen, V. W., 75
Bonnen, J. T., 438, 442, 448, 454
Brass products industry. *See* Nonferrous metals products industry

Break, G. F., 15–16
British Columbia, 7, 41, 144, 146–147, 166; agriculture, 222, 225, 464–465; economic development, 216–219; employment, 219, 223–225, 229–230; industry, 219–222, 225–226; labor force, 223–224, 227–229, 231–232; mining, 192, 222–225; population, 219, 228–231; transportation, 228
Brown, T. M., 83, 92, 100, 105
Buckley, K., 43, 102, 131, 317–318, 348
Burton, C. L., 257
Business services. *See* Service industries

Central Canada: defined, 144. *See also* Ontario; Quebec
Chemical industry. *See* Nonmetallic minerals and allied products industry
Clark, C., 257, 271, 616
Clothing and household goods industry, 68–69, 574–578
Coal: forecasting, 471–473, 481–498; production, 471–473, 481–494, 498; regional distribution, 192. *See also* Fuels and fuels industry; Nonmetallic minerals and allied products industry
Coats, R. H., 54
Communications. *See* Service industries
Construction: investment, 338–339, 341, 344–346; railway, 43; residential, 81, 104–105. *See also* Construction industry
Construction industry, 539–540
Consumption and consumption patterns, 85, 106–107, 111, 306–329, 437–439, 443–445; 539–541; forecasting, 306–329; and income, 83–85, 314–320, 326
Copper mining and industry: employment, 529–531; forecasting, 498–500, 502–505, 529–530; production, 37, 498–500, 502–505. *See also* Nonferrous metals products industry
Corbett, D. C., 143